FROM A SPEAKING PLACE

From a Speaking Place

Writings from the First 50 Years of
Canadian Literature

EDITED BY W.H. NEW

WITH RÉJEAN BEAUDOIN, SUSAN FISHER,

IAIN HIGGINS, EVA-MARIE KRÖLLER, LAURIE RICOU

RONSDALE PRESS

FROM A SPEAKING PLACE
Copyright © 2009 held by the authors herein

RONSDALE PRESS
3350 West 21st Avenue
Vancouver, B.C. Canada
V6S 1G7

Typesetting: To The Letter Word Processing Inc., in Sabon LT 10 pt on 12.5
Cover Design: Julie Cochrane
Cover Art: "Northern Lights with Communication Towers"
Paper: Ancient Forest Friendly Silva Enviro (FSC)

Ronsdale Press wishes to thank the following for their support of its publishing program: the Canada Council for the Arts, the Government of Canada through the Book Publishing Industry Development Program (BPIDP), and the Province of British Columbia through the Book Publishing Tax Credit Program and the British Columbia Arts Council.

Library and Archives Canada Cataloguing in Publication

From a speaking place: writings from the first 50 years of Canadian literature / editors: W.H. New; with Réjean Beaudoin ... [et al.].

Includes bibliographical references.
Includes some text in French.
ISBN 978-1-55380-064-4

    1. Canadian literature—History and criticism. 2. Canadian literature—20th century—History and criticism. I. New, W. H. (William Herbert), 1938– II. Beaudoin, Réjean, 1945– III. Title: Canadian literature (Vancouver, B.C.).

PS8077.1.F76 2008   C810.9   C2008-902248-3

At Ronsdale Press we are committed to protecting the environment. To this end we are working with Markets Initiative (www.oldgrowthfree.com) and printers to phase out our use of paper produced from ancient forests. This book is one step towards that goal.

Printed in Canada by Marquis Printing, Quebec

Contents

9. RELATIVE POSITIONS

DECORATIVE WOODCUTS BY GEORGE KUTHAN

Conversations: A Preface

From a Speaking Place celebrates both Canadian literature and *Canadian Literature* — the former because that is its subject, the latter because all but one of the essays and commentaries collected in this book appeared in the journal *Canadian Literature* during its first fifty years. The one exception is the essay by Laura Potter, who wrote "A Short History of *Canadian Literature*" especially for this volume. Recording her own experience working as an undergraduate intern and editorial assistant with the journal, her essay traces some of the changes and challenges that have shaped and reshaped *Canadian Literature*, and it begins by tracking the conversations that led Roy Daniells, Geoffrey Andrew, and others to establish the journal at the University of British Columbia in the first place, in 1959, and to persuade the internationally recognized writer George Woodcock to be its first editor.

Just to *imagine* a journal in 1959 that would devote itself solely to Canadian writers and writing was an act of faith. Perhaps even of political daring. A few people thought it was clever then, hearing the journal's title, to ask "IS there one?" and "What will you do in your second issue?" and laugh. No worries there. People with foresight, committed to reading and listening to the writers of their own community, found such questions ironic but not funny, which meant that common sense prevailed. Contributors had much to say; so did readers, both at home and away, who became participants in literary conversations that fastened increasingly on the strengths of Canadian writing. The two hundred issues that have appeared since 1959 amply demonstrate what the founders hoped for: information, insight, intelligence, inquiry. In 2009 it is time to celebrate the journal's achievements, to re-encounter what contributors have had to say, and in a new context to listen again to why it matters.

From these 200 issues, *From a Speaking Place* selects essays and articles on literature both written and oral; literature in French, English, and other languages; comic as well as serious; local as well as national; multicultural, intercultural, international, and more. This book also brings together novelists, short story writers, professional critics, actors, editors, translators, theorists, lay readers, scriptwriters, historians, sociologists, several poets — a couple of poets laureate, even — and ready raconteurs: they constitute a mix of the well known and the soon-to-be well known, and they bring to the reading of Canadian writing their flair for language, their passionate intelligence, their commitment to understanding, to *listening*, and to a civil exchange of ideas. Civil, yes. Not unargumentative, not without disagreements and contradictions. But always with an eye on *learning more* rather than *fastening on less*. *Canadian Literature* has resisted being a coterie journal. Through its five editors — George Woodcock, William New, Eva-Marie Kröller, Laurie Ricou, and Margery Fee, all with different visions of what they wanted the journal to accomplish — it has striven consistently to be a place where diverse views could be expressed: to be a "speaking place" for writer and reader alike. A place that speaks; a place where speaking openly is possible. Hence the title of this volume.

By singling out some sixty-three items from among fifty years of accumulated commentary, we are calling attention to only a few of the remarkable contributions that the journal has already published; each of the two hundred issues so far (with more to come) opens into a roomful of insights. Here we have chosen essays for both their intrinsic interest and their variety of perspective. We are also trying to hint at some of the directions that Canadian literature (and the journal as well) might choose to follow over the *next* fifty years. What further impact will technological changes exert? What forces (political, commercial, social) could decide what will be accessible to read — or be worth reading? What does "worth" even mean in this context — or what will it mean if a resistance to notions of authority also rules out the possibility of commonality? What social issues will come to take precedence over those that have preoccupied writers in recent decades? How will the language of literature change, in this increasingly multilingual country? And of what interest, under any circumstances, is the past?

Any selection such as this one, cumulative by nature, affirms that the past has ongoing relevance — here, both to writing and to commentaries on and about writing. As editors, we have tried, however, not simply to arrange essays in a lock-step chronology, for to do that would be to imply, even unintentionally, some sort of mechanically progressive model, with the "perfect" article hovering in the air somewhere in the future, perhaps in one of those rooms I've already alluded to, where — if the logic of this model holds — it waits to settle and make all subsequent writing unnecessary. The model I prefer is one of ongoing process rather than inevitable progress — of a constant but interrupted, interruptible, genuine conversation, each voice (among many voices) picking up on this idea or that, rethinking it, then giving it back to the community of reading.

Which is not to say that chronology is irrelevant, or that in this book we ignore it. We do not. At the end of each of the essays, readers can find its original publication date; and in the sections we have called "Gallery", appears a sequence of reviews in the order they followed when they first appeared in the journal. These reviews look at books by writers — from Callaghan, Lasnier, Levine, and Carrier, through Ondaatje, Atwood, Gallant, and Munro, to Kroetsch, Mistry, Majzels, and Clarke, among others — who have markedly shaped the course of modern Canadian writing. In these sections, too, appear reflections that extend how we understand what "literature" means, its larger contexts, its importance in our imaginations: Al Purdy writing on Sir John Franklin's *Polar Sea* narrative, Dorothy Livesay writing on the painter Jack Shadbolt, Philip Stratford writing about translators and translation, Thelma McCormack writing about McLuhan and mass society, Sherrill Grace writing about 1930s socialist theatre, Jerry Wasserman writing about the film industry. This sequence tracks not simply a short history of literature, but also a short history of the practice of critical reading: what does it focus on? what does it use as a criterion of value? Does it make some set of moral choices its touchstone — or character and plot, perhaps, or formal integrity, or innovation? What, parenthetically, do words such as "originality" and "experiment" mean? And what does "authenticity" mean, and how does it connect with other resonant nouns: *nationalism, nationhood, citizenship, creativity*? What is the *politics*, moreover — not just the geography — of whatever it is that goes by the name of the regional? Is "value" being reassessed as a commitment to social issues, marginalized voices, globalization? or are marketing strategies and technological possibilities governing what we take to be worth reading? The "Gallery" sections constitute a chronology of readings, yes — but also an implicit conversation about merit and selectivity.

The other five sections in this book are organized less as sequences and more as topical clusters — where a series of separate speakers address loosely related subjects. In the opening section, for instance — which we've deliberately, punningly, called "Open Range" — the subject is *voice*. Warren Tallman's affirmation of the need for laughter focuses directly on Mordecai Richler's ability to entertain, pillory, satirize, and at least suggest the possibility of reform; but it also leads to several reflections on the role of the ironic as a way of altering perspectives, a way of levelling presumptions in real life, a way of relating to (and not just presuming to write "about") the imaginative lives of ordinary people. The anti-hero becomes a spokesperson of the ordinary, the one who punctures or offsets pretension. It is a recurrent voice in Canadian writing. Thomas King uses comic narrative to expose injustices in the history of Canada's First Nations; Laurent Mailhot and Susan Knutson analyze the role that Québécois and Acadian monologists perform as reconstructive historians; Norman Shrive opens a re-evaluation of Pauline Johnson's romanticized role in literary history (a challenge that was to be taken up much later by contemporary critics and historians); and Audrey Thomas considers the language and the gendered indirections of romance itself: its popularity, its appeal, its sometimes subversive wit, and its often covert personal or political ends.

"Adjoining Rooms" takes up another general topic, that of critical discourse, embracing realist, formalist, and comparative critical methodologies and also ranging across literary histories in search of trends and what might be learned from trends. Two articles are by their nature overtly historical: Margaret Atwood's account of the history of James Reaney's mythopoeic journal *Alphabet* and Laura Potter's short history of *Canadian Literature*. Four other articles are specifically comparative: those by Antoine Sirois on Grove and Ringuet, by the translator and short story writer Joyce Marshall on the art of translation, by Louise Ladouceur and by Réjean Beaudoin and André Lamontagne on ways of representing comparison.

Laura Potter's history reveals how a move in critical method (away from national preoccupations and towards investigations and applications of theory) affected *Canadian Literature*. In its earliest years — in that first decade or so, before postwar babies had grown into adulthood, before the wave of 1967 nationalism re-animated Canada, and before technological change had freed publication itself from its received centres in Toronto, New York, Paris, and Montreal — before such events, that is, one of the main functions of a pioneering journal such as *Canadian Literature* was to find facts and name names. (In Australia and New Zealand, *Meanjin* and *Landfall* were performing a similar role.) When these journals began, too little was already familiar; much had to be learned afresh and then shared. Writers such as Hugh MacLennan were still having to assert the validity of setting a literary work in Canada (even though this fight had been going on for a century or more), and critics were finding it useful to chart the stages in writers' careers, demonstrate the recurrence of themes, assert (often restrictively, it seems in retrospect) the delineating characteristics of a national culture. All these methodologies were to come into dispute. Later critics and editors privileged formal textual analysis and the explication of such strategies as polyphony and mixed genres; these in turn would give way to studies of social politics, literary contexts, suppressed or repressed voices, and the intricacies of race, sexuality, poverty, and gender. Analyzing and theorizing the legitimacy or the consequences of critical assumptions became a new norm. But finding facts and naming names did not go altogether out of fashion. Fortunately.

So conversation continues. Reading these essays again, in a different time, in differing surrounds, is not merely to engage in a retrospective exercise; it's to encounter connections we might have been aware of only hazily, to consider the impact of sight and sound and the necessary resonance of silence, to distinguish "listening" from simple "hearing," engage with the poetry of words, and realize afresh the sheer size of the house of writing.

The three subsequent sections — titled "Studio," "Listening Posts," and "Relative Positions" — turn attention to tradition and genre, the twinned draw of history and geography, and the unshakeable spell of family. In the first of these, Gilles Marcotte, Malcolm Ross, and Sandra Djwa variously consider how the language of francophone writing in Quebec separates itself from Royalist Paris norms, how Anglicanism shaped a generation of poets in New Brunswick (and beyond), and how anglophone poets as recently as Pratt were composing within a "great [European] tradition." George Bowering, Canada's first Poet Laureate, can be seen to follow on from some of Djwa's argument, distinguishing between a mythopoeia founded in Hellenic, Germanic, and Judeo-Christian tradition and that which re-imagined itself in local dialect and local phenomena. Robin McGrath looks in yet another direction, demonstrating how Inuit poetry traditionally relies on the musicality of song and assumes that utterance — *inspiration, breath* — will have practical consequences. With these essays as context, the succeeding essays by David Solway, Tom Wayman, and Iain Higgins, together with Kevin McNeilly and Wayde Compton's interview with George Elliott Clarke, bring the "Studio" section to a close. Lively arguments about the nature of poetry abound: what is its value, has it lost its validity in an age of pop image and slang, has the language of working people on the contrary rejuvenated poetry, and what does race have to do with writing?

These topics recur in other ways both in "Listening Posts" and "Relative Positions," where writers such as Margaret Laurence, Basil Johnston, Nasrin Rahimieh, Robert Kroetsch, Claire Harris, George Ryga, and Ven Begamudré raise questions about ethnicity, literature, and language, and where a number of other writers seek accommodation with their own private past. Margaret Laurence, in "Illusions of Simplicity," seeks a way of reconciling herself, through Mannoni, with a colonized Africa; Basil Johnston, speaking out of his own Anishnaabe heritage, talks about the precarious survival of Native languages in contemporary Canada; Nasrin Rahimieh looks at the place of "le discours arabe" in Canadian literature. These are "historical" matters all — but *in place*, every one of them. Hence T.D. MacLulich's account of "Exploration as Literature" deals not only with the language of ostensible documentary but also at least implicitly with the ramifications of a colonial encounter.

Robert Kroetsch's characteristically provocative "The Grammar of Silence," the last essay in "Listening Posts," once again eloquently affirms the importance of "listening" to critical reading, even to notions of "silence." In doing so it also sets up the series of essays that are gathered under the rubric "Relative Positions." Here, writers tell about their own lives: what they inherit, what they learn, how they touch others, how they change. Through the strategies of autobiographical memoir, travel narrative, anecdote, and apologia, they make present that which had been seen as absent, and they make familiar that which had been seen as strange. The poet Claire Harris, writing an obituary for Sam Selvon in "nation language," rewrites what (up to that point) academic studies of "Canadian literature" might have too casually accepted as axiomatic — a "Quebec/Canada" duality, for instance, which Acadian, Franco-Ontarian, and other francophone literatures challenge; or a presumptive British source for Anglo-Canadian speech, when a variety of *englishes* is the communal reality. Harris's writings change the sense of being "foreign" in her environment by reassessing and therefore reimagining this environment. So, too, with other contributors. In "Another Country," the poet and novelist Janice Kulyk Keefer recuperates the perceived "foreignness" of her Ukrainian family past, and celebrates the recovery of a connection. Norman Levine explains why he felt he had to leave Canada in order to write; Rudy Wiebe, connecting with the Arctic, and George Ryga, venturing into Mexico, both discover why writing across borders matters.

Which leads me to the last essay in this section — and in this book — Ven Begamudré's "Greetings from Bangalore, Saskatchewan." This essay has much to say about language, transformation, and narrative, much to say about recuperation, accommodation, and affirmation. It appears where it does not just because of its worthy topic, however, but also because I like the fact that the *last* essay in a book — and in this book of celebration especially — should use the word "Greetings." The word suggests another chance at beginning ("love consists in this," writes the German poet Rilke, "that two solitudes protect, touch, and greet each other") — maybe especially another chance when declarations of ostensible "solitude" multiply. "Greet" is an active verb. It declares "encounter"; it signifies the act of recognizing, the utterance of welcome.

Like Begamudré's essay, *From a Speaking Place* offers both a glimpse of a complicated past and an invitation to a future. It celebrates the vitality of writing, whether then, now, or still to come. The likelihood, of course, that future history will also be complicated — what history is not? — is no impediment to celebration; neither should it stifle the imagination. Complication is more a place of creativity, an opportunity — like a closed door that opens into an unfamiliar room — for inventiveness and exchange. Simply put, *Canadian Literature* has always tried to *work towards* rather than to *work against*. That's why it's had the history it has, and that's why it continues to live. This book invites you to join in the conversation.

For the editors,
WN

Conversations en forme de préface

D'un forum d'échanges célèbre à la fois la littérature canadienne et la revue qui porte ce nom, l'une en tant que sujet d'étude et l'autre parce que tous les articles et les commentaires ici recueillis, sauf un, sont parus depuis cinquante ans dans le périodique appelé *Littérature canadienne*. La seule exception est l'essai de Laura Potter, « *Une brève histoire de Littérature canadienne* », spécialement rédigé pour ce volume-anniversaire. Ayant été étudiante-stagiaire auprès du comité de rédaction, l'auteure retrace l'évolution de la revue à travers certains des virages et des défis qui l'ont façonnée à maintes reprises, à commencer par le fil des entretiens qui amenèrent Roy Daniells, Geoffrey Andrew et d'autres à fonder leur projet à l'Université de la Colombie-Britannique en 1959, ayant convaincu George Woodcock, écrivain de réputation internationale, d'en devenir le premier directeur.

L'idée d'une revue uniquement consacrée aux écrivains canadiens et à leurs ouvrages était alors un acte de foi, sinon d'audace politique. Quelques-uns ne voulurent pas rater l'occasion de faire un bon mot en apprenant le nom du nouveau périodique : « Est-ce qu'il y en a une ? », demandèrent-ils, et « Qu'allez-vous faire au deuxième numéro ? » Ils rigolaient. Mais ceux qui discernaient mieux les voies de l'avenir et qui se montraient attentifs aux écrivains de leur milieu ne bronchèrent pas. Ils comprenaient l'ironie des rieurs sans la trouver aussi amusante. Le bon sens prit le dessus. Les critiques et les lecteurs avaient beaucoup à dire, tant au pays qu'à l'étranger, et ce sont eux qui nourrirent les échanges littéraires de plus en plus propices à appuyer l'écriture de nos auteurs. Deux cents numéros ont vu le jour depuis 1959, ce qui justifie amplement l'espoir des fondateurs : information, perspicacité, intelligence et recherche étaient leur programme. Il est maintenant temps, en 2009, de se réjouir du travail accompli, de rappeler les propos de nos contributeurs et de chercher à en comprendre l'importance dans le nouveau contexte où nous sommes aujourd'hui.

Ce volume présente un choix de textes parmi ces deux cents livraisons, réunissant des articles et des essais sur la littérature orale et écrite, en français, en anglais et en d'autres langues, écrits fantaisistes ou graves, régionaux ou nationaux, multiculturels, interculturels et quoi encore.

La matière de ce volume rapproche des romanciers, des nouvellistes, des critiques de métier, des comédiens, des éditeurs, des traducteurs, des théoriciens, des lecteurs, des scripteurs, des historiens, des sociologues, plusieurs poètes — quelques-uns couronnés — et des conteurs. On y trouve les noms connus et ceux qui le seront bientôt, tous apportant à la lecture de notre production littéraire leur finesse linguistique, leur intelligence passionnée, leur volonté de comprendre, d'écouter et de débattre les enjeux dans un esprit de courtoisie. Il faut insister sur ce dernier mot. Argumenter, inscrire son désaccord, confronter les pôles de discussion, certes, mais toujours en s'efforçant d'en apprendre davantage au lieu de réduire la question. *Littérature canadienne* a réussi son pari de ne pas devenir l'organe d'une clique. Ses cinq directeurs, chacun(e) à sa manière et avec ses visées propres sur ce que la revue devait réaliser, ont toujours été clair(e)s sur ce point : *Littérature canadienne* tend à accueillir des points de vue divers et librement exprimés dans un forum ouvert aux écrivains et aux lecteurs. Là-dessus, George Woodcock, William New, Eva-Marie Kröller, Laurie Ricou et Margery Fee n'ont guère varié. En un mot, la revue est un lieu de discussion où la liberté d'opinion dispose de tout l'espace possible. D'où le titre du volume qu'on va lire.

Le choix de soixante-trois textes, parmi cinquante années de commentaires, focalise le regard sur un assez petit nombre de contributions remarquables. Deux cents numéros font un vaste réservoir de pensées. Les textes retenus l'ont été à cause de leur intérêt intrinsèque et de l'éventail des orientations qu'ils ouvrent. L'intention était d'indiquer ainsi quelques-unes des directions que pourraient suivre la littérature canadienne et la revue dans le prochain demi-siècle. Quel sera l'impact des changements technologiques ? Quelles forces (politiques, commerciales, sociales) pourront déterminer ce qui sera accessible aux lecteurs ou ce qui vaudra la peine d'être lu ? Et qu'est-ce que la valeur peut encore vouloir dire dans ce contexte ? Quel sens prendra ce mot si le rejet de la notion d'autorité ruine toute possibilité de sens commun ? Quelles questions sociales s'imposeront au lieu de celles qui préoccupaient les écrivains des dernières décennies ? Dans ce pays de plus en plus multilingue, comment évoluera la langue littéraire ? Et de quel intérêt, dans n'importe quelles circonstances, peut être le passé ?

Tout choix comme celui-ci, récapitulatif par définition, ne peut qu'affirmer la pertinence prolongée de ce qui relève de l'histoire, tant pour l'écriture que pour le com-
mentaire critique et la réflexion sur l'acte d'écrire. En préparant ce recueil, on a tâché
toutefois d'éviter la seule séquence chronologique, parce que cela aurait reconduit,
même involontairement, une sorte de modèle mécaniquement progressif tendant à
localiser la perfection attendue au matin radieux d'un lendemain, peut-être dans
l'une de ces salles imaginaires où — si c'est possible — l'absolu de l'écriture serait en
instance d'avènement, rendant du coup caduque tout nouveau projet d'écrire. Je
préfère à cet inéluctable progrès le modèle d'un processus continu, tissé d'un entretien interrompu, interruptible mais authentique, chaque voix s'emparant d'une idée
ou d'une autre, la repensant pour la remettre ensuite à la collectivité des lecteurs.

Je ne soutiens pas que la chronologie n'a plus la moindre raison d'être, ni qu'elle
est ignorée dans les pages qui suivent. Il n'en est rien. À la fin de chaque texte, on
trouvera la date de sa parution; dans les sections nommées « Galerie », des comptes
rendus sont rangés dans l'ordre chronologique de leur première publication. Ces
recensions commentent les oeuvres d'écrivains qui ont décisivement marqué le vi-
rage moderne de l'écriture au Canada : de Callaghan, Lasnier, Levine et Carrier
jusqu'à Ondaatje, Atwood, Gallant et Munro, en passant par Kroetsch, Mistry,
Majzels et Clarke, entre autres. Dans ces sections se poursuit la réflexion sur la
compréhension qu'est la nôtre du sens de la littérature, sur ses contextes élargis,
son importance imaginaire : Al Purdy traite du récit L'Océan polaire de Sir John
Franklin, Dorothy Livesay du peintre Jack Shadbolt, Philip Stratford des traducteurs et de la traduction, Thelma McCormack de McLuhan et de la société média-
tique, Sherrill Grace du théâtre socialiste des années 1930, Jerry Wasserman de
l'industrie du film. Ces textes ne se contentent pas d'ébaucher la courbe historique
de la littérature, mais ils dessinent aussi l'évolution de la pratique des lectures critiques à travers ses objets et ses critères appréciatifs. La critique s'appuie-t-elle sur
quelque ensemble de valeurs morales ou s'en remet-elle, peut-être, à la figure des
personnages, à moins que ce ne soit la cohérence de l'intrigue ou encore l'unité
formelle, sinon l'innovation? Que signifient, incidemment, des mots comme « originalité » et « expérimentation »? Qu'en est-il de l'« authenticité » et comment re-
coupe-t-elle d'autres mots aussi vibrants que nationalisme, caractère national,
citoyenneté et créativité? Quelle dimension politique — allons plus loin — se trouve cachée par ce qu'on qualifie de régional, par-delà la géographie? N'assiste-t-on
pas à quelque revalorisation inédite, émergente dans l'engagement à l'intérieur des
débats de société et la défense des marginaux, sans parler de la mondialisation?
Doit-on comprendre que les stratégies de mise en marché et les possibilités technologiques déterminent entièrement ce qui est jugé digne d'être lu dans l'océan des
produits disponibles en librairie? Cette partie, « Galerie », établit une chronologie
des lectures, certes, mais elle nourrit aussi une discussion implicite sur les notions
de valeur et de choix.

Les autres parties sont organisées par regroupements thématiques plutôt qu'en
séquences linéaires et les auteurs y abordent librement des sujets plus ou moins

apparentés. Au tout début, par exemple, dans la section « Champ libre », la voix est au centre des propos. L'affirmation de Warren Tallman sur le besoin de rire débouche sur l'étude du talent de Mordecai Richler pour le divertissement, la dérision, la satire, autant de moyens de corriger les travers. Mais ce n'est pas tout : on est amené à diverses pensées sur le rôle de l'ironie comme instrument de modification de la perspective, d'harmonisation des attentes disproportionnées de la vie réelle et de saisie de l'imaginaire des gens ordinaires. Qu'on ne s'y trompe pas : l'anti-héros se fait alors le porte-parole du quotidien en éliminant toute affectation. La littérature canadienne utilise fréquemment cette voix moyenne. Thomas King recourt au récit comique pour explorer les injustices dont sont victimes les premières nations dans l'Histoire du Canada ; Laurent Mailhot et Susan Knutson analysent respectivement l'importance des monologuistes québécois et acadiens dans la réécriture de l'histoire ; Norman Shrive ouvre la voie d'une réévaluation du statut idéalisé de Pauline Johnson dans l'histoire littéraire (le défi ne devait être relevé que beaucoup plus tard par les critiques et les historiens récents) ; enfin, Audrey Thomas examine le langage de la romance et ses ambiguïtés à l'égard des rôles sexuels ; elle scrute la popularité du genre, son attrait, son esprit parfois subversif et ses dénouements souvent voilés dans leurs motifs personnels ou politiques.

« Chambres communiquantes » traite un autre sujet général : celui du discours critique dans ses méthodologies réaliste, formaliste et comparative, scrutées dans toutes les tendances et dans ce qui peut s'avérer instructif dans les modes, au-delà des faits attestés dans les histoires littéraires. Deux articles sont d'ordre historique par définition : la lecture que fait Margaret Atwood de l'histoire du journal mythopoétique *Alphabet* de James Reaney et la brève histoire de *Littérature canadienne* de Laura Potter. Quatre autres articles sont nommément comparatifs : ce sont ceux d'Antoine Sirois sur Grove et Ringuet, de Joyce Marshall (traductrice et nouvelliste) sur l'art de la traduction, de Louise Ladouceur ainsi que de Réjean Beaudoin et André Lamontagne sur les différentes façons de représenter la comparaison.

L'approche historique retenue par Laura Potter montre bien comment le mouvement de la critique s'éloignant des considérations nationalistes remplacées par la pensée théorique a touché la revue. À ses débuts, au cours du premier versant des années 1960, avant que les *baby boomers* n'aient atteint l'âge adulte, avant que la vague du nationalisme de 1967 n'ait soulevé l'âme canadienne et avant que les nouvelles technologies n'aient affranchi la publication des grands centres, tels Toronto, New York, Paris et Montréal — avant tout cela, l'une des principales tâches d'une revue comme *Littérature canadienne* était d'établir les faits et d'identifier les acteurs du milieu littéraire. (*Meanjin* et *Landfall* remplissaient le même emploi en Australie et en Nouvelle-Zélande. Quand ces revues ont commencé à publier, bien peu de choses était déjà connu ; tout était à découvrir et à partager.) Des écrivains comme Hugh MacLennan devaient encore se justifier de traiter un sujet canadien (même si le combat se poursuivait depuis plus d'un siècle), et les critiques trouvaient utile de tracer la courbe des carrières d'écrivains, de montrer la récurrence des thèmes afin de soutenir l'affirmation (souvent restrictive, semble-t-il rétrospectivement) des grandes caractéristiques d'une culture nationale. Toutes ces méthodologies allaient être remises en question. Les critiques et les éditeurs ont ensuite privilégié l'analyse textuelle et l'explication formelle de la polyphonie et du mélange des genres, ce qui ouvrit la voie aux études sociologiques et politiques, puis à l'analyse des contextes littéraires, des voix occultées ou réprimées dans l'enchevêtrement des notions de race, de sexualité, de pauvreté et d'identité sexuelle. L'examen systématique et la théorisation de la légitimité des présupposés critiques et de leurs effets devinrent la norme incontournable. Mais les données factuelles et les noms n'ont pas disparu pour autant. Heureusement.

Le dialogue continue. Relire ces essais aujourd'hui, dans un tout autre entourage intellectuel et technologique, ce n'est pas tant revenir en arrière que mettre au jour des rapports dont personne n'était vraiment conscient auparavant, c'est comprendre la différence entre écouter et entendre quand on s'engage dans la poésie des mots et qu'on saisit à nouveau l'étonnante vastitude du monde de l'écriture.

Dans les trois sections suivantes — ce sont « Studio », « Postes d'écoute » et « Positions relatives » —, l'attention se tourne vers la tradition et le genre, les motifs jumelés de l'histoire et de la géographie ainsi que l'inébranlable sort réservé à la famille. Dans la première, Gilles Marcotte, Malcolm Ross et Sandra Djwa se demandent diversement comment la langue française des écrivains québécois les distingue des normes littéraires parisiennes, comment l'anglicanisme a imprégné une génération de poètes et même au-delà au Nouveau-Brunswick, et comment des poètes anglophones, aussi récemment que Pratt, s'inscrivaient à l'intérieur d'une « grande tradition européenne ». George Bowering, premier poète officiel du Canada, semble donner suite en partie à l'argumentation de Djwa en retenant la distinction entre la mythologie poétique issue des traditions grecque, allemande et judéo-chrétienne, et celle qui se recrée dans le dialecte local et dans la phénoménologie d'un lieu donné. Robin McGrath explore une autre voie pour démontrer que la poésie inuite repose traditionnellement sur la musicalité du chant et postule que la prononciation — inspiration et expiration respiratoires — entraîne des conséquences pratiques. Ces essais fournissent un contexte aux études suivantes de David Solway, de Tom Wayman et d'Iain Higgins ainsi qu'à l'entretien de Kevin McNeilly et Wayde Compton avec George Elliott Clarke. La section « Studio » se termine là-dessus. L'intensité du débat sur la nature de la poésie n'y manque pas : en quoi consiste sa valeur ; devant la faveur de la langue populaire et de son imaginaire, la poésie conserve-t-elle encore sa validité ; le langage du monde ouvrier a-t-il plutôt rajeuni l'expression poétique ; et comment la problématique de la race affecte-t-elle l'écriture ?

Ces sujets se présentent encore, mais sous un autre angle, dans les sections « Postes d'écoute » et « Positions relatives », où des auteurs tels Margaret Laurence, Basil Johnston, Nasrin Rahimieh, Robert Kroetsch, Claire Harris, George Ryga et Ven Begamudré soulèvent les questions de l'ethnicité, de la littérature et de la langue, tandis qu'un certain nombre d'écrivains cherchent la réconciliation avec leur passé au plan personnel. Margaret Laurence, dans « Illusions de simplicité », trouve le moyen d'accepter son expérience vécue d'une Afrique colonisée, grâce à Mannoni; Basil Johnston, à partir de son ascendance anishnaabe, parle de la survivance précaire des langues aborigènes dans le Canada contemporain; Nasrin Rahimieh se penche sur la place du « discours arabe » dans la littérature canadienne. Tous ces sujets sont d'ordre historique, mais ils sont tous localisés. D'où l'exposé que fait T.D. MacLulich de « l'exploration comme littérature », ce qui l'amène à viser non seulement le langage nommément documentaire, mais aussi, au moins implicitement, les ramifications d'un choc colonial.

« La grammaire du silence » de Robert Kroetsch, texte typiquement polémique, le dernier des « Postes d'écoute », affirme une fois de plus, et éloquemment, l'importance d'être à l'écoute de la lecture critique et même de notions comme le silence, ce qui introduit la suite d'essais réunis sous la rubrique « *Positions relatives* ». Ici, les écrivains livrent leurs expériences personnelles; ce dont ils héritent, ce qu'ils apprennent, comment ils rejoignent les autres, comment ils évoluent en changeant. À travers la stratégie d'écriture des mémoires intimes, des récits de voyage, de l'anecdote et de l'apologie, ils rendent présent ce qui était vu comme absent et ils familiarisent le lecteur avec ce qu'il percevait comme étranger. La poétesse Claire Harris rédigeant la notice nécrologique de Sam Selvon en « idiome de Trinidad » révise un axiome apparemment trop aisément admis (jusqu'à présent) des études littéraires canadiennes : la dualité Québec-Canada, par exemple, bien qu'elle soit contestée par les littératures acadienne, franco-ontarienne et les autres littératures francophones du pays; ou bien l'origine prétenduement britannique de la parole commune des Anglo-Canadiens, alors qu'une grande diversité d'accentuations de l'anglais constitue plutôt la réalité de leur expression. Le point de vue de Harris change le sens du fait d'être étranger à son environnement en réévaluant celui-ci, c'est-à-dire en le réimaginant. Elle n'est pas la seule à le faire. Dans la section « Un autre pays », la poétesse et romancière Janice Kulyk Keefer récupère l'étrangeté perçue du passé de sa famille ukrainienne, et célèbre la reconquête d'un lien. Norman Levine explique pourquoi il a senti qu'il devait s'exiler pour écrire; Rudy Wiebe, s'installant dans l'Arctique, et George Ryga s'aventurant au Mexique découvrent tous les deux ce qui se passe quand on écrit au-delà des espaces familiers.

Voilà qui m'amène au dernier essai de cette partie et du livre — « Meilleurs voeux du Bangalore, Saskatchewan ». Cette réflexion est riche en observations sur la langue, la transformation et la forme narrative, sur la récupération, l'adaptation et l'affirmation. La place de ce texte en fin de parcours est significative par sa substance, mais aussi parce que j'aime que le mot « voeux » soit prononcé pour conclure, et plus encore dans un ouvrage festif comme celui-ci. C'est une autre chance de commencement (selon le poète autrichien Rilke, « l'amour consiste en ceci que deux solitudes se protègent, se touchent et se veulent du bien ») — et tout particulièrement, c'est une opportunité de plus sans doute, lorsque les déclarations de grande solitude vont croissant. Faire des voeux est un acte performatif qui instaure la rencontre, manifeste la reconnaissance et concrétise l'accueil.

Il en va tout à fait ainsi dans l'essai de Begamudré, « *Un forum d'échanges* », qui conjugue l'aperçu d'un passé compliqué à l'invitation à s'ouvrir à un certain avenir. Ce texte illustre la vitalité de l'écriture tant hier qu'aujourd'hui et aussi demain. Évidemment, rien n'assure que la suite de l'histoire ne sera pas encore plus compliquée — quelle histoire ne l'est pas? Est-ce une raison de s'en attrister et d'étouffer l'imaginaire créateur? Non, car la complexité défie l'inventivité, l'ingéniosité, stimule l'interaction comme une porte fermée s'ouvrant sur une chambre inconnue. En clair, *Littérature canadienne* s'est toujours efforcé d'aller dans le sens de la nouveauté et non contre elle. Telle est son histoire et telle est sa continuité actuelle. Le présent volume se veut une invitation à prendre part à la conversation qui se poursuit depuis un demi-siècle.

WN pour le comité de rédaction
traduit en français par RB

A Note on Style

Canadian Literature first appeared in hand-set type (using a Baskerville font, with coloured block letters, design by Robert Reid); thirty-five years later, the journal adopted a computer-set format (using a combination of Minion and Univers fonts, design by George Vaitkunas); these differences have disappeared in the current volume, which uses Sabon throughout. Some other differences, however, remain — patterns of documentation vary from early volumes to later, for example, and while we have simplified some formats, we have not attempted to impose a single contemporary bibliographic standard here. Nor have we erased all the variations in "house style" (affecting punctuation, layout, italics, and related matters) that occurred as each editor adopted a contemporary standard. We have chosen rather to let the variations reflect the journal's editorial history. On other matters, editorial changes have been introduced: to correct typographical errors, to alter punctuation for the sake of clarity, or to accede to the original author's request.

Acknowledgments

I am grateful first of all to my co-editors for their contributions to the planning, shaping, editing, and proofing of this volume; to our assistants, Laura Potter and Melanie Tiemstra, who handled correspondence and assiduously tracked down copyright holders, and to Julie Walchli and the Arts Co-op Program at UBC; to Donna Chin, Matthew Gruman, and Margery Fee, at *Canadian Literature*; to Shelley MacDonald Beaulieu, for typesetting and layout; and to Ron Hatch and his colleagues at Ronsdale Press, for their careful editorial advice.

Collectively, and with thanks, the editors wish further to acknowledge the offices of Stephen Toope, President of UBC, and Nancy Gallini, Dean of Arts at UBC, together with the UBC Program in Canadian Studies, for providing financial support to help publish this book.

We also wish to express our warm appreciation to the authors of these assembled essays for contributing their work to *Canadian Literature* in the first instance; and to the authors (and the executors of the estates of authors now deceased) for copyright permission to reprint their essays here. We are grateful also to Rudy Wiebe for the revised version of his essay: "'Passage by Land' extracted from *River of Stone by Rudy Wiebe*. Copyright © 1995 Jackpine House Ltd. Reprinted by permission of Knopf Canada." — WN

I. OPEN RANGE

Warren Tallman

Need for Laughter

As he writes *St. Urbain's Horseman* Mordecai Richler is thinking both comedy and music, and he's thinking them on what used to be called the grand scale. At the outset a number of major themes are introduced and they unite, as they alternate and recur, into his larger comic theme, call it the fortunate pratfall of Jacob Hersh. As theme gives way to theme, a shuttling weave, Richler adjusts the tone and tempo, calling on all of the writing secrets he has mastered over some twenty years in order to orchestrate his comedy of a sad yet exuberant and spiky Jew.

 beginsand

Jake's spikiness derives from the same Montreal ghetto in which Duddy Kravitz served his apprenticeship in the 1959 work that made Richler's reputation as an important novelist. Duddy figures in *St. Urbain's Horseman* as a minor motif, a childhood pal of Jake's who is now negotiating his talent for swindling into a fortune. This latter-day Duddy closely resembles his earlier self — up to a point. As a first successful step toward millions, he markets a remarkably effective diet pill, the secret ingredient of which is tapeworms. When a chemist cracks the formula, Duddy disappears into a maze of swindles within swindles, leaving the consequences to his partners and the complications to a large number of extremely thin customers. Same old Duddy. But not quite. For in diminishing him from a major to a minor figure Richler also diminishes his earlier potentialities. As apprentice, Duddy plunged so thoroughly into his attempts to out-con the world that he began to move beyond mere swindles to more interesting human possibilities. But in the *Horseman* the possibilities have vanished. He's all

millionaire, and not much more. His fondest latter-day aspiration is to get
his eyes and/or hands up those slopes which begin at the hem of every
passing London mini-skirt. And his rueful self-appraisal — "Who in the
hell could love Duddy Kravitz" — cancels his earlier potential as a young
man with a consuming appetite to gobble the whole world. It's, in little, as
though Falstaff were to grow thin, honest, and genuinely contrite.

Yet Richler robs Duddy of his large hunger for the world deliberately, in
order to hand it over to friend Jake in the form of a somewhat different
hunger. While minor figure Duddy is making his moves to where the money
is, major figure Jake makes his to where imagination might be, as a television
and film director of some distinction. Yet only some, for he is shown as good
but not all that good, successful but in curiously compromised ways, and
ambitious but given to fumbling his best chances away. At first glance this
might seem the portrait of a man who can't quite make it up the ladder to
where the sweet life begins, intense gratification of having reached the top.
But looking again, it becomes evident that Richler is searching elsewhere
through Jake's eyes, not the effort to get up, but a need to climb down. Jake
positively doesn't want the sweetness, deliberately insults important persons,
consciously consorts with film-world nobodies, and eventually cultivates the
malevolent Harry Stein. To make friends with Harry is like holding hands
with an unexploded stink bomb, sure to go off. When it does, a great stench
settles in around the good name Jacob Hersh. Yet the steps by which Jake
moves from respectability to disgrace are waystations of a deeper search, his
dream of his older cousin, Joey Hersh, the Horseman.

Joey grows up in Montreal as still another of Richler's nothing boys, son
of a disgraced father who deserts the family; of a mad and madcap mother
who also disgraces him, every other day; and brother of Jenny, who early
on establishes and then maintains a reputation as one of the more reliable
town pumps. As her outspoken mother says, "she's a whore," but for free,
come almost whomsoever. One miserable 1937 winter day her brother
disappears and for six years, no Joey. Abruptly, one fine 1943 spring day,
along shabby St. Urbain's Street, lo a fire-engine red MG. From which
steps a transformed Joey, with an endless supply of cash in hand. And a
dazzling procession begins, clothes from the most exclusive shops, mysterious, beautiful women from some posh, long-legged sexual heaven, brooding phone calls from faraway places — shades of Gatsby from over the
way in New York. And the whispered legend starts. Did Joey fight against
Franco in Spain, is he a communist, did he visit Trotsky in Mexico? Was
he, in between times, a pro ball player, a licensed pilot, an actor in Hollywood, a man with underworld connections at the far end of those phone
calls, in hiding, even being hunted down?

If adolescent Jake is fascinated by these intimations of an heroic life, he
is even more fascinated by a transformation in Joey from the typically

timorous St. Urbain's boy into an assertive, at times a dangerous Man. When Joey gets drunk, as he often does, he exudes hard-bodied, hard-eyed menace. When some French-Canadian toughs beat up a young Jew, Joey organizes a counter-attack which lands a local dignitary's son in the hospital. Vengeance is ours, saith Joey. But the Jewish fathers, frightened, apologize. When some other French-Canadian boys intimidate Jake and Duddy at the local ball field, Joey comes along and intimidates the French-Canadian boys. Later he will fight the Arabs in the 1948 war. Most crucial of all, he will become, in Jake's imagination, The Horseman, and also the Golem, in Jewish tradition a body without a soul, searching through the world to revenge the loss. It is the infamous Doktor Mengele, one of the monsters at Auschwitz, that Jake believes Joey is pursuing. The dreadful image at the heart of Jake's nightmares is of women in the outhouses while other women crouch, drinking contaminated water from an adjacent stream. Enter the good Doktor to bring in sanitation by destroying not the outhouses but the women.

Over the years it's become clear that Richler is essentially iconoclastic, almost invariably asserting tough-minded scepticism in the face, under force, of the modern world — kid me NOT! Letting cousin Joey be Jake's hero, his vision of a redeeming manhood for Jewish men, Richler consciously selects a sleazy hero, made up of the sleazy kitch boys dream along St. Urbain's street. Seeking revenge for Mengele's monstrous treatment of Jewish women, Joey himself mistreats women, deserts a wife and child in Israel, swindles another woman in London, and plays the petty cheat to each next town he passes through. Beyond adolescence Jake never does catch up with Joey except in dreams, Nazi-haunted nightmares into which, fleetingly, his cousin rides, mounted in a magnificent Plevin stallion:

> Neighing, the stallion rears, obliging the Horseman to dig his stirrups
> in. Eventually he slows. Still in the highlands, emerging from the dense
> forest to scan the scrub below, he strains to find the unmarked road
> that winds into the jungle, between Puerto San Vincente and the
> border fortress of Carlos Antonio Lopez.

This is Paraguay where 40,000 escaped Nazis are thought to live, Mengele included. But vengeance is not Joey's, saith Mordecai Richler. Beyond his dream of his cousin as Horseman and Golem, Jake falls into step with a London body even more lacking in a soul, Harry Stein, the Jewish Iago, pure venom, gratuitous hatred, malice incarnate. Ride along with Joey in your dreams and there will be a shift in which you tag along with Harry. All German girls beware.

To understand how Jake makes the transition from dreams of Joey to friendship with Harry, the reader needs to understand Harry's dim-witted mistress, Ruthy. And to understand Ruthy one needs to consider first, Jo-ey's sister, Jenny. Every good writer is likely to have at least one well that is always coming in, from which words will flow almost easily into place. For Richler this natural resource has always been Jewish lowlifers: in *St. Urbain's Horseman*, the Hersh family. And how Richler loves it, and how he hates it, the intense, hot, heavy interest that fathers, mothers, sisters, brothers, uncles, cousins and aunts all take in one another to the exclusion of every other interest. Jenny, the most intelligent of the Hershes, recog-nizes the almost incestuousness of such closeness when she tells Jake that brother Joey returned to Montreal that fabled spring of 1943 because "he wanted to fuck me," and that he left to avoid doing so. Jenny wants out of the hothouse, so she elects for self-education in art, literature and philoso-phy. As such, she becomes Jake's muse and he "her acolyte." Jake, grown up, remembers her solitary, back-bedroom study light gleaming through late St. Urbain's hours; remembers Modern Library books, a map of Paris, a drawing of Keats, Havelock Ellis, the *Saturday Review of Literature*, re-members how he "had revered her, how she had once excited him." Given the double pull, of reverence, as for a muse, and excitement, as for a mis-tress, it's all but inevitable that Jake will follow after when she makes her move to escape from Hershville.

But such an escape! Out of the family warming oven into the pale fires of the Toronto culture-establishment by way of a calculated marriage to Doug Fraser, whom Richler portrays as perhaps the most asinine play-wright CBC Radio ever encouraged in all its long history of encouraging asinine playwrights. However, Jenny marries Doug, not for the imagina-tion he doesn't possess, and not for a sexuality which he also doesn't pos-sess, but as a way to become reigning hostess for Toronto writers, artists, directors and producers. Much of her success as hostess consists in her willingness to go to bed with whomsoever, except her husband (reluctant-ly) and Jake (not at all). That woman who discovers she has become the eternal feminine for a particular man — Jenny for Jake — will realize that in order to be his muse she had best not be also his mistress. Swallow my cousin, cousin swallow. When adolescent Jake wants her she lets him fool around but then tells him to go home and grow up. When he does grow up and still wants her, she declines and sleeps instead with Duddy, driving Jake dotty. But it will be at one of her parties that he gains entrée to his career as a film director and meets his eventual best friend, the genuinely talented writer, Luke Scott. A career and a standard by which to judge that career. Fleet sweet swallow.

But enter Richler's scepticism, clipping her wings and pouring salt on her tail. Just as cousin Joey is a sleazy hero, cousin Jenny is a sleazy muse, the best that circumstances provide for St. Urbain's boys, but very much bar-gain basement, damaged goods. However, the scepticism is not to be understood as simply Doubting Mordecai with a moted eye for all the things that are under the sun. It's that he distrusts muses, at least the kind that Jake takes to be soul of his soul. There is a direct connection between Jenny in Montreal and Toronto, and Ruthy in London. For lame-brain Ruthy is the would-be-muse to end all muses, totally convinced as she takes on each next shabby lover that Goethe has re-occurred. And who is the first lover she takes on in these terms but cousin Joey, the Horseman. Who, having seduced and swindled her, rides off into the European sunset with her life-savings in his saddlebags. Enter her next lover — who else but Harry Stein, determined that Jake will make good for Joey, so that Ruthy will have savings *he* can swindle from her. Ruthy thinks that's super, since in her eyes Harry, who boasts a high I.Q., is at the level where "there's Gertrude, there's Ep and there's Ein." Moving from his pre-occupation with Joey and Jenny to his pre-occupation with Harry and Ruthy, Jake enters into some of the finest passages in the novel, in which he revels in their shoddiness as one might indulge a madness in order to be rid of it. Because muse Jenny still knocks at inner chambers of his being, Ruthy's atrocious capacity for adoration answers. Because hero Joe still rides his dreams, Horseman and Golem, Harry appears, vengeance incarnate. Before whom place a delectable dish, a statuesque German girl, Ingrid. Threaten her. Strip her naked. Rape her. Bugger her. Fellatio. Down on hands and knees. Put Joey's saddle on her back. Get out Joey's riding crop. Mount, whip, and ride to your revenge for Jewish women crouched by Auschwitz outhouses drinking their own shit-fouled water as prologue to the even more horrible gas chamber cantata, writhing and clawing their way to the very top of death's most vaulting ambition. Small wonder that Jake Hersh is a hypochondriac. Fears success. Marries a Goy.

But vengeance is mine, saith the Lord. Through the screen of lies Ingrid, Harry and Jake need to tell in court, it's clear that Jake is scarcely guilty as charged. His great mistake is to arrive home unexpectedly, get involved with the drunkenness of it all, and become understandably indiscreet. He does fondle her. He does pinch her, viciously, to his surprise. But when she goes suddenly onto her knees and fumbles at him, he pulls away. And when Harry begins the saddle and riding crop routine, Jake quarrels, gets angry, and shoves Ingrid rather roughly out of the house. All of which the jury comprehends. Also the judge, who is hard on Harry, whom he despises and sentences to seven years, and on Jake too, whom he deplores but lets off with a suspended sentence. However, the real judge of the event is a sceptic named Mordecai. And as he's wincing with the pain of it all, he's smiling, a benevolent scepticism. He knows that in depths of himself where the invisible worms fly in the night Jake is guilty, his dream of Joey leading him into league with Harry to heap humiliation on the tender flesh of the German girl. So he winces. But he also knows that by letting his creature Jake act out the nightmare, he, Jake, will arrive at knowledge of how ridiculous a nightmare it all is, how little he is actually interested in such revenge: a grope, a pinch, and a push. So judge Mordecai aids and abets the crime in order to cure the criminal, lets Jake follow Joey toward revenge and meet Harry, the exact man for the job, Iago come round again to arrange the denouement.

But what a fraud of a vengeful fellow this Harry Stein proves out, an inept Iago who selects, among other things an entirely wrong victim. Judge Mordecai makes it clear that pretty Ingrid is a mostly compliant baggage who assumes that anal, oral and genital intercourse are simply what people do on sexual occasions — as, indeed, they do. Iago Harry went too far and did hurt and humiliate her — for a while. Otherwise she experienced it all as another one of those odd evenings in a long series. The greatest damage to her pride was probably when Jake pushed her out of the house, Gott in Himmel, all this and no screen test too! And though it did seem weird to be down on her hands and knees with Joey's saddle on her not-so-pure Aryan back, ready to be whipped and paraded past wherever it is the shades of the Auschwitz women huddle, it doesn't seem at all weird to judge Mordecai, the smiling sceptic who arranged it all. He sees it as the ludicrous end point of Jake's bad dream. Under a law of rueful laughter, the sentence he imposes would seem to read, in the vernacular, come off it Jake Hersh, dark is not the colour of your true love's hair. You are no inverted Jewish Mengele, twisting toward revenge. You are what you actually are, a spiky Jew up from St. Urbain's street, needing to be a spike since modern times have small room for sensitive plants, as I, judge Mordecai, also spiky, can testify. But be a golden spike. And at the end, the ridiculousness burned deeply in burning the bad dream out, lo, friend Lucas Scott drives up in his shiny fire-engine red reputation, the best writer in town, offers his best script to best friend Jake to direct. The sweet life. And Jake hesitates, weeps for the death of cousin Joey, the Horseman, but accepts, for once malleable. And a golden thread takes over from the invisible worms now fled into some other night than the one from which Jake has awakened.

A comic world then, the spirit of which is not from dark to darker to darkest, but from dark to lighter to laughter, and release. Harry Stein is certainly the worst news Richler has given us to date, with his obscene phone calls, nasty put-downs and ugly feelings. But the passages that spell him out contain some of the most elated writing in the novel. If he were true Iago no one could laugh. But as a failed Iago he's a very funny nasty fellow. The portrait of Harry reveals the reality of Richler's scepticism, which has always been the main fact met in his novels. Just as it cuts against everybody's pretensions that they are better than they actually are, it cuts against fears that they are worse. A humane, a forgiving scepticism, then, the test of which is not in some officious pronouncement — I AM THE HUMANE SCEPTIC — but where it belongs, in the writing itself, the upbeat music that takes over when awful Harry and awful Ruthy make their appearances. They are unbearable — look the other way! — but the writing itself rescues them, allegro, so that, like Jake, the reader tags along. However, in other parts of the novel there are problems.

க

For an older generation of writers in Canada, young Mordecai Richler must have seemed rather markedly a wild one in much the same way as the older Irving Layton and younger Leonard Cohen seemed also wild — then. And so he was — then. His brash, wrong-side-of-the-tracks writing rushes make the more considered styles of Hugh MacLennan and Morley Callahan seem almost elegiac. But time plays funny tricks, and in our speeded-up world doesn't wait around very long before playing them. To a newer generation of writers, it's doubtless Richler's prose that seems elegiac, inviting comparison, not forward to the much more open, freely improvisational modes in which they work, but back to modes they have all but abandoned. This isn't enmity, a new wave of artists who would like to see Richler's ship sink. Surely, no serious writer or reader can fail to appreciate the magnitude of his attempt to create a symphonic novel, the four movements, the many themes that weave congruently through the entire work, the animated writing with which he attempts to achieve a comic triumph of spirit over some grim modern realities. But respect it as they may, it will doubtless be precisely the imposed superstructure from which a good many younger artists will flinch as being an unnecessary burden for any writer to carry on his bent and straining back. *Heavy, heavy* often does hang over his typewriter.

Never more so than when the upbeat writing he needs in order to sustain the upbeat intention of the work becomes strained, particularly in the burlesque passages that recur intermittently throughout the novel. These passages are an old and puzzling story in Richler's writing — fragments of film scripts, newspaper items, letters to Jake from pathetic, backwoods TV aspirants, a do-it-yourself I.Q. test — you too can be a Harry Stein — and, most important, a number of zany episodes that mock the social, sexual, marital lives and times of Toronto and London establishment sophisticates. These burlesques do double duty in the novel. Musically they occur as a kind of running scherzo, sounds of life's whirly-birds crooning through crazy days. Thematically they explore and present the public level of Jake Hersh's life, just what kind of wacky modern wonderland it is to which he (and all the rest of us) are more or less Mad Hatters. The difficulty occurs when such passages strain in their reach towards laughter and become insistent, unfunny. For instance, the evening that Jake and his wife have dinner at the home of his attorney, Ormsby-Fletcher.

It begins with Jake's awareness that given the conflicting lies he, Ingrid and Harry will be telling in court, the logic of their testimony will count for rather less than the presence on his behalf of an "upright plodding WASP" lawyer. With dull propriety itself at your side how could you possibly be guilty of unspeakable carnalities? If you grew up along St. Urbain's Street you know how to con, and Jake did and Jake does, deftly manoeuvring Ormsby-Fletcher into accepting his case. Which of course makes Jake eminently respectable in the eyes of Ormsby-Fletcher, positively his favourite Jewish sex pervert. And his wife's favourite too. Hence the invitation. Everybody knows that the English have the most revolting food sense in the civilized world so the meal becomes a series of soggy lumps. Afterwards Mrs. Ormsby-Fletcher enthuses (with fluted voice) over examples of (it's her special interest) paintings by cripples, teeth paintings, toe paintings, maybe even armpit paintings. Given Richler's bawdiness it's a little surprising that she doesn't bring in work by some paraplegic Modernist who has given up brushes entirely to become the first penis painter, now nurse if you'll just . . . When Jake goes to the John (vetting the hamper for glimpses of the lady's lingerie), the toilet — ah England — plugs. And what to do with the contents? Scoop it all up in his shorts and throw it out the window? Or smuggle it to the downstairs John, one hopes in working order? Or smuggle himself downstairs, establish his presence there, and let four-year-old junior take the rap for the mess upstairs? Which latter, Jake does.

Few readers are likely to object to bathroom humour per se — shades of Swift, Rabelais, Henry Miller, the human race generally, half the jokes we tell. Or to a demolition job on English uppah claws ridiculousness. In art there are always rooms to spare, including those furnished with hostility à la Freud insights into wit and laughter. Burlesque, by which the enemy is turned into a caricature of himself, has always been a favourite style for such furnishings. Richler's characteristic enemies are establishment people, the mad hatters at the top of the social heap, the insufferable ways in which they lord it shabbily over the rest of us. With lowlife vulgarity he is very much at ease. The true vulgar leads after all to the vulgate, that common tongue which the artist can then subtilize, humanize, liberate, a natural stamping ground for the comic spirit. But the highlife vulgarity of establishment people — Mrs. Ormsby-Fletcher — destroys subtlety, humanity and freedom by revelling in the shoddy, the banal, the pretentious. So the hostility that Richler feels does him credit. Nor can there be any objection to the burlesque masks he assumes in order to project that hostility; vengeance is mine saith the artist, slyly. It's the writing itself that poses the difficulty, the ways in which it tightens into a forced hilarity and loses comic resonance. This is very much like those evening gatherings at which people, laughing hysterically, demolish some common enemy. Played back the next morning, with all the giggles gone, the exchanges are likely to be singularly unfunny. For this reader, the Ormsby-Fletcher passage, and a number of others in the novel, are like that — the next morning.

The difficulty may be a double one. It takes a good hater to write successful burlesque, one able to revel in a happiness of malice made sweet. William Burroughs for instance — his savage joy. Richler never seems quite able to revel. Like his protagonist, Jake, he is perhaps too forgiving, gentle. Thus one of the funniest passages in St. Urbain's Horseman, the middle-aged film makers' soft-ball game on Hampstead Heath, is no burlesque at all, but delicious roly-poly slapstick. Strictly speaking, these film folk are much more dangerous enemies of art than ridiculous Mrs. Ormsby-Fletcher. They are establishment vulgarians who have long since converted film-making, which they control, into a shoddy game of wheel and deal, no mystery, no beauty, no power, just wheel, just DEAL. However, Richler writes them into place as a collection of huffing, puffing, show-off teddy bears for whom he feels not hostility but an amused affection. Hostility need not enter because he is seeing them as lowlifers, clowns to their own careers, whose wheeling and dealing takes on authentic comic resonance as they play ball in order to, like they say, play ball. My favourite is the one who can't decide whether to hit a single, a double or a triple because not sure whether it would be more politic to talk to the first, the second or the third baseman. So he strikes out. However, when hostility enters and the burlesque masks go on, Richler's writing tends to tighten into a more strained grimace. Which is to laugh — and write — the hard way.

But the more important difficulty must be traced to Richler's symphonic superstructure. Once he establishes burlesques of modern life as a major theme of the novel he must write a certain number of such passages, whether he feels like it or not. This is linear imagination at work, with a vengeance, since by page 10 he has committed himself to four such themes that he will need to sustain through what turns out to be a long 467 pages of writing. Or a short 467 pages if one considers the various economies he needs in order to keep any given theme in balance with the others. All writers know it is difficult enough to sustain the tone and tempo of even a single theme over a period of days, weeks or months. What happens when the feelings in which the theme is grounded just go away? Smoke writing. To sustain four themes, each with a somewhat different tone and tempo, and at the same time to shuttle back and forth in order to weave them into a larger, unified comic progression from movement to movement to movement to finale is a task for imagination that can be thought either heroic or over-burdened. A further difficulty in the writing, the frequent intrusion of expository asides in the midst of narrative passages, argues for the over-burdening.

Novelists are supposed to kiss and tell, but they are usually expected to dramatize, visualize or sound the kissing and telling, not simply to explain that Jake is happily married, has grown weary of modern literature, or is a small "l" liberal who realizes that his very comfortable life style scarcely squares with his feelings about world misery. Goethe said it long ago, critics are dogs, yapping at artists' Achilles tendencies, and it seems all but certain that Richler will be faulted for the too-frequent intrusion of this expository bridging. Which is what it seems to be, a shorthand way to keep one or another theme moving and evolving those times he is out of patience with direct presentation. Or, more likely, is struggling to keep one theme in balance with the others, a problem in harmonics. Thus, by simply explaining that Jake is "immensely pleased" or "enormously amused" Richler confirms the comic nature of the place without having to pause and present the pleasure or amusement. Yet when he must explain, it's clear that he realizes the reader might very well be concluding otherwise, say that Jake must be horribly depressed or not one bit pleased. However, the real issue is not the intrusion of the expository asides per se. There is no law that says a novelist cannot explain those times he isn't interested to present, just as there is no law that says a critic, or anyone else, cannot narrate, dramatize or sound his responses. All writing is art and all writers should have access to all of the possibilities that language affords. It's more *apropos* to ask, do the expository intrusions stay lively enough to sustain, even enhance, the general liveliness Richler is seeking in creating his comic vision of Jake Hersh. I think not. When they occur, it's a little like listening to upbeat music momentarily interrupted by someone talking, not from the audience, but from the midst of the music itself. Such intrusions mar that animation which is the soul of this novel. They occur least often in just those passages where Richler is at his lively best, the portraits of Harry Stein and Ruthy, and whenever Jake for old time's sake, or for need, goes on back home to Montreal.

When he is at home with the various Hershes (or they visit him) the tempo is held at a quick-handed fast, and the tone stays sceptical. But it all dips down — sweet chariot — to some undersurface where sad is singing to sad, laugh and chatter as they will. There is a beautifully modulated passage in which Jake, about to quit college, goes to a delicatessen with his father, divorced from his mother. The crass jokes — "fart smeller, I mean smart feller" — become muted sounds on some cracked harmonica that the father discovers he can no longer play for the son, try as he will. Similarly, when his mother comes to London the modulations are superb, the sweet chariot herself, patting her breasts, preening her body, seducing her grandchildren, cutting out the competition, effacing herself into the centre of attention, and my boy, my boy, my buoy. Who left his Maw long years ago, as her direct, accusing glance reminds him at the airport — the husband gone, the children gone, you Yankel too — what's left for hot-house eyes?

The passages that give us the mother and father open a way, perhaps, to where the comic genius that rules over this novel dwells. To follow Jake's feelings along lines that lead to inner chambers of their defeated but animated lives is to reach a place where there is no laughter at all but anguish instead that human existence needs be so grim an affair, *felt* as grim — the tawdriness of his father's life and reactions to life, the obsessive stupidity of his opposition to Jake's marriage, the ugly pathos of his illness and death, the even uglier travesty of his funeral. Nor is the father alone in this lower world, for shade comes to join shade, the defeated mother, Joey, Duddy, Jenny, Ruthy, Harry Stein, all as well afflicted by tawdriness, ugliness, stupidity, defeat. And for silent chorus, hooded, the Auschwitz women, the excremental lilies, in life less than excrement. It is from this grim region that the resonance flows which moves into the best, most elated writing in the novel as the desolation is redeemed into a comic vision. If Richler sends Jake to melancholy places, it's in order to arrive at a genuine, a felt need for laughter. It is when he moves away from the need into contact with merely social ugliness, stupidity and defeat — the world of the establishment whirlybirds — that the writing turns non-resonant and strains for its effects. There can be no desolation at heart over the Ormsby-Fletchers' foolishness. They are merely foolish. As Jake might well say, who needs them! And because need doesn't enter in, because there will be no second dinner at their home, no necessary third to still the voices of desolation, there can be no deep resonance to underlie the reach for laughter. So the writing strains because the comic superstructure moves in with its relentless insistence — and there must have been times when Richler wondered why — that he be a funny fellow.

∞

Swift, Yeats says,

> has sailed into his rest;
> Savage indignation there
> Cannot lacerate his breast.
> Imitate him if you dare.

It will be to Richler's everlasting credit, since works of art endure, that he does dare to imitate Swift, in more than a few ways. *Gulliver's Travels* was the first English novel to take advantage of symphonic form, inadvertently since the form itself was only just coming into being. In *Gulliver*, there are the four lively movements, liveliest of all being the third, a swirling prose scherzo, all over the geographical and thematic place. And the fourth movement, in Houyhnhnm-land, recapitulates and resolves the themes woven into the first three. Which is a way of saying that *St. Urbain's Horseman* is *Gulliver* come round again. Most of the writing devices Richler uses have sanction, in that Swift also used them. Just as Swift laces burlesque passages through *Gulliver*, Richler laces them through *Horseman*. Just as Richler intrudes expository asides into his narrative, Swift intrudes even more of them into his: passages concerning law, education, family life, written in over Lemuel's shoulder. And both writers hold to the crucial rule that, as their scepticism cuts the ground from beneath their protagonists' feet, redemption will occur not in pronouncements but in the act, the art of writing. If the human spirit is to prevail over the grimness of things, it will prevail in the interstices of the words themselves: "there is a music at the heart of things."

And there is another decisive similarity, though it leads to an even more decisive difference. Both novelists choose as protagonist a fool whom they then trap into experiences which will reveal and, they hope, cure the foolishness. Gulliver doesn't seem exactly cured at the last, since he's mad enough to believe that he's almost a horse and likes it that way — farewell mankind! Yet he's an awfully human horse. If you met him trotting down the street, you'd be less likely to weep for mankind lost than to smile. Jake isn't exactly cured either, since he does leave the question of Joey's death open, implying that he might some day climb back on to the nightmare desire that vengeance shall be Joey's, Harry's and his. But the similarity that leads to difference is a deeper one. Both Lemuel and Jake are atheists; Jake by direct acknowledgement of the fact that throughout his ordeals he never once calls on God's help, as his creator did every evening of his adult life. Which means that both fools must call on their human resourcefulness to outface or outfox the surrounding grimness. But Swift takes Lemuel's atheism as the basic foolishness that branches out into all his other idiocies, driving him finally outside human boundaries, to Horseville. Richler takes Jake's atheism as a source for his tenacious humanity, the stubbornness with which he clings to fair play for such sorry specimens as Joey and Harry Stein. Swift, then, is on God's side, laughing, while Richler is on man's side, needing to laugh, trying.

Because this is so, Swift would see Richler playing the fool to his fool by imposing on him an untenable proposition that mankind can go it alone. Yet were he to sail on out of his rest and re-appear on a sudden London to tell Richler so — fool Mordecai! — it would surely be a double sign. Sign of his belief that God forgotten is man abandoned. But sign also that the Horseman from Canadhnhnmland has written his way into the kind of company he, Swift, always did prefer. Which is a long way for a spiky boy from St. Urbain's Street to have travelled. Even Duddy, swindled out of his role as major figure, would be impressed. And one sees Horse Lemuel trotting briskly along, but turning solicitously to Horseman Jake, flat on his back again: You see Jacob, we Houyhnhnms have been doing this longer than you Canadhnhnms.

CL 56 (Spring 1973)

Thomas King

A Short History of Indians in Canada

Can't sleep, Bob Haynie tells the doorman at the King Edward.

Can't sleep, can't sleep.

First time in Toronto?

Yes.

Businessman?

Yes.

Looking for some excitement?

Yes.

Bay Street, sir, says the doorman.

Bob Haynie walks down Bay Street at three in the morning. He loves the smell of concrete. He loves the look of city lights. He loves the sound of skyscrapers.

Bay Street.

Smack!

Bob looks up just in time to see a flock of Indians fly into the side of a building.

Smack! Smack!

Bob looks up just in time to get out of the way.

Whup!

An Indian hits the pavement in front of him.

Wimp! Wimp!

Two Indians hit the pavement behind him.

Holy Cow! shouts Bob, and he leaps out of the way of the falling Indians.

Whup! Whup! Whup!

Bob throws his hands over his head and dashes into the street. And is almost hit by the van.

Honk!

Two men jump out of the van. I'm Bill. I'm Rudy.

Hi, I'm Bob.

Businessman? says Bill.

Yes.

First time in Toronto? says Rudy.

Yes.

Whup! Whup! Whup!

Look out! Bob shouts. There are Indians flying into the skyscrapers and falling on the sidewalk.

Whup!

Got a Mohawk, says Bill.

Whup! Whup!

Couple of Cree over here, says Rudy.

Amazing, says Bob. How can you tell?

By the feathers, says Bill. We got a book.

It's our job, says Rudy.

Whup!

Bob looks around. What's this one? he says.

Holy! says Bill. Holy! says Rudy.

Check the book, says Bill. Just to be sure.

Flip, flip. flip.

Navajo!

Bill and Rudy put their arms around Bob. A Navajo! Don't normally see Navajos this far north.

Is he dead?

Nope, says Bill. Just stunned.

Most of them are just stunned, says Rudy.

Some people never see this, says Bill. One of nature's mysteries. A natural phenomenon.

They're nomadic, you know, says Rudy. And migratory.

Toronto's in the middle of the flyway, says Bill. The lights attract them.

Bob counts the bodies. Seventy-three. No. Seventy-four.

What can I do to help?

Not much that anyone can do, says Bill. We tried turning off the lights in the buildings.

We tried broadcasting loud music from the roofs, says Rudy.

Rubber owls? asks Bob.

It's a real problem this time of the year, says Bill.

Whup! Whup! Whup!

Bill and Rudy pull green plastic bags out of their pockets and try to find the open ends.

The dead ones we bag, says Rudy.

The live ones we tag, says Bill. Take them to the shelter. Nurse them back to health. Release them in the wild.

Amazing, says Bob.

A few wander off dazed and injured. If we don't find them right away, they don't stand a chance.

Amazing, says Bob.

You're one lucky guy, says Bill. In another couple of weeks, they'll be gone.

A family from Buffalo came through last week and didn't even see an Ojibwa, says Rudy.

Your first time in Toronto? says Bill.

It's a great town, says Bob. You're doing a great job.

Whup!

Don't worry, says Rudy. By the time the commuters show up, you'll never even know the Indians were here.

Bob walks back to the King Eddy and shakes the doorman's hand. I saw the Indians, he says.

Thought you'd enjoy that, sir, says the doorman.

Thank you, says Bob. It was spectacular.

Not like the old days. The doorman sighs and looks up into the night. In the old days, when they came through, they would black out the entire sky.

CL 161–162 (Summer-Autumn 1999),
from *Toronto Life*, August 1997

Laurent Mailhot

Le monologue québécois

L'homme ne disait rien. Ce que nous nommons monologues sont des dialogues avec quelque part ignorée de nous-mêmes — GILLES HÉNAULT

Le monologue idéal serait silencieux — YVON DESCHAMPS

Le monologue est la forme la plus ancienne et la plus nouvelle du théâtre québécois (je ne dis pas de la scène canadienne ou canadienne-française). Il se situe à la fois en marge (au cabaret, dans les boîtes) et au coeur de notre théâtre. Des chansonniers aux dramaturges tous les hommes de la parole et du spectacle l'ont plus ou moins utilisé. Yvon Deschamps et Michel Tremblay l'ont rendu particulièrement significatif. Le monologue est peut-être, aujourd'hui comme au temps de Jean Narrache et de Fridolin, notre forme de théâtre la plus vraie, la plus spécifique, la plus populaire et la mieux engagée, la seule où puissent se retrouver ensemble travailleurs et chômeurs, intellectuels et bourgeois. Comment ? Et pourquoi ?

ⲟ⳥

Le roman nous avait habitués aux *voix* de Maria Chapdelaine, à la *folie* de Menaud, aux *jongleries* d'Alexandre Chênevert, au *vécrire* de Galarneau. Yves Thériault publiait des *Contes pour un homme seul*, Adrien Thério un *Soliloque en hommage à une femme*, Réal Benoît voulait *Quelqu'un pour m'écouter*, etc. Ces personnages sont maintenant sur la

scène, sous les feux. Ils n'ont pas fini de ruminer et de se bercer (d'illusions), mais l'humour (rose ou rouge, noir, corrosif ou grinçant) leur est
venu en même temps que le geste et la parole.

Adolescents ou quadragénaires, vieilles filles ou matrones, ivrognes ou
pédérastes, employés, manoeuvres ou intellectuels de gauche, ils sont plus
que diverses facettes de l'homme québécois. Presque tous « en-dessous de la
moyenne », comme Gratien Gélinas le disait de Fridolin, ils en dévoilent les
dessous, le conditionnement psycho-sociologique. Voix sans visages d'un
pays incertain, ils appellent, ils explorent, ils nomment. Le monologue est
un moyen de dépasser (sans tout à fait en sortir) la *jonglerie* hivernale, le
repliement méditatif sur soi. Le personnage est encore seul, mais il est seul
avec d'autres, solitaire-solidaire, puisqu'il *jongle* devant un public, et qu'on
découpe, on organise sa *jonglerie*. De *jongleux* mélancolique et sédentaire il
est devenu jongleur : joueur, rieur en même temps que révolté et tragique.

La Sagouine acadienne d'Antonine Maillet, admirable excroissance ou
rejeton naturel des *Crasseux*, est-elle une pièce, un discours, un récit? C'est
un monologue « pour une femme seule » qui a trouvé son auditoire et sa
mémoire :

> Ah! c'est point aisé de te faire déporter coume ça, et de crouère que
> tu y laisseras queques plumes dans ta déportation. Ca se paye ces
> voyages là. C'est vrai que tu fais parler de toi après : ils te dounont
> toute sorte de façon de beaux noms, coume Evangéline et les saints
> martyrs canadiens. Ils t'appelont un peuple héroïque et martyr et ils
> te jouquont quasiment dans la niche de l'Ecce Homo (. . .) C'était
> une belle histouère, c't'elle-là à Marie-Stella pis Evangéline; ben moi
> j'aimais encore mieux les contes de mon défunt père.

Citoyenne d'« En-bas », fille et femme de pêcheurs, née « quasiment les
pieds dans l'eau », un peu morue à l'occasion, la vieille femme de ménage
a pour tout décor « son seau, son balai et ses torchons », comme Fridolin
avait son chandail de hockey, sa fronde, sa chaise et sa casquette de travers.
L'anti-Evangéline s'adresse « à son eau trouble », elle se décrasse après
avoir décrotté tout le monde. La Sagouine, qui est à elle seule « un glos-
saire, une race, un envers de la médaille », un livre d'images et de *Jos Gra-
phie*, est une marée montante à la frontière de l'observation et du rêve, du
subconscient et de la lucidité. « La moman » et « La femme de 47 ans » de
Jacqueline Barrette (*ça-dit-qu'essa-à-dire*) sont des sagouines montréalai-
ses, durcies et rongées par la mécanisation, la publicité, les *vues sexées;*
plus gênées et plus gênantes parce que moins folkloriques : elles ne compo-
sent aucun tableau, aucun discours; elles se décomposent.

03

Si le monologuiste est un « raconteur bien ordonné qui commence par soi-même » (selon la formule de Jean-V. Dufresne), Yvon Deschamps est le mieux né et le mieux ordonné des conteurs. Il est né pauvre, *pogné*, imaginatif et un peu délinquant, typiquement montréalais, dans un quartier Saint-Henri qui évoque *Bonheur d'occasion* mais aussi le Plateau Mont-Royal de Michel Tremblay. « Mon personnage, c'est toute ma jeunesse. Et cette mentalité qui est mienne par moments. Ce sont des souvenirs du passé. Il faut que ce soit ça », dit-il dans une interview à Jean Royer. Il faut que ce soit ça au départ (*Dans ma cour* : « les seize portes s'ouvraient et les trente-deux bras se rabattaient sur les enfants »), un Deschamps refoulé a réapparu, mais aussi plus et moins que Deschamps.

Baptiste est l'ouvrier colonisé, aliéné, qui se repose et se complaît dans l'inconscience, l'asservissement, la servilité. Il se fait le domestique de son patron (« un bon *boss* »), allant jusqu'à tondre son gazon le dimanche et à accepter avec reconnaissance un verre de bière tiède. Niais, *niaiseux*, Baptiste l'est sans retenue; inspiré et bavard, il ira cependant au bout de son personnage, en découvrira les limites, les tares. Il est à l'origine d'un langage, d'un registre, d'un style, qui le traduisent tout entier, puis le trahissent, le dépassent, l'entraînent à se (re)définir. D'explication en explications, le personnage se noue et se délie, se déplie, se multiplie. Devant l'autorité, le travail, l'argent ou le bonheur, ses réactions sont attendues. Face à sa femme (morte) et à son petit, elles sont déjà plus ambiguës. Par rapport à la politique, aux mass-média, aux jeunes, à la nouvelle culture, le héros de Deschamps est nous tous, non seulement québécois mais américain, occidental. Par exemple dans *Nigger Black*, *Le Foetus*, *Cable TV*, sur la guerre et la vie, le racisme et les communications non-communicatives.

Les monologues de Deschamps naissent et se développent diversement, de l'observation aussi bien que de la mémoire, par l'écriture, le rythme, la musique. *Les Unions qu'ossa donne*, construit comme une chanson (six couplets séparés par un refrain musical), fut d'abord un sketch où Gilbert Chénier jouait l'employé et Deschamps le patron; après deux semaines, on renverse les rôles et l'improvisation fonctionne le plus naturellement du monde, si bien que l'interprète se retrouve auteur d'un texte qu'il n'a jamais rédigé. Il n'a pas écrit une seule ligne non plus du long *Cable TV* (« un *gag* », au départ). *Les Anglais*, pourtant assez subtil, fut improvisé cinq minutes avant d'entrer en scène pour le spectacle *Poèmes et chants de la Résistance*. *Le Honte* a commencé par une dizaine de phrases, enrichies peu à peu des ânonnements et des âneries de cette bonne femme (adepte des *hot lines* radiophoniques) qui trouve que les Canadiens français « i sont pas capa' d's'exprimer », et « quand i parlent, on les comprend pas ». *Pépère* et *Le Foetus*, par contre, furent rédigés d'un jet et d'une façon définitive. En général, un monologue atteint sa taille et sa forme après cinq ou six mois de vie publique. Certains se présentent comme de la provocation directe, l'agression d'un public trop bien assis, trop gentiment disposé.

« Comme la poésie de Gilles Vigneault, la prose populaire d'Yvon Deschamps se développe toujours à partir d'elle-même, sans jamais se disperser; et, avec une rigueur fascinante à saisir le fouillis presque désespérant du paradoxe et de la contradiction (. . .) Deschamps a inventé la logique pas-d'allure, l'anti-vérité, le contre-mensonge »[1]. Forçant la dose, il fait du poison un contrepoison, du somnifère un réveil. Utilisant les termes les plus terre à terre (une manifestation devient du « marchage en gang dans 'es rues »), un accent nasal, des évidences grossières, des contradictions apparentes et boiteuses — « Nous aut' on n'a jamais eu d'argent, mais ça nous a pas empêchés de travailler », où le lien causal est souligné par la coordination —, Deschamps les redresse et les fait parler. Ses pléonasmes sont délirants, ses onomatopées ont du sens, ses platitudes de l'épaisseur, ses piétinements du mouvement. Il rend audibles, presque tangibles, l'absurdité et l'absurde. *S'tessdrardinaire!* Au Père qui demande, d'une voix mal endimanchée : « Les petits gars, si on arait de l'argent, que ferions-nous-tu avec », l'enfant répond, imperturbable : « Peut-être que pourrions-nous-tu nous acheter une machine avec » (*L'Argent*). Remarquons enfin que le Bonheur et divers Proverbes ou Dictons se promènent en chair et en os, comme des vieillards fantomatiques, radoteurs, dans les monologues de Deschamps (*Le Petit Jésus* les assimile aux grands-prêtres). La personnification de l'abstrait est ici dénonciation des clichés, de la routine verbale impersonnelle.

On est pogné mais . . . ON VA S'EN SORTIR, ce titre déjà long et apparemment clair, Deschamps l'explique ou l'explicite ainsi : « On va aller se pogner dans autre chose, mais on n'a pas le choix. Et puis après, on recommencera à s'en sortir »[2]. Il n'y a d'issue et même de fait irréfutable pour personne sinon la mort, « épanouissement total de la vie », dira-t-il ailleurs. Il n'y a que des issues partielles, portes qui ouvrent sur d'autres murs et d'autres portes : l'indépendance du Québec en est une à ses yeux, comme la libération sexuelle, la syndicalisation, la tolérance, etc.

CB

François Hertel, qui fustigera plus tard le misérabilisme de Marie-Claire Biais et du groupe de *Parti pris*, se plaignait après *Tit-Coq* dans des termes analogues à ceux de Victor Barbeau, fondateur de l'Académie canadienne-française : « Notre culture est désespérément peuple! » et, ajoutait-il, « si passionnée! » Selon lui, on peut assister à des « vaudevilles » comme ceux de Gélinas (l'aurait-il dit de *Bousille*, sa meilleure pièce?) dans « n'importe quel cabaret parisien comme les Deux-Ânes ou le Théâtre de Dix-Heures ». Gérard Pelletier[3], qui rapporte ces propos de l'exilé, demande au critique de « faire la différence entre les blagues à fleur de peau des chansonniers montmartrois et le caractère profondément humain des sketches de Fridolin ». De même, le spectateur doit aujourd'hui distinguer entre des imitateurs ou chansonniers (au sens parisien) comme Jacques Normand ou Claude Landré, les Jérolas ou les Cyniques, qui s'engagent dans l'actualité la plus immédiate, et des auteurs-compositeurs comme Gilles Vigneault ou Georges Dor qui, à côté de leurs chansons, ont développé avec bonheur des monologues souvent très proches du théâtre. Ceux-là sont des caricaturistes ou des journalistes; ceux-ci sont presque des écrivains. Ils ont créé des types, des mythes, un ton. Leur *voix* est ailleurs que dans leurs cordes vocales; leur musique est dans le langage.

On pourrait encore citer des poètes, tels Miron, Chamberland, Péloquin, Duguay, Michèle Lalonde ou Michel Garneau, comme exemples de cette littérature orale et prophétique. *La Nuit de la poésie* n'était pas toujours poétique, mais elle était toujours théâtrale ou dramatique. Elle était le monologue à plusieurs voix d'un peuple[4] qui cherche à se reconnaître pour s'unir. Du libre et disparate *Show de vot' vie* (par la Quenouille bleue à la discothèque « Chez Dieu ») au *Show de la parole* où Péloquin fait reculer la mort, où Duguay fait vibrer à l'unisson, jusqu'au « boutte », jusqu'au « Toutte », la syllabe sacrée: Ommmmmmmmmmm . . . — d'un *show* à l'autre (et depuis *L'Osstidcho* de Charlebois, Forestier et Deschamps), chansons, jeux, monologues, parole et (du moins chez Duguay) silence s'intercalent et s'interpénètrent.

> J'ouvre la porte, rien.
> Je ferme la porte, rien.
> J'ouvre la porte, rien que moi-même,

gratte, frappe et joue Robert Charlebois (*Margot*).

> Car comment voulez-vous parler, chanter ou rire,
> C'que vous voudrez,
> Car comment voulez-vous c'que vous voudrez
> Quand la vie s'en est allée sans vous en parler . . . (*Le Mont Athos*)

Les « expressions occultes » du *Zirmate* de Péloquin, l'infonique ou infoniaque *Lapocalipso* de Duguay (infonie = « symphonie de l'infini »), *Sur fil métamorphose* ou *Les Oranges sont vertes*, de Gauvreau, sont-ils poèmes ou spectacles? Et les « Monologues de l'aliénation délirante » de Miron? Françoise Loranger cite justement ce poème en postface à *Médium saignant*[5] — à moins que ce ne soit en préface à cette pièce « avec un seul personnage ». (« une âme aussi nue que possible »), qu'elle rêvait d'écrire après deux pièces « collectives » :

> moi je gis muré dans la boîte crânienne dépoétisé dans ma langue et
> mon appartenance déphasé et décentré dans ma coincidence ravageur
> je fouille ma mémoire et mes chairs jusqu'en les maladies de la tourbe
> et de l'être pour trouver la trace de mes signes arrachés emportés pour
> reconnaître mon cri dans l'opacité du réel . . .

Le monologue, qu'il soit poétique, comique ou dramatique, est toujours «dépoétisé», «déphasé et décentré». Il est un mur sondé, un sol fouillé, ravagé, un cri sourd ou perçant, une blessure qui voudrait guérir sans se cicatriser.

Quand j'parl'tout seul (6000 exemplaires vendus) ou *J'parl' pour parler*, écrivait durant la Crise des années 30 Jean Narrache (pseudonyme transparent d'Émile Coderre). «J'écris pour être parlé» est le titre plus dynamique, déjà théâtral, d'un poème de jeunesse de Dubé:

> J'écris pour être parlé
> Et pour qu'il soit possible
> à mon frère inconnu
> D'entendre couler mes larmes
> et ma joie se débattre
> Entre les quatre grilles des prisons
> de mon rêve.[6]

Dire pour ne pas être dit, préfère pour sa part Gilles Derome (c'est le titre-poème de son recueil), auteur d'un *Qui est Dupressin?* qui fut, en 1962, après celles de Languirand, la première pièce antidubéenne, anti-psychologique et antiréaliste, du théâtre québécois. Dans tous les cas il s'agit cependant d'un écart entre dire et parler, entre écouter et entendre, entre écrire et créer:

> on n'ouvre pas les yeux sans tuer quelque mystère
> bénéficiant en silence
> de notre contumace,

déclare Gérald Godin dans son «Cantouque français dit du temps nouveau». Voir n'est pas regarder, n'est pas savoir. D'un oeil, d'une oreille, d'une bouche à l'autre, il y a un sous-entendu, un malentendu, un inter-dit et un interdit.

ᙯ

Le monologue joue un rôle important dans le théâtre proprement dit: dans les pièces de forme conventionnelle ou traditionnelle, davantage encore dans les structures éclatées du nouveau théâtre. Et je pense moins ici aux longues tirades, morceaux de bravoure ou professions de foi, qu'il est facile de repérer un peu partout, qu'à des recherches et expressions de soi totales, comme les confessions à la fois personnelles et historiques de la matriarche du *Temps sauvage*, de la Mère du *Marcheur*, de Jean à la fin d'*Un fils à tuer*, de *Brutus* enfin où on a l'impression que « les personnages se parlent non point pour se comprendre mais pour s'expliquer; et non point pour s'expliquer à l'autre, mais à soi ».[7]

Les drames réalistes de Dubé font une place de choix à l'oraison funèbre et amoureuse (*Zone*), à l'autoportrait des parvenus (*Bilan*), au plaidoyer quasi-judiciaire (*Au retour des oies blanches*), à l'allocution inconsciemment autocritique des séparatistes de salon (celui des *Beaux Dimanches* est célèbre). Plus significative est la courbe descendante que dessinent les dialogues des protagonistes : « l'échange verbal s'achève presque immanquablement en supplication, en aveu d'impuissance ou en cri de désespoir ».[8] La structure des pièces de Dubé est parallèle, symétrique : elle est d'ailleurs fondée sur le couple, aussi bien dans le cycle populaire que dans le cycle bourgeois de l'oeuvre. Les figures, le style sont ceux de l'inventaire, de la répétition, de la reprise, du « cercle qu'il faut rompre après en avoir fait le tour pour qu'il cesse d'être le tombeau, la cage et le vaisseau où les générations précédentes se sont trouvées emprisonnées ».[9]

La majeure partie ce de qu'on appelle le théâtre québécois n'est au fond que des monologues esquissés, esquivés, ou encore développés mais juxtaposés. Si l'intrigue (là où on en veut) est souvent lâche, le dénouement arbitraire, les dialogues maladroits et artificiels, les monologues, eux, sont le plus souvent réussis. C'est le cas non seulement de *Bien à moi, marquise* (Marie Savard), de *La Duchesse de Langeais*, de *La Sagouine*, de *Solange* (Jean Barbeau) ou du *Pierre Sigouin* de Jacques Hébert, pièces à un seul personnage, mais des *Grands Départs* et des *Violons de l'automne*, d'*Encore cinq minutes* et d'*Un cri qui vient de loin*, pièces élaborées à partir d'un ou de plusieurs monologues différés, entrecoupés, morcelés.

Ces déménagements sur place, ces transports interrompus, ces plaintes, ces espoirs, cette protestation, cette revendication, cette douleur complaisamment ou courageusement étalée, ces cris qui viennent de l'enfance, ces familles *en pièces détachées* (suivant le titre de Tremblay), ces femmes et ces hommes qui essaient de se donner un nom, un visage, ce sont des monologues en situation et en action. Leur désordre même répond à une nécessité, obéit à des lois. Le *joual* par exemple, le sacre, le blasphème, les gestes manqués, le travestissement (des sexes, des âges, des conditions sociales, des sentiments), l'auto-destruction par l'alcool, le suicide, la prostitution, l'exil. « On ne peut dire le mal, le pourrissement, l'écoeurement dans un langage serein, correct; il faut que mes paroles soient ébranlées dans leur fondement même, par le déstructuration qui est celle du langage commun, de la vie de tous ».[10]

Il devient de plus en plus évident, à mesure que ses pièces sont créées, que la production de Michel Tremblay n'est pas due au hasard ou au miracle. Des *Belles-soeurs* à *Marie-Lou* une unité et une progression organiques s'imposent au spectateur et au lecteur. Le théâtre de Tremblay a des principes de construction solides et précis : non pas d'abord le *joual*, le personnage féminin ou le cadre montréalais (cuisine, taverne, club), mais cette forme (thème et structure) qu'est le monologue. Lorsqu'il évoque les influences qui l'ont marqué, Tremblay mentionne Gélinas, Dubé, les choeurs grecs, Beckett, « le plus grand », et, inattendu, Shakespeare, « à cause de mon grand amour pour les monologues qui n'en finissent plus ».[11] La Duchesse de Langeais, « plus femme que toutes les femmes ! », commère, vaniteuse, perverse, masochiste, « une grande artiste » dans son genre, n'en finit plus d'imiter et de s'imiter, de faire du théâtre dans le théâtre et des oeillades, des apartés dans le monologue. La Berthe des *Trois petits tours* sait qu'elle ne sortira jamais de sa cage de verre de caissière. Le « Showtime ! Showtime ! » du *doorman* (au « Coconut Inn ») n'est pas pour elle, mais elle tient, sans illusion, à ce qu'on lui laisse ses illusions : « Qu'on me sacre la paix, pis qu'on me laisse rêver ! C'est tout ce qui me reste ! » Cela, elle le fait très bien, se donnant la réplique avec une verve triste, consciente de son retard et de ses limites, et pourtant capable de s'inventer « une vraie vie de vraie Star d'Hollywood ! » Dans *A toi pour toujours, ta Marie-Lou,* dédicace effacée d'une photo jaunie, le quatuor est divisé par couples : le père et la mère, l'un devant ses bouteilles de bière vides, l'autre son tricot sur les genoux ; les deux filles, la célibataire casanière et la chanteuse *western* soi-disant émancipée. Tous sont immobiles dans leur espace respectif (sauf cette dernière, Carmen) et fixés (au sens psychanalytique) sur une époque et des événements passés. Cadavres en sursis qui racontent, préparent et (re) vivent au ralenti leur mort. Manon répète sa mère, Carmen reprend le geste désespéré de son père : l'anéantissement du noyau familial (un accident-suicide emporte Leopold, Marie-Louise et l'enfant qu'elle portait).

Le phénomène est particulièrement visible dans les spectacles les plus récents, qu'il s'agisse de revues improvisées et éphémères comme *Finies les folies !* (contre le projet de loi 63) ou *Hello Police*, de créations (plus ou moins) collectives comme celles du Théâtre du Même Nom et du Grand Cirque Ordinaire, ou de pièces proprement dites, lues au Centre d'essai des Auteurs dramatiques : *Dimi*, de Marc-F. Gélinas, *Les Pigeons d'Arlequin*, de Michel Gréco, « western intérieur », « théâtre de la lucidité sur soi-même, théâtre d'introspection », *Triangle à une voix* ou ce *Geste parlé*, d'André Caron, qui présente son oeuvre comme « l'art de ne pas dire ce qu'on a à dire et prendre quarante millions de détours pour y arriver ». *Wouf Wouf* aussi, la machinerie-revue de Sauvageau, est un monologue intérieur traduit en parodies, en parades, en numéros de cirque, peuplé de rêves concrets, d'actions simultanées et contradictoires, parcouru surtout par un intense désir et des besoins élémentaires : la faim, la soif, l'envie d'aller pisser et de lancer, libre comme l'air, le cri de Tarzan : « Haaaaaaaaaaaaaa . . . !!! »

Nos monologues sont très proches des bulles et du trait des bandes dessinées, où l'important est ce qui est absent, suggéré, et que le spectateur ajoute, imagine, comme le reconnaît Deschamps. Jean Barbeau est l'auteur de *Solange*, confession d'une ex-religieuse, d'un *Goglu* immobile et masturbatoire, et d'autre part des quatorze stations au poste de police d'un *Chemin de Lacroix*[12] laïcisé, et d'un *Ben-Ur* (*Benoît-Urbain* Théberge) qui passe de l'album de famille à *Zorro, The Lone Ranger*, etc. « C'est de valeur que tous ces héros-là soient américains . . . Pas que j'en ai contre les Américains, mais . . . il me semble que ce serait plus l'fun si . . . si on avait les nôtres, nos héros . . . ».[13] En attendant qu'on se décide entre Dollard des Ormeaux et Chénier, Ben-Ur collectionne les joueurs de hockey et est bien content de jouer du revolver dans un uniforme gris-bleu d'agent de la *Brook's* (« Sécurité depuis 1867 . . . »).

03

« Notre theâtre, dans sa forme la plus spontanée, ressemble à une soirée de famille », observait Jean-Claude Germain, dont l'équipe, le T.M.N., produisit un *Diguidi, diguidi, ha! ha! ha!* où la « sainte trinité québécoise », *son* père, *sa* mère et *son* fils, est amenée à quitter sa chaise et à marcher à quatre pattes. Avant et jusque dans l'obscurité finale, la Mère prononce : « Je veux plus avoir pitié de personne . . . je suis tannée de passer ma vie à m'excuser . . . Je sais pas pourquoi je parle mais y faut que je continue (. . .) Je veux être libre tout court . . . je veux être liiiiibbbrrreeee . . . je veux être libre de le dire sans avoir à le crier . . . » *Laver son linge sale* (en famille) était d'ailleurs le titre d'un montage de scènes choisies par André Brassard, et qui allaient d'Henry Deyglun au T.M.N. Même dans un radiothéâtre aussi symboliste que *Les Invités au procès*, d'Anne Hébert, l'homme qui, « pour s'être réservé un seul petit placard pour son linge sale, se croit à l'abri de la crasse pour le restant de ses jours », devra admettre qu'on lave son linge sale en famille. « La Fête de Fridolin », un des meilleurs sketches sur le titi montréalais, se terminait par le rappel hygiénico-moral de la mère à son fils : « Fridolin, c'est samedi à soir . . . Ça fait qu'avant de te coucher, donne ton coeur au Bon Dieu, puis jette ton corps au linge sale ». *Corps* voulait dire maillot de corps, mais l'ambiguïté est savoureuse.

Une soirée de famille, c'est toujours un remue-ménage, un lavage de têtes et de sous-vêtements, un *brassage* du refoulé qu'on refoule encore. Ce sont des épanchements et des confidences, des retraites et des agressions, de longs silences brutalement rompus, des incompréhensions et des discours parallèles. Peu de véritables dialogues, conversations et discussions. On défend moins un point de vue qu'on ne se défend soi-même, globalement. Les affirmations sont des affirmations de soi. On raconte des histoires et on raconte son histoire. Avec attendrissement et fureur, gêne et sans-gêne, de façon aussi drôle que pathétique.

Faut-il rattacher cette façon de faire (ou de se représenter) à une tradition orale particulièrement riche, reprise dans le domaine du conte par un Ferron, un Thériault, un Carrier? Sans doute, mais cette tradition elle-même doit être reliée à certains aspects de notre géographie et de notre histoire: l'isolement des rangs et des fermes, la rigueur de l'hiver, la longueur des voyages, l'exil saisonnier des forestiers, etc. Les temps faibles et monotones étaient ici brusquement coupés par des temps forts, des fêtes, aussi rares que violents. La parole éclatait soudain après des jours, des mois de solitude et de silence. À ce propos, la mise en scène de *La Guerre, yes sir!*, de Carrier, contrairement à ce qu'ont noté des chroniqueurs, paraît tout à fait appropriée à la pièce et à la tradition. Cette alternance, voire cette coexistence sur le plateau d'une toile grisâtre, d'un espace vide, démesuré (à la Lemieux), et d'autre part de scènes intérieures débordantes de vie, de couleurs, de mangeaille et de passions (un Massicotte brueghelisé), rend très bien compte de ce double rythme: ralenti jusqu'à l'immobilité, accéléré jusqu'au tourbillon.

Nous pouvons passer sans transition de la guerre de la Conquête à la soumission, de la résistance passive à la Révolte de 1837–38, de la Confédération parlementaire aux plébiscites anti-conscriptionnistes, du duplessisme à cette réforme agitée qu'on a appelée la Révolution tranquille ou *The Not So Quiet Revolution*, comme du jeûne à l'ivresse, du cléricalisme à l'indifférence religieuse, de la glace au soleil. « Faire la révolution, c'est sortir du dialogue dominé-dominateur; à proprement parler, c'est divaguer. Le terroriste parle tout seul », explique Hubert Aquin; « au théâtre ne doivent monologuer que les personnages qui hésitent indéfiniment, qui se trouvent aux prises avec la solitude déformante du révolutionnaire ou de l'aliéné. Il n'y a de monologues vrais que dans l'incohérence. L'incohérence dont je parle ici est une des modalités de la révolution, autant que le monologue en constitue le signe immanquable ».[14]

☙

Le monologue est par excellence l'aire et l'art de l'antihéros, du sous-personnage, de l'individu émietté et perdu. Ses parcelles d'humanité sont d'autant plus émouvantes qu'elles sont dérisoires.[15] Ne cherchant pas à nous en imposer, la voix des monologues, cassée, rugueuse, répétitive et toujours chaude, s'impose à elle-même, se découvre une histoire, parfois un corps (pour la souffrance) et un visage (pour le rire). « J'ai l'impression que toutes les grandes tragédies québécoises vont être drôles (. . .), comme si notre plus grand malheur était arrivé en 1763 et que plus rien de pire ne peut maintenant arriver. Ça ne va peut-être pas si mal. Et c'est peut-être comme ça qu'on est universel. *Notre douleur voit grand.* On n'est pas tout seuls. On en voit d'autres qui sont mal pris », déclare Jean Barbeau dans la préface à son *Chemin de Lacroix*. « Bonheur, viens-t'en, viens-t-en vite, parce que moi je m'en vas! . . . », criait Deschamps à la fin de son monologue le plus naïvement tragique. Qui est menacé de disparaître? L'homme et son milieu, sa collectivité (sa nation) indissociablement.

Le monologue est toujours la voix de plusieurs en un seul, le silence de tous en chacun. Il est délesté et lourd, fragile et tenace, sorte de mémoire du futur au passé, ou d'imagination à partir d'un réel invraisemblable. Le monologue est tout entier présent et actuel, parole ou silence irrécusables, mais il déporte constamment l'attention vers ce qui aurait pu ne pas être, vers ce qui pourrait être autrement. Interrogation, exclamation ou points de suspension, il ne connaît pas le mot FIN. Noeud sans dénouement, sa structure est l'attente, le recommencement (donc l'espoir), même si son thème est la fatalité, l'impuissance, l'emprisonnement, l'angoisse. Le monologue québécois vit de ces contradictions entre la forme et le fond, l'instinct et la conscience, le quotidien et l'événement. Est-il destin ou libération? Il se nourrit du théâtre et de l'histoire (et il les nourrit) en attendant que ceux-ci, pour un temps, le remplacent.

Notes

1. Jean-V. Dufresne, « Deschamps quatre », dans *Actualité sur scène*, programme du spectacle de l'automne 1970 à la Place des Arts. — Voir, du même auteur, *Yvon Deschamps*, Montréal, Les Presses de l'Université du Québec, « Studio », 1971.

2. Programme du spectacle. Supplément de *Québec-Presse*, 6 février 1972, 3. — *On n'est pas sorti du bois* est le titre d'une comédie musicale distanciée, exorcisante, critique, de Dominique de Pasquale (Montréal, Leméac, « Répertoire québécois », 1972). Gilbert David note dans sa présentation : « Le Théâtre "québécois" n'en finit pas d'achever le Canadien Français : c'est un meurtre légitime qui ressemble à un suicide » (7). « Avec les sauvages, c'est le cri de guerre que je vais lancer », dit Pet-le-feu, un des trois personnages trop blancs, trop pâles de *Lendemain d'la veille*, monologues d'Odette Gagnon.

3. « Culture peuple », *Le Devoir*, 12 février 1949, 9.

4. Gérald Godin disait, à propos de la tournée « engagée » de Mouloudji (célébrant le Paris de 1870) et des *Poèmes et chants de la Résistance II* (après nos « événements d'octobre ») : « la différence c'est que notre Commune nous la vivons actuellement. »

5. Montréal, Leméac, « Théâtre canadien », 1970 — La critique du *Montreal Star* voyait d'ailleurs *Médium saignant* comme une non-pièce, un non-spectacle, « *a prolonged cry of frustrated rage* », « *an exorcism of fear and a litany of hate* ». « Si vous ne pouvez pas parler, criez! », conclut Loranger (139).

6. Marcel Dubé, *Textes et documents*, Montréal, Leméac, « Théâtre canadien D-I », 1968, 14.

7. Jean Éthier-Blais, « Le *Théâtre* de Paul Toupin », *Le Devoir*, 16 décembre 1961, 12.

8. Maximilien Laroche, *Marcel Dubé*, Montréal, Fides, « Ecrivains canadiens d'aujourd'hui » 1970, 100.

[9] *Ibid.*, 112.

[10] Paul Chamberland, « Dire ce que je suis », *Parti pris*, vol. III, no. 5, janvier 1965, 36.

[11] « Entrevue avec Michel Tremblay », *Nord*, vol. I, no. 1, automne 1971, 69.

[12] « Ça parle, la majorité silencieuse (. . .) Ça parle mal, ça parle pas fort, ça parle pas directement aux autres, mais ça parle . . . Si vous alliez dans les endroits où ça se ramasse, vous entendriez . . . » (*Le Chemin de Lacroix* suivi de *Goglu*, Montréal, Leméac, « Répertoire québécois », 1971, 49).

[13] *Ben-Ur*, Montréal, Leméac, « Répertoire québécois », 1971, 98. — Albert Millaire, directeur du Théâtre Populaire du Québec, rappelle le principal élément de sa mise en scène : « Nous avons assis le personnage de Ben à l'avant-scène, nous lui avons donné un carton plein de *comics*, nous lui avons réservé un bon projecteur, et c'est là que s'est engagé le grand monologue du début de la deuxième partie. *Ce grand monologue a été mis en pièces et nous nous en sommes servi au début et tout au long de la représentation* ». (*Ibid.*, 5–6. C'est moi qui souligne.)

[14] « Profession : écrivain », *Parti pris*, vol. I, no. 4, janvier 1964, 27.

[15] Récemment, chez *Sol* (Seul), doux et auguste clown de Marc Favreau.

CL 58 (Autumn 1973)

Susan Knutson

From Marichette to Rosealba and La Sagouine: A Genealogy au féminin for Acadian Theatre[1]

As the organizers of the celebrated booklaunch for *La Sagouine*[2] must have realized, Antonine Maillet's Sagouine can appear as a curious anomaly in Acadian theatre history; indeed, it can appear as an embarrassing reminder of the poverty and unremitting labour which once marked the lives of too many Acadian women. It is true that a theatrical tradition described in terms of a highly educated male élite — Marc Lescarbot, Senator Pascal Poirier, Mgr. Marcel-François Richard or Father Camille Lefebvre — cannot account for a Sagouine who is working-class, female, and educated strictly in the school of hard knocks. My essay, however, takes issue with Zénon Chiasson's suggestion that, "le théâtre d'Antonine Maillet demeure un cas à part du théâtre acadien. La dimension de cette oeuvre la propulse dans les rangs du répertoire universel et nous oblige à chercher . . . ailleurs les signes de notre identité théâtrale" ("Fragments" 63). On the contrary, the Sagouine is the most brilliant representative of a popular Acadian theatrical tradition which has flourished since the late nineteenth century, as Pierre Gérin and Pierre M. Gérin have suggested.[3] This essay seeks to contribute to a more complete understanding of this tradition.

Scholars, notably Jean-Claude Marcus and Roger Lacerte, have explored the rapport between Acadian collégial theatre and the popular, oral domain of *le conteur*, but the dynamism and the persistence of Acadian oral culture have yet, perhaps, to be fully appreciated. Academic accounts have also tended to overlook the fact that whereas the literary theatrical tradition is heavily dominated by men, the oral tradition has included women.

The oversight is not surprising, given that oral traditions and women's lives often escape documentation altogether. With respect to theatre history, it must be remembered that popular activities, theatrical in the broadest sense, are only historicized insofar as they encounter literary habits and institutions. As I shall show, it is precisely through such encounters that a vibrant Acadian tradition of Sagouinesque monologists can be discerned. While performances (apart from those of Viola Léger) are local and occasional, and scripts, if they exist, remain unpublished, this tradition is nonetheless a striking feature of contemporary, popular Acadian culture. Rosealba, the Sagouine of the Baie Sainte-Marie, as she has often been called, is of particular interest both because of the passionate following she inspires in her home community and because of the literary quality of her monologues. Other contemporary Sagouines include Lonice and Françoise, "les deux vieilles Sagouines [sic] de Pombcoup [Pubnico-Ouest])" (*Le Petit Courrier*, le 29 avril 1976, 1), and Sophie-Anne, "la Sagouine de Chéticamp" (*Le Courrier*, le 20 avril 1979, 10).

We must ask whether the existence of local Sagouines testifies more to the influence of Antonine Maillet than to that of a prior, or parallel, oral tradition. Certainly Maillet's Sagouine has been imitated; we read, for example, that "La Chandeleur se fête avec Gapi et la Sagouine" in Margeree, Cape Breton, with a photo of two local people dressed up and dancing in old-time costume (*Le Courrier*, le 8 février, 1979, 1–2).[4] Nevertheless, however brilliant her success, Maillet's character cannot have inspired all the Sagouines in Acadie. Rosealba came on the scene before her, in 1962, although the early Rosealba resembled Maillet's Sagouine less closely than the Rosealba of today.[5] Other, earlier monologists are comparable: Marguerite à Yutte, from L'Anse-des-LeBlanc; Marie-Marthe Dugas, from Station-du-Petit-Ruisseau; and, a generation before, Fannie Thériault, originally from Rivière-aux-Saumons, who lived for many years in Lower Saulnierville. Suzanne Deveau, "la grande Souqui" of Chéticamp, Cape Breton, is remembered by Anselme Boudreau as a "très bonne conteuse" known to him in his youth (193). Already elderly in 1908, Suzanne Deveau would have been a senior contemporary of Émilie Leblanc, the author of a remarkable series of monologues of which we have considerably more evidence, since they were published, under the *nom de plume* of Marichette. Pierre Gérin and Pierre M. Gérin have brought to light the story of how, from 1895 to 1898, Marichette signed a series of letters to Valentin Landry, the editor of *Évangéline*, while her creator, Emilie Leblanc, resided in Chéticamp (Saint-Alphonse), Clare. Marichette's kinship with Maillet's Sagouine is clearly noted by the scholars who rediscovered her:

> Ces lettres sont une mine d'or pour le linguiste, pour l'historien, pour
> le sociologue, car elles exposent les problèmes de l'instruction, de

> l'assimilation, du chômage, la corruption politique, le rôle de l'Eglise,
> la misérable condition et les aspirations de la femme. Le style, la
> truculence de la langue, les thèmes, la rhétorique de la protestation
> annoncent la Sagouine. (P. Gérin 38)

It may seem paradoxical that an enterprise which seeks to describe an oral
theatrical tradition should take as evidence the non-theatrical writing of a
highly-educated, middle-class woman such as Emilie Leblanc. Marichette's
literary medium, however, does not so much set her apart as confirm the
fact that the female monologists of whom we have any knowledge each
signify in some way the complex but fruitful encounter between women,
the oral traditions in which women played an important part, and the
predominantly masculine domain of higher education.

In this context, it is worth recalling that both Antonine Maillet and Viola Léger began their careers as professors at Notre-Dame d'Acadie; both
were, therefore, among the first generation of women to have a real impact
on the classical theatrical traditions within the colleges.[6] Antonine Maillet,
in *Les Confessions de Jeanne de Valois*, describes the theatre classes held at
the first *collège classique* for girls, in Memramcook, New Brunswick, as
the professors and students alike immersed themselves in their French
heritage and made it their own:

> Les images qui me trottent dans la mémoire sont celles d'un François
> Villon qui bat les pavés de Paris en égrenant les plus beaux vers
> français; celles de la farce de Maître Pathelin que nos comédiennes
> montaient comme si la pièce leur avait été dédiée. (184)

Zénon Chiasson points out the accomplishments during the late 1950s of
the award-winning theatre company of Notre-Dame d'Acadie, under the
direction of Antonine Maillet ("L'Institution" 752–53).

Émilie Leblanc, the creator of Marichette, also studied at Memramcook.
"Puis elle était allée à l'École normale de Fredericton, où elle avait eu la
chance d'être l'élève du célèbre professeur Alphée Belliveau" (Gérin and
Gérin, *Manchette* 39). She must have been impressed with his enlightened
views regarding the authenticity of Acadian French, as with the ideas of
Pascal Poirier who at that time was publishing his first monographs on the
parler franco-acadien. A writer and an intellectual, Emilie Leblanc lived at
a time when women, and perhaps particularly Acadian women, had almost no access to the public world, yet she was a natural leader of the
Acadian cultural revival taking place in her generation. She was the only
woman to succeed in having her views in support of women's suffrage
published in *Évangéline* (Gallant 5). Her upbringing and her education
must have given her the sense that a new era was dawning, but a tragic

love affair led her abruptly to a brutal encounter with the common lot of women (Gérin 1984). It was after this that she took up her pen to write in the name of Marichette, speaking through the persona, and in the popular idiom of an uneducated woman, as Antonine Maillet would choose to do eighty years later.

As Pierre Gérin remarks, Marichette's use of popular or colloquial language takes on sharp significance in passages treating of politics, myth, or religion, where the subject matter locates her unmistakably in the discursive domain of the educated elite. It is in such passages that her parodic audacity becomes clear: "La belle ordonnance ronflante de la langue classique, dans laquelle se complaisaient les orateurs et les écrivains de cette époque, est brisée, disloquée" (Gérin, "Une Écrivaine" 44). If the violence with which some of Marichette's detractors denounced her writing is thus made more understandable,[7] we can equally better appreciate from this perspective the contribution Emilie Leblanc made to an Acadian Renaissance which would eventually lead to greater respect both for local varieties of French and for women (Gérin, *Une Écriviane* 44). Marichette's use of Acadian French is no more folkloric or sentimental than la Sagouine's triple disruption of the classical theatrical traditions which — from the neo-classical masque of Marc Lescarbot to the century of collégial theatre documented by Laurent Lavoie, Roger Lacerte, Jean-Claude Marcus, René LeBlanc and Micheline Laliberté — had elided any representation of women, working-class life, or non-standard French.[8]

Rosealba, too, has evolved through the encounter between popular, oral traditions and those of the colleges and the Church. The first Rosealba performance which I have been able to locate took place around a campfire at the Colonie de la Jeunesse Acadienne (C.J.A.), at the Baie Sainte-Marie in the summer of 1962, the year the camp was first open to girls. On that occasion, Rosealba was played by Sister Thérèse Robichaud, who based her performance on a script written by an unidentified person (Robichaud). Cécile LeBlanc Poirier learned it there, and later performed it herself (Poirier). A little later, someone, probably a nun, passed the text to Anne-Marie Comeau, who performed it a number of times (Comeau). Michel Thibault heard it as a child, in the spring of 1964, and later, in 1973 or '74, he began to collaborate with Anne-Marie Comeau to recreate Rosealba as an older woman with nineteen children (Thibault, Personal Interview). The Rosealba productions of 1994 and 1995 were collaborations of Anne-Marie Comeau, Michel Thibault, Charlene Déraspe and Marie-Adèle Deveau, and the texts also drew on a series of community interviews. As theatre, Rosealba draws on a wide range of talents and skills, but it is also true to say that the monologues are inspired by an entwining of the oral traditions of Saulnierville Station with the influences of the Church, specifically of *Les Filles de Jésus* in Saulnierville, and with modem educational practices generally. That this influence is characterized in the monologues as both negative and positive — both humiliating and uplifting — underlines the extent to which we are looking not only at instances of influence and education but also at difference and resistance, equally evident in the monologues of Marichette and *La Sagouine*.

The encounter between women, higher education and oral tradition is also evident in the theatre of "les deux vieilles Sagouines [sic] de Pombcoup." Lonice and Françoise are dramatizations of traditional Acadian women. They are played by two modern women, Caroline d'Entremont and Lucile d'Entremont, who see their theatre as a means of educating and entertaining their community while preserving traditional knowledge and skills such as butter-making and weaving (d'Entremont and d'Entremont).

The Chéticamp storyteller known to Anselme Boudreau as "la grande Souqui" was another highly literate participant in oral Acadian traditions. As a young person, Suzanne Deveau read a great deal, and later in her life, although she was visually impaired, she could still recite Molière by heart. Boudreau comments, "Elle ne contait pas seulement des contes; elle racontait presque mot à mot des histoires qu'elle avait lues durant sa jeunesse. Je me rappelle de deux: *Le médecin malgré lui*, de Molière, qu'elle appelait l'histoire de Sganarelle et Martine, et le roman *Un de perdu, deux de retrouvés*, qu'elle appelait l'histoire de Pierre et saint Luc" (193). Insofar as Suzanne Deveau was a storyteller and not, like Rosealba or Maillet's Sagouine, the dramatization of a storyteller, she seems closer to a predominantly oral tradition. We can only speculate, however, on the paths she might have taken were it not for her disability.

Of the monologists and storytellers whom I am examining in this essay, only Fannie Thériault (b. 3 April 1886) could be said to belong to a truly oral tradition. Curiously, she describes herself not as a *conteuse*, and even less as an actress, but as follows: "moi, je suis une personne qui est intense — je parle beaucoup, je grouille beaucoup, je chante beaucoup" (Thériault). Significantly, Fannie — unlike the others — has no persona but speaks in her own name. In effect, she is closer to the reality which Rosealba and the Sagouine represent, a discovery which suggests that ultimately, one aspect of the oral heritage is this character-type: the poor, old woman who speaks in the idiom of her people. We might say that insofar as Fannie was innocent of this character-type, she was closer to the reality it replaces and recreates. As for Émilie Leblanc, insofar as she animated the character-type, she can be unproblematically placed in proximity to the oral tradition we are tracing.

Antonine Maillet has always described herself as a "conteuse, directement issue d'un lignage de conteurs oraux, j'appartiens à la littérature orale" (1977: 207). She has explained clearly, and René LeBlanc has underlined, the extent to which her work stands at the crossroads of the oral and the written traditions: "je me situe à la jointure de la tradition orale et de l'écriture" (cited in LeBlanc 1985: 58). She has many times insisted on the reality of the Sagouine's referents. In a 1973 interview with Anne Girard, she delineates the major themes which circulate around the question of her famous character's origins: first, the question of class ("les gens d'en bas"), and the imperative to give a literary voice to those who have been silenced; second, the reality of the Sagouinian referent which is affirmed on two levels, that of the individual, and that of the type, "parce qu'elle est à multiples exemplaires." In another interview, Maillet explains that the Sagouine is based on two or possibly three actual women (see Scully). Local tradition at the Baie Sainte-Marie has it that the third model for the Sagouine is none other than Marguerite à Yutte (Belliveau), to whom Antonine Maillet and Rita Scalabrini refer in *Acadie pour quasiment rien* (11). Maillet interviewed Marguerite à Yutte in the late sixties, during the period when she interviewed several other people at the Baie, including Capitain Sullivan, of Meteghan, who was, of course, a model for her character, Sullivan (Muriel Comeau).

Maillet has explained that the Sagouine represents a disinherited class of people, which is clearly the case. In the context of this enquiry into Acadian monologue traditions, however, it is clear that she also re-presents the character-type of the older, working woman who has the vision, energy and language to articulate reality on behalf of her community, and who therefore enables that community to affirm its Rabelaisian heritage, and laugh. Fannie Thériault, it seems, was in fact that type of woman, suggesting that the type is in one sense an objective referent, and that such women live within the community with a relatively low degree of self-consciousness. Marguerite à Yutte may be another example;[9] and Antonine Maillet has created several fictional counterparts such as "la veuve à Calixte" in *Mariaagélas*. On another level, however, the type is a consciously adopted persona which gives permission for some individuals to speak, and to speak freely, about what they know most deeply. Clearly the persona serves as a strategy in this sense for Anne-Marie Comeau, Marie-Adèle Deveau, Michel Thibault and Charlene Déraspe, who become Rosealba; for Caroline and Lucille D'Entremont, who become Lonice and Françoise, and for Émilie Leblanc, who became Marichette. The shared referent and common experience associated with this character-type are responsible for the strong sense of correspondence which unites the monologues of *La Sagouine* with Marichette's letters and Rosealba's monologues, and which explains the immediate recognition of connection and similarity experienced, for example, by Anne-Marie Comeau when she was introduced to the letters of Marichette (Anne-Marie Comeau).

It is worth noting, too, that to a significant extent the monologists share the subject matter of Acadian daily life from a woman's perspective. Maillet's Sagouine and Rosealba, in particular, describe life during the Depression, when many people lived on the threshold of subsistence. Rosealba gives a comic description of this period in the following monologue from the 1994 spectacle, "Rosealba nous parle":

> J'avions point de welfare dans mon temps. Si tu pouvais point t'occuper
> de toi-même t'allais à la Poor House. Nous autres faulait que ça
> raguernit et rien que tu tires là-bas. C't'affaire de recycling, là . . . ce
> n'est pas les Anglais qu'ont commencé ça! Ça fait des années que je
> raccommode, que je rapièce, que je raguerne pour épargner! J'en ai lavé
> des sacs à scallop pour faire des lavettes ou des caneçons. J'en ai teindu
> de la cottounade avec du jus de bettes pour faire des rideaux. J'ai même
> fait des chemises avec des sacs de farine, quand j'pouvais en trouver qui
> étaient encore faits de butonne. Y avait un des enfants qui était assez
> grous — je crois que c'était Nastasse — . Pour une chemise pour lui ça
> prenait deux sacs de 100 livres. Une de ces chemises ça dit PURITY en
> avant et ROBIN HOOD en arrière. Il était faraud de ça! Y savait point
> quoi ça disait. Y pouvait point lire. (Thibault and Déraspe)

Rosealba's monologue communicates not only the economies and life-skills of a leaner time, but also the humour that sees her through. She has a sweeter personality than the Sagouine. Maillet has commented that, "la Sagouine est une révolutionnaire sans aigreur contre l'injustice qu'elle reconnaît. Elle est debout mais elle accepte son rôle. C'est ce qui fait à la fois sa grandeur et sa misère" (Royer 47). Rosealba, too, is "sans aigreur," but she is perhaps less revolutionary and certainly not as grand. Indeed, she can seem quite childish, yet her observations are often profound.

Curiously, she is less accepting of injustice. This can be seen in the 1995 monologue which recalls her brother who died in the war (Thibault and Déraspe). Of his induction, she explains, "A c'te temps là on avait besoin de passer des tests pour sawoir si t'avais assez de compernure pour aller te battre." When she accompanies him to Halifax on the train, she wonders "pourquoi c'qu'on célébrait de même pour envoyer nos hoummes se battre dans les vieux pays . . . se faire estropier." These comments, delivered quite innocently, are initially comic. However, when the letter announcing her brother's death arrives, the monologue ends in searing empathy with "Mamme [qui] pourrait jamais accepter ça." The silence which follows in effect reframes Rosealba's earlier remarks about the war, first seen as slightly ridiculous, but now recognized as an outbreak of unacceptable violence within the social order. Rosealba also expresses anger at other injustices: when her son loses a job as a Bingo caller because he doesn't know English — "there's no E in BINGO!" (English in the original) — or when she herself, as a young girl, misses her confirmation basically because her family was so poor. As Michel Thibault notes, her anger is both astute and comic. "Through the laughter run . . . poverty and tragedy. Her innocent comments convey such a strong social message" (Thibault, Telephone Interview). The Sagouine recognizes herself to be "une citoyenne à part enchère (ce qui est moins gros que la part 'entière')" (Royer 47). Rosealba does not express this class consciousness, although her monologues overflow with details of daily life as a poor member of a minority culture. The world she projects is, for the most part, whole and warm and funny. As the cliché would have it, she is rich in the things that matter most.

Behind the figures of Marichette, the Sagouine and Rosealba, we discern the intelligence, strength and humour of Acadian women. Acadian working- and middle-class class women prior to the mid-twentieth century performed a tremendous amount of work daily, as Anselme Boudreau explains in his chapter on "L'ouvrage des Femmes": "Autrefois, à Chéticamp, les femmes travaillaient bien plus que les femmes d'aujourd'hui" (130). Among other tasks, such as working for the church and educating their children, they produced wool fabric by hand, beginning with the care of the sheep; and from this they sewed and knitted; they made quilts and carpets for their large families. In addition to helping with the farm labour, harvesting and plowing, for example, they grew large kitchen gardens, and put aside and stored all kinds of food; they took care of pigs, chickens, and cows; they milked, and made cheese and butter, sausage and headcheese; they washed all the clothing and bedding by hand, and they scrubbed their houses, floors and walls; they made soap; and of course they cooked, washed dishes, and bore many children. It is astonishing that in addition to all this, some women found the time and the energy to play the violin or the organ,[10] or to read widely.

Yet they did. Suzanne Deveau, for example, was married to Polite à Marine LeBlanc, a man whom Boudreau describes as "pas très . . . industrieux" (193). Susanne raised her four sons in extreme poverty; at the time that Anselme knew her, she did not have a home of her own but lived and eventually died in the homes of others. One of her sons was somewhat lacking in "compernure" — to borrow a word from Rosealba, who has the same problem with her son Thaddée — but the other three went on to become well-educated and successful. Unfortunately, all three moved to the United States. In her old age, Anselme would read to her, and Souqui, in exchange, would tell him stories that sometimes went on for days. While some women played music and others made beautiful quilts, many, like Suzanne Deveau, turned to an art which could be practised at the same time as domestic work — talking.

In this context, it is worth noting that the most exuberant exploit mentioned by Fannie Thériault during her interview was performed during a "quiltine" of women working together to clean the Saulnierville Church:

On faisait une quiltine pour laver l'église, et p'is, y avait une chaise
pour prêcher, là, vous savez.

[Quelqu'un dit]: "Qui ce qui va laver la chaise?" Bien, c'est Fannie
qui va laver la chaise.

Père Castonguay [s'est dit]: "Je vais aller me cacher dans la sacristie
parce qu'elle va faire quelque bassesse."

J'ai monté dans la chaise, j'ai commencé à décrier les vendeux de
grog, p'is, mon ami, j'la contais ça d'Iong et d'travars . . . Quand j'ai
bien fini là, quand j'ai commencé à laver la chaise, il a sorti de là-
dedans . . . (Thériault)

This spontaneous celebration of popular theatre reveals several noteworthy
characteristics. The first is the fact that it occurs within the context of communal work. As was often the case, the work was gender-specific; here, the
women are working together to clean the Saulnierville Church. In the story
of Louise à Dan, below, it is the men who are working together in the
woods. Second is the fact that the church occupies a central place in the
culture. Third, and bearing in mind that Fannie was a well-known bootleg-
ger, we note the presence of parody. It is a very gentle parody, however,
since apparently not even the priest was offended.

In Louise à Dan's story, the parodic element is equally delicately posed;
in fact, the occasion could just as well be described as a "messe blanche,"
the sincere celebration of church ritual in the absence of a priest:

J'étions à Darthmouth à logger p'is du temps de la messe tous les
dimanches avant-midis, Freddie à William disait le chapelet. Je nous
mettions tous de genoux, parce que je pouvions point aller à l'église. Je
savions pas où était l'église. Après dîner ils alliont su' un nègre à
Preston s'acheter un gallon de bière p'is ils amenions ça à la camp. Y
boivions ça et Dan disait à Freddie de nous faire un prône. Freddie
allait dehors . . . y avait des buches . . . C'te gars-là pouvait prêcher. Les
hoummes alliont dehors demi grogués . . . Ils arrachiont leurs calottes
de su' leur tête . . . et ils écoutiont Freddie. (Louise à Dan Comeau)

Parodic imitation of the "gens d'en haut" has always been the prerogative
of the "gens d'en bas," and such is the case here. These two parodies, however, have their end not in revolution, but in laughter.

A parodic element is more evident in the monologues of Rosealba than
in either Marichette or the Sagouine, perhaps because live theatre lends
itself more easily to parody than the written word or the radio monologue.
Mime, mimicry and dance are masterfully handled by Anne-Marie Comeau
who, as Rosealba, easily slips from one persona to another. For example,
during the 1995 monologue on the Festival Acadien, she recalls the visit of

Princess Margaret to the Baie Sainte-Marie, and then, simply becomes her:

> Croireriez-vous que je me souvonne du Premier Festival en 1955?
> J'm'en souvonne par rapport que c'était l'année que Princesse
> Marguerite de l'Angleterre avait venu.
>   [Rosealba devient Princess Mar.: chapeau-tiara]
>   "So nice to be here among you loyal Acadian subjects.
>   "I just adore your purée de râpure.
>   "Je suis très contente d'être ici en cette occasion de fierté, de festivité,
> de loyauté, de bonté et de Red Rose thé . . .
>   Elle n'avait pas vraiment dit ça mais c'est de-même que j'm'en
> souvonne. (Thibault and Déraspe)

There is also, in Rosealba, a good deal that is not parodic but is simply funny and familial, representing the kind of talking that mothers do with their children. Indeed, Michel Thibault has suggested that for him, his mother is a primary influence in the creation of Rosealba:

> Les histoires que je raconte, ce sont des histoires que j'ai entendues
> de ma mère. . . . Le sens de l'humour de Rosealba, c'est le sens de
> l'humour de ma mère. Ma mère était très comique. Elle faisait rire tout
> le monde . . . elle pouvait beaucoup, beaucoup rire . . . On n'a jamais
> eu beaucoup d'argent. Ma mère économisait, nourrissait ses enfants,
> mais en même temps elle réussissait à monter quelque chose de solide;
> elle voyait l'importance du village, de la famille. . . . C'est ironique,
> mais ma mère ne saura jamais jusqu'à quel point elle a participé aux
> monologues. (Thibault, Personal Interview)

The important family context is typical of oral tradition.
Anne-Marie Comeau, too, recalls storytelling as a family activity:

> Ma mère me contait des histoires, beaucoup. Mon père itou me
> contait des histoires de tchômes, du diable qui venait à des *games*
> de cartes, des *bootleggers*, toute de quoi qui faisait peur. Des
> histoires, on en avait tout le temps . . . chez nous. Je me souviens de
> ces *gatherings* icitte, puis je faisions des boules de *fluff* et du *fudge*,
> puis ça parlait . . . j'avions un poêle à bois et des lampes; j'avions
> point de lumière . . . ma mère n'avait pas le temps de s'assire et
> conter des histoires: elle avait onze enfants. . . . ma mère [contait]
> des affaires qu'ils faisions quand elle était jeune, c'était plus
> comique; Mamme n'avait point de peur, point de tristesse. (Anne-
> Marie Comeau)

Anne-Marie Comeau grew up in a family with strong oral traditions. Both parents participated, and it is interesting to note the different styles of each: whereas the father told the stories which are usually classified as "contes," the mother told tales which were more anecdotal and domestic and less highly structured. Her stories would be easier to break off and to pick up again, as the rhythm of the day permitted. Her stories would more resemble monologues, transmitting important but not necessarily breathtaking information about the family and the extended family, the kind of genealogy which is still the bread and butter of conversations at the Baie Sainte-Marie today. Rosealba participates as a matter of course in this community activity, and Antonine Maillet has immortalized it, not so much in the character of the Sagouine, but in that of Pélagie-la-Gribouille. The maintenance of family histories is part and parcel of the work of the *conteuse*.

Maillet's Sagouine and all of her sisters are central to the evolution of a theatrical identity in Acadie. Belonging wholly neither to the collégial nor to the popular camp, they are able to elicit response from an unusually broad spectrum of society, as James de Finney has shown with respect to *La Sagouine* (26, 27). This response has also, he argues, an important social function, in that "la rencontre du public et de l'oeuvre a permis de réunir et de valoriser esthétiquement des fragments d'une culture populaire sous-estimés jusqu'alors" (41). Bearing these insights in mind, and remembering that the Sagouine, Rosealba and other Sagouines are contemporary, popular phenomena, let us return, in conclusion, to the scholarly accounts of Acadian theatre history. The importance of oral tradition to Acadian theatre history has been noted. Roger Lacerte, in 1978, emphasized that the theatre of the classical colleges was preceded by amateur theatre in the parishes, and in 1980, Jean-Claude Marcus argued that the ancestor of Acadian theatre is the art of storytelling. These discoveries were prompted, at least in part, by the necessity to resolve the apparent contradiction between the assertion — made by René Baudry, Pascal Poirier and others — that the Acadians are a theatre-loving people, and the fact that Acadian theatrical tradition, in the accepted sense of a native dramaturgy and a consistent and professional theatre, begins about 1960. Jean-Claude Marcus suggests a generous interpretation of theatrical activity which takes as its key element an "échange d'émotions entre acteurs et spectateurs" (634). In this light, Acadian theatre can be seen, he argues, as a rich and ongoing tradition. In the same vein, Roger Lacerte suggests that we interpret the expression, "tradition théâtrale" in a broader sense than usual.

> Lui qui ne fut par le passé ni jamais assez nombreux ni assez stable ni
> assez riche pour bénéficier de troupes permanentes de professionnels
> mais qui a néanmoins toujours eu un goût prononcé pour le spectacle

comme pour le conte, la légende, la chanson, enfin, pour toutes les
formes de littérature parlée, orale, populaire. (119)

Lacerte distinguishes between the "théâtre de société" and the "théâtre
d'école" (127), commenting that the Acadian classical colleges have a solid
theatrical tradition which goes back to the 1850s and which is preceded
and paralleled by amateur traditions based in the communities. Local
theatrical and variety shows held to raise funds for the parishes and schools
are too numerous to count (127).

Marcus also distinguishes between theatre in the parishes and theatre in
the colleges and convents. Local theatrical events, described as "séances
dramatiques et musicales," or "soirées récréatives," should be envisioned,
he argues, as a somewhat structured and enlarged extension of "'la veillée,'
qui dans l'ancien temps, réunissait, au cours des longues soirées d'hiver, les
membres d'une famille et leurs voisins" (635).

Citing Père Anselme Chiasson, who writes in his history of Chéticamp of
the repression of dancing as an acceptable social pastime, and of its repla-
cement by "des parties de cartes, de jeux de société, des chansons, des
contes et des histoires drôles" (210), Marcus makes a critically important
formulation:

> En Acadie, plus qu'ailleurs, l'ancêtre de l'acteur est le conteur. Pour
> capter et conserver l'attention de son public, le conteur se devait de
> rendre son "histoire" . . . dramatique, et déployer pour ce faire
> certaines techniques qui, sans qu'il en eût conscience, ressortissaient à
> l'art dramatique. (635)

Marcus places this oral tradition in a chronological context: in the
1870s, with the development of Acadian national consciousness and the
founding of such important institutions as the *collèges classiques* and
L'Assomption, domestic traditions declined and were replaced by developing national institutions which reflected the structural transformations of Acadian society.

> De familiale qu'elle était, la "veillée" devient paroissiale, et l'on quitte
> peu à peu la cuisine pour aller s'ébaudir ou pleurer, le plus souvent les
> deux, à la salle paroissiale, à celle de la C.M.B.A. (Catholic Mutual
> Benefit Association), de la Société des Artisans Canadiens-français, ou
> plus tard de l'Assomption, etc. L'époque du conteur décline, celle du
> théâtre s'amorce. . . . (637)

Both collégial and community theatrical traditions, in other words, are
indebted to the powerful oral tradition of the conteur, which accounts for

the fact that in the newly formed theatrical academies, both the faculty and the students were sufficiently at ease in a theatrical idiom that they were regularly able to supplement the French repertoire with original compositions. Scripts, however, were rarely published and the literary imperative to preserve texts was even more neglected in the domain of community theatre, of which little is known because no texts have survived.

If Marcus is prescient in noting that behind the Acadian taste for the theatre we can discern the presence of *le conteur*, he is hasty in assuming that the storyteller faded away, as he implies, in the 1860s. After all, as Zénon Chiasson has demonstrated, it would be another hundred years before Acadian literary dramaturgy would get off the ground; another one hundred and ten years until *La Sagouine*. Antonine Maillet herself makes the claim — cited by Marcus — that prior to 1960, "la tradition littéraire en Acadie est presque uniquement orale" (636). In fact, when Marcus suggests a chronological movement from the kitchen to the parish hall, he inadvertently points to a larger reality: the Acadian elite may have been busy rebuilding Acadie, but the kitchens remained, as they still do, and kitchens are the locus of family life and the traditional domain of women. The *conteur* is still in the kitchen, the *conteur* may be a *conteuse*, and Acadian oral traditions are still in dialogue with the classical theatrical traditions of the educated elite.

The entire matter can finally be related to the predominant and most difficult issue facing Acadian culture today: the question of language. As Pierre Gérin remarks of Marichette, the use of a popular, colloquial language has significant symbolic value: "comme les femmes, le parler franco-acadien a été confiné dans les cuisines et les basses-cours. C'est avec elles qu'il en est sorti" (Gérin 44). Gérin is describing the world of the late nineteenth century, but — with respect to the location of the *parler franco-acadien* if not with respect to that of women — the situation remains virtually unchanged one hundred years later. It is perhaps to the endurance of this popular language that we can attribute the astonishing survival of the oral traditions which are embodied in it. In this sense, from the perspective of theatre history rather than from the perspective of linguistics or of politics, Acadian French can be freshly perceived as the difficult treasure that it is, the irrepressible music of a people.

Notes

[1] This paper is based on research carried out within the framework of *Hommage à Rosealba*, an action-research project dedicated to researching and supporting popular theatrical traditions at the Baie Sainte-Marie, and to discovering as much as possible about the Acadian monologue tradition. The research project is described more fully in the *Humanities Research Fiches*, No. 11, 1995, published by the Canadian Federation for the Humanities. Many people have supported this project and its goals; in particular, Marie-Adèle Deveau contributed enormously both to the

research and to the 1994 and 1995 Rosealba performances. The Explorations
Programme of the Canada Council, the Cultural Affairs Department of the
Government of Nova Scotia and Université Sainte-Anne all provided funding.
Thanks are also due to Anne-Marie Comeau, Michel Thibault, Muriel Comeau,
René LeBlanc, Normand Godin, Jean Daigle, Père Anselme Chiasson, Murielle
Comeau, Neil Boucher, James Quinlan, Gérald Boudreau, Harley d'Entremont,
Martine Jacquot, Edwin Doucet, Marcel Weaver, Raymond Gaudet, Sylvestre
Muise, Jean-Louis Belliveau, Chris Meuse, Imelda Amirault, James de Finney,
Willemine Mathieu and all of the wonderful people who gave interviews.

2 *La Sagouine* was launched at the Université de Moncton, in 1971. Alain Pontaut, in
"Les Sortilèges de la Sagouine," describes how Viola Léger, in the character of the
Sagouine, quietly scrubbed the floors, breaking anonymity only when she stood up
to deliver the opening monologue of Maillet's text. "Comme surprise, mais pas
dérangée, par les invités, une femme de ménage, que sans doute on avait oublié de
chasser, frottait le plancher et déplaçait son seau. Elle osait même adresser la parole
aux notables ainsi réunis. . . . [I]l avait . . . fallu quelque temps pour que les invités
s'aperçoivent qu'il ne s'agissait pas d'une pauvresse égarée dans ce lieu distingué
parmi l'élite du savoir et de la société, mais qu'ils venaient de rencontrer la vedette
de ce brillant lancement" (7–8).

3 La Sagouine "n'était pas tombée du ciel. Toute une tradition la préparait de longue
main, discrètement" (*Manchette* 13).

4 The pervasive influence of Antonine Maillet's *La Sagouine* can be seen, for example,
in the fact that during the 1970s, the French-language weekly *Le Petit Courrier de
la Nouvelle-Écosse* (a.k.a. *Le Courrier de la Nouvelle-Écosse*) featured some
twenty-two articles, interviews and photos of either Viola Léger or Antonine Maillet
in connection with *La Sagouine*.

5 For a more detailed discussion, see Susan Knutson, "The Evolution of a Community
Archetype: A Look at the Origins of Rosealba," and "Interview avec Michel
Thibault."

6 The acquisition of a Bachelor of Arts Program at the convent Notre-Dame du Sacré-
Coeur, in Memramcook, in 1943, followed by the founding of Notre-Dame
d'Acadie, in 1949, meant that the classical course of higher education as offered in
the French-Canadian institutions of the period became accessible to women for the
first time, and after this point it is impossible to speak of an elite theatrical tradition
which is exclusively male (Couturier Leblanc 575; Gallant 17–24.)

7 "[L]es fameuses lettres . . . furent si mal reçues par la soi-disant élite que la
malheureuse auteure finit par renoncer à écrire" (Pierre Gérin, 39).

8 Acadian theatre had a noble beginning: a neo-classical masque, composed in
alexandrines, staged on the waters of the Annapolis Basin on 14 November 1606,
to honour the return of Sieur de Poutrincourt to Port Royal. Composed and
directed by Marc Lescarbot, a young Parisian lawyer and Acting Governor of the
Habitation (in Poutrincourt's absence), "Le Théâtre de Neptune" was staged and
performed in an exclusively masculine world and was, of course, written in Parisian
French.

This extraordinary initiation was followed by a silence of almost two hundred
and fifty years. In the words of Laurent Lavoie, "avant le 'Grand Dérangement' de
1755, les Acadiens vivaient paisiblement, défrichant leurs terres et se rencontrant
pour fêter certains anniversaires et événements particuliers; après la déportation et
pendant une centaine d'années, c'est le néant" (452).

The documented tradition begins again in the mid-1850s, in Memramcook, NB,
where L'abbé François-Xavier Lafrance opens le Séminaire Saint-Thomas. In 1866
the Seminary is incorporated into the Collège Saint-Joseph, directed by Père Camille
Lefebvre; this first Acadian *collège classique* is joined in 1874 by the Collège Saint-

Louis at Saint-Louis-de-Kent, NB; in 1890 by Collège Sainte-Anne, in Pointe-de-
l'Église, NS, and in 1899 by the Collège du Sacré-Coeur at Caraquet, NB. As
Laurent Lavoie, Roger Lacerte, Jean-Claude Marcus, René LeBlanc and Micheline
Laliberté have documented, the colleges, and the theatrical academies they fostered,
regularly invited the public to enjoy theatrical performances, tragic and comic, in
French and in English — sometimes as often as five times during the academic year.
Lacerte celebrates the century-long tradition of collégial theatre while lamenting the
failure to survive of many original scripts written by both students and teachers.
"Les Acadiens de Philadelphie" (1875) and "Les Accordailles de Gabriel et
Évangéline (Saynette Champêtre)" by Senator Pascal Poirier; "Scène Acadienne à
Rogersville," by Mgr. Marcel-François Richard; "Subercase," by Père Alexandre
Braud (1903), and "Le Drame du Peuple Acadien" (1930), by Père Jean-Baptiste
Jégo, have been preserved: these texts are strongly nationalistic and often nostalgic
in tone. All of these scripts use exclusively the French of the Academy.

Until the 1940s, in the boys' colleges, all of the participants in theatrical events
were boys or men. Even the female roles were eliminated from plays taken from the
standard repertoire, and the creators of a certain "Vercingétorix," which was
performed at the Collège Sacré-Coeur in 1906, reportedly denied permission to a
French director who wished to stage their play in Paris, because he wanted to
introduce female characters. "[L]es auteurs refusèrent," comments Laurent Lavoie,
"sans doute pour éviter la 'pollution morale' causée par la présence maléfique de la
femme" (454). The author of "Subercase" manages a misogynist allusion to the
feminine sex which contradicts everything that is known about Acadian women:

> Forts les corps! Forts les coeurs! et viriles les âmes!
> Purs de toute souillure, allez laissant aux femmes
> Les larmes de faiblesse et jusqu'au dernier jour
> De votre vie, aimez à dire avec amour
> Ce double cri qui doit rester votre devise:
> Vive la France! L'Acadie et l'Église!
> (cited in Lavoie, 453)

9 Pascal Poirier is noteworthy in that his surviving plays include female characters.
On the other hand, they were written and performed after he had left Collège Saint-
Joseph. "Les Acadiens en Philadephie" was performed in Ottawa, in 1875.
René LeBlanc refers to Marguerite à Yutte as "la Rosealba de son temps," noting
that she performed at Christmas concerts, picnics and parish halls from one end of
Clare to the other, and that her monologues, which were extremely funny, dealt
with daily life and were delivered in the French of the region (LeBlanc, 1997).
Charelle Saulnier reports that according to her father, Fidèle Thériault, Marguerite à
Yutte knew everybody, was a matchmaker, and a genealogist (a *défricheteuse de
famille*) (Saulnier, 1997). Nadine Belliveau adds that Marguerite was somewhat
moqueuse, and that the location of her family home, adjacent to the general store
and the road leading down to the wharf, allowed her to keep an eye on affairs in
her village. Nadine's impression is that Marguerite did not create a distinct persona
for her monologues: "il n'y avait pas de décalage entre le personnage dans la vie
quotidienne et le personnage sur l'estrade" (Belliveau, 1997).

10 *The Courrier*, October 16,1975, carried two photos of such women: the first page
features Madame Lydie Melanson, who at 91 "joue encore son violon avec
confiance"; Madame Eva Melanson, an accordion player, is also featured (15). The
paper covered another remarkable woman, Mme. Elizabeth Fournier (née Deveau),
of Saulnierville Station, photographed at 91 years of age with her axe and the wood
she has cut (Robicheau).

Works Cited

"À propos de La Sagouine: entretien avec Jean-Michel Lacroix." Études canadiennes/
    Canadian Studies: bulletin interdisciplinaire des études canadiennes en France?,
    (1977): 101–111. Antonine Maillet: Dossier de presse. 3 Vol̩s. Bibliothèque du
    Séminaire de Sherbrooke, 1981, 1986, 1988.
"Antonine Maillet: Entretien avec André Major." Cahiers Renaud-Barrault, écriture
    romanesque, écriture dramatique 91 (1976): 104–23.
Belliveau, Nadine. Personal interview with the author. Pointe-de-l'Église, 12 June
    1997.
Boudreau, Anselme. Chéticamp: Mémoires. Réécrit et annoté par Père Anselme
    Chiasson. Moncton: Éditions des Aboiteaux, 1996. Chiasson, Père Anselme.
    Chéticamp, histoire et traditions acadiennes. Moncton: Éditions des Aboiteaux,
    1961.
Chiasson, Zénon. "Fragments d'identité du/dans le théâtre acadien contemporain
    (1960–1991)." Studies in Canadian Literature/ Études en littérature canadienne
    17.2 (1992/3): 61–69.
——. "L'institution théâtrale acadienne." In L'Acadie des Maritimes. Moncton: Chaire
    d'études acadiennes, 1993: 751–88.
Comeau, Anne-Marie. Personal interview with the author. Saulnierville Station, 13
    September 1995.
Comeau, Louise à Dan. Personal interview with Marie-Adèle Deveau and Anne-Marie
    Comeau. Hectanooga, 1 November 1993.
Comeau, Muriel. Personal interview with the author. Pointe-de-l'Église, 30 June t994.
"Connaissez-vous 'Sophie-Anne'?" Le Courrier de la Nouvelle-Écosse, le 20 avril
    1979:10.
Couturier Leblanc, Gilberte, Aleide Godin et Aldéo Renaud. "L'Enseignement français
    dans les Maritimes, 1604–1992." In L'Acadie des Maritimes. Moncton: Chaire
    d'études acadiennes, 1993: 543–85.
De Finney, James. "Lecteurs acadiens d'Antonine Maillet: réception littéraire et
    identité." Revue de l'Université de Moncton 21.1 (1988): 25–41.
D'Entremont, Caroline and Lucile D'Entremont. Personal interview with the author.
    Quinan, 10 February 1993.
Gallant, Cécile. Les Femmes et la renaissance acadienne/ Women and the Acadian
    Renaissance. Moncton: Les Éditions d'Acadie, 1992.
Gérin, Pierre. "Une Écrivaine Acadienne à la Fin du XIXe Siècle: Manchette." Atlantis
    10.1 (Fall/Automne 1984): 38–45.
Gérin, Pierre M. and Pierre Gérin. "Une femme à la recherche et à la défense de
    l'identité acadienne à la fin du XIXe siècle, Manchette." Revue de l'Université de
    Moncton 11. 2 (mai 1978): 17–26.
Gérin, Pierre M. and Pierre Gérin. Marichette: lettres acadiennes 1895–1898, édition
    commentée. Sherbrooke: Éditions Naaman, 1982.
Girard, Anne. "Antonine Maillet et la Sagouine." Le Droit, le 26 mai 1973: 23.
Knutson, Susan. "The Evolution of a Community Archetype: A Look at the Origins of
    Rosealba." Mélanges offerts à René LeBlanc.
——. "Interview avec Michel Thibault." Mélanges offerts à René LeBlanc.
"'La Chandeleur' se fête encore." Le Courrier de la Nouvelle-Écosse, le 8 février,
    1979:1–2.
Lacerte, Roger. "La tradition théâtrale en Acadie." Revue de l'Université de Moncton
    11.2 (mai 1978): 119–28.
Lavoie, Laurent. "Le théâtre de langue française au Nouveau-Brunswick." Le théâtre
    canadien-français. Vol. V of Archives des lettres canadiennes. Montréal: Fides, 1976:
    451–66.

LeBlanc, René. "Conteuse de l'Acadie." *Québec français* 60 (1985): 58–60.

——. Personal interview with the author. Pointe-de-l'Église, 15 May 1997.

LeBlanc, René and Micheline Laliberté. *Sainte-Anne: collège et université, 1890–1990.* Université Sainte-Anne: Chaire d'étude en civilisation acadienne de la Nouvelle-Ecosse, 1990.

"Les deux vieilles Sagouines [sic] de Pombcoup." *Le Petit Courrier de la Nouvelle-Ecosse*, le 29 avril 1976:1.

Maillet, Antonine. *Les Confessions de Jeanne de Valois.* Québec: Leméac, 1992.

——. *La Sagouine, pièce pour une femme seule.* Introduction by Alain Pontaut. Québec: Leméac, 1971,1990.

——. "Littérature acadienne." *Mémoires de la Société Royale du Canada.* 4e série, tome XV (1977): 207–14.

——. *Mariaagélas.* Ottawa: Lémeac, 1973.

——. *Pélagie-la-Charrette.* Québec: Leméac, 1979.

Maillet, Antonine and Rita Scalabrini. *L'Acadie pour quasiment rien.* Ottawa: Leméac, 1973.

Marcus, Jean-Claude. "Les Fondements d'une tradition théâtrale en Acadie." *Les Acadiens des Maritimes: Etudes thématiques*, sous la direction de Jean Daigle. Moncton: Centre d'études acadiennes. 1980: 633–66.

Mélanges offerts à René LeBlanc. Ed. E.M. Langille et al. Antigonish: The Centre for Regional Studies, forthcoming.

Poirier, Cécile LeBlanc. Personal interview with the author. L'Anse-des-LeBlanc, 14 July 1994.

Pontaut, Alain. "Les Sortilèges de la Sagouine," introd. *La Sagouine, pièce pour une femme seule.* By Antonine Maillet. Québec: Leméac, 1971,1990.

Robichaud, Soeur Thérèse. Telephone interview with the author. 14 September 1995.

Robicheau, Harold C. "93e anniversaire de naissance." *Le Courrier de la Nouvelle-Ecosse*, le 22 septembre 1977: 3.

Royer, Jean. "Un personnage universel qui prend ses racines dans l'enfance acadienne d'Antonine Maillet." *Le Soleil*, 14 octobre 1972: 47.

Saulnier, Charelle. Personal interview with the author. Pointe-de-l'Église, 12 June 1997.

Scully, Guy. "Le Monde d'Antonine Maillet." *Le Devoir*, samedi 29 septembre 1973.

Thériault, Fannie. Personal interview with Edward Gesner. December, 1975. Collection of Murielle Comeau.

Thibault, Michel. Personal interview with the author. L'Anse-à-l'Ours. 7 July 1994; forthcoming as Susan Knutson, "Interview avec Michel Thibault." *Mélanges offerts à René LeBlanc.*

——. Telephone interview with the author. 16 August 1995.

Thibault, Michel and Charlene Thibault Déraspe. "Rosealba nous parle" and "Rosealba, 1995." Unpublished draft manuscripts. Used with permission.

Audrey Thomas

A Fine Romance, My Dear, This Is

"Does the man in this book have hawklike features?"

"Aquiline. He has aquiline features. And dark hair, as usual."

"Same thing," Alice said. "A fancy name for hawk-like. What colour are his eyes?"

"He's blind. He wears dark glasses all the time."

"He's blind? They're never handicapped. He won't stay blind, you wait and see. That's just to get Nurse Prue to Ceylon" — INTERTIDAL LIFE

It's probably not the "done thing" to quote from oneself but I began reading Harlequins at about the same time I started on the second draft of *Intertidal Life*. The store at the government wharf at North Galiano has a free library of books discarded by weekenders and summer people and, as one might suspect, most of these books fall into the category of popular fiction, books by Richard Ludlum, Harold Robbins, Arthur Hailey, mysteries, romances. I had never read a romance until I went to Galiano. My mother and the women I baby-sat for when I was a teenager read the *Ladies Home Journal*, the *Women's Home Companion*, *Redbook*, and the serials in *The Saturday Evening Post*. If they had romantic fantasies they kept them well hidden and frankly I think they were much more inclined to fantasize about post-war kitchens and RCA Home Entertainment Centres. I read the Bobbsey Twins, Nancy Drew, Charles Dickens and later, in plain wrappers, books like *God's Little Acre* and *The Chinese Room*. I had plenty of romantic daydreams but I didn't read romances. So I picked up a couple of Harlequins from the store, more out of curiosity than anything else, and my daughter and I read them out loud to one another. The first two were Nurse books — *Nurse Sally's Last Chance* and *Nurse Prue Goes to Ceylon* — and they were pretty much as I expected. The girls were pretty without being beautiful (the rival girls, the scheming connivers, were the beautiful ones); they had, however, vulnerable mouths and lovely eyes and were decent girls, nice girls, who, in the end, won through to their hearts' desire (a man with hawk-like features and an income of £5,000 a year — or I should say the 1950s equivalent of Mr. Darcy's income). These books seemed innocent enough, silly, but innocent and the sexual awakening of these girls (we finished those two and went back for more, and more) was described in such flowery language, often using images from nature — fires, floods, acts of god, clouds, rainbows, etc., etc. — that it was great fun reading bits out loud.

> Something within her seemed to melt, to deliquesce,[1] a sensation like vertigo seized her; she felt as if she were adrift in a strange, multi-coloured cloud, frightened and yet filled with delight. (*Next Stop Gretna*, Harlequin 1970)

> Oh Symond, please, it's more than enough. I only want what you want, and it's been that way for some time. (*The Black Knight*, Harlequin, 1977)

> This was madness, Diana thought wildly and fought with all her strength. Then somehow she was free. She swallowed convulsively.
> "But how can you behave like this when you are going to marry Felicena?" The tears fell.
> He frowned. "Who says so?"
> "Everyone knows."
> "Except me." (*A Kiss in a Gondola*, Harlequin, 1969)

> Debby looked very young and very vulnerable lying in the warmed bed with the elevated feet and the protective cradle around her. She was on plasma and saline, and according to Kevin's notes on her chart was on oxygen inhalation and morphine injections. (*Nurse Deborah*, Harlequin, 1970; Perhaps this one should have been re-named *High as a Kite?*)

So, these girls started out with careers, usually but not always in the bud stage, they were perky and smart, often fought with the hero — usually only verbally in the early stages — experienced strange unfamiliar sensations whenever the hero was around, symptoms similar to a heavy attack of "flu" but which they came to recognize, after many setbacks and much anguish as love love love. Often, as in the case of Nurse Deborah, they suffered an

accident, nothing *disfiguring* you understand, and, through approaching un-
consciousness — or the haze of oxygen inhalation with morphine injections
— they heard the hero cry out "Darling!"

They meet, give up their careers, marry the hero and presumably live
happily ever after. For whatever the setbacks (and Harlequin romances are
real comedies of errors, everything from mistaking the brilliant, wealthy
architect for an ordinary worker on a building site to mistaking the heroine for a boy) the Harlequin Girl, like the mythical Mountie, always got
her man. This is one of the dogmas of Harlequin Romance — there is *always* a happy ending. The settings of these books were usually exotic,
Greece, Italy, and Spain being really popular — but nothing east of Athens
unless the hero is a Caucasian working in Saudi Arabia or Africa — in
other words, as the English would say (and these books originated in England) "no wogs." Scotland was also considered exotic, Holland was, and is,
very popular, and hospitals were exotic as well. (Mainly because of all
those handsome, unattached surgeons running around or, rather, striding
through corridors, their white coats flying behind them.)

We read them and we laughed, tried to see who could find the worst image (I won with "she melted against him like butter on a hot biscuit") but
spent most of our reading time on the "good stuff," the stuff that would
excite a child's imagination and enlarge her love of language: *The Wind in
the Willows*, *Alice in Wonderland*, C.S. Lewis, Tolkien, the Beatrix Potter
books, Edward Lear.

The old romances were touted as "heartwarming" and they were so obviously silly that I couldn't see that they were doing us, either of us, any
harm. It did bother me that the heroine, if she wasn't a nurse, worked always as a secretary or an assistant of some kind; she was never an executive, she was never actually *in charge* of anything, or nothing larger than a
hospital ward. The hero, whether doctor, lawyer (never Indian Chief),
architect, or artist was definitely in charge of his life; he was successful. If
he had to work for a living he had worked hard and had arrived.

The heroes and heroines, whatever their names (and an entire essay
could be written on the names of romance characters. Henry James would
love it. How do you like Jason Carver, for a famous artist? Almost as good
as Caspar Goodwood, wouldn't you say?) always played the same roles.
Like Holiday Inns (whose motto is "we never surprise you") or McDon-
ald's hamburgers, they were absolutely predictable. They are like the
cheapest panty hose which declare on the package, "one size fits all." In a
recent guideline for the writing of a Harlequin Romance ("our original
and longest-running romance line") the editors say:

> The plot should not be grounded in harsh realities — Romance readers
> want to be uplifted, not depressed — but at the same time should

make the reader (and "the reader" is always female) feel that such a love is possible if not probable. (Why the "but"? They seem to imply that love is more probable when grounded in harsh realities. Probably just a slip of the word processor.)

℃℥

So the reader knew, when she went into the drugstore or supermarket or second-hand bookstore that if she bought a Harlequin Romance she was guaranteed a "good read" with a happy ending. And because of this an interesting psychological phenomenon took place. *The reader knew more than the heroine.* The heroine might be out on a sheep ranch in New Zealand or in a fabulous villa on a Greek island but she was crying her eyes out because she thought the hero didn't love her. The heroine was extremely confused, about her own feelings and the feelings of the hero. She sorts out her own long before she ever understands that the hero is in love with her. The hero, who is recognizable to the reader the minute he steps on stage, *is* in love with the heroine, and the reader, curled up in bed or in an easy chair, knows that all the rudeness, hostility, and patronizing remarks are just a cover for the growing awareness of his own vulnerability where the heroine is concerned. ("'I was a swine,' he admitted apologetically.") The hero — his remarks, his general attitude — makes the heroine feel young, foolish, inadequate, and very very vulnerable on her part. ("Vulnerable" is a very common word in these romances, as is melting, even when disguised as "deliquesce." All the heroines eventually deliquesce.) The reader, who knows the ending, feels superior to the heroine even if the reader is sitting in a shabby chair in a room she doesn't like married to a man who is neither a prince nor charming. At least *she* knows where she stands.

One might mention at this point that we do expect, when buying or borrowing a detective novel, that the book will have a pre-ordained, "positive," if not exactly happy, ending — the murderer will be found out, justice will triumph. And if we like murder mysteries we probably have a favourite writer — Ngaio Marsh, Dorothy Sayers, Simenon, Nicholas Freeling, Agatha Christie — and even a favourite detective. I can't think of anyone who would be ashamed to admit to reading detective stories or even adventure or intrigue. These books are read by both men and women and, I would guess, men and women from all walks of life. Yet who among our acquaintances (and it would have to be a woman, males simply don't read Harlequins) would admit to reading Harlequin Romance, or even some of the newer, presumably more modern, more "realistic" lines — Harlequin Presents, Harlequin Temptation, Harlequin Intrigue (a kind of "detective" story), Harlequin American Intrigue. Who would write her name on the inside of the book under the statement: "This Harlequin Romance belongs in the personal library of . . . N . . ."? Yet there are millions of women who do, 20 million Harlequin readers in the U.S. alone, and, in our country, Harlequins account for 28 per cent of all paperbacks sold.[2] Harlequins are translated into twelve languages and sold in 98 countries. That's a lot of women; that's a lot of books. As Bob Dylan would say, "Somethin's Happening Here." But why? Asking why is becoming almost as popular as reading the things. And not only asking why but asking the question I began to ask myself, as Harlequin introduced its new lines and the action became more violent as well as more explicitly sexual (but never *described* too explicitly of course. He touches her "moist femininity"; she feels his "force" pressed against her) — are these books doing actual harm?

In her interesting examination of the Harlequin industry, *Love's $weet Return* (which was originally written as a Ph.D. thesis I believe) Margaret Ann Jensen seems at first to take the position that the criticism of romance fiction is unfair and sexist "based as it is on acceptance of males and their fantasies as the measure of worth." This may or may not be so — it's certainly something to think about. Is criticism of romances just one more example of the general put-down of literature written by women (and 99 per cent of Harlequins are written by women)? If so, the criticism, that they are "Trash," doesn't seem to inhibit all these millions of women who snap up Harlequins every month, as soon as they appear on the shelves, or sooner if they belong to the Harlequin Reader Service — "take these four books and Tote Bag FREE" — and I assume that they do this quite openly, don't hide them in bottom drawers beneath the underwear or sweaters, as men often do with pornography; I assume they don't rush home and wrap them in brown paper. I doubt if they see the reading of romance fiction as an act of defiance on their part ("you can call this trash but I'll read it anyway"); I doubt if husbands feel threatened if they see their wives looking at them over the top of *Dear Conquistador* or *A Kiss in a Gondola*. I doubt if Harlequins have ever been named in divorce suits and yet some women, what Jensen calls "heavy" users, read as many as sixty books of popular fiction (romance readers read all kinds of popular fiction) a *month*. They are addicts. Most of these women are full-time housewives/mothers, women in the labour force, elderly women who don't get out much. Reading these books is what Jensen calls a "removal activity." This is an activity which "allows one to be physically present but mentally absent" and is "one of the few luxuries that women can afford to give themselves." (They come as low as 25¢ at the Sally Ann and I am sure there are other places, like the store on Galiano, where they are traded or given away for free. Jensen tells us that McDonald's gave them as a gift one Mother's Day and they have been known to turn up in boxes of laundry soap or sanitary napkins.) If a housewife/mother sits down to watch television when anybody else is home the chances are pretty good that she won't be able to watch the program of her choice. If she buys something sweet and self-indulgent (jelly do-nuts, a box of *Turtles*) she'd better eat it sitting on a bench in the park. But supposing she has something that *she* wants and nobody else wants? Why then she's home free. Her husband isn't interested in Harlequins nor are her children (and anyway teen-aged girls now have their own romance lines to choose from, *Wildfire* "for girls 12 to 15 years old," *Sweet Dreams* and. *First Love* "for 11–16 year old girls," and several others. This is like giving young girls root-beer flavoured chapstick. They'll get addicted to having something on their lips and be buying lipstick at $4.50 before you know it). Traditionally men have always been able to "get away" physically. Work took them away during the week and their leisure activities either had to be done away from home (golf, fishing, "pub night") or were dangerous ("don't touch Daddy's table saw!"). And even when families were all for mother having a "room of her own" it rarely worked out that way (unless it were a sewing room or laundry room). Read Doris Lessing's "To Room 19" to see to what terrible extremes a woman will go to have privacy and peace; read Alice Munro's "The Office." So women have to "make walls," to do, as one Harlequin ad puts it, their "disappearing act." I don't think romance readers care one bit that the situations are repetitive or even, all claims to the contrary with the new lines, that they have very little to do with real life. They hold something in their hands that is not only cheap (and therefore a forgiveable personal indulgence on mother's part) but easily recognizable by the rest of the family as non-threatening. I know that satisfied readers do write in to the Harlequin company ("Thank you for bringing romance back to me. J.W., Tehachape, Calif." "Harlequins are magic carpets . . . away from pain and depression . . . away to other people and other countries one might never know otherwise, H.R., Akron, Ohio") and give an assortment of reasons why they are so satisfied. But underneath it all they know that they can sit down, put their feet up, keep an eye on the kids or the oven, and indulge in something that is uniquely theirs, something safe, yet fun, something they like which doesn't have to be shared.

∞

So are they harmless or maybe even *helpful* to women? (I'm not talking about the women who *write* them. As Jensen points out, the successful Harlequin writers, "anathema of feminists," make as much as corporate executives and are doing what they like doing at the same time.) I no longer think they are harmless. I think, in fact, they are more and more approaching pornography, if they have not already arrived. If by pornography I mean stories containing sex and violence then the new Harlequins are full of it. They are ostensibly "new compelling stories of passionate romance for today's women." But when I started looking at the newer ones — and I think the change started in the mid–1970's — I was appalled at the element of fear and violence, if not actual violence, that occurs. In *Duel of Desire* (1979) by Charlotte Lamb (!), the heroine, Deborah, who was left an orphan when her parents died in a fire and she was found crying in the garden in her pram, is a high-profile well-paid, executive assistant to Alex St. James, a music-industry executive. The plot is the usual far-fetched nonsense. Suffice it to say that Alex and Deborah (who gradually discovers, to her horror, that she loves this arrogant womanizer) ends up having to spend several days in an upstairs bedroom of Alex's mother's French farmhouse. Mama has left because of a flood threat which becomes a reality after Alex and Deborah arrive. Alex at one point kisses Deborah so hard he bites through the skin on the inside of her mouth, he pulls her hair, he shouts "you lying little bitch," says "damn you" several times, scares her by his violent behaviour and yet she agrees to marry him — because she has fallen in love with him. Later on he explains that it was her seeming coldness towards him that "drove" him to such behaviour. Also, at the end, when he suggests that now she's his wife she'll have to find another job and she doesn't see it, he frowns. "Damn you, my wife isn't working, especially in the same office as myself." And he uses, as an excuse, the rationalization, "How the hell would I get any work done." Kiss (passionately) and fade out. This is really old wine in new bottles. The language is coarser and hero and heroine go to bed at least once (*de rigueur* now in the more spicy lines, Harlequin Presents and Harlequin Temptation as well as Harlequin Intrigue) but *he* is always in the power position, seems in fact to be ruder, cruder, and nastier than ever. Jensen says "concern about economic security, loneliness, powerlessness and sexual violence against women pervades romances" but then you get the inevitable happy ending.

I have read perhaps two dozen of the "modern" romances and they scare me. The happy ending simply doesn't make up for all the fear. Jensen says "the romances we get are a product of literary history, contemporary social changes, and the corporate drive for profitability." It's that last bit we should pay attention to. Harlequins were slipping financially so they "modernized" the plots a little, followed current trends in T.V. and film, and now their sales are up again. Harlequin's heroines are older but not necessarily wiser. They still melt under the aggressive sexuality of the hero. They may have wonderful careers but they give them up at the drop of a panty. I have *yet* to read one when the heroine is going to continue to work after marriage. The hero, who wants her at any price, may say she can work but she, on her own (ha ha), has decided she's fed up with the lonely life at the top. She is, in short, a R.E.A.L. woman again.

I don't know how one can stop all this. It worries me that millions of women are buying the violence and abuse, the *humiliation*, along with the happy ending. He didn't really mean it; I drove him to it anyway. I'm still thinking about all this and have no real conclusion. There's a lot of anger against women right now, perhaps more than there has ever been (who gets beaten up or verbally abused when a man loses his job. It's often "women and children first," not the boss). *Women* are writing these books for other women to read. You've come a long way baby, sure you have. A long way down. These aren't really "light reading" any more and the messages coming through are very disturbing. I have no answers at the minute, only questions. Why are women exploiting other women in this way and what's to be done about it all?

Notes

1 In the old Harlequins you got a lot of this sort of language; one didn't "mow the lawn" for instance, one "trimmed the verdant sward." Or the gardener did; the gardener trimmed the verdant sward. This isn't the world of *Lady Chatterley's Lover*; Harlequin heroes were, until very recently, rich, rich, rich. Was that, to the Harlequin reader, the moral equivalent of my mother looking at the ads for Kelvinators and Wallace Sterling?

2 These figures and many of the quotations (identified as such) are from Margaret Ann Jensen, *Love's Sweet Return: The Harlequin Story* (Toronto: The Women's Press, 1984).

CL 108 (Spring 1986)

Norman Shrive

What Happened to Pauline?

As everyone interested in Canadian literary history knows, the Pauline Johnson centennial was celebrated *last* year; indeed, the more obvious activities connected with it took place during or close to her birth-month, March, and are therefore well over a year into the past. But neither in 1961 nor in the time since has there appeared in print — at least, to my knowledge — any reasonably searching evaluation of the real place in Canadian letters of this internationally famous versifier and story-teller. Marcus Van Steen's introduction to a new McClelland and Stewart edition of *Legends of Vancouver* was inclined to repeat the usual commonplaces, although with a refreshing suggestion of doubt here and there. Ethel Wilson's memoir in *Canadian Literature*, delightful as it was, was really a book review of the same new edition.

Recognition of another type was, of course, ample. It included a special five-cent stamp, testimonial dinners, articles in weekend supplements and pilgrimages to Stanley Park, to Mohawk Chapel and to Chiefswood, the old Johnson home on the Grand River. The International Conference on Iroquoian Studies, which drew scholars from all over North America to McMaster University, had as part of its three-day programme a public lecture on "The Place of Pauline Johnson in Canadiana." Perhaps the most important expression of respect for Miss Johnson's memory (judging by the dignitaries present) was a special dinner in Brantford. As reported by the *Expositor*, "Chief Red Cloud (Fred Williams), with his grandson, Little White Bear (Perry Williams), performed a number of traditional dances." Mohawk songs "were sung by the Wright Quartet," and "decorating the tables were paper models of canoes and tepees." Miss Ontario, of the Six Nations Reserve, was there, perhaps very appropriately, and so was Dr.

George F. Davidson, Deputy Minister of Citizenship and Immigration, to give the main speech of the evening. Miss Jessie L. Beattie, author of *The Split in the Sky*, read her poem, "A Message from Pauline" (as her ardent supporters invariably refer to her), and, unaccountably, Mordecai Richler wandered in, retaliating a week or so later, one senses, for the discomfort he felt, by writing a squib for *Maclean's* which, Miss Beattie told me, did not please her at all.

But the learned journals seemed blandly indifferent to Miss Johnson. Yet Pauline Johnson is material for interesting controversy. If we accept her as Indian (which, technically she was not, even when given her Indian name, "Tekahion-wake"), how did she and the people who claim her as their own differ from their brothers and cousins on the other side of a man-made border? What necessarily makes her part of Canadiana rather than of Americana or of North Americana? And then there is perhaps the most searching of all questions: was Pauline Johnson really a poetess — Indian, Canadian, North American or otherwise?

At the Brantford dinner, Dr. Davidson, deploring the fact that the recently published *Oxford Book of Canadian Verse* contained not one word of Miss Johnson's writings, took a verbal swipe at academic critics who believed such an anthology gave "a truly representative and completely adequate picture of all the facts of our Canadian craft and skill in this important literary art without including a single word from the pen of the person who, more than anyone else, must be regarded as the main truly Canadian writer of our time." But many literary scholars would disagree with this assessment of Pauline Johnson. A.J.M. Smith, for example, the editor of that same *Oxford Book of Canadian Verse* and himself a poet of international reputation, suggests that although the poetry of Miss Johnson was much admired in Canada, "the romantic fact of her Indian birth, played up by critics and journalists, has been accepted as convincing proof that she spoke with the authentic voice of the Red Man." Pauline Johnson, he continues, had a vigorous personality and an excellent sense of the theatre, as well as the good fortune to be praised by "a fashionable London critic," Theodore Watts-Dunton. But, says Professor Smith, the claim that her work is genuine "primitive poetry, or that it speaks with the true voice of the North American Indian will hardly be made by responsible criticism. . . . Her best known pieces are decorous imitations of . . . [Tennyson and Swinburne]. They have a graceful and easy-flowing cadence, which presents admirably vague impressions of pellucid waters and shadowy depths, but they are as empty of content as any devotee of pure poetry could wish. . . ." They are "minor Victorian escape poems"; and when Miss Johnson tried to portray the feelings and aspirations of the aborigines, she became "theatrical and crude." The rhythm "is heavy, the imagery conventional, and the language melodramatic and forced. Her best work is not to be found in her Indian poetry at all but in one or two pretty and very artificial little lyrics."[1]

Here, certainly, are two assessments that if not diametrically opposite appear to have little in common except sense of conviction. And perhaps Canadian literary critics, feeling that Smith had said all there was to be said on Pauline Johnson, could not be bothered to tell Dr. Davidson to stick to his portfolio and leave literary judgments to the qualified. Yet, by interpreting Miss Johnson and her objectives in terms of the literary, social and nationalistic climates in which she lived, we can bring closer the professional and non-professional viewpoints and show why neither side can dismiss out of hand the other.

In the first place, the responsible literary critics of whom A.J.M. Smith speaks, with their comparatively wide knowledge of the struggle of Canadian letters for national and international recognition, have felt that much of Miss Johnson's work falls into a particular, all-too-characteristic pattern. Only three years after she was born, the Reverend Edward Hartley Dewart, in his introduction to British North America's first anthology of verse, intimated the sense of urgency that he and others were beginning to feel over the need for a truly Canadian literature. "There is probably no country in the world," he remarked, "where the claims of native literature are so little felt, and where every effort in poetry has been met with so much coldness and indifference as in Canada."[2] It is not important here that we note the reasons that Dr. Dewart offers for this neglect; most of them are familiar by now. What is significant, however, is the self-conscious attitude reflected by poet and critic alike at the time, the desire to be *Canadian* as distinct from British or American. The fact of Confederation, of course, served to increase the enthusiasm, and soon the newspapers and periodicals were publishing a veritable flood of verses supposedly Canadian. The poets concerned are known now only to the more devoted student of Canadian letters; the verse, from the intrinsically literary point of view, is undistinguished. But most of it is notable for one or two aspects in particular. In its reflection of national aspiration it both exudes sentimental idealism and implies a sense of colonial inferiority. In short, it is thoroughly romantic, even to deriving much of its imagery and technique from the English Romantic poets of half-a-century before. In it we see significant illustration of the attitudes that determined the way poetry was written in later nineteenth-century Canada. The example set by the English Romantic poets directed it towards the depiction of native landscapes and, sometimes, native people, and although those landscapes and people were viewed as through an English filter — for example, by referring to them by the use of English instead of Canadian idiom — the verse was nevertheless considered "Canadian." And herein lies a source of confusion. To be dependent upon the literary tradition of England, as Smith has emphasized, surely cannot be a defect. If it is, perhaps all American poets except Whitman are to be dismissed with their Canadian cousins. But in post-Confederation Canada it was more important that the verse be written by a Canadian than that it be poetry; the comparison was more often between the poet and an accepted English master than between poetry and non-poetry. This approach to criticism is, of course, still with us; it reflects, in fact, an attitude that is sometimes expressed by a type of Canadian nationalism still very much alive. Professor Smith wrote in 1946 that "when it is recognized that the claims of nationalism are less important than those of universality and that a cosmopolitan culture is more valuable than an isolated one, our twentieth-century criticism will be prepared to approach contemporary Canadian poets."[3] And as late as 1957 he could remark, "the question of national identity still seems to underlie our thinking and haunt our imagination."[4]

ભ

How all of this is relevant to Pauline Johnson should be reasonably clear. During her most impressionable years the literary influences upon her were similar to those upon dozens of other versifiers of the eighteen-seventies. And despite her insistence upon her father's importance in her learning "the legends, the traditions, the culture and etiquette"[5] of the Indian, her literary education was English. Walter McRaye, her business manager and companion, reports quite objectively that she read the standard poets and was especially fond of Scott, Byron, Tennyson and Adelaide Ann Proctor — the latter achieving a somewhat dubious fame as the author of *The Lost Chord*. And Miss Johnson herself reveals how she fits squarely into a particular manifestation of Victorian romanticism when she describes her parents. "Their loves were identical," she writes:

> They loved nature, the trees best of all, the river and the birds. They loved the Anglican Church, they loved the British flag, they loved Queen Victoria, they loved beautiful, dead, Elizabeth Elliott. They loved music, pictures and china with which George Johnson filled his beautiful house. They loved books and animals, but, most of all those two loved the Indian people, loved their legends, their habits, their customs, loved the people themselves. Small wonder that their children should be born with pride of race and heritage, and should face the world with that peculiar courage that only a fighting ancestry can give.[6]

There is certainly nothing reprehensible in such an outpouring of love. Unfortunately, however, when many Canadian poets of the time, Pauline

Johnson among them, attempted to express their various loves in verse, they did so in a rhetorical, overly sentimental, often self-indulgent, way. In short, they reflected those aspects of flabby Victorian romanticism so familiar in much of the fiction, music, architecture and art of the period. In the United States Mark Twain was scornfully to denote the period as the "Gilded Age," illustrating his derision, for example, by the tragi-comic story of the Grangerfords and Shepherdsons in *Huckleberry Finn*; Canada, characteristically, had to wait a few more decades for Stephen Leacock and a similar satirical perspicuity. Yet, how can we appreciate what these poets were trying to do unless we are also aware of the contemporary tastes and norms that influenced them? One of Miss Johnson's many concerts was given at Prince Albert. Here is the programme of another evening of culture sponsored by the PAYMLAC (the Prince Albert Young Men's Literary and Athletic Club) as it is recorded in the Prince Albert *Times* of November 23, 1883:

> SONG: — "A Flower from my angel mother's grave" very prettily sung by Miss Mackenzie.

> READING: — By Mr. Fitz-Cochrane, "Gray's Elegy on [sic] A Country Churchyard."

> SONG: — By Mrs. Col. Sproat, "Jock o' Hazeldean," which was so acceptably delivered as to call for an unanimous encore, which produced that ever-popular old song "Comin' thro' the Rye," also very nicely sung.

> The next number was a reading by Mr. J.O. Davis, but he was prevented by illness from appearing.

> *   *   *   *   *   *

> Mr. Joseph Hanafin read the celebrated speech by Sergeant Buzfuz from Pickwick, in very good form.
>   Mrs. Brown then favoured the audience with the song "Twickenham Ferry" in such acceptable style as to demand an encore, to which she kindly responded with "Two is Company, Three is None," which was also well received.

> *   *   *   *   *   *

> The programme was well wound up by a comic song, "Patrick, Mind the Baby," by T.O. Davis, given in his best style, which brought down

the house, and he was obliged to respond with "When McGinnis Gets a Job," which also took the house by storm.

It may be noted that Charles Mair, a man who considered himself of superior cultural tastes and who within a few months was to be widely praised for his closet drama, *Tecumseh*, was one of the officers of the PAYMLAC. I do not wish to suggest by this example, however, that the level of literary taste throughout Canada was of a consistently low level. Two periodicals in particular, the *Canadian Monthly* and the Toronto *Week*, reflected, through the editorship of men such as Mercer Adam and Goldwin Smith, and the contributions of writers such as W.D. LeSueur, Sara Jeannette Duncan, Charles G.D. Roberts and Archibald Lampman, a standard of excellence that the Canadian literary periodical has probably not attained since. It is significant, however, that both magazines had died from lack of support before the end of the century, thereby supplying evidence (not that it was needed) of the gap between the literary critic, the poet and the popular taste. Pauline Johnson herself, determined as she was to write, realized that she could earn no more than a few cents when she was fortunate enough to have work published; she therefore embarked upon a career that essentially catered to that taste. Dressed in Indian costume she went from city to city, town to town, even barn to barn, reciting her verse and reading her interpretations of the Indian legends. And despite the protests of those who see her as "a true poet," we must describe these tours as being in the tradition of the music-hall, not of the concert recital, nor even of the peripatetic bard of old, as has been rather romantically suggested. Walter McRaye, writing in 1946, notes that there "were no movies, or radio or Chautaquas" in the 'nineties:

> Entertainment was given either by professionals or local talent. These were usually designated "concerts" or "shows." The professionals were brought in from Toronto, Montreal or Hamilton. Singers, violinists, cartoonists, comedians and lecturers — Pauline Johnson was of such a company. She read from her own poems and appeared in costume, a beautiful buckskin dress trimmed with ermine skins, and with silver brooches scattered over the bodice. These were very old and had been hammered from silver coins by the native Indian silversmiths. Two scalps hung suspended from her waist, a Huron scalp and one that had been given to her by a Blackfoot Chief. Around her neck was a beautifully graded cinnamon bear-claw necklace, and on her wrists bracelets of wampum beads. Draped around her shoulders was . . . [a] red broadcloth blanket . . . ; in her hair was an eagle feather. This costume was laid aside in the second half of the programme when she appeared in conventional evening dress.[7]

The picture is a striking one; one feels, indeed, that Miss Johnson could have carried at least part of the audience by merely standing on stage. And for those interested in symbolic acts and gestures, the change of costume for the second part of the programme may be of significance.

Cʒ

We should note that much of the popular interest in Miss Johnson today is still stimulated by the essentially non-literary aspects of her career — her Indian heritage, her dress, her skill as a stage performer and her personality. Even the fact that she, a woman, would engage in such an arduous and unusual venture might still raise a post-Victorian eyebrow — although, admittedly, to a very limited extent now. But she was unusual, and the fact that her poetry echoed the mellifluous cadences of Tennyson and Swinburne, the Victorian sentimentality of Adelaide Proctor, and the self-conscious nationalism of her own Canadian contemporaries, was ignored by her audiences. They probably were not aware of these borrowed and assimilated characteristics; if they were they probably did not care anyway. They *liked* Pauline Johnson and what she said, and that was enough. But, unfortunately, that is not enough for the literary critic. It is his business to do more than take his seat in the Orpheus theatre or before the hastily improvised stage in a western barn and merely listen to an Indian princess talk about her father's people. In short, he knows too much for his own popularity.

To talk about her father's people. This statement has, perhaps, unfair implications. Let us accept Pauline Johnson as she herself wished to be accepted — as a Canadian Indian. And in her own time this role was the very one in which her audiences *wished* — almost desperately, one feels at times — to see her. Psychologists might even say that her enthusiastic followers would have *projected* this role upon her, whether she wished it or not. For while Pauline Johnson was growing up, the popular image of the Indian was undergoing a significant change. He was no longer only the tomahawk-wielding, scalp-adorned aborigine of earlier times. Nor was he only the noble savage of the eighteen-thirties and 'forties. He had become more than noble; he was also the down-trodden, dispossessed — and vanishing — victim of the ruthless white man. And perhaps most significant in this era of urgent nationalism was the fact that the role of the Indian in preserving Canada herself was apparently being forgotten. Here, for example, are Mercer Adam's comments in the Toronto *Varsity* of March 5, 1886:

> It is important that the heroic deeds of the faithful Indian allies of Britain, in the struggle to plant and maintain the flag of the Empire on this continent, should be treasured, and a fitting memory preserved of their

loyal services and staunch friendship. Nor should gratitude be lacking, particularly in the Canadian nation, which owes so much to the Indian tribes for the heritage it now peacefully enjoys, and from which it has rudely dispossessed the children of the woods, and done much to make them what they are now — a poor emasculated, vanishing race.

These remarks were written almost exactly one year after the outbreak of the North-West Rebellion. Yet they reflect no antipathy towards, for example, Chief Poundmaker and the Indians who had joined Riel against the Queen's authority. Many Canadians in Ontario felt, in fact, that the tribes had been goaded by the half-French Riel; many in the West sympathized with both Riel and the Indian. And Mercer Adam was only one commentator among many — including essayists, novelists, poets — who were reflecting a depiction of the Indian in rather stereotyped and often self-indulgent terms. Self-indulgent because one cannot help feeling at times an almost patronizing attitude towards the Indian, at times even a reflection of a guilty conscience.

Pauline Johnson actually was one of the few people who saw through the new popular image of the Indian and who said so in writing. Aside from certain prose pieces in *Legends of Vancouver* some of the most perceptive, the most unaffected writing she did was in private letters to friends and in fugitive newspaper articles, writing that reflects an author of distinction more than the Pauline Johnson of the stage and of "The Song my Paddle Sings." The term "Indian," she noted,

> signifies about as much as the term "European," but I cannot recall ever having read a story where the heroine was described as "a European." The Indian girl we meet in cold type, however, is rarely distressed by having to belong to any tribe, or to reflect any tribal characteristics. She is merely a wholesale sort of admixture of any band existing between the MicMacs of Gaspé and the Kwaw-Kewlths of British Columbia, yet strange to say, that notwithstanding the numerous tribes, with their aggregate numbers reaching more than 122,000 souls in Canada alone, our Canadian authors can cull from this huge revenue of character, but one Indian girl, and stranger still that this lovely little heroine never had a prototype in breathing flesh and blood existence!

This conventional, seemingly invariable and inevitable maiden, Miss Johnson continues, is known as Winona or Wanda.

> She is never dignified by being permitted to own a surname, although, extraordinary to note, her father is always a chief, and had he ever

existed, would doubtless have been as conservative as his
contemporaries about the usual significance that his people attach to
family name and lineage.

Above all, however, she is to be recognized by two distinguishing characteristics: her suicidal mania and her misfortune in love. She is, Miss Johnson notes,

> always desperately in love with the young white hero, who in turn is
> grateful to her for services rendered the garrison in general and himself
> in particular during red days of war. . . . Of course, this white hero
> never marries her! Will some critic who understands human nature,
> and particularly the nature of authors, please tell the reading public
> why marriage with the Indian girl is so despised in books and [yet is]
> so general in real life?

Mercer Adam's Wanda, she notes, is much in love with Edward McLeod,
"makes all the overtures, conducts herself disgracefully, assists him to a
reunion with his fair-skinned love, Helene; then betakes herself to a boat,
rows out into a lake in a thunderstorm, chants her own death-song and is
drowned." Jessie M. Freeland's Winona is also the unhappy victim of violent love that is not returned. She assists young Hugh Gordon, "serves him,
saves him in the usual 'dumb' animal style of book Indians, manages by
self-abnegation, danger, and many heart-aches to restore him to the arms
of Rose McTavish, who of course he has loved and longed for all through
the story." But Winona also finds the "time-honoured canoe, paddles out
into the lake and drowns herself."[8]
   There is a temptation to give further exemplification of this quite delightful critical perspicuity, but the point is clear enough. Pauline Johnson,
the person, knew the Indian and could perceive the artificiality that had
become associated with him. The irony is, however, that she in some respects became part of that artificiality, either deliberately or unknowingly.
That it was the latter is perhaps indicated by the lapse in her powers of
discrimination when she applied them to poetry. For example, in the glow
of her enthusiasm for Charles Mair's verse-drama depiction of the Indian,
a depiction she felt to be far more realistic than that of any other Canadian
author, she reveals the romantic tendencies of both her own nature and of
the age. "Oh! happy inspiration vouchsafed to the author of *Tecumseh*,"
she exclaimed, "he has invented a novelty in fiction — a white man who
deserves, wins and reciprocates the Indian maiden's love — who says, as
she dies on his bosom, while the bullet meant for him stills and tears her
heart:

Silent for ever! Oh, my girl! my girl!
Those rich eyes melt; those lips are sunwarm still —
They look like life, yet have no semblant voice.
Millions of creatures throng and multitudes
Of heartless beings flaunt upon the earth;
There's room enough for them, but thou, dull fate —
Thou cold and partial tender of life's field
That pluck'st the flower; and leav'st the weed to thrive —
Thou had'st not room for her! Oh I must seek
A way out of the rack — I need not live
. . . . but she is dead —
And love is left upon the earth to starve,
My object's gone, and I am but a shell,
A husk, an empty case, or anything
That may be kicked around the world.[9]

This rhetorical, melodramatic homage to Shakespeare Pauline Johnson found "refreshing," thus indicating, perhaps, the standards she set for herself in verse-writing. Mair became one of her closest friends: "Oh!" she wrote to him, "you are half an Indian, I know — the best half of a man, anyway — his heart." She invariably addressed him as "My Dear Tecumseh" and on one of her tours she wore an exquisitely made costume that Mair had sent her from Prince Albert. He frequently insisted that if ever his play were brought to the stage only Pauline Johnson could play his Indian heroine. She was, he said, a "true poet," one "of a race knit up in the noblest way with our history," the "Canadian Sappho" whose poetry would live "even in this dark age."[10]

The "dark age" referred to was that period just before and after Pauline Johnson's death. Perhaps at no other time has the prospect for Canadian literature been bleaker than what it was then. As Desmond Pacey has aptly suggested, if the last three decades of the nineteenth century could be termed "the golden age" of Canadian literature, "the first two decades of the twentieth were without a doubt the age of brass."[11] Said Mair, referring cynically to the work of Ralph Connor, "No one reads poetry except the poets themselves; the whim of the flimsy day is the novel."[12] Even most of the verse writers were considered in some quarters as mere dilettantes and not poets at all. Mair, for example, regarded Service, MacInnes and Drummond as "jinglers, coarse rhymesters or worse."[13] And the story of how Pauline Johnson's days were made reasonably happy ones only through the generosity of devoted friends is a well-known one. By the end of the war she, like so many personalities of another era, was virtually forgotten.

ﻼ

This nadir in the history of Canadian letters introduces one last significant
aspect of Pauline Johnson's reputation — its quite remarkable re-ascend-
ency in the nineteen-twenties. Why this should be can be partly and certainly interestingly explained by reference to another literary personality
— John W. Garvin.

Garvin is surely one of the most fascinating figures in Canadian letters. A
stockbroker by profession, he had evidently decided during the war that his
ability as a businessman and his enthusiasm as a student of literature could
be combined to sell Canadians an awareness of their literary achievements.
He admitted to having written "about 130 poems," but, he said, "I have
greater confidence in my philosophical theories and in my capacity as a literary critic."[14] Beginning modestly by an edition of Isabella Valancy Crawford's poems and some articles on poets in the *Public Health Journal*, Garvin
was by the early nineteen-twenties a well known anthologist and booster of
Canadian writing. These achievements, however, were to exact in the next
decade a large price from both the man and his reputation. Garvin's "pet
hobby," as he called it, was to bring him (and his wife, Katherine Hale) financial ruin. Even worse, perhaps, it was to identify him in the minds of later
rebelling poets and critics as one of F.R. Scott's "expansive puppets" who
"percolate self unction" when the "Canadian Authors Meet." For Garvin
and his literary pretensions seem no more at home than where "the air is
heavy with 'Canadian' topics," where one is mixing with the *literati* and the
maple leaf is praised "beneath a portrait of the Prince of Wales."

But none can deny that Garvin (and others like him) helped to generate
a new awareness of Canadian literature. Garvin's circle of enthusiastic *literati* in Toronto indicated the beginning of a movement such as Canada
had not beheld since Confederation. Garvin edited anthologies, undertook
lecture tours, even organized newspaper controversies over such topics as
"Who was the real Father of Canadian Poetry?" or "Who are our greatest
poets?" Today we cannot help flinching before some of his superlatives. In
one of his letters he wrote: "I and other discriminating critics rate Charles
Mair and Isabella Valancy Crawford as the greatest poets Canada has
produced."[15] In other correspondence he styled Charles G.D. Roberts, his
son, Lloyd Roberts, Albert Durrant Watson, Pauline Johnson and Robert
W. Norwood as also "great." After a careful reading of Norwood's "Song
of a Little Brother," he reported that he "unhesitatingly ranked him" as
great too. It may not be irrelevant here to note that Norwood, an Anglican
minister, had other talents as well. As Garvin described him: "He is such a
splendid fellow, so brilliantly versatile; read[s] Browning's 'Calaban' in a
masterly manner and sings comic songs incomparably. He could make a
fortune on the vaudeville stage."[16]

The posturing extravagance of these people in both their verse and criticism has had a rather curious influence upon the history of Canadian let-

ters. For this whole literary movement of the early 'twenties had an anachronistic affinity with that of the post-Confederation period. As then, the poets of the later time, supported by patriotic critics, seemed obliged, as A.J.M. Smith has noted, to gather "their singing robes about them to hymn the mysteries of Life and the grandeurs of Empire,"[17] to regard their craft as one of a very high "high seriousness." But, as Desmond Pacey has remarked, with their nineteenth-century emphasis upon nature and love, they seemed unaware that a new age had come into being, and that even it was changing rapidly.[18] The revolutionary trends that were influencing poetry elsewhere in the world were barely reflected in Canada; here again this country had to wait another decade. The poet and man of letters of the time, in fact, stood apart from the restless world around him; he was fastidious or affected in his dress, even to celluloid collar, ribboned pince-nez and stick-pin in his cravat; new members of the group were "new singing voices" who would "surely be heard afar"; if they were female, they were "brilliant daughters" of Toronto or Montreal; if male, they were "sons of Apollo." And if they reflected the changing currents of the world outside, they did so esoterically. Albert Durrant Watson, for example, had a medium by whom he aspired to communicate mystically with voices of the past, and he was a keen follower of the adventures in spiritualism of Oliver Lodge and Conan Doyle. One of his works, *The Twentieth Plane*, Garvin described as "a remarkable book, a product of psychical research seances." Other poets were similarly souls apart.

These remarks will introduce one last paradox concerning Pauline Johnson. She became one of those Canadian poets chosen for immortality by the literary boosters of the 'twenties, and whereas she herself had encountered difficulty in having her verses published during her lifetime, her name and somewhat romantic career now assured space for those verses in a large number of text-books and anthologies. "The Song my Paddle Sings" and "In the Shadows" became familiar to pupils of elementary and secondary schools throughout Canada, pupils who, significantly enough, were undergoing, it will be recalled, what the jargon of today would call an indoctrination programme, by which the maple leaf, the beaver and Jack Canuck became almost holy symbols and Empire Day and Victoria Day occasions for nationalistic reverence. In their enthusiasms to apotheosize Canadian writers, however, the critics did themselves and their subjects more harm than good, for when more sober, less chauvinistic judgment viewed many Canadian poets as being somewhat less than great, the consequent reaction tended to sweep all our early poets aside, along with the whole corpus of what has become known as the Maple Leaf school of criticism. Thus we have the remarks of Woodcock, MacLure and Levine, which were quoted in *Canadian Literature* last summer, but are humorously significant enough to bear repeating: "Victorian versifiers like Heavysege and Sangster and

Mair were dead before they reached the grave," "Lampman is a good old cheese, but Roberts and Carman belong on captions in the New Brunswick museum (Carman's verse is to poetic speech what Baird's Lemon Extract used to be to Demerara Rum)" and "the dead wood of the nineteenth century."

But such criticism is just as invalid as that of Garvin and his friends of the 'twenties. Pauline Johnson has suffered from both. The time has long since come, surely, for what she as an intelligent woman would have most wished, an unprejudiced, dispassionate assessment not of her verse in isolation, but of her verse in reference to the conditions by which it was written. If we attempt this, I think we shall see that she is to be neither unrestrainedly praised nor sneeringly scorned. For she tells us something about what it was like to be a writer in the eighteen-eighties and 'nineties in Canada; she tells us something about what became the fabric of our literary history. She herself, certainly, had none of the pretensions to that greatness so romantically ascribed to her by over-enthusiastic critics and well-meaning schoolmarms and schoolmasters. Nor did she wish anyone, one can infer from her private correspondence, to make apologies — or even anthropologies — for her. Perhaps what she was, what she tried to do and what effect she has had upon the enlightened, contemporary Canadian are reflected by Ethel Wilson's reminiscence in, ironically, the same number of this periodical as were the remarks quoted above:

> Many years later I saw her in a crowded street. She was much much older, yet she had a sad beauty. She was ill, walking very slowly and lost in sombre thought. Memory rushed in and, stricken, I watched her as though I had done it.

Notes

[1] "Our Poets: A Sketch of Canadian Poetry in the Nineteenth Century," *UTQ*, 12 (October 1942), 89–90.
[2] *Selections from Canadian Poets* (Montreal: John Lovell, 1864), x.
[3] "Nationalism and Canadian Poetry," *Northern Review*, 1 (December-January 1945–46), 42.
[4] *The Book of Canadian Poetry* (3rd ed. Toronto: Gage, 1957), 36.
[5] Walter McRaye, *Pauline Johnson and her Friends* (Toronto: Ryerson, 1947), 19.
[6] *Ibid.*, 20.
[7] *Ibid.*, 61–62.
[8] Toronto *World*, March 22, 1892.
[9] *Ibid.*
[10] Public Archives of Canada, Denison Papers, 6001, Charles Mair to George T. Denison, April 19, 1913.
[11] *Creative Writing in Canada* (1st ed. Toronto: Ryerson, 1952), 82.
[12] Denison Papers, 4454, December 28, 1901.
[13] *Ibid.*, 4424, October 15, 1901.

[14] Queen's University Library, Mair Papers, Garvin to Mair, May 23, 1913.
[15] *Ibid.*, November 17, 1915.
[16] *Ibid.*, December 14, 1915.
[17] *The Book of Canadian Poetry*, 2.
[18] *Creative Writing in Canada*, 84.

CL 13 (Summer 1962)

2. GALLERY ONE

Robert Weaver

Stories by Callaghan

Morley Callaghan IS the most important novelist and short story writer in English Canada, and he is the only prose writer of an older generation who might have much influence on the young writers of today. Yet his reputation in his own country has been a curiously fugitive one, and although his stories have been published in all sorts of anthologies and most of the influential magazines of our time, the bulk of them seem now to be surprisingly little known. Two early collections of the stories, *A Native Argosy* and *Now That April's Here*, have been out of print for many years, and recent essays about Callaghan's work by Canadian critics — Malcolm Ross, Hugo McPherson — have dealt with the novels, which lend themselves more readily than the stories to an intellectual framework.

Callaghan's stories *are* hard to write about: their odd, wistful, lyric quality keeps escaping definition; they require from the reader a kind of quiet, unhurried sympathy that most of us are too impatient to give. And I want to write an appreciation of them — a difficult thing for any critic to do. But the occasion for some kind of appreciation is certainly here in this new collection, *Morley Callaghan's Stories*. It's a fine, impressive book, and its publisher ought to share some of the credit for being willing to risk a big and nearly comprehensive collection when volumes of short stories are notoriously difficult to sell in hard covers.

One test of a writer is whether he has the ability to create a complete fictional world, and in the fifty-odd stories in this book Morley Callaghan shows us a whole world. It isn't a wide, wide world. It's the narrow, stifling world of a few small towns in Southern Ontario and one section of Toronto — the old, downtown area of the city spreading a couple of miles east and west of Yonge Street and ending a few blocks south of St. Clair Avenue. One of the incidental virtues of *Morley Callaghan's Stories* is that it captures forever the spirit of much of this crowded and lonely heart of the city before the wreckers moved in.

The people who live in Callaghan's part of the city inhabit some shadowy boundary line between social classes: they are not solidly middle class but they do not consciously belong to the working class. I suppose that a sociologist might define them pretty clearly, but I once described them as marginal people, and I still can't discover a better way of identifying them. They are the students, the landladies, the waitresses, the young clerks and their wives, the slightly failed and faded older couples, who belong to the rooming houses and furnished flats of the aging residential streets downtown. (The people in the stories about the small towns aren't much different in status and expectations.) In many of the stories we meet the old, tired priests and the eager, young priests of the city parishes. There are no really wealthy people in this world, and Callaghan has a wry comment about that in a brief introductory note he has written for the book. On summer nights Callaghan's people are likely to be out wandering through the streets, and in the cold weather they hurry to the restaurants and bars and other amusements of a city that has always had its own, very strong texture but (until lately) no sharp and decisive character. They are city people, yet they are uneasy, alien, not really settled in to the city; you sense that the city frightens them, that they feel vulnerable — and they are indeed vulnerable.

For one characteristic of Callaghan's world is that it stifles or wears away the people who inhabit it. The atmosphere of his stories often reminds me of the atmosphere of the Italian neo-realistic movies (especially De Sica); it isn't surprising that many of the stories have been translated and published in Italy since the war. Most of Callaghan's people are caught, sooner or later, in one of those small tragedies that are so appalling simply because they are never over. Or they attempt a tiny rebellion against the restrictions of life. But even the rebellions are subdued and fumbled a little from the beginning. Yet I don't want to give the impression that there is nothing but tragedy and sorrow in this world, and Callaghan does not subscribe to that Catholic heresy that gives the work of Mauriac and Graham Greene its joyless and obsessive quality. There is a great deal of sweetness and innocence and love, an eager, yearning, uncertain reaching out for life, in all these stories. Again I am reminded of De Sica.

The first story in the book is called "All the Years of Her Life." It has been given the place of honour, and it establishes at once one of Callaghan's favourite themes. A boy, Alfred Higgins, has been working in a drugstore, and one night the owner stops him with the evidence on his person of the petty thievery that has been going on ever since he began to work there. The owner calls the boy's mother, and when she arrives at the store, Mrs. Higgins, with her quiet pleading and painful composure, persuades the owner not to call the police. Alfred is fired, and the mother and son go home together. Alfred swears that it will never happen again, but it has happened many times before, and it will happen so many times in the future. There is nothing for Mrs. Higgins to do when they arrive home but to drink a cup of hot tea and try to compose herself to face all the years of her life.

In the story called "A Wedding-Dress" there is rebellion: a tiny, only half-conscious rebellion of the spirit against drabness and restriction. Miss Lena Schwartz lives in a boarding house on Wellesley Street in Toronto (almost the exact centre of the area of the city I described earlier as Callaghan's special preserve). She has been waiting for fifteen years to marry Sam Hilton; now she was "thirty-two, her hair was straight, her nose turned up a little and she was thin." But at last she is going to be married, and she quits her job to spend the day shopping before going to Windsor for the wedding. Her spirit, so meek and drab, has come alive on this day, but she hasn't much money, and the dresses she can afford to buy dampen her fine feeling. She looks at some French dresses; they are beautiful and far too expensive, and she has a dream of men watching her on the street as she walks with Sam in one of these fine dresses. And in her dream, almost unaware, she slips a dress from its hanger and into the wide sleeve of her coat.

The next morning Lena Schwartz is in court, in the dress which does not fit her thin figure, charged with shoplifting. Sam has come from Windsor, and there are the lawyers and the magistrate, who find Miss Schwartz pitiful and a little amusing. Sam agrees to pay for the dress, and she is released to leave the city and be married. And where is the dream of the sly glances of men as she goes walking in her fine, French dress?

There are more dramatic stories such as the well-known "Two Fishermen" about the hangman come to do his job in a small Ontario town. But most of the fifty stories in this book quietly explore some common happening in the life of the city or one of the Ontario towns. A young priest tries unsuccessfully to bring solace to an unhappy, hysterical and important woman member of the parish ("The Young Priest"). A father and son discover themselves through a lost baseball cap ("A Cap for Steve"). Two English boys trace out their little tragedy as misfits on a Toronto newspaper ("Last Spring They Came Over"). A whole way of life in an Ontario town comes painfully alive in "Ancient Lineage." The Depression wears away at young couples with too little money and older men insecure in their jobs. Young people make a try at love, and there are other small rebellions like that of Miss Lena Schwartz that somehow just flicker out.

These stories are North American, but they don't connect Callaghan with Ernest Hemingway as many people would like to do. They are quieter, more human, and less optimistic than most American fiction. If Callaghan's stories are good evidence (and I think they are), we Canadians are far less hopeful than Americans about altering circumstances. There is a sweetness and an eagerness for life (and a failure to make connection) in much of Callaghan's work that has a good deal in common with the stories of Sherwood Anderson. But there is an acceptance of life that seems more European than North American, and that may help to account for the interest in Europe in Callaghan's work in recent years. This book has an odd and appealing quality of seeming at once to come from another time and to be perfectly contemporary. It is the best we have in the tough *genre* of the short story, and it is very good indeed.

CL 2 (Autumn 1959)

Gérard Bessette

Un grand poète

Mademoiselle Rina Lasnier vient de nous donner son meilleur recueil de poésie.

Avant toutefois d'analyser le groupe de poèmes qui constituent la valeur de *Mémoire sans jours*, disons un mot des pièces médiocres, plutôt nombreuses, qui déparent le recueil.

Il y a d'abord les poèmes qui figurent sous le titre général de « Le Christ aux outrages ». Ils rappellent fâcheusement *Madones canadiennes* et *Le chant de la montée*, dans lesquels la poétesse nous avait chanté en un style farci d'images conventionnelles la vie de Rachel et les vertus de la Vierge. Je ne blâme pas Rina Lasnier d'avoir échoué dans ces tentatives. Rien n'est plus difficile que de renouveler des sujets séculaires qui ont pu fleurir à une époque de foi collective intense comme le moyen âge, mais qui, au XXe siècle, requièrent le talent cosmique d'un Claudel ou la fraîcheur d'imagination d'un Péguy pour nous toucher poétiquement.

Rina Lasnier n'est guère plus heureuse dans la section intitulée « Petit Bestiaire familier » où elle nous sert un mélange indigeste de descriptions réalistes et de religiosité :

> Culs-de-jatte assoupis sur leurs moignons,
> 　[il s'agit de carcasses d'automobiles]
> Amputés des vols et des élans voyageurs,
> Refuge des chats, des lapins et des oignons,
> Arches de Noé de nos jardins potagers. (134)

Il est toujours dangereux de vouloir édifier un symbole à partir de données essentiellement prosaïques. Sur le plan de la logique, on aboutit à un échec analogue quand on essaye de tirer une conclusion générale de prémisses particulières. L'image ne colle plus à sa base; elle flotte, désincarnée, dans le vide : cela devient une fantaisie nouménale ou du bel esprit.

Il est également inutile de nous arrêter à « Silves ». Quoique à un moindre degré, les poèmes de cette section souffrent des mêmes défauts que « Petit Bestiaire . . . » et que « Le Christ aux outrages ».

Au contraire, « Malemer » et « Poèmes haïtiens », que l'auteure a placés au début de son recueil, comptent parmi les plus beaux poèmes de notre littérature. Non seulement éclipsent-ils le reste de *Mémoire sans jours*, mais ils laissent loin derrière eux les meilleures pièces d'*Escales* et de *Présence de l'absence*.

« Malemer » est, en effet, un poème symbolique dans le vrai sens du terme, un poème qui, sans jamais sombrer dans une obscurité absolue, dans un chaos indifférencié à la façon de la plupart de nos poétereaux contemporains, suggère plusieurs

« solutions » sans en imposer aucune. La mer profonde, c'est le sein maternel, le principe de la vie, le subconscient, la poétesse elle-même, etc. mais, à la surface, dans le déroulement de ses vagues, c'est aussi l'ensemble du monde extérieur avec ses multiples séductions, c'est le danger de se laisser emporter par le verbalisme, de disperser en vocables superficiels l'unicité inexprimable de toute conscience. Il faudrait une exégèse à la Noulet ou à la Madaule pour rendre pleinement justice à ce poème polyphonique.

Moins vastes, moins cosmiques que « Malemer », les « Poèmes haïtiens » compensent leur relative minceur par un rythme plus pulsatif, par des images plus immédiates et par un primitivisme sauvage et touffu. Il m'est impossible de juger le degré d'originalité de ces poèmes, car je n'ai pas lu les ouvrages de Louis Maximilien et de Jacques Roumain que Rina Lasnier, avec une admirable honnêteté intellectuelle, mentionne au bas des pages comme sources d'inspiration.

Pour donner une idée de la beauté de « Poèmes haïtiens », je citerai quelques lignes de « Ountougni » (il s'agit d'une batterie de tambours vaudouesque):

Sur la peau tendue du silence, ountogni,
pulsion solitaire sans paix ni appel, . . .
socle du son insulaire au centre de la solennité,
passe rocailleuse dans la liquidité d'une fête.

Secret serein de la durée par le bris sonore du temps,
insistance horizontale de la corde raide tendue aux dieux,
sommation sans surcharge de signes, d'exil ou de transes;
mailles du filet neuf aux genoux écartés du tambourineur,
et sous ses paumes, étoffe vaste de l'ombre indivise;
césures blanches avant le coloris impur du chant,
os dur du son sans oscillations de plumages;
voix égale des morts sans écho sépulcral,
sonorité du sang lié au sang, levée processionelle de la négritude. (23)

Que faut-il penser du métier, de la technique de Rina Lasnier? — Tout comme pour la valeur et la qualité de ses poèmes, quelques distinctions s'imposent. Dans les rares pièces comme « Chansons » où elle emploie la versification classique (sauf pour la rime), elle réussit fort bien:

Lève du coffre de velours
Lève ta viole sous ta main
Murmure d'amante ou d'amour
À coeur battant dès le matin (48)

Au contraire, quand ses « vers » ne font que se rapprocher de la prosodie traditionnelle sans tenir compte du nombre de pieds ni de la césure, Rina Lasnier produit des textes bâtards, illisibles à haute voix :

Quand nous cherchons une foi vulnérée,
Quand nous cherchons, plus humble que l'espérance,
Le tison d'une foi trois fois humiliée,
C'est Pierre . . . et sa face fait pénitence.

C'est lui, coq rouge et credo de la lumière,
Et le soleil bondit pour une autre évidence,
C'est lui le pas infaillible de la croissance
Et la tête du blé honore la poussière, (38)

Heureusement, ce qu'elle pratique la plupart du temps, c'est le vers libre, sorte de
verset claudélien où les « rimes » et les assonances irrégulières sont étayées par de
nombreuses allitérations et par une gamme subtile de sons vocaliques. Voici un
extrait de « Malemer » :

Malemer, aveugle-née du mal de la lumière — comment sais-tu ta
nuit sinon par l'oeil circulaire et sans repos de paupière ?
    pierrerie myriadaire de l'œil jamais clos — malemer, tu es une tapis-
serie de regards te crucifiant sur ton mal ;
    comment saurais-tu ta lumière noire et sans intimité — sinon par le
poème hermétique de tes tribus poissonneuses ?
    ô rime puérile des étages du son — voici l'assonance sinueuse et la
parité vivante,
    voici l'opacité ocellée par l'œil et l'écaillé — voici la nuit veillée par
l'insomnie et l'étincelle . . . (16–17)

On peut fort bien se passer de régularité et de rime classique quand on les
remplace par un si souple et si subtil éventail d'assonances et d'allitérations.

Je devais aussi parler dans cet article de *Miroirs*, ce recueil de « proses » paru en
même temps que *Mémoire sans jours*. Mais à quoi bon ? A quoi bon éreinter un
écrivain de talent, peut-être de génie, comme Rina Lasnier, parce qu'elle a commis
un livre médiocre, presque nul ?

Il est vrai que les trois premières « proses », qui notent les impressions d'enfance
d'une fillette du nom de Messalée, sécrètent une poésie mineure, un peu mièvre, susceptible de charmer les adolescentes et les romantiques attardés. Mais le reste est nul.

Voulez-vous une élucubration sur la neige ? La voici :

La neige ne raisonne pas car elle est pure voyance ; elle regarde sans
juger et sans connaître . . . La neige a des yeux pour voir car elle n'a

pas péché contre la lumière, mais elle ne dit rien de ce qu'elle a vu en haut ni de ce qu'elle découvre en bas . . .

Préférez-vous un étrange extrait de la vie de la Vierge?

Approchez-vous, moinillons et enfants de choeur qui ébranlez la Trinité à coups de clochettes; et vous, ma soeur sacristine qui pleurez vos burettes cassées, approchez.

Il serait cruel d'en citer davantage. Ces enfantillages sont d'autant plus pénibles qu'ils veulent exprimer des sujets augustes, sacrés pour la plupart des lecteurs. Mais ce n'est malheureusement pas avec de bonnes intentions que l'on fait nécessairement de la bonne littérature. Autrement Nérée Beauchemin, Pamphile LeMay et William Chapman seraient les princes de notre poésie.

Arrêtons-nous ici, et concluons en disant que, grâce aux vingt premières pages de *Mémoire sans jours*, Rina Lasnier se révèle peut-être le plus grand poète du Canada français contemporain.

CL 8 (Spring 1961)

Donald Stephens

Ordinary People

Canadian fiction needs more writers like Norman Levine who will lift the short story from its secondary place in Canadian letters to a position of prominence. Callaghan has given some good short stories, and now there is Levine who has consciously shaped his stories into compact pieces of construction, economy, and apt characterization. In them manner and matter are closely linked, and are an end in themselves. Levine's stories are not associated to a larger scheme as are those of many short story writers (Katherine Mansfield's New Zealand stories are an example of this). Rather, when his stories are finished, he has said all that he feels is necessary. Finely wrought, carefully explained, Levine's stories are complete; the reader does not wonder what happened before the action began, or what will occur in the future. There is never a vagueness about the stories; never is the reader left in obvious doubt. This certainty, or lucidity, in his work, is his most compelling quality, the factor which makes Levine a distinguished writer among the many new Canadian writers. He is a sincere and simple teller of tales; in an age which boasts of being astute and knowing in experience, Levine's unsophisticated stories appeal, if only because they are always readily understood and unequivocal.

Levine does not experiment with the story form, as a novelist frequently does. Nor does he develop and strengthen the theme as the story progresses; it is completely thought out before he begins. In *One Way Ticket* there are eight short stories and one long one, each dealing with a number of journeys. The long story is the poorest, where the focus is more on character and the episodes are selected to display the character's personality. In the others, however, the character is selected to point out a significant episode. It is hoped that Levine will stay with the story form, for this collection indicates that if he were to write a novel the quality of sustainment would be lacking, as it is in this book in "The Playground."

The title of the book is misleading. The publisher tells us, on the jacket blurb, that these are stories where the narrator holds a return ticket; it is the other people who have to remain where they are, who have only "one way tickets" that the book is about. But even the narrator at times has a "one way ticket." He seems to want to leave what he finds, but he never does; he finds similar things each time.

There is, however, a diversified picture of life in Levine's stories; he moves from one extreme to another in attitude and is careful not to merge these into an ineffectual medium. On one level his stories are complete with strong realism, ordinary simplicity of common men, and graphic actual description. On the other level there are the fantasy and psychological studies, as in "Ringa Ringa Rosie," interspersed with lyrical passages and subtleties which are interesting in themselves.

Levine is a sincere author who writes stories showing a unique ability to tell a complete tale. Showing does not necessarily mean displaying. Levine's stories, indeed, make little obvious display at all. That, perhaps, is why many people would prefer the stories of a Lawrence or a Huxley. Levine's work is free from affectation. His full appeal is not immediate. The reward with the stories of Norman Levine lies not merely in the number of separate examples of fine stories in this volume, but in the way that they go so well together to produce a wonderfully rich and varied picture of ordinary people.

CL 12 (Spring 1962)

Thelma McCormack

Innocent Eye on Mass Society

I used to think that Marshall McLuhan was an innocent who had discovered depth psychology and called it "television." Since depth psychology is as good an approach as any to the mass media, a great deal better than some, McLuhan with all his mannerisms was working in the right direction. This impression is borne out in *Understanding Media* where what he has to say about the mass media of communication is contrived, autodidactic, amusing, occasionally right and occasionally dangerous. But below the surface of his comments about the media is an insight and system which bear serious attention whether one is interested in the media or not. McLuhan has now gone well beyond discovering depth psychology; he has discovered mass society.

The metaphors he draws upon are from preliterate societies. In particular, he is entranced by the group cohesion and group consciousness of an "oral" culture, a term which summarizes a closed, static, tradition-bound social structure where relationships are face-to-face, where there is scarcely any individual differentiation and only a rudimentary division of labour. In urban industrialized societies, consensus on such a scale is an artifact, achieved by the sacrifice of critical judgment, sustained internally by anxiety and externally by manipulation. To paraphrase McLuhan's most famous dictum: the medium is history: the message is the mass movement.

Content of the media is irrelevant, according to McLuhan. Thus he refuses to be drawn into discussions of Kitsch and popular culture that have so engaged intellectuals in recent years. By "content," he means the manifest content of any particular news story, feature article, TV documentary, etc. The real stuff of the media are not facts, opinions, concepts, but the structure of symbols that emerge cumulatively. Imagine the American constitution rewritten by Joyce and analyzed through structural linguistics and you have approximately what McLuhan regards as the substance of the media. Imagine, also, *Finnegans Wake* rewritten by Thomas Jefferson and analyzed by John Stuart Mill and you have the mistake McLuhan thinks we make.

Our mistake belongs to the age of mechanical technology which produced individualism, scientific detachment, democratic pluralism, nationalism, the sequential analysis of cause and effect, the class struggle, competition, the market mechanism, critical intelligence, a rational approach to social change and a high degree of self-conscious awareness. All of them divisive. Electronic technology of the twentieth century is unifying, communal, demanding commitment and involvement. It submerges individual personality, obliterates social differences and de-nationalizes the world, restoring the ethos of the oral society. The great modern revolution for

McLuhan, seen most clearly in the mass media of communication, is the shift from divisive to unifying ways of perceiving and organizing experience, from "explosion" to "implosion."

No field of science I know of has not moved in the direction of configurational concepts, and in that sense McLuhan is a popularizer of contemporary science though he appears to be unaware of these developments. His hypothesis that technology is responsible for this historical change is something else again. It is legitimate to regard technology as a causal variable, but its weight in relation to other factors, material and non-material, in the social matrix, and the precise nature of its social and psychological impact, direct and indirect, are exceedingly complex problems. For McLuhan, however, this is not a provisional hypothesis. Technology is the Prime Mover, and everything, large or small, becomes its consequences. Wherever he looks, from ladies' hair-dos to weapons, he finds corroboration.

The immediate model for this is depth psychology where all behaviour awake or asleep, trivial or important, accidental or planned, expresses the motivational key — a key, moreover, which we do not, will not, cannot consciously recognize. McLuhan draws upon this model further by locating the source of technology within the individual. Technology is nothing more than the externalization of our feet, hands, eyes, brain, skin, teeth, etc. The correspondences he establishes between body and machine are cruder and more arbitrary than those of a Freudian since McLuhan is not guided by a theory of motivation, least of all by one based on conflict. For Oedipus, he offers Narcissus, who having created his own image fails to recognize it.

The Narcissus myth eliminates the dichotomy between consumer and producer just as the modern economy eliminates the price mechanism. The "audience" of the media is not the consumer; it is the producer. We are not sold General Motors cars in McLuhan's system; we are shareholders, producers of transportation. Looked at one way, he is simply saying that audiences are not passive, that communication is a reciprocal process, and the fact that communication is now mediated, conducted through a technology, does not alter this. This is one of the cornerstones of current media research, and it is characteristic of the older media as well as the newer ones. We not only select the books we read, but read into them and read out anything that is threatening. Looked at another way, this is an argument for public ownership of the media, for it is, as McLuhan says, as absurd for us to "lease" to others the media of communication as it would be to "lease" speech.

Either way, this new producer role does not solve any better than the old consumer role the problem — no problem to primitive societies — of how we control the media. Being told that we own or produce the media of communication can be as politically disingenuous as Henry Luce's concept of "the people's capitalism," as dishonest as thinking that letters to the Soviet press or, closer to home, open-line radio where the housewife and folksy disc jockey exchange generalities are genuine forms of participation. McLuhan does not suggest that these problems constitute another area of inquiry or that they do not properly belong in a general theory of communication. On the contrary, to raise them at all, he maintains, is to misunderstand the media. This is not arrogance on his part, for it is inherent in this theory, essentially an historical theory, that these and similar questions belong to an earlier epoch.

Much of McLuhan, including his style and his penchant for anthropology, is reminiscent of Veblen who similarly began his analysis with technology and expected that its rational logic would spread to the business class and ultimately throughout social life. Engineers were Veblen's vanguard of the revolution. Instead, we got the "managerial revolution," for Veblen, like McLuhan, underestimated our capacity to use technology without being influenced by it. Technological determinism, like all forms of determinism, is never able to cope with discrepancies and must rush in concepts like Ogburn's "cultural lag," Marx's "false consciousness," and McLuhan's psychic shock or "numbness."

Historical determinism is the mystique of all modern ideologies. However, what distinguishes the ideologies of mass society is their response to alienation, their disillusionment with the democratic "left," their idealization of provincial anti-intellectual and anti-secular values. They combine, as J.L. Talmon says, two contradictory notions: social cohesion and self-expression. McLuhan and McCarthy, vastly different in every other respect, intuitively grasped the same thing. McLuhan is not interested in restoring the values of a secular-rational cosmopolitan *Anschauung*, for it destroys the cohesion of tribal life and is as obsolete as the assembly line in an age of automation.

The more passive, alienated and uncommitted we are, the more we yearn for, the more strongly we respond to ideologies of "effectiveness" provided they make no demands on us. The most successful ideology is the most ambiguous one which we structure ourselves with our infantile and wish-fulfillment fantasies. Applying this principle to the media, McLuhan distinguishes between "hot" media, like print and radio, which are highly structured, and "cold" media, like TV, which are relatively unstructured. The latter, he claims, involve us; the former, do not.

Actually, they both involve us, but in different ways, the difference being the distinction between "identification" — when you cry with the martyred Elsie who is forced to play the piano on the Sabbath — and "projection" — when you see your mother's face in the clouds. Identification is the mechanism of social learning; it is growth, strengthening and broadening the ego. Projection is regression, the absence of controls and capacity for problem-solving. When McLuhan talks about "involvement," he means projection. For the alienated with their impoverished or damaged egos, projection is the only means of involvement. It goes a long way toward explaining why changes in a party line scarcely disturb the true adherent, and why, as Lasswell pointed out many years ago, logical consistency is not the criterion of ideology. The race is to the vaguest.

McLuhan goes even further, equating projection or "participation in depth" with "maturity." As he describes "participation in depth" it is the furthest extreme from introspection, the latter being private, inner-directed, self-critical, leading to a sense of apartness, a capacity to live comfortably with relative truths, to resist group pressure, and, if necessary, to endure isolation. McLuhan's definition of "maturity" is "belief," collective belief.

All historical determinism faces the problem of leadership. According to McLuhan, the group best qualified to lead us into the Promised Land are the artists who "can show us how to 'ride with the punch'." Taken at face value, this is a puzzling choice to make since no group has had a sorrier record in the past century for its inability to understand or accept technology than artists. The explanation lies, I think, in understanding that McLuhan is talking not so much about artists as about art. He is attempting here to develop an aesthetic theory which abolishes the distinctions usually made between (1) "highbrow" and "lowbrow" art; and (2) "lowbrow" and "folk" art. In his system, folk art and popular art ("lowbrow") become the same, a rationale that Marxist writers used to give years ago for going to Hollywood. In a limited sense, he and they are right. Structurally, popular art and folk art are both highly simplified and repetitive. They may move us at the level of universal archetypal images. Both have a social function; in the case of folk art or religion, it is to provide the closure of ritual. But, if in mass society, there is, as Malraux says, no "folk," the closure is delusional; its function is escape or pseudo-closure, harmless enough under certain circumstances, even necessary, but disastrous as a fixation and dangerous in a period of confusion and rapid social change which calls for the highest degree of political intelligence.

The distinction between "highbrow" and "lowbrow" art is minimized by recognizing that great art, too, tells us something about the "human condition." The distinction becomes even more blurred by art styles which have no cognitive content and communicate solely by involving us. In McLuhan's system, then, there is no difference between abstract art and a television screen. "Pop art," which is, on the one hand, a parody of folk art, and, on the other hand, a parody of what we have traditionally meant by the term "creative," carries this to its logical conclusion. Aesthetic theory thus becomes the science of communication. It is as if we were asked to judge art by the same criteria we would use in judging snapshots of our children, and if this sounds foolish, it is no more so than the reverse fallacy which intellectuals usually make in approaching the media; that is, to judge family snapshots by the same criteria they would use for judging art. When McLuhan turns to the specific media of communication, he runs into difficulty. First, because he is forced to deal with "content" in the same terms as anyone else does, e.g. "the success theme." Second, because it is almost impossible to isolate what is unique about a medium from the policies of the people who run it. For example, the diffuseness of TV, its avoidance of controversial subjects, may have as much to do with the costs of TV and the cautiousness of TV executives as it does with the intrinsic nature of the medium. We can be sure it will become even "cooler" with colour. Radio, he tells us, is a "hot" medium and so can deal with ideas, personalities (Hitler, Fred Allen) and empirical data (the weather). At the same time, since it is an electronic medium, it is intimate and tribal, or, as we are more apt to say, it is the intellectuals' ghetto, just exactly what we have been hearing from TV executives. Is it because they understand the medium and we do not? Finally, whatever distinctions may be made among the different media, the distinction between "hot" and "cold" breaks down. All of the media, taken together or separately, are nothing if not flexible; radio and print are as capable of surrealism as realism; the seven types of ambiguity are as much in poetry as they are in television.

Still, McLuhan is a godsend to the TV producer who because he is often young wants recognition and who because he is an *arriviste* to the media wants status. In McLuhan he can find a basis for claiming that TV is unique, different from the older media; above all, different from print. Long impatient with the psychological ineptitude of most do-good preachy broadcasting and equally frustrated by the complexities of modern thought, he finds in McLuhan a mandate to experiment without worrying too much about "content." His banner is television for television's sake.

Watching TV is a revelation. More and more public affairs programs resemble Rorschach cards, each one different but no objective content in any; each one involving us, but leaving us none the wiser as citizens. One politician differs from another in the way one piece of abstract art or one page of Joyce differs from another. Just how cynical this is is revealed by McLuhan's suggestion that had Jack Paar produced Nixon the election results might have been different. As it was, Kennedy with his more diffuse image was better suited to the medium. In other words, McLuhan is saying that TV depersonalizes and de-intellectualizes politics. The depersonalization of politics could be the hopeful start of politics based on issues in which the elected representative is held accountable for his ideas rather than his morals or character. But a de-intellectualized politics is its antithesis. Combined, they are the politics of ideology in mass society, an ill wind that blows some good to the young eager TV producer who thinks that political theory is in the hand-held camera.

TV producers are not the only ones to welcome McLuhan. Canadians in general have become more susceptible to the charms of an intellectual exploring the cultural demimonde without the usual class biases. It is an attractive egalitarian avant-garde image for a country that has not yet had its Whitmans, Sandburgs, or Pounds; a country that has only begun to face the fact that it is urban and industrialized, its quickest and best minds straining at the leash to break away from an intellectual Establishment which has been singularly obtuse, Mandarin-minded and peculiarly punitive. Bright young men will find in McLuhan's enthusiasm for the media a populist realism, his distrust of intellectualism a revolt against dead scholarship and the demands of specialization, his approach through technology an unsentimental toughness, his removal of the issue from a context of values a liberation from petty Philistine censors, his rejection of social criticism a long overdue break with the tiresome futile leftish politics of the thirties. It is an ideal formula for the 1960s, and to his disciples — and they are legion — McLuhan is a prophet. From a longer perspective, he is the first, original, genuine Canadian *ideologue* of mass society, but his sense-ratios were shaped by the irrationalism, determinism, and folk romanticism of the nineteenth century.

CL 22 (Autumn 1964)

Ronald Sutherland

Faulknerian Quebec

Three Canadian novelists have written books which take the William Faulkner approach to characters in a rural setting. George Ryga's *Ballad of a Stone Picker* and Sheila Watson's *The Double Hook* both effectively dramatize the grotesque consequences of clinging to false values, of inverted or perverted ideas which have become life forces. It is the French-Canadian writer Roch Carrier, however, who comes closest to the significance, power and artistry of Faulkner at his best.

There are, of course, many contrasts between rural Quebec and the American Deep South, especially when the former is pictured under several feet of snow; but despite these contrasts and despite the book's striking originality, *La guerre, yes sir!* has much in common with *As I Lay Dying*. It has an atmosphere and flavour peculiar to Quebec, but it offers insight into the quirks and crudities of human nature with the subtle penetration characteristic of Faulkner's work. It has the same kind of black humour and devastating irony, and it also focuses on the central image of a coffin.

In Carrier's story the coffin contains the body of a soldier, Corriveau, who was killed in action and has been returned to his home village for burial. Complicating the situation, the Canadian Army has sent along a seven-man contingent of English-speaking soldiers to provide Corriveau with an appropriate military send-off. The railway station is quite a distance from the tiny, totally French-speaking village, and the soldiers have to carry the coffin the whole way along an unploughed road. On the same road at the same time, a local soldier on leave is carrying his new bride, a former Newfoundland whore called Molly, on his shoulders through the snow.

Roch Carrier has the capacity to bring extraordinary and convincing characters to life with a minimum of description. Besides those already mentioned, several others end up in the Corriveau house to sit through the night with the corpse. There is Amélie, whose husband Henri deserts from the Army when he discovers that his wife is sheltering a draft dodger. A simple soul, Henri nevertheless becomes disturbed upon learning that Amélie has given birth to two sets of twins since his departure years before. She carefully explains to him how the twins had simply developed inside of her "et puis, ils sont sortis." "Ce qui m'intéresse," Henri replies, "c'est de savoir comment ils sont entrés." Then there is Joseph, who has calmly chopped off his hand in order to avoid the draft, thus inadvertently providing the local boys with something to use as a puck in their hockey games.

The story proceeds in a series of scenes, each seemingly more fantastic than the previous one. The English-Canadian soldiers, like creatures from another planet, sit stone-faced while the villagers get drunk on cider and eat "tortières."

Speaking about *La guerre*, Carrier once remarked that the events of the book take place in the Middle Ages — the Middle Ages of French Canada. The novel examines a variety of attitudes, prejudices and superstitions which warped the lives of the characters involved, just as they have warped and continue to warp the lives of many Quebeckers. The influence of the Church in every aspect of life is underlined repeatedly. Throughout the wake, chanted prayers alternate with blasphemies and curses based upon the prayers. The reader witnesses a society turned in upon itself, a society seething with frustrations and inhibitions, ready to explode at any moment. Traditional outlets for these frustrations, in Carrier's novel as in Quebec itself, are in the process of breaking down.

With regard to French-English relations, Carrier's main point, of course, is that the language barrier, the absence of communication, constitutes a formidable obstacle. Despite prejudices and fears on both sides, the Corriveaus want to be hospitable to the English-Canadians who have come to bury their son, and the soldiers want simply to fulfill their duty to a fallen comrade, but because effective communication is impossible, the situation deteriorates and the old prejudices are heightened rather than weakened.

If at all possible, Carrier's *La guerre* should be read in the original French. The distinctive style is likely to lose a lot in translation. In fact, if the superb colloquial language of the book were to be rendered in the same way as similar diction in Gabrielle Roy's *Bonheur d'occasion* was rendered in the English translation, then a major part of *La guerre's* appeal and virtuosity could be lost entirely. But whatever happens in translation, Roch Carrier is a young writer with remarkable skill and originality. He might well be able to do for French Canada what Faulkner did for the American South. *La guerre, yes sir!* is certainly an impressive start.

Philip Stratford

Circle, Straight Line, Ellipse

Do you believe in signs? Here are three groups of translations on a common subject — French-Canadian poetry — whose different characters are described by the geometric figures that the typographer has chosen to present the contents in each case.

The back cover of John Glassco's *The Poetry of French Canada in Translation* shows the names of 47 French poets circumscribed by the names of 22 English translators; Fred Cogswell is presented in straight line relationship to the *One Hundred Poems of Modern Quebec* that he has translated, title and author drawn up flush to the righthand margin; while in Doug Jones's quarterly of writers in translation, subject and translator are represented as the twin centres of an *Ellipse*.

But before plunging into mathematical speculation, let's look at the total accomplishment. Taking these three sources together, never has so much French-Canadian poetry been so readily accessible to the unilingual reader. In the past, as John Glassco mentions in his preface, translation in Canada was almost an underground art, circulated in mimeographed pamphlets, in little magazines, or in limited editions. Now over 300 poems by 60 poets are available, translated by two dozen English-Canadians, most of them skilled poets themselves. That's not much compared to what remains to be done, but compared to what we had last year, it's riches.

I have already named the three prime movers. Each has played a slightly different role, the most composite going to John Glassco. Besides editing the volume, he has supplied a fine preface, as interesting for its insights into the nature of French-Canadian verse as for its seasoned reflections on the art of translation. It's a pity it isn't longer, for Mr. Glassco is a master of both subjects, but as a classicist he has also mastered the art of brevity. So we must be content.

He has, in addition, translated about one-third of the book himself, trying his hand at thirty-eight different poets. Such versatility has its price; all translations are not equally happy, though none is exactly sad. He excels at the urbane and witty couplet, as in this variation on the *carpe diem* theme (from Paul Morin):

do not insist on gathering roses
it leads to arteriosclerosis

But he also has lyric sweep and can deliver a solid surrealistic wallop. Occasionally, in order to produce a representative anthology, he has had to include samples of high banality, but this is rapidly and blandly done.

His eclecticism makes it difficult to distinguish his true voice. I seem to hear it best in his new translations of Saint-Denys Garneau, or in some of the light verse, for example, in his translations of de Grandmont and Godin (with A.J.M. Smith). But do I think I detect him here, in the faultless ease of this verse, because, as Glassco says, "poetry marked by clarity of thought and expression, spare and striking imagery and a simple internal movement" lends itself better to translation, or is it simply because I am partial to these poets? One thing certain: it is a real tour de force to be able to change into half-a-dozen poetic idioms as gracefully as a well-dressed man casually displaying his wardrobe.

Personally, I prefer translations where the translator's own frame shows through the cloth. And other members of Glassco's team, freer to choose only what suits them, come through with their own tone and idiosyncrasies intact. The Horatian irony of A.J.M. Smith, the dark romanticism of Eldon Grier, the controlled colloquialisms of George Johnston, the fragmented melancholy of R.A.D. Ford, the linguistic intricacies of Ralph Gustafson — all these survive a close rendering of the originals. In some translations (I am thinking of A.J.M. Smith's version of the ballad "Right You Are, My Brigadier" — of most of his work for that matter), the question of authorship becomes inverted, and one finds oneself wondering, "How in the devil could you ever turn *that* into French?" All this contradicts the theory that the translator should be some kind of invisible, tasteless, odourless medium, and backs up Glassco's claim that his book is not so much a collection of poems-in-translation as one of translations that are poems in themselves.

In this connection, special recognition is given to F.R. Scott as pilot and pioneer in the translation of Quebec verse. His own spareness and deftness are well adjusted, as we know, to the lean stride of Saint-Denys Garneau and the surgical swiftness of Anne Hébert.[1] But it is good to see collected here his translations of Hénault and Trottier, and to find the same style applied as successfully to translations of younger poets like Brault, Giguère, Pilon and Ouellette.

There is no space to comment on the performance of all the other poet-translators who complete the circle. At any rate, the last word must by rights come back to John Glassco who has so proficiently marshalled this round-up of talent. Three-quarters of these translations have never before appeared in print and were solicited or hunted down by this industrious and self-effacing editor. Typographically, his name should appear where it really belongs — right in the centre of the circle.

Fred Cogswell's single-handed translation of *One Hundred Poems of Modern Quebec* is a much more straightforward affair. The verse, too, is plainer, more direct, often less mannered, but less spectacular too, less rich in allusion, and sometimes lacking in syntactic sinew.

Four of Cogswell's poems appear in Glassco's collection; of the rest, only sixteen overlap, and he has added a dozen new poets. So this volume is a valuable complement to the other. In quality, too, it stands up well. From one poem to the next Cogswell's translations are less even; some of the more abstract originals are almost unintelligible in his versions, but whenever simplicity is required, or native strength and, yes, let's say it, a kind of prosaic humility in expression, his verse is better. In the two cases where Cogswell translations coincide with ones by F.R.

Scott for instance — in Saint-Denys Garneau's famous "Birdcage" poem and in "The Time Corrected" by Pierre Trottier — I prefer Cogswell. The differences are small. Cogswell is a little more explicit, a little more personal, more homely. Scott is more formal, stiffer, more enigmatic. He makes calculated use of certain French-type constructions which give his translation a somewhat eccentric gait, while Cogswell's rhythms are more natural.

One can't be categorical; it would be possible to prefer Scott for almost the same reasons. Whatever the result, I recommend the game of comparing translations as a fast and fascinating way to get into the heart of the poetry, the French as well as the English. With poems repeated in the two collections, and using Cogswell as yardstick, one can also compare the inspirations and techniques of Colombo, Downes, Ford, Glassco, Grier, Gustafson, Johnston, Smith and Sparshott.

One can even attempt the subtle sport of comparing Fred Cogswell with himself, for the same poem (e.g. Rina Lasnier's "The Body of Christ") sometimes appears in the two collections with mysterious variations. As a rule, one Cogswell seems to be more polished and well-rounded, while the other, when confronted with a problem in translation, takes the shortest distance between two points.

An objection that could be levelled at both books is that they contain so little verse by really young poets. Generations now in their thirties and forties are liberally represented, and the first quarter of Glassco's anthology is given over to French-Canadian classics. But Glassco includes only two poets in their twenties, Cogswell only four. Another sign of typical Canadian conservatism is the long publishers' parturition period for both books: Fred Cogswell did most of his work on these poems in 1967–68, and John Glassco's preface is dated October 1968.

Both objections and some others are countered by Doug Jones's quarterly *Ellipse*, which for the past year has been presenting translations of two Canadian writers, — one French and one English — in each issue. Until now the emphasis has been on poetry, though the latest number, *Ellipse 4*, was devoted to short stories by Roch Carrier and Dave Godfrey. The twin-centred elliptical principle is followed throughout the book: the original poem appears on the left, the translation on the right; an article or interview in English introduces the French writer, one in French the English, and so on.

To illustrate how it works, take *Ellipse 3*, which double-bills Michèle Lalonde and Margaret Atwood. A bilingual Editorial / *Avant-propos* situates and relates the two centres. Then come translations of nine Lalonde poems (four by Jones), a poetic tribute by Raymond Souster, "Michèle Lalonde, Reading," and a long interview with her conducted by Doug Jones. In the back half of the book Margaret Atwood gets equivalent treatment (fourteen poems and one prose text translated, plus an article by Tom Marshall).

Such thorough consideration is usually beyond the scope of an anthology, but it represents the kind of deep study that any translator worth his salt is ready to undertake. As a result, Jones's translations of Lalonde are supple and new, with a rhetoric of their own but one that does not betray his model.

Ellipse is a kind of running continuation of the two collections reviewed. Its regular appearance and flexible format permit it to be more experimental and to feature younger writers. It is an excellent sign to see writers like Jacques Brault, Roch Carrier, Gilles Marcotte and Guy Robert (all of whom translated Atwood poems) discovering for the first time in its pages the stimulation and challenge of the art of translation.

Notes

[1] Scott's exchange of correspondence with Anne Hébert over difficulties experienced in translating *Le tombeau des rois* has just been republished in book form by HMH in Montreal.

CL 49 (Summer 1971)

A.W. Purdy

Rock Gothic

In 1819, under orders from the British Admiralty, an expedition commanded by Captain John Franklin set out to map the shores of the polar sea, from the Coppermine River eastward. Franklin's party consisted of five Englishmen, including a Mr. Wentzel, clerk of the North West Company; seventeen Canadian "voyagers," these probably being of mixed French and Indian blood; and three interpreters, all Indians. In addition, two Eskimos, plus a large number of Copper Indian hunters, were employed by the Franklin expedition.

Franklin's principal base was Fort Providence on Great Slave Lake. His final jumping-off point for the Coppermine River was Fort Enterprise on Winter Lake. In 1820, two years after leaving York Factory on Hudson's Bay, the Franklin expedition proceeded north in birch canoes to the arctic sea — achieved overland by only two white men previously, Samuel Hearne and Alexander Mackenzie.

Copper Indian hunters and their chief, Akaitcho, provided game along the route. The Hudson's Bay Company and the North Westers supplied both food and other necessary provisions. Wentzel, the North Westers' clerk, accompanied Franklin to the Coppermine River's mouth, and returned south. Then the birch canoes, which had traversed inland rivers and countless portages, took to the northern seas, hugging the coast, which was mapped for 550 miles east to Point Turn-again.

Franklin's original plan, after mapping the coast eastward as far as possible, had been to return west to the Coppermine and travel south along the river to Fort Enterprise, where supplies would be stored for him. However, if the summer was too far advanced or they ran short of food, plans would be changed, and the expedition would journey south across the barren ground from some undetermined point along the sea coast. As it turned out, they did run short of food, and at a time when the season was far advanced toward arctic winter. Coronation Gulf and the newly-named Hood's River was the route taken to Fort Enterprise.

It was a man-killing trip across the barrens! In fact, six men died: four of starvation, one murdered, one executed for the murder. The battered birch canoes were abandoned shortly after leaving Coronation Gulf. Caribou (which Franklin calls "deer") were nearly nonexistent; any that were sighted proved too fleet of foot for the weakened, near-starving barren ground hikers. "Tripe de roche" (edible lichen on rocks), putrid animal carcasses and wolves' carrion were their food. Along the way, Michel Teroahaute, an Iroquois Indian, killed an English officer and was himself killed by another of Franklin's officers. It seems likely that the Indian, perhaps driven insane by hunger, had been eating the bodies of some of his dead companions.

Fort Enterprise was reached eventually, but the expected food supplies were not there. With total catastrophe in sight, Lieutenant Back travelled farther south, searching for Akaitcho and his Copper Indian hunters. After finding the Indians, sleds of food were sent back to rescue the main party at Fort Enterprise from starvation. At which point, in the fall of 1820, the long journey that took four years was really at an end.

This book — Narrative of a Journey to the Shores of the Polar Sea — is a reprint of Franklin's original volume, and a very impressive reprint. It has thirty pages of plates (reproductions of the early steel engravings), many in colour, and includes four detached maps, plus several long appendices relating to flora and fauna, etc. If not quite a work of art, the book comes close to being one.

But reverting back to the expedition itself, Franklin's narrative leaves me very unsatisfied. Apart from being a lousy writer (Back was much better), Franklin's conduct of the expedition seems to me (and others) an ample explanation of his later tragedy — a tragedy that sent dozens of English captains searching westward for the vanished Franklin as well as the North West Passage.

For instance, why weren't the food supplies more efficiently arranged? Everyone, including Franklin, knew that travelling over the barren ground was no English tea party. And why didn't Franklin rely on travelling west by sea (according to his original plan), and returning on the basis of his *actual* food supplies on hand, rather than relying on problematical game along the route? Why, why, why? All this being hindsight, of course.

In addition, the curious story of Michel, the cannibalistic Iroquois, seems to pose more mysteries in Franklin's narrative than it solves. Probably Lieutenant Back and the Copper Indian chief, Akaitcho, were — as some historians have asserted — the reasons the entire expedition didn't perish. Back nearly died himself on this desperate journey south in search of supplies to aid Franklin. Akaitcho and his hunters provided the most vital necessity of all: food.

Here's what Franklin said of Akaitcho and his people: "the art with which these Indians pursue their objects, their avaricious nature, and the little reliance that can be placed upon them when their interests jar with their promises . . ." And later: "Dr. Richardson, Hepburn and I, eagerly devoured the food, which they imprudently presented to us, in too great abundance, and in consequence we suffered dreadfully from indigestion." Also Dr. Richardson: "we placed no confidence in the exertions of the Canadians who accompanied him (Franklin, that is) . . ." Contrast this against the Copper Indian chief, Akaitcho's own words (Englished by Franklin): "I know you write down every occurrence in your books; but probably you have only noticed the bad things we have said and done, and have omitted to mention the good."

On the evidence of this book, Akaitcho, the long-dead Indian chief who accompanied the long-dead English captain, John Franklin, may have had a point. Franklin and the officers under his command seem to me a bunch of upper-class English snobs lording it over what they suspected might not be an inferior race. But because Franklin and his men both endured and achieved much — are in some sense underlying rock-gothic in Canadian history — I suppose they were also heroes.

3. ADJOINING ROOMS

George Woodcock

A Cycle Completed:
The Nine Novels of Robertson Davies

GLENDOWER: *I can call spirits from the vasty deep.*

HOTSPUR: *Why, so can I, or so can any man, / But will they come when you do call to them?*

GLENDOWER: *Why, I can teach you, Cousin, to command The Devil.*

HOTSPUR: *And I can teach thee, Coz., to shame the Devil / By telling truths: tell truth and shame the Devil.* (WILLIAM SHAKESPEARE, *HENRY IV, PART I*, III.I.53–59)

With the publication in the autumn of 1988 of *The Lyre of Orpheus*, Robertson Davies has completed the third of his fictional trilogies, each centred on a different Ontario town, and each dominated by a central group of characters through whose varying perceptions and memories the current of events that characterizes the trilogy is perceived.

The completion of the triple triad is, as Davies has undoubtedly recognized, an event that stirs a multitude of numerological, folkloric, and mythological echoes. Nine was one of the three mystical numbers of the Pythagoreans, and though three was a perfect number which Pythagoras made the sign of the deity, nine had its specific significance as a trinity of trinities, the perfect plural. For Pythagoras, and later for the great classical

astronomer Ptolemy, the universe moved in nine spheres. In various contexts we find the number particularly associated with inspiration and imagination. There were nine Muses, nine Gallicenae or virgin priestesses of
the Druid oracles, and nine Sibylline books transmitted from Cumae to
Rome. Echoed constantly in Davies' novels is the ancient concept of a nine
day's wonder: as the old proverb has it, "A wonder lasts nine days, and
then the puppy's eyes are open." But most relevant of all in considering *The
Lyre of Orpheus* as the last Davies novel to date — and perhaps the last of
the kind to which we have become accustomed since *Fifth Business* appeared in 1970 — is the role which nine plays in music, for nine was the
Pythagorean *diapason*, man being the full chord, or eight notes, and nine
representing the deity, ultimate harmony.

The Lyre of Orpheus is not merely a novel about music; it is a novel
about the nature of art in general and its relation to reality and time and
the human spirit. But the main plot carrying this theme concerns a musical
event, and in doing so it takes us back with striking deliberation to the first
group of Davies novels, the Salterton series. For, like the last of that series,
A Mixture of Frailties (1958), *The Lyre of Orpheus* is built around a family
trust which offers a phenomenally generous grant to a young woman musician from a Philistine background, and finds itself sponsoring a controversial opera, so that a contribution is made to the art of music in a general
way at the same time as the young musician, aided by wise teachers, undergoes an inner transformation that opens to her what in Davies' terminology one might call "a world of wonders"; in Jungian terms she is taken out
of the anonymity and personal incompleteness of common life and achieves
individuation.

There are indeed important ways in which *The Lyre of Orpheus*, written
thirty years later, goes beyond *A Mixture of Frailties*. While Monica Gall
in the earlier novel is a singer whose talents are trained by inspired teachers, and the opera in which she becomes involved is the original work of
another — a wayward modern genius — in *The Lyre of Orpheus* we edge
nearer to the creative role, for the musician, Hulda Schnakenburg (generally called Schnak), is a composer engaged not in an original composition
but in a task of inspired reconstruction. She is making an opera, *Arthur of
Britain*, out of scattered fragments left by E.T.A. Hoffmann (better known
as a Gothicist tale-teller than as a musician) of an opera he was unable to
complete before his early death from the nineteenth-century endemic,
syphilis. At the same time the priestly scholar Simon Darcourt (one of the
narrators of an earlier Davies novel, *The Rebel Angels)* constructs the li-
bretto around which the score that Schnak develops from Hoffmann's
fragments is built up. Schnak and Darcourt, with their various collabor-
ators, manage to recreate an authentic sounding early nineteenth-century
opera which pleases the spirit of E.T.A. Hoffmann who makes a ghostly

appearance in the comments from the underworld that appear as interludes between the narrative chapters.

Related to this major plot is a strikingly similar sub-plot devoted to the visual as distinct from the audial arts. As well as acting as pasticheur-librettist, Simon Darcourt is engaged on a biography of Francis Cornish, the celebrated connoisseur and art collector whose bequest has funded the preparation and production of *Arthur of Britain*. Darcourt stumbles on the clues which reveal to him what readers of *What's Bred in the Bone* already know, that Cornish was actually the painter of a famous triptych, *The Marriage of Cana*, done so authentically in the fifteenth-century German manner that it has been plausibly attributed to an unknown painter working five centuries ago who was given the name of the Alchemical Master.

Simon Darcourt manages to convince everyone involved, including the owners of the painting and the reluctant mandarins of the National Gallery to which it is eventually given, that a work done sincerely and without intent of fraud in the style of a past age is not a fake and can be as authentic as the best work in a contemporary manner. The argument put forward by Darcourt's colleague Clement Hollier, an expert on myths, is not only interesting in itself but important for what it tells us about Davies' own attitudes towards the arts and about his own literary achievement. Here is Darcourt's paraphrase of Hollier's statement:

> If a man wants to paint a picture that is intended primarily as an exercise in a special area of expertise, he will do so in a style with which he is most familiar. If he wants to paint a picture which has a particular relevance to his own life-experience, which explores the myth of his life as he understands it, and which, in the old phrase, "makes up his soul," he is compelled to do it in a mode that permits such allegorical revelation. Painters after the Renaissance, and certainly after the Protestant Reformation, have not painted such pictures with the frankness that was natural to pre-Renaissance artists. The vocabulary of faith, and of myth, has been taken from them by the passing of time. But Francis Cornish, when he wanted to make up his soul, turned to the style of painting and the concept of visual art which came most naturally to him. Indeed, he had many times laughed at the notion of contemporaneity in conversation . . . mocking it as a foolish chain on a painter's inspiration and intention.
>
> It must be remembered . . . that Francis has been brought up a Catholic — or almost a Catholic — and he had taken his catholicity seriously enough to make it a foundation of his art. If God is one and eternal, and if Christ is not dead, but living, are not fashions in art mere follies for those who are the slaves of Time?

In musical terms the chapter in which these matters are resolved can be regarded as a coda, a concluding passage after the main pattern of the work has been developed and completed; it states the theme of the novel more definitely and succinctly than in early renderings. *Arthur of Britain* has been completed and successfully launched as a new work in the operatic repertoire, Schnak had found herself and her career, and now, three years later in a chapter free of the ghostly voice of E.T.A. Hoffmann (a ghost now actually laid), we can consider what is the meaning of it all, assisted by our reflections on Francis Cornish's strange master work. And so, just as *The Lyre of Orpheus* as a whole, with its deliberate reordering and retelling of the plot of *A Mixture of Frailties*, completes the circle of Davies' mature fiction, so this final chapter of the latest of his novels acts, I suggest, as a veiled *apologia pro vita sua*, a justification for the uncontemporary aesthetic underlying Davies' life work.

∽

George Orwell once remarked on the striking fact that the best writers of his time — and among them he included the great apostles of literary modernism — have in fact been conservative and even reactionary in their social and political attitudes. This is certainly true of most of the great moderns in the Anglo-American tradition; Eliot, Pound, and Wyndham Lewis were all to be found politically somewhat to the right of old-style Toryism, and James Joyce failed to join them only because of a massive indifference to anything outside his own linguistic experiments.

Robertson Davies has not spoken of his political views in any detail or with much directness. I have no idea how he votes, though it is clear that he has the kind of Tory mind which judges politics ethically; his treatment of Boy Staunton's political career in *Fifth Business* suggests that he probably has little patience with what passes for a Conservative cause in late twentieth-century Canada.

What distinguishes Davies from the reactionary modernists is that his Toryism runs into his art as well as his political ethics. He is an unrepentant cultural elitist. "There is no democracy in the world of intellect, and no democracy of taste," he said in *A Voice from the Attic* (1960) and he has not since shown a change of attitude. He has never posed as an avantgarde writer of any kind. In spite of occasionally expressed admiration for *Ulysses* as a great comic work, he has never followed Joyce's experiments in language, and despite a loosely stated interest in Proust, he has never tried to emulate Proust's experiments in the literary manipulation of time and memory. Indeed, in this respect he has been far less experimental than other writers we do not regard as particularly avant-gardist, like Margaret Laurence and Marian Engel. Though in his two later trilogies he may view the same sequences of events in different novels through different eyes, he still tends within each novel to follow a strictly chronological pattern, with effect following cause, whether the causes are the inner ones to be dragged out by Jungian analysis or the outer ones which we see a character's social ambiance and physical environment imposing on him.

Not that, even taking into account the clear, serviceable and declarative prose that Davies writes, we should regard him as a plain realist. If he is a realist, it is not in the documentary sense, but in the theatrical sense of wishing to give plausibility to the implausible, in his early novels to farce and in his later ones to melodrama. There is always in his writing a heightening of the use of language that goes beyond the demands of ordinary realism, and, given his special interests, Davies might justly be called a magic realist rather than a surrealist. It is true that he shares with the surrealists a preoccupation with depth psychology and its resources of imagery, but while most of the surrealists tended to put their faith in Freud, Davies has found Jung a richer source.

Just as his magicians are technicians of illusion rather than true thaumaturges, so Davies himself takes a pride in artifice, yet he is too conservative a writer to fit in with the postmodernists, metafictionists and destructionists of our own day. Far from being destructionist, indeed, his novels are as Edwardianly well-made as Galsworthy's Forsyte novels or Arnold Bennett's fictional chronicles of the Five Towns, while among his contemporaries the one novelist he has regarded as undeniably great, and whom he has admitted to be an influence, is Joyce Cary, whose virtues lay not in his experimental daring, but rather in a zest for the language, "a reaffirmation of the splendour and sacredness of life," and the same kind of restless and active erudition as Davies displays in his own fiction.

While recognizing that a novel is a work of artifice in which verisimilitude is part of the illusion, and often using contrived fictional devices, Davies manifests little of that preoccupation with the relationship between writers, readers, and the work which has led metafictionists ever since Cervantes and Sterne in their smoke-and-mirror games with reality. He is too didactic, too much concerned with developing lessons about life, and with displaying knowledge and expertise, to subordinate the central narrative, the line of purpose in his works, to any speculative process that might seem to weaken its validity. He is, essentially, a novelist in the central English tradition of Fielding and Dickens and Cary, intent on using artifice to entertain and to instruct. He is brilliantly inventive and has an extraordinary power of assimilating information and presenting it acceptably. But he has little formal originality, little of the power of imaginative transfiguration, so that his novels are still influenced by the conventions of the theatre where he began his writing career, and large sections of them are dominated by the kind of didactic dialogue we used to associate with Bernard

Shaw and his disciples. Art comes, when it does, at the end of the process, in the accidental way which also accords with the main English fictional tradition. The kind of deliberate artistry that distinguished the main French tradition from Flaubert onwards, and the tradition of deep social criticism that distinguished the central lineage of Russian fiction from Turgenev onwards, find no place in Davies' books.

Nor, for that matter, does one find much in common between Davies' novels and those of the writers, like Hugh MacLennan and Sinclair Ross and Margaret Laurence, whom we regard as most faithful in their projection of the climate and character of Canadian life and its relation to the land. Davies' novels are restricted geographically to a tiny fragment of Canada — Toronto and the small towns of western Ontario — and to a restricted social milieu of Old and New Money, of the false and true intellectual and artistic aspirations of the middle class, and working-class people are introduced only for comic relief, as in the case of the Morphews in *Leaven of Malice* or the elder Galls in *A Mixture of Frailties*, or on condition that they become transformed and find their way into the cultured bourgeoisie, as Monica Gall does in *A Mixture of Frailties* and Hulda Schnakenburg seems about to do at the end of *The Lyre of Orpheus*.

Davies did indeed define his attitude to Canada in an interview in *Maclean's* in 1972, two years after *Fifth Business* was published, when he replied to the complaints he had heard that "my novels aren't about Canada":

> I think they are, because I see Canada as a country torn between a very
> northern, rather extraordinary mystical spirit which it fears and its
> desire to present itself to the world as a Scotch banker.

Davies and his critics tend to use the term "mystical" in a rather loose and general way which has nothing to do with the genuine experiences of mystics like St. John of the Cross or Jakob Boehme, but if we interpret this statement to mean that Canadians hover between an intuitive acceptance of their environment which leads them to see their history in mythic terms, and a grey and materialist attitude in everyday life, I think we have perhaps a good point at which to begin a reconsideration of the triple fictional triads of which *The Lyre of Orpheus* represents the conclusion.

೮೩

Looking back at *Tempest Tost* (1951), the first of the early novels of manners which Davies set in the small town of Salterton (Kingston transmogrified), we notice how limited is the range of situations in Davies' novels, for here already we have the theatrical producer, Valentine Rich, coming into a Canadian town to direct the amateur actors of the Little Theatre in a production of *The Tempest*, just as in *The Lyre of Orpheus* the formidable Dr. Gunilla Dahl-Soot will descend on Toronto to preside over the Canadian metamorphosis of Hoffman's *Arthur of Britain*. And in the very choice of the play that is produced in the earlier novel — *The Tempest* — we have the favourite Davies theme of the interchangeability of life's pretences of reality and art's frank and open illusionism.

The main satirical device of *Tempest Tost* is a relatively simple one: the effort to find among the inadequate citizens of Salterton the types who will adequately project Shakespeare's characters. The results of the casting are ludicrous: Prospero is played by an arrogant and insensitive pedant, Professor Vambrace, Ferdinand by a young army officer whose aim in life is to seduce as many girls as he can, and Gonzago by an owlish middle-aged schoolteacher, Hector Mackilwraith, who falls lugubriously in love with the rich man's daughter Griselda Webster, who is half his age and plays Ariel.

As this is a novel of manners, people are rarely illuminated from within, but are seen usually as they react to each other in social situations. At this stage Davies was still obviously much affected by the theatrical world in which he had recently been so closely involved, and the dialogue reads like a cross between that of early twentieth-century English farce and — when ideas are uppermost — that of Thomas Love Peacock's conversational novels. All the Davies novels give off a perceptible whiff of Peacock, though I have been unable to find any reference that might show Davies took a direct interest in him; the way of transmission may have been through Aldous Huxley, whom Davies certainly read with attention, since in *The Rebel Angels* — with oblique acknowledgement — he made extensive use of W.H. Sheldon's theories linking temperament with physical types which Huxley had already introduced extensively into his later books.

The disadvantage of this kind of dialogue, as Hugo McPherson pointed out in an early issue of *Canadian Literature*, is that it reveals very little of the private as distinct from the social personalities of the characters, and this creates an extraordinary formal awkwardness, since Davies then saw no other way to reveal his people in depth than to explain them in long narrative passages; in one instance, twenty pages of narrative are spent giving the history of Hector Mackilwraith so that we know how this amorous clown — the would-be lover of Griselda — came to be what he is. The shallowness of this approach to characterization ends in simplistic contrasts; Valentine Rich strikes us as being much too good and Professor Vambrace much too bad to be true.

Yet *Tempest Tost* prefigures in its own way much of the later Davies: the preoccupation with mystery as illusion, with art as artifice and — personified in those who variously court Griselda — the absurd complexities of the emotional life — with love and sex as rich sources of comedy.

Like *Tempest Tost*, *Leaven of Malice* anticipates the later novels with the kind of display of practical knowledge that often makes one think, while reading a Davies novel, of Zola and the naturalists. Davies is not so brutally obvious as Zola in presenting his characters as the products of material circumstance; even in his later novels when he shows his characters strongly conditioned by childhood experience and social ambiance, he allows them ways of liberation for which the iron determinism of the naturalists left no space.

But he does share with the naturalists the urge to present very circumstantially the activities and interests in which his characters become involved; it is part of the verisimilitude on which convincing illusions depend, as his magicians constantly insist. He began — and this perhaps shows the caution of a writer who is craftsman by intent and artist by good fortune — with areas where he already had knowledge through experience. His involvement in the theatre — both professional and amateur — gave him the background for *Tempest Tost*, and his occupation of editing a newspaper, the *Peterborough Examiner*, gave him that for *Leaven of Malice*, which combines a satirical picture of small-town feuds with the tension of a rather mild detective mystery, for the plot centres on a false and maliciously placed newspaper announcement of the coming marriage of Sollie Bridgetower and Pearl Vambrace. Like the Montagues and the Capulets, the academic families of Bridgetower and Vambrace are ancient enemies, and the notice results in splendid histrionics as Professor Vambrace threatens legal action in all directions. However, in the end all is well, since, by the kind of glib twist that was common enough in London West End comedies at the time, Solly and Pearl fall in love during the feuding process, and after the perpetrator of the hoax is discovered the malicious announcement is in fact fulfilled when they marry.

Leaven of Malice, though a more tightly constructed book, is flawed in the same ways as *Tempest Tost*. The satire moves at the surface level of manners, so that the characters are two-dimensional, and the didacticism of the book is largely unassimilated; Davies will break up the action for several pages at a time to give — say — a disquisition on who reads newspapers and why. Thus the novel moves haltingly as a series of dialogues and slapstick encounters interrupted by essays. At best it and *Tempest Tost* are reasonably good entertainment, but like most mere entertainment they seem very dated a third of a century after writing.

A Mixture of Frailties is an altogether more satisfying book — and much more of a real novel — than its predecessors, as Davies himself seems to suggest by repeating its essential situation in *The Lyre of Orpheus*. There are several reasons for this. First, though satire is not absent, it is given depth by the comparison of two worlds of manners and taste, those of Salterton and those of Britain. Then, through the concentration on the training of Monica Gall and the emotional adventures that accompany it, we are shown for the first time not merely a character getting wise to his own inadequacy, as with Hector in *Tempest Tost*, but the awakening and development of a whole personality as her various masters introduce Monica to the splendours and miseries of life and art. In the process a deeper and less facile element of romance enters into *A Mixture of Frailties*, and the tension between satire and romance, between comedy and the tragedy that eventually breaks in, gives the narrative an element of dramatic *chiaroscuro* and a depth of perspective that the earlier novels lacked. *A Mixture of Frailties* broadens because of its multiplicity of locale, and deepens psychologically because we are no longer seeing people merely in terms of their behaviour, but as individuals who feel deeply and speak their feelings. They also speak their knowledge, and sententious in a sub-Wilde way as Sir Benedict Domdaniel may be when he talks of life and artifice and art, his aphorisms are an improvement on the interpolated essays of the earlier works.

◖◗

With *A Mixture of Frailties* in 1958 Robertson Davies seemed like a novelist who after some clever failures was really beginning to find his way, and yet he waited twelve years before publishing his next novel, *Fifth Business*, in 1970. During the intervening period he moved from the newspaper world into that of academe, becoming Master of Massey College at the University of Toronto in 1961 and shortly afterwards he began to teach dramatic literature as a graduate study. During this interlude his writing was very scanty and almost entirely journalistic. Whatever the reason for the silence, it was a productive one. The world changed, and Davies changed his mind with it. He paid attention to the deep theological and political debates of the 1960s, and though he became no easy convert to any novel doctrine, he quietly modified his attitudes to life and kept his mind open to anything he might be able to use when he returned to fiction again. It was a time of rapidly growing permissiveness both in behaviour and in the ways in which people expressed themselves, and though Davies was too conservative at heart to make any great changes in his use of language, he was ready, by the time he came to write *Fifth Business*, to write openly of things he had not even hinted in his earlier novels, so that while both *Tempest Tost* and *Leaven of Malice* were devoid of any active sexual irregularities, and *A Mixture of Frailties* contented itself with a little heterosexual living in sin, such hitherto unmentioned pursuits as sodomy began to find their place in later Davies books, and invariably as negative manifestations of the quasi-Gnostic dualism that had turned the novels from 1970 onwards into the skirmishing grounds of good and evil.

Good and evil, truth and falsehood, reality and illusion — the oppos-
itions continue through the rest of Davies' novels, and there has never been
a resolution of the struggle. There is much calling up of "the vasty deep,"
much conscious and unconscious seeking for God, but, as Dunstan Ramsay admits in *Fifth Business*,

> I had sought God in my lifelong . . . preoccupation with saints. But all
> I had found in that lifelong study was a complexity that brought God
> no nearer.

In practice, Davies' characters are much nearer to Hotspur than to his own
fellow Welsh sage, Owen Glendower; they too seek to "shame the devil,
and tell the truth." In fact the whole of the so-called Deptford trilogy
(which extended so far beyond Deptford), beginning with *Fifth Business*,
is an attempt by three different people, Ramsay himself, David Staunton
(the son of his friend Boy Staunton), and Paul Dempster, to discover the
truth about themselves and about the strange series of events in which they
are involved. All their enquiries proceed on a human level. The wonders
that occur among them, at the hand of Paul Dempster metamorphosed
into the magician Magnus Eisengrim, are man-made illusions, not supernatural marvels. Mary Dempster, the "fool saint" through whom Ramsay
seems to get a whiff of the divine, is in fact a woman turned half-witted by
misfortune, and the miracles he attributes to her are not such as the church
would accept. In the end the wise and eccentric old Jesuit, Father Blazon,
calls upon him to abandon his quest for saintliness if not for saints:

> Forgive yourself for being a human creature, Ramezay. That is the
> beginning of wisdom; that is part of what is meant by the fear of God;
> but for you it is the only way to save your sanity. Begin now, or you
> will end up with your saint in the madhouse.

Similarly, when the devil appears to Ramsay, it is in the form of a human
being, the rich Swiss woman Liesl who is Eisengrim's impresario and eventually becomes Ramsay's friend.

In all this, Davies is not suggesting that the good represented by the
saints or the evil represented by the devil does not exist. What he tells us is
that — unless we belong to the privileged and scanty ranks of the mystics
who have been vouchsafed the ecstatic vision of deity — we see both the
divine and the diabolical in fleeting manifestations in our human existence,
hinted rather than stated in dreams, in myths, in puzzling personal encounters. That is why Ramsay, like Clement Hollier in the third trilogy that
begins with *The Rebel Angels*, will operate as a scholar in the interface
between history and myth; why Jungian analysis with its underworld of

archetypical beings mysteriously residing in the collective unconscious which we all share will play such an important role in the novels; why the illusions that Marcus Eisengrim creates by mechanical means will shadow forth a different "world of wonders" as mysterious and inaccessible as the world of Plato's Forms. In the end, one is left after reading Davies' later novels with a sense of the enormous ambivalence of one of the key phrases of the religious quest: "Seek, and ye shall find." Davies' characters, or at least the significant ones, seek and indeed they find, but what they find is not the Grail of which they have gone in search. If they are fortunate they find self-realization, and often it is in some way self-realization through creation. The individual may not find God in the whole and all-consuming way of the great mystics, but he will realize the fragment of God, the creative spark, that is within himself.

All this represents an enormous thematic advance on the early Davies novels, and it is clear that the twelve years of literary silence were spent in much study and thought. Still, in the last resort the success or otherwise of the novels lies not in what they tell us, which an intelligent tract could probably do as well, but in how they tell it. And here also *Fifth Business* is a great advance on even *A Mixture of Frailties*. Indeed, there are some who say it represents the peak of Davies' achievement, the best of all the nine novels, and, as we shall see, there is some justification for such an opinion.

In *Fifth Business* Davies departs from the old-fashioned form of third-person narrative with somewhat theatrical dialogue which he used in the Salterton trilogy. Now he uses a direct and rather aggressive first-person approach as Ramsay, a retiring master at Colborne College, protests to the Headmaster about the patronizing farewell notice accorded him in the *College Chronicle*. His letter of protest extends into a whole book, but once we accept this basic implausibility we find ourselves involved in the account of a strange life told with a becoming idiosyncrasy and with a vigour of language and imagery, and a grasp of the grubby glory of life, that is quite beyond anything in the Salterton stories. What makes the book so successful is a remarkable unity of tone which extends into an appropriateness of speech to character and character to action that rarely lapses.

With the ingenuity of a dedicated mythographer, Ramsay traces how a mis-aimed snowball, intended for him and wickedly loaded with a stone, set the three main characters of the novel, and of the rest of the trilogy, on their often parted but always interweaving paths in life.

The stone-laden snowball, intended by Boy Staunton for Ramsay, knocks down Mary Dempster and brings on the premature birth of her son Paul. It also results in her permanently losing her reason and becoming what the local Catholic priest calls a "fool saint," eccentric in her behaviour and indiscriminating in her generosity, up to the point when she scandalizes the town by giving herself to a wandering tramp, whom the trauma of their discovery by a search party in the local hobo jungle turns into a missionary in the city slums.

Ramsay, whose evasion of the snowball resulted in Mary Dempster's misfortune, not only feels a lifelong guilt towards her, but, in observing actions he can only interpret as saintly, is started on his career as a high-class hagiographer, tracing the various kinds and conditions of sainthood, and treating the phenomenon of hagiolatry as one of the points where myth and history most illumine each other and where illusion may lead to the recognition of truth.

Ramsay's other boyhood passion is the deceptive magic of conjuring; himself too ham-handed to succeed, he passes his knowledge on to young Paul Dempster who has the necessary manual facility. And when Paul has endured enough of his Baptist minister father's fundamentalist disciplines, and of the mockery to which his mother's actions subject him at the hands of Boy Staunton and the other Deptford children, he lets himself be seduced into a freak show by the homosexual conjuror Willard, one of Davies' most chilling personifications of evil. After years of virtual slavery during which he learns his art, Paul falls in with the formidably ugly and intelligent and also very rich Liesl Naegeli, who establishes him as the internationally famed magician Magnus Eisengrim. Meanwhile, Boy Staunton, the author with his hard-centred snowball of all these strange metamorphoses in the lives of others, goes on blindly with his self-obsessed career as financier and politician, impervious to the sufferings of others until, in a fatal encounter where he and Paul and Ramsay for the first time come together as a trio, he gains a kind of enlightenment into the emptiness of his life, goes off with the stone which Ramsay has religiously preserved, and dies mysteriously, drowned in his car with the stone in his mouth.

It is the single, consistent, idiosyncratic, eloquent voice of Ramsay that gives *Fifth Business* its impressive and convincing power and unity, which neither of the later volumes in the trilogy projects to the same degree. Bizarre as much of it may seem to him, the reader is aware of the essential, devil-shaming truth of *Fifth Business*, its authenticity as the account of a failed search for the divine. Ramsay's letter, of course, is a piece of artifice, a literary contrivance, but it is a contrivance that we accept as easily as we might accept a magnifying glass as an aid to reading a difficult text. The character evoked by it seems to live with his own inner vigour, and so all that happens to him seems fictionally authentic.

In his trilogy Davies sets out to show the consequences of the snowballing from the standpoints of the three Deptford boys who were most affected, but in *The Manticore* he actually circumvents the problem of how to perceive and present the insensitive and monstrously self-conceited Boy Staunton by showing Boy's life through the eyes and feelings of his son, the brilliant and alcoholic lawyer David Staunton, "who had a dark reputation because the criminal world thought so highly of him, and who played up to the role, and who secretly fancied himself as a magician of the courtroom."

Realizing that the shock of his father's dramatic death has pushed him to the edge of a mental breakdown, David decides to subject himself to psychoanalysis, and it is this analysis, conducted in Zurich by the Jungian Dr. Joanna von Heller, that forms the frame of the book. It consists of conversations with Dr. von Heller, interspersed by sections of a narrative of the past which the analyst requires David to write. In the process we are given not only a picture of the kind of upbringing that by middle age had carried Boy Staunton's son to the verge of madness, but also a portrait of that startlingly soulless man, his father, who was evil by default of goodness.

But the framework is too rigid for events to move easily and too awkward to be evocative of character. Neither of the Stauntons stands in the mind's eye as a living person with the same kind of depth and complexity as Ramsay in *Fifth Business*. One of the reasons is that in *The Manticore* Davies is even more eager than in previous novels to perform as the Canadian latter-day Zola, exhibiting too painfully and at times all too dully his Jungian scholarship and his carefully acquired knowledge of the working of the Canadian legal system.

The third novel of the series, *World of Wonders*, tells of the transformation of Paul Dempster, the wretched Deptford boy, into the famous and accomplished stage magician, Magnus Eisengrim. Again there is a rather contrived frame, for the story is told when Eisengrim is playing the role of an earlier magical illusionist, Jean-Eugène Robert-Houdin, in a film directed by the famous Swede, Jürgen Lind. Evening after evening, at the urging of Ramsay who wishes to prepare an authentic biography of Dempster as well as the lying life of Eisengrim he had earlier written to give his friend publicity, the magician tells of the terrifying experiences in the lower levels of the entertainment world by which, like an ancient shaman being ceremonially reborn, he was transformed from a parson's tyrannized son into a wonder-worker. The framework gives the narrative a formality that does not always accord with the spirit of what is told, and acts as a kind of hobble to the narrative. Yet the content is so dark and compelling in its evocation of evil and so fascinating in its use of the illusory wonders of the magician's art to suggest by analogy the true wonders of existence, that the knowledge so broadly displayed of early twentieth-century English theatre and of the life and crafts of American show people becomes far more thoroughly assimilated into the narrative than happened with Jungian analysis in *The Manticore*. In form, as in content, *World of Wonders* impresses one as a work of consummate artifice, in which the protagonist, Paul Dempster, is barely perceived as a human being through the multitude of bright mirror images and the endless argumentative evasions he displays in offering his conversational autobiography. One feels that this is Proteus, and that his creator has never really got him by the heels. At the end of the novel it is not Paul Dempster but once again canny old Ramsay who emerges as the one thoroughly convincing, because thoroughly revealed, character. Such are the perils to a novelist of entering too deeply and deliberately into the world of illusion.

ॐ

A different kind of writer's peril emerges in the third group of Davies novels, the Toronto campus trilogy as one might call it. For these books — *The Rebel Angels*, *What's Bred in the Bone*, and *The Lyre of Orpheus* — are partly at least *romans à clef*, based on Davies' experiences of educational and cultural institutions, so that readers in the know have had no difficulty recognizing some of the people whom Davies has embellished into often bizarre characters: John Pearson transmogrified into John Parlabane in *The Rebel Angels*, for instance, and Alan Jarvis made over into Aylwin Ross in *What's Bred in the Bone*. Such mergings of fact into fiction always arouse doubts in one's mind about the writer's motives and ultimately about the nature of his achievement. Is he playing metafictional games with the reader? Or is he lazily offering us memory half raw? As distinct from the youthful autobiographical novel, which is a *rite de passage* many readers undergo in the development of their fictional imagination, the *roman à clef*, in the hands of an experienced novelist, is always an equivocal achievement in which the power of imagination remains in doubt.

Still, the three novels are more than *romans à clef*; if the Deptford series is concerned with the relationship between illusion and reality as mediated by artifice, this later group tends to be dominated by the relationship between true art and artifice, played out, as in the earlier novels, against the shifting scenes of a stage where history and myth are seen as merging.

In a literal way the central figure is Francis Cornish, whose life is told in the middle novel, *What's Bred in the Bone*. Cornish is known to the world as a discriminating connoisseur and a voracious collector of art. In the first volume, *The Rebel Angels*, he has just died and left to three professors the task of sorting the great accumulation of objects he has acquired and of distributing them in accordance with his will. The narrative is a curiously divided one, part of it being written by one of the three professors, Simon Darcourt, as a gossiping journal of academic life he called "The New Aubrey," and alternating chapters forming a kind of interior diary of Maria Theotoky, a half-Polish, half-Gypsy graduate student; she thinks herself in love with Clement Hollier, the second of the professors, a great mythographer who has seduced her in a fit of absent-mindedness. The third professor, the leading villain, is an unprincipled academic poseur, Urquhart

McVarish, who steals from the Cornish collection a remarkable unknown Rabelais manuscript after which Hollier lusts academically.

These high eccentrics, consumed by scholarly passions and academic greeds, and reinforced by such colleagues as the sinister ex-monk John Parlabane, present academe as the terrain of such strange conflicts that one feels often Davies is trying to compensate for his frustration with the dullness of real Canadian academic life. The action mounts to a suicide (Parlabane's) and a bizarre murder (of McVarish by Parlabane) among sexual orgies as strange in their own way as anything in Petronius. The novel slides — as so many of Davies' do — into the serene harbour of a happy ending, out of tone with the rest of the book, in which Maria, having recovered from her infatuation with her professor, marries Arthur Cornish, the rich nephew of Francis and the real administrator of the Cornish estate.

Once again we are treated to displays of knowledge. There is a fascinating oddity about the arcane lore of gypsies rejuvenating and faking old violins which provides some of the most entertaining pages of the book. There is also an unfortunate bit of stale derivativeness when the Sheldonian theory of the effect of physique on temperament is warmed up in a weakly humorous scene when Ozias Froats expounds his theories on the qualities and virtues of human excrement. It is a more disunited novel than any of Davies' previous works; the central intrigue over the Rabelais papers is too weak to carry the burden of so many extraneous interests, and no character — not even wicked Parlabane or the brooding offscene presence of Francis Cornish is sufficiently realized to sustain one's interest.

Francis Cornish comes fully onstage in *What's Bred in the Bone*, which is really a classic *Bildungsroman*, in form, language, and in the handling of the trilogy's central theme, the relationship between artifice and art. A whimsical structure, in which the chapters are interspersed with angelic conversations, does not disguise the fact that the novel is told in a very conservative third-person narrative. Cornish's life begins in Blairlogie on the Ottawa River, which is clearly a fictional presentation of Renfrew, where Davies spent much of his childhood, and the money that will eventually finance Francis as a collector comes originally from the destruction of the northern Ontario forests. Like Ramsay's, his childhood is dominated by an obsession, in this case with "the Looner," his idiot brother, the first Francis, whose survival has been concealed and who becomes one of the earliest subjects of the second Francis's pencil when he begins his lonely apprenticeship as an artist.

Following a picaresque line, the novel takes Francis to Oxford, where he falls in with the famous restorer of classical paintings, Tancred Saraceni; he eventually joins Saraceni at a castle in Bavaria where their task is to restore — and improve in the restoring — a cache of German late medieval paintings which are passed on to the credulous Nazis in exchange for authentic

Italian masterpieces from German collections. Here — and the opportunity is not lost for a display of the knowledge Davies has acquired of the
methods of the old masters and how their effects can be reproduced in
materials now available — Francis perfects his grasp of the technique of
painting. When he has reached this point Saraceni proposes to test his aesthetic imagination by leaving him to paint — on an old ruined altarpiece
— the work that will show he is a true artist as well as a fine artisan. The
result is *The Marriage of Cana* which, when it surfaces before a commission established to send European paintings back to their proper homes,
Saraceni proclaims to be an original by an unknown early painter, whom he
calls The Alchemical Master; later Aylwin Ross publishes an analytical essay that seems to set the picture firmly in the political and social context of
the times. What we — as readers — know to be the work of a modern man
has been accepted by the artistic establishment as the work of a man five
centuries before, and we enjoy the ironies that our knowledge allows us.

But Davies is after more than irony. There is serious business on foot
here, as *The Lyre of Orpheus* reveals. I have already shown, in opening this
essay, how in plot *The Lyre of Orpheus* circles back to the early Davies
novels, as if to signify that a cycle is being closed, and how, thematically, it
brings to a conclusion questions regarding the nature of literary art that
are implicit in Davies' fiction from the beginning.

Here, in this most recent novel, the artistic conservatism of Robertson
Davies is clearly displayed, in argument and in practice. Once again the
narrative is a traditional third-person one, given a touch of metafictional
contrivance by the introduction of the beyond-the-grave commentaries of
Hoffman, which in fact deepen the conservatism of the narrative by presenting the views on art of a nineteenth-century musician, which the twentieth-century musicians in the novel are seeking to bring to fruition. The
enthusiastic account of Schnak's dedicated toil in completing another
musician's work abandoned so long ago is a clear denial of the cult of originality that has dominated western art and literature since the days of the
romantics. Allied to the cult of originality is that of contemporaneity, the
idea that the true artist must speak of his time in its own verbal or visual
language; Darcourt's triumphal assertion of Francis Cornish's genius,
which finds in *The Marriage of Cana* an expression that is neither original
nor contemporary but is true to his talents and his life, is a negation of that
doctrine too.

Thematically, *The Lyre of Orpheus* projects a viewpoint that is reactionary
rather than classicist in formal terms, for, though Davies has adhered increasingly in his most recent English novels to the traditional methods of mainstream English fiction, his interests have placed him on the verge of Gothic
romanticism in selecting his content, while his approach to characterization
has brought him close to a comic tradition in fiction that, as we have seen,

runs from Fielding through Peacock and Dickens to Joyce Cary. In denying the importance of originality and contemporaneity he is in fact guarding his own territory, for he is neither a strikingly original novelist, nor, in the sense of representing any avant-garde, a notably contemporary writer.

Here lie the main reasons for the popularity of Robertson Davies, which some critics have found offensive to their ideas of what Canadians should be expecting of their writers. It resembles the current popularity of realist painters like Alex Colville, Christopher Pratt, Ivan Eyre, and Jack Chambers. Most people, in Canada and elsewhere, are artistically conservative; only the avant-gardes of the past are — though not invariably — acceptable to them. It is true that the permissiveness of the 1960s made the broader public open to certain kinds of content that were once unacceptable. But, as the totalitarians have always known, it is in the formal aspects of a work that the deepest rebellion declares itself, and it is at this point that general readers, feeling the boundaries of normal speech and perception slipping away, become disturbed; the nihilism of much of modern art and literature bewilders and repels them. They need reassurance, and the novels of Robertson Davies, which present no real formal challenges, and whose essential optimism is shown in upbeat endings, with quests completed, wishes fulfilled, evil routed, and villains destroyed, are admirably suited for the calming and comforting of uneasy Canadians. They exist on the edge of popular fiction, where Pangloss reigns in the best of possible worlds.

CL 126 (Autumn 1990)

Antoine Sirois

Grove et Ringuet:
Témoins d'une époque

Deux romans parus dans la troisième décade du 20e siècle, *Trente arpents* de Ringuet, en 1938, et *Fruits of the Earth* de Grove, en 1933, venaient à la fois couronner et défier une forme de littérature qui semblait bien installée depuis le milieu du 19e siècle, celle du roman du terroir.

Cette bonne littérature, comme on le sait, dépeignait habituellement une vie idyllique où les protagonistes, à force de volonté et de bras, atteignaient à un bonheur ignoré des citadins. Les héros, robustes et vertueux, vivaient au rythme des jours et des saisons et finissaient par conquérir et dominer la nature dans l'espace rural qui leur avait été dévolu par l'auteur.

À la suite de Zola dans *la Terre*, Grove et Ringuet, importants dans leur littérature respective, témoignent d'un monde en transition, passant de l'époque agraire à l'époque technique. Grove décrit une période qui s'étend de 1900 à 1921 dans *Fruits of the Earth*, et Ringuet de 1887 à 1930 dans *Trente arpents*. La première histoire se déroule dans l'Ouest, au Manitoba, l'autre dans l'Est, au Québec.

Les auteurs continuent, sous un aspect, le genre traditionnel, décrivant des héros enracinés dans leur terroir, à la psychologie un peu mince, qui tiennent plus du type que de l'individu. Mais les héros triomphant des forces de la nature sont devenus tragiques, leur règne est passager et illusoire. Ils sont esclaves du sol qu'ils croyaient dominer.

Dans l'étude qui suivra, je me restreindrai aux deux romans cités plus haut, qui ont une valeur esthétique certaine et qui m'ont paru significatifs et de l'accélération de l'histoire et de la transformation d'un genre romanesque.

La composition même de l'œuvre exprime la transformation du genre. *Trente arpents* narre l'histoire d'Euchariste Moisan. Ce paysan typique prend graduellement possession de ses trente arpents de terre, les fait rendre au point de pouvoir cumuler chez le notaire des sommes de plus en plus rondelettes. À cet accroissement de biens correspond une considération grandissante qui se manifeste par son élection comme marguillier à l'église et comme commissaire d'école. Il se sent béni en son fils prêtre qui vient auréoler sa réputation. Jusqu'ici, c'est le destin de Jean Rivard, modèle bien connu du roman du terroir. Mais au printemps et à l'été, succèdent l'automne et l'hiver. L'auteur, par une autre série de temps forts, décrit le déclin du héros : dissensions dans sa famille, mort du fils prêtre, désertion de ses enfants pour la ville et les usines, dépossession par son aîné, perte de son argent, feu de sa grange et enfin départ pour les États-Unis, où il finit, lui si attaché à ses animaux, comme gardien de nuit dans un garage de machines considérées comme autant de bêtes dangereuses. Abe Spalding, dans *Fruits of the Earth*, connaît un destin analogue, coloré seulement par le contexte géographique et social différent. Il met en valeur graduellement les lots qu'on lui a cédés. Sans liarder comme Moisan, il joue surtout avec son crédit pour accroître ses possessions. Son succès commande le respect des fermiers qui l'élisent comme chef du district et président de sa « commission scolaire ». Après une récolte extraordinaire en 1912, il bâtit la maison de ses rêves, symbole de sa réussite. Scénario jusqu'ici digne encore des meilleurs romans idylliques. Mais le fils aîné sur lequel Abe comptait meurt. Les autres enfants s'éloignent. Il connaît des difficultés financières et l'échec aux élections. Le deuxième fils sur la succession duquel il comptait se désintéresse du sol, passionné par la mécanique ; Abe restera sur la terre, mais désormais dépassé lui aussi par les événements. Son succès matériel n'aura pas été une bénédiction dans le sens biblique, car il a causé et masqué un échec personnel intérieur et une faillite familiale.

L'on ne peut s'empêcher de penser à *La Terre* de Zola où l'auteur joue aussi sur deux volets, celui de l'ascension du fils et du déclin du père, avec la différence que Zola conduit les deux de front, alors que Grove et Ringuet centrent surtout l'attention sur la montée et la chute du même protagoniste.

Les paysans-types de Grove et de Ringuet sont dépassés par leur temps. Ils avaient vécu dans un espace fermé, physiquement et moralement, bercé au rythme même des saisons, axé sur les récoltes et porteur de valeurs traditionnelles. Voilà que, désormais, à la suite des innovations techniques, de l'industrialisation accélérée par la guerre, une série de forces nouvelles vont menacer les traditions conservatrices qui sont propres aux civilisations agraires. Le choc est d'autant plus sensible que l'espace rural est bien clos, replié sur lui-même. « Cette société étroite . . . », dit Ringuet, « cette société circonscrite au voisinage et pour qui l'homme de la paroisse contiguë est déjà un dembétranger qui ne s'agrège jamais quelqu'un venu du

dehors, ni même ses fils. Il n'y a vraiment fusion qu'après deux générations ». « La petite patrie restreinte que seuls connaissent les paysans », dira-t-il encore.

L'espace rural manitobain, bien que plus vaste et moins auto-suffisant à
cause de sa dépendance des marchés extérieurs pour l'écoulement de son
blé, contient quand même le paysan dans des limites réduites. Grove déclare de son héros : « His vision had been bounded by the lines of his farm
. . . » Il ajoute : « More and more the wind-break surrounding his yard
seemed to be a rampart which, without knowing it, he had erected to keep
out an hostile world ».

CS

Dans *Trente arpents* l'envahissement de l' « étranger » se produit de multiples façons, prend différentes figures. Il apparaît par exemple sous la figure d'Albert, le Français engagé par Moisan pour l'aider sur sa ferme.
D'une autre origine, il ne parle pas le français des paysans, il ne se rend pas
à la messe dominicale, il refuse de se laisser lier à trente arpents de terre.
On le considère alors comme un être « anormal », « presque inhumain »,
« suspect », pour employer les termes de l'auteur, et qui crée dans ce monde
familier un « sentiment d'insécurité ». Il représente pour les campagnards
des valeurs différentes et troublantes. L'étranger prend aussi la figure de la
science et de la technique. Les forces du paysan, dépendant jusqu'ici de ses
bras, seront multipliées par la machine; dans le roman, l'on passe de la
faucille à la faucheuse, du râteau à main à la lieuse, du cheval au tracteur.
Le rythme des communications s'accélère par les premières automobiles :
« On était loin des dimanches d'autrefois . . . L'automobile était venue qui
avait changé tout cela ». L'agronome, représentant de la science, commence
à être consulté par le fils, au scandale du père. L'espace qui était statique
devient dynamique. Mais ceci ne se fait pas sans résistance : l'oncle Éphrem
s'oppose au passage de la faucille à la faucheuse, le père Moisan craint de
passer de la moissonneuse-lieuse au « tracteur à gazoline », comme il dit, de
l'élevage des poules à la culture des champignons. Pourquoi ces résistan-
ces? Sentiment de crainte pour des instruments qui semblent maléfiques : le
« tracteur à gazoline » a déjà ruiné une terre, dit Moisan à son fils. Un vieux
paysan déclarait à Moisan : « Si on faisait la culture comme dans le vieux
temps, ça donnerait pas aux jeunes le goût des mécaniques qu'est bonnes à
rien qu'à amener des accidents ». L'auto que croise Moisan « est lancée à
une allure de démon ». Autant d'attitudes qui démontrent l'opposition du
milieu qui voudrait que les choses se fassent comme « au bon vieux temps ».
Désir de retour au temps sacré parfait, immobile, qui n'est que reprise de
lui-même, désir de perpétuer les valeurs anciennes, avec la nostalgie de ce
qui bouscule l'ordre permanent et la sécurité.

L'étranger, perturbateur de l'ordre, prend encore une autre figure, celle de la ville. Facteur extérieur qui vient déraciner les enfants du sol. Pour le père Moisan elle revêt un visage hostile, crée des sensations d'étouffement, de désarroi, et même d'épouvante. Mais pour plusieurs de ses enfants elle devient un pôle d'attirance éblouissant. Trois des enfants finiront par travailler dans les usines ou les filatures. Éphrem est ravi par «les grosses gages» et les femmes provocantes; Lucinda, par «les douze dollars de gages», en argent liquide, les fanfreluches, les robes de couleur vive. Napoléon est «leurré par l'appeau de la ville, ébloui par les facettes des affiches lumineuses, par l'argent facile, facilement gagné, facilement dépensé». C'est la grande désertion du sol, combattue par tant de romans du terroir voués à la conservation de la tradition garante du bonheur de l'homme.

L'étranger comme personne ne joue pas un rôle dans le monde des pionniers de l'Ouest qui viennent tous forcément d'ailleurs et, dans le cas présent, de nombreux pays. Mais il semble que malgré cette diversité des expériences et des origines, un milieu paysan se reconstitue avec des valeurs déterminées qui tiennent plus au genre de vie qu'à l'origine ethnique. Abe Spalding, qui vient ouvrir des espaces nouveaux, après avoir brisé avec le monde paysan traditionnel en Ontario, se résigne seulement à l'utilisation de la machine parce qu'elle est l'unique solution pour conquérir ces vastes plaines: «There was only one, power-farming as it was called: machinery would do the work of many men. But Abe liked the response of living flesh and bone to the spoken word and hated the unintelligent repetition of ununderstood activities which machines demanded. Yet sooner or later he must come to that; he would have to run the farm like a factory; that was the modern trend . . . » Les fermiers du district expriment leur étonnement et leur scepticisme devant les innovations techniques d'Abe tel que l'éclairage des poulaillers la nuit ou l'utilisation de la trayeuse mécanique. Eux aussi, comme les paysans de Ringuet, affichent un mépris pour la science agronomique; «college farming» dit l'un. Spalding, comme nous l'avons exprimé, se voit surtout commandé par la nécessité, car il ne croit pas que la technique vienne améliorer le sort de l'homme: «Labour-saving devices galore; and they did save labour; but did they save time? »

Mais Spalding est bien lucide sur le phénomène nouveau dans l'évolution humaine. Il comprend qu'il est dans l'âge de la machine — « machine age » —, qu'il y a un esprit correspondant au «machine age», mais il juge que cette époque nouvelle contribuerait plus à l'information qu'à la formation du caractère: «The imparting of information would be the paramount aim, not the building of character». Il constate surtout qu'il n'a pas lui-même l'esprit de cette ère mécanique: «What is needed is the mechanical mentality and this he did not have». Grove comme Ringuet signalent tous les deux ce nouvel aspect qui oppose les générations: l'existence chez les fils d'une mentalité correspondante à l'ère mécanique qui envahit maintenant

le Canada de l'est à l'ouest : Éphrem et Jim sont attirés par les garages.
Grove insiste pour nous montrer comment Jim est doué de cet esprit : il est
un « born mechanic », il a le « spirit of the machine ». C'est lui qui entraîne
son père pour la première fois dans une automobile.

La ville joue également dans *Fruits of the Earth* un rôle perturbateur qui
corrompt les jeunes esprits. Facteur d'attirance, elle arrache les enfants à
leur milieu : « children taken from the farm and transplanted into the environment of town tended to grow away from the land and the control of
their parents ». Le séjour dans les villes, pour les études par exemple, donne
encore naissance à un « commercial spirit » : « the boy had the commercial
spirit . . . an effect of his stay in town ».

Cet éloignement physique et moral du monde agraire traditionnel est surtout activé pour Grove par la Première Guerre mondiale. Le paysan de
Ringuet s'en souciait peu, il ne vendait que mieux ses récoltes. Grove perçoit ce grand tournant au retour des militaires. La guerre a créé toutes sor-
tes de besoins, a bouleversé l'esprit des hommes. L'argent fait son apparition.
Le paragraphe suivant est plus éloquent que toute dissertation : « The war
had unsettled men's minds. There was a tremendous new urge towards immediacy of results; there was general dissatisfaction. Irrespective of their
economic ability, people craved things which they had never craved before.
Democracy was interpreted as the right of everybody to everything that the
stimulated inventive power of mankind in the mass could furnish in the
way of conveniences and luxuries. Amusements became a necessity of daily
life. A tendency to spend recklessly and to use credit on a scale hitherto
unknown was linked with a pronounced weakening of the moral fibre. In
the homes of the Hartleys, McCreas, Wheeldons, Topps, gramophones and
similar knick-knacks made their appearance; young men wore flashy
clothes, paying or owing from forty to a hundred dollars for a suit. Girls
wore silk stockings, silk underwear, silk dresses; and nothing destroys mod-
esty and sexual morality in a girl more quickly than the consciousness that
suddenly she wears attractive dessous. This orgy of spending had been
enormously stimulated by the easy money of the flax boom; and the rate of
expenditure was hardly retarded by the subsequent disaster of the slump. A
standard of expenditure once arrived at is not so easily abandoned as established! » La fille même de Spalding est rendue enceinte par un ancien militaire. Le dernier geste d'Abe Spalding aura une valeur symbolique face aux
valeurs nouvelles en gestation. Il fermera l'ancienne école du district devenue à ses yeux un endroit de dévergondage de la jeunesse.

L'argent, les filles, l'alcool, les amusements, autant d'éléments reliés à la
ville dont l'image, dans ces deux romans, correspond à celle que peignait
le roman paysan traditionnel. Et le lecteur n'est pas certain que Grove et
Ringuet, dans leur analyse presque clinique, n'endossent pas tous deux la
perception que les vieux paysans se font eux-mêmes de l'urbanisation et de

l'âge nouveau. Ils nous semblent adopter une même perspective. Ringuet brosse une image très déprimante de Montréal ou de White Falls à la fin de son roman. Grove par son héros semble prévoir une décadence des valeurs morales.

ଔ

Si Grove et Ringuet se rencontrent dans la composition de leur roman, s'ils se rejoignent dans leur témoignage sur une ère en pleine mutation, ils partagent aussi des conceptions analogues dans leur vision de l'homme. Les romanciers du terroir étaient jusqu'ici assez optimistes, assez idéalistes, sur le destin des hommes ; nos deux romanciers s'engagent à contre-courant et en proposent une vision tragique. Celui que l'on croyait un maître est en réalité un esclave.

Ringuet, tout au long de son roman, nous fait sentir la condition dépendante du paysan par rapport à la nature : « Et cela, dit-il, suivant l'ordre établi depuis des millénaires, depuis que l'homme abdiquant la liberté que lui permettait une vie de chasse et de pêche, a accepté le joug des saisons et soumis sa vie au rythme annuel de la terre à laquelle il est désormais accouplé ». Moisan perçoit « que toutes les choses de la terre et lui-même ne dépendraient plus rien que de la terre même et du soleil et de la pluie ». Mais ce semble surtout l'auteur qui parsème son récit de réflexions sur le destin de l'homme sans emprunter le truchement d'un personnage. Elles réfléchissent un sentiment d'impuissance de l'homme face aux éléments. Ses décisions sont « conditionnées par la pluie, le vent, et la neige ». Il a une « chétive intervention dans l'ordre des choses » ; ses gestes sont futiles dans « l'immensité indifférente des éléments ». S'il peut vaincre parfois, il a aussi la sensation, et ici c'est le cousin de la ville qui réfléchit, que la nature champêtre est si grande qu'il se sent « annihilé par son immensité même ». Quelle sera la réaction du paysan de Ringuet face à cette fatalité qui l'écrase ? Quand les campagnards virent Éphrem Moisan, le fils, se rebeller, ils ne pouvaient comprendre qu'on « n'acceptât point l'état de choses éternel et fatal et qu'on pût vouloir lutter contre ; que l'un d'eux essayât de prendre le chemin de traverse des décisions humaines qui ne sont pas imposées par la nature ou la coutume. Mais ils n'en avaient pas moins une espèce d'admiration étonnée pour le rebelle, pour cette mauvaise tête d'Éphrem Moisan ». On peut tout au plus ruser, « apprendre en quoi il faut obéir à la nature et comment profiter d'elle ».

Le paysan de *Trente arpents* accepte donc sans révolte l'ordre des choses. Cette attitude semble même normale : le paysan développe une *passivité*, celle « dont sont imbus ceux, hommes et bêtes, dont les décisions ne sauraient jamais être que conditionnelles : que conditionnées par la pluie et le vent et la neige pour les hommes . . . »

Nous ne sommes pas étonnés que le héros conserve cette disposition passive, lorsqu'il croupit chez son fils aux États-Unis. Voici les ultimes réflexions à la dernière page de l'oeuvre. « Il n'a pas renoncé à retourner là-bas à Saint-Jacques; renoncer cela voudrait dire une décision formelle qu'il n'a pas prise, qu'il ne prendra sans doute jamais, qu'il n'aura jamais à prendre. Ce sont les choses qui ont décidé pour lui, et les gens, conduits par les choses ». L'homme passe, la terre demeure. Le roman se termine ainsi : «. . . à des hommes différents . . . une terre toujours la même ».

Le paysan de *Fruits of the Earth* connaît-il un destin analogue? Comme Moisan, Spalding est asservi par le sol, et il en a nette conscience : « il lui avait donné le pouvoir de la faire ».

Il se voit, comme Moisan, soumis aux caprices des éléments, à la pluie, au blizzard, à la sécheresse, au feu qui sont en conflit perpétuel avec l'homme : « Now he fought because farm and weather ruled him with a logic of their own ».

Lors de la grande inondation, Abe et ses compagnons prennent figure de héros et de géants « fighting the elements ». Il se sent particulièrement vulnérable à l'occasion de la grande récolte sur laquelle il a tout misé. « Unless some major disaster interfered this crop would place him at the goal of his ambitions. But could it be that no disaster was to come? He felt as though a sacrifice were needed to propitiate the fates. He caught himself casting about for something he might do to hurt himself, so as to lessen the provocation and challenge his prospect of wealth must be to whatever power had taken the place of the gods ». Abe Spalding a réalisé plusieurs de ses grands rêves, surtout matériels : il a obtenu les deux milles carrés de terre désirés, il a misé et gagné sur la grande récolte de 1912, il a bâti la maison qui dominerait la plaine. Mais il a aussi pris conscience « of the futility of it all », dans un retour sur lui-même, car il avait éloigné de lui son épouse et ses enfants. Cinq ans après avoir élevée son château, il s'est aperçu que celui-ci se désagrégeait déjà. « The moment a work of man was finished, nature set to work to take it down again ».

Le pionnier de Grove est manifestement lucide face à son sort. Il sait faire des retours sur lui-même et juger de sa situation tragique. Peut-être est-ce à cause de cela qu'il est plus *actif*, en affrontant sa destinée. À la résignation passive du paysan de Ringuet qui ne comprenait pas qu'on « n'acceptât point l'état de chose éternel et fatal et qu'on pût vouloir lutter contre . . . » il oppose une résignation active. Eucharistie Moisan n'a pas pris de décisions; les choses ont décidé pour lui. Abe Spalding qui avait démissionné un temps, décide lui, d'accepter consciemment son sort, et aussi de lutter contre lui. Prométhée enchaîné, il ne se rendra pas aux dieux. L'école qu'il avait fondée est devenue à la fin du roman « an abode of iniquity ». L'esprit d'après-guerre envahit le district. Il décide de prendre ou de reprendre ses responsabilités, de réparer ses erreurs avec sa famille

« True resignation meant accepting one's destiny; to him, it meant accepting the burden of leadership . . . I'll go on . . . To the end . . . Wherever it may be ». Il se lève et va fermer l'école.

Conception analogue chez Grove et Ringuet du destin de l'homme-paysan, livré à la nature, même résignation, mais réaction plus lucide et active du pionnier de Grove.

Ringuet et Grove se sont dégagés des idylles régionalistes en vogue. Chacun à leur manière, dans des espaces éloignés l'un de l'autre, ils ont reflété de façon analogue la grande transition de l'ère agraire à l'ère technique au Canada.

Ils ont su aussi et surtout se dégager des particularismes ou des régionalismes pour porter leurs thèmes sur un plan plus universel, celui du destin de l'homme face à la nature. D'origine ethnique et de milieu différents, à l'intérieur d'un même pays, ils se rejoignaient sous des aspects dont l'importance m'a paru justifier une comparaison.

CL 49 (Summer 1971)

Joyce Marshall

The Writer as Translator: A Personal View

I once read that all writers should in the course of their careers write at least one book for children and translate at least one book from another language. (I believe the exact words were "owed it to the profession" — a daunting phrase.) I haven't yet written my book for children (though I have one or two excellent ideas and have been waiting for years for something — myself? — to set me going) but I have translated seven books, as well as a number of shorter pieces, from French, the only other language I know. I'm not at all sure that this was in any sense a gift to the profession of letters — I don't think in such terms and, anyway, someone else would have translated the books — but it was certainly a gift of tremendous value to me as a writer, a writer in English.

Of the seven books only three were works of fiction — *The Road Past Altamont*, *Windflower*, and *Enchanted Summer* (to give them their English titles), all by the late Gabrielle Roy — and as I am myself a writer of fiction, I propose to deal specifically with these. Though I learned something about the languages from my translation of the three non-fiction books, and though my work on *Word From New France: The Selected Letters of Marie de l'Incarnation* plunged me into the heart of an alien seventeenth-century society and a personality unlike my own in every respect (a huge and exciting leap of the imagination), I shall leave these more or less to one side.

My translation of the three Gabrielle Roy books, which concluded with close, extremely demanding sessions during which she and I went over my translations word by word and sentence by sentence, not once but several times, gave me the inestimable privilege of friendship with one of our greatest writers (and finest and most elusive human beings). We were already acquainted, in fact vaguely friendly when I undertook the work but I would never have known her so well if I had not seen her at work and, by working with her, learned much about the methods and imaginative texture of an extraordinarily disciplined and original mind. As I have described these revision-sessions more than once, in other places, emphasizing to some extent their amusing aspects, I shall not repeat these descriptions here, just say that they were great fun and, because we were both exceedingly stubborn people, often exasperating as well and that in my frequent need to defend myself, often turning my mind inside out to do so (for though of the two of us she was the unquestioned authority on her own meaning and intention, I was just as unquestionably the authority on English syntax and idiom), I learned things about the English language I might not have learned in any other way, learned what it could do and couldn't do and above all learned to value it more than I had ever done before. I've often thought that every translator, especially every translator who was just beginning to learn the craft, should have had to work at least once with Gabrielle Roy — particularly if that translator hoped or was trying to be a writer. It was a stimulating, if at times excruciating, process but having been through it three times, I was glad finally to decide not to go through it again. I learned much from these sessions and what I learned I know. I am grateful for this and for the friendship that survived all differences of opinion and added so much to my life. But I am getting ahead of myself. I propose to write in general as well as particular terms about the writer (in this case myself) as translator: what are (or might be) the disadvantages, the advantages, and the ultimate gains.

⚃

I became a translator by accident. I had done some writing and it was known that I'd grown up in Montreal and thus knew French, so when some time in the late 1950s Robert Weaver wanted a story by Gabrielle Roy translated for broadcast over the CBC he asked whether I'd give it a try. I said I would and learned whatever I've learned about the craft of translating by doing. I'd never met anyone who'd done even a single translation — in fact, there were few such people in this country at that time. I'd never (nor have I yet) taken a course in translating. (I don't think that in those days there were any such courses.) I'd never read a single book — or for that matter an article — on the subject. After I decided in the late 1970s not to translate any more books, having grown weary of scraping my mind raw over thoughts that weren't mine, I encountered a few books and sometimes read them even now, thinking rather wistfully how useful they'd have been when I was trying to teach myself to be a translator.

At the time, however, I undertook the job of translating one of our most important and, for some reason that I'd never quite managed to put my finger on, one of our most intractably difficult writers, without knowledge, theories, or skill. And soon after I'd completed that first story, Harry Binsse, who'd translated Gabrielle Roy's most recent books, was no longer available for freelance work and I was asked to translate *La Route d'Altamont*, of which the story I'd already translated was a tiny part. I happened to be bored with my own writing at that time; I felt that I knew what I would say before I said it since I'd been saying the same things, or at least the same sorts of things, for years. So I agreed to translate the book.

For me it was a gruelling and desperately difficult undertaking. I simply set down the English equivalent, as nearly as I could discover it, of every word in pretty much the order in which they occurred in the French, then tried to turn the resulting curious sentences into English. At this point it was the similarities rather than the differences between the languages that troubled me. It might have been easier to work with a language that didn't have subjects, objects, prepositions, conjunctions, etc. (if such languages exist), at any rate from a language that didn't make even wild, clumsy sentences when translated more or less word after word. As a matter of fact, I never got much beyond this first stage of translating fairly literally then fighting the results into English. If there are tricks I never discovered them or problems with easy solutions I never found them, and when I did find a solution to a problem, any relief I might feel was quickly wiped out by the looming of some new equally formidable problem. I learned a great deal by this fighting; what effect it had upon the outcome I cannot say. As I'm discussing this matter from the point of view of a would-be translator who was already a writer, the fact that I did know, at least essentially, how an English sentence went was an advantage. But even so I found, and continued to find whenever I was translating, that I had to spend some time every day reading English — not the newspapers but the most immaculate English I could find. Otherwise I simply forgot, or was at least in danger of forgetting, how an English sentence was put together and why it was put together in that way. I also had to examine very carefully, not only every word of the French but every word of my English rendition, deciding not only what it meant but also what it weighed and how it affected other words and phrases in the sentence. (This last was important. English words do condition, even tinge, one another as French words do not do to the same extent.) Another useful discipline was that I was forced to follow Gabrielle Roy's thoughts and intentions in every way. I'd tended in my own writing (as I imagine most writers tend) to try to get an effect in one way and, if this failed, strike it out and try some other way. As a translator I had to get Gabrielle Roy's effect in the way she had chosen to obtain it. This was complicated by the fact that much as I admired her writing, and continued to admire it, I did not always like, or perhaps it would be more exact to say I didn't always find congenial, the way she obtained an effect — by which of course I mean her emotional, dramatic, or structural effect. But I was bound to use her way.

ひ

And now we come to what might have been the disadvantages (or at least difficulties) of the writer (myself) as translator. People often asked me, and in fact continue to ask me, "Weren't you tempted to convert the French into an equivalent of your own English style?" The answer to that is No — not only was I not tempted to do this, I would have found it impossible. (I have a style presumably although I'd be at a loss to try to describe it; it seems to be a sort of rhythm that comes, in some way I can neither control nor analyze, from my head to my fingers.) I suppose if there were a writer whose thoughts and imaginative processes were identical, or almost identical, to my own, I might slip into this rhythm without realizing that I was doing it. But when, as with Gabrielle Roy, not only the thoughts themselves but the structure of the thoughts, the use or withholding of detail, in fact the entire attitude, were idiosyncratic and unique, these thoughts, coloured as they were by the mind that inspired them, could not fit themselves into my particular way of forming sentences but had to find their own arrangement of words, vocabulary, and stress. I never found this in itself much of a problem. As a writer of fiction, I was accustomed to writing dialogue, in other words to recording the speech of people who expressed themselves in characteristic ways. Translation is simply an extended exercise in dialogue-writing. I didn't describe it to myself as such at first, I simply did it, or at least tried to do it, reminding myself when necessary that this was someone else speaking, not I myself. And an entire novel, or linked series of stories, was a more extensive piece of dialogue than any I'd tackled before, and the fact that it came from a mind that was very much subtler than any I could possibly invent was not only a tremendous challenge to me as a writer but a marvellous holiday from myself.

I've been asked, by the way, whether the intensity and prolongation of the work — the solitary struggling and the final discussion-sessions with Gabrielle Roy of which I've already spoken — tempted me or even caused me unknown to myself to try to write like Gabrielle Roy, structure events as she structured them, attempt to copy her style. I don't believe so. Our minds were too different, as going right down into the bones of her writing would have shown me even if I hadn't been aware of it before. The experience made me not only more disciplined as a writer but, by taking me right away from myself, more conscious of how I wanted to write, what I wanted my style and approach to be. In other words it taught me to accept my own individuality, even to know, dimly at least, what this individuality involved.

So much for the benefits and disadvantages. Now for the discoveries. I suppose the chief of these, and the one that sums up all the others, was the realization that my thinking, my attitude, in fact everything that influences my way of expressing myself, as well as my choice of what I want to express, is completely bound up with the English language — and with this realization came my awareness that I was glad that this was so. It is easy for anyone who was taught to speak French, as I was by a native speaker of the language, to acquire an inferiority complex about English. I certainly did and I even have a record of the way it started, in a diary I kept when I was twelve. Into the usual record of childhood doings, ornamented with the usual high-flown and egotistic sentiments, comes the announcement that "today Mademoiselle —— told us that no one could write good prose in English because English words can mean more than one thing." "Damn her and her French!" I added, apparently already determined to prove her wrong. Though I never referred to the incident again, the memory must have rankled. In fact I know it did. Certainly Mademoiselle ——'s pronouncement was not the last such comment I heard. French-speakers are taught not only to value but to extol their own language as English-speakers are not and I always had a sneaking fear that English could never achieve the *clarté* French was said to possess and to possess by its very nature. The trouble was that I loved French and kept up my reading of the language through all the years when my life in Toronto gave me very few occasions to speak it, loved it not only for its *clarté* but for the marvellous lightness of its sentence structure, the neat adroit phrasing and connections between phrases that often made me, as a lover of language, want to cry aloud with delight. Can English ever do this, I sometimes wondered.

Perhaps not that. Or not precisely that. But what it can do, it does to a considerable extent because English words, in Mademoiselle ——'s immortal phrase, "can mean more than one thing," are influenced by other words, spread, are never static. And we have so many — the Latin words so formal and heavy often, or at least abstract, the Saxon words so much quicker, so evocative, so much closer to the heart. (We've never after all these centuries quite accepted these Latin intruders, I often think.) After years of working with French, getting right down into the sinews of the language while doing no original writing of my own, staring at words whose meanings, though perhaps not subject to change, were often so wide that they swallowed up a good half dozen of our small bright English words (and needed a variety of set phrases — *pour ainsi dire, malgré tout,* etc. — to tie them down), looking at conclusions when I wanted to see process — for French is to a considerable extent a language of nouns, English a language of verbs — and discovering that a sentence of great *clarté* in French wasn't at all clear in English (and this often because it didn't tell me the things I wanted to know), I began to feel less apologetic about English. I have even praised its merits to French-speakers on occasion, to their great surprise. Perhaps "merits" isn't the right word. Perhaps no language can be said to possess merits as such. Perhaps all I mean is that English suits me as a medium of expression, multiple meanings and all, and that I'll cheerfully damn, as I did with such lack of knowledge when I was twelve, anyone who suggests that it can't produce "good prose."

CL 117 (Summer 1998)

Louise Ladouceur

A *Firm Balance: Questions d'équilibre et rapport de force dans les représentations des littératures anglophone et francophone du Canada*

L'étude des discours critiques portant sur la relation entre les littératures canadiennes d'expression anglaise et d'expression française révèle une présence importante d'emblèmes et de symboles chargés de représenter cette relation. Exprimant les positions, les présupposés et les aspirations propres à chaque ensemble discursif, ces figures symboliques mettent en scène un rapport de force qu'elles contribuent d'ailleurs à façonner.

Issus d'abord des études en littérature comparée canadienne, ces emblèmes ont exprimé un idéal égalitaire fort louable mais très éloigné de la réalité. Avec l'élaboration d'un discours critique et théorique sur la traduction littéraire canadienne à la fin des années quatre-vingt, les façons de représenter la dynamique des échanges entre les littératures anglophone et francophone mettent en lumière un autre type de relation. Délaissant l'analyse des différences et des ressemblances entre les répertoires, ce discours donne à voir un rapport de force avoué entre littératures majoritaire et minoritaire, un rapport dont les enjeux sont de taille puisqu'il s'agit de donner sa propre voix et sa propre langue à la parole de l'autre.

L'étude qui suit propose d'examiner les symboles et les désignations attribués aux littératures anglophone et francophone du Canada par la littérature comparée canadienne en premier lieu et, par la suite, dans le discours portant sur la traduction littéraire en contexte canadien. Issus en grande partie du discours critique anglophone, ces emblèmes sont peu connus des francophones, pour qui ils ne constituent pas une tradition critique. Par conséquent, cette étude invite un lectorat francophone à prendre connais-

sance d'une activité emblématique importante au Canada anglais et fort
révélatrice des perceptions et des conceptions qui contribuent à définir les
littératures écrites dans les deux langues officielles du Canada.

Solitudes en équilibre

Dans « Canada's Two Literatures: A Search for Emblems » (1979) et dans
l'ouvrage intitulé *All the Polarities: Studies in Contemporary Canadian
Novels in French and in English* (1986), Philip Stratford propose une étude
des emblèmes attribués aux littératures anglaise et française du Canada
depuis environ un siècle. Dans cet article, qui me servira de point de départ, Stratford cite Pierre-Joseph-Olivier Chauveau, éducateur, homme de
lettres et homme politique québécois qui, en 1876, déplorait le manque
d'échange entre ce qu'il appelle alors les « deux races » (335). Chauveau
compare cet état social à l'escalier du château de Chambord, « construit de
manière que deux personnes puissent monter en même temps sans se rencontrer » (335):

> Anglais et français [sic], nous montons comme par une double rampe
> vers les destinées qui nous sont réservées sur ce continent, sans nous
> connaître, sans nous rencontrer, ni même nous voir ailleurs que sur le
> palier de la politique. Socialement et littérairement parlant, nous
> sommes plus étrangers les uns aux autres de beaucoup que ne le sont
> les Anglais et les Français d'Europe. (335)

Selon Stratford, cette vision plutôt pessimiste était compensée par
l'enthousiasme d'un William Kirby qui, dans son roman *The Chien d'Or:
A Legend of Quebec*, publié à Montréal en 1877, exprimait le souhait de
voir « the two glorious streams of modern thought and literature united in
New France, where they have run side by side to this day — in time to be
united in one grand flood stream of Canadian literature » (268).
    Au milieu du siècle suivant paraît à Toronto le roman de Hugh MacLen-
nan dont le titre, *Two Solitudes* (1945), deviendra l'emblème consacré de
la relation entre les cultures anglaise et française du Canada. L'auteur commente le titre de l'ouvrage en lui faisant porter en épigraphe ces vers de
Rainer Maria Rilke: « Love consists in this, / that two solitudes protect, /
and touch, and greet each other ». Ici, la métaphore évoque le rapport
amoureux unissant un couple. Dans sa préface, MacLennan apporte ces
précisions sur les désignations employées dans l'ouvrage:

> No single word exists, within Canada itself, to designate with
> satisfaction to both races a native of the country. When those of the
> French language use the word Canadien, they nearly always refer to

themselves. They know their English-speaking compatriots as Les
Anglais. English-speaking citizens act on the same principle. They call
themselves Canadians; those of the French language French-Canadians.

Suivant la logique des désignations attribuées aux deux groupes linguistiques, les oeuvres littéraires écrites dans l'une ou l'autre langue appartiennent à ce qu'on appelle alors les littératures canadienne-anglaise et
canadienne-française, désignations qui se sont imposées depuis que la Loi
constitutionnelle de 1867 a reconnu la coexistence des deux langues au
sein de la fédération canadienne.[1] La figure des « deux solitudes » s'impo-
sera autant en français qu'en anglais et elle donnera lieu à de nombreuses
reprises qui vont témoigner de l'évolution du couple en question dans le
discours critique littéraire.[2] Ce qu'il faut retenir de la métaphore inaugurée
par MacLennan, c'est qu'elle exprime des vœux de rapprochement qui
vont devenir un important leitmotiv au sein d'un discours critique occupé
à démontrer que « les deux littératures nationales du Canada [. . .] ont
suivi une évolution parallèle et qu'elles ont plus de caractères communs
qu'on ne le croit habituellement » (Sylvestre et al., v).

Dans cette foulée émerge en 1965 un symbole géographique qui mar-
quera profondément la critique littéraire canadienne-anglaise. Il s'agit de ce
que Northrop Frye appelle « a garrison mentality » et qu'il décrit en ces
mots : « a garrison is a closely knit and beleaguered society, and its moral
and social values are unquestionable » (830). Selon Frye, c'est une attitude
commune aux deux littératures puisque « Canada has two languages and
two literatures, and every statement made in a book like this about 'Canadian literature' employs the figure of speech known as synecdoche, putting
a part for the whole. Every such statement implies a parallel or contrasting
statement about French-Canadian literature » (*Literary History* 823).

À la même époque, du côté francophone, la double spirale de Chauveau
a cédé le pas à l'antagonisme spatial dessiné par Jean-Charles Falardeau
dans *Notre société et son roman* (1967). Il explique : « La littérature canadienne-anglaise, selon ses critiques, est tendue selon un axe horizontal : la
relation homme-milieu ou homme-société. Pour le critique de langue française, l'axe de sa littérature est, à l'inverse, vertical : il est donné par la
relation homme-destin ou homme-absolu » (58). Cette représentation an-
tagonique n'est sans doute pas étrangère à l'esprit de la Révolution tranquille, le mouvement d'émancipation qui emporte alors le Québec vers
l'affirmation d'une identité culturelle spécifique.

Malgré la divergence des points de vue adoptés par Frye et Falardeau, les
dénominations auxquelles ils ont recours pour désigner les littératures re-
lèvent toujours du principe voulant qu'elles aient en commun d'être canadiennes et se distinguent par la langue. C'est un principe dénominatif que
Clément Moisan analyse dans *L'âge de la littérature canadienne* (1969) :

> Le Canada comprenant deux langues et deux cultures, l'expression
> littérature canadienne ne peut jamais recouvrir toute la réalité. Il faut
> toujours ajouter une épithète et former un adjectif composé:
> canadienne-anglaise, canadienne-française ou encore, ce qui semble
> plus juste, dire littérature canadienne d'expression anglaise ou
> d'expression française. On va même jusqu'à inverser les termes: anglo-
> canadienne, franco-canadienne. (17)

Déplorant la lourdeur de cette terminologie, Moisan précise que les auteurs
ont en général « adopté une solution très simple : selon qu'ils sont Canadiens
français ou Canadiens anglais, l'expression littérature canadienne désigne les
oeuvres écrites dans leur propre langue » (18). On retrouve ici une attitude
analogue à celle décrite auparavant par MacLennan. Dans son étude, qui a
comme intention de « démontrer la parenté des deux littératures canadiennes » (*L'âge de la littérature* 13), Moisan leur reconnaît une problématique
commune, celle d'être marginale et de devoir « résoudre des problèmes de
croissance avant d'atteindre à [leur] pleine maturité » (163). Si, à l'instar de
Moisan, les critiques s'astreignent à examiner les fondements et la portée des
désignations auxquelles ils ont recours pour nommer les ensembles littéraires anglais et français du Canada, c'est que ces désignations sont devenues le
symbole d'enjeux littéraires et politiques importants.

Dans le climat d'effervescence et de changement que connaît le Québec
des années soixante, la question identitaire est au centre des préoccupations
et on interroge la pertinence d'une désignation qui attribue le même déno-
minateur à chaque littérature. Représentative de ce mouvement, auquel elle
a fortement contribué, la revue *Parti Pris* (1963–68) publie en 1965 un numéro intitulé « Pour une littérature québécoise », dont Pierre Maheu décrit
le sujet en ces termes : « nous pensons que la 'littérature canadienne d'expression française' [. . .] est morte, si jamais elle a été vivante, et que la littérature québécoise est en train de naître » (2). Selon les auteurs, ce
déplacement prend des sens divers : pour Laurent Girouard, « [l]a littérature
québécoise prend possession du pays, de l'enfance, de la modernité » (11).
André Major y fait l'expérience de la liberté devant « un passé qui nous
écrase » (16) et à partir duquel il faut découvrir « le sens de notre vérité
propre » (17). Dénonçant sa « situation dans ce pays, qui est [s]a réduction
au regard de l'altérité anglo-canadienne » (27), Gaston Miron affirme que
la « littérature ici [. . .] existera collectivement [. . .] le jour où elle prendra
place parmi les littératures nationales, le jour où elle sera québécoise » (30).
De son côté, Paul Chamberland conçoit le « malheur canadien-français »
(38) comme « un universel qui consacre notre folklorisation » (38), pendant
que Jacques Brault convie la littérature « à aller de l'avant par ses moyens
propres et [à] projeter pour tous les hommes cette liberté que nous ne sommes pas encore » (51).[3] Ce déplacement onomastique prend donc racine

dans un discours qui affiche ses orientations indépendantistes, ce qui a pour
effet d'investir le nouveau qualificatif d'un fort coefficient politique. Cette
reconfiguration des désignations attribuées à chaque ensemble littéraire met
en évidence leur caractère politique, ce qu'a éloquemment démontré Cynthia Sugars dans l'article qu'elle consacre aux façons dont la critique littéraire canadienne conçoit les deux littératures et aux prises de position
politiques que recouvrent les désignations employées.[4]

Dans le contexte de l'époque, le recours au qualificatif « québécois » pour
désigner la littérature produite en français au Québec offre l'avantage de
représenter cette littérature sous un angle majoritaire, puisque le français
est au Québec la langue de la majorité. Par conséquent, on renverse ainsi
l'effet d'une dénomination fondée sur la langue au sein d'une fédération
bilingue où le français occupe une position minoritaire. Cela a toutefois
pour résultat d'exclure les oeuvres issues des communautés francophones
canadiennes non québécoises, qui occuperont désormais le champ sémanti-
que désigné par l'appellation « littératures canadiennes-françaises ». Les littératures dites « canadiennes-françaises » vont toutefois emboîter le pas et
se doter de désignations qui mettent l'accent sur leur particularisme en se
qualifiant de franco-terreneuvienne, acadienne, franco-ontarienne, franco-
manitobaine, fransaskoise, franco-albertaine, franco-colombienne, franco-
ténoise et franco-yukonnaise,[5] constituant ainsi des ensembles littéraires
distincts dont le trait commun serait une condition d'exiguïté.[6]

Ces glissements définitoires se sont faits graduellement de telle sorte que
la désignation « littérature québécoise », née de la Révolution tranquille et
mise de l'avant au cours des années soixante, est maintenant d'usage cou-
rant et s'est délestée de la connotation idéologique associée au projet politique qu'elle exprimait il y a trente-cinq ans. C'est ce qui incite Pierre
Nepveu à en questionner le sens : « cette appellation ne recouvre plus rien
d'essentiel ou de substantiel, [ce] qui pourrait nous entraîner à parler désormais, avec un certain à-propos, d'une littérature post-québécoise » (14).
D'autre part, la littérature écrite en langue anglaise au Canada a continué
de se définir comme canadienne-anglaise ou canadienne, selon le désir des
auteurs de distinguer ou non les corpus écrits dans chaque langue.

Si les emblèmes anglais et français s'attachaient auparavant à relever les
points communs entre les littératures tout en insistant sur la distance qui
les séparait et leur isolement respectif, les événements de 1970 inciteront
les critiques anglophones à mettre de l'avant une symbolique du rapprochement pendant qu'on se fera silencieux du côté francophone. Comme le
fait remarquer Clément Moisan :

> [a]lors qu'avant cette date on traitait des deux littératures par hasard
> ou accident et qu'on faisait porter l'attention sur leur existence et
> surtout sur leur ignorance réciproque, après 1970 on semble vouloir

élucider le pourquoi de cette ignorance et rechercher des points de ressemblances ou de dissemblances qui seraient révélateurs de leur situation de littératures marginales. (*Comparaison et raison* 114)

Dans cette veine, s'élabore une réflexion sur le lien entre les littératures qui privilégie d'abord la recherche de thèmes et de mythes fondateurs communs. Après avoir fondé en 1969 la revue de traduction littéraire *Ellipse*, dont le titre est une figure géométrique courbe comprenant deux centres de force égale qui représentent les deux littératures jointes en un objet unique, D.G. Jones publie *Butterfly on Rock: A Study of Themes and Images in Canadian Literature* (1970). Il y soutient que le développement de la littérature canadienne, incluant celle du Québec, va d'une condition d'exil et d'aliénation vers la redécouverte et l'affirmation d'une identité propre. Deux ans plus tard, Margaret Atwood fait paraître *Survival: A Thematic Guide to Canadian Literature*, une étude dans laquelle « Canada is a collective victim » (36) dont les fictions dans les deux langues officielles ont pour préoccupation centrale la survie de héros en position de victimes. Tel que l'indiquent leurs titres, ces études, à l'instar de celle de Frye, traitent de la littérature francophone en tant qu'élément constituant du grand ensemble littéraire canadien.

Poursuivant la réflexion amorcée dans l'article « Twin Solitudes » (1967) où Ronald Sutherland attribue aux deux littératures « a common national mystique, a common set of conditioning forces, the mysterious apparatus of a single sense of identity » (22), l'ouvrage *The New Hero: Essays in Comparative Quebec/Canadian Literature* (1977) propose un symbole connu sous le nom de « mainstream » et décrit ainsi : « the mainstream of Canadian literature [...] is a matter of sphere of consciousness, an author's awareness of and sensitivity to fundamental aspects of both major language groups in Canada and of the inter-relationships between these two groups » (94). Ici, la métaphore fait écho au vœu exprimé presque cent ans auparavant par Kirby, une aspiration qu'on a dotée déjà de quelques fondements thématiques.

À la fin des années soixante-dix et dans la décennie qui suivra le Référendum de 1980, on s'intéressera davantage à ce qui distingue chaque littérature tout en insistant cependant sur le lien indivisible qui les unit. Le principe emblématique du parallélisme connaît alors son apogée. Dans l'article « Canada's Two Literatures: A Search for Emblems » (1979), Stratford soutient que « [i]n Canada, literatures in French and in English have grown up side by side in roughly parallel fashion as far as their rhythms, types, and conditions of development are concerned » (131). Pour parler de ces littératures, Stratford utilise plusieurs dénominations et, dans le même article, parle des « Quebec and English-Canadian novels » (135) à partir d'un corpus représentant «[t]he English-Canadian novel » et « [t]he

French-Canadian novel » (135). On évite donc ici de trancher en faveur de l'une ou l'autre dénomination.

Dans cet article, Stratford conteste la valeur du « mainstream » de Sutherland, de la « vertical-horizontal or separatist theory » de Falardeau et de l'ellipse de Jones en tant que symboles du rapport entre les deux littératures et propose plutôt un emblème emprunté à la génétique : la figure du « double helix which proved to contain the secret of life » (138). Il explique ce choix en mettant l'accent sur deux propriétés importantes des lignes parallèles. En premier lieu, elles ne se rencontrent jamais, si ce n'est dans l'infini : « the two literatures have developed quite independently. There has been next-to-no sharing of experience on critical, cultural or creative levels » (132). Ensuite, les parallèles ne peuvent exister qu'en se définissant l'un par rapport à l'autre : « one parallel fixes and defines the other » (137). Ainsi, conclut Stratford, les parallèles géométriques ou littéraires, bien qu'ils ne se rencontrent jamais, agissent l'un sur l'autre dans un rapport de nécessité symétrique et réciproque.

Jugeant les modèles précédents insensibles à la fragile complexité du rapport entre les deux littératures, E.D. Blodgett propose en 1982 de représenter ce rapport en empruntant le titre d'un recueil de poèmes de Paul Celan, *Sprachgitter*. Il explique ainsi son choix : « A Gitter is a lattice-work fence, a grid of interwoven strands whose common threads relate and distinguish, but do not unify. The grid divides according to language, distinguishes according to culture, history, and ideology » (33). Résolument opposé aux symboles unificateurs, Blodgett insiste sur la nécessité de préserver un pluralisme qui est à la fois source de fragilité et de vitalité pour le Canada. C'est un pluralisme dont, selon lui, ne rendent pas compte les recherches en littérature comparée canadienne, trop souvent restreintes à des études binaires Canada/Québec et mal équipées au niveau méthodologique pour effectuer la comparaison avec d'autres littératures. Blodgett soulève aussi la question fort pertinente de l'idéologie inhérente à toute théorisation :

> What we have been reluctant to assert is not only that literary theory
> is ideological, but that any literary theory that tries to resolve the
> problems of nation-states that are at least bilingual in an official sense
> must be clear about its ideology. A bicultural policy, of course, always
> implies a central question, namely, whose culture, and this question is
> always answered by the dominant group. (32)

Dans l'article « Our Two Cultures », publié en 1984, Patricia Smart déplore l'hégémonie des approches thématiques ou sociologiques de la critique comparative canadienne et rejette les emblèmes existants. Elle commente les représentations du rapport entre les deux cultures dans les œuvres de Hubert Aquin, Margaret Atwood et Jacques Godbout en insistant sur l'inégalité des langues officielles canadiennes et la spécificité de chaque tradition littéraire. Inspirée par la vitalité du dialogue et des échanges amorcés à la fin des années soixante-dix entre les écrivaines et les critiques canadiennes francophones et anglophones, Smart suggère alors de concevoir le rapport entre les deux cultures selon un modèle tiré d'un texte de Nicole Brossard, « La femme dos à dos ». Elle explique :

> Brossard's striking image of two women standing back to back [. . .] is
> one of touching but not of fusion, of separate identities respected and
> shared as both partners look not at each other, but — supporting each
> other — out to the world. Transposed, it becomes an image of two
> nations and two projects, an adjacent but not common space, a border
> shared in which both cultures find strength in difference. (17)

Tout comme le *sprachgitter* de Blodgett, l'emblème retenu par Smart propose d'illustrer le rapport entre les deux systèmes culturels et littéraires à l'aide d'un emprunt linguistique fait à l'allemand dans le premier cas et au français dans le second. Témoignant d'une volonté de prendre l'altérité linguistique en compte et de transgresser les frontières de la langue anglaise, le recours à des termes allemand et français comme matériau emblématique atteste aussi l'assurance d'une langue dominante qui ne se sent nullement menacée par ces emprunts à des langues étrangères.

S'inpirant de l'emblème de Stratford, qu'elle modifie afin de dé-polariser les deux littératures, Cynthia Sugars suggère un nouvel emblème qu'elle inclut dans le titre de son article « On the Rungs of the Double Helix : Theorizing the Canadian Literatures » (1993). Elle propose alors de concevoir les littératures non pas comme si chacune d'elle composait un des rubans parallèles de la double hélice mais plutôt comme si elles étaient réparties de façon analogue aux séquences génétiques elles-mêmes le long d'une chaîne : « in contiguous or split intervals depending on where the critic chooses to slice it at any given time » (39).

A Firm Balance

Dans cette abondante activité emblématique pratiquée par les comparatistes canadiens quelques recoupements s'imposent. Ce qui frappe, en premier lieu, c'est la prédilection de la critique anglophone pour ce genre d'exercice. Poursuivant la réflexion de Blodgett, on pourrait voir dans cette pratique une prédisposition du groupe dominant à non seulement témoigner de l'existence d'un rapport entre les cultures, mais aussi à le sonder pour en imposer une lecture que l'emblème est chargé d'illustrer. En second lieu, on peut observer dans plusieurs de ces symboles la récurrence d'un présupposé qui leur sert de prémisse. Explorant ce qu'ont en commun les doubles escaliers en spirale de Chauveau et l'ellipse de Jones, les parallèles de Stratford, le treillis de Blodgett et la femme dos à dos de Smart, Margery Fee constate : « What these images figure is equality and difference at the same time, sometimes with the addition of a kind of abstract interdependence. English and French in Canada are 'equal partners' in these metaphors » (5). On pourrait en dire autant des métaphores voulant que les deux littératures évoluent au rythme d'une « garrison mentality » commune et qu'elles se rejoignent dans un « mainstream » littéraire réunissant « both major language groups ». Toujours selon Fee, ce présupposé serait peu représentatif d'une réalité où « anglo-Canada has most of the territory, most of the population, and most of the votes in the House » (5).

Que les symboles fondés sur ce présupposé soient l'expression d'un idéal souhaité n'empêche pas qu'ils aient pour effet d'évacuer une réalité pourtant fondamentale : la relation qu'entretiennent les littératures en question est un rapport de force marqué par l'inégalité des langues officielles du Canada.[7] Concevoir que le rapport entre les littératures canadiennes anglophone et francophone puisse reposer sur l'égalité ne peut être qu'une illusion d'optique inhérente à la position occupée dans l'équation. D'un point de vue anglophone et majoritaire, il est aisé de concevoir l'égalité comme acquise et allant de soi. Fort de la position qu'on occupe, on prône un équilibre illusoire entre deux littératures qui sont loin d'avoir le même poids en termes de territoire, de nombre et de moyens. On pourrait concevoir cette symétrie forcée comme un état de « firm balance », une sorte d'équilibre imposé dans lequel on maintient les deux littératures. C'est une fausse conception dans laquelle les francophones ne se reconnaissent pas. Confrontés de façon quotidienne et factuelle à une toute autre réalité, ils vont plutôt se dissocier d'un discours où est occultée une asymétrie qui fait pourtant toute la différence. La réelle inégalité du rapport de force entre les littératures française et anglaise du Canada s'affiche toutefois quand on se déplace vers le territoire de la traduction littéraire, autant dans la façon dont on la pratique que dans les discours critiques qu'elle alimente.

L'épreuve de la traduction

Lieu de rencontre et d'interpénétration des littératures qu'elle met en contact, la traduction est façonnée par le rapport qu'entretiennent ces littératures. Plus qu'un regard qu'on pose sur l'autre, le texte traduit propose une substitution de sa langue et de sa voix à celles de l'autre. Cette commutation ne va pas sans aménagements qui agissent en profondeur sur le texte traduit. Puisqu'il est impossible de reproduire exactement le texte original, les moyens linguistiques de chaque langue n'étant pas identiques et interchangeables, on doit faire des choix qui privilégient nécessairement certaines interprétations. Ces choix doivent en outre s'inscrire dans un contexte social, culturel, historique et politique qui donne au texte des valences autres que celles du contexte d'origine, ce qui demande aussi des ajustements. Enfin, la traduction est le produit d'un agent qui fait une lecture subjective d'une œuvre et en propose une interprétation informée par les rapports conscients et inconscients qu'entretient le sujet traduisant avec le texte et le contexte sources. En fin de parcours, le texte traduit porte les marques d'une lutte dont le résultat est la représentation de l'autre par et à travers soi. Il s'agit donc ici d'un rapport de force avoué dans ce qui se présente comme une joute identitaire.

Activité auparavant discrète, la traduction littéraire prend vraiment son envol avec la création du programme de Subvention de traduction du Conseil des arts du Canada en 1972, lequel a pour mission d'encourager le dialogue et l'échange entre les communautés anglophone et francophone du Canada à une époque où leur relation est particulièrement tendue. Le programme est d'ailleurs exclusif : on ne subventionne que les traductions d'oeuvres canadiennes d'une langue officielle à l'autre. Selon l'étude menée par Ruth Martin sur l'impact de ce programme de 1972 à 1992, il y avait en 1977, soit cinq ans après sa fondation, presque deux fois plus de livres traduits que dans toute l'histoire de la traduction au Canada (54). Fait à souligner, alors qu'on s'attendrait à ce que la minorité francophone emprunte en plus grand nombre à la majorité anglophone qui, en principe, a plus à offrir, c'est l'opposé qui se produit. Ce phénomène est particulièrement marqué dans le domaine du théâtre puisque 60 des 62 traductions théâtrales recensées par Martin sont des oeuvres francophones traduites en anglais. Cette nette différence dans le nombre d'emprunts s'explique de plusieurs façons.

Avec la canonisation du joual comme langue littéraire québécoise en 1968, le théâtre devient un haut lieu d'affirmation identitaire et se voit chargé de faire résonner sur la place publique une langue qui se distingue par sa spécificité orale. Grâce à cette nouvelle norme linguistique, l'écriture théâtrale franco-québécoise connaît un essor sans précédent. Dans cette foulée va s'ouvrir le marché de la traduction théâtrale puisque les pièces étrangères, qui devaient auparavant passer par la France, sont désormais traduites sur place dans une langue locale populaire. Toutefois, on privilégie alors les prestigieux répertoires britanniques et américains plutôt qu'un répertoire canadien qui suscite peu d'intérêt et qui est encore bien timide. Les pièces traduites ne sont donc pas admissibles au programme de traduction du Conseil des arts.

Si on s'intéresse peu au répertoire du Canada anglais, ce n'est pas uniquement par indifférence ou par méfiance. A cette époque, le théâtre canadien-anglais emprunte massivement aux répertoires britannique et américain qui lui servent de modèles et s'investit peu dans la création. Il faut attendre la mise en place du réseau des « alternative theatres » dans les années soixante-dix pour que commence à se constituer un répertoire canadien-anglais auquel on empruntera volontiers à partir de 1980. Ainsi, il n'y aura pas moins de six pièces canadiennes-anglaises produites en traduction au Québec entre 1980 et 1983, soit l'équivalent de toute la décennie précédente.

Pour ce qui est du programme d'appui à la traduction du Conseil des arts, il semble donc qu'il ait surtout contribué à la traduction du répertoire français en anglais par des traducteurs chargés d'établir des ponts entre les deux cultures. Comme le fait remarquer Kathy Mezei, « [s]ince the 1950s, particularly in the context of the Quiet Revolution, the 1970 October Crisis, and the rise of the Parti québécois, English-Canadian translators have proclaimed a political mission to 'bridge' the two solitudes (« Translation as Metonymy » 88). Dans la ferveur nationaliste qui accompagne les célébrations du Centenaire de la Confédération au Canada anglais, la métaphore du pont, déjà présente dans le discours portant sur la traduction, est mise à l'honneur et connaîtra une longue carrière. Dans les textes anglophones, la traduction littéraire se voit alors attribuée la mission d'offrir « a possible bridge over the gap of language between English and French Canadian writing » (Dudek et Gnarowski, cités dans Mezei « Translation as Metonymy » 89).

Employée, entre autres, par Louis Dudek et Michael Gnarowski en 1967, par John Glassco en 1970 et par G.V. Downes en 1973 pour présenter la poésie en traduction (Mezei 89), cette figure sera reprise par Philip Stratford en 1983 pour le titre de l'article, « Literary Translation: A Bridge Between Two Solitudes ». Par la suite, elle apparaîtra dans l'intitulé bilingue de l'ouvrage de Jean Delisle *Au coeur du trialogue canadien: Bureau des traductions 1934–1984/Bridging the Language Solitudes: Translation Bureau 1934–84*. Il est à noter ici que la métaphore n'est conservée que pour la version anglaise du titre. Alors qu'on invite les anglophones à une cordiale rencontre des solitudes linguistiques, le titre français insiste sur le rôle de la traduction comme tiers agent nécessaire au procès de communication, une communication plutôt singulière du reste puisqu'on doit la désigner par un néologisme. Mezei empruntera à son tour l'image du pont pour l'article intitulé « A Bridge of Sorts: The Translation of Quebec Literature into English » (1985), dans lequel elle conçoit la traduction comme une des rares formes d'interaction entre les écrivains anglophones et francophones, lesquels demeurent le plus souvent isolés dans une indifférence mutuelle. Sherry Simon questionne toutefois la représentativité de cette vision de la traduction comme agent de fraternisation:

> Too closely associated with humanistic ideals of transparence and
> tolerance, too obviously linked to the political sphere (the final resting
> place of language issues in Canada), the subject of translation for a

long time conjured up pious images of bridges and brotherhood,
clearly out of sync with the realities of Canadian cultural politics.
("Rites of Passage" 96)

Il faut dire que la figure du « pont » offerte par la traduction, chère aux
anglophones, ne suscite pas le même enthousiasme de l'autre côté de la
rive, où la traduction est perçue comme un symbole de domination politique et un agent d'assimilation linguistique.

Dans le contexte politique canadien, où les rapports de force sont inti-
mement liés à la dualité linguistique, la traduction et son discours se char-
gent nécessairement de fortes connotations politiques. Selon Larry
Shouldice, non seulement elles n'échappent pas au politique, elles en sont
les outils. Dans l'étude qu'il consacre au programme de Subvention de
traduction du Conseil des arts, Shouldice soutient que le succès relatif de
la traduction vers l'anglais ne peut s'expliquer uniquement par les arguments habituels voulant que le dynamisme de la littérature québécoise des
années soixante et soixante-dix attire l'attention, même à l'étranger, que les
Canadiens français sachent lire l'anglais et qu'ils achètent moins de livres
que les Canadiens anglais. Il maintient plutôt que « much of English Canada's interest in Quebec literature stems from a political impulse, and that
this helps explain the relative proliferation of translations from Quebec.
As Hubert Aquin might have expressed it, literary translation in our federal system is a form of cultural appropriation » (80). Shouldice exprime
ainsi les motivations politiques auxquelles obéirait la traduction littéraire
au Canada à cette époque :

> It is not uncommon, I think, for English Canadians to view translation
> as a means of fostering national unity; and while this is no doubt true
> of some French Canadians as well, one senses in the latter a more
> pronounced impulse to intelligence gathering for strategic defence
> purposes: "love thy neighbour" on the one hand, and "know thy
> enemy" on the other. (75)

Il ne faut pas s'étonner, en effet, que la fonction et les enjeux de la traduction littéraire puissent être perçus de façons fort divergentes de part et
d'autre. Cette activité qu'on voudrait conviviale du côté anglophone suscite une grande méfiance chez les francophones pour qui elle a incarné, dès
le début du régime britannique, la nette supériorité hiérarchique de l'anglais par rapport au français. Selon Ben-Zion Shek,

> les documents-clés de l'histoire du Canada, tels la Proclamation royale
> de 1763, l'Acte de Québec, l'Acte constitutionnel, le rapport Durham,
> l'Acte de l'Union, l'Acte de l'Amérique du Nord britannique, le Statut

de Westminster, ainsi que les textes des deux référendums sur la
conscription, ont été rédigés d'abord en anglais puis *traduits* en
français [. . .]. La traduction à sens unique a reproduit les rapports
réels dominants-dominés de la conjoncture militaire, en premier lieu,
puis et par conséquent, politique et économique. (111)

Cela fait en sorte que la traduction française d'œuvres littéraires canadiennes-anglaises est ressentie selon Shek « à la fois comme une menace et
comme une perte d'efforts dans une entreprise marginale, du point de vue
de la lutte pour la survie d'une langue et d'une culture minoritaires » (112).
Pour les francophones, la monumentale activité de traduction par laquelle
doit passer le bilinguisme canadien ne fait pas que mettre en relief la di-
glossie des langues officielles du Canada, elle porte aussi préjudice au français, langue d'arrivée constamment soumise à l'influence de la langue de
départ qu'est l'anglais. Selon Sherry Simon, les effets néfastes de la traduction sur la langue française forment un leitmotiv important au Québec où,
devenue « [t]opique de la défaillance, rappel de l'obligation dans laquelle
le Québec se trouve par rapport à autrui, la traduction est souvent un sujet
pénible » (*L'inscription sociale* 31).
 C'est dans le climat de grande tension linguistique du début des années
soixante-dix que Jacques Brault entreprend de traduire des poètes cana-
diens-anglais et publie, en 1975, le recueil intitulé *Poèmes des quatre côtés*,
dans lequel il expose une conception de la traduction fort inusitée au Québec pour l'époque. En la dégageant de sa responsabilité d'imiter, elle pourrait, selon lui, acquérir une certaine autonomie créatrice dont bénéficierait
la langue d'arrivée, « suspendue entre deux certitudes maintenant problé-
matiques, langue qui reconnaît alors sa difficulté d'être. Et sa raison d'être.
Une langue qui se refuse à pareille épreuve est d'ores et déjà condamnée »
(15). L'argument habituel voulant que la traduction porte préjudice à la
langue cible exposée aux influences de la langue source se trouve ici ren-
versé, ce qui a pour effet de réhabiliter une activité souvent jugée douteuse,
comme le souligne le traducteur au début de son ouvrage : « Les clefs de la
traduction appartiennent aux puissants. S'il n'y a pas de langue mondiale,
il y a des langues colonisatrices » (16). Cette vision salutaire du traduire
qu'il propose alors, Brault suggère de la nommer : nontraduction (15-34).
Ainsi donc, lors même qu'elle désigne une activité constructive, chose rare
au Québec, la traduction se voit affublée d'un préfixe de négation et ne
peut prendre une valeur positive qu'en niant sa propre action.
 Au niveau des procédés privilégiés, l'étude que fait Sherry Simon de la
traduction littéraire pratiquée au Canada dans *Le trafic des langues. Traduction et culture dans la littérature québécoise* (1994) met en relief l'opposition qui informe les représentations de l'altérité véhiculées de part et
d'autre dans les textes en traduction. Selon Simon, les versions anglaises de

romans québécois font preuve d'une « surconscience de la différence » et obéissent à une « visée ethnographique » (55) voulant qu'on insiste sur les marques d'appartenance culturelle au contexte source. La même tendance se manifeste dans les versions canadiennes-anglaises de plusieurs pièces de Michel Tremblay, le dramaturge le plus traduit au Canada, où on affiche l'altérité du texte source au moyen de nombreux gallicismes qui ont pour fonction d'accentuer la saveur française du texte traduit. Il suffit de penser aux nombreuses traductions anglaises de ses pièces qui conservent le titre original français : *Les Belles-Soeurs* (1973), *Bonjour, là, Bonjour* (1975), *Surprise! Surprise!* (1975), *En Pièces Détachées* (1975), *La Duchesse de Langeais* (1976), *Trois Petits Tours* (1977), *Damnée Manon, Sacrée Sandra* (1981) et *La Maison Suspendue* (1992). Ces gallicismes difficilement compréhensibles pour un auditoire unilingue anglophone proposent une lecture exotique d'un texte et d'un propos que leur incommensurable altérité rendrait intraduisibles.

Pour ce qui est de la traduction française du répertoire canadien-anglais, Simon prend appui sur la recherche menée par Annie Brisset, laquelle expose la « visée identitaire » de la traduction québécoise du répertoire de langue anglaise, surtout américain et britannique, entre 1968 et 1988.[8] Selon Brisset, la traduction était alors chargée de mettre à distance le texte original afin de donner au texte traduit une couleur locale et lui permettre de contribuer à l'élaboration d'un répertoire québécois. Dans cette veine, il faut souligner le grand succès qu'a connu le phénomène de l'adaptation théâtrale au Québec entre 1969 et 1990 dans la traduction du répertoire canadien-anglais. Évacuant les marques d'appartenance au contexte source au profit de références géographiques et culturelles québécoises, ce mode de traduction occultait complètement le texte original canadien-anglais.[9] On peut donc observer un important phénomène de polarisation dans les procédés appliqués à la traduction littéraire selon le sens qu'elle emprunte d'une langue officielle à l'autre.

Avec les nombreux échanges et l'abondante traduction que pratiquent les auteures féministes francophones et anglophones canadiennes à partir de 1983, le discours sur la traduction littéraire esquisse un autre déplacement. Sans offrir d'emblème chargé de représenter les deux littératures, on met de l'avant certaines métaphores qui servent de modèles à une pratique féministe de la traduction littéraire. Dans un article intitulé « Theorizing Feminist Discourse-Translation » (1989), Barbara Godard met au point un néologisme qui conjugue les notions de transformation et de performance dans un processus de « transformance ». Insistant sur la visibilité de la traductrice dans un travail de recréation du texte, cette modalité de traduction a pour effet d'inscrire le féminin dans l'ordre symbolique du langage. La traduction est donc présentée ici comme un phénomène de transformation du texte, ce qui a l'immense mérite d'échapper aux clichés voulant que le texte traduit puisse être une reproduction fidèle du texte original. Puis, signalant l'émergence de nouvelles images issues de l'échange de textes en traduction entre les auteures féministes francophones et anglophones, Kathy Mezei met l'accent sur une figure à caractère erotique empruntée à Nicole Brossard dans un texte où il est question de « [s]a langue dans la bouche de l'autre » et qui porte le titre « French Kiss » :

> The use of an English expression containing the adjective "French" to describe a sexual act in a French text is a multi-layered parody in which stereotyped perceptions of sexuality (English puritanism versus French hot-bloodedness) reflect cultural positions. (English wariness of the French difference; French alienation and subordination under the English.) This inversion of French/English also mirrors the sexual inversion of the traditional heterosexual binary male/female romance in Brossard's tale of lesbian love. ("Translation as Metonymy" 94)

La rencontre des langues envisagée ici apparaît donc dans un texte critique anglais qui s'inspire d'un texte de fiction français portant un titre anglais dans lequel figure le mot « français » en anglais. Cette mise-en-abîme témoigne non seulement de l'intrication des positions occupées par chaque littérature mais aussi des aspects ludiques et spéculaires dont l'échange est investi.

Contredisant les emblèmes décidément égalitaires mis de l'avant en littérature comparée, la traduction littéraire canadienne et le discours qu'elle engendre mettent en relief l'inégalité des deux langues officielles du Canada et l'asymétrie des ensembles littéraires qu'elles circonscrivent. Du côté anglophone, le symbole par excellence demeure le pont, par lequel on traverse aisément d'une rive à l'autre. Si l'on tient ainsi à préserver l'accès à l'autre rive, c'est que cet accès ne constitue pas une menace d'invasion. C'est aussi qu'il permet de ramener chez soi des œuvres empruntées à l'autre et chargées de le révéler de façon exacte et identique puisque le pont suppose un passage mais non une transformation. On prétend ainsi représenter l'autre sans agent ni intermédiaire qui pourrait en altérer l'image. À cet effet, le néologisme proposé par Barbara Godard rend compte du travail de la traduction de façon beaucoup plus juste puisque l'opération traduisante repose sur une transformation multiple qui agit sur l'œuvre littéraire dans ses aspects linguistiques, culturels et sociaux selon l'interprétation qu'en fait et qu'en propose la personne qui traduit.

Du côté francophone, on propose de nier une activité perçue comme néfaste en la dotant d'une désignation qui exprime un refus de reproduire l'autre ou de prétendre en offrir une image fidèle. Ici, la traduction se vit comme une épreuve dont l'issue est la mise à distance de l'autre jugé menaçant pour sa survie. Loin d'inviter à une rencontre cordiale par l'entremise du pont, on invite plutôt à brûler les ponts en réfutant l'emprunt initial afin de créer une nouvelle œuvre. La traduction est ainsi dépouillée de son ancrage dans une littérature source pour être mise au service de la création dans une littérature cible.

Parce qu'elle ne fait pas que jeter un regard sur les langues et les cultures, mais les oblige à une interpénétration, la traduction est un lieu d'interaction par excellence où on peut observer les comportements et les stratégies dictées par le rapport de force propre aux langues et aux cultures qu'elle met en contact. En ce sens, la traduction littéraire est un enjeu de taille puisqu'elle est à la fois miroir et instrument d'une relation linguistique et culturelle qu'elle donne à voir en la mettant à l'épreuve.

Notes

Une première version de cette étude a fait l'objet d'une communication présentée au colloque de l'Association des littératures canadiennes et québécoise, tenu à l'Université d'Ottawa en 1998. Je tiens à remercier Clément Moisan, qui a gracieusement accepté de lire et de commenter ce texte.

[1] Auparavant, les francophones étaient qualifiés de « canadiens » alors que les anglophones se définissaient avant tout comme sujets « britanniques ».

[2] De nombreux titres d'ouvrages, de colloques ou de produits culturels mettent en scène l'illustre emblème, dont l'emploi dessine à lui seul le profil d'une dynamique à l'œuvre dans la représentation du rapport entre les littératures du Canada.

[3] Pour une étude des circonstances dans lesquelles s'est imposée cette dénomination, voir Nepveu.

[4] Sugars identifie quatre conceptions des ensembles littéraires anglophone et francophones en littérature canadienne comparée : un modèle séparatiste qui conçoit la littérature canadienne et la littérature québécoise comme des entités non reliées; un modèle centraliste qui les englobe sous la désignation littérature canadienne; un modèle bifocal qui allie deux littératures canadiennes d'expression anglaise et d'expression française; et, enfin, un modèle « sovereignty-association » (29) qui situe les deux littératures dans une sorte de « co-operative separatism » (29) au sein d'un contexte multiculturel.

[5] Chacun de ces groupes s'est par ailleurs doté d'un drapeau qui apparaît sur les programmes d'événements réunissant les « communautés francophones vivant en situation minoritaire au Canada » (Semaine internationale de la francophonie, Québec, 1999).

[6] Sur cette notion, voir l'ouvrage de François Paré intitulé *Les littératures de l'exiguïté* (1992).

[7] Selon le portrait statistique des communautés de langues officielles établi par Stacy Churchill d'après le recensement de 1996, la population canadienne comprend une majorité anglophone unilingue estimée à 67,1 p. cent, un groupe bilingue correspondant à 16,3 p. cent et une minorité francophone unilingue évaluée à 15,2 p. cent (1998).

[8] Voir Brisset.

[9] Voir Ladouceur.

Works Cited

Atwood, Margaret. *Survival: A Thematic Guide to Canadian Literature*. Toronto: Anansi, 1972.

Blodgett, E.D. *Configurations: Essays on the Canadian Literatures*. Downsview: ECW, 1982.

Brault, Jacques. « Notes sur le littéraire et le politique ». *Parti Pris* 2.5 (1965): 43–51.

——. *Poèmes des quatre côtés*. Saint-Lambert: Noroît, 1975.

Brisset, Annie. *Sociocritique de la traduction. Théâtre et altérité au Québec (1968–1988)*. Longueuil: Les Éditions du Préambule, 1990.

Chamberland, Paul. « Dire ce que je suis ». *Parti Pris* 2.5 (1965): 33–42.

Chauveau, Pierre-Joseph-Olivier. *L'instruction publique au Canada: précis historique et statistique*. Québec: Augustin Côté, 1876.

Churchill, Stacy. *Nouvelles perspectives canadiennes. Les langues officielles au Canada: transformer le paysage linguistique*. Ottawa: Patrimoine canadien, en collaboration avec le Programme des études canadiennes et le Programme d'appui aux langues officielles, 1998.

Delisle, Jean. *Au coeur du trialogue canadien: Bureau des traductions 1934–1984/ Bridging the Language Solitudes: Translation Bureau 1934–1984*. Ottawa: Ministre des approvisionnements et services Canada, 1984.

Falardeau, Jean-Charles. *Notre société et son roman*. Montréal: HMH, 1967.

Fee, Margery. « Imagining Quebec ». *Canadian Literature* 148 (1996): 4–9.

Frye, Northrop. « Conclusion ». *Literary History of Canada: Canadian Literature in English*. Ed. Carl F. Klinck. Vol. 3. Toronto: U of Toronto P, 1967. 821–49.

Girouard, Laurent. « Considérations contradictories ». *Parti Pris* 2.5 (1965): 6–12.

Godard, Barbara. « Theorizing Feminist Discourse-Translation ». *Tessera* 6 (1989): 42–53.

Kirby, William. *The Chien d'Or (The Golden Dog): A Legend of Quebec*. Montreal: Lovell, Adam, Wesson & Company, 1877.

Ladouceur, Louise. « Du spéculaire au spectaculaire: le théâtre anglo-canadien traduit au Québec au début des années 90 ». *Nouveaux regards sur le théâtre québécois*. Halifax/Montréal: Dalhousie French Studies/XYZ, 1997.185–94.

MacLennan, Hugh. *Two Solitudes*. Toronto: Collins, 1945.

Maheu, Pierre. « Présentation ». *Parti Pris* 2.5 (1965): 2–5.

Major, André. « Ainsi soit-il ». *Parti Pris* 2.5 (1965): 13–17.

Martin, Ruth. « Translated Canadian Literature and Canada Council Translation Grants 1972–1992: The Effect on Authors, Translators and Publishers ». *Ellipse* 51 (1994): 54–84.

Mezei, Kathy. « A Bridge of Sorts: The Translation of Quebec Literature into English ». *The Yearbook of English Studies: Anglo-American Literary Relations Special Number 15* (1985): 202–26.

——. « Translation as Metonymy: Bridges and Bilingualism ». *Ellipse* 51 (1994): 85–102.

Miron, Gaston. « Un long chemin ». *Parti Pris* 2.5 (1965): 25–32.

Moisan, Clément. *L'âge de la littérature canadienne*. Montréal: HMH, 1969.

——. Comparaison et raison. *Essais sur l'histoire et l'institution des littératures canadienne et québécoise*. Montréal, HMH, 1986.

Nepveu, Pierre. *L'Écologie du réel. Mort et naissance de la littérature québécoise contemporaine*. Montréal: Boréal, 1988.

Paré, François. *Les littératures de l'exiguïté*. Hearst, ON Le Nordir, 1992.

Shek, Ben-Zion. « Quelques réflexions sur la 'traduction' dans le contexte socio-culturel canado-québécois ». *Ellipse* 21 (1977): 111–16.

Shouldice, Larry. « On The Politics of Literary Translation in Canada ». *Translation in Canadian Literature: Symposium 1982*. Ed. Camille La Bossière. Ottawa: U of Ottawa P, 1983. 73–82.

Simon, Sherry. *L'inscription sociale de la traduction au Québec*. Québec: Office de la langue française, 1989.

———. « Rites of Passage: Translation and Its Intents ». *Massachusetts Review* 21.1–2 (1990): 96–110.

———. *Le trafic des langues. Traduction et culture dans la littérature québécoise*. Montréal: Boréal, 1994.

Stratford, Philip. *All the Polarities: Comparative Studies in Contemporary Canadian Novels in French and English*. Toronto: ECW, 1986.

———. « Canada's Two Literatures: A Search for Emblems ». *Revue canadienne de littérature comparée* 6.2 (1979): 131–38.

———. « Literary Translation: A Bridge Between Two Solitudes ». *Language and Society* 11 (1983): 8–13.

Smart, Patricia. « Our Two Cultures ». *Canadian Forum* 64 (1984): 14–19.

Sugars, Cynthia. « On the Rungs of the Double Helix: Theorizing the Canadian Literatures ». *Essays on Canadian Writing* 50 (1993): 19–44.

Sutherland, Ronald. *The New Hero: Essays in Comparative Quebec/Canadian Literature*. Toronto: Macmillan, 1977.

———. « Twin Solitudes ». *Canadian Literature* 31 (1967): 5–24.

Sylvestre, Guy, Brandon Conron et Carl F. Klinck. *Écrivains canadiens/Canadian Writers*. Toronto: Ryerson, 1972.

Réjean Beaudoin and André Lamontagne

Official Languages and Their Literatures

The changing relations between the two official languages of Canada are like those of an ill-matched couple who live under the same roof but sleep in different beds. Our two founding literatures have a similar relationship: the more they share, the more constrained they are by old boundaries. It may seem illogical, but the fact remains that the cohabitation of Canada's two official languages has simply resulted in a union of resistant differences. How could it be otherwise?

The scene: a restaurant in downtown Vancouver. We are sitting at a table, waiting for our order of beer. The conversation is in French. Our waiter arrives. He apologizes for not being able to serve us in French, struggling to do so in a few words of this language that he has studied but not mastered. He explains the situation very courteously. No one takes offence, and the whole matter would end there if one of our group did not feel obliged to add: "One doesn't hear too many foreign languages in this part of the city." His remark is obviously intended to acknowledge the waiter's apologies and to put him at ease.

Some people around the table bit their mother tongue. No one dared reply that French is not a foreign language, according to Canada's Official Languages Act. It was evident that the remark had been made without malice. The speaker was an eminent scholar, a professor with an international reputation. Here he was, a man who had spent many years of his life mastering the subtleties of French (and with such skill that no francophone would be able to detect the fact that he was not a native speaker), and yet he still felt very profoundly that his acquisition of

French was a kind of graft from a foreign body. What should one make of this?

It is not so irrational or inexplicable. The way in which each one of us internalizes our language perhaps accounts for why only one language seems completely natural and entirely suited to the reflexes of one's personality. An individual is capable of learning several languages, of course, but the political symbolism of multilingualism doesn't quite match up with the psychological truth of a mind that remains attached to its first unilingual experiences. How do languages cohabit in the mind of a polyglot? The status of official languages in a bilingual or multilingual state constitutes a phenomenon of quite a different order. The unilingual waiter seemed more aware of this than the distinguished bilingual scholar.

Our experience in the restaurant was quite recent. As we sat around the table that night, we remembered a similar experience from some thirty years before. It was in the early 1970s. At the end of a conference in Vancouver, the delegates were going back to their hotel in a taxi; they were chatting amongst themselves in French. The driver (a member of a visible minority) was intrigued, and asked, "So what language are you speaking?" He was obviously frustrated at not being able to take part. That he wasn't able to follow the conversation didn't shock anyone, but not to be able to recognize the sound of French, and to confuse this official language with the foreign noise of some cacophonous Babel — that was too much. The person who recollected this incident was Québécois and did not hide his anger. Imagine his surprise, then, to hear himself warmly supported in his anger by the very person who had defended the waiter, and who, scarcely an hour before, had spoken of French as a foreign language. Would one not say that this kind of francophilia was in fact closer to the taxi driver's attitude than to that of the waiter? But we will not come to any conclusions too quickly. After all, it takes many conferences and many fine talkers to make a country, bilingual or otherwise.

It's not so much a matter of the ability to speak another language as it is of the political valence appropriate to each language that is spoken. Learning the vocabulary and the grammatical constraints of a new linguistic code is not the only challenge; internalizing the various strategies that a language invents to translate reality in its own distinct fashion — that is what is really difficult and yet it's in that respect that each language is unique. It follows that every language exercises a kind of absolute sovereignty over the organization of its universe and in the expression of its own relationship to reality. Comparatists like Clément Moisan and Philip Stratford have shown how anglophone literature and Québécois literature render a Canadian reality that is not the same in every respect. If each language tends to make itself into a self-sustaining system, then by definition how could two languages share equal official status? What would this mean in practice? Can they share anything more than their legal status, which amounts to saying that one of them loses what was, in the beginning, its genuine political significance?

This is precisely where language and literature are profoundly connected. Today, there is a general tendency to believe that this link is outdated, and that one can acquire another literary culture without having to go through the process of learning a foreign language. This is a complex debate and we don't intend to get involved in it here, except to question whether one can ever know a literature without knowing the language in which it is written.

If we have two official languages in Canada, what then about the relations between the literatures that represent their highest expression? Why not call them our official literatures? What became of the work of a scholar like Henry James Morgan and the project of Canadian unification set in motion with his *Bibliotheca Canadensis: or, A Manual of Canadian Literature?* The nationalist dream has turned into a complex polysystem of unstable intersections and surfaces that still awaits the analytical work of specialists to render it into an intelligible whole. It is certain that there is still work to do in building institutional links between anglophone literature and Québécois literature; as for the Canadian book market, well, the links between the two literatures are almost non-existent. Clearly, there is a profound gap between the professional readers of Canadian literature and the average readers who buy their own books in bookstores or borrow them from the public library. The researchers, literary critics, and teachers in the two languages communicate with each other, exchanging research tools and sharing the same interests. More and more there is the feeling that we all participate in the same Canadian literary institutions. This is a development in part imposed by the mechanisms controlled by Ottawa: SSHRC, the Canada Council, and the Aid to Scholarly Publishing Programme. All these have a significant impact on the system of university research and teaching. Moreover, one can observe the same phenomenon in colloquia, conference banquets, journals, and joint research projects, but all this is perhaps less imposed than chosen. The publishers also play their role when they are offered grants to subsidize the costs of translation. Are all these players consciously or passively responsive to pressure from federal sources? In any case, the question remains: is there an identifiable market of bilingual readers? Or is there just a tiny elite catered to by public money? Ask the waiter, not your librarian.

To create a market of bilingual readers will be a long-term task for our education system. At a time when immersion programs have lost ground, the future does not look too rosy. The universities could do their part by strengthening French programs, but it is instead the opposite that one observes: the numbers are not in favour of language teaching. Why? More and more French specialists prefer to teach literary theory in English in order to fill their classes. Academic administrators have been known to reassure potential students by telling them what they want to hear: that it isn't necessary to know how to read or speak French in order to have the pleasure of discussing Foucault or Lacan. André Brochu puts it bluntly in his *La Grande Langue: Éloge de l'anglais:* "The Being, as everyone knows . . . speaks English." As Claude Hagège has rightly observed in *Halte à la mort des langues*, languages are at war. Enforced cohabitation leads only to the erosion of the minority language or to its creolization. And if one also cre-olizes minds and spirits? But no, we must not tell students that every idea is first embodied in the language in which it is expressed.

A final anecdote. A few years ago, a professor was flying from Ottawa to Vancouver on the now-defunct Canadian Airlines. He was leafing through the airline's complimentary magazine and came across an article celebrating Canada's Top Ten "must-read" authors. Nothing too surprising: Margaret Atwood, Robertson Davies, Mordecai Richler, and so on. Not a single Québécois writer appeared on the list — not even Gabrielle Roy, even though she was born in Manitoba and has been translated into English and read from one end of the country to the other. And so the professor realized what Canadian literature meant in this context: literature written in English. But when he started reading the French version of the same article on the following page, he could hardly believe his eyes: the translation was literal. The francophone reader, who in this case happened to be a professor of Québécois literature, found himself being offered a summary in French of his literature, without the name of a single Québécois author. The editor of the publication and his staff, in their innocence, would probably have been very surprised to learn that, in translating this article without paying attention to cultural context, they had managed to wipe out an entire literature. Bilingualism without cultural adaptation or context never achieves its announced objectives. Since the merger of Air Canada and Canadian, we notice that this magazine has sunk without a trace. It is consoling to know that *Canadian Literature* will outlive it.

Works Cited

Brochu, André. *La Grande Langue. Éloge de l'anglais*. Montréal: XYZ, 1993.
Hagège, Claude. *Halte à la mort des langues*. Paris: Odile Jacob, 2000.

CL 175 (Winter 2002)

Laura Potter

A *Short History of* Canadian Literature

In the autumn of 1958, Roy Daniells and George Woodcock consolidated their plans for a University of British Columbia quarterly devoted to the critical discussion of Canadian writing.[1] They chose *Canadian Literature* for its title — asserting their belief that Canada had its own distinct literature. When the first issue of *Canadian Literature* appeared in 1959, critics pounced. "*Is* there a Canadian literature?" became the question *du jour*. The *Canadian Forum* noted that the name of the new journal could be "ominous depending on your response to 'Canadian' as a literary term" (125). *The Tamarack Review* praised the journal while gently mocking its focus: "[o]n the whole, *Canadian Literature* miraculously avoids being Can. Lit." (4). Many predicted the journal would run out of material after only a few issues. Fifty years later, however, *Canadian Literature* is one of Canada's most respected literary journals, and its subject has won acclaim both at home and abroad.

Oddly, Canadian literature and *Canadian Literature* entered my life when I was studying at the University of East Anglia in Norwich, England, during the 2005 Fall term. In my third year studying for an English degree at UBC, I had decided that I wanted to spend a term reading English literature in England. I wasn't too sure how this would benefit my understanding of Austen, Milton, or Shakespeare but I believed that all would become clear once I was surrounded by crumbling castles, Gothic cathedrals, and "England's green and pleasant land."

I learned a lot about England — and about Canadian stereotypes of England — in those three months, but I learned even more about my own country and its culture. Immersed in a new environment and different experiences, I suddenly found home foreign and intriguing. My enthusiasm for Canada manifested itself most prominently in a new interest and pride in its literature. I hunted down Canadian authors in bookstores for the simple pleasure of seeing their books on the shelf, and I delighted in informing my flat mate that Yann Martel, winner of the 2002 Booker Prize, is Canadian. I chose, despite the difficulties of locating books in libraries across the UK, to write my essays on Michel Tremblay's *Les Belles Soeurs* and Margaret Atwood's short story "Uncles." Around this same time, *Canadian Literature* posted the position of book reviews assistant on UBC's Arts Co-op website. I sent off a cover letter and resumé, felt awkward being interviewed by a panel of editors on a speaker phone, but wonderfully, perfectly, got the job. In January 2006, I returned to Vancouver and began work, which the posting stated would make me "familiar with the entire book review process, including book ordering, and corresponding with reviewers and publishers." *Canadian Literature* and its editors gave me much more — a comprehensive course in Canadian writers and writing.

I was aware of the reputation of the journal when I began that January but I did not appreciate how extensively the journal had documented our literature. Northrop Frye accurately predicted this achievement in 1967: "As Canadian literature develops and matures the journal will have a role of increasing significance, apart from the fact that its early issues will become historical records of unusual interest in their own right." Preserved in its 200 issues is the work of Canada's foremost writers — from Thomas King, Al Purdy, and Dorothy Livesay, to Margaret Atwood, Yves Beauchemin, M.G. Vassanji, and Margaret Laurence. Anglophone Canadian literary critics, ranging from the established to the newly emerging, contributed — Janice Fiamengo, Fred Wah, Northrop Frye, Stephen Slemon, and Lisa Grekul, to mention only a few — as did *Canadian Literature*'s own editors: George Woodcock, William New, Eva-Marie Kröller, Laurie Ricou, and Margery Fee.

The initially skeptical reception of *Canadian Literature* indicates the general climate of Canadian letters in the 1950s. A popular colonial metaphor for Canadian writing at the time was that, as the "daughter" of the English or French "mother" literature and as the "younger sibling" of American literature, it needed to "grow up" (New, Interview). This model further claimed that Canadian literature could only exist once the country's culture had fully developed; until then "real literature" happened elsewhere. The Massey Report of 1951 had reinforced this view, answering "no" to the capitalized heading "IS THERE A NATIONAL LITERATURE?" (222–3).[2] The commission praised homegrown periodicals for "remaining resolutely Canadian" (65), but lamented that a lack of funding imperiled their existence; Toronto's *Here and Now* (1947–49), Montreal's *Northern Review* (1945–56), and Vancouver's *Contemporary Verse* (1941–1952) had all stopped publishing by 1956. Even finding Canadian books to read was a challenge. English-Canadian publishers were not interested in the high risks and low profits associated with publishing Canadian books. In 1952, the Canadian Retail Booksellers Association had only 35 member stores (MacSkimming 35).

However, attitudes were changing. The July 1955 conference at Queen's University, entitled "The Writer, His Media and the Public," stirred excitement about Canadian writing that had previously been lacking.[3] The conference brought together the nation's literary professionals, writers, academics, and publishers, to discuss how together they could develop Canadian literature. The resulting recommendations helped shape the future Canada Council's system of grants, services, and awards for professional Canadian artists and arts organizations (Djwa 312). The CBC's literary programs *Critically Speaking*, *Canadian Short Stories*, and *CBC Wednesday Night* were beginning to air to audiences of 25,000 to 50,000 across the country (MacSkimming 39). Producer Robert Weaver became involved in publication as well, co-founding *The Tamarack Review* in 1956. Two years later, McClelland and Stewart launched its New Canadian Library (NCL) series. The first of its kind, this paperback reprint series, with a retail price of $1 a volume, significantly increased accessibility to the best of Canadian fiction.[4] Just as the NCL produced the number of editions sufficient for the study of Canadian fiction in universities and high schools across the country, *Canadian Literature* became the venue for the literary criticism that would support and extend this endeavour.

The success of the Canadian Writers' Conference inspired Roy Daniells, Head of UBC's English Department, and George Woodcock to think that a new journal was called for. In the *Dalhousie Review* of Autumn 1955, Woodcock described the dearth of Canadian criticism and the resulting negative effects on the growth of a national literature ("A View"). He concluded that the situation would not improve without the founding of a critical journal (219). "[S]o far as I was concerned," he later observed, "[this article] was the beginning of *Canadian Literature*" ("Getting Away" 7). Daniells was thinking along similar lines. In September 1955, he wrote to Dean Geoffrey Andrew, "The question of a University Quarterly keeps popping up. . . . What I [have] learned about QQ [*Queen's Quarterly*] and UTQ [*University of Toronto Quarterly*] makes me think that the time here may be riper than we have admitted to ourselves."

A casual conversation among Roy Daniells, Dorothy Livesay, and W.C. McConnell, on their flight home from the Kingston Conference, began a chain of events that would lead to the 1959 founding of both *Canadian Literature* and *Prism*, UBC's creative writing magazine (Djwa 312). The airborne discussion centred on British Columbia's need for a similar conference. Six months later, Daniells chaired the inaugural Conference on BC Writing, held 27–29 January 1956 at UBC; Woodcock spoke at the panel discussion, "How Does the Writer Reach his Audience: The Critic's View."[5]

At a mid-February meeting, organized by colleague Earle Birney to discuss a lecturing opportunity at UBC, Daniells briefly touched on the possibility that Woodcock would be a good editor for a university quarterly (Woodcock, *Beyond* 65). One was an experienced and skilled administrator, the other a respected editor and writer. Together they had the abilities, experience, and determination to make the journal a success. Though Woodcock began lecturing at UBC in July 1956, plans for the journal were deferred for two years.

Woodcock spent the 1957–58 winter in France. Meanwhile, Daniells, English professor Stanley E. Read, and university librarians Inglis Bell and Neal Harlow began preparations for a quarterly that would publish criticism solely on Canadian literature. Such a journal, they hoped, would reassess literary works and periods, and so chart the history of writing in Canada. According to Carl F. Klinck's memoirs, the committee initially considered Reginald E. Watters, then the university's only specialist in Canadian literature, for the editorship. However, they approached Woodcock instead when he returned to Vancouver.[6] Woodcock was particularly suited for this position because of his extensive literary connections and editing experience as founder and Editor of *NOW*, a politically radical literary magazine published sporadically in England from 1940 to 1947. Despite Woodcock's lack of a university degree, his reputation in English literary circles helped him to be recognized by Canada's literary community after his return to Canada in 1949.[7]

Woodcock later emphasized that *Canadian Literature* succeeded because it arrived "at the right moment in the development of a Canadian literary tradition, and created its own ground swell of critical activity" (*Beyond* 292). The "baby boom generation" came of age in the 1960s and 1970s and their youthful enthusiasm and rejection of tradition drove an emerging Canadian cultural nationalism. Woodcock proclaimed in a 1960 editorial that "literature in Canada is a growing art" (6). Small presses and literary communities sprouted across Canada, resisting the traditional dominance of publishers in Toronto and the United States. Publications multiplied. By 1964, *Canadian Literature* had to abandon its initial determination to review all Canadian books — by then, too many were being published.

Other literary institutions and publications had their beginnings in this decade, including the Readers Club of Canada (1959), Carl F. Klinck's *Literary History of Canada: Canadian Literature in English* (1965), and new Canadian and Québécois literary magazines, such as the *Journal of Canadian Studies* (1966), *Mosaic* (1967), *Open Letter* (1965), *West Coast Line* (1966), and *Voix et Images* (1967). As talented new writers appeared on the literary scene, *Canadian Literature* responded with reviews and articles on such books as Mordecai Richler's *The Apprenticeship of Duddy*

Kravitz (1959), Leonard Cohen's *The Spice Box of Earth* (1961), Sheila Watson's *The Double Hook* (1959), and Margaret Laurence's *The Stone Angel* (1964). New literary magazines continued to appear in the 1970s. The arrival of *Essays on Canadian Writing* in 1974 signalled the great increase in Canadian literary criticism over the preceding 15 years; not only had *Canadian Literature* not run out of material, but now the journal had a competitor.

When Woodcock resigned as Editor in 1977, he proudly noted that the 73 issues he had supervised constituted "a cumulative oeuvre in its own right" (*Beyond* 292). W.H. New became his successor. An assistant Editor since 1965, a respected voice in Canadian literary criticism, and a good friend, New was Woodcock's first choice for Editor. Woodcock marked his departure from the journal with an unassuming acrostic poem spelling out, "George Woodcock hands over to Bill New," which begins:

> Bill New in fact takes over; Woodcock goes.
> If names have meaning, or if puns have point,
> Let's have no doubt the future is renewal. ("Finis")

Renewal indeed. New's first years as Editor were a transitional time for the journal and for Canadian literature. 400 serious new writers emerged in the period 1960–1985 (New 214). *Canadian Literature* had played an active role in this growing assertiveness, gathering information or arguing for the Canadian qualities of a particular text. New strove for a thorough examination of the connections between cultural and intellectual history. Many issues during his editorship — *Science and Literature*, *Poets and Politics*, *Literature and the Visual Arts*, *Writing & Cultural Values* — reflect his interest in different literary forms and in interdisciplinary investigation. Canadian writing was also moving in new directions. Changes to immigration laws in the 1970s led to an increase in non-European immigrants and, later, to the emergence of such writers as Rohinton Mistry, M.G. Vassanji, and Anosh Irani (New 219).[8] In 1959, Woodcock had stated that "from time to time [*Canadian Literature*] will investigate the smaller minority literatures of Canada — Ukrainian, Icelandic, etc" ("Tentative Confessions" 21). New and his Associate Editors pushed for articles on Asian Canadian and Caribbean Canadian literatures, which had been under-represented in Canadian criticism. The resulting special issues examined the links to different cultural backgrounds in this generation of younger writers, which included Fred Wah, SKY Lee, Roy Kiyooka, and Claire Harris. Equal priority was given to First Nations writers whose emerging strong voices roughly coincided with the 1980s movement for Aboriginal nationhood (New 214). The substantial *Native Writers and Canadian Writing* issue (1990) was the first collective inquiry into this field and received warm recognition among Native writers across Canada. W.H. New edited the journal for almost as long as Woodcock. He retired from the editorship of *Canadian Literature* in 1995, having written 55 editorials and edited 72 issues — one short of Woodcock's 73 issues.

In the following 13 years, Canadian literature gained an increasingly international readership as many Canadian authors rose to global stardom. In 1992, Michael Ondaatje became the first Canadian to win the Booker Prize with his novel *The English Patient*. Atwood's *The Blind Assassin* and Yann Martel's *The Life of Pi* won the Booker in 2000 and 2002 respectively. Alistair MacLeod was awarded the 2001 International IMPAC Dublin Literary Award for *No Great Mischief*. In 1995, Carol Shields received the Pulitzer Prize for Fiction for her novel *The Stone Diaries* and in 1998 she won the Orange Prize for *Larry's Party*. In 2007, Atwood, Ondaatje, and Alice Munro were all nominated for the Man Booker International Prize in recognition of their contributions to contemporary fiction. Canadian francophone writing garnered international attention in 1979 when Antonine Maillet's novel *Pélagie la Charrette* won the prestigious Prix Goncourt. *Canadian Literature*'s international readership similarly increased during this period, buoyed by these authors' successes and the presence of Canadian Studies programs in Europe, the United States, Africa, South America, Asia, and the South Pacific nations. In 2007, *Canadian Literature*'s subscribers were 45% Canadian, 36% American, and 19% international.

New's successor as Editor, Eva-Marie Kröller raised the journal's profile abroad by establishing an international editorial board and further formalizing the peer-review process for article submissions, already begun by the previous Editor. The peer-review process challenged *Canadian Literature*'s longstanding commitment to a general readership. However, non-specialist readers too continued to enjoy the journal; Tom Wayman's reflections on teaching poetry to students (in Winter 1997's *Contemporary Poetics* issue) won favour with high school English teachers, and the 1999 special issue *On Thomas King* is often featured on course reading lists (Kröller). The journal also changed in another way during the 1990s. To keep up with new technological opportunities, Managing Editor Donna Chin successfully negotiated *Canadian Literature*'s involvement with online publishing at this time, and she developed for the journal a sophisticated website.

Canadian Literature strengthened its commitment to Canada's francophone writers during Kröller's editorship, with the appointment of Alain-Michel Rocheleau as Associate Editor of francophone writing. Woodcock had originally intended to make the journal bilingual but, despite his best efforts, French-language submissions were rare. Quebec nationalism and separatist sentiment characterized the 1960s and 1970s; francophone writers refused Governor General's awards and intellectuals scorned the opportunity to publish in what they perceived to be an English Canadian magazine. After 10 years, in which French-language material never amounted to more than 10% of an issue's content, Woodcock dropped the pretence of bilingualism with regret (*Beyond* 85). However, Canadian Studies programs have opened up dialogue between researchers in French-language Canadian and English-language Canadian literature. Since the 1980s, francophone content has gradually increased in Canadian Literature. Associate Editor Réjean Beaudoin has energetically promoted French-language content, with such special issues as *Littérature francophone hors-Québec/Francophone Writing Outside Quebec* (issue 187) and *Gabrielle Roy Contemporaine/The Contemporary Gabrielle Roy* (issue 192).

The immense growth of Canadian literature since 1959 has brought with it a diversification of academic specialties, and the journal has invited Guest Editors to develop special issues in their area of expertise. This process continued under Acting Editor Susan Fisher (2003–4) and Editor Laurie Ricou (2003–2007). The result has been diverse special issues and variation in the editorial voice. The 2006 *Literature of Atlantic Canada* issue, for example, was the first to be guest edited by scholars — Coral Ann Howells and Marta Dvořák — located outside Canada.

At the time I joined the *Canadian Literature* team, I was largely unaware that I had become a part of one of Canada's most influential literary institutions. For me, working at *Canadian Literature* was a booklover's dream. Stuffed into brimming bookshelves or stacked in orderly piles, books and literary magazines overwhelmed the three modest offices located on the UBC campus. I loved going to work. Each week, I devoured the tantalizing descriptions of forthcoming novels found in glossy publishers' catalogues, ordered review copies, and waited. Two weeks later, packages greeted my arrival at work and I spent my mornings coveting books that, though they would be later sent off to reviewers, could have their opening pages (or more) first "sampled" by me. But a girl cannot survive on books alone — conversation rounded out my experience. Only a bookcase divided me from Editor Laurie Ricou's desk and, as he wandered in and out of our shared office or sat reading submissions, he regularly fell prey to my questions about Mazo de la Roche, Guy Gavriel Kay, Lisa Moore, and any other Canadian author who sparked my curiosity during those twelve months. With the same bemused patience and deadpan humour that packs his classes each term, he indulged the voice piping up from the other side of the bookcase and shared with me his insight into the discipline. I like to think he enjoyed these interruptions.

Though I no longer work at *Canadian Literature*, Canadian literature has not disappeared from my life. In 2008 I completed an Honours thesis on Sara Jeannette Duncan's *Cousin Cinderella: A Canadian Girl in Lon-*

don — a book unknown to me until an article in Issue 177 caught my eye. Considering my own experiences in the U.K., I doubt my interest in literary representations of Canadians in England is surprising. In Summer 2007, Laurie Ricou passed on the role of Editor to Margery Fee, Associate Editor from 1995–2000. Under her leadership and the guidance of an international editorial board, *Canadian Literature* continues to publish quarterly issues containing reviews, poems, interviews, personal essays, and the best in recent scholarship. Having achieved its 50th birthday, it shows no signs of slowing down.

I am grateful to Eva-Marie Kröller for her guidance, editing, and encouragement as I wrote this "short history." Never too busy to answer my questions or to resolve my worries, she inspired in me new confidence in my writing. Many thanks also to Laurie Ricou and Bill New for their further advice.

Notes

1   Daniells was Head of UBC's Department of English from 1948 to 1965. Woodcock was hired as a lecturer in 1956.
2   The Massey Report came to be the popular name for the Report of the 1951 Royal Commission on National Development in the Arts, Letters, and Sciences, a government-funded publication that examined and made recommendations for Canada's cultural institutions and agencies. Headed by Vincent Massey, the Report was an endorsement of the power of arts to define and build a nation's sense of identity. Its concluding recommendation for a government council and funding body led to the 1957 founding of the Canada Council for the Arts. Fifty years later, this Crown Corporation continues to provide the Canadian arts scene with funding.
3   Poet, lawyer, political activist, and professor, F.R. Scott was the prime mover behind this 1955 conference, commonly referred to as the Canadian Writers' Conference or Kingston Conference (MacSkimming 25).
4   The first four titles published for the NCL were Frederick Philip Grove's *Over Prairie Trails*, Morley Callaghan's *Such is My Beloved*, Stephen Leacock's *Literary Lapses*, and Sinclair Ross's *As For Me and My House*.
5   The Conference on BC Writing concluded with the unanimous vote of 60 delegates in favour of the creation of a BC literary magazine and the establishment of a periodical committee for this purpose. As the committee's chairman, Woodcock submitted a brief to the Koerner Foundation requesting a grant to help found a journal of criticism, creative writing, and book reviews. However, the Foundation denied funding ("Prism"). The project stalled until, in the summer of 1958, UBC English professors Jan de Bruyn and Jacob Zilber gained the support of Dean Geoffrey Andrew for a UBC magazine of creative writing. Their efforts resulted in the 1959 founding of *Prism*, which continues to publish today as *Prism International*.
6   Watters had taught UBC's first ever Canadian literature course the year prior and was compiling the innovative *A Checklist of Canadian Literature* (1959) at the time. According to Klinck, only when Watters received a fellowship to study in Australia in June 1958 did the committee approach Woodcock (98). As Fetherling notes in *The Gentle Anarchist*, Woodcock's memory of his appointment conflicts with Klinck's, and the UBC archives provide no insight into the matter (89). Since he was not a specialist in Canadian literature, Woodcock initially felt ambivalent

about Daniells' offer. Though he strongly believed that Canada needed a critical journal, his earlier plan had been for a journal of general criticism, a broader field with which he felt better acquainted. Nonetheless, Daniells' promise that the committee could advise him when necessary and his own confidence in the "art of editing," led Woodcock to accept the first editorship of *Canadian Literature* in Fall 1958 (*Beyond* 83).

7   Born in Winnipeg on 8 May 1912, Woodcock moved to England that same year with his homesick mother. He returned to Canada 35 years later with his wife Ingeborg to settle permanently in British Columbia.

8   From 1951 to 1981, the percentage of Canadians born in Asia increased from 2 percent to 15 percent of the total number of foreign-born Canadians. By 1991, 25 percent of foreign-born Canadians were born in Asia (Statistics Canada).

Works Cited

"A Canadian Literary Review." *The Canadian Forum.* 39 (September 1959): 125.
"A Point of View." *The Tamarack Review.* Editorial. 13 (Autumn 1959): 3–4.
"Minutes of Meeting of Canadian Literature Committee." 1 December 1958. UBC Archives. *Canadian Literature* fonds. Box 72.
Report. Royal Commission on National Development in the Arts, Letters and Sciences. 1951.
Daniells, Roy. Letter. To Geoff Andrew. 6 September 1955. UBC Archives. Roy Daniells fonds. Box 36–11.
Djwa, Sandra. *Professing English: A Life of Roy Daniells.* Toronto: U of Toronto P, 2002.
Fetherling, George. *The Gentle Anarchist: A Life of George Woodcock.* Vancouver: Douglas & McIntyre, 1998.
Frye, Northrop. Letter. To George Woodcock. 28 February 1967. UBC Archives. *Canadian Literature* fonds. Box 71.
Klinck, Carl F. *Giving Canada a Literary History.* Ed. Sandra Djwa. Ottawa: Carleton UP for U of Western Ontario, 1991.
Kröller, Eva-Marie. Personal Interview. 23 November 2006.
MacSkimming, Roy. *The Perilous Trade: Publishing Canada's Writers.* Toronto: McClelland & Stewart, 2003.
New, W.H. *A History of Canadian Literature.* 1989; rpt. Montreal: McGill-Queen's UP, 2001 [2nd ed. 2003].
——. Personal Interview. 4 December 2006.
"*Prism*: A Brief History." [1960] UBC Archives. *Prism* fonds. Box 13. Folder 1.
Statistics Canada. 1951. Population by birthplace, Canada, 1871–1951 (table). Population, General Characteristics, 1951 Census. Census of Canada
——. 1984. Population Born Outside Canada by Place of Birth and Sex, for Canada and Provinces, 1981 (table). *Population, Place of Birth, Citizenship, Period of Immigration, 1981 Census of Canada.* Statistics Canada Catalogue no. 92–913 (Volume 1 – National Series). Ottawa.
——. 1992. Immigrant Population by Place of Birth and Sex, for Canada, Provinces and Territories, 1991 (table). *Immigration and Citizenship, 1991 Census.* Statistics Canada Catalogue no. 93–316. Ottawa.
Woodcock, George. "Summer Thoughts." Editorial. *Canadian Literature.* 5 (Summer 1960): 3–6
——. "Finis — An Acrostic" *Canadian Literature.* 74 (Autumn 1977): 4.
——. "Getting Away with Survival." Editorial. *Canadian Literature.* 41 (Summer 1969): 5–9.
——. *Beyond the Blue Mountains: An Autobiography.* Markham, ON: Fitzhenry and Whiteside, 1987.

———. "The Tentative Confessions of a Prospective Editor." *British Columbia Library Quarterly.* 23.1 (July 1959): 17–21.

———. "A View of Canadian Criticism." *The Dalhousie Review.* 35.3 Autumn 1955. 216–223

———. "Brief on a Proposed Journal of Canadian Writing." To the Leon and Thea Koerner Foundation. February 2, 1957. UBC Archives, *Canadian Literature* fonds. Box 72.

(2009)

Margaret Atwood

Eleven Years of Alphabet

Now the young intellectual living in this country, having gone perhaps to a Wordsworth high school and a T.S. Eliot college, quite often ends up thinking he lives in a waste of surplus USA technology, a muskeg of indifference spotted with colonies of inherited, somehow stale, tradition. What our poets should be doing is to show us how to identify our society out of this depressing situation. — JAMES REANEY, "EDITORIAL," *ALPHABET* #8

Searchers for a Canadian identity have failed to realize that you can only have an identification with something you can see or recognize. You need, if nothing else, an image in a mirror. No other country cares enough about us to give us back an image of ourselves that we can even resent. And apparently we can't do it for ourselves, because so far our attempts to do so have resembled those of the three blind men to describe the elephant. Some of the descriptions have been worth something, but what they add up to is fragmented, indecipherable. With what are we to identify ourselves? — GERMAINE WARKENTIN, "AN IMAGE IN A MIRROR," *ALPHABET* #8

All this is connected together, by the way — JAMES REANEY, "EDITORIAL," *ALPHABET* #16

With the appearance this year of its combined eighteenth and nineteenth issues, *Alphabet* will be over, and its small but faithful audience can only mourn and collect back issues.[1] While it lasted, it was perhaps the most remarkable little magazine Canada has yet produced. Many literary magazines are group or movement oriented: they publish certain people or certain styles. Others, if they have "professional" pretensions, are greyish collections of goodish writing. *Alphabet* was different; its editorial decisions were based not on last names or idiosyncracies of punctuation, or even on "literary" standards, but on a set of premises about literature — or rather art of any kind — and therefore about life that was in application all-inclusive.

The premises themselves were set forth in the initial issues. The first *Alphabet* was subtitled "A semiannual devoted to the iconography of the imagination." Each issue was to concern itself with a "myth," the first being Narcissus, the second the child Dionysos, the third Prometheus, and so forth. To those unfamiliar with *Alphabet's* actual methods, the terms "iconography" and "myth" may suggest rigidity and a tendency to collect and categorize. But the editor's faith in the correspondences between everyday reality (life, or what *Alphabet* calls "documentary") and man-made symbolic patterns (art, or what *Alphabet* calls "myth") was so strong that in practice he left interpretation and pattern-finding to the reader. He merely gathered pieces of writing, both "literary" and "non-literary," and other subjects (an article on Narcissus, a real-life account of what it was like to be a twin, the Tarot card of the Fool) and let the echoes speak for themselves; coincidences were there, he insisted, not because he put them there but because they occur. The "myth" provided for each issue was only a kind of key:

> . . . Actually the same thing happens if you take the face cards out of a
> card deck; then put a circular piece of cardboard near them. Curves
> and circles appear even in the Queen of Diamonds and the Knave of
> Spades. But place a triangular shape close by and the eye picks up
> corners and angularities in even the Queen of Clubs. What every issue
> of *Alphabet* involves, then, is the placing of a definite geometric shape
> near some face cards.[2]

The reader never knew when he picked up an issue of *Alphabet* what would be inside. It might be anything, and the announced "myth" for the issue was not always an obvious clue. In eleven years and nineteen issues *Alphabet* published or mentioned, among other things, an article on Aztec poetry, a list of the Kings of England reaching back to the Old Testament, Indian rock paintings, an article on *Christabel* which identified Geraldine as Wordsworth, James McIntyre the Mammoth Cheese poet, the Nihilist Spasm Band, an early review by Bill Bissett in the form of a poem, the music of the Doukhobors, schoolboy slang and hand puppetry, the Black Donnellys, and a cantata about Jonah. Academic and pop, "traditional" and "modern," verbal and visual, "local" and "international": *Alphabet* had no snobberies.

Because Reaney cheerfully acknowledged an interest in Frye, hasty codifiers stuck him in a Myth School of their own creation and accused him of the sin of "being influenced," without pausing to consider that for an artist as original as Reaney "influence" is taking what you need because it corresponds to something already within you. Others, who preferred a glossier, more Cream-of-Wheat-like "professional" consistency of texture in their magazines, found it easy to sneer at *Alphabet* for being one man's magazine (which it was), eccentric and eclectic (which it also was), and provincial, which it wasn't. Surely it's much more provincial to turn out second-rate copies of the art forms of another culture (what price a TV variety show with Canadian tap dancers instead of American ones), than it is to create an indigenous form, and *Alphabet* had something much more important than "Canadian Content"; though it was catholic in content, it was Canadian in *form*, in how the magazine was put together.

What follows is hypothetical generalization, but it is of such that national identities are composed. Saying that *Alphabet* is Canadian in form leads one also to say that there seem to be important differences between the way Canadians think — about literature, or anything — and the way Englishmen and Americans do. The English habit of mind, with its preoccupation with precedent and the system, might be called empirical; reality for it is the social hierarchy and its dominant literary forms are evaluative criticism and the social novel. It values "taste." The American habit of mind, with its background of intricate Puritan theologizing, French Enlightenment political theory and German scholarship and its foreground of technology, is abstract and analytical; it values "technique," and for it reality is how things work. The dominant mode of criticism for some years has been "New Criticism," picking works of art apart into component wheels and springs; its "novel" is quite different from the English novel, which leans heavily towards comedy of manners and a dwindled George Eliot realism; the American novel, closer to the Romance, plays to a greater extent with symbolic characters and allegorical patterns. The Canadian habit of mind, for whatever reason — perhaps a history and a social geography which both seem to lack coherent shape — is synthetic. "Taste" and "technique" are both of less concern to it than is the ever-failing but ever-renewed attempt to pull all the pieces together, to discover the whole of which one can only trust one is a part. The most central Canadian literary products, then, tend to be large-scope works like *The Anatomy of Criticism* and *The Gutenberg Galaxy* which propose all-embracing systems within which any particular bit of data may be placed. Give the same poem to a model American, a model English and a model Canadian critic: the American will say "This is how it works"; the Englishman "How good, how true to Life" (or, "How boring, tasteless and trite"); the Canadian will say "This is where it fits into the entire universe." It is in its love for synthesis that *Alphabet* shows itself peculiarly Canadian.

"Let us make a form out of this," Reaney says in the *Alphabet* #1 Editorial. "Documentary on one side and myth on the other: Life & Art. In this form we can put anything and the magnet we have set up will arrange it for us." The "documentary" aspects of *Alphabet* are as important as the "myth" ones, and equally Canadian. Canadian preoccupation with and sometimes excellence in documentaries of all kinds — film, TV, radio, poetry — is well known. *Alphabet* was addicted to publishing transcriptions from life: accounts of dreams, conversations overheard in buses, Curnoe's Coke Book, a collage of letters from poets, known and unknown across the country. The documentarist's (and *Alphabet*'s) stance towards such raw material, and thus towards everyday life, is that it is intrinsically meaningful but the meaning is hidden; it will manifest itself only if the observer makes the effort to connect. Give our model Englishman a hamburger and he will tell amusing anecdotes about it (his great aunt once tripped over a hamburger, hamburgers remind him of Winston Churchill); the American will make it into a symbol by encasing it in plastic or sculpting it in plaster. The Canadian will be puzzled by it. For a while he will say nothing. Then he will say: "I don't know what this hamburger means or what it's doing in this particular place — where is this, anyway? — but if I concentrate on it long enough the meaning of the hamburger, which is not *in* the hamburger exactly, nor in the hamburger's history, nor in the mind of the onlooker, but in the exchange between the observing and the observed — the meaning of the hamburger will reveal itself to me." The Canadian, one notes, is less sure of himself and more verbose about it than the other two, but he is also more interested in the actual hamburger.

Such theories, like all theories, are questionable, but the joys and graces of *Alphabet*, luckily, are not: its variety, its enthusiasms, the innocent delight it took in almost everything. Above all, one is amazed by its uncanny ability to anticipate, sometimes by five or ten years, trends which later became fashionable, Canadian cultural nationalism among them. "Who would have thought seven years ago," says Reaney in *Alphabet* #14 (1967) "that pop culture would catch up to *Alphabet?*"

The reasons for *Alphabet*'s demise are partly personal — "In ten years," comments Reaney, "you say what you have to say" — and partly financial. The first ten issues were handset by the editor who taught himself typesetting for this purpose; the last five needed grants to help pay the spiralling printing costs. But it's ironic that *Alphabet*, never in any way commercial, should fold just when a potential market for it is appearing in the form of large Canadian Literature classes at universities. If every serious student of Canlit acquires (as he should) a set, *Alphabet*, like beavers and outlaws, may soon be worth more dead than alive. Searchers for the great Canadian identity might do well to divert time from studying what also occurs here, like Ford motor cars, and pay some attention to what, like *Alphabet*, occurs *only* here. *Alphabet's* light is done; we can only hope that someone else with an equally powerful third eye, coupled with the desire to start a little magazine, will happen along soon.

Notes

[1] Back issues and facsimiles available in 1971 from Walter Johnson Reprint Company, 111 Fifth Avenue, New York 10003, New York, USA.
[2] *Alphabet* #2.

CL 49 (Summer 1971)

4. GALLERY TWO

Andreas Schroeder

The Poet as Gunman

Had Michael Ondaatje not come out with his lyric/dramatic *The Man With Seven Toes* in 1969, I would have said that nothing in his previously published work really prepared me for his recent award-winning *The Collected Works of Billy the Kid*. In fact, in terms of the quite considerable improvement in Ondaatje's recent verse as compared to the earlier *Dainty Monsters*, I'd say the statement still holds true. The many lamely constructed similes of *Dainty Monsters* and the often lurid lyric excesses of *The Man With Seven Toes* are a far cry from the more carefully crafted, casually understated material of *Billy the Kid*. Negotiating this book, I sensed a sure-footedness, a control which I have never felt in Ondaatje's earlier books. Indeed, if he hadn't used the historic framework of the adventures of Mrs. Fraser (*The Man With Seven Toes*) in a manner somewhat prophetic of his similar technique in *The Collected Works of Billy the Kid*, I would have found little area for comparison whatsoever.

The rather unusual choice of an old Wild-West saga — the story of Billy the Kid — as a literary vehicle struck me at first as dubious, but strikes me now as quite an intelligent choice to have made. For one thing, though much has been written about the incidents surrounding the Kid's life — the early shootings, the cattle rustlings, the Lincoln County wars and finally his fatal shooting by Sheriff Garrett in Fort Sumner in 1880 — very little record remains (or has existed) of the Kid's own version of his story, of anything which might have given the reader more of an insight into his character than the descriptions of those who claimed to know him. Somehow, even after each of these people has had his say, the Kid still remains essentially a silent, mysterious puzzle, an assemblage of pieces of hearsay and history representing a man whose deeds were clear, but whose reasons for perpetrating them were not. For this reason there was plenty of room for Ondaatje to develop and amplify, with few restrictions, an entire personage to whatever specifications he pleased, and, on top of this, to plunge quickly into deep water without having to waste unnecessary space with lengthy explanations and introductions, since the exterior, physical realities of his subject were already general cultural property.

In *The Collected Works*, then, Ondaatje projects himself into the minds of the Kid and Sheriff Garrett to retell the saga from the inside, writing down the reminiscences, jokes, casual thoughts, answers to simulated questions and even hallucinations which may have passed through the two men's minds. Using poems, prose sketches, "eyewitness" reports, diary-like notations and an ostensible newspaper interview with the Kid, Ondaatje restores to the saga the third dimension it had lost by having become an old tale always told from a single storyteller's point of view. Ondaatje's "new version," in fact, becomes one of the most intimate kinds of documentary imaginable, the camera having completely free access to both public and private sides of the subject(s); i.e., the incidents themselves as well as the minds of the men who provoked them are open to inspection.

Of course, the value of *The Collected Works* as a colourfully reconstituted account of the history of Billy the Kid has only little to do with the value of the book as such, and even less with its winning of the Governor General's Award. The success of the poetry and prose between its covers goes well beyond its subject — a telltale hallmark of good literature in any style. And if the person of Billy the Kid consequently evolves into a character almost too sensitive to be a believable gunman, well — history must remain the slave of Art. Frankly, if Billy the Kid had ever really managed to describe a fever-ridden week spent in an abandoned barn in the way Ondaatje has him describe it on page 17 of this book (unfortunately much too long to quote), he had no business being a gunman in the first place, and probably would have known it.

Indeed, one is always conscious of Ondaatje speaking through the mask of Billy, Garrett, or any of the other characters in the book, but this never detracts from either the story or the verse; the characters, in fact, flourish by this method in a truly dramatic way. Whether any of the historic persons really appeared the way Ondaatje recreates them simply becomes irrelevant; they make a very credible amount of sense within the context of Ondaatje's version of the tale. His story takes on its own rhythms, entirely outside the realities of history.

While I keep itching to quote passages to demonstrate many of the above-mentioned points, *The Collected Works of Billy the Kid* is the kind of book which generally defies quoting anything less than the entire section or poem being referred to, particularly since these sections tend to be cumulatively successful as well as individually so. Only a very few, like this oblique little description of Sheriff Garrett, are short enough and can fairly be pulled out of context:

You know hunters
are the gentlest
anywhere in the world

    they halt caterpillars
    from path dangers

lift a drowning moth from a bowl
remarkable in peace

in the same way assassins
come to chaos neutral

The clean simplicity, the uncluttered, toned-down, almost easy precision demonstrated in this poem and generally characteristic of the book is probably the happy
result of Ondaatje's being forced to assume, at least to some degree, the simplicity
of speech his characters themselves would have used. This little exercise has done
Ondaatje a world of good, and *The Collected Works* reflects it. Only occasionally,
in precisely five poems, does he let his lyric overdrive run away with him to the
detriment of the poem, which becomes not only non-believable in context, but
simply bad or mediocre poetry outright. That's not a bad average for a 105-page
book. Mind you, I don't mean to imply that the rest of the work is therefore necessarily all undiluted genius, but it's certainly strong enough to keep one reading
voluntarily and continuously, from cover to cover, without the incentive of a six-
shooter in the back.

CL 51 (Winter 1972)

Stephen Scobie

A Dash for the Border

bp nichol's *Monotones* opens with a quotation from *The Writings of Saint And*,
one of the saints on whom Nichol has built the personal mythic structure of *The
Martyrology*, in which the saint dreams that he "foresaw the imminent end of all
speech." This quotation reflects a kind of doubt or obsession about the limits of
language, which runs through much contemporary poetry. Consider also this short
piece, from David Rosenberg's *Paris & London*:

WHITE CURTAINS

It's all a matter of getting past words to the language outside our head,
either visually like art or orally like poetry. Because words are inadequate, in this programmed space, to get through the machines, you

have to come out from behind them and make a dash for the border
just as they stop at the first security check. This is what is commonly
known as "Checkpoint Charlie."

This kind of doubt is one of several possible approaches to concrete poetry, and
to the kind of annihilation of language which we find in much of the work of Bill
Bissett, such as *Drifting Into War*. But the poet's feelings that "words are inadequate" do not always extend so far; often the doubt resolves itself into being, not
so much about language itself, as about a particular kind of discursive language, a
language which talks *about* experience rather than attempting to reproduce or
reenact it directly. At another point in *Monotones*, Nichol rejects "all this cold
fucking dispassionate 'discourse'" in favour of "just to be able to open the mouth
and scream." This view, however, has its limitations. Rosenberg's statement is oddly
reminiscent of Eliot's "words, after speech, reach / into the silence"; these words
come from *Four Quartets*, which is a supremely logical and discursive poem, yielding as little as possible to any supposed "inadequacy" of words. Not only is "discourse" not necessarily "dispassionate"; it is also, as Eliot shows, a fully viable
technique for making that "dash for the border" and across, into the silence.

Gary Geddes's *Rivers Inlet* stands out from the other books under review, mainly because it uses a much more conventional, traditional mode of "discourse." In
their varying degrees, Nichol, Rosenberg, Gardiner and Bissett are attempting a
different kind of poetry, a poetry which presents the process of perception in a very
direct and (apparently) undiluted manner. One reads them for the qualities of
grace, precision, wit, and energy in the movements of their perception and its struc-
turing, rather than for any great interest in the substantive experiences they are
talking *about*. Geddes, on the other hand, is conventional enough to present us
with a communicable subject matter, and with thoughts, emotions, and perceptions
which clearly relate to it. His is a much more public voice: he has things he wants
to tell us, and writing the poems is as much a way of discovering what these things
are as it is the way of telling.

Rivers Inlet concerns the poet's return to scenes of his childhood, and memories
of his parents — a common enough theme, and one which holds our interest only
in so far as its *particular* realization, in terms of its images, rhythms, and perceptions, can come alive for the reader. Geddes succeeds admirably in giving his ideas a
location, a place and a habitation in a real and convincing world; he is able to
present Rivers Inlet both in its physical appearance and in its emotional ambience:

No fooling around with beaches
and pleasant meadows, the only
way to go was up.

(As an east coast Scot myself, I also appreciate the exactitude of "a dozen / grey
stone houses holding back / the North Sea.") Geddes is also able to extend this

particular experience into more generalized statements, though some of his lines on such occasions come dangerously close to cliché:

> This birth is an end
> and a beginning, a place
> we all come back to,
> are never far from.

Particularly strong are the images of water, "an element / that, having none, distorts / the shape of things," an awareness which, together with the setting, reminded me at times of Margaret Atwood; I am sure that this book would find its place in her schema of Canadian literature. *Rivers Inlet* is modest in scope and intention, traditional in approach and form; not a book to praise extravagantly, but a book to enjoy quietly.

In contrast to the way in which the subject-matter of *Rivers Inlet* is fully realized and made available, the substantive experience of *Monotones*, *A Book of Occasional*, and *Paris & London* is always kept at a remove, distant and slightly elusive. The poets are writing of the movements of their own minds and the connections they make, without worrying too much if these connections remain absolutely private and inaccessible to the reader. Gardiner's self-deprecatory aside —

> God you guys talk abt weird
> boring things. Yourselves.
> And your friends.

— does not completely answer the objections which a frustrated reader may raise. There is always a potential emptiness, or sterility, in this type of writing, a point where the reader tires of even the most graceful movements of perception and demands to share something of the substance of what is being perceived.

Of these three books, by far the best is Nichol's *Monotones*; and this is due mainly to the poet's absolute command of sound and rhythm. bp has lost nothing of his ear, and *Monotones*, like all his work, is a joy to read. At times the rhythm is indeed so authoritative that it creates in the reader a profoundly emotional response, even if we are not always absolutely clear just what it is we are feeling emotional about. For all that, *Monotones* still seems to me a minor work, and interesting chiefly as a prelude to the much more massive and satisfying achievement of *The Martyrology*.

Dwight Gardiner's *A Book of Occasional* has its moments too, though these are mostly moments of intellectual appreciation of the cleverness with which the poems are being turned, as line creates line and images from one poem link up with others. The poems are entertaining to read, but there is a certain tenuousness about them: the structure and the connections keep the emotion at bay. In the same way as Nichol needed the imagery and mythic structure of the saints to make his work cohere, so I suspect that Gardiner needs something more than just the idea of the serial poem form to focus his talents.

Rosenberg's *Paris & London* is the least satisfactory of these works. He sets up connections and references so allusive and personal that they continually exclude the reader from his poems, and Rosenberg's rhythms, the movements of his language, are simply not interesting enough, over a large body of poems, to compensate.

In Bill Bissett, we continue to find a tremendous energy of form, directed almost against itself. Bissett reaches to the edges of language and destroys it, yet keeps returning. The visual forms on the page (and how curious to see the determined untidiness of Bissett's gestetnered productions faithfully reproduced in the normally immaculate Talon format) always tend towards the destruction of any form they set up, while in sound Bissett returns to the strict and revivifying form of the chant. One tends to think of Bissett as a romantic artist, with a strong innate capacity for self-destruction, but he is also (at what I think is his best) capable of the strong control of his chants, or of the almost classical understatement of poems like "Killer Whale" and "Th Emergency Ward." Thus, for me the best things in *Drifting Into War* are the simple, controlled typestracts, produced by overtyping certain spaces within squares and rectangles of letters, which present clean, abstract visual designs. At other times, as in "A warm place to shit," Bissett proves that he is better than anybody else at parodying the worst of Bill Bissett.

Drifting Into War is not a book which will produce any converts to Bissett, nor is it really a good introduction to his work: both these functions are best served by Anansi's *Nobody Owns Th Earth*. It ranges widely in quality, some of it being rather awful, some of it splendid; as always, Bissett needs a good editor, though it has to be admitted that a good editor might take away from the total impact of his work, which perhaps depends as much on the bad as the good.

Whatever "inadequacies" language may have, it is still the material of poetry: there is no other. For a poet working clearly and gracefully in the centre of a tradition, like Geddes, the resources of the word are still amply sufficient; for those like Nichol and Bissett, working at the limits, there are always new discoveries, new routes leading simultaneously back into language and on into silence.

Dorothy Livesay

Painter into Poet

At the Toronto Art Gallery in the late 1920s and early 1930s there was an air of excitement which drew students of all ages. We were enthused by the Group of Seven, by Lawren Harris, and later by the West Coast painter whom he so helped, Emily Carr. As a "beginning" poet I remember well going to a lecture given to the Theosophical Society by Lawren Harris, during the course of which he read from his newly published book of poems, *Contrasts*. It was a fascinating experience, comparing the words with the paintings. I remember thinking that Harris's free verse was very close to Imagism, but that he did not have the feeling for the rhythm and music which was a part of that movement. His poems were, it seemed to me, a stage removed from poetry: linguistic guides to the painter's vision.

Something of the same impression must have hit me when, after coming to Vancouver in the mid-Thirties I first met Jack Shadbolt at a writers' group. His painting had exhilarated me with its daring, dash and originality. The influences were strong: forest, rock and sea, the insignia of British Columbia; but undoubtedly there was also the painterly influence of Lawren Harris's abstract impressionism and of Emily Carr's vibrant anthropomorphic vision. To these painters the British Columbian landscape, whether on Pacific shores or in northern mountain country, became a living organism that somehow grew roots right into the painting — illustrating Harris's key theme — "the North as a source of beneficent informing cosmic powers behind the bleakness and barrenness and austerity of much of the land." The same response was to be evoked in poetry when, in the Forties, Earle Birney and Malcolm Lowry began publishing. But at that time little did anyone realize that the painter Shadbolt was also attempting to translate the thing seen into the thing communicated through language. Today, when I remember him reading his poems aloud, I think that none of us listening (Ethel Wilson, Bill McConnell, myself) understood what he was trying for; perhaps because his rhythms were rough and his language too often was searching for "poetic" effects and philosophical abstractions.

Now that all of Shadbolt's poetry is available [in *Mind's I*] — some 60 poems interspersed between 35 black-and-white drawings pulsing with life, vibrant with trees, roots, branches, rocks, ocean waves and the small creatures that inhabit them — it is possible to appreciate what evocations Shadbolt is capable of, in language.

First, though, a sour note. It seems a pity that the artist saw fit to include the early efforts at confessional love poetry, for these have little relationship to the paintings or to the natural world that has inspired them. Occasionally there is a successful poem like the one which begins:

> I'm told a man new blind
> shaving with no mirror
> cuts himself
> His mirror fetched
> habit controls
> and he continues easily
>
> Since you are gone
> habit and I go on
> but sometimes when by thought
> you are not here
> who mirrored me
> who blind as I?

Here the metaphysical dialectic works, exemplifies Shadbolt's credo that "my form always develops from a dialogue of opposites." But unfortunately few of the poems from this early period achieve this effect: rather there is a sense of strain, as in this stanza:

> Whatever may be scanned
> in the morning edition of me
> when I am proof-read for the truth
> by the unsparing day

with its disastrous last line: "She left her print on me." This is bad verse.

Happily Shadbolt gets into his stride as a poet when he is concerned not with his human relationships but with what his outer and his inner eye see in the objective world:

> Down I go by
> red shed on bleak rocks to
> Hidden creviced beach
> Heart on foam-flower stalks feeding
> dead in leaf

In his book, *Mind's I*, we reach this stage with the lovely imagist poem "Beech Groves" (version II) dated 1934, where

> Tonight again is starless
> Fall has bared an ice-fang

gleamed with light
The proud beeches wear
moon's agony
of shining rain

until

Forest veins
the sweet sap-hunger
know no longer
but remember
axe blades' gash
and sap-gush stain
Now these bronze glades will know
the solace of snow

These short two- and three-beat lines really work. The only puzzle is the rationale behind the poet's use of capital letters. Why?

From the 1930s also come poems like "December Woods," in which a favourite symbol, the scarlet bird, appears:

Near me on a limb
perched tensile with
the held-breath skill
of fragile things
this scarlet
jet-eyed
flick-winged mystery

The drawings are charged with these birds, these mysteries; as are poems like "Strange Tale," "November Afternoon," "Quarry" and the beautiful reminiscence of childhood, "Metchosin," which calls to mind Roberts's "Tantramar Revisited." But this is the West Coast, Vancouver Island, and the time is 1938:

These were the gold-grained fields
whose memory fretted
the long years of trying to forget
this land of sweet yield
with the plow's ridge wheeling
clear to the sea
followed by gulls' screaming
the white lips of foam
silently sighing . . .

> But oh that aching roll
> downfield and over
> to the slow grey crumpling of the bay
> threshing those silvered logs
> the oak groves gyrating
> out to meet the rocks
> in the late breeze — these
> could be a start

Perhaps Shadbolt's happiest, most lyrical poems are those which evoke flowers, such as "Spring Rain," "Anniversary," "Looking Across." In the last-named poem the artist-poet looks across the sea to the island where he was born:

> Always facing me
> the brooding Island
> with its sombre conic evergreens
> its dark openings inward
>   . . .
> calling me across the heads
> of pink opiate poppies
> just above the windowsill
> and blue spurts of larkspur thrusting up

Beyond them he sees "along the very level / of the riffled racing water" the "beckoning mysterious rim." And when he moves north he meets the power and mystery of "Agamemnon Channel" and "Princess Louise Inlet." Exciting poems! Many of the illustrations in this book are of birds: ravens, larks, gulls, "blue heron's frightful cry." The poems too are peopled with birds, but it is the horned owl who emerges as the key feathered figure both in the drawings and the poems. The longish dramatic poem "To a Young Horned Owl" (1971) should be forever anthologized. The language is clinical, that of a naturalist: "Rope-like muscles contract down / spine and / sword-unsheathed wing feathers," but it is also charged with metaphor, "fan bristlingly / . . . in panzer grip to / steel talon clenching." Owl becomes "King of dreams . . . lord of near field / mouse terror . . ." More poems such as this could transform the unforgettable painter into an unforgettable poet.

CL 60 (Spring 1974)

Herbert Rosengarten

Urbane Comedy

Margaret Atwood's new novel *Lady Oracle* is a compound of domestic comedy, Jungian psychology and social satire, stirred with wit and flavoured with the occult. Its narrator-heroine, Joan Foster, tells the story of her ugly-duckling progress from unhappy childhood in suburban Toronto to literary success and fame (reviews in the *Globe and Mail*, CBC interviews), and a personal crisis which sends her into hiding in Italy. As a child, Joan suffers from excessive fatness, and the tortures which this condition causes her are intensified by her prim mother's frustration and despair at having produced such a monster. At school, at dancing-class, at Brownies, she is made to feel an outsider, and learns to hide her feelings, even to fear them. Though a drastic diet reduces her to normal size, the adult (and attractive) Joan is still tormented by a lack of self-confidence, a fear of exposure and failure, and she is driven to hide behind other identities: mistress of a Polish émigré, wife of an immature student radical, adulterous lover of an artist — in each relationship she acts a role determined for her by her partner, seeking to be what he desires, too insecure to be herself. (Allegorists of national identity please note.) Joan's deeper emotional needs find some outlet in her writing, where she can parade her yearnings in the fancy dress of "costume Gothics" with such titles as *Stalked by Love*, *Love — My Ransom* or *Storm over Castleford*, published (not surprisingly) under an assumed name. She understands the importance of escapist literature to the thousands of bored women who share her frustrations; more importantly, she recognizes the danger of allowing her fantasy to subdue her real, waking life; and the novel is in large part the account of her efforts to bring the two sides of her personality into a harmonious and fruitful junction.

Atwood means to give her heroine a quality of helpless vulnerability, but endows her with an ironic sensibility so keen as to make her seem the strongest character in the book, a cool and amused observer rather than the chief sufferer. This is a minor failing, however, and it is a relief to turn from the humourless intensity of *Surfacing* to the urbane comedy of *Lady Oracle*. In the former novel, the heroine's grim entry into a primeval world and her determined rejection of human contact conveyed a kind of superior contempt for the equivocations and compromises of everyday life, as well as a feminist hostility to a society which reduces women to the level of sex objects. In some respects the pattern is repeated in *Lady Oracle*: the heroine, trapped in an identity she detests, searches for some meaning in her life; shedding men along the way, she undergoes a ritual death and rebirth, flirts with dark powers in her psyche, and emerges to a new awareness of self. Also reminiscent of *Surfacing* is the book's attack on the crassly materialistic concerns of North

American life, on the vulgarity of a society dedicated to show. Yet in *Lady Oracle* these themes become largely a source of satiric humour; there is none of the morose self-righteousness which marks the tone of the earlier novel. Atwood has not lost her seriousness of purpose, but her vision has broadened, and she has developed a maturer sense of the possibilities inherent in any given situation.

This is evident in her treatment of the occult, which is presented both comically (who could be frightened by a spiritualist medium called Leda Sprott?) and convincingly: Joan's experiences with automatic writing are disturbingly inexplicable. These last give the book its title; Joan gathers the products of many hours of trance-script into coherent poetic form and publishes the collection under the title *Lady Oracle*, a phrase from one of the poems. The work, described by her enthusiastic publishers ("Morton and Sturgess") as a cross between Rod McKuen and Khalil Gibran, is a great success; and the process of marketing the book and its author provides Atwood with the opportunity for some telling satire at the expense of the Canadian literary establishment. Joan "receives" the poems by staring into a mirror before which is placed a lighted candle. They tell the story of an unfulfilled love between a woman possessed of great but unhappy power, and an evil male figure with icicle teeth and eyes of fire; clearly they enact the conflicting emotions within Joan herself.

> She sits on the iron throne
> She is one and three
> The dark lady   the redgold lady
> The blank lady   oracle
> of blood, she who must be
> obeyed forever
> Her glass wings are gone
> She floats down the river
> singing her last song

The allusion to the Lady of Shalott is clear: Joan must break the mirror if she is to find herself; she must face life directly instead of creating images or disguises. When the novel begins, we find her hiding, having faked her death in order to begin life anew; at the end she literally breaks through the glass, to an acceptance of herself as she is.

The heroine's search for emotional fulfilment and psychic integration gives coherence and direction to a plot that might otherwise seem rather creaky and disjointed. As is often the case with fiction cast in autobiographical form, the narrative follows an episodic line, and parts of the action are sometimes very tenuously connected. Why, for instance, does Joan suddenly decide to go to England? In life, the cause might be quite obscure or trivial; in fiction, we need to feel that such decisions relate to theme or character, that there is some point, but Joan's choice of England as the place for a new start seems quite arbitrary. Still, such weaknesses seem slight beside the deftness with which Atwood handles each episode in Joan's career and introduces so many unusual and interesting characters. She has, too, an admirable control of style; her ability to insert the telling phrase and her eclecticism of reference give her writing a liveliness and polish that are unusual in Canadian fiction. Diana of Ephesus and Bertrand Russell rub shoulders with Joan Crawford and Kentucky Fried Chicken; this may offend purists, but it makes *Lady Oracle* a readable and (dare it be said of *serious* writers?) entertaining book. And should Atwood ever be short of money, she can always fall back on Gothic romances; the excerpts she provides here reveal a talent that would be the envy of any Harlequin novelist.

CL 72 (Spring 1977)

Clark Blaise

At Home in All Voices

You remember the old Storyland Limited? Half an hour, there and back. Little stops along the way, quaint stations, scenery like a picture postcard, friendly passengers, velvet banquettes, polished mahogany trim. Redcaps always helpful, conductors who knew their business, announcing the stops in plenty of time, taking your elbow as you edged out the door — remember that? You felt good after every trip, relaxed, respected.

Then the Twentieth Century Express roared into town. They cut the staff, ripped out the upholstery and left a blind old man in blue rags behind, who cursed as he punched the tickets. No more porters. No more little stops. Washed-out scenery too — just the backs of tenements where, approximately, lonely men in shirt sleeves flicked the butts of loosely-rolled cigarettes into the dust swirls left by retreating winter ice, exposing the brownish clumps of dying grass feebly fed by the anemic turds of sullen pets.

After the bankruptcy came the Great Reorganization. Sleek wagons of vinyl and plastic — amazing what they can do with old cattle cars. But confusion reigns. Computers prove whimsical. So many conductors, so many uniforms. Sometimes they help, mostly they babble snatches of poetry and philosophy mixed with lyrics of old dog food commercials. You've got to be sharp to make any sense at all. I end up taking tickets or wearing a red cap and *schlepping* (how did I even learn that word?) heavy bags. No one knows where we are, or the names of towns. Acrylic posters block the windows. The ticket destination reads only: THERE.

Which brings me, approximately, to Leon Rooke, at home in all conventions, in all uniforms, all voices. Twenty-one stories are reprinted in these two collections; with inevitable overlaps the thirteen stories in the Fiction Collective selection [*The Broad Back of the Angel*] reduce to ten not available in the Oberon [*The Love Parlour*]. The O selection has a "modern" bias; the FC is more "postmodern," a little zingier and more American in feel. If you like Leonard Michaels, Max Apple, some of Russell Banks, some Barth and Barthelme, give the FC edition a try. Both are bargains.

I'm slightly biased towards the Oberon selection. I'm predisposed, as is Rooke's friend and selector-of-stories, John Metcalf, to the ominous landscape, the single, apt detail ("The sun, obscured though it might be, was hot on the side of her face and a fly was crawling on her neck — or perhaps it was sweat . . ."), and I like the voice of untethered consciousness as it shuffles and deals — I like those things more than incessant wit and parody. (The three "Magician" stories and the two "Friend-ship" stories in the FC selection are sometimes funny but I didn't reread them. Clear them away and there's still more honest *fiction* in that edition than you're likely to encounter in any book of stories currently on the market.) The Oberon selection, by contrast, has only one story I'd remove — "If Lost Return to the Swiss Arms" — which, despite its O. Henry Award some years back, seems to have been conceived in a pre-modern idiom. The rest of the book is gold.

I'm much taken with the Mexican-set "For Love Of —" ("— Madeline, Eleanor, and Gomez") series of stories and Oberon reprints all three. With FC you get only two panels of what is obviously a triptych: two of the three is a mutilation. FC, however, will give you a scarey, deadpan gem called "Wintering in Victoria" (Rooke's home, incidentally) which is available in Canada only in an Oberon an-nual. It should be permanently gathered in this country, with the best of his work.

Even as it stands, I judge the Oberon collection of Rooke's short fiction to be the most technically accomplished, most perfectly realized and easily the most psycho-logically sophisticated ever published in this country. I only wish Oberon had a way of distinguishing this book from the dozens of drab, perfunctory efforts they've published in the past. And should an FC editor be reading this, it's only fair to point out that he/she did something far worse: in "Dangerous Women" (known as "Call Me Belladonna" in Canada) a character's perfectly reasonable allusion to Water-gate ("Here it was 1973 . . .") has been . . . what, freshened? . . . to "Here it was 1977 . . ." thus transforming a sluggard into a catatonic.

What should be emphasized is this: in both collections there is more than one masterpiece. FC's title story would qualify, plus "Wintering"; Oberon's little vol-ume is a feast. "If You Love Me Meet Me There" and "Memoirs of a Cross-Coun-try Man" are so intense, so perfectly implanted as *voice* (post-Modernism's victory over Modernism) as to be un-paraphrasable.

One doesn't "enter" such stories in the conventional sense. Instead, they enter you.

CL 81 (Summer 1979)

W.H. New

The Art of Haunting Ghosts

The title story in *From the Fifteenth District* is an odd piece. In three anecdotal sketches, it tells three separate stories of haunting: but in the turnabout world of Mavis Gallant it is the ghosts who are haunted. People who remain alive pursue, perceive them, and so perpetuate the images they have created of them, which are always external, and therefore always inaccurate. Major Emery Travella wishes to be rid of "the entire congregation of St. Michael and All Angels on Bartholomew Street," who pursue him with tape recorders and "burn incense under the pews"; Mrs. Ibrahim, mother of twelve, wishes to be rid of the doctor and social worker who refuse to agree on the truth of the treatment they have accorded her; and Mrs. Carlotte Essling wishes to be rid of a husband who keeps insisting she is an angel (whereas angels, she says, are either "messengers" or "paramilitary," and always "stupid"). Such sketches amply display Gallant's sardonic asperity and the precision of her social conscience. Yet what, as fiction, do they signify? One answer to this question might well be that they don't have to signify anything; they just have to exist, as artistically turned objects for us to marvel at and pass by. But that won't do. Insistently the stories call attention to themselves, and then to something else; the nature of human relationship, perhaps — but that is too bland; more closely, our human compulsion to visit ourselves upon the past, in order to secure a significance we fear we might otherwise be unable to possess.

By chance, I read this book at the same time as I read Margaret Atwood's *Life Before Man*, a brittle elegy for the 1970s in which egocentricity triumphs over affection, demonstration over ceremony, and distance over relationship. Much about the old traditions ridiculed and rejected in Atwood's book is shown clearly to be ridiculous and rejectable, yet the empty generation of the story — despite sex and intellect: despite either Reason or Passion — can find no way to escape its own emptiness. Even the narratorial voice is aloof, cautious, caustic at critical moments as though insecure. About what? Presumably about what it all signifies. For ultimately the characters don't matter; they are *would-be* urban sophisticates, chocolate rabbits without centres. Readers are invited to watch them, but there is no life with which to engage; and all that does seem finally to matter in the book is the texture of the language itself, an inwardly spiralling evocation of an attitude that in turn epitomizes an elusive decade.

In Gallant's world characters *do* matter, despite the fact that their lives seem often as bone-barren as any in Atwood's case studies. I think this is so because, however insignificant the lives, in each of them something of *consequence* happens. The textures of Gallant's stories — all as third-person as Atwood's — work to expose the fabric of consequence rather than the tissue of appearance. And the fictionality of "From the Fifteenth District" points to the process whereby such revelations happen.

The stories are set in Europe. French, Italian, Swiss, German, the characters are variously survivors, exiles, émigrés, border-crossers, visitors, and prisoners-of-war. But most of all, if we can trust the title story, ghosts. In "The Moslem Wife," for example, a woman named Netta Asher inherits a hotel and a world in the south of France, marries her cousin Jack Ross, and sets out to live an ordinary life. When World War II intervenes, catching her there and Jack in America, each develops separately, and when later she writes to him she wants to send the truth of her own experience:

> 'I suppose that you already have the fiction of all this. The fiction must be different, oh very different, from Italians sobbing with home-sickness in the night. The Germans were not real, they were specially got up for the events of the time. . . . Only in retreat did they develop faces and I noticed then that some were terrified and many were old. . . .'
>   This true story sounded so implausible that she decided never to send it. She wrote a sensible letter asking for sugar and rice and for new books; nothing must be older than 1940.

But she cannot pass into new territory; his memory will not let her. He sends food but forgets about books, and then returns, asserting that a walk with her *before the War* was "the happiest event of his life." Despite all her intentions, all her experience, all the changes in her tangible self, she is haunted by this foreign presence that lays claim to the reality of a previous existence. Gallant then closes the story with one of those magnificent, moodily detached sentences which characterize her writing. In the face of Jack's flat declaration, no matter how unconvincing it is, Netta surrenders: "Having no reliable counter-event to put in its place, she let the memory stand."

One questions, of course, the satisfactoriness of such a relationship. But what the story does is make us aware of the inadequacy of any relationship, the nature of its genesis, and its undeniable reality. As with the finest of the other stories in the book — "The Remission," for example, in which a sick Englishman takes longer than expected to die on the Riviera, with an impact of an unexpected kind on his family; or "The Latehomecomer," in which a German prisoner-of-war is held longer than normal in France because his papers have been lost, and finally returns home unfulfillingly, wanting a prewar mother, who herself wants a postwar son — "The Moslem Wife" takes the present, twists it sharply with the past, and watches the exchange of ghosts. The picture that emerges is not a jolly one, though it is not without wry amusement, but it is intensely compassionate. To be human in Gallant's world is to be touched almost always by durations of distress, but it is not as a consequence to be out of reach of love. As a result, the book is an enormously satisfying one. Neither flamboyant nor slick nor particularly easy to read, it is a splendidly written work, full of nuance and personality and compellingly evocative detail. It draws us slowly into the vortices of human behaviour, and asks us to observe more faithfully than we might have thought possible the intricate simplicities of our fellows and ourselves.

CL 85 (Summer 1980)

E.D. Blodgett

Winging It

A few years ago I came across Munro's "Dulse" somewhat by chance in a copy of the *New Yorker*. As I recall, it was a puzzling experience, and I began to wonder what new shape her work might be taking. I was somewhat apprehensive. There was no question that the story bore the imprint of Munro's style, particularly the unprepared shifts of point of view, the interweaving of several lives, the general sense of abandonment, all skilfully captured by choosing a setting in a guest house on an island in the Bay of Fundy. It had, of course, its little odd sides, in this instance an old man in pursuit of Willa Cather's past. But where, I asked myself, was the word that would edge the story, willy nilly, toward the kind of quirky epiphany so clearly manifest in her earlier fiction, the word that would suggest, as the narrator remarks in "Marrakesh," how "there was in everything something to be discovered"? Perhaps there was none; and I was apprehensive as one would be for any writer who has unquestionably reached the mastery of her craft. Would the next step run such risks that one could not predict the outcome? The question is apposite, for there was no doubt in my mind that Munro was capable either of remaining a mere success or of finding some way deeper into the mystery she has chosen to explore. She has chosen neither to abandon what she does so well nor to continue in quite the same vein; and her new collection, *The Moons of Jupiter*, is an achievement that surpasses her previous work, and for one reason: for the former clarity, didactic in its purity, she has substituted a will to surrender to whatever the story might suggest in its own demands to discover itself. Such a change implies a change with regard to Munro's understanding of her art; and while new narrators no longer radiate with the same wit, it now appears as if the wit belongs wholly to the design of the stories, a design to which both author and reader must yield.

Because Munro has chosen to explore a mystery, she faces more than the usual problems of craft that writers of short stories face: the figure through which the several levels of her fictions connect is at once the vehicle and the obstacle. It was the vehicle so long as the narrator was permitted to appear in control of the narration and to be the object toward which discovery aims. When, as in her recent collection, the story itself is the discovery, then the vehicle becomes obtrusive in a competitive way. What happens is that the figure, particularly some revelatory metaphor, is dropped. To drop what is often perceived as the mark of the short story requires incredible assurance, for it means that one must surrender to something beyond skill. That Munro has been aware of the risk — that something must follow upon skill — has been apparent at least since the concluding story of *Something I've Been Meaning to Tell You*, in which the narrator, a relatively clear autobiographical persona, observes of her mother that "she has stuck to me as close as ever and refused to fall away, and I could go on, and on, applying what skills I have, using what tricks I know, and it would always be the same." It is that act of surrender that gives her new stories their power: they adhere not so much because of the narrator's telling, but because of the author's persistent yielding to what the story is telling her. So far as I am aware, Munro's method is not one that "works a story up," but rather one that pares away to what can minimally remain and still survive the pressures of its implications. This means that the burden of the stories is borne by the material gaps on the page as well as by the concession to multiple focus, while staying within the limits of the traditional bounds of the form.

Thus, if one must speak of a special kind of loss, the loss of a somewhat obtrusive narrator impelled to identify, to display, often with dazzling grace, her awareness how all action conduces to metaphor, what can one say of what remains? Now that the narrator finds herself on a par with other characters in the story, suddenly characters that formerly appeared peripheral, those marvellous gestures that could be tossed off because they were needed for discovery, what were once hardly more than rhetorical figures are now indispensable in themselves. Such are David and Kimberly in "Labor Day Dinner," Albert's wife and sister-in-law in "The Visitors," the wonderful infiltration that Kay makes in "Bardon Bus." A whole story, "Pure," is dedicated to such a figure. Readers of Munro will not be surprised by figures like these; but what is new is their gain in definition that follows upon the narrator's self-effacement. Where they were once drawn with whim, sympathy, and even a slight condescension, subsumed as they were by the narrator's more privileged position, they now appear with an overwhelming gust of compassion. Consider the wonderful, epiphanic conclusion of *Lives of Girls and Women*, when Bobby Sheriff did "the only special thing he ever did for me" and danced "like a plump ballerina." The narrator's comment on the dance, no matter how adolescent and how appropriate to the narrative, implies the sense of the old style in high relief: "People's wishes, and their other offerings, were what I took then naturally, a bit distractedly, as if they were never anything more than my due." That this is a tendency, focusing either the narrator in first person or some central protagonist, would be difficult to deny; and it inheres in Munro's understanding that figures of fiction are not symbols but metaphors of identity whose enactment is in the telling, in how the story sets forth to find Del or Rose or whatever other masks "I" would choose.

I have said that this new collection is characterized by Munro's willingness to yield to the demands of the story, and I am aware how close this borders upon cant. I want, however, to emphasize the apparent lack of focus in *The Moons of Jupiter*, for it is this lack, the frequent absence of protagonist or guiding narrator, that allows her text to emerge polyphonically; and the absence of that particular pressure allows one to slip from the object of discovery to the process of discovery itself. This shift of perception is one that enhances the author at the narrator's expense, and we are almost allowed to see how the author goes about the assembling of sequences, almost permitted to know when a character will enter and for what reason. I say "almost," for part of the delicacy of Munro's art is the pressure it puts upon the traditional short story without becoming overwhelmed by post-structural play. Munro never seems to refine her art without first earning title to the refinement: to be merely new would not seem sufficient. But the effect of her gradual move away from emphasizing ends and endings is such as to make of her fiction a meditation upon both her craft and the life within which it dwells, a life whose language is honed and loved well. One thinks of the late essays of Montaigne when whoever "I" signifies is drawn inevitably into its text, its shape bent to fit whatever shape its fiction assumes. I want to mention "Dulse" again as a story of such capability, and "Bardon Bus" and the exquisitely wrought "Labor Day Dinner," its voices continually drifting into minds and through the air of windows. And how do the ephemeral sequences of "Hard-Luck Stories" cohere? Simply because of apparently shared themes, or because of their quality of being so accurate — I almost said "classic" — that their ending is only arbitrary? And they do not end, for their telling is only an occasion for further meditation, further unknowing. As the narrator observes of one of the listeners, "Something unresolved could become permanent. I could be always bent on knowing, and always in the dark, about what was important to him, and what was not."

It has become a commonplace in the criticism of Alice Munro to speak of her as always suspended between the conventions of fiction and confession. The change that these stories witness, I would suggest, no longer permits such a distinction and for what may appear a paradoxical reason. The mark of a documentary (or confession) is its reliance upon artifice to suggest the real. Fiction, by contrast, requires but art to produce the real. Munro, by abandoning her will to order through identity, her desire to urge pattern into metaphor, by shifting the weight of perception from narrator or protagonist to the endless surprise of plot, has chosen to make us believe that the real yields only to art and not to some unresolved collusion between fiction and quasi-autobiography. What, then, are we to make of the word "connection" that, one way or another, is used in several of these stories, and as a sub-title to the first half of the initial story? The narrator herself of the title story furnishes an answer, and it is an answer that could be used as a commentary on the technique of the whole collection: "I ask my mind a question. The answer's there, but I can't see all the connections my mind's making to get it." That willingness, however, to distinguish "I" so from "mind," to let "I" articulate while "mind" invisibly and independently connects, is at once magnanimous and decisive, for it has released Munro from the tyranny of "meaning." To choose to explore mysteries one must be prepared for certain sacrificial acts, and also incalculable discoveries, where one must be prepared, as Munro remarks in "The Turkey Season," to "Never mind facts. Never mind theories, either." It is to enter a country where contradictions, lacunae, even the unwanted come with the territory. It is the art of the meditation: to lay bare as part of the routine exercises of the spirit.

CL 97 (Summer 1983)

5. STUDIO

Gilles Marcotte

Une poésie d'exil

Le lecteur français n'éprouvera généralement, devant la poésie canadienne-française d'aujourd'hui, aucune impression de dépaysement. Il peut lire un recueil d'Anne Hébert, par exemple, ou d'Alain Grandbois, sans même soupçonner qu'il a paru outre-Atlantique, c'est-à-dire dans un climat physique et spirituel fort différent du sien. Entre la poésie qui s'écrit à Paris et celle qui s'écrit à Montréal, il n'existe assurément pas de cloison étanche. Les mêmes influences littéraires s'y retrouvent, et si l'on peut définir, quant à la France, une aventure poétique commune, cette aventure est partagée par les poètes du Canada français.

On peut donc se demander s'il est permis — et si oui, dans quel sens — de parler d'une poésie canadienne-française. Au début du siècle, encore, plusieurs de nos poètes se distinguaient aisément: par un bric-à-brac de thèmes patriotiques et régionalistes, insérés avec plus ou moins de bonheur dans des formes passe-partout. Ces signes tout extérieurs sont aujourd'hui révoqués, et l'on convient qu'avec Saint-Denys Garneau la poésie canadienne-française s'est résolument tournée vers l'homme, vers l'universel. De là à dire qu'elle n'a plus rien de canadien, il n'y a qu'un pas. Mais, pour le faire, il faudrait ignorer les liens très étroits que gardent entre elles les oeuvres les plus significatives d'aujourd'hui; entre elles, et avec ce qu'avait donné de plus vrai la poésie canadienne-française du siècle précédent. Notre poésie n'est plus enfermée dans ses frontières; mais cette liberté même qu'elle a conquise l'a conduite à explorer avec plus de conscience et de rigueur un paysage spirituel qui lui appartient en propre. En ce sens, elle révèle, au-delà des différences de formes et de filiations littéraires, une très profonde unité. Dans la mesure même où elle échappe aux facilités du pittoresque local, la poésie canadienne-française rejoint une interrogation fondamentale, qui est celle de son enracinement, de sa réussite humaine dans un *lieu donné*.

∞

Cette interrogation, on l'entend déjà chez l'ancêtre Crémazie, qui écrivait, aux environs de 1850, des poèmes effroyablement lourds, enchifrenés, soumis à des influences étouffantes. Mais les vers de sa *Promenade de trois morts*, si maladroits soient-ils, disent avec sincérité une difficulté de vivre, qu'on aurait trop vite expliquée par le tempérament personnel et quelques circonstances pénibles. La première voix poétique qui s'élève au Canada parle de la mort; de la mort, non pas comme un repos, une paix, un au-delà, mais de celle qui pourrit de l'intérieur tout espoir d'enracinement. Une interdiction de vivre ici. Le témoignage de Crémazie, d'ailleurs, sera bientôt corroboré. Son contemporain Alfred Garneau avoue la même hantise des cimetières, la même désaffection à l'égard de l'existence. Quelques années plus tard, Albert Lozeau:

> Je sens en moi grandir une âme d'étranger.

Quand la poésie de cette époque renonce à ses alibis patriotiques, sentimentaux ou religieux, c'est cela qui reste : un sentiment d'étrangeté à la vie, d'exil radical. Ses paroles les plus justes sont paroles d'effroi, de regret, de désespoir, et elle s'abandonne, sous divers prétextes de fiction littéraire, à d'étranges malédictions.

On peut s'en étonner; voire, s'en scandaliser. Il ne semble pas normal que les premiers chants d'un peuple jeune, réputé jovial et sain, engagé dans une rude aventure de survivance, soient autres qu'héroïques. Mais c'est là se faire une idée un peu simple de la réalité canadienne-française. Nos premiers poètes n'avaient rien de primitifs; c'étaient des Européens déracinés. Par toute leur culture, par les fibres essentielles de leur être moral, ils continuaient d'appartenir à la France. Ils n'étaient plus totalement français, pourtant. Un autre style de vie, d'autres appartenances, un autre sol les requéraient. Un autre « paysage », qu'ils n'avaient pas encore reconnu, et dans lequel ils ne s'étaient pas encore reconnus. Le Canada ne pouvait être, pour ces poètes, un lieu humain parfaitement suffisant. Faire un pays, ce n'est pas seulement défricher, bâtir des villes, édicter des lois, c'est aussi — et surtout — réinventer l'homme, dans un réseau de coordonnées nouvelles. L'Américain n'y est pas encore arrivé : Alfred Kazin a pu parler dans son récent essai sur les lettres américaines, d'une « impression de dépaysement ressentie sur notre propre sol ». Si l'Américain souffre, aujourd'hui, d'un tel dépaysement, qu'en sera-t-il du Canadien français, affronté à la même tâche d'humanisation, mais replié sur lui-même, isolé en Amérique par sa langue même, privé des secours qu'offrent le nombre et la richesse à ses voisins du sud?

Et comment, dès lors, s'étonner que notre poésie s'interroge, avec une constance et une angoisse toutes particulières, sur sa condition d'exil?

ඏ

Non pas qu'elle en évoque fréquemment la figure extérieure, qu'elle se retourne avec nostalgie vers ce qu'hier encore on appelait, au Canada français, la « mère-patrie ». Elle ne peut recevoir son humanité d'ailleurs — et la France, dans un certain sens, lui est un ailleurs. L'exil que subit la poésie canadienne-française est celui, sans forme ni visage, qui se loge au coeur, et nourrit la tentation de l'absence. Absence à la réalité extérieure, à la réalité sociale: à mesure qu'elle se dégage des clichés patriotiques et régionalistes, cette poésie se découvre sans voix devant les hommes, devant les paysages qui devraient être siens. Très rares, parmi nos poètes, sont ceux qui ont affronté les grands espaces américains; et ils n'en ont tiré qu'une impression de néant, ce « silence des neiges aux épousailles sèches de vide », qu'évoque la poésie d'Yves Préfontaine. Mais le plus souvent, les paysages, les choses, sont à peine évoqués. On se tient à l'écart, dans une intimité douloureuse, où l'extérieur n'est admis qu'après avoir perdu sa qualité *d'autre*. Ce qu'on a coutume d'appeler le réel devient ici un jeu d'images pures, sans autre appui, sans autre titre à l'existence, que leur résonance intérieure. À l'extrême, voyez *Le Tombeau des rois*, d'Anne Hébert: on y parle de fontaines, d'oiseaux, d'arbres, de maisons, de villes, mais les images évoquées par ces mots sont privées de coloration individuelle. Le particulier n'existe pas pour cette poésie. Elle ne *nomme*, elle ne possède que le plus général, ce qui commence tout juste d'exister. Elle naît en même temps qu'un monde; ou plutôt, elle renaît, dans le sentiment que tout lui a été enlevé, interdit, et qu'il faut tout réapprendre à partir des éléments.

Tout réapprendre, et soi-même d'abord. Car si la possession des choses paraît menacée, le poète n'éprouve pas moins de difficulté à se posséder lui-même, à réaliser sa propre unité. La figure définitive de l'absence, nous la trouverons ici: dans une aliénation intérieure, dont la poésie canadienne-française n'a jamais cessé de porter le témoignage. On pense aux vers de Saint-Denys Garneau:

Je marche à côté d'une joie
D'une joie qui n'est pas à moi . . .

C'est pour avoir fait éclater en pleine lumière, pour avoir vécu et exprimé, avec une sincérité bouleversante, cette aliénation, que Saint-Denys-Garneau a exercé une influence décisive sur la récente évolution de la poésie canadienne-française. Avant lui, beaucoup de choses avaient été dites, mais par échappées seulement, avec des réticences, des hésitations; et aussi, il faut l'avouer, dans des formes poétiques surannées, peu propres à libérer l'expression. Chez Saint-Denys-Garneau, libération de la forme et libération de la parole vont de pair. Désormais, il sera de plus en plus difficile d'éviter quelque dur affrontement. La poésie canadienne-française a trouvé son centre: avant toutes choses, elle confesse une division intérieure, un profond malaise à vivre. D'Anne Hébert à Alain Grandbois, de Jean-Guy Pilon à Roland Giguère, il n'est pas aujourd'hui, au Canada français, de poésie digne de mention, qui ne se mesure d'abord au péril de l'absence. C'est dans ce combat qu'elle affirme, de plus en plus largement, son humanité, et qu'elle rejoint les poésies contemporaines les plus significatives.

cs

On ne manquera pas, en effet, de remarquer que plusieurs des caractères attribués à la poésie canadienne-française pourraient, tout aussi bien, s'appliquer à plusieurs poètes français de l'après-guerre. Une différence subsiste, cependant, qui fait que les mêmes mots, en France et au Canada, ont mêmes sens . . . et ne l'ont pas. Le poète français est *armé* comme le canadien ne l'est pas. Il *possède* un langage — quelque difficulté qu'il éprouve à le recréer; une culture — quelques dures secousses qu'elle ait subies. Il habite une maison, même menacée de ruine, où il se reconnaît aussitôt, où les moindres objets lui offrent un sens immédiatement recevable. Le poète canadien-français commence plus bas, dans une pauvreté plus nue. Ses pessimismes — ou ce qu'on désigne souvent de ce nom — ne sont pas les pessimismes européens. Il en est encore à reconnaître sa demeure, à conquérir son droit à la vie, ses libertés avec lui-même et avec les choses. La poésie canadienne-française est une poésie des premières démarches.

CL 2 (Autumn 1959)

Malcolm Ross

"A Strange Aesthetic Ferment"

When one looks down over Fredericton from the hills where Charles Roberts and Bliss Carman once took their long hikes with George Parkin, one still sees the spire of Bishop Medley's Cathedral rising above a city hidden in elms. Old Frederictonians, whether they be Anglican or Roman, Baptist or Marxist, think first of their Cathedral whenever they think of home.

George Goodridge Roberts, the father of Charles and Theodore (and Bliss Carman's uncle) was Canon of the Cathedral and Rector of the parish church of St. Anne's. George Parkin, headmaster of the Collegiate School in Fredericton, was an active Cathedral layman. Something should be said about the coincidence at just the right time of the Tractarian Bishop, his Gothic Cathedral, the great teacher whose classroom had no walls, "the new music, the new colours, the new raptures of Pre-Raphaelite poetry,"[1] and the young and eager spirits ready to respond to the peculiar genius of this place and this time.

"The Fredericton of those days," Charles G.D. Roberts recalls, "was a good place for a poet to be." It was "stirring with a strange aesthetic ferment." Tiny as it was, with no more than six thousand inhabitants, Fredericton was nonetheless a capital city, a university city, a cathedral city:

> She had little of the commercial spirit, and I fear was hardly as
> democratic as is nowaday considered the proper thing to be. But she
> was not stagnant, and she was not smug. Instead of expecting all the
> people to be cut of one pattern, she seemed to prefer them to be just a
> little queer. . . . Conformity, that tyrant god of small town life, got
> scant tribute from her. There was much good reading done, up-to-date
> reading, and if people wrote verse, they had no need to be apologetic

about it. To Fredericton it did not seem impossible that some of them might turn out to be *good* verses.

Good verses, Roberts avers, were indeed being written not only in "the big red rectory" on George Street, and in the Carman house, but also in a house not far from the Cathedral where "a slim, dark-eyed and black-browed youth by the name of Francis Sherman . . . was dreaming with William Morris and Rossetti over old romances of Camelot and Lyonesse."

There is no easy explanation of this "strange aesthetic ferment" in the little city of the Loyalists in the last quarter of the ninteenth century. Both A.G. Bailey[2] and the late Desmond Pacey[3] have drawn attention to the civilizing presence of the university. Bailey also points to "societal" influences, particularly the "lawless and speculative spirit of the lumber trade" which had made of Fredericton an island unto itself:

> The expansion of the trade brought hordes of poverty-stricken Irish
> to New Brunswick, decimated the forests and bled the province of its
> wealth, but provided a modicum of revenue for the support of the little
> body of civil servants, lawyers, judges, clergymen and professors who
> made up the governing class of the capital. Those Anglicans and Tories
> survived the loss of their political dominance because the establishment
> of responsible government was delayed in New Brunswick, and did
> not, in any case, mean a sharp break when it did come. . . . Moreover,
> it was a closely knit company of experts and adepts in administration,
> education, and religion, and the Province continued to depend upon
> it for some of these services long after confederation. To this circle of
> professional people the Carman and Roberts families belonged.[4]

Bailey argues convincingly that whereas in Nova Scotia "Howe and Haliburton had met a political challenge,"[5] in New Brunswick "Carman and Roberts experienced a crisis of the spirit after the political battle was lost, and something of the world along with it." Howe and Haliburton had Man for their argument; Roberts and Carman, perforce, turned to the landscape.

I think this is so. Certainly "the little society of professional people" in Fredericton could not for ever nourish its brood of poets, and they were soon to be off to Toronto and Boston, New York and London, Cuba and Montreal, taking their landscape with them. However, the actual advent of the "creative moment" itself (and Bailey, of course, agrees) has its own inner urgency not to be understood solely in terms of the shape and stress of a society as such. Something happened that might not have happened. It happened in the context of a cultural phenomenon that could not have been predicted of a society of professional people already outliving their usefulness.

Roberts[6] attributes the advent of "the creative moment" to "the vitalizing influence of George R. Parkin, falling upon soil peculiarly fitted to receive it." Much has been made of Parkin's influence — and who can doubt it? But nothing has been made of Parkin's Anglicanism, his devotion to Bishop Medley, his friendship with Canon Roberts — a friendship which had much to do with those long hikes over the hills with Charles Roberts and Bliss Carman, and those rapt recitations of "The Blessed Damozel," a poem which Parkin "loved so passionately that Bliss sometimes suspected him of saying instead of his prayers."[7]

One wonders what would have happened in this "little society of professional people" if an evangelical had been sent as first Bishop of Fredericton, if there had been no Gothic Cathedral on the river, if between the teacher and his "favourite two" there had been no band of friendship in the faith?

What was the soil "peculiarly fitted" to receive Parkin's influence? In part, at least, it was New England soil. A.G. Bailey puts it thus:

> The poetry of Fredericton represented the flowering of a tradition that had been four generations in the making on the banks of the St. John; and behind that, across the divide of the Revolution, lay the colonial centuries.[8]

This is not to say that Roberts and the others were conscious of belonging to and fulfilling a native tradition in poetry. Bailey makes this clear:

> Charles G.D. Roberts, who perhaps more than any other fathered the national movement in Canadian poetry, considered that he was writing on a tablet that no one had written on before. He showed little awareness of the work of Sangster and Heavysege, nor that of Jonathan Odell, the Tory poet of the Revolution, who had been among the founders of his own city of Fredericton.[9]

Nevertheless, the influence on taste and manners of men like Odell — and other founding fathers like Ward Chipman and Edward Winslow — made Fredericton, from the start, heir to the culture of colonial America. The well-stocked private libraries, the university itself, the urbane and cultivated air of this remote frontier town, owed as much to the American tradition as it did to college professors from Oxford and transplanted British officials.

The place took something of its actual look from the older colonies. Just across the way from Medley's Gothic Cathedral stands Jonathan Odell's handsome colonial house. In the shadow of the Cathedral spire was the house where Benedict Arnold once lived. The mark of New England craftsmen was evident on houses throughout the city, on the white pine churches and farmhouses along the river, on the chairs and tables, dressers, and clocks and highboys of even the simplest Fredericton homes.

Roberts and Carman grew up in mind of their ancestor, the Reverend Daniel Bliss, pastor of Concord at the time of the Revolution. A.G. Bailey, in a tape recording of his literary reminiscences prepared for the Harriet Irving Library of the University of New Brunswick, shows how vividly the New England memory lived on in Fredericton. He traces the ancestry of Carman and Roberts to one Peter Bulkeley, "The founder of Concord in the Massachusettes Bay Colony":

> It was Peter's granddaughter, Elizabeth Bulkley, who married Joseph Emerson, and two descendants, thus necessarily cousins, Hannah Emerson and the Rev. Daniel Emerson, became espoused in the year 1744. Both were ancestors of the Baileys of the University of New Brunswick and Hannah was a great aunt of Ralph Waldo Emerson, and sister-in-law of Phoebe Bliss, who was, in turn, sister of Daniel Bliss, forebear of Bliss Carman and Charles G.D. Roberts. These families, Baileys and Bliss's, so early connected, were to meet again and mingle in ways that had, in the fulness of time, a significance for the development of a Fredericton literary tradition.[10]

In 1861, Loring Woart Bailey, the grandfather of A.G. Bailey, came from the United States as Professor of Chemistry at the University of New Brunswick. "His friendship with the Carman and Roberts families in Fredericton brought together once again two families that had been connected away back in Revolutionary days in Concord."

Then, too, there was something "native to the blood" of these Loyalist New Englanders in the Maritime terrain itself. Roberts, writing of canoe trips with Carman, captures the feeling they both had of being three hundred years in the wilderness:

> I have never seen Carman so happy, so utterly at home, as in those wilderness expeditions. He was essentially native to the woods and the lovely inland waters. He paddled and handled his canoe like an Indian. He trod the forest trails like an Indian, noiseless, watchful, taciturn, moving with long, loose-kneed slouch, flat-footed, with toes almost turned in rather than out — an Indian's gait, not a white man's! That love of the sea that was later to show itself in so much of Carman's poetry was perhaps atavistic — an inheritance from some of our New England and approximately "Mayflower" ancestry.[11]

CB

One need not subscribe to notions of "atavism" to recognize a congeniality of place that wells out of time past but still present. The political break with the American past was only in part a cultural break. Even the Anglican parsons who fled to New Brunswick from the Revolution brought with them ways that smacked of American Congregationalism. Until quite recently in New Brunswick the rector answered a "call," the Bishop appointing only after the congregation had chosen their "minister." And, in the main, Anglican churches were built in the style of the New England meeting-house. Bishop Medley, in horror at what he saw of New Brunswick church architecture, said to one of his laymen: "Mr. R.—, when you build a church, build a church but when you build a barn, build a barn!"[12] And Ketchum tells us that in the days before Medley

> the Church buildings and church services were alike of a dull and dreary sort. New churches were built but more after the plan of the meeting house. In the public services there were no responses — that all-important part of divine service fell to the lot of the clerk. The parish church of Fredericton — the pro-Cathedral — had its galleries and square pews. The altar stood in a narrow space between the reading desk and the pulpit. . . . church music was little understood or attended to.[13]

The Loyalists had brought with them their books and their crafts and a deep-down instinct for forest, river, and sea. But they had also brought a Puritan distrust of the senses. For even among the Anglican Loyalists there was evident and active what A.S.P. Woodhouse once called the Puritan "principle of segregation" which put apart, and far apart, the order of nature and the order of grace. The austerity of the sacred was to be preserved from any taint of the profane. Skills that went to the shaping of fan-windows and Chippendale chairs were not to be employed on altar-pieces and lecterns. To stain a window was perhaps to stain a soul.

This is not to say that learning was not valued, and for its own sake. (The college on the hill could not be hid.) There was pride, too, in the houses and public buildings of mid-century Fredericton. The red-coated garrison gave sparkle to the streets and the convivialities of Government House. There was a love of fine horses, and parades; there was canoeing or iceboating on the Saint John, the hunting party deep in the forest. But there was also the prim white church with square pews, galleries and blank windows — a place apart from the life of town and river.

In 1845, into this mixed society of Loyalist New Englanders, British bureaucrats and soldiers, lumber kings and small merchants came John Medley, first Bishop of Fredericton. It was the year of Newman's secession to Rome — not an auspicious moment to proclaim Tractarian doctrine and to build Gothic churches![14]

Medley, an Oxford man, was not only a friend of Pusey, and Keble. He was also an ecclesiologist, the author of an influential book, *Elementary Remarks on Church Architecture* (1841). He was a musician, the composer of choral settings for the *Te Deum* and the *Benedictus* as well as a number of hymns. It was his great (if not his greatest) achievement to give to Fredericton, to the diocese, and, in no small measure, to the whole ecclesiastical province of Canada, a sense of the kinship of beauty and holiness. His strenuous effort to reclaim for the sacred all of the outcast glory of the profane was begun in Fredericton almost a generation before the birth of Charles G.D. Roberts and Bliss Carman, who were to come of age in Medley's city, reared and taught by men who were Medley's friends, his allies, his disciples. The Bishop in what he built, in what he said, in what he did, altered a climate of the mind.

One need not here say much about the pastoral and doctrinal concerns of Bishop Medley. One must note, however, his Catholic insistence on the apostolic sanction for his high office, his Catholic sacramentalism, and his affirmation of the classical Anglican doctrine of the *via media*, an affirmation made persuasively enough to win him, in the end, the support of both High Churchmen and Evangelicals. Then, too, there was his solicitous care for the poor (he abolished pew-rents on arrival in Fredericton), and his astonishing travel by ship, canoe and horse to the farthest outposts of his diocese. No Yankee circuit rider rode farther than this intrepid Englishman who was to become the most ardent of New Brunswickers and, after 1867, without forsaking his Englishness, became a committed Canadian, pleading for full self-government in the Canadian Church while advancing the spiritual claims of the universal Church beyond any possible reach of the secular arm.

With generous financial aid from England, the practical help of Frank Wills, a young English architect, and the advice and collaboration of William Butterfield, the noted English Gothicist, the Bishop, on arrival, began to build his Cathedral. The spire soon rose above the town, giving high point and focus to what had been a jumbled prospect of Georgian houses, British barracks and lumbermen's palaces. At the other end of town he built his Chapel of Ease — St. Anne's, consecrated in 1846, six years before the Cathedral. Also designed by Frank Wills, it is, says Phoebe Stanton, "the finest small North American parish church of its date in the English Gothic style."[15]

Even before the completion of his Cathedral, Medley was on the move about the diocese, exhorting his people to build churches, not barns. Soon new churches, of wood, but built under the guidance of the Gothic ecclesiologists, were consecrated at Newcastle, Burton and Maugerville. Later, the Bishop's son Edward, who had studied with Butterfield, designed several wooden Gothic churches, the most notable of which are at St. Stephen and Sussex.

In making possible through architecture a renewal of Catholic practice in Anglican worship, the Bishop had also effected a revolution in sensibility and taste. After the blank meeting house with the pulpit rising like a mountainous idol above the speck of a "communion table," St. Anne's, with its rood-screen, stained glass, and tiled reredos, and Christ Church Cathedral, cruciform, in dim religious light, pulsing with the music of the Bishop's own *Te Deum*, struck the mind and imagination of the Loyalist town like an apocalypse.

It is not surprising that the Bishop's sermon in stone and painted glass and lighted altar was not at first, and by everyone, happily heard. There were those among the meeting-house men of Fredericton who saw idolatry as well as extravagance in these "Romish" structures. The Bishop met the charge of extravagance by paying for St. Anne's out of his own pocket and by raising large sums in England for the construction of the Cathedral. Rebutting the charge of idolatry, in sermons, in addresses to lay audiences, in admonitions to his clergy, he argued with Ruskinian fervour and Tractarian point against that inherited Loyalist, Puritan bias which would allow splendid dwellings for governor, merchant and soldier, but which refused to the church all delight of eye and ear.

"Are they who despise the Church of God, and lay out all their substance in the decoration of their houses, of necessity the most holy?" He was fully conscious of that "principle of segregation" which had kept the order of grace wholly aloof from the order of nature: "if there be no necessary connexion between external beauty and spiritual religion, is there any close connexion between spiritual and external deformity?"[16]

From this sermon, preached at the consecration of St. Anne's in 1847, to the very end of his days (in 1892), it was among the Bishop's chief tasks to baptize beauty, to give beauty back to the Giver of it. In so doing he proclaimed not only the beauty and, for the Christian, the *congeniality* of the natural order. He was to affirm, as well, the integrity of the natural order and the full and proper dignity of the life of the senses.

The consecration sermon in itself was intended as a defence of beauty in worship. Alarmed at the puritanical bigotry of the evangelicals and the "high and dry" Churchmen alike, Medley was at great pains to protect the imagery of traditional Christian worship from the rigours of these latter-day iconoclasts. But he does not stop with a defense of beauty in worship. He calls upon his people to venerate and to enjoy as Christians the sensuous beauty of all creation:

> For let us consider to what did God vouchsafe us *form, colour,*
> number and harmony? . . . why does the Book of God answer to the
> work of God, and dwell so often and so vividly on external nature? . . .
> Did God make all these works for nought? Or are we intended to

suppose them only for sensual enjoyment, that the animal man may be gratified, while the spiritual man is neglected?[17]

It follows that, in worship, "if the tongue praise him, why not the heart, the feet and the hands? What difference is there in principle between reading or singing the praises of God with the lips, and engraving those praises on wood, or stone, or glass?"[18]

The senses which respond to the beauty of creation are validly employed in praise of the Creator. But if art is indeed a suitable handmaiden of religion, it has its own province too. The lecture on "Good Taste," delivered in 1857 to a lay audience of churchmen in Saint John, is a nice distillation of Medley's thought on the secular implications of his aesthetic principles. Here, in little, is a doctrine of beauty, art and nature which the Bishop propounded almost daily in private discourse as well as public, with consequences not only for the life and look of the church and the city, but also for that "strange aesthetic ferment" of which Roberts speaks.

℃ß

Fredericton as it is today owes much to the man who had talked like this about city streets and houses:

> In laying out a town, it is common in North America to avoid the crooked lanes and devious ways of our ancestors, and to provide wide and spacious streets. So far so good, but it is not breadth or length only which gives a street a fine commanding appearance. The houses, if not of uniform height, should certainly not present an astonishing difference, one mansion towering to the skies, and the next a shanty of eight feet from the ground. The colouring and ornamentation of a house require great consideration. It is a safe as well as an ancient rule that nothing should form part of the decoration of a building, which is also not part of its construction. . . . Then as to colour. It is either as if men had no eyes, or lived in a colourless world. Their houses glare with white paint, and the same idea is repeated again and again, without variation, while there is not a hill, nor a lake, nor a flower which is not without its variety.[19]

Even now, the Cathedral with its varied and lovely architectural brood, defies the government "planner" who so often proposes, but still in vain, to erect around this priceless place his ugly monotones of steel and glass.

While I am not sure that the Bishop had read the Second Book of *Modern Painters* (although I suspect he had) he seems, like Ruskin, to discern in nature's teeming variety what Ruskin called "divine attributes," the mark of the Maker on things. The order of nature is given its own governance, its own integrity. It lives by laws unto itself, is lovable in itself and by itself, even as it gives witness to Other than itself.

Medley lifts the imagination to the restless, kaleidescopic configuration of clouds in language that suggests the art of Constable:

> What exquisite beauty lies in *water* and *light*, and in their mutual
> relation to each other. The clouds present an endless variety of form and
> colour, sometimes in streaks like the finest pencilling of the artist . . .
> sometimes like balls of snow or crystals, sometimes piled up like the
> everlasting hills, disclosing huge cavernous recesses, lighted up with a
> bronze colour, like the interior of a volcano, sometimes resembling cities
> whose top reached up to heaven, then melting into spacious plains,
> sometimes so transparent that we would seem to pierce them through
> with the hand, then gathering suddenly into a thick, fierce and angry
> mass, bursting into forked flames and threatening destruction.[20]

But in this "wide awe" of cloud and storm there is hidden wisdom to be pondered. For this infinitely unpredictable conduct of the natural order is still lawful conduct, and wonder at it is the beginning of human wisdom and the fountain-source of art. One must also observe that Medley takes no terror from those angry masses of clouds "bursting into forked flames and threatening destruction." There is in him, it must be insisted, "no terror of the soul at something these things manifest."[21] Quite the contrary. The Bishop "accepts the universe." He was, of course, not unaware of the "wrath of God." He never forgot that men were too often prone to bask under the sun of Satan. In his sermons he had much to say of original sin, of the Fall, and of the deep wound left by the Fall in the heart of things. But he had much more to say about the redemptive sacrifice of the Cross. It was Medley's Tractarian orthodoxy which protected him from all dark notions of the "total depravity" of the natural order and the natural man. Freed from fear by faith, he opened his church door and let beauty in — and nature.

Little wonder that there can be found in the Bishop's flock no trace of what Frye calls the "garrison mentality." Nor is there evident, in young churchmen like Roberts and Carman and the others who gathered at the parish Rectory on George Street, anything like the working of that old puritan "principle of segregation" which had isolated the sacred from the profane. Through Medley's Gothic door there entered, as it had not entered the door of the old Loyalist meetinghouse, all of the New Englander's active love of woods and sea and river.

The Rector of the parish, George Goodridge Roberts (a Bliss of Loyalist lineage on his mother's side), had come to Fredericton in 1874 to serve close to his Bishop. He was a man after Medley's own heart and had, before coming to Fredericton, rearranged his little church at Westcock in accordance with Medley's liturgical principles. In his new charge at St. Anne's he was equally faithful to Medley and had to contend manfully with nervous parishioners who saw in lighted candles on the altar the dire threat of "popery."

It was in Canon Roberts' rectory that Charles and Bliss Carman, the Stratons, and, later, Francis Sherman, gathered after the canoe trip and after family prayers or evensong to read their verses to each other and to talk of Rossetti and Tennyson and Swinburne. Parkin was often among them, and Canon Roberts himself. The young poets were, in those days, active churchmen. Charles sang in his father's choir at St. Anne's. Carman served at Medley's cathedral altar and assisted Parkin in the Cathedral Sunday School. Francis Sherman was to become the fast friend of Tully Kingdon, the coadjutor Bishop and his next-door neighbour.

It might be said, then, that "the soil" which Roberts tells us was "peculiarly fitted" to receive "the vitalizing influence of Parkin," was New England soil which had been "Gothicized." It was from this soil that Parkin himself drew his own first strength. Born in Salisbury, New Brunswick, of Anglican parents, he received his early religious training from the Baptist Church because there was no Anglican Church within miles. According to his biographer, Sir John Willison,[22] Parkin, when he came to Fredericton, was soon drawn to the Cathedral, and "his family tradition, his instinctive love of seemliness and dignity in worship, and above all the character and influence of the Bishop brought him back to the Church of England." When he went to Oxford on leave from the Collegiate school, he bore from the Bishop "letters of introduction to several prominent men in the church." Parkin went to Oxford ready for Ruskin (whose first Slade Lecture he heard), ready for Pusey (whom he visited as well as heard), ready for Gothic England and for a past made present in the bright colours of Pre-Raphaelite poetry. It was as though he had come upon the very source of what he had already loved most. When he returned to his own country as a prophet he was a prophet honoured. For his country had been made ready for his prophecy.

ᴄᴣ

The soil had indeed been prepared. Here was "the fair beginning of a time." But the "strange aesthetic ferment" that began in Rectory and Cathedral with Parkin's return from Oxford to this Gothicized colonial soil was to have unpredictable issue. Carman and Roberts soon went their own and very different ways. There are traces of Pre-Raphaelite colours and images in some of their earlier work but other influences were soon to gain ascendancy. Neither, of course, was to be a "Christian" poet. Carman's early "Easter Hymn" was never published and, by the time he wrote "Low Tide on Grand Pré," he was closer to New England transcendentalism than to any force or fashion coming out of England. The mark of the Gothic and the Christian was to be stronger and more enduring on the work of the younger poets of the group, Francis Sherman and Theodore Goodridge Roberts.

The directions eventually taken in the poetry of Charles Roberts and Bliss Carman can be explained in part, at least, by the loss of that faith in which the ferment of the first creative moment had begun. The actual drift away from the faith — Parkin's faith, Medley's faith — is another story and not to be attempted here. Even in his college days Charles Roberts had admitted religious doubts and reservations to his father (who was disturbed but tolerant). Dorothy Roberts once told me that her uncle, for all his scepticism, had clung for years to a faint hope, at least, in "the permanence of human identity," and he seems always to have been nagged by "the religious question." In at least one remarkable poem, "When Mary the Mother Kissed the Child," he seems magically for a moment to be back at Christmas time in his father's choir at St. Anne's.

I remember having dinner with him once in Fredericton in the late 1930s. Rather mischievously, I asked him if he intended to go to the Cathedral in the morning — or perhaps to St. Anne's. "No," he said, "No, I'm afraid not." There was a twinkle in his eye and, I fancied, a rather wistful smile on his lips as he added, "Nowadays, I carry my church within me." I remembered that I had once seen him in the Cathedral, not many years before, at the state funeral for Bliss Carman.

Theodore Goodridge Roberts, younger than Charles by almost eighteen years, was no church-goer either, but, much more than his brother or his cousin Carman, he retained a fascination for the chivalric Christian tradition, for Saint Joan and her "banner of snow,"[23] and for the Love who tells the Young Knight

> I am the spirit of Christ
>   High and white as a star.
> I am the crown of Mary
> Outlasting the helmet and war.[24]

It was not so much to the pageantry of Pre-Raphaelitism that Theodore Roberts was drawn. His daughter, Dorothy, has spoken to me of his veneration of the suffering Christ and of his symbolic use of the sacrificial Indian hero Gluskap as a kind of Christ-figure in some of the tales and poems.

Francis Sherman, eleven years younger than Charles Roberts, wrote poetry which is often thoroughly Pre-Raphaelite in style and specifically Christian in theme. The titles of not a few of the poems in his volume

Matins are quite liturgical — "Nunc Dimittis," "Te Deum Laudamus." (He had first thought of calling his book *Lauds and Orisons* and then *The Book of the Little Hours*.[25]) His best work seeks to reveal a Christian dimension in the order of nature and in the love of man for woman.

Carman himself, after his Fredericton years, was to be close for awhile in Boston to Phillips Brooks, the eminent Rector of Trinity Church. Among his other Boston friends were Ralph Adams Cram and Bertram Goodhue, the Gothic architects, and Louise Guiney, the devout Roman Catholic poet. But the drift which had begun in his college days with an enthusiasm for Emerson and Thoreau (and soon for Josiah Royce) carried him irreversibly towards transcendentalism in its late New England twilight, and very far from the Tractarian teaching of his boyhood. By 1903 he could write like this:

> Surely the soul of man is the only tabernacle of the veritable God. The
> sense of living humanity as to what is true, what is good, what is
> beautiful to see, is the only sanction for belief. You and I, standing
> outside the reach of an obsolete authority, believe and cherish the
> words of the Sermon on the Mount not because Christ uttered them
> but because we cannot help assenting to their lofty truth.[26]

The truths of Christianity, he goes on, need "only to be separated from superstition to appeal to us in all their charm and power." (Emerson might well have written this!)

But if Carman was to leave the church through Medley's open door and find his way back to New England (the New England not of his puritan ancestor, the Reverend Daniel Bliss, but of Ralph Waldo Emerson) he was never to become one of Frye's "garrison" men. If he was one day, as Frye puts it (unfairly, I think) to utter "prayers of a stentorian vagueness to some kind of scholar-gypsy God,"[27] the prayers were not to be uttered "in stark terror." D.G. Jones is one of the few critics since the 1930s to be perceptive enough to recognize in Carman's poetry a loving acceptance and a celebration of the natural world:

> More than any other Canadian writer he has the kind of faith in the
> goodness or justice of life that is implied in Christ's parable of the lilies
> of the field which neither toil nor spin, and yet are clothed in a glory
> greater than Solomon's. . . . Throughout his career he was able to write
> poems in which we glimpse an authentic sense of the joy and
> poignancy of being alive — of what it means to love a woman or the
> world.[28]

If Mary Perry King was to replace Medley as Carman's mentor, and if Carman was to put aside Christian dogma in favour of a kind of transcendentalism, he was never to lose the slouching Indian gait, or the sense of kinship with all created things that Medley's door had opened to him. He had known early the awful presence "swift and huge / of One who strode and looked not back." When his cousin, and close friend of Cathedral days, Andy Straton, died suddenly and young, Carman turned for solace, however, not to the hopes of Christianity but to Josiah Royce's *Religious Aspects of Philosophy*. In Royce's thoughts, as J.R. Sorfleet so aptly summarizes it, "evil is no more than a momentary dissonance in the organic unity of God's good act, and is soon resolved into God's goodness."[29] From Royce, from Mary Perry King and from George Santayana, Carman sought to build a system of ideas which could sustain and justify his faith, early and everlasting, in the holiness of beauty and the integrity of nature, a faith which he had first come to hold, with such different Christian sanction, in Medley's Cathedral city.

Fredericton, for awhile, had been "a good place for a poet to be," but not for ever a good place for a poet to stay. Charles Roberts soon found that not even Toronto could support a writer. Carman could not resist the New England of his forbears (after a few months in Boston, like many a Maritimer since, he could not imagine himself living anywhere else). Only Theodore Roberts returned later in life and after much wandering, to live in Fredericton and the Maritimes.

John Medley would have been grieved to know of the "unchurching" of his young churchmen. He would at least have been perplexed by Carman's curious New England heterodoxies. But in Theodore's Young Knight, and "The Maid," and in all that he had loved and known "on that far river" of the early years, in Roberts' uncommon songs of the common day as well as in "Mary the Mother," in much of Sherman's *Matins*, he might have recognized something of the gifts which he had himself once given. With Carman's proclamation, early and late, of the holiness of beauty and the sense that his poetry imparts "of the joy and poignancy of being alive," the first Bishop of Fredericton would have had no quarrel. He would, one is sure, have been gratified rather than dismayed.

Notes

[1] This quotation and the quoted passages which follow immediately are from Charles G.D. Roberts, "Bliss Carman," *Dalhousie Review*, 9 (March 1930), 409–17.

[2] "Sir Charles G.D. Roberts," in *Essays in Canadian Criticism* (Toronto: Ryerson, 1969), 180–87.

[3] "Creative Moments in the Culture of the Maritime Provinces," in *Culture and Nationality* (Toronto: McClelland and Stewart, 1972), 54–55.

[4] *Ibid.*, 54.

[5] *Ibid.*, 56.

[6] Roberts, 417.

[7] Roberts, 413.

[8] Bailey, 56.

[9] "Evidences of Culture Considered as Colonial," in *Culture and Nationality*, 184.

[10] This and the brief passage which follows are quoted with permission of the author and the library from a manuscript revised from typescript "Literary Memories of Alfred Goldsworthy Bailey: Part 1," 2–3, and 5.

[11] Roberts, 415.

[12] "John Medley." By W.O. Raymond, in *Leaders of the Canadian Church*. First series, ed. W.B. Heeney (Toronto: Musson, 1918), 121.

[13] W.Q. Ketchum, *The Life and Work of the Most Reverend John Medley*. Saint John: McMillan, 1893. Pp. 26 and 64. This is still the only full account of Medley's career. A fine chapter on Medley is included in Christopher Headon's unpublished doctoral thesis *The Influence of the Oxford Movement Upon the Church of England in Eastern and Central Canada, 1840–1900* (McGill U, 1974).

[14] The point was made by Eugene Fairweather in "A Tractarian Patriot: John Medley of Fredericton," *Canadian Journal of Theology*, 6.1 (1960), 17. This is the best approach to Medley in print.

[15] *The Gothic Revival and American Church Architecture* (Baltimore: Johns Hopkins UP, 1968), 130. Professor Stanton devotes a full chapter to Christ Church Cathedral and St. Anne's and I am indebted to her for information about Medley's Gothic churches in wood. The most thorough architectural study of the Cathedral is to be found in Douglas Richardson's unpublished master's thesis *Christ Church Cathedral, Fredericton, New Brunswick* (Yale U, 1966).

[16] *The Staff of Beauty and the Staff of Bands*. Saint John: Church of England Young Men's Society of the City of Saint John, 1847, 14.

[17] *Ibid.*, 12.

[18] *Ibid.*, 13.

[19] *A Lecture . . . Subject "Good Taste."* Saint John, 1857, 21.

[20] *Ibid.*, 18–19.

[21] Northrop Frye, Conclusion to *The Literary History of Canada* (Toronto: U Toronto P, 1965), 830.

[22] *Sir George Parkin* (London: Macmillan, 1929), 26–7.

[23] "The Maid," *The Leather Bottle* (Toronto: Ryerson, 1934), 71. Theodore Goodridge Roberts was lost for a while in the shadow of his brother's fame and in the reaction against the romantic tradition which began with "McGill Movement." He is a fine poet with his own very distinctive voice.

[24] "Love and the Young Knight," *The Leather Bottle*, 65.

[25] See *The Complete Poems of Francis Sherman*, ed. Lorne Pierce (Toronto: Ryerson, 1935). Information about Sherman's search for the title of his volume of poems was derived from his letters in the Hathaway Collection of the Harriet Irving Library, the U of New Brunswick.

[26] *The Friendship of Art*. Boston: L.C. Page, 1903, 265.

[27] "Canada and its Poetry," *The Bush Garden* (Toronto: Anansi, 1971), 134.

[28] *Butterfly on Rock* (Toronto: U Toronto P, 1970), 95–6.

[29] "Transcendentalist Mystic, Evolutionary Idealist: Bliss Carman, 1886–1894," *Colony and Confederation: Early Canadian Poets and Their Background* (Vancouver: UBC P, 1974), 205. The most persuasive study we have yet had of Carman as a serious and consistent thinker. The discussion of "evolutionary idealism" and the comment on Santayana's influence I found particularly helpful.

Sandra Djwa

Canadian Poets and the Great Tradition

In the beginning, as Francis Bacon observes, "God Almightie first Planted a Garden . . . the Greatest Refreshment to the Spirits of Man."[1] It is this lost garden of Eden metamorphosed into the Promised Land, the Hesperides, the El Dorado and the Golden Fleece which dominates some of the sixteenth- and seventeenth-century accounts of the New World reported in Richard Hakluyt's *Principal Navigations, Voyages, Trafiques and Discoveries of the English Nation* (1598–1600) and the subsequent *Purchas His Pilgrimes* (1625). References to what is now Canada are considerably more restrained than are the eulogies to Nova Spania and Virginia; nonetheless there is a faint Edenic strain in the early reports of the first British settlement in the New World.

John Guy implemented the first Royal Patent for settlement at Cupar's Cove, Newfoundland, in 1610, a settlement inspired by Bacon and supported by King James, who observed that the plantation of this colony was "a matter and action well beseeming a Christian King, to make true use of that which God from the beginning created for mankind" (Purchas, XIX). Sir Richard Whitbourne's "A Relation of the New-found-land" (1618) continues in the same Edenic vein as he describes Newfoundland as "the fruitful wombe of the earth":

> Then have you there faire Strawberries red and white, and as faire
> Raspasse berrie, and Gooseberries, as there be in England; as also
> multitudes of Bilberries, which are called by some Whortes, and many
> other delicate Berries (which I cannot name) in great abundance.
> (*Purchas*, XIV)

Many of the first Planters in Canada saw themselves, at least initially, as new Adams beginning again in the garden of the New World reserved by

"God . . . for us Britaines,"[2] which, if not Eden itself, was at least a Golden
Fleece sufficient to show the "wayes to get wealth, and to restore Trading."[3]
Yet, as the first poetry and the journals of exploration assert, the upper half
of North America was not a garden but a wilderness. Newfoundland was
a rocky and unprofitable fishing station, no Eden even for the soaring
flights of the seventeenth century imagination. Hayman in 1628 writes
that the island is "wild, salvage . . . rude, untowardly." As a remedy, he
proposes "neat husbandry," that combination of physical and moral endeavour which will transform a "plain, swarth, sluttish lone" into a virtu-
ous matron, "pretty pert, and neat with good cloathes on."[4] Lacy, writing
a century later in 1729, turns the satirical eye of Restoration comedy on
the bleak land and inhabitants:

> Most that inhabit are a fearful Tribe, / Whose Characters I cannot well
> describe; / Who, like *Siberians*, lonely here reside, / And, in a willing
> Banishment, abide. / It is this sottish People's common use / To warm
> their Veins with an Infernal Juice, / Both Men and Women do this
> Liquor choose, / And rarely keep the Bottle from their Nose.[5]

As Lacy's unpromising reports might indicate, the Adamic impulse which
had led England to foster the plantation of settlers in Newfoundland was
quickly diverted after the first quarter of the seventeenth century into
settlement of the more promising colonies of Virginia and New England.
The consequence for the Canadian section of British North America was a
cultural silence which settled down for almost two hundred years.

ℓ ℏ

As a framework to the literature which was slowly to emerge from these
colonial beginnings, I would like to suggest the following points: first, English Canadian literature has been characterized by a literary dependence
upon British models and by a distinctively moral tone; secondly, the English great tradition, as reflected by Canadian poets, has been essentially
Royalist rather than Puritan; and thirdly, the introduction of Darwinism
into Canada coincided with the emergence of Romanticism. As a result of
all these factors, that vision of nature and of society reflected in English
Canadian poetry differs sharply from that written in the United States or
Great Britain.

Historically, Canadian poetry has been both imitative and didactic. The
first original poetry written in English in the new world, R[obert]
H[ayman]'s *Quodlibets, Lately Come Over From New Britaniola, Old
Newfound-Land* (1628), consisted of "Epigrams and other small parcels,
both Morall and Divine." The first four books of this volume were Hay-

man's, the others were translated from the Latin of the English epigram-
matist, John Owen, and others, concluding with "two Epistles of that
excellently wittie Doctor Francis Rablais." *Quodlibets* is, of course, written from within the seventeenth-century literary tradition which sanctions
both imitation and the moral function of literature. Consequently, it is
questionable whether we can accept Hayman as the progenitor of a distinctively Canadian poetry rather than a minor figure in the British tradition, versifying abroad.

However, this distinction cannot be applied two hundred years later
when the Canadian Oliver Goldsmith (grandnephew of the celebrated Oliver Goldsmith) writes a lengthy narrative poem, *The Rising Village*, to
show the fate of those suffering English countrymen who left the "sweet
Auburn" of his uncle's *The Deserted Village* for North America where
"Wild Oswego spreads her swamps around, / And Niagara stuns with
thundering sound."[6] This poem focuses upon the conquering of the wilderness and the rising of the Canadian village but has an apparently disjointed
middle section, a tale of sweet Flora and her faithless lover Albert. Goldsmith's reasons for including this moral tale of "Vice as a warning to Virtue" are not at all clear until we recognize that "sweet Flora" is analogous
to Wordsworth's "Ruth" and her faithless lover to the impetuous, but
amoral, young man from Georgia's shore. It then becomes apparent that
the purpose of the interlude is to express Goldsmith's Deistic belief that
there is a necessary connection between the ordered laws of nature and the
laws which must control human passion; without such moral dictates the
rising village of Acadia cannot hope to progress in emulation of Britain's
"laws and liberty." As this summary might suggest, the political, moral and
literary aspirations of the young settlement are described by Goldsmith as
immediately directed towards a following of the colonial vision of the British tradition.

Quodlibets and *The Rising Village* may be taken as representative specimens of early Canadian verse until approximately 1890. The emphasis on
moral teaching in relation to the development of community and the as-
criptions of these values to Great Britain is characteristic of later epics such
as Thomas Cary's *Abram's Plains* (1789) and of William Kirby's *The U.E.:
A Tale of Upper Canada* (1859), while the whole question of the social
compact of people, King and God is particularly explored in the heroic
dramas of Charles Heavysege, especially in *Saul* (1857) and *Jephthah's
Daughter* (1865). In addition, much verse written in Canada in the eighteenth and early nineteenth century can be characterized as a response to
the picturesque landscape of Canada filtered through the prevailing British
model. Hayman borrowed from Owen, Goldsmith from his English grand-
uncle, Heavysege from Shakespeare and, on the basis of internal evidence,
from Charles Lloyd's 1815 translations of the Italian dramatist, Alfieri.

Isabella Valancy Crawford and Sir Charles G.D. Roberts, often hailed as Canadian originals, were actually highly indebted to their contemporaries and predecessors. Crawford borrowed from Tennyson, Longfellow and Dante; Roberts' *Orion* (1880) is modelled on the *Orion* (1843) of Richard Henry (later Hengist) Horne, an English Victorian. It is not until E.J. Pratt's parody, *The Witches' Brew* (1925), a farcical inversion of *Paradise Lost*, which manages, incredibly, to combine an Adamic sea-cat, an alcoholic apple, and a satire on Temperance, that Canadian poetry begins to move away from the English stream; significantly, this movement is initiated by parody. Ironically, the book was first published in Great Britain as Pratt's Canadian publisher, Lorne Pierce of Ryerson Press, regretfully refused the manuscript, explaining that this "sparkling" brew was a little too strong for an United Church publishing house.[7]

The most attractive rationale for the general practice of literary imitation is given by Thomas Cary in the preface to his *Abram's Plains*:

> Before I began this Poem I read Pope's Windsor-Forrest and Dr.
> Goldsmith's Deserted Village, with the view of endeavouring, in some
> degree, to catch their manner of writing; as singers in country-churches
> in England, to use a simple musical comparison, modulate their tones
> by the prelusive sound of a pitch-pipe.

The most dogmatic assertion of the Canadian allegiance to the English tradition is given nearly one hundred years later in 1883 by Charles G.D. Roberts, then a rising young poet, in an Alumni Oration at Fredericton entitled "The Beginnings of a Canadian Literature":

> Now it must be remembered that the whole heritage of English Song is
> ours and that it is *not* ours to found *new* literature. The Americans
> have not done so nor will they. They have simply joined in raising the
> splendid structure, English literature, to the building of which may
> come workmen from every region of earth where speaks the British
> tongue.

Implicit here is the assumption that the Canadian poet is addressing himself to an English audience, a pervasive view of the poet's function which would not encourage the development of an indigenous Canadian tradition.

Not only was eighteenth- and nineteenth-century Canadian verse a colonial reflection of the English tradition but it was directed towards one aspect of this tradition which we might provisionally describe as the Royalist strain. Unlike the first poetry of the United States in which the Puritan insistence upon the supremacy of the individual spirit culminated in political and cultural independence, Canadian poetry, which originated in a brief Royalist period and then began again under eighteenth-century Deism, is essentially hierarchical, positing a social compact of subject, King and God, reflecting the monarchical vision of the moral and social order. The first Planters of Newfoundland were prominent Royalists — Lord Baltimore, Lord Calvert, the learned Lord Falkland — and as there was no leavening influx of Puritan immigration, there is no seventeenth-century English Canadian literary heritage of Puritan verse. French Acadia did not become British Nova Scotia until the Treaty of Utrecht (1713) and Quebec did not fall to the English until 1759. Consequently, those English poems produced in the newly conquered Quebec after 1770 are primarily an exposition of eighteenth-century Deism with handy political encomiums to the surpassing virtues of the British monarch, the British moral order and the British God. Furthermore, after 1776 this view of society was substantially reinforced by the wholesale emigration to Nova Scotia and Quebec of some 40,000 United Empire Loyalists who shared the same belief in the essential interdependence of subject, king and state as did their seventeenth-century Royalist forebears. The Loyalist code was, in turn, interpreted by their nineteenth-century descendants (in particular, by William Kirby in *The U.E.: A Tale of Upper Canada*, 1859) as a legacy of moral and social behaviour:

> Religion was with them more deed than word;
> To love their neighbour and to fear the Lord;
> Honour their King and yield his high degree.

As Kirby's epic demonstrates, the Loyalist emigration was to provide the intellectual matrix for the nineteenth-century flurry of Confederation verse which developed between 1860 and 1890 around the political vision of Canada as the "New Nationality" within the "Vaster Britain" or so-called "Imperialist" movement. Because the dominant literary vision of Canadian nature developed during the same period which saw the emergence of the new nationalism, several of the literary nationalists, in particular Charles Mair, Charles Sangster and Charles G.D. Roberts, tended to view Canada's struggle to maintain her political sovereignty against the United States from the perspective of the Darwinian struggle for survival. The encompassing political myth, as Carl Berger has pointed out, proclaimed that Canadians were the "Northmen of the New World," associating freedom, law and moral rectitude with Northern nations (as distinguished from the effete, degenerate South), and maintaining that Canadian freedom and moral order lay in the continued connection with Great Britain.[8] In verse, Mair's drama *Tecumseh* (1886), the Canadian national anthem "O Canada" with its lines "the true north, strong and free," Roberts' meretricious poem "Canada"

("O Child of Nations, giant-limbed"), and W.D. Lighthall's anthology, *Songs of the Great Dominion* (1889) are all reflections of this prevailing Darwinist myth.

ੴ

The framework, then, for the evolution of an English Canadian tradition has been political and cultural; it may be described as "Royalist" in the seventeenth century, "Loyalist" in the late eighteenth century, and "Imperialist" in the latter part of the nineteenth century. After 1870, the dominant thematic concern of the poetry, that vision of moral and social progress which transforms the rude wilderness into the cultivated garden, is to be contained within a modification of Romanticism as dictated by Darwin.

Darwinism had a profound effect on English Canadian Romanticism because *The Origin of Species* (1859) appeared just as the first "native" poetic group, that of the Confederation of 1860 poets, was emerging. Because the Canadian mythos was the product of a hard, sparsely populated country and because the literary vision of Canadian nature developed after Darwin and after the loss of Sir John Franklin at the North Pole, it was already too late in time to gloss successfully the struggle for survival with the Edenic vision of an Emersonian transcendentalism as had been done in the United States some thirty years earlier. As a result, Canadian Romanticism was infused from its inception with overtones of Darwin's nature, an accident of literary history which strongly distinguishes the Canadian view of nature from those of the United States and Great Britain.

Consequently, although the poets of the Confederation do attempt to write in the old Romantic mode — in fact, the transcendental dream is the dominant metaphor of the period — such poetry often breaks from within because it is attempting to hold in reconciliation two opposing views of nature. As we read through the poetry of the 1880's and 1890's we can see the Roberts' uneasy reconciliation between the Romantic world spirit and the Darwinian germ of life must ultimately break down, as it later does, into glimpses of a fearful and amoral nature in the poetry of Archibald Lampman and Duncan Scott. By the mid–1890's, especially in the poetry of Lampman and Scott, the dream as metaphor has become an indicator of a schism in Romantic sensibility because it functions in a failed attempt to transcend a Darwinian world. Still later, in Duncan Campbell Scott's poem "The Height of Land" (1916), the transcendent vision becomes a "Something [that] comes by flashes" and the poet's eye is directed out towards the Northern landscape:

> Upon one hand
> The lonely north enlaced with lakes and streams,

And the enormous targe of Hudson Bay,
Glimmering all night
In the cold arctic light. . .

The earlier, Darwinist-inspired, political vision of Canada as a Northern land is to continue into the 1920's and 1930's with the efforts of the *Canadian Forum* to promote a new and virile art worthy of the young and powerful Canadian nationality. This new art had already been signalled by the strong Northern landscapes of the Group of Seven and was soon to be paralleled in poetry by E.J. Pratt's "Newfoundland," by A.J.M. Smith's "The Lonely Land," and by F.R. Scott's "North Stream." This new Canadian nature described by Smith as "The beauty of strength / broken by strength / and still strong" first appears in Pratt's *Newfoundland Verse* (1923). The title lyric asserts the powerful crash of sea on rock and presents a people as strong as the nature they resist. The tides of Newfoundland flow

   with a lusty stroke of life
   'Pounding at stubborn gates,
   That they might run
   Within the sluices of men's hearts.

In Pratt's view, man, evolving from the sea, still carries part of the sea with him; this primitive inheritance can lead him to fall backward into atavism, or, guided by Christian ethics, he may move forward along the evolutionary road. In his post-Darwinian view of nature and in his stress upon an ethical interpretation of Darwinism, Pratt is characteristic of the Canadian tradition.

That the Darwinian debate in Canada was largely ethical is evident from a survey of articles published in the relatively popular *Canadian Monthly and National Review* for the decade 1872–1882.[9] Articles such as "Darwinism and Morality," "The Evolution of Morality," "The Ethical Aspects of Darwinism: A Rejoinder," and "Evolution and Immortality," indicate that the Canadian attempt to adapt evolutionary theory to existing religious and social structures is far closer to the English debate between Darwinism and religion which culminated in T.H. Huxley's "Evolution and Ethics" (1893), than it is to the popular reception given to Herbert Spencer's "survival of the fittest" in the United States during the same period. For example, Goldwin Smith's essay, "The Prospect of a Moral Interregnum," which developed one aspect of Spencer's *The Data of Ethics*, was largely accepted when published in the United States in the *Atlantic Monthly* in 1879; in Canada, it was greeted with a storm of protest when re-published in the same year in *Rose-Belford's Canadian Monthly and National Review.*

The poetry of the period manifests a similar yoking of evolution and ethics. Isabella Valancy Crawford's poem, *Malcolm's Katie* (1883), may be read as a rejoinder to Goldwin Smith's essay "Pessimism" of 1880, also reprinted in *Canadian Monthly*. Smith had introduced Hume's speculations on a malignant Deity and eloquently described "fatherless" man as "the sport of a blind but irresistible force."[10] Crawford's poem, a Victorian love triangle set against the clearing of the soil and the rising of the Canadian settlement, assigns similarly compelling but ultimately discredited statements to the villain, Alfred,[11] gives the voice of evolutionary progress to the hero Max, and places the whole struggle for survival in the human and natural world within God's hand:

> In trance of stillness Nature heard her God
> Rebuilding her spent fires, and veil'd her face
> While the Great Worker brooded o'er His work.

Equally, in Roberts' poetry and prose we find a consistent attempt to bring the Darwinian struggle under divine plan, as is explicit in the title of his first animal story, "Do Seek Their Meat from God."

E.J. Pratt's relation to the English stream was even closer than that of the poets of the Confederation yet, ultimately, he was to move out of it entirely. Born in 1882 in Newfoundland, then still a British colony for reasons best expressed by that popular Newfoundland ballad, "The Anti-Confederation Song" ("Our hearts turned to Britain, our backs to the gulf / Come near at your peril, Canadian wolf"), Pratt was the son of an English Methodist minister. His early reading included Shakespeare, Carlyle's *French Revolution* and Milton's *Paradise Lost*.[12] But his integral relation to the English stream is best indicated in a cursory survey of his first verse: *Rachel* (1917), a narrative, is a Newfoundland version of Wordsworth's "Michael"; *Clay* (1917), a badly written verse drama, contrasts evolutionary pessimism derivative of Hardy's *The Dynasts* with Christian evolutionary ethics suggestive of "The Paradox" by Alfred Noyes. However, with the parody of *The Witches' Brew* (1925) and the realism of *The Roosevelt and the Antinoe* (1930), Pratt began to move away from the English stream. The latter poem, a moving account of an actual 1926 rescue at sea, seems to have led Pratt away from literary imitation into the documentation of life.

Strongly influenced by his Newfoundland experiences of continued struggle against an implacable nature, a struggle which he characterizes in his "Memories of Newfoundland" (1937) as "the ironic enigma of Nature in relation to the Christian view of the world," and by his early training in theology, much of Pratt's poetry can be seen as the attempt to equip man with an evolutionary ethic to counter Darwin's nature. In an address given at Cornell University during the 1940's he remarked that he could not reconcile the Romantic vision of nature with the Victorian need "to put man in his evolutionary setting." At that time he stated: "We look upon life with the eyes of a Thomas Huxley who saw the ethical and the cosmic in perpetual struggle."

As his acceptance of Thomas Huxley's evolutionary ethics implies, Pratt felt a strong moral revulsion to some of the implications of social Darwinism; in particular, he could not agree with the ethical sanction given by Herbert Spencer to "the survival of the fittest." The early poem, *The Great Feud* (1926), described by him as a "fantastic picture of some stage in the evolutionary struggle for existence," was written "to show how near to extinction a race might come, if the instinct to attack and to retaliate upon attack were given absolute rein without any moral considerations." The poem, an uneasy mixture of jocular beast fable and satiric allegory (of World War I), nonetheless firmly asserts that a perversion of morality and reason, resulting in the destruction of community, must inevitably accompany the survival of the fittest individual. The protagonist of this poem, a female ape, "the cleverest of her time," distorts both truth and a newly evolved moral law as she takes upon herself "the strain / Of descent." This punning conclusion to *The Great Feud* implies not only the ape's descent to a neighbouring valley where her brood lies hidden, but also the perverted "reason" of the descent of evolutionary man.

In his Romances lecture, "Evolution and Ethics," T.H. Huxley had argued "the ethical progress of society depends, not on imitating the cosmic process, ... but in combating it ... by the substitution of what may be called the ethical process; the end of which is not the survival of those who may happen to be the fittest, ... but of those who are ethically the best." It is essentially this view of evolution that E.J. Pratt adopts. The whole struggle on the *Titanic* (of the 1935 poem of the same name) is summarized in the conflicting impulses of the passengers just before the ship goes down: "self-preservation fought / Its red primordial battle with the 'ought'." Red and primordial, this battle is an internalization of the struggle of the survival instinct against the ethical sense. Similarly, the significance of Brébeuf's magnificent endurance under torture in the 1940 epic, *Brébeuf and his Brethren*, is the triumph of moral man in moral community against amoral nature; in the largest sense it is an allegory of western man at the outset of World War II.

Huxley had also suggested in the Romances lecture: "It may seem an audacious proposal thus to pit the microcosm against the macrocosm; and to set man to subdue nature to his higher ends." In "The Truant" (1943), Pratt's most characteristic poem, this ethical paradigm is explored. Here, the microcosm, truant man, is pitted against the macrocosm of the natural order (or cosmic process) jocularly described by Pratt as "a grand Panjandrum" (a false God or pretender to power). Opposing the natural process of mere survival, the truant affirms the grandeur and spiritual dignity of man's heroism in the service of the Christian ideal. In the last epic, *Towards the Last Spike* (1952), a narrative of the building of the Canadian Pacific Railway, Pratt turns back to the concerns of the earliest pioneer poetry, the conquering of the land. With this poem, Pratt's evolutionary thought moves full-circle: from Huxley's dominantly pessimistic view of natural process (as expressed in the first narratives) to a dominantly optimistic view of the relation between man and nature in *Towards the Last Spike*. This optimistic view of evolution is highly suggestive of Jan Christian Smuts' *Holism and Evolution* (1926). Smuts had argued that all parts of the evolutionary process work for the good of the whole, whether the organism is rock, cell, man, or the nation state. By adapting Smuts' holism in *Towards the Last Spike* (especially as revealed in the metaphors of metamorphosis which transform Scots labourers to Laurentian rock), Pratt is able to integrate man with nature. Man, composed of the same elements as the rest of nature, is also equipped with "Mind" which, in Smuts' view, has the capacity for directing ethically the whole. As in the earlier poem *The Roosevelt and the Antinoe*, the ethical triumph is the result of human co-operation as opposed to Darwinistic competitive individualism. It is characteristic of Pratt's poetry that there are no individuals as such; even Brébeuf is generic man, and representative of group idealism. Pratt's insistence on man's capacity to make an ethical choice and so shape his own evolutionary development, is as representative of the Canadian interpretation of Darwinism as Robinson Jeffers' pessimism regarding human progress and his insistence on man's depravity is characteristic of the American.

In his presentation of a moral and hierarchical society, Pratt reflects the historical development of English Canadian poetry. His poetry, from *Newfoundland Verse* (1923) to *Towards the Last Spike* (1952), spans, both topographically and aesthetically, Canada's development from colony to nation, from the Newfound-Land origins of Hayman's *Quodlibets* (1628), still firmly rooted in the English tradition, to the entry of British Columbia into Confederation in 1871 and the beginnings of a distinctively Canadian view of nature. Darwin's nature and T.H. Huxley's cosmology may have provided the intellectual outlines of Pratt's poetic world, but Canadian history, Canadian geography and Canadian cultural experience, as well as Pratt's good heart and his moral vision, give substance to this world. The major narratives, *Brébeuf and His Brethren, Behind the Log, Dunkirk* and *Towards the Last Spike*, all recapitulate Canadian experience — the struggle against the wilderness, the building of the railroad which united the country, Canadian participation in the Second World War — in terms which Canadians have understood and with which they have identified. It may be that the evolutionary myth is particularly suited for adoption by a developing country where the vision of progress still remains a powerful one and where the struggle against nature has always been a constant feature of life.

Notes

1   Francis Bacon, "Of Gardens," *Essayes or Counsels, Civill and Morall.*
2   William Vaughan, *The Golden Fleece*, 1626.
3   *Ibid.*
4   R[obert] H[ayman], *Quodlibets, Lately Come Over from New Britaniola, Old Newfound-Land*, 1628.
5   B. Lacy, "A Description of Newfoundland," *Miscellaneous Poems*, 1729.
6   Goldsmith quotes these lines from his uncle's "The Traveller," in his introduction to *The Rising Village and Other Poems*, 1834.
7   Letter from Lorne Pierce to E.J. Pratt, Lorne Pierce Collection, Douglas Library, Queen's University.
8   Carl Berger, "The True North Strong and Free," *Nationalism in Canada*, ed. Peter Russell. Toronto: McGraw Hill, 1966.
9   Index to the *Canadian Monthly and National Review* and *Rose-Belford's Canadian Monthly and National Review*, Marilyn G. Flitton, "The Canadian Monthly, 1872–1882," unpublished M.A. thesis, Simon Fraser U, 1973.
10 Goldwin Smith, "Pessimism," *Rose-Belford's Canadian Monthly and National Review*, IV (March 1880).
11 Isabella Valancy Crawford, "Malcolm's Katie," *Old Spookses' Pass, Malcolm's Katie and Other Poems*, 1884. Alfred's assertions regarding human mutability and the existence of earlier worlds, now destroyed, are directly suggestive of the arguments of Lucifer in Byron's *Cain* (1821). In effect, Crawford merges Lucifer's Manicheanism with Darwinian pessimism.
12 Henry W. Wells and Carl F. Klinck, *Edwin J. Pratt, the Man and his Poetry*. Toronto: Ryerson, 1947.

CL 65 (Spring 1975)

George Bowering

Why James Reaney is a Better Poet:
(1) than any Northrop Frye Poet
(2) than he used to be

By now it is apparent that the mainstream of today's Canadian poetry (in English) flows in the same river-system as the chief American one — that (to change figures of speech in mid-stream) nurtured first-hand or second-hand by followers of William Carlos Williams and Ezra Pound. The *Contact* people in Toronto of the 1950s, and the *Tish* people in Vancouver of the 1960s are in the middle of what has been happening in Canadian poetry, mid-wars.

But there is a small group of poets in Ontario who arose after World War II, and who remain outside the contemporary mainstream. They may be said to descend not from Williams and Pound, but from T.S. Eliot and Robert Graves, especially, to bring it on home, as those figures from an earlier time are reflected in the literary theory of Northrop Frye of the University of Toronto. The poetry produced by this group has not had any noticeable influence on younger Canadian poets and their magazines, possibly because it takes literary criticism as an important source; it tends to find its audience in the universities of Canada, or more precisely, of Upper Canada. To speak of something perhaps not as relevant, the work of these poets looks more British than American — one could say more bookish than American.

The poets I am writing of are Jay Macpherson, Douglas Le Pan, and James Reaney. Eli Mandel was once drafted into this tradition by some critics, but has lately opted out. James Reaney, as I will want to show, is also of late finding a separate way.

Northrop Frye has written a lot of literary theory, which is best known from his *Anatomy of Criticism*. A few years ago he chose to popularize his critical thoughts in a short series of CBC talks, published by the CBC as *The Educated Imagination*, which title suggests one main belief to be found in the poetry written by the members of the "Frye School," that they are dealing with a knowledgeable and critical rendering of discoveries made through the imagination, usually thought of in terms of archetypal mythology.

There, too, is their principal weakness and contradiction, that while they want to tap the enormous resources of the unconscious to body forth their poetry, they appear rather as super-conscious and architectural poets, making verses with too much obvious eye for critical theory. Critical theory of Frye's sort is interesting as long as it remains a game (in the philosophical sense) but when it begins to shape poetry, then it defeats its own proclaimed premises, as the unconscious becomes a thing mocked. Poets who operate this way can look like upper-middle-class adults doing teenage dances at a rock-blues dance.

But I will look at Frye's *Educated Imagination*, and some of the poems of the "mythopoeic" poets, and see whether and how Frye's pronouncements describe (or prescribe) what has been happening.

ও

Frye's major concerns, of course, seem dated, no matter what truth may lie in them. They are filled with nostalgia for the critical rape of the unconscious that happened in the 1920s and 1930s. And they are sometimes, for all Frye's talk of the imagination, quite turgidly clerical.

The first thing man notices, says Frye, is that nature is objective, apart from man's sense of himself. Then he makes or sees a series of consequent splits, between his emotions and his intellect, between the world a man lives in and the world he wants to live in. So man sets to work in this context and tries to make the world over, to create a humanized world. Frye seems to me to be calling for the maker as one who imposes his desires on the world of nature — and that is the conventional Christian/Western conception, regarding the settlement of America, for instance.

Developing his argument in a classical way, Frye then speaks of a third level of the mind, beyond the simply emotional or intellective levels — the imagination, where a man sees a vision or a model of a world beyond present accomplishments. That vision has nothing to do with time, with the future. It is nothing like the scientist's or engineer's plan, which is only a progressive improvement of the present accomplishments. Literary people, says Frye, are left in the cold by things, like science, that evolve. Artists could never run the objective world. Poets are superstitious, living by the evidence of their senses — a flat earth, for example. As in most of his pronouncements Frye is here half right, as Freud was. He agrees with Freud in associating the artistic and neurotic minds. He agrees with many other professors that the artist has to be a luddite. The "limit of the im-agination is a totally human world," he says, but here he is led astray by his original opposition of human and objective, the subject-object split, which may be conceived only by the self-appointed "subject."

So he says that the poet's job "is not to describe nature, but to show you a world completely absorbed and possessed by the human mind." This is where the poets of the Frye school are outside the Canadian mainstream. A poet who would possess the world with his mind writes his poetry from the mind, the possessor. He begins by subjecting the rest of his faculties and responses to the admiral mind. Get a hold on yourself, is his advice to himself. Then reach for everything else. The ego rules, or thinks it does. As Eliot treated history, Frye's poet would treat nature, as organizer and pos-sessor of it. Today my quatrains, tomorrow the world. This is different from the poets outside this particular myth — they would rather become possessed *by* nature, to *discover* their natures, by exploring with all their faculties, the mind as one among them. Frye speaks many times of the poet seeking identity of mind with nature. The un-Fryed, or "raw" poet, is likely to *surrender* identity (as in a psychedelic awakening) as a step toward communion with the rest of his self (see Whitman's use of that last word).

Frye tells how his poets (he tends to generalize his ideas to cover all poets) seek identity of mind and nature. Men create gods, creatures who are simi-lar to both men and objective nature — hence the wind-god and the wolf-god. Then when men no longer believe in those creatures, they become part of literature. Poets, says Frye, do not literally believe the things they write, but rather make codes. When, as with Hemingway and his bullfights, the writer seems to believe in the truth of his rituals, Frye says that he is ac-tually imitating previous literature. Frye would not accept that Allen Gins-berg actually saw the face of Moloch on the skyscraper wall. But Jay Macpherson, Frye's most ardent follower, obviously agrees that the names and events in poems are myth-charactered codes of experience:

> I'm Isis of Sais,
> If you'd know what my way is,
> Come riddle my riddle-mi-ree.

Frye's point is that Aristotle's arrangements hold; there is a universe of things and a universe of ideas, and a universe of literature. To write litera-ture, the poets draw from the universe of literature. Forms, he says, come only from earlier literature, but by forms he appears to mean ideas and events. (He says that Canadian writers imitate the models of D.H. Lawrence and W.H. Auden — and he says this on the radio in 1962! His being that far out of touch with Canadian writing helps to explain the distaste for Frye among most Canadian writers.)

I don't want to give the impression that I thoroughly disapprove of all that Frye says. I agree with many of his words. He seems to agree with Williams, for instance, by saying that "it isn't what you say but how it's said that's important," but then he moves to something I can't agree with when he speaks of poets' *"transferring* their language from direct speech to the imagination." (Italics mine.) Once again the human mind as separate from and superior to the materials of the natural universe.

Primitives feared the animals and their spirits, so they donned their skins in dance and poetry. Frye would say that we now make poetry by pretending to do the same thing, while scientists and others study primitives and animals among other things. But today we fear our own technology and not nature, because we have subdued and understood nature, or so we are told. In modern dance and poetry it is the skin of the technology we wear, including the skin of Relativity and Quantum. The poets are the unacknowledged shamans of the world. They do not get their forms from literary code alone. Literature is not myth with belief removed, though it may be written as though it were, as witness Miss Macpherson.

Frye says that the great theme of English poetry is the desire to regain paradise, and James Reaney says that is what Jay Macpherson is trying to do. The poet who wants to possess the world with his mind often writes of that desire as his subject material. The poets who want to become possessed *act* like primitives, hoping to know paradise in their poetic forms, all the faculties engaged, as in dance with music and incense. It is not what you say that's important but how you say it. The poetry of Eliot's age and mode was ironic in tone as it spoke *of* the terror in this fallen world outside paradise.

So the raw poets think of poetry's words as action, often ritual action. Frye's poet thinks of it as code of thought. In Frye's view, characters in literature are different from characters in history in that they are typical or universal manifestations, representatives, representing parts of our lives. Allegory has crept in. All images are symbols — Frye says that. Williams distrusted symbolism as an act of the overbearing intellect. To go to the extreme of this line of thinking, Frye says that knowledge of literature cannot grow without knowledge of the main stories in the Bible and classical literature. That would come as a surprise to many readers of the *Tale of Genji*. Of course Frye probably had only a Western literate in mind. That is one of the limitations of his argument.

I have said something to the effect that Frye sees the poet gathering materials of life, nature, literature, to himself and his poem, much as Eliot's persona is seen trying to do at the end of *The Waste Land*, and that the raw poets see it another way around. It is not surprising then, that Frye embraces the old favourite notion of the writer's detachment, that he favours things in literature to be removed just out of reach of action and belief. Of course we know that we are hearing about two ways of viewing poetry written, when we hear from Frye and his opposites. Frye could likely make a logical case for Blake as detached, much to the dismay of some other writers.

I think, though, that we can fault Frye especially for his generalizing on the process of writing literature. Related to that is his overstressing of literature as inspiration for literature. (Much of important new writing may be seen as attempt to provide alternative for literature.) And related to that is his confusion between the writing of lyric and the writing of its criticism. Anyone who has too much Graves and Frye on the mind might plead for myth rather than creating it, asking readers to see with the eye rather than through it. Witness Jay Macpherson, who often jams together homely observations and spooned-on myth-figures:

> My mother was taken up to heaven in a pink cloud.
> My father prophesied,
> The unicorn yielded to my sweetheart,
> The white bull ran away with my sister,
> The dove descended on my brother,
> And a mouse ran away in my wainscot.

Why, no one ever sees or mentions a "wainscot" in Canada!

☙

But in the frye mind, literature is a game. Literature, says Frye, has no moral referent (all these remarks are secularizations or diminishings of Keats' remarks about the poetical character), and so in that endless debate about the topic, he stands opposed to Pound and Williams and their followers, tenuous as that following may be. In fact he goes so far as to say that "literature has no consistent connection with ordinary life, positive or negative," though later he calls the world of literature a model to be striven after. (But the self-contradictions in Frye have been a topic of conversation in the learned journals ere now.) He carries on the closet fiction of the New Criticism, the idea that the poem is entirely self-contained, which may be a good system for criticism, but lousy for literature. As a poet, I feel it impossible to agree with Frye that my writing looks either up toward heaven or down to hell, never horizontally at life. I find that horizontal view possible as soon as my self begins to expand outside the bounds of the ego, the "subject."

But literature, says Frye, is there to refine the sensibilities, always with knowledge of the artifice foremost. That is literature as a game. Games have counters, players, rewards, all totally symbolic, with no referents save in the psyche. The reader, as well as the literary character, exists "only as a representative of humanity as a whole." So it is that Jay Macpherson may declare that her first person in the poem is Isis. I find that a reasonable stance, but shallow compared with Olson's "Maximus" or Williams' "Paterson" — and I will not accept it as the only possible way. I think Raymond Souster, for example, walks through the Toronto streets of his poems in no one's skin but his own, perceived through, not by, the literary imagination.

But, says Frye, "how dangerous the emotional response is, and how right we are to distrust it." Distrust rhetoric, his opposers would say, for he does not, and distrust reason at least more than you distrust emotion. Emotion, at least, makes for better dance, and the primitive mind is in the head of the best dancer in the world. Frye is right to say that poetry is the first primitive writing, but he wants, he says, a poetry of impersonal nexus, the poem as dance removed from the dancer. The beginning of reason, where it is not primarily intuitive, causes awkward stumbling, as seen in the poetry of Auden or Spender.

Or of Jay Macpherson, for instance. Her verses tend toward closed form, with the ever-present threat of disorder — that is fine, a creditable imitation of the primitive. But the jungle dance seeks to evoke a favourable response from nature (external or internal), not to cow it. Miss Macpherson's syntax and vocabulary are awkwardly and deliberately "literary," poetic diction as an attempt to make magic — thus to impose her will on nature. The ordering ego hulks over Miltonic inversions:

> In the snake's embrace mortal she lies,
> Dies, but lives to renew her torment,
> Under her, rock, night on her eyes.
> In the wall around her was set by one
> Upright, staring, to watch for morning
> With bread and candle, her little son.

There is no doubt that Miss Macpherson is Frye's most faithful follower (her book is dedicated to him), especially concerning his notion that all literature is imitation of earlier literature. In reading a poem such as her "The Marriage of Earth and Heaven," one encounters metrics and philosophy copied from an earlier century.

But I don't find a real encounter with myth. Such real encounter would be a here-now fright or swoon or rapture. Myth is the imaginative base of culture, and culture is not alive if it is not being formed with the materials and shapes available to the senses. The literary mind thinks about past culture, but to copy the modes of past culture is to give oneself over to time, where gods and giants are only reported, never met. They must be met in the here and now, where their faces and limbs are seen through eternity's film. (In "The Rhymer" Miss Macpherson uses 1940 slang in the 1950s, and is false even to time.) Miss Macpherson should look to Robert Duncan, the great American Romantic, who understands these things in his poems of Osiris and Set, not as literary gentlemen but as fleshy shadows in his room's corners.

In his article[1] on Jay Macpherson's book, James Reaney says that she is trying to return to Paradise, an effort that fits into one of the major themes of English poetry. But Paradise is straight ahead, not somewhere on the trail we have made since the Fall. (Incidentally, in that article Reaney points out the most important contribution of Miss Macpherson, her attempt to make a book rather than a collection of poems. The suite of poems was a valuable artistic innovation in Canada, and Miss Macpherson and James Reaney seem to have led the way with theirs.)

Reaney also mentions Miss Macpherson's care for the "myth of things within things" — which may be a way of avoiding the horizontal view, but which may also be an illusion disguising a bookish isolation. The poet makes the choice of either the easy acceptance of that old pattern or trying to make metaphor from contemporary discoveries and views, in his own skin.

I catch, in the poetry of Miss Macpherson, as well as in that of Le Pan and Reaney, Frye's disinterest in or distrust for science and technology. The poets in what I've called the Canadian mainstream hearken in their various imaginations to Whitman's decree that science and art are no enemies, which extends from Blake's pronouncement that the body and the spirit are one.

Douglas Le Pan gives his view of the result of man's technology in his poem "Image of Silenus," where in contrast to the wilds he sees the city, and calls on his reader to look at how men shrink the gods in themselves, to

> See them, the shrunken figures of desire,
> Swarming complete as when they were first here deposited,
> But not heroic, filling all the sky,
> Miniatures rather, toys in a toy shop window.

There is Eliot's detestation of his surroundings, which is finally a detestation of self, a useful Christian emotion, but poor starting view for a poet, unless he really does feel that literature looks only up or down, in this case down, where "The figures fashioned out of desperation / . . . all throng behind the ironic mask." The pun says that our technology will not permit myth-figures anywhere but in literature. The romantic fallacy holds that the city destroys magic, a sentimental and reactionary view. I suspect that Douglas Le Pan doesn't like Marshall McLuhan's books, for the wrong reasons.

The opposition of wild nature and ugly city, and the diminishing of myth are two consistent themes in Le Pan's poetry. He seems to be resentful that the Canadian forests were not found filled with nymphs and sprites and their chroniclers. In "A Country Without a Mythology" he begins to lament that no mythology has been fashioned, as "No monuments or landmarks guide the stranger," but a reader begins later to see that it is history that's not here in (presumably) frontier Canada, that mythology dances in its wild danger, figured by a war-painted "lust-red manitou." God enough for any land. But there Le Pan is stuck, in the wilds. Canada confronts the explorer with waterfalls and tangled forests that a man must find his mind in. Le Pan seems to be trying to do what Frye suggested — to identify himself or his mind with the external world, to choose where he will pretend that he sees gods. As man separates his self and the "objects" of his sight, he here separates the areas of those "objects," into untouched nature, to which the poets looks upward, and the city of man's technology, to which he looks down, with irony.

In falling easily to the romantic fallacy (truth and beauty and innocence in nature — all opposite in cities), Le Pan (punning on his name?) also takes refuge in literature as alternative to common life, answering another Frye description and stepping out of the mainstream, into the forest preserve.

I invite you to read these titles: *The Boatman*, *The Net and the Sword*, *The Wounded Prince*, *A Suit of Nettles*. They all make reference to standard literary myth, hoping to suggest universal archetypes. But any reader knows that he has to be prepared by books to know what the universalities are, before reading the poems. In so doing he knows that he has made himself a specialist. He is aware of that irony. He is so aware due to the knowledge in his conscious and civilized mind that has forever removed all possibility of stepping into the world of the child or the primitive. That is likely why Frye thinks that poetry is myth with belief removed.

⚃

James Reaney was once a Fryed poet (*A Suit of Nettles*, 1958), but has in most recent years broken loose to make myth from local materials rather than spooning it on from the golden bowl of literary materials. In the later poems and theatrical experiments he has sought a way of understanding myth and myth-making not as alternative to history and politics and commerce and city-planning, but as the register made on the emotions and unreason by all those things. He is not the reader encountering Icarus in

book or painting, and observing his after-images in contemporary flights
and minds. He observes the materials in Winnipeg or Stratford, and shines
the infra-red light on them, revealing their own vibrations that are in the
present act of producing myth. He is the man on the ground, seeing Icarus
while he flies, and understanding the meaning without gloss.

The process really got under way, I believe, in *Twelve Letters to a Small
Town*, and has continued, despite misunderstanding by CBC actors, in the
recent radio suites, and is best apprehended in the latest forms Reaney uses
— amateurs and children, the actual human materials produced by the
soil, speaking the words discovered by both the poet and themselves, not
simonized by the wax of literature.

Reaney begins to move beautifully away from Frye's strictures with the
first quatrain in *Twelve Letters to a Small Town* (Reaney may deny all
this), where the poet tries to see under the literary name laid on the "Avon
River Above Stratford, Canada":

> What did the Indians call you?
> For you do not flow
> With English accents.
> I hardly know
> What I should call you
>   Because before
> I drank coffee or tea
>   I drank you
>   With my cupped hands
> And you did not taste English to me

I find two things important here — the *personal* pronoun and the determination to find myth with the senses, the taste of water in cupped hands,
not the idea of a sacred Greek or English stream. So that when Reaney
comes to say

> The rain and the snow of my mind
> Shall supply the spring of that river
>   Forever

he has moved inside, he has made the world human, as Frye would say, but
he has done so by finding out that what is human is in the world as surely
as the stream's water is in his body, here and now. Not Noah of the book,
but Reaney of the river, is the prototype of this myth's beginning (and
middle, anyway).

And that river, the river running through Stratford, runs into the Canadian mainstream at last, enriching it. Not that this is final aspiration or

subjective concept of good. Just a view of how it is to this horizontal sight.

Notes

[1] James Reaney, "The Third Eye: Jay Macpherson's *The Boatman*," *Canadian Literature* 3 (Winter 1960): 23–34.

CL 36 (Spring 1968)

Robin McGrath

Reassessing Traditional Inuit Poetry

In July of 1745, Dr. Samuel Johnson, as virtual editor of *The Gentleman's Magazine*, published a "Greenland Ode," an Eskimo-language poem with an English translation (qtd. in Sherbo 575). This ode celebrates the birthday of King Christian of Denmark, and was the first Inuit poem to be available to the English-speaking world. In the two and a half centuries since the "Greenland Ode" appeared, more and far better Inuit poetry has been published, but it has received little scholarly attention. Only Rudy Wiebe's article in *Canadian Literature*, "Songs of the Canadian Eskimo," and a handful of articles by the anthropologist Sven Frederiksen, make any attempt to examine this aspect of Inuit culture.

Canadian scholars and teachers have been curiously reluctant to approach Inuit poetry on any level, perhaps because they think they will not understand it. This paper will look at the history of Inuit poetry in English, and will examine a number of fairly typical poems in an effort to show that Inuit poems in English are not just anthropological enigmas, but are works that are accessible to anyone who brings curiosity and a little imagination to their reading of poetry.

Inuit song is immensely old, but it has only really been available to English-language readers in any quantity since 1925 when Diamond Jenness published *Songs of the Copper Eskimos* (Roberts and Jenness), an academic work with interlinear translations from the Inuinaqtung dialect. Jenness was not a poet, nor was he fluent in Inuktitut, and it is clear that he realized the limitations of his translation, yet many of the works are deeply moving and powerful. Vilhjalmur Stefansson made an attempt to popularize the works in 1929, and he arranged for a Canadian singer, Juliette Gaultier de la Verendrye, to sing them at Town Hall in New York. She performed against a backdrop of totem poles and aurora borealis, and although the *New York Times* reported that the songs were very well received, being "decidedly melodious and an entire novelty to the audience" ("Songs of the Copper Eskimos Given"), there was no sudden recognition of the joys of Inuit poetry on the part of the general reading public.

Knud Rasmussen's massive *Report of the Fifth Thule Expedition*, with its extraordinary collection of songs and legends from across 5,000 miles of Arctic coastline, appeared in ten volumes between 1928 and 1945. Rasmussen was not just an accomplished linguist, theologian and ethnographer, but was also an Inuit poet himself. In addition, he was highly photogenic, and perhaps because of his native background he attracted considerable attention from the press; but unfortunately Rasmussen died the year after returning from the expedition, leaving his work incomplete. After a brief popularity, the poetry he translated was ignored. The translations he produced are likely never to be rivalled, and he set the standard by which all subsequent translations and collections of Inuit poetry are measured, but English readers still had not acquired a taste for work that was ambiguously labelled "primitive" even by its promoters.

In recent years, traditional Inuit song has fared somewhat better. During the 1950s, Edmund Carpenter wrote an article for Marshall McLuhan's journal, *Explorations*, in which he drew upon the Jenness material; and he followed this with *Anerca*, a small volume of Rasmussen's translations, in 1959. Inuit poems were often included in collections of Indian poetry in the 1960s, and volumes of Inuit poetry were edited by Lewis in 1971, Houston in 1972, Lowenstein in 1973, and Hoffman in 1974. In 1976, Rasmussen's ten-volume *Report* was reprinted at prohibitive cost, and in 1981 John Robert Colombo edited *Poems of the Inuit*, a compilation of some of the best of the ethnographic collections. Colombo's meticulous and sensitive editing and his discussion of Inuit poetics now make it possible to introduce these works to students at the high-school or university level.

There has been a tendency for those writing about Inuit poetry to stress the magical, ritualistic, and musical aspects of the compositions, or to assure the readers that if the poems do not make any narrative or lineal sense that is because they are not intended to. The implication is that for Inuit poets, how a thing is said is more important than what is said. There is some truth in this assertion, but it is usually taken too far. The poems are songs and in many cases the music predominates, so that when it is removed or lost, what is left is sparse and repetitive. In many of the incantations, the meaning is deliberately obscured or key words were changed when the chants were sold or given to the collectors. Sometimes an anthropological knowledge of the culture is needed for the reader to be able to decode the embedded meaning and the obscure metaphors used by Inuit poets. However, many Inuit poems, possibly even the majority, are quite straightforward and can be read and understood with very little effort by English speakers.

 times

Rasmussen identified four basic categories of Inuit poetry: songs of mood, hunting songs, charms, and songs of derision. These four categories are not mutually exclusive; it is possible for a hunting narrative to be combined with the philosophical musings of a mood poem, but identifying the dominant thrust of the works makes it a little easier to understand them. The following four extracts from sample poems give some idea of what can be found in Inuit poetry. The first, "Ptarmigan," is a mood poem. Mood poems are songs of reflection which do not involve a central story or action; they are like Imagist poems which try to give a visual impression which involves the perception of relationships. This particular example, by the poet Umanatsiaq, has an unexpected though typical twist:

> On the top of a snowdrift
> In the tundra
> Stood a little ptarmigan
>
> Its eyelids were red,
> Its back was brown,
> And right between its buttocks
> Sat the sweetest little arse. (Lowenstein 51)

This poem has been the subject of considerable discussion among Danish scholars. Inuit poems are frequently very literal and it is all too easy to develop complex interpretations that cannot be justified. In the case of "Ptarmigan," it is best to concentrate on the almost photographic detail used to convey the mood in the poem.

The ptarmigan's brown back indicates that, despite the presence of a snowdrift, summer is finally on its way. The ptarmigan is an amusing little bird, and a fine harbinger of spring, and after a long, dark winter the sight of its back feathers turning from white to brown might very well produce one of those moments Wordsworth called "spots of time." It doesn't do to wax too lyrical, though; the poem might be better understood if you see Inuit smacking their lips over the last line. A ptarmigan's *itiq* might more properly be translated into English as a "pope's nose" or a "parson's nose" rather than the cruder "arse" that is usually used. The *itiq* on a ptarmigan is a sweet, literally sweet, oily morsel that is greatly appreciated by gourmets. Umanatsiaq was likely aiming a rock at the bird as he admired it and composed his song, just as William Carlos Williams reached for the plums with one hand and the pen with the other.

Charms and incantations are often fragmented, incomprehensible, or in magical language; they are similar to nonsense verse, sound poetry, or even concrete poetry, where the form the poem takes dominates its meaning. "Who Comes" is a classic; it is credited by Carpenter to Ohnainewk, who recited it on his death bed, but Colombo points out that it is a variation of a longer poem, "Against Sickness," known among the Greenland Eskimos (Colombo 113).

> Who comes?
> It is the hound of death approaching
> Away!
> Or I will harness you to my team. (Colombo 100)

This poem or chant is relatively simple; it follows the traditional dialogue or question/answer sequence of the song-duel or flyting; it makes reference to the dog-husband of the sea goddess Nuliajuk (also called Sedna), who fathered the people of this world, and it pivots on the use of dogs for transportation, a cultural practice not used extensively anywhere in the world except the Arctic. But a reader needn't know any of this to appreciate this little poem. When the hound of death comes for us, be it Cerberus or some domestic mutt of our own imagining, we would all like to be able to challenge him so boldly.

Hunting songs can be reflective but are more likely to be narrative and full of incident. Success in the hunt is a favourite theme of Inuit song and for Orpingalik it is his life. The great hunter had been seriously ill and composed the poem "My Breath" during a fit of despondency. In a widely quoted remark, he explained that he called the poem "My Breath" because "it is just as necessary for me to sing as it is to breathe" (Colombo 109). Internally, however, the poem reveals a strong emotional connection between hunting and sexuality. Orpingalik sees the polar bear's attack as a challenge to his manhood, claiming that the bear "really believed / He alone was a male," and the seal he recalls harpooning is also "an old and cunning male." In his depression, he wishes his wife would go to a better man who could be her refuge. He is also surprised at his own reaction to illness:

> Knowest thou thyself?
> So little thou knowest of thyself!
> While dawn gives place to dawn,
> And spring is upon the village. (Colombo 39)

Derisive songs are satiric and are often monologues or dialogues; they are like Old English flyting poems in which verbal assault is part of the intellectual game. Netsit's song, "Men's Impotence," links hunting and sexuality in a derisive song. The full title, given in the literal translation Rasmussen generally provided of his interpretations, is "A Song of Men's Impotence and the Beasts They Hunted." In "Men's Impotence" we meet a hunter who cannot function at all:

> Perhaps — well
> It may not matter!
> Perhaps — well.
> I sing merely of him,
> "The Boiling One,"
> Who sat, fearful, his mouth fast closed,
> Among women. (Colombo 31)

He is isolated, silent, not just fearful but frightful, a danger to others. His face is described in terms of male hunting implements, a mouth bent like a kayak rib, eyes shaped like horn cut into leisters, his mouth is closed fast and his eyes bode ill. Like Wiebe's Almighty Voice, he is described as having a face like an axe. The man who cannot hunt becomes a danger to his fellows, a man who cannot sing becomes a danger to himself, and by implication, a man who cannot love women will hate them.

CB

It is evident even in the four sample poems just discussed that there are thematic links between various types of Inuit poetry. The act of composition is also a major subject of Inuit poetry and is also linked to hunting. Akjartok, like Orpingalik, feels that to breathe is to sing and to sing is to recall the hunt. The poets usually recall killing male animals, which are larger and a real challenge to their prowess. Here is a typical example:

> I call forth the song
> I draw a deep breath
> My breast breathes heavily
> As I call forth the song.
>
> I hear of distant villages
> And their miserable catch
> And draw a deep breath
> As I call forth the song.
>
> I forget altogether
> The heavy breathing of my breast
> When I call to mind the olden days

When I had strength enough
To cut up mighty bulls
I call forth the song.

While the sun was on his upward way
Across the sky
A song I call forth
As I draw a deep breath. (Colombo 44)

Sometimes, of course, the song does not come forth, just as sometimes the seal refuses to surface or the fish refuses to take the hook. Ikinikik sings

I have only my song
Though it too is slipping from me. (Colombo 83)

Ivaluardjuk's lament is that

. . . songs
Call for strength
And I seek after words. (Colombo 43)

Piuvkaq observed that it is

A wonderful occupation
Making songs!
But all too often they
Are failures. (Colombo 36)

In another poem he admits that he prefers fist fighting to singing because

Words melt away
Like hills in fog. (Colombo 41)

Apparently, breaking someone's nose occasionally produces more lasting satisfaction than composing a poem does.

Although these works frequently explore man's sense of fragility and insecurity, images of the land in Inuit poetry provide a sense of stability and continuity. The poet may be overwhelmed by the power of nature, he may not survive his encounters with it, but the land is always there. Kaneyioq begins his chant:

My thoughts went constantly
To the great land
My thoughts went constantly. (Colombo 100)

Padloq's magic charm, to be recited when in sudden danger of death, says:

You earth
Our great earth
See, oh see
All those heaps
Of bleached bones. (Colombo 66)

Uvavnuk's trance song also depicts man as small and insignificant in his confrontation with the land:

The Great Sea
Has set me adrift
It moves me as the weed in the river
Earth and the great weather
Move me
And move my inward parts with joy. (Colombo 21)

Uvavnuk might just as easily have sung Keats's

. . . on the shore
Of the wide world I stand alone, and think
Til Love and Fame to nothingness do sink. (Abrams 1830)

Padloq, too, would have given a nod of recognition to Blake's

Oh Earth, O Earth, return
Arise from out the dewey grass. (Abrams 1327)

Like Wordsworth, whose mountain strode after him "with purpose of its own" (Abrams 1458), Uvunuaq, too, sees the land as reflecting her inner turmoil. When she heard that her son had killed a man, she sang

Earth became like a mountain with pointed peak
And I stood on the awl-like pinnacle
And faltered
And fell. (Colombo 51)

Birney's bushed trapper was not the first Canadian to feel the great flint come singing into his heart.

Death is a frequent theme in Inuit poetry, for obvious reasons, but even this is handled much as it is in some non-Inuit works. Netsit's "Dead Man's Song" and Paulinaq's "Song of Aijut After his Death" both explore fear of death and a simultaneous longing to escape life. Like Archibald Lampman, they imagine what it would be like, but the Inuit composers use stock phrases from the oral tradition and impart their own particular understanding of the experience. Netsit sings:

> I am filled with joy
> When the day peacefully dawns
> Up over the heavens. (Colombo 96)

Paulinaq similarly sings

> I am filled with joy
> When the big sun up there
> Rises up over the vault of the sky. (Colombo 98)

Both tell of feeling the maggots in the hollows of the collarbone, and of being buried in a snow-hut. Paulinaq, however, projects his fears onto the hunter Aijut and does not have the same need as Netsit to end with a consolation or positive statement. He ends as a corpse buried in the igloo:

> And I felt horror
> There on the freshwater ice
> And I felt horror
> When from the great sky out there
> Came the loud cracking of the ice. (Colombo 99)

By dwelling on the horrors of death and his failure to enjoy life, Netsit manages to revive his interest in the new day:

> Now I am filled with joy
> For every time a dawn
> Makes white the sky of night,
> For every time the sun goes up
> Over the heavens. (Colombo 97)

Dawn seems to be a dangerous time for Inuit poets — it can mark the new day, and renewal, but sometimes Nauliajuk's dog husband is referred to as the "hound of dawn" as well as the "hound of death" (Colombo 113), so it has ambiguous implications. Netsit's version of the vision of death, with its question/answer sequence, feels more complete, a true inner-debate, an internal song duel.

The famous satiric song duels, in their purest forms, were a remarkable judicial and cultural achievement but very few examples have survived intact. Perhaps it was because every duel had a winner and a loser and nobody wanted to take the time to memorize a losing song. The satiric songs that have been transcribed and translated into English are often directed against the self. In the Ammassalik Eskimo "Song of an Old Man About His Wife," the poet reflects on the fact that his wife's face, wrinkled and blotched with age, is a mirror of his own, and they are neither of them young and handsome anymore (Lewis 84). In the traditional "Song of Longing" the poet mocks his own infatuation with other men's wives (Colombo 29). In "The Old Woman's Song," the poet mocks her own lost youth and appeal, and sings:

> Virtue is only to be found in old women
> And therefore it is my sorrow
> Oh, I am so sad
> Because I am old. (Colombo 48)

The ability to laugh at one's own sexual intemperance, and to puncture one's own pretentiousness, is something the Inuit poets share with a number of contemporary Canadian poets. Al Purdy, who travelled with the people of Baffin, is one who comes immediately to mind. The composer of "The Old Man's Song," like Purdy, makes fun of his own intellectual musings:

> I have grown old
> I have lived much
> Many things I understand
> But four riddles I cannot solve
>
> The sun's origin
> The moon's nature
> The minds of women
> And why people have so many lice. (Colombo 48)

Of course, Inuit poets frequently mean the opposite of what they say, and when they list all the things they cannot do they are sometimes simply making sure that people know that they are, in fact, highly accomplished men and women who are simply too polite to brag.

⊰⊱

Comparing Inuit poetry to English poetry stresses the universal nature of the works; the world inhabited by the Thule people is far away in time and space, but they were expressing their responses to the human condition in ways that have been used by many other cultures in many other times. Poems about birth, work, sex, and death are bound to touch chords in everyone.

It is well to remember, though, that there is one major difference between the contemporary Canadian poetic tradition and that of the traditional Inuit. Inuit believed in the practical application of poetry. While our own poets composed verses describing their feelings about the weather, Inuit poets believed that if they got the words of their poem just right, they could actually affect the weather. If there is any one cultural element that is foreign to English-language readers, it is this. Our nearest equivalent would be a belief in the efficacy of prayer. Bad weather was more than just an inconvenience to Inuit, and the song that could improve it was often all that stood between life and death. Such a song had as much practical importance as a sharp knife or an antibiotic. When Aua sang "This is blood that flowed from a piece of wood. Dry it up!" (Colombo 59), he believed that the words, and the words alone, could actually stop a wound from bleeding.

Such a belief in the power of words must produce poems of tremendous endurance. A frequently quoted explanation comes from the Inuit explorer and poet Knud Rasmussen:

> These works don't arrive like fragile orchids from the hot houses of professional poets; they have flowered like rough, weather beaten saxifrage which has taken root on rock. And they ought to matter to us. For do we not hear through them something that reminds us of the original features of our own old songs — the same teasing humour, the same quiet melancholia — and sometimes in glimpses, a simple but grandiose pathos which grips us by virtue of its immediacy. (qtd. in Lowenstein 109)

It was this sense of our own tradition that Dr. Johnson recognized when he published the "Greenland Ode," and it is this, too, that Rudy Wiebe and John Robert Colombo hope we will all recognize.

Works Cited

Abrams, M.H., ed. *The Norton Anthology of English Literature: The Major Authors.* New York: W.W. Norton, 1986.

Carpenter, Edmund, ed. *Anerca.* Toronto: J. M. Dent, 1959.

——. "Eskimo Poetry: Word Magic," *Explorations* 4 (1955), 101–11.

Colombo, John Robert, ed. *Poems of the Inuit.* Ottawa: Oberon, 1981.

Hoffman, Charles. *Drum Dance*. Toronto: Gage, 1974.

Houston, James., ed. *Songs of the Dream People*. Don Mills: Longman, 1972.

Lowenstein, Tom, ed. *Eskimo Poems From Canada and Greenland*. London: Anchor, 1973.

Lewis, Richard, ed. *I Breathe a New Song: Poems of the Eskimo*. New York: Simon and Schuster, 1971.

Rasmussen, Knud. *Report of the Fifth Thule Expedition — The Danish Ethnographical Expedition to Arctic North America*, 1921–24. 10 vols. Copenhagen: Gylden-dalske Boghandel, Nordisk Forlag, 1928–45.

Roberts, Helen H., and Diamond Jenness. *Songs of the Copper Eskimos*. Ottawa: King's Printer, 1925.

Sherbo, Arthur. "The Making of *Ramblers* 186 and 187," *PMLA* 67 (1952), 575–80.

"Songs of the Copper Eskimos Given," *New York Times* (9 April 1927), 7.

Wiebe, Rudy. "Songs of the Canadian Eskimo," *Canadian Literature* 52 (1972), 57–69.

CL 124–125 (Spring-Summer 1990)

David Solway

The End of Poetry

Our native Muse, heaven knows and heaven be praised, is not exclusive.
Whether out of the innocence of a childlike heart to whom all things are
pure, or with the serenity of a status so majestic that the mere keeping
up of tones and appearances, the suburban wonder as to what the strait-
laced Unities might possibly think, or sad sour Probability possibly say,
are questions for which she doesn't . . . in her lofty maturity any longer
. . . care a rap, she invites, dear generous-hearted creature that she is, just
tout le monde *to drop in at any time . . .*
— W.H. AUDEN, *THE SEA AND THE MIRROR*

I.

Despite the state of fratricidal strife that exists among poets and the schools
they are associated with, there is a common and implicit assumption about
the poetic calling in the modern world that unites them. It has now attained to the status of an unchallenged dogma, which can be syllogized as
follows. First, if a poem is to be a vital and meaningful comment on or
analysis of experience, it must to some extent reflect that experience. Secondly, experience in and of the contemporary world is a reductive phenomenon, fragmented, anarchic, pulverized. Consequently, any poem that
pretends to authenticity or authority must reflect the discontinuities of the
life we are compelled to live by virtue of the fact that we are living *now.*

This series of postulates has much to recommend it and is obviously
persuasive. For one thing, who can doubt the critical placebo that poetry
must, in one way or another, reflect the structure, quality, or contours of
the age in which it moves and has its being if it is to retain its vitality?
Otherwise, must it not be hospitalized, kept alive by elaborate life-support
systems, surviving intravenously in a state of archival nostalgia? Poetry

must be *in* its time in order to be *of* its time, and it must be of its time if it
has any intention of lasting since only through a vigorous participation in
the temporal can it presume to achieve eternity.

For another thing, the analysis of contemporary experience as disinte-
grative is now little more than a blatant truism. Hardly anyone questions
any longer the psychological commonplace that a sense of alienation, loss,
and despair is the essential factor in the modern experience of the world.
The only absolute we acknowledge is the speed of light; as for the rest, the
Heraclitean flux has escaped the confines of a pre-Socratic apothegm and
threatens to swamp us all in every aspect of our lives. If God died in the
nineteenth century, as Nietzsche tells us, Religion promptly followed in the
twentieth, taking with it our only viable guarantee of a now mainly worthless moral currency. The spectre of instant annihilation robs us of our seriousness in our dealings with one another and with posterity. Political life
has broken down as has the humanist faith in Reason, and even the ultimate cohesions of speech have been syntactically undermined. It is not just
that monologue has replaced dialogue but that the monologue has become
largely unintelligible. The precarious balance of whatever ecology we wish
to consider has been upset beyond, as many suspect, the possibility of restoration.

If this is the condition of life which the poet confronts, then (assuming
that the creative élan has not abandoned him, that he has not been reduced
to silence, which may be the only honest response to such irremediable
devastation) it follows that the poem he sets about composing, repressing
the conviction of its futility beneath the surface of his narcissism, must
reflect the chaos, the rootlessness, the violence, the disruptions, the spiritual centrifugalities of the world he is condemned to die in. And this evidently means that the poem he is condemned to live in must rid itself of all
historical ballast and of all those traditional beatitudes of form, order, and
intelligibility invoked by the more fortunate poets who still lived in the age
of innocence between Pericles and Hitler.

Such, put simply, is the modern poetic creed. Obviously, the issues it
raises are more complex than its mere formulation might indicate. For
example, does not a poetry which *resists* its time, opposing lucidity to obscurity, order to chaos, sense to senselessness, by that very token indirectly
or elliptically participate in its time, if only through the medium of a problematic recognition? Is not its actual practice implicitly diagnostic? May
not rhyme, let us say, constitute a plea for harmony and not an atavistic
ineptitude? May not the very existence of, if not metre, a discernible cadence suggest the need for internal continuity and psychic momentum
rather than the ineffectual hope of dim arcadian symmetries? In short, may
there not be historical periods in which poetry if it wishes to survive is
compelled to live *in partibus infidelium*, carrying on a sort of guerrilla

warfare against the pervasive assumptions and dominant 'realities' of the day? The relation of literature to its time is not necessarily one of strict equivalence and the commitment of the former to the latter is often paradoxical or rebellious.[1]

We are touching on the insoluble dilemma of the relation between art and life, which I do not want to resurrect here. Suffice it to say that neither pole of the equation can substitute for the equation itself. The self-contained world of art is at best a dubious refuge from the confusions and banalities of raw experience, bringing with it the dangers of inanition and preciosity. On the other hand, the sheer, voluminous flux of experience into which the artist is regularly advised to plunge in order to revitalize his flagging energies will more likely than not leave his literary corpse washed up on the beaches of respectability, academia or, if he is thorough, in the churning surf of an African exile. But the artist must nevertheless judge which pole of the equation he should diffidently approach in the service of his unforgiving muse if his work is to avoid becoming parodistic or inconsequential.

To return to the development of our theme. Despite the almost infinite permutations which the subject permits, the theory of poetry reduces as does that of art in general to the theory of imitation taken in its widest conceivable sense. And imitation is conceived in basically two ways. The artist is required either to imitate "nature," which can mean anything from landscape to manners to interior or psychological configurations. Or he is exhorted to the imitation of the traditional forms of literary endeavour in appropriate language, in which case he "copies" not "nature" but one or another of the formally established ways in which it has been agreed that nature may be copied. In the first instance, his imagination must be governed by his apperception of reality or, in the complex refinements of later speculation, by its own intrinsic laws as it conspires with the external *materia* to produce reality itself. In the second case, imagination must be subordinated to a social and critical consensus regarding the appropriate forms of literary representation, whose pedigree dates from the *Republic* and the *Poetics*.

The operative terms are, of course, to be understood with a certain generous latitude. Literature is not slavishly mimetic, it is also inventive and analytic, and no genuine writer is concerned with photographic verisimilitude. He does not copy so much as interpret. Similarly, the antithetical terms "nature" and "tradition," notwithstanding the venerable polarity into which they have been historically locked, are susceptible of endless modification. But the two "moments" of the antithesis can never be entirely eluded and the thrust of the writer's creative temperament moves in one or another of these ancestral and inevitable directions. In this sense it may be valid to claim that beneath the profusion of individual modulations we can distinguish these two fundamental impulses toward the imitation of "nature" on the one side or the imitation of established "form" on the other. That is, we may speak either of the "laws" which the creative temperament must obey or of the "norms" to which it must conform.

The two impulses are not at bottom diametrically opposed, as the social doctrine implicitly assumes that reality is not infinite and there accordingly exists a definable number of expressive forms which correspond to its limited permutations. Of course, the classical world is extinct and the neoclassical sensibility was hijacked by Industrial Capitalism, but the simple fact that we continue to accept the rhetorical distinction between poetry and prose, that poets (somewhat heedless of their innovative practices) tend to leave the customary margins on either side of the page, and are also given to declaiming or chanting their verses rather than merely *reading* them, is evidence of an abiding belief in the formal difference between the two media and therefore in the general validity of the classical idea. "Form" is grounded in "nature" and is solidly associated with a repertoire of legitimate strategies for the expression of different kinds of experience.

2.

The blunt fact remains that the theory of poetic convention has fallen on evil days and is widely regarded as superannuated. The classical idea of poetry as requiring elevated diction — as commanding a unique language distinct from both prose and ordinary speech, equipped with a peculiar set of rules, conventions, and formal exclusions — is now considered as an exercise in brahmanic arrogance or anachronistic fatuity. It simply does not meet the brazen imperatives of contemporary experience and is as unseasonable or ludicrous as mixing a Molotov cocktail in a Ming vase. When Ortega defines poetic language as a "hovering" medium, raised above the abrasions and rugosities of current speech, he is looking back to the traditional conceptions of epic, drama, and the prophetic literature. But even the conversion of the hoary emblems of the winged steed or magic carpet into that of the lexical helicopter does not redeem his formulation from the charge of antiquarianism. Poetic conventions are *passé:* rhyme is obsolete (did not Milton consider it a barbarism?); metre is infantile, and even the stress-count is a throwback to Anglo-Saxon artlessness; the stanza form continues to be used but more as a logical convenience, an adaptation of the prose paragraph, than as a part of the traditional architectonic; and the language itself must avoid archaic "heightening" or "point" as it scrupulously democratizes its mandarin inclinations in the direction of the idiomatic, the colloquial, and the ubiquitous. Poetry can now be dialed on the telephone and read on the buses sandwiched between advertisements, as if Wordsworth's Preface were actually to be taken seriously.

The prevailing dogma is clear and unmistakable. The doctrine of the imitation of traditional form is defunct, relegated to the limbo of a classical irrelevance. A poetry which honours the canons and attitudes of its masonic past, which reveres the illustrious predecessor, which recognizes degree and precedence, and which deploys a complex, formally appropriate, and distinctively memorable language is dismissed as either hieratic snobbishness or creative senility. The proper use to which this kind of poetry can be put was determined by Congreve's Mrs. Millamant, who curls her hair with love letters, but "only with those in verse . . . I never pin up my hair with prose." And the poets who continue to practice these ancestral sanctities are patronized as elegant but pitiable old fogies mourning the end of their feudal prerogatives. The world has passed them by. The careening motorcar has flung the yellow caravan into the ditch and the poet who wishes to survive must shake the dust out of his knickers and dream of magnificent onsets into a levelling future. Thus the principle of mimetic form is no longer adequate to the explosiveness and terror of the modern world and must be abandoned if we are to come to terms with the nature of our experience, the superluminal chaos of our event-horizon. Otherwise, along with religious faith, good craftsmanship, diplomatic immunity, and other such vestigial remnants of a vanished order, poetry cannot hope to escape obsolescence. This, more or less, is the creed to which the majority of poets now subscribes.

But if the imitation of form, the hallowing of poetic convention, has been tossed onto the scrapheap of outmoded pieties, we are left with the imitation of nature as the only theoretical foundation on which to ground the poetry of the modern era. The forms we must devise or discover in order to mirror, contain, or inflect the volatilities of our experience must inevitably *correspond* to that experience. In consequence, form moves toward the paradoxical assimilation of formlessness and the poet begins to conceive of his work as a sequence of ambiguous strategies to reflect the sense of confusion, homelessness, and disruption (or of mere indifference) with which the world persecutes him. Honesty, he asserts, compels him to write directly — eloquence is suspect, stable form the result of quaint artisanal compulsions, and time too valuable and fugitive an inheritance to waste on laborious composition. A poem can no longer claim the luxury of evocativeness, and the sense of its commitment to pressing, immediate needs invalidates its allegiance to its own constituent materials, an activity it can only regard as an untenable hedonism or technical encapsulation. The predictable effect of all this is that poetry comes increasingly to resemble prose.

The poetic modes which flourish in this climate of misinformation are clearly the descriptive narrative, the documentary, and the personal reminiscence (often deflected pronominally into the third person to evade the accusation of lyrical infatuation). These modes of poetic discourse are seen as unobjectionable from the standpoint of the contemporary milieu and even as adventurously experimental. And they are accompanied by the feverish search for structural models: the memoir or diary is high on the list of acceptable templates, but a quicksilver backing can be scraped together from almost any paradigmatic quarter, provided it is non-poetic in origin, such as the TV script, the recipe, the memo, or even the telephone book. (The fact that Villon, among others, used the testament in precisely this way partially explains his resurgent popularity.) The point I am making is that today the tendency is almost universal and by no means a maverick or eccentric gesture. The technical vacuum left by the extinction of conventional form has been surreptitiously filled by the substitution of prosaic or documentary prototypes, since the poet must get his structural patterns from somewhere. The element of disingenuousness arises from the conflict between the proclaimed conviction that form must be internal and organic and the obsessive practice of ransacking (to use Johnson's word) the world of common, unmediated experience for exemplars and paradigms. There is no escaping the ironical conclusion that the contemporary notion of form is at least as external and artificial as the literary conventions for the application of which the traditional poet is routinely denounced.

But there is a further and more corrosive irony at work in the matter under discussion. The imitation of form is widely construed as archaic, reactionary, and inappropriate; heightened language is regarded as artificial (once a term of approval, now dyslogistic); order and restraint are dismissed as hangovers from a pastoral and genteel state of mind, now understood as historically incongruous or irrelevant. But the imitation of nature or of the given state of affairs which underlies contemporary practice is in effect the province of the novel, as has been the case since Robinson Crusoe domesticated his island and Moll Flanders picked the pockets of the contemporary scene. And when it comes to holding the mirror up to nature on Stendhal's dusty highway or in Hamlet's theatre, poetry is out of its league and cannot compete with its formidable opponent. The novel is just too compendious, too all-embracing, too versatile and flexible and omnivorous a genre to defer in its analysis of experience to the right of poetic primogeniture. Moreover, to add injury to insult, it is capable in its lyrical mood of actually swallowing and digesting its traditional rival, so that the only place where we may still encounter poetry in its old-fashioned guise of evocative speech is in the body of the novel itself — an irritable Jonah, a lying Pinocchio, whistling in the depths of the Leviathan. And as if to administer the *coup de grace*, modern criticism has deposed that the novel is not a continuation of the classical tradition, the descendant of the epic, but is the unique literary expression of modern society deriving ultimately from the Puritan reformation of the sixteenth and seventeenth centuries and the industrial upheavals of the eighteenth.

This irony is not only inescapable but possibly terminal as well. Poetry, in approximating to the novelistic parallax, ceases to be "poetic" and grows more and more prosaic in structure, content, and language. The idea of "decorum" did not wither away, however, with classical and Renaissance literary values. Decorum may be defined as style accommodated to subject, means to ends, idiom to intention. Thus the idea of poetic decorum in today's literary environment exacts an extortionate price from the practicing poet because he must now bring his poem into line with the novelistic perspective on the world and adopt the techniques and strategies of an alien genre if he is to retain or regain credibility. So the truth stares us glumly in the face. The poet goes on multiplying narrative upon description upon documentary in odd linguistic constructs called poems that scarcely anyone bothers to read except other poets and an entrenched minority of academic critics — without whom, be it said, the medium would quickly succumb to literary entropy. Meanwhile it manages to maintain itself prosthetically.

If the imitation of nature is the privilege or the proper sphere of the novel and the imitation of form has been consigned to oblivion, it seems reasonable to assume that poetry is confronted with only two options, namely, it must be either prosaic or irrelevant. There is no *tertium quid*. It reflects and participates in the modern experience of universal chaos and predictably disintegrates, becoming discontinuous, haphazard and aleatory, or variously smuggles an extraneous concept of order into its performative ambience and so reduces itself to a parasitical and undistinguished existence, encroaching on the terrain of the novel only to be wiped out or incorporated. This is where the imitation of nature inexorably leads it. The other alternative is equally depressing: it opposes the experience of violence and anarchy and stays equally clear of the giantocracy of the novel, setting up a small, countervailing linguistic system predicated on order and continuity. Thus it becomes instantly obsolete and intensely private, the formal expression of nostalgia for a lost coherence.

The modern poet navigates in the straits between the Scylla of the irrelevant and the Charybdis of the prosaic, and there is every sign in the apocalyptic moment we inhabit that his epic journey is about to be cut short, if it has not already ended. And if, as many believe, the novel is itself endangered by the graphic and electronic revolutions inspired by a triumphant technological barbarism, prose will soon confront its own set of complementary options: to become irrelevant as its predecessor, or somehow cinematic and instantaneous as its successor. In which case it is possible that poetry will be deprived of even its posthumous survival in the body of the novel, one more minor, unremembered casualty in the collapse of the past.

Note

[1] This is a point stressed, perhaps overstated, by Wilde in *The Decay of Lying*, which claims that art in no case reproduces its age. "So far from being the creation of its time, it is usually in direct opposition to it. . . ."

Concluding Note

In a certain sense poetry (or the improbable act of writing and reading it) has more in common with Science Fiction than with any other branch of prose literature, given the 'Coleridgean' proviso that Science Fiction (of the cruder sort at any rate) is popular since it relies on the familiar operations of fancy and poetry is paradoxically remote since it is based on the rigorous principles of the imagination. The traditional poem and the SF story construct codified worlds which in terms of consistency and intelligibility provide a fleeting alternative to the feeling of dispersion and the experience of triteness we associate with contemporary life. At the same time, it is obvious that Science Fiction cannot be diffracted through the medium of verse (although this has been inadvisedly attempted) without the reciprocal annihilation of the two genres. The poem in its quest for poise and equilibrium is immediately crippled by an orthopedic self-consciousness while the Science Fiction story in its need for spectacle and narrative expansiveness chafes in frustration at the formal and rhetorical limitations imposed upon it. But it might be worth suggesting that poetry was the Science Fiction of the ancient world, not in the sense of detailing implausible adventures in the epic (or even Lucianic) mode but rather in describing an implicit trajectory that overarched and to some extent negated the world of daily experience. Poetry once provided, as Science Fiction does today, the significant alternative to the commonplace.

We might also note that poetry has been crowded out of the aesthetic field not only by its brawny, mimetic competitor, the novel, but by its once-pliant, former handmaiden, music. Eric Havelock tells us in his *Origins of Western Literacy* that as the written word gained its identity and became "increasingly prosaic," it was freed from its previous bondage to mnemonic verse rhythm. But this emancipation had the concomitant effect of releasing rhythm from its subservience to poetry, allowing it to be conceptualized in pure sound independent of diction and "increasingly thought of not as an accompaniment to words but as a separate technology with its own laws and procedures." Thus both the mimetic and phonetic functions of verse have been taken from it by the disciplines of fiction and music, which are better adapted to the respective modalities of verbal imitation and rhythmic sound than is their ostensible predecessor.

CL 115 (Winter 1987)

Tom Wayman

Why Profess What is Abhorred: The Rescue of Poetry

I.

As I gathered up my papers at the end of class, a young man approached my desk. I was five weeks into teaching a freshman introduction to literature/composition course at a four-year college in the BC Interior. "Well, Tom," the student said. "You did the best you could."

His hand indicated my notes for the four-week-long unit on poetry we had just completed; we would begin a unit on short stories the next class. "But in spite of your efforts," the young man continued, "I haven't changed my mind. I still hate poetry."

How can anyone hate poetry? Do they hate sonnets, ballads, villanelles? Rhymed or unrhymed verse? Elizabethan, eighteenth-century, Victorian poets? Robert Frost, Robert Lowell, Robert Creeley? Lyric, imagistic, conversational, language-centred techniques? Narrative or non-narrative strategies? Federico Garcia Lorca, Cesar Vallejo, Pablo Neruda? Sound poetry, concrete poetry, prose poetry? Gwendolyn MacEwen, Susan Musgrave, Erin Mouré? Aboriginal, South Asian, revolutionary, feminist, Rasta, work, black, Hispanic, Nuyorican (New York Puerto Rican) poems? Zbigniew Herbert, Tomas Tranströmer, Yehuda Amichai? Those Australian migrants: Thalia, Jeltje, π.O.?

The statement *I hate poetry*, which I hear in one form or another whenever I teach an introduction to literature class, is like claiming: "I hate music." Anybody can ferociously dislike Rap or Rachmaninoff, Country and Western or John Cage. But I've never heard someone completely dismiss any other form of cultural expression.

Nor are creative writing classes exempt. At the start of each post-secondary introductory creative writing class I teach I outline the genres we are going to cover. Inevitably in response I am informed: "Ugh. Not poetry. I hate poetry."

Why does this emotion arise? How is it perpetuated? In my collection of essays *A Country Not Considered: Canada, Culture, Work*, I argue that one important origin for our attitudes to literature is our formal education — "since school is the only place most of us ever meet people whose job it is to try to show us the worth of literature" (30). What events occur in elementary, secondary and post-secondary classrooms to cause women and men to decide they detest an entire art form?

In my case, I was blessed with a few teachers who managed to communicate — at least to me — a deep affection for literature. This reinforced the enormous delight in poetry evinced by my father during my childhood. Although my father was a pulp mill chemist, he was passionate about reading, and reading aloud, English poets like A.E. Housman and Alfred Noyes, and Canadian poets like Wilfred Campbell and E. Pauline Johnson. Our house while I was growing up in the 1950s and 1960s also contained well-worn editions of *contemporary* Canadian poets — F.R. Scott, Dorothy Livesay, Earle Birney, Irving Layton, Miriam Waddington. The latest volumes by these and newer writers such as Eli Mandel, Al Purdy, and Leonard Cohen continually arrived.

The enthusiasm that my father and to a lesser extent my mother demonstrated for poetry convinced me that the art mattered, that it had a past, a present, and a future that held value. Constrasted to these beliefs was the dreary mechanistic attitude to poems taken by some teachers I encountered. In these classrooms, we were directed to closely examine lines for the sole purpose of ascertaining stress patterns and rhyme patterns in order to conclude whether a fragment of verse — irrespective of meaning or any other artistic consideration — was trochaic or anapestic, whether rhyme schemes were ABBA or ABAB or LSMFT. And even in university, many instructors insisted on one correct interpretation of ambiguous sections or whole poems: all other possible readings were decreed null and void. Studying poetry thus was like auto shop or the rifle disassembly/assembly drill in army cadets. Full marks were obtainable if you could name the parts correctly as you took the apparatus apart, and full marks were assigned if you could follow the approved method of reattaching the pieces speedily back into working order. The only difference was that a reassembled poem could not fire a bullet, any more than the poem could be driven someplace. Instead, the lines of words squatted inertly on their white page, blanketed literally or metaphorically with comments superimposed in red pencil. A distorted, hideous thing.

My discussions with my current students lead me to conclude that for the *majority* my worst experiences match their recent interactions with poetry in institutions of learning. During early adolescence these students often sought to express their feelings about their emerging selves in a free-form style of writing they called poetry. At times the lyrics of certain popular songs, the words bolstered by effects generated by the accompanying music, speak to them with unusual force or meaning. Yet encounters like these that suggest the incipient power of words presented in a non-prose format are light-years distant from the way poetry was inflicted on them in school.

Exposure to poetry was used as a measure against which the student was pronounced stupid, unimaginative, a failure. Who would not hate an activity or artifact that authority utilizes to brand us with these labels? Formal schooling in many subjects frequently diminishes a student's self-respect in this manner. Mathematics, history, science classes can be taught so as to primarily instruct us that we are brainless, lazy, worthless. Yet at least in these subjects the teacher can indicate how our shortcomings in these fields will have direct and dire consequences in adult life: these areas of instruction are clearly necessary to succeed on many jobs, or to comprehend what is happening in the world in which we are supposed to be citizens. But poetry? Why are we made to feel badly about ourselves over a subject which no instructor bothers to even *try* to claim has the slightest use outside of school? We can grudgingly admit that we cannot escape the influence on our lives of biology, physics, geography — regardless of how badly taught in school, and of how our reaction to that pedagogy may have damaged our self-esteem. But if there is one subject in which we were pronounced incompetent on which we can *afford* afterwards to vent our anger and dismay at how school labelled us, that subject is poetry. Like any powerless minority lacking status in the larger world, poetry is the perfect receptacle for our rage and frustration, is safe to despise, loathe, abhor.

As a poet, I am not happy with the present situation. Can poetry be taught so that it is not detested, not asked to bear the sins of mass public education? After all, a hatred of poetry does not even restore the self-respect of the despiser. Rather, this abhorrence when expressed serves as a restatement or reminder of the perceived inadequacies of the person uttering the emotion. So this venting reinforces the pattern that equates the art form with a poor self-image. And the expression of this dislike obviously does poetry no good.

I believe effective change proceeds from root causes of inappropriate or inadequate behavior. We have to ask, then, two radical questions. First: what do we teach poetry *for*? That is, what is our *aim* in including poetry as part of the English curriculum at any level? The second question is: what do we teach *poetry* for? In an era when poetry is a thoroughly marginalized art form, what positive contribution can a poem make to human existence? Whatever poetry's usefulness to society might have been in the past, why seek to encompass the art now in our educational system? My two main questions here are obviously interrelated, although I will consider them in sequence.

2.

When I walk into a classroom to instruct people about poetry, what should my intention be? I am convinced that my achievement as an instructor must be judged by whether those who experience my pedagogy leave the class with a love of the art. According to this standard, the student I refer to at the start of this article represents a defeat on my part. But ideally any material I introduce to my students, or any artistic technique I draw to their attention or expect them to become proficient in understanding and describing, will contribute to initiating or affirming an *affection* on their part toward poetry.

I want the students to emerge from the class as enlightened amateur readers of poetry: amateur, where the word means "lover of." Even when we teach creative writing, educational administrators and others are often startled when I insist that our fundamental goal is to produce careful, knowlegeable *readers* rather than professional writers. How much more true is this for the instruction of poetry. Upwards of 98 per cent of those we teach will never become professional critics of poetry (or become poets). So our pedagogy must be shaped toward this reality.

Just as very few students in the fine arts will continue on to become professional painters or sculptors, and just as few people who take guitar lessons will become professional rock or classical guitarists, so the overwhelming majority of those we instruct in our poetry classes will not embark on a career as professional responders to — or writers of — poetry. The foremost objective of our teaching consequently must be to produce an interested and informed *audience* for poetry.

The foundation of any curriculum in poetry should be to provide students with a wide exposure to examples of the art — whatever the historical era or theme or other focus of the course. Students then need to be encouraged, in as open an atmosphere as possible, to articulate and defend their responses to these poems. This goal requires that students have the tools with which to examine their own reaction to a poem. Students also need the tools to successfully communicate that response to others. Each student has to be able to show — not just tell — others why she or he responds as she or he does to a poem (and thus defend her or his reaction). These same analytic skills allow students to thoroughly absorb lessons gathered from their reading, or from hearing the comments of classmates or the instructor about such poems. The student can then more readily adapt or incorporate these lessons into her or his appreciation of the art.

A poetry curriculum therefore must involve a safe, supportive, and informed environment in which students can critique the writing of contemporary or historical authors as well as the response of other class members to these poems. By so doing, the student excercises and refines skills in thinking, writing and reading.

At the very least, a course in poetry should not leave students with a dislike — or *increased* dislike — of the art form. What conceivable use can such a pedagogical outcome be? Yet at present this is the curriculum's net effect on most students. How does this result help the student? Help the art form? Help the arts or humanities or the community or any larger reality or abstraction? To me, a course of studies in poetry instead should improve the student's ability to recognize and enjoy the subtleties as well as the more evident achievements of the art. The student should discover or further augment within himself or herself an awareness of the power of the written word to describe and even to initiate ideas and emotions. The result of the course's accomplishments should be a feeling of pleasurable wonder at what the human race, via this art form — via *words* — has wrought.

I believe that the negative reaction to poetry created by pedagogies employed today arises from a different, unstated curriculum objective: to develop professional critics. My teaching experience convinces me that unless students understand why this or that critical method enhances their delight in an art form, the application of any critical theory becomes an exercise in drudgery, in irrelevant make-work. Inculcating and/or preserving a love of poetry must be the intent of any application of critical thought to the art. The danger in proceeding otherwise is that as each new generation of teachers at any level is trained, these men and women are trained to dislike or despise poetry and poets.

I have certainly witnessed firsthand the consequence of the existing pedagogy not only as a student but as an instructor. BC Interior colleges during the past decade have suffered an inflow of new English PhDs produced in graduate seminars that appear to be steeped in either vicious competitiveness or competitive viciousness. Far from producing teachers with a love of the art or the artists in their chosen field, these graduate schools unleash new instructors who behave very much like abused children. Smarting from some series of crushing blows to their self-esteem, the new professors seek to vent their anger on any target they deem powerless — from their hapless students to any colleague they conclude is vulnerable to some form of academic scorn or punishment. Supersaturated themselves with the jargon of the critical stance favored at their alma mater — a jargon which will date the would-be scholars more rapidly than they imagine — these instructors attempt to drench any and all within their academic reach with a language comprehensible only to a highly specialized few. The effect of such behavior on anyone's appreciation of the art form they supposedly profess is no factor for consideration. I can recall one newly minted colleague spluttering in opposition to a curriculum proposal, opining that the suggested approach was wrong because it "would privilege the writer over the critic." Multiply such comments by a thousand and you can imagine the atmosphere in which poetry continues to be studied in many classrooms.

So bitter is the environment generated by the latest generation of PhDs that it affects not only the future of poetry but that of the English departments in which these hurting and hurtful men and women find themselves employed. I know of one BC Interior department which as a last resort recently sought en masse professional counselling. Since the departmental vote to seek such help was 21 to 7, I am dubious about the ultimate results of this initiative.

Despite such developments, I retain my belief in a syllabus whose goal is to achieve and sustain a love for poetry. As I note above, central to this pedagogical approach is to familiarize students with the broadest possible scope of the art. Regardless of how a course is organized — historically, thematically, or concentrating on technique — the aim here is to ensure that a student does not conclude poetry inhabits only a narrow band of the art's actual spectrum. The more expansive the student's exposure to poetry is, the more likely the work of some poet will engage the sensibilities of the student.

The women's movement, the new self-consciousness of various minorities, the increased attention to literary translation all have helped make available poetries supplementary to the established canon. A revelation of the full literary context — historical or modern — in which a poet plied her or his art also helps illustrate for the student poetry's immense range.

This need to impress upon students the multifariousness of poetry is subverted, however, by the standard teaching anthology. With rare exceptions, teaching anthologies are generated from existing anthologies rather than from primary source research. As a result, the same set pieces tend to appear over and over. This selection process shrinks poetry to a smaller presence than that required to improve the current circumstances of the art. Anthology editors would claim they are distilling the essence of poetry; I would propose they are desiccating poetry. The endlessly-taught "important" poems become the clichés of teaching: the original power of the poet's expression wears extremely thin after far-too-frequent repetition in classroom after classroom.

Finding alternatives or supplements to the teaching anthology of course involves skill and ingenuity. Technically, the photocopier is an instructor's chief ally in the rescue of poetry (although somewhat threatened by the federal government's new misguided copyright provisions). Also, where the syllabus permits, assigning as a text an entire book by a local writer, or by an author who will be reading in the community or school during the semester, is another means to boost students' awareness of poetry's rich texture and extent.

Discovering *what* to photocopy or assign remains a vital task for teachers wishing to adopt new materials. Obviously if an instructor hates poetry herself or himself, such professional development will be regarded with distaste. I fear in a great many cases this is another result of our existing pedagogy. And if a teacher has been persuaded by his or her own wretched experiences in school that she or he is unable to discern value in any poem not previously approved by others, such a teacher also is unlikely to choose material that will effectively inspire delight or affection in students.

For those with enough self-confidence in their enjoyment of the art to seek fresh poems, at present only a wide reading with an open mind can provide pedagogically useful examples of writing. I would like to see a more formal expansion of the informal sharing of teachable poems that exists among poetry-friendly colleagues who already know each other. Some form of mandatory continuing education in the pedagogy of literature could serve in a more organized way to provide teachers at all levels with a source of poetries that work well in the classroom to ignite a love of the art in students. This requirement might reinforce the concept that instructors need to expand their pegagogical repertoire throughout their careers in order to continually improve their teaching. Or maybe upgrading should be mandatory only in subject areas where present teaching styles and syllabuses produce demonstrably negative results, as with poetry.

3.

Yet, whatever our pedagogical goal, why bother teaching poetry at all? Given that time is at a premium in our educational process, why is poetry a fit subject when the art's current marginal status is attested to by various measurable standards? For instance, small press publishers have complained to me that whereas 30 years ago a new collection of poems by a Canadian author routinely sold a pitiful 1,200 copies, a similar book these days is lucky to sell 500. And this despite a surge in the size of the population, and three decades of phenomenal growth in post-secondary institutions — each of which makes literature courses a requirement for a degree. To the mystification and shame of my colleagues who teach creative writing, during this same period the number of graduates from our programs in imaginative writing also has escalated, without affecting these sad statistics. Even in the U.S., if books by contemporary poets sell more readily, the authors almost invariably are known to the public for having achieved celebrity in other fields: as novelists — Margaret Atwood, for example; or as musicians — Leonard Cohen; or as incarnations of cultural postures or concepts — Sylvia Plath as tormented genius/woman-as-victim, or Robert Bly as a founder of the men's movement.

One societal trend at the dawn of the new millennium is for us more frequently to be spectators instead of participants in our life — to be listeners to music, for instance, rather than singers or performers ourselves. In accordance with this development, I encounter less and less frequently people who enjoy the memorization and recitation of poems. The generation that delighted in knowing by heart Robert Burns or Robert W. Service is vanishing, and is not being replaced. Nor is verse by other poets committed to memory by such an extensive cross section of people as once could recite work by these two bards. Where attraction to types of poetry among a larger population has recently surfaced — for example, cowboy poetry, or the poetry competitions known as "slams," or Rap with its insistent rhyming couplets — these forms of the art with greater appeal are primarily oral. Plus, the basis for the more widespread response to these manifestations of poetry is spectacle — consumption of a public performance. With rare exceptions, these versions of the art do not repay close reading; whenever the verse is considered outside of the spectacle (or in the case of popular music, when separated from the musical accompaniment), the words' emotional power weakens noticeably or disappears. Books by these poets, or by poetry performance artists, do not sell in significant numbers. This is not art one takes home in written form.

The Internet is sometimes lauded as the locale of a renaissance of interest in publishing poetry. As nearly as I can ascertain, though, the establishment of electronic magazines and the enormous opportunity for self-publishing that the Net offers remains a matter of "give" rather than "get." Staring into a cathode ray tube is a notoriously stressful way to receive information of any kind. I have never experienced and cannot imagine reading for pleasure from a monitor screen. Downloading writing from the Net, printing it off, and then attempting to read it offers more benign possibilities. But a sheaf of printer paper is in effect an unbound book: a loose collection of sheets, and of an awkward size with regard to portability or ease of perusal. Although I am in close contact with a number of fellow writers, teaching colleagues and students who are Net afficionados, I have never yet heard a single one recommend enthusiastically a *poem* they discovered on the Net. These Net surfers frequently are excited and fascinated by *information* they glean among the electrons. The literature posted at so many sites, though, seems to be scanned simply *as* information, in the Net users' characteristic coasting and skipping over the endlessly unscrolling acres of words in search of a jolt, a charge, some astonishment.

Body hunched forward, face inches from a screen, does not appear to be a posture conducive to a leisurely and careful reading of a literary text. The

Net may well serve as the depository for poems which formerly the lonely and socially inept consigned to their desk drawer. But of all the literary arts, poetry least rewards the act of browsing, and browsing is the quintessential human interaction with the Internet.

So if poetry today is firmly marginalized, why involve it in our curriculums? My answer originates with the rapt expression of wonder and joy I encounter each term when a student truly connects with a poem. "Wow," the student will effuse, "I didn't know a poem could be about this." Or: "This poem really touched me in a way I haven't felt before." A power exists in these words that completes an emotional circuit between author and reader.

Certain assemblages of words we call poems succeed beyond question at bridging the core solitude of human existence. Each of us is alive in a fleshly and perishable body, linked however tenuously to family and community, to a social past and present, and still each of us labors basically alone to experience and process our life. What *relief* — for surely that is the root of the exhilaration we feel when a work of art overwhelms us — to sense that another human voice possesses the ability to stir us, to reach the ear or eye of our innermost being. We are buried alive in our own personality, but from time to time a poem or sculpture or painting is able to speak reassuringly, wisely, disturbingly, lovingly about the human adventure we share.

Meaningful art is a profound act of solidarity: a declaration, via the artist's wish to communicate her or his vision to me, of my essential participation in the human story. Just as a tree heard to fall in the forest confirms the sound that event causes, so my acknowledgement of a specific poem's efficacy at engaging me validates the poet's imagination and toil. And where a literary artifact successfully achieves the transfer of an emotional or intellectual stimulation from the author to me, I have enriched my life. As long as a poem is able to enhance a man's or woman's perception of what it means to be human, the art form proves its worth. Each time I observe the face of a student shine with a radiance not evident before a poem was read and absorbed, my faith in the value of poetry and the teaching of poetry deepens.

The very definition of the art, though, poses problems as well as reasons for instruction in it. I consider poetry to be the most intense possible use of language. Traditional poems employ regular patterns of stress, sound and/ or stanza in order to create linguistic intenseness, to call attention to the difference between what the poem wishes to communicate and everyday speech. But the very regularity of these patterns implies predictability, and predictability can lessen the reader's attention, can detract from intensity.

Regular patterns were largely abandoned by poets early in the twentieth century. Belief in set arrangements and hierarchies in social, religious, scientific and artistic life was crumbling around the poets. And any concept of predictible orderliness in these spheres continued to be challenged as the highly irregular century proceeded.

Yet when poets discard regular templates (whether for metre, rhyme or stanza) the problem of creating intensity increases. Poets have to draw attention to the difference between their discourse and everyday speech without resorting to predictable patterns. Language somehow must work harder than with conventional prose — or else why call what is written poetry? — and the reader's passage through the words must be slowed down enough that the reader becomes aware of the way language is working. Since the methods of solving the problem have to be unpredictable, however, a second difficulty arises: in effect, the poet invents the art form every time he or she writes. A reader is asked to enter unfamiliar ground each time she or he is invited to read a non-traditional poem.

This double challenge offers the greatest opportunity for poets to generate intensity, even while simultaneously the poem's fulfillment of this potential may enormously discomfit the intended audience. The strategies chosen to alert the reader that she or he must read the poem differently than prose can include playful, fractured and/or ambiguous use of sense, grammar, spelling, sound. The page can serve as a canvas: indents, typography, and stanza and line breaks may impart meaning visually. Extensive use of metaphors or similes, hyperbole, and image banks that draw on esoteric knowledge are other compositional devices contemporary poets may adopt.

Meanwhile, the experimental nature of many attempts to distinguish this discourse from conventional prose can alienate readers if the *purpose* of adopting a particular compositional technique is not understood, or is deliberately mystified in a defensive gesture on the part of the writer. When poetry is already disliked by the population for reasons discussed above, and then poetry is further cloaked in an aura of difficult access, the combination can only be bad news for the art. The BC poet and publisher Howard White describes an Amnesty-International-sponsored encounter between Canadian and foreign writers in Toronto:

> At a bull session later some CanLit prof asked why poetry was less
> marginalized in so many developing countries and about 17 third-
> worlders tried to answer at once. The general drift was, western poets
> have done it to themselves because all they do is write for each other.
> They consider it corruption of true art to write for common taste, but
> they're never done whining that the public fails to appreciate them.
> And even when poets from developing countries show how well the
> public responds to poets who write for common taste with serious
> purpose, western writers fail to get the message. Somebody tried to
> make a case that western writers didn't have the kind of big social

challenges poets in developing worlds did, but gave up when
somebody else yelled, "Try taking your culture back from Hollywood
and Madison Avenue!" (10–11)

A variety of approaches to creating an intense use of language is *bound*
to produce artistic disagreements, though. Intensity, after all, is not a quality capable of objective measurement. The Chilean poet Nicanor Parra
cautions against claims that one specific technique will be the salvation of
poetry, or that any such strategy is the only correct one for whatever reason. His poem "Young Poets" is here translated by Miller Williams:

Write as you will
In whatever style you like
Too much blood has run under the bridge
To go on believing
That only one road is right.

In poetry everything is permitted.

With only this condition, of course:
You have to improve on the blank page. (143)

I regard the uncertainty swirling around the corpus of contemporary poetry — and, by extension, historical poetries — as a marvellous and unique
opportunity for learning. This situation constitutes for me a further justification of poetry's inclusion in our schools. Poetry raises an abundance of
questions about linguistic expression, about the purpose and function of
art, about the formation of personal judgment, about the skills necessary
to form and defend in words an opinion or idea. Revealing the craft of
poetry can initiate students into the craft of other artistic media — music,
cinema, clay, fibre arts. Issues of marginality and the mainstream, of the
role of cultural gatekeepers, of speech and silence are inherent in any study
of poetry. Where students are shown poems that successfully enlarge their
sense of the world, of the myriad possibilities of human life, of other ways
of envisioning the challenge of being human, the art has unquestionably
earned its place in any curriculum designed to educate minds rather than
merely train them. Indeed, an inquiry into the very basis of much of the
educational process — labelling, categorizing — is subsumed by an examination of poetry. How can there be both prose poems and poetic prose? In
the latter case, if poetry is writing at its most intense, is the "small dream
about time" (140) in Annie Dillard's non-fiction *Pilgrim at Tinker Creek*
— the riveting sequence where the book's narrator views all the temporal
content of the Earth at a single glance (140–43) — not poetry? Or what
about the splendidly evocative image that closes Sid Marty's non-fiction

Men for the Mountains, where the narrator listens to the shade of legendary Jasper Park warden George Busby?

> He leaned forward then and held his gnarled hands out to the firelight, and the flames threw his shadow, magnified, onto the thick logs of the cabin wall. Then he began to weave a tale of high mountains and of proud men that rode among them, like princes surveying their estates, like lords high up in their strongholds, where only the wind could touch them, and where the world was free of pain and sorrow, and we were always young. (270)

If such prose can be termed poetry, what is the purpose of nomenclature? What does it mean to exist at a time when boundaries between the various arts are collapsing, when even some sciences are apparently converging?

In our culture at present, the most widely accepted means of determining value is cash: anything that cannot attract dollars is judged worthless. Yet poetry exists entirely outside the money economy. Almost no book of poetry makes a profit; virtually no poets can live on sales of their art. To continue to honor poetry — to deem the art culturally significant — is to instruct students that some things on this planet have value even if those things cannot be assigned a monetary equivalent. Few people would attend a church that lacked a building, that was so poor the congregation met in the open air. Few sports or games — even among children — are now played without prior purchase of expensive equipment. But poetry insists that there *is* a worth beyond dollars, that some human activities and creations are literally priceless.

Not that poetry lacks a defense even in terms of its usefulness to commerce, to the pursuit of money. For instance communications consultant Cheryl Reimold, in a four-part series published in the magazine of the U.S. Technical Association of the Pulp and Paper Industry, explains why reading poetry would be helpful to business people. In introducing her first article, she urges:

> To your regular diet of technical or business material, add a little poetry. Wait, please — don't stop reading this yet! I'm not suggesting this only to offer you the aesthetic and spiritual gifts of poetry. Poetry will help you write better memos, letters, and reports.
>
> Great poetry releases the power in ordinary words and makes them resonate. The poets take all the principles of writing — persuasion, clarity, organization, force — and exploit them to the maximum. In a few words, they can tell the story of the world. To discover the possiblities in language and use it to transmit your message with real clarity and power — you must read poetry. (97)

I locate poetry's merit as a subject for study at considerable remove from Reimold's claim that exposure to some poems will spice up a corporate executive's memos. But I certainly endorse her praise for the best poets: "In a few words, they can tell the story of the world." Whatever small amount most of us know about the Elizabethans or Victorians, we know from poems that have lasted. The mighty armies, fleets, battles, social unrest have faded with the kings, the queens, the wealthy, the desperately poor. Some words were scratched on paper by one particular human, on a Thursday afternoon when a rainstorm seemed imminent and a couple of domestic responsibilities — involving a rip in a coat and a diminished household fuel supply — were being evaded. Improbably, those words are what has endured. The noisy among us today are certain that the sense of our own time we will bequeath to the future will involve movies, television, the latest pop music star. Perhaps. But so far among humanity's achievements, poems have proven among the most effective time travellers.

I believe that when we teach our students affection for poetry, we teach them affection for the human story as it has been, as it is, and as it will be. Which is to say that as we rescue poetry for love, we teach our students love for their own species, and so for themselves. Surely that deserves our best efforts as teachers; surely our profession has no more crucial task.

Works Cited

Dillard, Annie. *Pilgrim at Tinker Creek*. New York: HarperCollins, 1988.

Marty, Sid. *Men for the Mountains*. Toronto: McClelland and Stewart, 1978.

Parra, Nicanor. *Poems and Antipoems*. New York: New Directions, 1966.

Reimold, Cheryl. "Principles from Poetry. Part 1: Persuasion." *Tappi Journal* 68.12 (1985): 97.

Wayman, Tom. *A Country Not Considered: Canada, Culture, Work*. Concord, ON: Anansi, 1993.

White, Howard. *Ghost in the Gears*. Madeira Park, BC: Harbour, 1993.

Iain Higgins

A First Chorus on Poetics

— How to start? One way would be to admit there is no coming to terms with *poetry*, *poetics*, and *criticism*, and there is only coming to terms: etymologically, for example, which gives us "something made," "about something made" (*peri poietikés*, in Aristotle's phrase), and "judgment."

— Very neat, but not very helpful: origins are hardly binding on posterity, which in any case usually has trouble locating them, and a term's meaning inevitably shifts over time. Semantic fields are no less worked over, expanded, abandoned, recolonized, enclosed, contested, and so on than any other sort of territory.

— So take a historical view, then?

— That would be another way, certainly, and one which would acknowledge that what a poem is, or is understood to be, has never been constant, nor has what people choose to do with it or use it for: Aristotle, Longinus, Geoffrey de Vinsauf, Dante, Boileau, Goethe, Wordsworth, Mallarmé, Pound, and Milosz, amongst others, differ considerably on this subject, and that's staying within the Western traditions, which, rich as they are and affected as they occasionally are by, say, Arab or Chinese influences, still share the same watershed.

— Not what is a poem, then, but when?

— Perhaps, but what about, where is a poem? A disciplinary (that is, a conceptual) approach might be another way here: a poem is found amongst those things that aim to please, and so poetics would be a branch of aesthetics, and criticism a cicerone or a pander, depending on your point of view.

— But would poetics really be a branch of aesthetics? That's only one possible conceptualization, even if it has much to recommend it; poetics, after all, no less than the poems it aims to describe, prescribe, or even proscribe, can just as well and just as usefully be allied with or subsumed under anthropology, biology, ethics, gender studies, literary criticism, psychology, rhetoric, semiotics, or sociology.

— Which is a way of recognizing that just as criticism can do many things (judge, elucidate, explicate, comment, converse), so too can a poem, and it typically does more than one thing at once: instruct, delight, baffle, know, express, imitate, communicate, be, contain, answer, sound. Any adequate poetics would have to account for this multi-facetedness, which undoubtedly explains why there have been and still are so many poetics.

— So let's just admit that there is no poetry without poetics, and recall the paradoxical fact that it must precede poetry before it can follow after, since without poetics not only would there be no comprehension and no sustaining commentary, there would be no originating composition.

— Maybe so, but a poetics needn't be and usually isn't made explicit before anyone goes about composing, reading, or formally responding to a poem.

— True, but only where the poetics in question is shared, or not in competition or conversation with other conceptions of the poem, text, word-thing, thoughtsong, or whatever. The very fact of variable nomenclature points again to different conceptions of poetics, the products of each of which will have their own distinctive purchase on the face of things.

— Except of course that the face of things, like language itself (which is what helps us both create and come to know that face), is multi-faceted, and so any poetics and its poems necessarily leave larger or smaller gaps where they fail to get a handle on certain of the word's or the world's ways.

— And a good thing too: otherwise there'd be no more poems to make, and commentary would be redundant.

— Well, I'm not sure most poets or readers give much thought to poetics, which is about as interesting as talking of tofu instead of eating beancurd, and even if some poets do give it thought, very few of them are any more articulate about the whole business than your sweaty hockey player is when someone shoves a mike in his face at game's end and asks about how he scored the winning goal: stuff about the muses or voices or images arriving from out of the blue or cadences felt in the forearms is hardly any more satisfying an explanation than someone's saying, "the guys played good tonight and I was just in the right place when the puck came my way; after that, I put my head down and shot, and in she went."

— But that's such a male metaphor, though at least it makes clear that a poem and therefore the poetics that enables it are gendered and social constructs as well as someone's own makework.

— Oh, come on, this poetics stuff is just a lot of academic post-hockery: the poet simply sets the poem down on the page and the reader reads it.

— It's not quite so simple as that, you'd have to agree, since no one ever wants to write without first having read; and if the poem on the page looks or sounds different from what they're used to, many people just turn away from it, as a large body of readers has been doing for a good century now: I don't know much about poetry, runs one well-travelled line, but I know what I like — and yet that espousal of tasteful ignorance cannot be made without an implicit poetics.

— Can't say I agree at all, unless you want to make majority opinion defective whenever it conflicts with minority views.

— You may not agree, but I do, and I'd add that if there's any post-hockery it's played mainly in commentary, though the twist here is not only that poems made according to emergent or archaic or little-known poetics will find no or few readers without commentary, but also that there's no such thing as poetic immortality without this secondary activity, since almost all poetic hosts would die without their critical parasites.

— Even translators, whose business it is to multiply the possible worlds and wordways that exist within a given tongue, rarely work without the aid of commentary and criticism, and can easily be thought of as participating in the latter tasks.

— And why not go further? Isn't "Progressive Insanities of a Pioneer" at once a poem in its own right and a translation of and commentary on "Bushed," Atwood's poem extending the afterlife of Birney's in its independent dependency? And couldn't the same be said of Bringhurst's "Anecdote of the Squid" in relation to Klein's "Portrait of the Poet as Landscape"?

— There's no escape from secondariness, it seems, a point all the easier to concede when we recognize that from the very start poems have often made a habit of commenting on their own or other poetics: think of the bards who show up on Homer's epic stage or of Chaucer's sharp theoretical turns in narrative mid-flight, not to mention poetic treatises on poetry, such as Lu Ji's or Sikong Tu's. Some of those old boys may have reached a popular audience but they certainly knew that theirs was a learned pursuit with its own conceptual groundwork.

— Point after point inadvertently proved in the making: references to "the page" and "reading" already imply a textual rather than an oral poetics, which signals our inescapable cultural belatedness: if it's true that we can craze print with the trace of talk — and that has been the explicit aim of many poets in recent decades, so much so that ecritural countermovements have sprung up against demotic poetics — it's also the case that our spoken words inkstain the air almost from the time we first plunge into language, since in a culture with writing mother and father tongues cannot help but entwine like caducean serpents around some prior and usually taken-for-granted axis.

— But isn't "immortalizing" commentary needed only when poets and their work no longer have an integrated social space? Like now.

— If so, then Leonard Cohen's your mythical merman, and his seachange from poet to popstar is epoch-making, for it means that his afterlife — largely because he's gone so savvily in for the widely shared poetics of mass-market culture and in pseudo-ancient fashion energized his world-weary lyrics with electrified music — won't be confined to classrooms and quarterlies. A movie star, after all, edited his last selected.

— Let it be said again, you mean, only with a further claim for good measure: poem and poet alike are social and gendered constructs, and the creatures of marketing and media as well.

— So, if it's not quite post hoc, poetics is still necessarily in hock to its particular organs of dissemination?

— Precisely the point of so much marginal composing since Mallarmé blanked out the invisible page and the homemade demi-mondes of para-publishing made space for those few readers left undigested by book-of-the-munching.

— Enough said. Look, any poem that matters remains unsullied by such circumstantial slings and arrows, since it occupies its own as-it-were transcendent space in which we can sail whenever we read or hear it.

— We? Who's we?

— Here by way of illustration is a centuries' old scrap: "Dronken dronken y-dronken / Dronken is Tabart at wine / Hey . . . sister, Walter, Peter, / Ye dronke all deepe, / And I shall eke! / Stond alle stille — / Stille as any stone: / Trippe a littel with your foot / And let your body go."

— Perhaps you've got a point there; for the funny thing is, a poem both is and is not the sum of its confluent contexts; knowing those things might enhance your pleasure or understanding in the reading, but they are no substitute for a direct encounter, or for a further poetic response.

— "We all have our altars & icons," as Mouré says, unexempt herself.

— You mean, then, that the present (and hence the poetics) of any given culture is always asynchronous with itself: the more so, the longer and more layered a culture's historical memory or the broader and more aggregate its multicultural and multilingual reach. Even the mainstream, which in the cultural freemarketplace might as well be called the maelstrom, contains strong residual and emergent strands of flow variously entwined with the dominant, which in Canadian anglophone poetics might be called the "trivial anecdotal."

— And if the dominant flows mixed with the residual and the emergent, it also meets unpredictably with any number of current-altering eddies, shoals, falls.

— But wait: here's a postcard dropped in from out of the blue.

Moses supposes his toeses are roses,
but Moses supposes erroneously. This
from one of the apocrypha, the prophet
as vaudeville poet. And a toe by any
other name? — one of the bronchial tubes   First Chorus on Poetics
through which we breathe the earth;   c/o *Canadian Literature*
a clitoral homologue rubbing us right   #155
whenever we move (hence the wearing   Page Proof, BP
of shoes in civilized cultures); a stylus   VOX oNo
shared by all legged creatures, though each
steps in with its own brand of choreogra-
phy. [signed] *Worden Edgewise*

— [*Omnes*, out of synch] Well, what can you say to that? Maybe "on words and up words."

CL 155 (Winter 1997)

Robert Bringhurst

Singing with the Frogs

I.

In September 1996, a small group of poets, students and scholars met at
Trent University, in Peterborough, Ontario, for what I think was the first
colloquium ever held to address the practice of literary polyphony. Our
hosts were Sean Kane and Stephen Brown. Our moderator was Stan Dragland. Our guest of honor was Dennis Lee. The other invited speakers and
performers were Roo Borson, Kim Maltman, Don McKay, Jan Zwicky and
Clare Goulet. Nine months later, I am still repeating some of the things I
said there, still recanting others, and still learning what I learned.

The basic terms here — polyphony, monophony, homophony — are all
names for musical phenomena, and music more than anything will teach
us what they mean. All the arts are specialties, but all the arts are one. No
branch will fruit for long when it is severed from the tree.

Polyphonic music is music in which two or more interrelated but independent statements are made at the same time, creating a statement that
none of these statements makes on its own. The statements that are made
may imitate each other (as they do in a canon or a fugue), or they may go
their separate ways with one eye on each other (as they usually do in a
motet). But they retain their independence either way. Their relation is that
of coequals, not of musical servant and lord. That coequality is *why* what
they say can exceed the sum of the parts.

Polyphony, in short, is singing more than one song, playing more than
one tune, telling more than one story, at once. It is music that insists on
multiplicity — instead of uniformity on the one side or chaos on the
other.

266   From a Speaking Place

Listening to two or three or four interrelated but independent melodies at once has an immediate effect. "You can see their minds expand!" Jan Zwicky says — speaking as poet, violinist, teacher and philosopher all at once. Polyphony creates a kind of musical and intellectual space absent from music of all other kinds.

Playing separate melodies in sequence does not create polyphony. Playing one melody supported by accompaniment, no matter how complex, doesn't create polyphony either. Music that consists of one melody at once with its accompaniment — one statement at a time, with harmonic supports and defenses — is not polyphonic nor monophonic either. It is *homophonic* music.

There are polyphonic scores for modern dance and for ballet, but in the dance hall and ballroom sense, polyphony is not the stuff to dance to. Its multiplicity of statement interferes with the two stock themes of loneliness and fusion and with most of the other stock emotions pop music now conveys.

In fact, though it surrounds us all, many people living now have evidently never listened to polyphony. Much present music seems designed to drown it out instead of making it more audible. Most of what pours out of tape decks and radios now in every corner of the world — pop music, rock music, country music, twentieth-century folk music, opera, and most of the classical hit parade — is homophonic music. One melody sounds at a time, and is varied or developed or repeated over time, while all the other voices shore it up or hold its coat or hold its hand.

Most of the polyphonic repertoire in the European tradition is written for small ensembles of skilled singers, for chamber groups, and finally for soloists skilled enough with lute or keyboard to play two tunes at once. The greater part of this repertoire was written during the Renaissance. Its heyday ends where many people's sense of European musical history begins: with the work of J.S. Bach.

Polyphonic music and homophonic music are different in design, different in construction, and different in effect, though the boundary between them is frequently a wide and fuzzy line. It can be difficult to say precisely at which point a secondary voice asserts its independence or gives it up again — and yet the difference overall is one no listener can miss.

I have heard very intelligent people suggest that every poem is polyphonic — because a poem is a simultaneity of syntax, breath rhythm, speech rhythm, rhetoric, metaphor, the interplay of phonemes against morphemes, and all that. This isn't wrong, but it misses the point. An aria played on a solo violin is likewise a simultaneity of rhythm, intonation, musical syntax, dynamics, and so on. But that one melodic line, no matter how richly intoned or inflected, does not create the perceptual space and the sense of multiplicity that real polyphony does. Roland Barthes obscures the point as well when he defines theatricality as *une véritable polyphonie informationelle*. Polyphony does not mean merely information density or information overload. It does not mean *une épaisseur de signes*, "a thickness [or stupidity] of signs," to borrow Barthes's deliberate phrase (1964: 258). It means a space-creating dance of insistent and persistent multiplicities. The fuel of polyphony is time, from which it makes the space it needs.

Polyphony, like other borrowed words — *color, surface, shadow, tempo, frame* and even *voice* — is certain to acquire new and different *shades* or *hues* of meaning as a literary term. But if we use the word too loosely, we may find we only use it when it's not the word we need. Then we will have to coin another to mean what it once meant — unless we lose its meaning too.

2.

What is a polyphonic poem? It is a poem that is kin in some substantial way to polyphonic music. It is a cohabitation of voices. A poem that (to borrow two good verbs from Dennis Lee) *enacts* and *embodies* plurality and space as well as (or instead of) timelessness and unity. A poem in which what-is cannot forget its multiplicity. A poem in which no one — not the poet, not the reader, not the leader, and not God — holds homophonic sway.

The concepts of homophony and polyphony, and their underlying principles of harmony and counterpoint, are taught in every school around the world that teaches the European musical canon. But there are many more polyphonies than that. In Indonesia, India and Africa there are rich and deep indigenous traditions of polyphonic music. Inuit *katajjaq* (throat-song) is polyphonic too. What native North American music was like before the Europeans came is now not easy to find out, but the earliest recordings prove that it was often polyrhythmic. Much of it, in other words, was polyphonic music in which every voice but one is restricted to percussion. (Rhythmic more than melodic independence of the parts, according to Simha Arom, is the structural foundation of Central African polyphony as well.)

3.

The "invention" of polyphony can be a problematic turn of phrase, like the "discovery" of America. It simply isn't true that either music or polyphony is confined to the human realm. The assertion that it is — still often made — is all too reminiscent of the once-familiar claims that art and poetry or culture and morality are exclusively the property of city-dwelling Christians with a certain shade of skin.

Songbirds sing. That is fact and not a metaphor. They sing, and in the forest every morning, when a dozen or a hundred or a thousand individuals of six or ten or twenty different species sing at once, that is polyphonic music. What city dwellers frequently call "silence" is the ebb and flow of birdsong and the calls of hawks and ravens, marmots, pikas, deermice, singing voles, the drone of gnats and bees and bee flies, and the sounds of wind and rain and running water. The world is a polyphonic place. The polyphonic music and the polyphonic poetry and fiction humans make is an answer to that world. It is mimicry of what-is, as much as it is statements of what might be.

I am a rank amateur musician, with only a little experience playing jazz, European chamber work, and Indonesian gamelan. But night after night in Indonesia I have walked between the village, where the humans boomed and chirped with their bogglingly complex polyphonic tuned percussion, and the rice fields, where the frogs, just as earnestly and skillfully, were polyphonically croaking. Nothing but human arrogance allows us to insist that these activities be given different names. Bird songs, like human songs, are learned. They are cultural traditions. If some parameters of birdsong and frogsong are genetically preprogrammed in ways the string quartet, sonata and gamelan are not, so what? Bird *flight* too is genetically preprogrammed in ways that human flight is not. Does that entitle us to say that only we can really fly, and birds cannot?

If I'm allowed three musical wishes, two of them are these: I hope to learn to sing one half of a few *katajjait* myself; I also hope to meet the thinker from Pond Inlet (quoted but, alas, not named by Saladin d'Anglure) who said that humans learned the *sounds* of these songs from wild geese but learned the *meanings* of the sounds from the aurora.

4.

Music, dancing, storytelling, poetry are means by which we can and do embrace and participate in being, not tricks by which we prove our independence from or our superiority to it. Intrinsically, I think, the more power-hungry forms of homophonic music shut the polyphonic truth of the world out. This seems to me the case regardless whether the power comes from an amplifier, an orchestra pit or a military band. And intrinsically, I think, polyphonic literature and music acknowledge and celebrate plurality, simultaneity, the continuing coexistence of independent melodies and rhythms, points of view and trains of thought.

In homophonic music, lovely though some of it is, and written by geniuses, as some of it certainly is, only the leader has any substantial freedom of action. Melodies may follow one another, but they cannot coexist. Where the leader's voice leads, the accompanist's must follow. The laws of harmony demand that every tone or note or body have its own space or its own time or both. If two notes want the same space at the same time, the two must fuse and lose their independence, or one must move harmonically aside.

Polyphonic space is non-Newtonian or non-Aristotelian or both. In polyphonic art, two bodies can indeed occupy the same space at the same time without ceasing to be two. Two melodies, or three, or eight, can live their separate lives, with equal pay for equal work, and still eat at the same table and sleep in the same bed.

There are in consequence no polyphonic fanfares. Music played to celebrate the glory of the state or the triumph of the hero is always homophonic. But the equation is not simple. It is plainly not the case that every piece of homophonic music is politically unhealthy, nor that polyphonic music will put an end to war, religious bigotry or sexual oppression.

Most of the repertoire of Renaissance polyphony consists of musical settings of Christian texts. Many of these works are meditations on the trinity and on other enduring conundrums of coexistence: carnal and spiritual, sacred and secular, grief and forgiveness, weakness and strength, the church and the state. I would prefer a pagan polyphony — but that, after all, I am free to create, and I find the example of Christian polyphony quite helpful to that end.

I also cannot shake the sense that polyphonic literature, for me at least, is somehow now more urgent than polyphonic music. There is, I suppose, a simple reason for that: I see much more to speak of than to sing of in the self-entranced and self-destructive culture by which we are engulfed. Polyphony, like poetry, exists in many forms. Not all of it is sung; not all of it is lyric.

5.

Literature, say Socrates and Plato and Archibald MacLeish and Northrop Frye, is absolutely mute. I say so too. I say it speaks but doesn't talk. It is the gestural, or musical, not verbal, use of words. Music is to literature as poetry is to prose, and each is, in its own way, eloquent and mute.

The difference between polyphonic literature and polyphonic music is that literature in general — dumb and untalkative though it is — speaks louder than it sings. The languages of music, like the languages of literature, have grammars, but the languages of literature have dictionaries too. No lexicon or thesaurus will tell you the meaning of C-sharp. That seems to me the only crucial difference between literature and music. Music is what literature becomes when it escapes from under the dictionary; literature is music that must wear that web of reference and that weight of definition almost everywhere it goes.

We are taught, of course, to write with a single pencil, in one voice at a time, the same way we are taught to speak and sing, because one mouth is all we have. If writing were *instrumental* rather than *vocal* — if we spoke with our two hands, the way musicians play the lute or the piano — we could write as a good lutenist or pianist can play: in two, and on occasion even three or four distinct voices at once.

But could we read it? Could we hear it? Trained musicians read motets and fugues with ease, and even nonmusicians learn to hear and sometimes understand them.

We have, in fact, a lot of practice hearing polyphonic speech. It surrounds us in the woods, and it surrounds us in the street and the café. It's what we hear wherever we can listen to the world. It's also what we hear where people speak with neither fealty nor fear, and where their speech is not drowned out by their machines.

If we wrote poetry the way Josquin des Prez and Nicolas Gombert — two masters of polyphony — wrote music, we could write for four or eight. The mind is *capable* of that plurality. We are capable of polyphonic thought and polyphonic speech, as polyphonic music proves. We are capable, that is, of multiplicity of mind in a healthy form. Why is it that the only multiplicity of mind in fashion now is a crippling disease? Polyphony made audible is music. Schizophrenia made audible is noise.

6.

Cantata, sonata and toccata, like villanelle and sonnet, have become the names of forms. Some artists (Beethoven, Rilke) find them useful to dismantle and rebuild, while others find them useful to ignore. But the names point first of all not to differences in structure but to distinctions of instrumentation: *cantatas* to be sung; *sonatas* to be sounded (with such things as bows and horns); *toccatas* to be played by touching keys or valves or plucking strings. Compositions of this kind for speaking voice, I guess, should be *parlatas*, but that is not a word I want to coin. I am happier, most of the time, thinking of language in instrumental and gestural terms. Sonata and toccata are incongruous terms for works that are meant to be spoken, yet these names suit me fine. Something Don McKay said at the Polyphony Colloquium helped me understand why this is so. I quote here from the short working paper he sent around to other participants just before the colloquium convened:

> I take it to be obvious to anyone who raises nose from book: language is completely inadequate to the real. . . .
>
> Poetry is language used with an awareness of the poverty of language.
> . . . Poetry remembers that language is shaped air; it remembers ashes

to ashes, dust to dust, wind to wind; it knows we don't own what we
know. It knows the world is, after all, unnameable, so it listens hard
before it speaks, and wraps that listening into the linguistic act.

Dennis Lee, who plays a mean piano when he isn't writing poems, says
that when he writes he feels the poem, or the cadence out of which the
poem comes, largely in his forearms. One might think that a poet with a
tactile or somatic sense of poetry would feel the poem in his mouth or in
the fingers that he wraps around the pen. Perhaps some do. I think, myself,
that poetry is a *langue sans parole*, sometimes disguised as pure *parole*. I
think that I do not *write* poems at all. I think that I gesticulate with beak-
less lips and wave my stunted limbs.

7.

In the twentieth century Hermann Broch, T.S. Eliot, James Joyce, Thomas
Mann, Ezra Pound, Gertrude Stein, Louis Zukofsky, William Gass and no
doubt many others have knowingly embodied musical forms in their prose
and their poems. Some have been drawn to the structural principles and
techniques of string quartets and piano sonatas. Others — Joyce, Pound
and Zukofsky, for instance — were attracted to the polyphonic structures
of the fugue. How well they succeeded at composing polyphonic literature
is a question I will sidestep for the moment. It is important to me that they
tried. And it is important to me that composers reached for literary forms
at the same time. Samuel Barber's *Essays for Orchestra* and Charles Ives's
Four Transcriptions from Emerson are of a piece with T.S. Eliot's *Four
Quartets* and Hermann Broch's big prose sonatas.

Unknown to these writers, the Russian critic Mikhail Bakhtin had decided in the 1920s that polyphony in literature begins with Dostoevsky.
Bakhtin's brief book arguing this thesis was published in St Petersburg
(then Leningrad) in 1929. Soon after that, Bakhtin was arrested and im-
prisoned, as Dostoevsky had been eighty years before. His reputation and
his ideas vanished with him. But Bakhtin, like Dostoevsky, was saved by a
reprieve. He published his book again, after heavy revision, in Moscow in
1963. By then, unknown to Bakhtin, the literary use of polyphonic structures was on many European artists' minds, and on the minds of other
theorists as well. Claude Lévi-Strauss, to take an interesting example, had
begun to teach his students that the structures of myth and of music were
fundamentally the same. He attempted in particular to show that Native
American myth is structurally akin to the classical music of Europe. He
taught that European classical music shows what happens when the structures inherent in myth are denied, by the authority of the church or the
iron law of reason, every chance to express themselves in words. The four

thick volumes in which Lévi-Strauss unfolded this idea were published between 1964 and 1971.

Literary polyphony as Bakhtin understands it does not mean simultaneous multiple texts in the literal sense of the phrase. It means the continuous independence of the voices and viewpoints of the characters. We read their speeches and their dialogues line by line and voice by voice in sequence, but their visions live together in our heads, and their theses do not fuse. No final synthesis is attained. What Bakhtin sees in Dostoevsky

> is not a multitude of characters and fates in a single objective world, illuminated by a single authorial consciousness; rather *a plurality of consciousnesses, with equal rights and each with its own world*, combine but are not merged in the unity of the event. (1973: 6–7; 1984: 6)

Bakhtin insists that this plurality is strictly nondramatic. He speaks of Rabelais, Shakespeare, Cervantes and Balzac as precursors of Dostoevsky, but only the latter, he claims, created truly polyphonic literature — and polyphonic theatre, he claims, cannot exist. The theatre, he says,

> is by its very nature alien to genuine polyphony; drama may be multileveled, but it cannot contain *multiple worlds;* it permits only one, not several, systems of measurement. (1973: 41 /1984: 34)

It is true and significant that polyphony differs from dialogue. I think, however, that Elizabethan plays with two or more distinct simultaneous plots are among the clearest and most important examples we have of literary polyphony. And I think that admitting the existence of polyphony in Shakespeare takes nothing away from the richness of Dostoevsky's fiction.

Sometime in the 1930s, Bakhtin wrote another lengthy essay known as *Slovo v romane*, "Speech in the Novel." This has been translated, pretentiously, as "Discourse in the Novel," but *slovo* is an unpretentious word. A better rendering would be "How People Talk in Novels." Not that the essay is untroubled in the original by pretension of other kinds — for here again, Bakhtin insists that only the novel can be truly polyphonic.

> The world of poetry, no matter how many contradictions and insoluble conflicts the poet develops within it, is always illumined by one unitary and indisputable discourse. Contradictions, conflicts and doubts remain in the object, in thoughts, in living experiences — in short, in the subject matter — but they do not enter into the language itself. In poetry, even discourse about doubts must be cast in a discourse that cannot be doubted. (1975: 286/ 1981: 286)

It is hard to understand, reading statements such as this, how Bakhtin has remained so long the darling of contemporary criticism. It is true that he had little opportunity to read the poetry of T.S. Eliot and Ezra Pound, and none at all to read the poetry of Dennis Lee. That does not entirely absolve him of his arrogance in claiming no such poetry could possibly exist.

Doubt is not, in any case, the issue. The polyphonic structure of a mass or a chanson or a motet by the poet and composer Guillaume de Machaut or Josquin or Gombert does not require us to doubt a single word in any of its voices. What it does is enable us to hear and accept these voices all at once — and to hear what their simultaneity says that they don't say.

Polyphony is possible in poetry, drama, fiction, and in literary criticism too, though Bakhtin is no example. Like many Russian critics, he stakes out his position and argues it in fervent and combative and exclusionary terms. *Monologic* terms, as he himself would say. Even when praising and preaching polyphony, his practice is intensely homophonic.

8.

A few Canadian poets and critics — Jan Zwicky and Northrop Frye are important examples — are or have been trained musicians. They have learned the word polyphony first-hand, in a practical rather than theoretical sense, and in its original, musical context. But the term was rarely used by anyone discussing Canadian literature, so far as I'm aware, before the end of the 1970s. It was then that Dennis Lee began to speak about polyphony with his own peculiar twist. Both the subject and the word appear in his mock interview "Enacting a Meditation" (1979), and they are central to his essay "Polyphony: Enacting a Meditation" (a different work, despite the similarity in titles) which was published in 1982.

Lee does not demarcate and defend a theoretical position in his essay on polyphony. He accounts as best he can, as a working poet, for his own gut-level and deeper decisions. The result is more a spiritual confession than a literary manifesto, and it is all the more valuable for that. Now that there is a danger of polyphony becoming just another skilled procedure or technique — the hallmark of a Polyphonic School — Lee's fifteen-year-old hunches serve as powerful reminders of why a multiplicity of voices mattered in the first place:

> The discursive voice embodies one narrow human strain, of editorial-izing urbanity, and excludes all other currents in the speaker's makeup.
>   But it is not just the speaker's personal nature which is straitened by this voice. People and wars and trees and multifarious aspirations all go de-selved, within a vocal range that cannot embody their indigenous

tonalities. The whole world is shrunk down to a single repertoriai wave-
length. . . .

   . . .

Polyphony is the art of orchestrating more than one voice across a
work. The polyphonic shift from inflection to inflection, the clash and
resonance of vocal timbres from one moment to the next, is what
traces out the trajectory of a meditation.

   . . .

The plot of a meditation is enacted by the shifting inflections of the
meditative voice.

   . . .

To write polyphonically is to contest 'poetry' as it is now written.
Perhaps even to repudiate it altogether; to walk off that field, and try
to find the real one. (Lee 1982: §§3–7)

Lee's writings on polyphony owe nothing to Bakhtin. One may ask how
they could if Canada is really a free country, not a Stalinist regime. But polyphony for Lee, as for Bakhtin, is a matter of huge political import. The
reason is laid bare in an earlier essay, "Cadence, Country, Silence," published
in 1973. That essay rests in part on Lee's close reading of George Grant:

The prime fact about my country as a public space is that in the last
25 years it has become an American colony . . . [and] in a colony, the
simple act of writing becomes a problem to itself. (Lee 1973: 38)

The answer to this problem, as Lee knows, is not a revolution in which
one voice ousts another. The answer is not to shift the prisoners from one
cell to the next. But what about a space in which the doors are all unlocked
and there is no controlling voice? The polyphonic poem for Lee, like the
polyphonic novel for Bakhtin, is a space in which to breathe, not just a
space in which to speak. Polyphony, he says, "permits an openness to the
textures of being which is, for me, the *sine qua non* of writing at all"
(1985:191).
    Poets are not the only creatures who think and talk this way. A century
ago — before Bakhtin began to hear a real ecology of voices in the novels
of Dostoevsky — the biologist Jakob von Uexküll (1864–1944) taught that
the relation between any living thing and its environment is always contra-
puntal. Polyphony in Uexküll's terms is the quintessential form of the relation between species: life is polyphonic; death is not.
    Still, and again, the equation is not simple. It is not that a dominant voice
is always bad and a plurality of voices always good. And multiplicity of
voice as a spiritual goal is quite a different thing from multiplicity of voice

as a technical device. That is why Lee's writings on polyphony are haunted by the ghost of Ezra Pound — who is, in Lee's understanding of the term, a great polyphonist himself.

> It was as if [Ezra Pound] could go into a room, with a little hammer; strike each particular thing; pick up the frequency it emitted — and register that directly onto the page. (Lee 1985: 206)

The Cantos, Lee admits, is a treasure house of voices. What appalls him is its pointillist, imperative technique. The only way from one voice to the next is to close your eyes and cling to the demented poet's shoulders while he makes another leap.

Demented or not, that method of construction is one Pound shared with many other artists. The shifts of voice in Béla Bartók's Sonata for Solo Violin (Sz. 117), and in countless other works of modern music, are equally abrupt. Few poets or composers leap from voice to voice as agilely as Pound; few have his range; but the jump-cut may be the twentieth century's favorite artistic device.

Polyphony for Lee is a trajectory of voices, intuiting the grain of meditative space. One voice speaks at once, but in finding its trajectory, that voice actually *becomes* other voices as it goes. The self enacts its many selves, or is possessed by many selves, sliding or gliding more often than jumping from one to the next.

But Lee is also a musician, and musicians are familiar with sequential shifts of voice. They call them *modulation*, not polyphony. Dostoevsky, writing to his brother in 1864, described his own procedure in precisely the same terms: as modulation. Why did Lee choose Bakhtin's loaded (maybe overloaded) word instead of Dostoevsky's? There are, I think, two reasons. First, the essential end result of Lee's shifts from voice to voice is not the shift itself but the accumulating whole, an ecology of voices, and a silent voice that arises from the others, speaking on its own of the plurality of being. Second, Lee's kind of modulation is not the conventional musical kind. It is not modulation from established key to key along an equal-tempered path. It consists of unpredictable, often incremental shifts of tone or voice instead. That kind of modulation is found in music too, but in music as in literature, it lacks a proper name. It is close to being standard procedure in certain kinds of jazz and in some of the classical music of India. Anyone who listens to John Coltrane or old Ben Webster playing horn can learn to hear it. But in that tradition, no one writes it down — and at the moment, evidently, no one can. Those incremental shifts of voice and tone are musical phenomena for which we have no musical notation.

9.

Up to now, we've been discussing *metaphorical* polyphony in literature: polyphonic thought confined within the bounds of monophonie speaking. In the poetry of Ezra Pound and Dennis Lee, and (if we accept Bakhtin's evaluation) in the novels of Dostoevsky, voices may accumulate and finally coexist within the reader's mind, but one voice at once is what confronts us on the page, and one voice at once is what we hear when the work is read aloud. Even in the plays of Shakespeare, one voice at once is what we read and what we usually hear, and for the greater part of any given play, the several plots unfold by turns.

There are, however, literary works in which the polyphonic structure is as literal and real as in any work of polyphonic music. At the risk of sounding like a partisan — and therefore like Bakhtin — I must say that the finest examples I know of true polyphony in literature happen to be Canadian-made. They are, of course, not present in any anthologies, nor are they taught in any conventional course in Canadian literature, yet they are known and admired by students and composers of polyphonic literature in Canada and abroad.

Glenn Gould's three so-called "documentaries" — *The Idea of North* (1967), *The Latecomers* (1969) and *The Quiet in the Land* (1977) — are known collectively as the *Solitude Trilogy*. All these works are polyphonic through and through, but they are works for polyphonic speaking voices, not compositions written to be sung. They do not, in fact, exist except in the form of acoustic recordings. There are no written scores nor was there ever a coherent live performance. Scores and staged performances could both be created after the fact, but overdubbed and spliced magnetic tape is the real original medium.

The texts of the *Solitude Trilogy* are partly composed by Gould himself, partly contrived (by Gould's asking leading questions or creating situations which his microphone records), and partly found. But the found, contrived and custom-made components are laced with immense precision into stable compositions.

Gould played Bach throughout his life, but the polyphonic textures of the *Solitude Trilogy* are not Bach's textures. They are closer by far to the textures in Gould's own densely polyphonic String Quartet, published in 1957.

I didn't live in North America in 1967 nor in 1969, when the first two parts of the trilogy were broadcast. And I was somewhere in the bush at the time of the third. So I not only missed them all; I heard nothing about them. Entirely by accident, I was in Toronto in 1982, on the night Gould died — but all I knew about him then was that he was a master at elucidating Bach with a piano. In 1986, when the CBC recorded *The Blue Roofs of Japan* — a poem of mine scored for two simultaneous voices — Dennis

Lee brought Gould's much more accomplished work to my attention. The only way to hear the trilogy then was acoustic samizdat: pirated tapes of the radio broadcasts, but these were not very hard to obtain. In the three or four years between *The Blue Roofs of Japan* and *The New World Suites*, I did a lot of listening. I began, then, to understand that Gould was the most colossally improbable of all Canadian poets — and that he was, more improbably still, one of the greatest. To say this is also, perhaps, to contest what "poetry" means. I use the word as I must, and not as a name for the quaint little versified or verse-like bursts of verbal nostalgia, amusement and confusion that pass without remark in oral cultures but in literate cultures often get written and printed.

10.

For people like me, convinced not of the evil but of the impermanence and finally the irrelevance of industrial technology, the thought that full-fledged polyphonic literature might be dependent on the microphone, the tape deck and the splicing bar is not completely welcome. I am told that no such worries haunted Gould, but they haunt me. I use the fancy tools when they're here, but only on condition that I live at least part-time in the older world, where I do my work without them.

There is a lot of metaphorical polyphony in the works of preindustrial oral poets — mythtelling poets in particular. A mythology never consists of a series of stories told in a fixed and tidy sequence. A mythology consists, like a science, of potentially innumerable stories that are present to the mind *all at once*. But is there any real and literal polyphonic literature in the preindustrial world, or do we have to go all the way back to the frogs and the songbirds to hear it?

I first learned the answer to this question from Roy Franklin Barton, a gifted anthropologist who died in 1947, leaving on his desk several nearly finished manuscripts based on his life among the Ifugao of northern Luzon.

The culture of the Ifugao, like the culture of their uphill neighbours the Ilongot, survived five centuries of Portuguese, Spanish, Dutch and American colonization in the Philippines, and at least half a century of autocolonization by the Filipinos themselves. It was irrevocably altered by the Second World War: the invasion of Luzon by the Japanese, then the American counter-invasion, then Filipino independence and the increased missionization and forced modernization that rapidly followed. A similar story can be told, with local variations, for a hundred languages and cultures dotting the Pacific, from the Solomon Islands to the Aleutians.

Barton saw the older culture of the Ifugao in its final years. He worked in Ifugaoland first in the 1920s, learned the language well, was there again for eight years in the 1930s, and was, to his subsequent regret, still there when the Japanese landed in 1941. In those days, according to Barton, there were "at least 1500 deities known by name, . . . divided into about 40 classes." With that many spirit-beings to name and a similarly rich oral literature used to invoke them, the Ifugao had evolved a practical means for telling a number of stories at once.

> Before the myth recitation begins, there is an allotment of the myths among the priests. At a mock-headfeast I saw in Bitu in 1937 over forty myths were recited by 16 priests. Each priest recites his myth simultaneously with the rest and when he has finished one myth, he begins another. The result is a babble in which the words are indistinguishable. Boys or youths sometimes snuggle alongside a priest, turn their ear to him alone so as to listen only to his myth and in this way begin their education for the priesthood. The Ifugao man who is not a priest is an exception.
>
>   The myth recitation consists of short phrases barked out by the priest in two or three musical intonations — those of the young priest probably in a falsetto, those of an elderly priest in a deep rumble. If you should approach one of the little villages in which a myth recitation is going on, you would first hear a faint hum like that of swarming bees. As you come nearer, the hum would grow into a murmur and the murmur would grow into a roar like that of an approaching mob on the stage. Arriving in the village you would note that, despite the fact that [to a foreign ear] the stories were all being lost in a general jumble, there would nevertheless be an audience of women and children sitting underneath neighboring houses, gathered to listen. (Barton 1955: 6–7)

In the days before a feast, Barton says, he sometimes met the mythtellers sitting by the streams, talking with the water. Talking with the water, not lecturing the waves, was the favored method for training the voice. And some became particularly proud of their mythtelling skills and their voices.

> I have often noted that as a myth-recitation draws to an end, so that voices begin to drop out, some priests are timid and bring their recitations to a hurried close while others, bolder, contrive to prolong their myths, delighting in the chance of making a solo display of their voices and of their energy of recitation. (1955: 7)

It is too late now to hear those stories told as richly as they were in 1937, or to know how they were told 400 years before, or to cross-examine Barton, but I wonder if everyone there found the words as indistinguishable as he did. I think about those feasts among the rice fields now when I am listening to Gould and Josquin, and to Thomas Tallis's motet *Spem in alium*, for forty separate voices. I think about them too when I am listening to Orlando di Lasso's polyphonic setting of the penitential psalms, written about 1560, when the European ships were still discovering the harbours of North and South America, New Guinea, Indonesia, the Philippines — and when those who sailed on the ships were still just beginning to give lessons in the fear of God and the horror of man to half the peoples of the world. I think about the feasts, and I wonder if the words weren't perfectly clear, to those who knew them best, when they were still allowed to hear them.

The equation is not simple, but it holds. All truths are true: the ones that were, the ones that are, the ones we hear, the ones we don't, the ones that will be.

II.

It would clarify the nature of polyphony in literature if we knew more precisely what it is not. It is not, on the one hand, monophony or monody: it is not a single voice, whether lyric or narrative, melodic or prosaic, discursive or dramatic. It is also not homophony. But is there such a thing as homophony in literature? Are there literary works in which one voice leads and others strum the chords or otherwise supply harmonic background? Most songs (using the term in the popular sense) are that exactly. The singer sings the melody; the piano or guitar or orchestra or chorus does the backup. But song in this sense is a hybrid: verbal text coupled with musical composition. Are there any purely literary works that do the same? *The Blue Roofs of Japan* is as much homophonic as polyphonic, in my opinion, but Stan Dragland has pointed out to me a clearer and plainer example. It is found in James Reaney's chapbook *Twelve Letters to a Small Town* (1962). Not all of Reaney's letters have epistolary form. The eighth is cast as a dialogue between a piano student and teacher. An exercise is set. The student is to play a homophonic composition whose theme is the four seasons. The teacher tries a standard pedagogical technique. She asks the student first to play the lefthand part (the accompaniment), then the righthand part (the melody), and then the two together. All this is written out, or acted out, in words. The accompaniment, because it is just an accompaniment, includes no independent statements. It is written in nonsentences. A brief example will do:

Bud bud budling
Bud bud budling
    . . .

Leafy leafy leafy
   Leaf leaf leaf . . . (Reaney 1962; cf. Dragland 1991: 37)

The melody is equally mundane, but it does make statements of a kind. That is, it is written in sentences. Such as:

The spring winds up the town
The spring winds up the town.

After trying out the two parts separately, the student plays them both. Accompaniment and melody go marching in two columns down the page. Reading the text aloud would take two voices, just as playing it, if we could, would take two hands. But one voice speaks the melody, the other speaks the harmony. One voice follows where the other leads.

There is, then, I think, a simple test for polyphony in literature, analogous to the test for its musical counterpart. These are the usual conditions:

(1) There are two or more voices, which are *or are made to seem* simultaneous. (In imitative polyphony, the voices say more or less the same thing, though they say it out of frequency and phase with one another and may contradict each other in other ways. In independent polyphony, there is not only more than one *voice;* there is more than one *text*. These may be in different languages and move at different tempi or otherwise diverge.)

(2) At least two of the voices could stand on their own. They have something to say as well as a voice in which to say it. In literary polyphony, this normally means that the voices are *written in sentences*. They aren't saying things such as *oompah oompah oompah* or *me too yes me too*.

(3) One voice may have many more words than another, but no voice really steals the show. There is no soloist, no star.

(4) A space is created by these voices, and the space is claimed by a dance or pattern or form. That form does not exist in any of the voices by itself, but it emerges from their conjunction.

12.

Polyphony is not a literary or musical technique; it is a complex property of reality which any work of art can emphasize or minimize, or notice or ignore. Palestrina's polyphony is different from Carlo Gesualdo's, and both of these are different from Josquin's. We needn't be surprised if there are equally large differences in polyphonic practice in the literary world. Some of these differences are highly individual, and some are linked to genre. A mass is not a fugue. The Polyphony Colloquium at Trent confined itself to poetry and music, but some of the best polyphonic writing I have seen in recent years is polyphonic fiction.

I have not seen a novel or short story in which the reader is really expected to read more than one prose text at once. So all the polyphonic fiction I'm familiar with is, if you like, metaphorical polyphony. Some of it is nonetheless convincingly polyphonic. This again needn't come as a surprise. Metaphorical polyphony exists in music too. It represents, in fact, an eminent and durable musical tradition.

Metaphorical polyphony means using one voice skillfully enough to suggest the continuous presence of two or more. By alternating voices, a ventriloquist gives the illusion of speaking for two. Metaphorical polyphony functions by similar means. Music for piano doesn't normally involve metaphorical polyphony. Two hands really can play two tunes at once. So can the lutenist's five right fingers while the others stop the strings. But one voice at once is technically the limit for a bowed string instrument — a violin, a cello, a viola. There are, nevertheless, three fugues in Bach's three sonatas for solo violin, and three corresponding fugues in Britten's three suites for solo cello. Bartôk's sonata for solo violin includes a fugue as well. Each fugue has two voices, but the instrument it's written for has one. Each voice has to interrupt the other to be heard. The player has to shuffle back and forth between the voices, articulating each with clarity and force and continuity enough that both are heard — and both retain their independence. The voices interact without depending on each other. Polyphony is not the same as dialogue.

This again is polyphonic *thinking* embodied within monophonic *speaking*. Something similar occurs in plays like *Twelfth Night*, where two related plots unfold in alternating scenes.

Many of the stories of Guy Davenport are richly polyphonic in this sense. Several plots, threads or voices interweave. They may or may not touch at any point in the story. And just as in a Renaissance motet, one voice may be focussed on the sacred and another on the secular.

"The Meadow" is the first of several linked stories forming Davenport's sixth book of fiction, *The Jules Verne Steam Balloon* (1987). Three voices speak by turns here, in addition to the voices of the characters. The tenor voice is gleefully attentive to the sex life of several adolescents on a camping trip, unchaperoned. The bass — the cantus firmus — is a botanist, every bit as ardent in his way, who is noting in meticulous detail everything he can about the lives of flowering plants. The third voice — alto or soprano, I suppose — reports the actions of three very brainy, young and hyperactive angels known as Quark, Tumble and Buckeye. They are travelling by steam balloon, scouting out the scene and now and then reporting to a listener whose name we never learn.

What *happens* in the story? Not much more than happens in a song. But this is three songs. That is what happens. This is three songs sung together so they fit to make a fourth song, unlike any song a monophonic ear has ever heard.

In the elevated floor around the altar in the Baptistery at Pisa, something similar occurs. Laid in the mosaic are repeating sets of geometric lattices. Each is built from four sets of fivefold interlocking figures. The pattern they create — a long organic crystal, orthoclastic and hexagonal in symmetry, shimmering in its two-dimensional bed — does not exist in any of the figures, sets or lattices themselves. It exists in their conjunction: there alone. I do not know the name of the artist who created this mosaic. It was not evidently Deotisalvi, the Baptistery architect, nor Guido da Como, who built the font. The Baptistery's records suggest that the elevated floor was built around the time the roof was closed, toward the end of the fourteenth century. If so, the mosaic was laid about the time Guillaume de Machaut was writing his equally crystalline motets, polyphonic songs and hockets, and his intricately geometric four-voice mass.

The coincidence of music, crystallography and fiction is nothing strange to Davenport, who in one of his stories calls one of Mozart's quartets (K 575) "a polyhedral fragrance of light."

13.

Forms, and therefore meanings, are achieved through the conjunction of other forms and meanings. That principle is basic to biology and chemistry and physics and the history of art. In polyphonic structures, the conjunction is *nondestructive*. The component forms and meanings survive — within and beside and beneath and on top of the meanings and forms their conjunction creates.

Some of the oldest known artworks on the planet were rediscovered in December 1994 in a cave in the Ardèche — between the Rhône and the Cévennes in southern France. The site has since been named for one of the speleologists who found it, Jean-Marie Chauvet. If the published radiocarbon dates are correct, the paintings at Chauvet are 30,000 years of age: twice as old as the oldest dated paintings in Lascaux and Altamira.

There are a number of large murals in the cave. One of the most impressive, to judge from the reproductions (Chauvet et al 1996: 106–14), is the Lion Panel. Several dozen figures — lions, mammoths, bison, rhinoceros and horses — are rendered with great clarity in black, white and red on the undulating tawny limestone wall. The figures are in clusters. Patterns form where the outlines overlap. The result is both emphatically pictorial and powerfully abstract.

This is visual polyphony. It is the oldest known method for doing static, two-dimensional justice to moving forms in three-dimensional space. It was displaced, as a basic method, at a later date by geometrical perspective. But geometrical perspective has no working counterpart in music. Polyphony, therefore, remains the fundamental means in music of creating and elucidating space. (And visual polyphony persists, even within the realm of perspectival painting. It remains, I think, the quintessential means of representing or embodying a quintessential fact: that forms can coexist, creating space, and forms are born where others intersect.)

The mind, say good ethologists, including Konrad Lorenz, is just as biologically explicable — as *natural*, that is — as any other organ, like the liver or the forepaw or the fin, and its phylogeny can be just as clearly traced. We learn to think — not just as individuals but as species, and as genera and families of species — by accumulating sensory experience of three-dimensional space. That experience is achieved by several means, including echolocation, binocular vision and voluntary motion. (Involuntary motion yields far less feedback information.) The mind, in fact, consists of abstract patterns formed from concrete sensory perceptions. A work of polyphonic art — the Lion Panel, for example — has better things to do than represent a mental state; it represents the ground of mind itself.

These days, when I think about Glenn Gould fitting voices into voices in a basement in Toronto, I also often think about the hunter-painter-gatherers who made the murals of Chauvet. I think the painters might have liked to hear the pianist-turned-poet play some Bach, and that the painters in their turn might have shown us quite a bit about the subtleties of polyphonic speaking.

Leads and Sources

Works quoted or alluded to are itemized below. Those I especially recommend to people with an interest in polyphony are asterisked.

*Arom, Simha. 1985. *Polyphonies et polyrythmies instrumentales d'Afrique centrale.* Paris: SELAF.
*——. 1991. *African Polyphony and Polyrhythm.* Trans. Martin Thorn, Barbara Tuckett, and Raymond Boyd. Cambridge: Cambridge UP.
Bakhtin, Mikhail Mikhailovich. 1929. *Problemy tvorchestva Dostoevskogo.* Leningrad: Priboi.
——. 1973. *Problemy poetiki Dostoevskogo.* 4th ed. Moscow: Rossiia.
——. 1975. "Slovo v romane." In *Voprosy literatury i estetiki.* Moscow: Khudozh.
——. 1981. "Discourse in the Novel." In *The Dialogic Imagination: Four Essays.* Trans. Caryl Emerson and Michael Holquist. Austin: U of Texas P.
——. 1984. *Problems of Dostoevksy's Poetics.* Ed. and trans. Caryl Emerson. Minneapolis: U of Minnesota P.
Barthes, Roland. 1964. "Littérature et signification." In *Essais critiques.* Paris: Seuil.
*Bartók, Béla. 1947. *Sonata for Solo Violin* [Sz. 117]. London: Hawkes & Son.
*Barton, Roy Franklin. 1955. *The Mythology of the Ifugaos.* Philadelphia: Memoirs of the American Folklore Society 46.
*Bringhurst, Robert. 1986. *The Blue Roofs of Japan: A Score for Interpenetrating Voices.* Mission, BC: Barbarian.

*——. 1995. *The Calling*. Toronto: McClelland & Stewart.
*Chauvet, Jean-Marie; Éliette Brunei Deschamps; Christian Hillaire. 1996. *Dawn of Art: The Chauvet Cave*. New York: Abrams.
*Davenport, Guy. 1987. *The Jules Verne Steam Balloon*. San Francisco: North Point.
Dragland, Stan. 1991. *The Bees of the Invisible*. Toronto: Coach House.
*Gombert, Nicolas. 1951–75. *Opera omnia*. Ed. Joseph Schmidt-Gorg. 12 vols. Rome: American Institute of Musicology.
*Gould, Glenn. 1957. *String Quartet, Op. 1*. Great Neck, NY: Barger & Barclay.
*——. 1992. *Solitude Trilogy*. 3 compact discs. Toronto: CBC Records.
*Josquin des Prez. 1925–69. *Werken*. Ed. Albert Smijers. 25 vols. Amsterdam: Alspach.
Lasso, Orlando di. 1990. *The Seven Penitential Psalms and Laudate Dominum de caelis*. Ed. Peter Bergquist. Madison, Wisconsin: A-R.
*Lee, Dennis. 1973. "Cadence, Country, Silence: Writing in Colonial Space." *Open Letter* 2–6: 34–53.
*——. 1979. "Enacting a Meditation: An Interview with Dennis Lee." Prologue by Jon Pearce. *Journal of Canadian Poetry* 2.1: 5–23.
*——. 1982. "Polyphony: Enacting a Meditation." *Descant* 39: 82–99.
*——. 1985. "For and Against Pound: Polyphony and Ekstatic Form." *Open Letter* 6.2–3: 191–212.
*——. 1996. *Nightwatch*. Toronto: McClelland & Stewart.
* Leech-Wilkinson, Daniel. 1990. *Machaut's Mass*. Oxford: Clarendon P.
Lévi-Strauss, Claude. 1964–71. *Mythologiques*. 4 vols. (*Le Cru et le cuit*, *Du Miel aux cendres*; *L'Origine des manières de table*, *L'Homme nu*). Paris: Pion.
——. 1969–81. *Introduction to a Science of Mythology*. Trans. John and Doreen Weightman. 4 vols. (*The Raw and the Cooked*; *From Honey to Ashes*; *The Origin of Table Manners*; *The Naked Man*). New York: Harper & Row.
Lorenz, Konrad. 1973. *Die Rückseite des Spiegels*. Munich: Piper.
——. 1977. *Behind the Mirror: A Search for a Natural History of Human Knowledge*. Trans. Ronald Taylor. London: Methuen.
*Machaut, Guillaume de. 1956. *The Works of Guillaume de Machaut*. Ed. Leo Schrade. 2 vols. Monaco: L'Oiseau-lyre.
Reaney, James. 1962. *Twelve Letters to a Small Town*. Toronto: Ryerson.
Saladin d'Anglure, Bernard. 1978. "Entre cri et chant: Les katajjait, un genre musical féminin." *Études inuit* 2.1: 85–94.
Smith, Christine. 1975. *The Baptistery of Pisa*. New York: Garland.
*Tallis, Thomas. 1989. *Spem in alium*. In Tallis, *Latin Church Music*. Vol. 1. Taverner Consort & Choir. Compact disc. Hayes, Middlesex: EMI.
Uexküll, Jakob von. 1921. *Umwelt und Innenwelt der Tiere*. 2nd ed. Berlin: Springer.

CL 155 (Winter 1997)

George Elliott Clarke

in conversation with

Wayde Compton and Kevin McNeilly

from *The Crime of Poetry*

This interview consists of excerpts from a conversation, sponsored by *Canadian Literature*, in front of an audience at Green College, UBC, in late July 2002.

Kevin McNeilly (KM): George Elliott Clarke's poetry offers us an enticing tangle of contradictions and confrontations, things like a vicious delicacy or a brutal lyricism or — I've taken a phrase straight from his poetry — a "sweet hurt." Clarke provokes and challenges his readers' false comforts of culture, or of language, or of race, all the while immersing us in a kind of verbal balm. Wayde Compton's acclaimed first book of poems, *49th Parallel Psalm*, and his recent anthology *Bluesprint* have done great things to establish the presence and history of black British Columbian literature and orature. . . . Could you comment a little bit on your views about the cultural role of anthologists? . . .

Wayde Compton (WC): Well, I was wondering what inspired you [George] to start [your] bibliography [*Africana Canadiana*], because it's kind of the same question. For me, doing *Bluesprint* was just to get a sense of what is out there, to find the lay of the land. Because there's no foundation for what I'm doing in BC, I felt I needed to know what has come before. In terms of history, and also in terms of the writing. Is that a reason for doing a bibliography?

George Elliott Clarke (GEC): What happened was, in fall 1994, I got a letter from Professor [Doug] Killam at the University of Guelph, and
he asked me to do this article on connections between African
Canadian writing and African writing. And I said, "Sure . . ." So I
started looking for material to write about. . . . I just got interested, and I asked myself, so what else has Austin Clarke done, for
instance? What about books in translation? Who was the first
black playwright in Canada? Who was the first black novelist?
People were walking around saying, "Austin Clarke is the first
black novelist." And yeah it's true, but only in terms of the first
black novelist published in Canada. But if you looked at books
published outside of Canada, then you talk about people like
Amelia E. Johnson, who published her first novel [*Clarence and
Corinne; or, God's Way*], in 1890, but in Philadelphia. So does she
count? Yeah, because she was born in Montreal, and grew up in
Toronto. But Canada didn't exist yet. I count her as an African
Canadian foremother, and I think she should be read in that way.
She may never be very important in terms of African American
literature, but I would argue that for African Canadian literature
she's absolutely important, and partly because of the fact that in
none of her three novels does she use black characters. They're all
white characters because the people who were publishing her —
an American Baptist society — figured nobody was going to read
them. They did advertise her as a coloured woman writer, but they
realized there wasn't going to be a market for black characters. So
as long as their black woman writer wrote about white characters,
everybody would be happy. But what's fascinating for me is what
A.E. Johnson did to counteract that: she uses Black English. She
gives her white characters black English. It's like, thank you! The
illustrations are of white characters, and they have what is demonstrably black plantation English going on in the text.

I place someone like Suzette Mayr against her, and the whole
context of racial identity and so on . . . I want to honour those
who went and wrote and published when they had no expectation
of being received or even read. I mean, Truman Green, for instance, *A Credit to Your Race*, a fantastic work, and who read it
in 1973? . . .

KM   What kind of an audience do you envision for your work? . . . I
mean, who's reading this stuff?

GEC   I am hoping that everybody is. [Laughter.] That's my hope. I'm
interested in an audience of anybody who can read English. Because that's the only way my work is accessible, in that particular
language. On the other hand, yes, I am trying to communicate

specifically to black Nova Scotians, black Canadians, as well. I'm hoping that a black Canadian audience might find my work interesting, and a black Nova Scotian audience would find it interesting. But I also know that there is no way I can confine my writing to only those audiences, because there are very few publishers who, in the first place, will say "Okay, how many readers, how many identifiably only black readers can we guarantee your book?" Also, like many of us, I'm also . . . not didactic, but I am an educator. I am hoping that people pick up *Beatrice Chancy* and when they read that work, they'll say, "Oh yeah, there was slavery in Nova Scotia, and in Canada, and it wasn't necessarily a nice thing."

As someone just tried to argue recently in the *Globe and Mail*, in a letter to the editor: "Yeah well you know, our slavery wasn't as bad as American slavery." And I was like, "Oh really, tell that to the slaves." It was apparently a "kinder gentler slavery in Canada." [Laughter.] I'm trying to address those national myths that we tell ourselves, for the fundamental purpose of making ourselves seem better than Americans. There are a lot of things we do better than the Americans, maybe, like delivering health care; on the other hand, we can learn from them about addressing, despite our great multicultural society, our problem around race and racism. At least Americans talk about it. They may not solve it, but at least they talk about it. We don't even do that. I'm also trying to signal to the rest of the world, whoever may come across these texts in some obscure venue somewhere, that we exist! We exist! We've been here for a long time and for what it's worth, here's our literature. Take a look at it.

KM   I know in the introduction to *Eyeing the North Star* . . . you distinguish between African American and African Canadian literary practices or contexts. Could you elaborate on that?

GEC   . . . I think the greatest difference between African Canadians and African Americans is that African Canadians are not a monolithic group. And even though African Americans are composed of many different kinds of black people, who come from all over the world, there is really only, I would argue, one overriding African American identity, to which everyone is expected to subscribe, no matter where you come from.

In the same way that no matter where you come from in the world, to join the American republic is to accept certain ideas, values, principles, without dispute. To be an American is to accept certain fundamental values: you take an oath of allegiance to the revolution in effect — to what the American Revolution stood for

— when you become an American citizen. In the same way, African America also has a kind of expectation of immigrants to its body, so to speak, to become African American and to accept the major culture, the heroes, the history, . . . simply to identify with all of that.

Whereas in African Canada, there is no such overriding determination of what it means to be a black Canadian. You are black Canadian as you wish, more or less, in our context. And that makes for a far more heteroglot, far more diverse, far more democratic kind of community, I feel, and far more diverse community than you have with African Americans. On the other hand, that's not always completely good. Because it also means it's much more difficult to organize. . . . There isn't a single national black organization in Canada. Now there are national ethnic organizations . . . of Trinidadians, Jamaicans, Barbadians. But the difference is that here, one's ethnicity, national origin, home, root, culture still continue to have some prominence, and some importance, so one may easily identify oneself as being Somalian or Ethiopian or Trinidadian, as opposed to being Canadian, or as opposed to being African Canadian.

Another handy illustration of this principle comes from the 1991 census, and the analysis that was done in 1997 by James L. Torczyner at McGill University [*Diversity, Mobility and Change: The Dynamics of Black Communities in Canada*]. With a team of black sociologists, he looked at the 1991 census data; from an African American point of view, it's astonishing, because according to their analysis, 43% of black Canadians did not self-identify as black. In the 1991 census! Now, in the US, that's impossible. You could never get a figure like that. But in Canada, what happened, according to their analysis, was that people who came from majority black nations, in the Caribbean and in Africa, chose to identify themselves as being either British or French. So people from Jamaica, Trinidad or Nigeria said, "We're British," and people from Haiti and Senegal said, "We're French." From an African American point of view, again, this would be almost insane . . . But from their point of view, it made perfect sense, because the context is British, or the context is French, from which these respondents were coming.

Althea Prince in her introductory essay to *Being Black* talks about coming from Antigua, a majority black nation, where she's been schooled in British traditions (Wordsworth, daffodils, all that), and she flies to Toronto. She has come into another part of the British Commonwealth where she is now going to live with her sister, who's already been in Canada for a while, and she gets off the plane at Toronto International Airport, and everybody's staring at her. It's 1965, by the way; she is twenty years old. And she asks her sister, "Why is everybody staring at us?" And her sister says "Because you're black," and she had no idea. [Laughter.] No clue what her sister is saying to her: "What do you mean I'm black? That doesn't make any sense. This is stupid! I'm Antiguan! I'm a student! Why are you telling me I'm black?"

When one comes to North America from majority black culture, you don't grow up thinking of yourself as being black, you think about yourself in other ways. And so when you come to the US, to Britain, to France, to Europe in general or North America, you're suddenly in a minority, and a racialized minority at that, where you have a black identity thrust upon you. But then you have to decide, is that who you are, or not? Is that an identity that you really feel comfortable with? And not everybody does, nor should they. To suddenly have to think of yourself as being a minority, as being somewhat disempowered because of that status in this society and because of all the stereotypes that go along with that, is a tricky thing to ask people to do. For first generation immigrant writers, you see a working out of that exact dilemma: of either an adoption of something called black identity, or a rejection of it, as something very artificial and strange.

And I think you see this quite clearly in [Dany] Laferrière's *How to Make Love to A Negro*, which is a wonderful refutation of that attempt to impose a stereotype, even though he's using the stereotypes in that book. He can afford to make fun of those stereotypes because they are completely alien, artificial, antithetical to where he's coming from, where he's come from literally. And so he sees North Americans talking about black men and white women. For him this is actually a lot of fun. It's so silly in terms of his context, his own native context, that he can afford to have all kinds of fun with things that people like Eldridge Cleaver had to take seriously.

One of the phrases I use in my writing, I revised from Shakespeare: "Some are born black, some achieve blackness, and some have blackness thrust upon them." And I think that's really the Canadian way, so to speak.

Whereas in African America, it's simply imposed. I was given this lesson in very clear terms one bleak, rainy Friday night just outside Durham [North Carolina]. I was driving in my used 1990 Miata, towards the coast, and I was speeding, I admit it, I was speeding, and it was a lot of fun, and I got pulled over in the rain. Well, first of all, remembering that I'm a black male, no matter what, I keep both hands on my steering wheel. So I never move them off the steering wheel; they're always there, just in case there's any question of where my hands are, or what I might be doing. I don't want to get shot in the back of the head and all the rest of it. So the officer comes up; he takes a lot of time to approach the vehicle, and finally does. I admit: "Yes, you got me, yes I'm way over the speed limit." But anyway, he said, "Okay (I think he was mollified by the fact that I admitted my guilt), I'm going to mark you down as being only five miles over the speed limit so you'll only have a $100 fine instead of a $200 fine." Okay, I really appreciate that, officer: and I took the ticket and I was really happy. But when I finally looked at it the next morning, I realized there were two boxes on it, "B" and "W" and he'd checked off "B" for black, on a speeding ticket! But it reminded me, viscerally, that this is a society where in every single fundamental way, I was being determined. I was saying I'm Canadian, but I'm a "B" to him. Okay, I accept that, I'm happy, I identify, it's not a problem, I even identify in traffic court. [Laughter.] So there's much less space for discussions of mixed race identity, hybridity, than there is here. I mean here, here there's a lot more space. . . . Afrocentrism in Canada has to be lived intellectually, spiritually, psychologically, but it can't be lived politically, not in the ways it can be in the United States. In the United States you have blacks in numbers: in particular places, they can control the political network, the political system, including in some major cities. It's just not possible here, unless you are able to go off, settle, and form your own community someplace. . . .

KM   Both you and Wayde have produced anthologies with other kinds of conceptual frameworks that have to do with region: could either of you address the idea of region?

WC   When I realized that *Bluesprint* was being published, one of the things that I thought was strange (because I knew about *Fire on the Water* and was using that as kind of a model) — and it seems odd, but it was nicely symmetrical — was that on both ends of the country, the first regional anthology had come out of Nova Scotia, and the second had come out of BC. But it seems strange because the designation "black British Columbian" seems a little arbitrary. The whole time I was struggling with it: is this the body of people that I should be looking at, or should it be Western Canadian, or Alberta and BC, or what? Because the term "black British Columbia" isn't something that people own. Which is just what George is saying, on a sort of micro-cosmic level. But in Nova Scotia there is that sense, because it is a longer history I guess, of something more deeply rooted. But the black population in BC is actually larger than the black population in Nova Scotia today, by thousands. But still, there isn't a centrally located black community. I wonder what you have seen in terms of regionalism in Canada. We have regional issues among the general population of Canada, the way Canada breaks down, as Western Canada, the Maritimes, Quebec, Central Canada. In terms of black people, or black literature, do the regions have significance to the writing, or the way that black people formulate themselves? In BC sort of, but it is hard to say.

GEC   The answer to that is yes. I will, to my dying breath, say that black Canadian writing is as regional as Canadian writing in general. I do think there is a distinctive black BC school: now that you have put out *Bluesprint*, we all know there is one. And whether it existed before or not, it does exist now. That is one of the functions of an anthology, to say "this is who we are." Whether anybody agrees or not, the editor says, this is who we are. Even though you are being very cautious, and so on, and gentle, about imposing any kind of definition on people. The fact that the book is there, and the fact that you claim Sir James Douglas as a black writer, thank you, you are making some very real claims about territoriality, and what this body of literature consists of. What's going to happen now, Mr. Compton, is that younger black writers coming up, ten years younger than yourself, who may not have even started writing yet, when they start writing, and they're living in Vancouver or Surrey or Kamloops, and they go to the library, they will pick up *Bluesprint*, as they will whether you know it or not, and say, "Yeah, I'm a black BC writer, and when I am older and I pick up *Bluesprint*, we're all going to be included." And so when you set up those regional anthologies, you are setting up a tradition. All anthologies are basically saying a tradition exists. Whether you are talking about queer and lesbian writing, whether you are talking about women's writing from the 16th century, as soon as that scholar comes along and says, "Here is the anthology folks," *boom*, you've got a tradition, you have a canon. And the other anthologists are going to come along and say, "Well I don't really consider so and so to be a part of this; they are not really that kind of writer." But it's too late: you've already claimed it! It's already happened.

    I do think that the writers you've collected are in some ways different from writers, say, in central Canada. And I think one of the major differences is the fact that there's more space in BC to talk about racial hybridity than there is say in Toronto, or than there is in Nova Scotia. I think that in these places, the mixed race black person, to use that phrase, is racialized to a certain extent, much more so than perhaps may be the case in BC, as black. I also think BC is different because you have someone like James Douglas, as the founding father of the literature. There isn't another black community in Canada that can say the governor of the colony was a member of the establishment and got their literature started. . . .

KM   Maybe we can talk for a minute about the nature of the writing practice, or the textures of these conversations or the reconfigurations you're talking about. I borrowed today's title . . . from the author's disclaimer at the end of *Execution Poems*, where you talked about the crime of poetry. Although the book itself is about a crime, it's a very interesting move to hear poetry described as criminal. In what ways is the act of writing transgressive, perhaps, or criminal? How do you address that phrase, and why did you use it?

GEC   Wayde?

WC   Well, speaking at all seems to be breaking that, breaking a prohibition point in terms of black writing.

GEC   I think when you are coming from a minority perspective there is always a grain of transgression: the fact that you're speaking up, the fact that you are talking about injustice as you perceive it, as you see it. The fact that you claim that the white government in British Columbia is black is transgressive. It can be viewed as a kind of crime, of literature, of statement, of being, of saying. And also too, the fact that often we are trying to speak the unspeakable, we're trying to say what has not been said before, at least not in Canada in certain ways — trying to disturb the very idea of what is a Canadian identity. Can Canadian itself be centralized as white, or Anglo-Saxon, or Gaelic? Can it, really? Is it really possible to do that legitimately? And I think that a lot of the writing that we've been doing is an attempt to say no.

6. GALLERY THREE

Sherrill Grace

Theatre of Action

Until recently Canadians have believed not only that a native theatre didn't flourish here until the late 1960s, but also that there was little or no Canadian theatre worthy of the name until that time. As late as 1977 Brian Parker could call an important analysis of plays by three Canadian playwrights "Is there a Canadian Drama?" and the question seemed to make sense. But things are rapidly changing. Since 1974 (and the University of Toronto Conference "Canadian Theatre Before the Sixties"), there has been a growing critical interest in Canadian drama, particularly in its history — and regardless of what we mean by "Canadian drama" (whether we are "localists," "regionalists," "nationalists," or "internationalists"), the dramatic archeology of the past few years has gone a long way toward qualifying the idea that, prior to the 1960s, Canada was a dramatic wasteland. That a native theatre has been slow in developing and beset by a wide variety of problems is true. It is also true that the 1960s and 1970s witnessed an exciting upsurge in the writing and production of Canadian plays. But things *were* happening in the Canadian theatre during the 1920s, 30s, and 40s, and the story of these years is an exciting one.

One of the most recent efforts to tell this story is Toby Gordon Ryan's memoir, *Stage Left: Canadian Theatre in the Thirties*. Ryan's memoir of the years from 1929 to 1940 deals with the organization of Workers' Theatres in Toronto, Vancouver, Winnipeg, and Montreal, and it explores the various elements of these amateur groups which, together, constitutes a truly alternative, agit-prop theatre. *Stage Left* is, in fact, less Ryan's personal memoir than a collective recreation of the personalities, social issues, and theatre activity of the time. Interspersed with Ryan's own remarks are the recollections of many people who were active in the Workers' Theatres — people such as Harold Griffin (a founding member of the Vancouver Progressive Arts Club who reported on the PAC Players' successful production of *Waiting for Lefty* in 1935), Joe Zuken of the Winnipeg Workers' Theatre (recalling the defeat of a government ban on *Eight Men Speak*), Rose Kashtan of Montreal's New Theatre (recalling performances of *Bury the Dead* and *We Beg to Differ* as well as harassment from Duplessis's watchdogs), and Wayne and Shuster, who as

students were active in Toronto's Theatre of Action. The driving force behind all
these groups was the belief in a social theatre directly involved with current affairs
and the social inequities of the period. Although Irving Myers is speaking of Montreal's New Theatre Group, his remarks are representative of the "stage left" movement as a whole: "It was inept in many places, it was gauche, it was young, it was
awkward sometimes. But it had a dynamic and it had a goal that was absolutely
right. The things we were fighting against absolutely had to be fought."

Because she was instrumental in the formation of the Toronto Workers' Theatre
in 1932, and its continuation in a more permanent group called Theatre of Action
(formed in 1935), Ryan devotes several chapters of her book to the history of Toronto social theatre. And many aspects of this history are fascinating. While studying theatre at Artef (Workers' Theatrical Alliance) in New York, Ryan saw the
German agit-prop group, Prolet-Bühne. She was so impressed by their structure
and techniques that when she returned to Toronto in 1932 she and Jim Watts modelled their Workers' Theatre upon the German troupe.

Workers' Theatre was an informal organization in which all the members participated in as many ways as possible and in this, as in other ways, it foreshadows
the contemporary Theatre Passe-Muraille. The later Theatre of Action, however,
had a director (imported from New York), a regular core of members and a summer school. Its productions of plays such as *Waiting for Lefty* (1936), *Bury the
Dead* (1936), and the powerful *Steel* (1938) were staged at Hart House or Margaret Eaton Hall, but the troupe also toured southern Ontario towns in an effort
to bring social theatre to the people. For example, despite the strong union propa-
ganda, *Steel* was well received by local audiences and reviewers who praised the
power of the play and the clever expressionist sets of a massive steel plant. Theatre
of Action won at the Central Ontario Regional finals in 1938 with *Steel* and took
the play to the Dominion Drama Festival finals in Winnipeg that year. Although
they did not win in the finals, their work was praised, as *Bury the Dead* had been
in the 1937 finals (when John Coulter's *The House in the Quiet Glen* received the
Bessborough trophy). But Ryan remembers feeling ostracized by the regular Festival crowd and it is not surprising, as Ryan points out, that Betty Lee all but ignored
the Workers' Theatres in her history of the DDF, *Love and Whiskey*.

Ryan's method for putting *Stage Left* together is appropriate, in that the book
(like the theatre it chronicles) is a joint effort by many socially active and aware
Canadians. But this collage approach makes for a fragmented text which is not
always easy to follow. What is gained by the sense of immediacy and the enthusiasm of personal voices remembering is at times undercut by the lack of organization. Although there is a wealth of information here, and although the several very
fine and useful photographs of personalities and stage sets are supplemented by
appendices with press comments and a list of major productions, there is no index.
Given the book's structure and content, an index would have been invaluable.

However, I want to conclude on a positive note because *Stage Left* is a fascinating
record of the Canadian theatre past. In addition to recreating the activity of a unique

theatre of the time, Ryan sheds light upon the problems facing the development of a Canadian theatre in the 1930s. The plays performed by Theatre of Action were American plays and their directors were American because, as Ryan explains, there were very few Canadian plays around, especially socially relevant ones, and there were no schools to train Canadian actors and directors. When Syd Banks, a long-time Canadian member of the Toronto group, did take over in 1939, Theatre of Action was reaching the end of its short but vibrant life because a new world war drew energies and talents in other directions. Nevertheless, in its group structure, social ideals, summer schools, and devotion to Canadian theatre, Toronto's Theatre of Action was a forerunner of the alternative theatres of today. If it did not produce a Canadian repertoire in five short years, it did provide the place for talented Canadians (among them Lorne Green and Lou Jacobi) to practise their art. It was, in Toby Ryan's words, a unique and important theatre, "a dissenting voice, a true alternative theatre," and its story is one "that needs to be heard" today.

CL 98 (Autumn 1983)

Linda Hutcheon

Ex-Centric

It is interesting that the form which postmodernism has taken in Canadian fiction has been that of simultaneously taking seriously and challenging the conventions of realism, arguably our dominant novelistic tradition. One of the most common modes of this paradoxical postmodern use and abuse of conventions is what I have called "historiographic metafiction" — works which are self-consciously grounded in social and political history. *In the Skin of a Lion* is a good example of this kind of fiction and, like *Beautiful Losers* and many others before it, it is also a poet's novel, with carefully structured image patterns (here, based on earth, air, fire, and especially water) and narrative motifs (damaged arms and painted bodies, among them). It mixes the historical and the fictional, and offers to the reader a now characteristic Ondaatje blend of the surreal and the terribly real that leaves certain scenes lingering in the reader's memory long after finishing the novel: insect-like lights (sheaves of cattails alight) in the dark, held by Finnish loggers skating on a frozen river; a nun blown by the wind off the Bloor Street viaduct; an allegorical dramatic production in the illicit darkness of Toronto's R.C. Harris Water filtration

Plant; tannery dyers with their white heads and coloured bodies; the thief, Cara-vaggio, ironically painted blue to match the prison roof from which he then es-capes; the tour of smells in the Garden of the Blind. The power of these scenes resides at once in the imagination of both novelist and reader and in the clear con-nection of the novelistically imagined with the historically known — here ranging from the material history of the Toronto cityscape to the ethnic history of the Macedonian community that Lillian Petroff has been unearthing for us.

It does not take us long to realize that, despite the historical setting and person-ages, we are in the realm of overt metafiction. An opening disclaimer announces: "This is a work of fiction and certain liberties have at times been taken with some dates and locales." And, we might add, certain fates have been imagined where the historical record has remained silent: the end of famous Canadian missing person, Ambrose Small, for instance. The second of two epigraphs of the novel also points us to the metafictive orientation of this text: "Never again will a single story be told as though it were the only one." This is from John Berger, one of the most commit-ted historiographic metafictionists writing today, one whose own fiction contains the same mix of history, class commentary, political analysis, subverted realist nar-rative, and metafictive self-reflexivity as does *In the Skin of a Lion*. As in the fiction of E.L. Doctorow, class is an important issue in this novel; so too is race and ethnic difference, as it also is in the work of Maxine Hong Kingston.

I mention these two other novelists because Ondaatje is one of the few North American writers who address the issue of our immigrant, working-class history, a history silenced by official versions of public events. As both historiographers like Dominick LaCapra and novelists like Rudy Wiebe have recently been arguing, the version of the past that survives is the history told by the written documents and photographs that name and picture those deemed central. We know today the names of the rich (Ambrose Small) and the politically powerful (R.C. Harris, city commis-sioner), but we do not know the names of the peripheral, of the women of the rich (Small's mistress), or of the anonymous workers (who built the structures ordered by Harris). These are among the outsiders, the "ex-centrics," that are made the para-doxical (and very postmodern) centre of the novel. The protagonist, Patrick Lewis, may belong to the centre in terms of race and language, but he is working class and from the country. He also, of course, works hard to alienate *himself*, in order to protect himself from contact and from having to act. The novel is the story of his insertion into community and responsible action. As an ex-centric, Patrick comes to find a place among the others who populate the east end of Toronto early in the century: the nameless immigrants who make possible the dreams and visions of the powerful (the Bloor St. Viaduct, the Harris waterworks). Forced to cope with both danger and anonymity, these immigrant workers exist but remain unrecorded, de-nied their part in the historical process. Lacking the language of power, they cannot even symbolically name themselves and thus construct their own identity.

This is a novel about identity as defined from a position of ex-centricity and mar-ginalization. It is also a story of love and politics, and both are related to language and the power to name. Alice Gull (who has ironically named herself after a parrot) is an actress, a woman of many faces but no past. But it is Alice's love that breaks through Patrick's protective shell of silence, behind which he watches, reflects, but does not act. Her absent past, however, provokes him into a kind of activity, a seeking for historical evidence of her identity. What he learns is not only relevant to Alice:

> His own life was no longer a single story but part of a mural, which was a falling together of accomplices. Patrick saw a wondrous night web — all of these fragments of a human order, something ungoverned by the family he was born into or the headlines of the day. . . . [T]he detritus and chaos of the age was realigned.

And that realignment is this novel, the narrative that we too, as readers, have been piecing together.

Patrick goes from his alien position as an observer to a new role as actor: "Each person had their moment when they assumed the skins of wild animals, when they took responsibility for the story," and Alice's death is that moment for him. His skin is the lion's skin of the novel's first epigraph ("The joyful will stoop with sorrow, and when you have gone from the earth, I will let my hair grow long for your sake, I will wander through the wilderness in the skin of a lion"). He ceases to be "nothing but a prism" that refracts the life of others. That Alice's death coincides with his learning of the past of Canada, of the union battles of workers silenced by history, is not unrelated to his radicalization.

Patrick's entry into the world of action is destructive, yet necessary. He pays for his crime in prison and upon his release, in 1938, commits his final political act: the attempted destruction of Harris's waterworks. Here the theme of power that has been building up in the novel comes to its climax. Harris faces the threatening intruder with "How dare you try to come in here!" — to which Patrick replies: "I'm not trying this, I've done it." He confronts Harris with his (and his class's) forgetting of the workers who made their civic visions possible. When Harris says he fought tooth and nail for the waterworks' luxury, Patrick responds with: "*You* fought. *You* fought. Think about those who built the intake tunnels. Do you know how many of us died in there?" The reply is damning: "There was no record kept." In an attempt to save his life and his plant, Harris lectures Patrick on power: "You don't like power, you don't respect it, you don't want it to exist but you move around it all the time." That there is considerable truth to this accusation is ironically conditioned by the fact that Patrick is at that moment carrying a blasting-box in his hands.

This discussion links the notion of imagination and creation to power. Harris tells of dreams he has had, dreams that turn out to be of plans of places which could have existed in Toronto, but had been rejected: "These *were* all real places. They could have existed." The rich and powerful city commissioner, in fact, has been given the vision that is a *mise-en-abyme* of the entire novel's mixing of history and fiction in the context of class politics:

> You must realize you are like these places, Patrick. You're as much of the fabric as the alderman and the millionaires. But you're among the dwarfs of enterprise that never get accepted or acknowledged. Mongrel company. You're a lost heir. So you stay in the woods. You reject power. And this is how the bland fools — the politicians and press and mayors and their advisers — become the spokesmen for the age.

The responsibility for historical silencing lies not only with the rich and powerful, then. This is part of Alice's legacy to Patrick, as is clear when he chooses this moment to accept responsibility for her death in a bombing accident he might have prevented.

Harris comes to understand why he was chosen for Patrick's final assault: "he was one of the few in power who had something tangible around him. But those with real power had nothing to show for themselves. They had paper." But so too does the novelist. This is the power to change how we read fiction and history, to alter our awareness of the way we think we can draw lines between the imaginary and the real. The silenced ex-centrics on the margins of history — be they women, workers, immigrants (or writers?) — must take the responsibility and accept the power to change the perspective of the centre. This is the power given voice in *In the Skin of a Lion*.

This is a novel about ex-centricity and its power through naming, through language. As the work of Michel Foucault has shown, power is an ambivalent force, neither totally negative nor totally positive: it can build as it can destroy; it can be used to combat injustice as easily as to induce complacency. Literalized as dynamite in Ondaatje's novel, power allows the conquering of nature in the so-called name of civilization and yet also brings about the destruction of human life. Yet, the creative power of the novelist, the power to name the unnamed of history, may offer a somewhat less compromised model for yet another kind of blasting power, the power of postmodern fiction.

CL 117 (Summer 1988)

Manina Jones

Roses are Read

Any attempt to describe the work of Robert Kroetsch must inevitably end — or even begin — in contradiction. Kroetsch's prose fictions (it is dangerous to call them novels or narratives — perhaps ... even "prose" and "fiction" are risky terms) tend to be both genetically and linguistically equivocal. Thus, the seemingly simple act of summarizing Kroetsch's prose fiction to date unavoidably participates in the kind of playfulness the works themselves provoke: *Alibi* (1983) is a journal-novel that might be classified as documentary evidence against documentary evidence; *What the Crow Said* (1978) is a whimsical philosophical elucidation of be (e) ing and nothingness (and as such is anything but sweetness and light); Kroetsch's "archaeological treatise," *Badlands* (1975), becomes its own self-consuming artifact; *Gone Indian* (1973) is a sort of doctoral anti-thesis; *The Studhorse Man* (1970) is simultaneously an epic and the epic's epicedium; in *The Words of My Roaring* (1966), reading and speaking make and break the e-*lect-oral* promise, and the title of even Kroetsch's first and most conventional novel begins in an act of equivocation that simultaneously interpolates and alienates both reader and speaker: *But We are Exiles* (1965).

Given our experience with this beguiling body of prose fiction, it would surely be an understatement to say that we approach the title of Kroetsch's recent work, *Excerpts from the Real World: a prose poem in ten parts*, with a certain degree of scepticism. The real world is surely something that has never been very closely associated with Kroetsch's fiction. His writing, however, is *always* associating itself with the "real world" by invading and undermining the discourses that constitute that world, discourses we think of as "true" or "natural" or "real."

Excerpts from the Real World is certainly no exception to this (mis) rule. It is, for example, a "prose poem." Any dictionary of literary terms will tell us that prose poetry is a form of prose that makes extensive use of the figurative language and imagery characteristic of poetry. If we uphold such a definition with relation to *Excerpts from the Real World*, however, the term "prose poem" begins to sound redundant. This work violates the generic boundaries its subtitle implies, boundaries that seem to distinguish between poetry (writing that works by tropes and figures), and prose (writing that is, presumably, somehow transparently referential). In doing so, it also transgresses the boundary that distinguishes between the "literary" work and the "critical" discourse that comments on it. *Excerpts from the Real World* is selfconsciously cryptic, bizarre, and often opaque. Written in the form of a dated journal, it confronts us with such puzzling entries as this:

14/4/85

Here in the Highlands the budded trees, obscenely mauve, ache to
blossom. How do man and woman, in these blocky houses, speak
against such arrays of stone? Thinking of you, I forgot to pack a
sweater. Tell your new lover to wear glass pyjamas when he sets out
from Winnipeg to transport bull semen around the world.

One might tend, on first reading, to respond to such a passage with, "If this is the
'real' world, then it is a strange one indeed!" But is it? There is something strangely
familiar about the language of the preceding passage. There is nothing out of the
ordinary about its syntax or vocabulary. It is the way familiar language has been
arranged, the ways we are forced to read it that makes it strange.

   Kroetsch's poem is surrealistic in its use of a sort of dream logic, its strategy of
placing ordinary words, phrases, and images in incongruous juxtaposition so that
the reader feels called upon to "interpret" them as metaphorical (that is, to read
them as poetry) in order to make any sense of them at all. A section of one entry
takes us through this process: "Blue apricots are rare. Perhaps the apricots are
plums." We have no conventional referent for "blue apricots," but we can provisionally explain the unfamiliar conjunction of adjective and noun as a metaphor
for "plums." As readers we are being made aware of the process of interpretation
that goes into *any* act of reading, indeed any act of perception *as* an act of reading.
Excerpts from the Real World leads us down the garden path of conventional realism by using familiar situations, places, and dates, but that garden path is consistently exposed as a textual rug, and pulled out from under our naïve reading
practices. For example:

17/7/85

The hawk on the telephone pole, folding its wings like an angel at rest,
is planning a gopher's visit to the blue sky. The grasshoppers hit our
windshield like hail. You raise your head from my lap, asking what the
sound is. This is called writing a landscape poem.

Perhaps the best counsel for the confused reader is inscribed in the poem itself:
"Relax, and you'll kitsch yourself laughing." This is playful language that calls attention to its own pretentiousness, to the fact that by attempting to treat it strictly
and simplistically as "referential" we are taking it too seriously.

   Or not nearly seriously enough, for it is language that *creates* what we call the
"real." Without attempting a comprehensive interpretation of the passage quoted
earlier (the poem precludes such interpretations), one can not help but notice that
it is "bull semen" that is being transported around the "real" world. Could it be
that blatant fictions (bull) are being *disseminated* here? Is there a world market for
prairie bullshit? And why is it important to wear glass pyjamas? So we can witness
the "dissemination process"? *Excerpts from the Real World* may in many respects

be opaque, but it reveals its own processes of signification in a way that "real" realist texts never do.

Kroetsch's work takes the conventionally "referential" prose forms of the autobiographical journal, travel diary, and love letter and turns them inside out. They refer, we must conclude, not outward to an external pre-textual reality, but to the "reality" constructed by texts themselves, the fictions they make real. Saskatoon, for example, one stop on the traveller's excursion, is a place "invented" by the writer Don Kerr, "by growing up inside a movie palace," another source of texts. In the same excerpt the "speaker" (the term must . . . be used with extreme scepticism) comments, "I've applied to the Canada Council for a pair of running shoes and a whistle," perhaps so that he can be a "refer-ee," both a mediator in the play of signs (he "blows the whistle" on them, catches them out, draws attention to them), and also a subject of discourse, the one who is referred to in the context of the poem, who is himself mediated *by* the poem's language.

While the conventional speaker in a journal seems to act as a "medium" between world and word, as a sort of messenger, in this case it becomes clear that the medium *is* the message, that we can make no easy distinction either between the spoken and what it speaks, or between the speaking speaker and the spoken speaker. "His" enunciation in the poem is equivalent to a birth, an "entry" — as both an ingress and an item in the journal — into the world of the poem: "I liked the telegram, the one you sent me announcing my birth." In *Excerpts from the Real World*, it becomes increasingly obvious that the speaking "I" is a creation of discourse, and is dependent on discourse. Each time the pronoun is enunciated its context changes. It is, therefore, never self-identical, and we can hardly expect a coherent speaking "voice" for the poem. In one excerpt, then, we witness the literal fragmentation of the speaker: "Even as I lay down, I heard myself walking away." Kroetsch's poem begins with the words "I want to explain why I didn't answer the door." "I" didn't answer the door because any other use of the pronoun "I" necessarily makes it an other. Emile Benveniste elaborates on this contingent nature of the speaking subject: "I signifies 'the person who is uttering the present instance of the discourse containing I.' This instance is unique by definition, and has validity only in its uniqueness."

"I" is always defined in relation to an other, to a "you," which is, in one sense, a souvenir, the trace of the absent "I," seen from the outside, after the fact: "Like the ashtray I bought in Edinburgh (the castle, the castle), *you* remind me of where *I* once was" (my emphasis). *Excerpts from the Real World* deals with the traditional subject matter of the love letter, the relationship between an "I" and a "you," but the "you" of the poem is as indeterminate as its "I." How, for example, can either be established as a stable entity in such an ironic formulation as this: "'But most of all I luv you cuz yr you.' If you see what I mean"? "You" may be both lover and alienated self as in Rimbaud's *"je est un autre"* or the *autre* of the formulations of Lacanian psychoanalysis: *"L'autre.* The author. I'm not myself today. The other is a tramp. Con-floozied." The other is a tramp, perhaps, because it is unstable, like a vagabond. It has no firmly established conventional signified; its meaning varies according to context, and is therefore "unfaithful" to any particular referent: it refers "promiscuously," like a "floozie," a "tramp."

In another excerpt, the "speaker" asks his lover, "When will you leave your retailer of bull semen, there on the outskirts of Brandon, and buy a ticket to the Equator." The alternative presented is, perhaps, "dissemination" as defined by contemporary literary critics like Jacques Derrida, a dispersal of meaning over the web of signifiers that constitutes a text, producing "a non-finite number of semantic effects," as opposed to a one-way trip from word to meaning that somehow "equates" one with the other. The very possibility of "getting the message across" in the latter fashion is being questioned at every turn in *Excerpts from the Real World*. One entry reads, "Everything recurs (more or less). Consider, for instance, spring. Or transmission problems" (35). The problem of "transmission," conveying meaning unchanged from one place to another is, it seems, at the very least problematic. Even recurrence happens only "more or less." Spring is never the same spring: even in the context of that sentence there are two non-identical *springs*.

Like "I" and "you," "here" and "there" signify only in context, so that we must, as one entry says, "Let place do the signing for us." Place, therefore, in *Excerpts from the Real World*, may be defined as discursive space. The travelogue, rather than being a narrative of travel, becomes a record of its own changing meaning, its "travelling *logos*" and the journal "entry" can therefore no longer function simply as a "passage" to or from its author's meaning or pre-textual events. The poem's first line, "I want to explain why I didn't answer the door," is supplemented by the information that "Doors, in a manner of speaking, are descriptive. Otherwise we wouldn't be here now." The journal entries ("doors," in a manner of speaking) are both entrances and exits. Appropriate to a travelogue, they are places where meaning is "just passing through."

The reader of *Excerpts from the Real World* comes along for the ride. She is drawn into a "relationship" with the text, since in any reading situation its "you" may allude to her: "The affair I never mention, the one that turns out to be with you, was occasioned by an ice storm that toppled power lines and brought angels crashing into the frozen fields." Any reading of such a passage necessarily sounds reductive, but a possibility exists that the "affair" never mentioned is one between reader and text, an implicit relationship that takes place intertextually, rather than along the simplistic "power lines" of author and reader. In such a situation, "transcendental" meaning (the angels?) comes toppling down into the fields (of the play of signification?). One thinks of such complex intertextual relationships as those that occur in another passage: "Peter Eastingwood quotes John Cowper Powys to me. 'I like a chaotic strung-along *multi-verse*'." The "real world" is not a monolithic *uni*verse "out there." It exists within the polysemic world of the poem as "multi-verse."

"A chaotic, strung-along *multi-verse*" is a good way of describing the "real world" of *Excerpts from the Real World*, multiple both in meaning and form (the poem's numerous "excerpts"), and "verse" in its strategic *turn* of "realistic" discourse back on its own "poetic" or rhetorical status. *Excerpts from the Real World*, then, is a per/versely realist work. It exploits what Jerome Klinkowitz calls "the ultimate realism of words on the page and signs at play."

CL 119 (Winter 1988)

Glenn Deer

Heroic Artists

In her new volume of essays and autobiographical reflections, *Memoirs of a Book Molesting Childhood*, Adele Wiseman quotes Robert Kroetsch's comment to a group of writers in China: "where writing is concerned 'Our heroic men are women'." The accomplishments of Canadian women writers have indeed been heroic, achievements often realized while under the pressure of domestic, social, and moral responsibilities that men are allowed to elude. Wiseman writes that "it is considered somewhat heroic and even a sign of genius in a man if he behaves with irresponsible selfishness in his personal life. He is considered redeemed by his utter devotion to his art. The exact reverse is usually true for a woman artist. The writer who also wants to live her life fully as a mother and wife is constantly faced with largely artificial choices and has her guilts set out for her." These three books highlight the achievements of three Canadian women artists.

Ruth Gowers' *Emily Carr* is a compact biography in the Berg Women's Series and it invites comparison with Maria Tippett's authoritative and superbly researched *Emily Carr: A Biography* (1979). Tippett, writing as a native of British Columbia, and having grown up with the work of Carr and the landscape of Vancouver Island around her as a child, enters the mind of Carr and the people of her life with a novelist's passion and precision. But while brilliantly diagnosing the psychological development of Carr, Tippett still writes as a Canadian who takes some knowledge for granted: she expects that we already know such simple facts as where Vancouver and Victoria are located on the map.

Ruth Gowers, a cautious British scholar, never enters as fully as Tippett does into the life of her subject, never offers psychological diagnoses of Carr's "hysteria," and never assumes that we already know the geography of the West Coast: she includes a map of the West Coast and like a conscientious travel guide tells us where in

"Victoria today one can visit the home of James Douglas's daughter and son-in-law, Dr. and Mrs. Helmcken — a log-built house lovingly preserved with the furniture and fittings installed in the 1850's, complete with piano brought round Cape Horn." Gowers hopes to reach a different audience than Tippett seeks: she acknowledges that while in "North America, [Carr] has been the subject of both large- and small-scale biographies, as well as a mass of chapters in collective biographies, memoirs, sketches, notes, reminiscences, and articles . . . ," in Britain "she has received little notice in print from critics or art historians."

Admirably concise, clear, and informative, Gowers' treatment of Carr emphasizes the artist's determination and indefatigable attempts to educate herself and develop as an artist. Gowers' account de-emphasizes Carr's psychopathologies and loneliness, the self-deprecating persona that Gowers would contend was a fictional creation in Carr's autobiographical writings — she shows how Carr was often busier with her art work and more active in the social circles of the art community than Emily the autobiographer would have us believe. Gowers reports on the artist's resourcefulness and endurance in creating her work under living conditions that were often uncomfortable and inconvenient for artistic activity. What endures in this excellent introductory biography is a compelling picture of a stubborn, durable individual who succeeded in climbing over many barriers to achieve independence and the rights of adulthood.

Barbara Hill Rigney's *Margaret Atwood* is a concise monograph that is meant to introduce the newcomer to Atwood's work in broad outline and from the perspective of a feminist critique of male ideology. The intended audience, the undergraduate and the general reader, is presented with Atwood's critique of politics, sexuality, and the psychological self-entrapment that causes the victims of oppression to comply with and surrender to the oppressor. Hill Rigney sees Atwood as a moral and prescriptive writer who is able "not only to describe her world, but also to criticise it, to bear witness to its failures, and, finally, to prescribe corrective measures — perhaps even to redeem." The first chapter, "Maps of the Green World," argues that the moral lessons taught by Atwood are "through negative example"; the narrators in novels like *The Edible Woman, Surfacing,* and *Lady Oracle* are actually subjected to Atwood's ironic critique and are distanced from the author's own position. In this introductory chapter Hill Rigney surveys Atwood's deconstructive use of fertility myths, artist archetypes, sisterhood roles, victimization and the increasingly political vision developed in later works like *Bodily Harm, True Stories,* and *The Handmaid's Tale.*

Five subsequent chapters treat Atwood's novels and poetry in chronological order, with a final chapter on "Atwood as Critic; Critics on Atwood." Hill Rigney proceeds in each chapter to summarize selectively each novel, focusing on theme and character; she connects, very briefly, the concerns of the novels to those of the poetry, considers relevant critical material, and offers some defence of her own readings. However, she does not break substantially new interpretive ground in this book, and often the critics she cites for support, or to highlight an interpretive disagreement she has with them, demonstrate a more richly developed interpretation of Atwood's accomplishment than the one she herself offers: Sherrill Grace's *Violent Duality: A Study of Margaret Atwood* and Frank Davey's *Margaret Atwood: A Feminist Poetics* still present more convincing structural and narrative analyses of Atwood's work.

A major problem in Hill Rigney's approach is that it evades the description of Atwood's narrative craft and control of language. We can sympathize with the intention of the author, to present an enthusiastic and compact guide that can be comfortably read in one or two sweeps, but the thematic generalizations based on character analysis without rhetorical or narratological framing go begging for proof. Often Hill Rigney overlooks the important Canadian works that Atwood is dialogically addressing: for example, in the third chapter that features *Surfacing* and *The Journals of Susanna Moodie* only three pages are devoted to the *Journals* out of a total of twenty-three; more troubling than this lopsidedness is that the critic never mentions important Canadian statements on the documentary long poem as a genre — for example, by Dorothy Livesay, Eli Mandel, Michael Ondaatje, or Frank Davey — nor does she direct the potential student to Susanna Moodie's *Roughing It in the Bush*.

Other irritations in this book raise nationalist hackles, especially in this time of Free Trade jitters north of the forty-ninth. Hill Rigney, a Professor of English at Ohio State University, patronizingly refers to our literary debates over the merits of Atwood's *Survival* as "largely uninteresting quibbles over which authors ought to have been included." This dumping of the political struggles of distinctive regional writers and writing groups into a melting pot that disperses differences of aspiration and point of view is inexplicable for a critic who writes for a feminist series of books that hopes to disrupt the male-dominated canon of literature — for it is the politics of literary institutions and the use of canonical texts that is at the heart of the *Survival* debate, and this is now one of the major questions of contemporary literary theory and feminism: it is not simply an "uninteresting quibble."

I would be cautious in recommending this book to my students. It shows the proper enthusiasm for Atwood's considerable achievement, but it falls short in describing Atwood's superb control of voice and irony; and while casting our Canadian political habits into such lofty phrases as the "vaster concept of the Canadian mind," it stumbles into such factual lapses as when a character is described running in "circles around Toronto's *Parliament* Buildings."

Adele Wiseman is one of our most supple yet eloquent stylists. Winner of the Governor General's Award for the epic *The Sacrifice*, her collection of essays is an exquisite blend of meditations on her development as a woman and Jewish writer; she was among the first generation of women, along with Margaret Laurence, to break into the special ranks of distinguished post-war writing. Here we have Wiseman's powerful feminist reading of Henry James, reflections on ethnic marketplaces, travel notes on China, and contemplations of Canadian landscape in an age of ecological crisis. In some of our most energized prose, earthy, robust, crackling with humour both bawdy and delicately ironic, her enthusiasm for language and experience is seductive and inspiring. The essays and reflections presented here add up to a mixed autobiographical album, taking the reader in jagged chronological order from the rites of childhood and initiation into the pleasures of literature to later poignant explorations of human suffering. To prevent this collection from lapsing into too dark a pitch, Wiseman concludes with her angry, comic, and defiant complaint against the incompetencies and injustices of civic life and property inspectors in Toronto.

Wiseman's prose signals the distance that women writers have come since Emily Carr's generation, a generation that could not speak with Wiseman's ebullient and colourful confidence about sexuality, political life, and the morality of literature. Wiseman has the ability, rare in any writer, both to tell us what it feels like to be gripped by the pleasures of the book and to engage us in her passionately moral vision of literature's purpose. Here is the conclusion to the title-essay of a book that anyone interested in superb writing should own:

> Books have continued to be the other worlds I live in, primarily because I still adhere to the hope that I may yet be able to create my own true magic model for the spirit of a more humane world among them. But I have no more illusions about the world of books than I have about any other world. In books as in life, the greatest burden on the future is the past. Literature is a holding tank for the worst as well as the best in our culture. The lessons we learn are too seldom the lessons ostensibly being taught. Nevertheless, I still approach every new work with a hesitation that is like a preliminary washing of hands, and the profound conviction that I am about to learn to read. I enter books as I enter days, with respect and hope; each a chapter each a part of the passion, the continued yeagon of my life.

CL 120 (Spring 1989)

Lola Lemire Tostevin

Elizabeth Smart

According to Alice Van Wart's foreword to *In the Meantime*, thirty-two years separated the publications of Elizabeth Smart's first book, the now classic poem-novel

By Grand Central Station I Sat Down and Wept in 1945, and her poetic prose
work, *The Assumption of Rogues and Rascals* in 1977, which also saw the publication of a slim volume of poetry, *A Bonus*. In spite of this relatively small output, by
the time Elizabeth Smart died in 1986 at the age of 73, Canada had claimed her as
one of its most distinctive literary stylists. If there are still a few people who do not
know about Smart's personal history, they might ask themselves, given her talent,
why her literary yield was not more abundant. These three books, recently and
posthumously published, undoubtedly provide several answers.

One answer is that during and in between the events of her turbulent life Elizabeth Smart continued writing. When her cottage in England was sold, a mass of
letters, diaries, scrapbooks and MSS was discovered. According to *Autobiographies*,
she won a dollar for a poem when she was ten and became convinced then that
words would always be her chief preoccupation; she admits that she often read for
style rather than story.

Juvenilia, also edited by Alice Van Wart, documents the first eight years of
Elizabeth Smart's writing life covering the years 1926 to 1933. It includes stories,
letters, photographs, drawings, poems and reproductions of some original manuscript pages which show a neat, uniform print. From the age of 12, it would seem
that Smart was already concerned with visual and literary style and form, and her
obsession with words is apparent in a delightful short story "The Last Dictionary," in which two male bachelor friends go shopping for their fifty-sixth dictionary, because in them you can find "the most absolutely elegantly beautiful words."
There is also ample evidence in these early pieces of the thematic thread that was
to run throughout her work. The first line of the first story, "Heartless Baby,"
reads: "The woman came weeping into the room; her baby had died just yesterday." From the time she was 12, Smart was concerned with the relationship between love, pain and loss.

While it is obvious that the pieces gathered in *Juvenilia* were written by a youthful mind, it cannot be denied that as a child and young adult, Smart was very pre-
cocious. She had a vivid imagination, a keen sense of humour, was already working
with satire and irony, especially in the stories that revolve around the social stra-
tum in which she was brought up. Nor was her affluent upbringing lacking in exposure to literature, music and travel, and Smart's astute intelligence never stopped
capitalizing on all that her privileged family offered. The letters at the end of the
volume indicate that her relationship with her family, especially her mother, was a
close and mutually devoted one.

In the Meantime is a collection of poetry and prose, much of which was unpublished or no longer accessible. The selection spans a period of forty years from
1939 to 1979, and contains some of Smart's most revealing and moving work.
From the first lines of "Scenes One Never Forgets," in which a 63-year-old narrator
admits that she still wakes up in the middle of the night screaming for her mother,
to the lesbian eroticism symbolically identified with mother/daughter figures in
"Dig a Grave and Let Us Bury Our Mother," to the questioning of the mother

theme of "In the Meantime: Diary of a Blockage," all deal with a figure that Smart wrestled with all her life.

It is impossible to read these pieces and not be reminded of various recent feminist texts, such as Adrienne Rich's *Of Woman Born* in which she states that the two-person, mother-child relationship is circular and unproductive, or Nancy Chodorow's *Reproduction of Mothering*, which claims that often daughters do not abandon their mothers as love objects, but remain deeply identified with them. Because a daughter begins life psychically merged with her mother, as she gets older she may fear annihilation of the self, but she also longs for that primal oneness, a oneness that Smart sought in all her relationships and which she admits always evaded her. It is an astounding discovery to realize that while Elizabeth Smart's most famous work, *By Grand Central Station I Sat Down and Wept*, was loosely based on her relationship with the poet George Barker, it would appear that at least in her writing, she came closest to retrieving the primal oneness of the mother/daughter relationship through a lesbian episode, as depicted in "Dig a Grave and Let Us Bury Our Mother." It is a powerful story which not "only the body's language can say," but which also "join[s] the mind and the heart that overflow with sympathy to action." While the book comes full circle in many of the poems, such as "Rose Died," a flawless and moving poem about her dead daughter, and in the last story, "In the Meantime: Diary of Blockage," one cannot help but wonder if perhaps Smart's question "Was the Mother idea a dead-end, a mistake?" isn't valid. Although she asserts that a relationship between mother and daughter is more lasting than the most passionate sexual love, one wonders after reading all of Smart's writing if the struggle to retrieve that first love, the search for an equivalent to the impossible maternal fusion, was not regressive.

Autobiographies is the kind of book that you cannot put down, not only because of its literary merit, but also because, as Smart herself writes, "People are greedy for details. A set scene establishes order." In a recent issue of *Brick* (Spring 1988) Alice Van Wart claims that because Smart was most concerned about craft, the events of her life did not necessarily correspond to those in her writing, and that it is fallacious to interpret her life from her art. The art of self-invention has played too large a role in twentieth-century literature for the reader not to be aware that autobiography is not necessarily based on verifiable facts of a life history. For some writers (I am thinking of Sartre and Nabokov) the writing of an autobiography is a process of self-creation, a process through which one gets to know oneself and even change oneself, if that is what is desired. Smart was too aware of language not to know that knowledge of the self is inseparable from the practice of language. She might have been aware that her writing was not an attempt to provide an image or picture of who she was in "real life," but surely she was aware how the recording of certain facts would be perceived and interpreted, and the picture we are left with in *Autobiographies* is unmistakably clear.

While *Autobiographies* is fascinating in that it contains notes and early drafts of what became Smart's two masterpieces, it was also one of the most exasperating and frustrating experiences I have had while reading autobiographical material. More than half of the book consists of journal entries and letters written between 1940 and 1947 when Smart was involved with the poet George Barker. There are a few instances early in their relationship when Barker appears to have been loving and supportive of her work, especially in a letter to her in which he suggests changes in an early draft of *By Grand Central Station*. Other than that letter, however, Barker can only be *perceived* as "cagey," "insulting," "abusive," without "respect or consideration," "hateful," "selfish," "callous," given to "betrayals and repudiations," and "lying." Smart on the other hand is *perceived* as a woman who was willing to subsume not only her art but her entire life to the whims of George Barker. One gets weary of reading how she continuously supplied him with money, how without him she could only "be a deadweight," how if he left her she "could no more write a book . . . than a fish on the deathbrink," how as a mother of his children she can only sit by and wait for his "instructions for the conduct of their hours and lives" — the list goes on and on.

When, at the age of 30, Smart writes "I need a house, a husband, money, a job, friends, furniture, affection, someone to look after the children, clothes, a car, a bicycle, a destination," we realize that perhaps what Smart wanted above everything else was the realization of some notion of perfect passion, love, marriage, harmony. By the time I came to the end of this book, where the last line written shortly before her death reads "a consenting adult moves on," I truly wished that this courageous woman, blessed with such a formidable talent, had moved on just a little sooner.

CL 122–123 (Autumn-Winter 1989)

Margery Fee

Double Discourse

When Daphne Marlatt and Betsy Warland read from *Double Negative* at Mrs. Dalloway's Books in Kingston, they explained the book's origin as a way to share the experience of travelling from Sydney to Perth along the railway line that contains "the longest stretch of straight railway in the world." Each wrote two poems a day and then they exchanged, discussed, and revised the results — at first with no thought of publication. Although Marlatt's poems alternate with Warland's, whose poem is whose is not clearly indicated, only one of the violations of convention in this collection:

> walking into the diner
> 'are you ladies alone'
>   'no'
>   'we're together'

Here are the two female negatives that make a positive, two lesbian lovers who rewrite the train from inside as a womb, rather than from the outside as a phallus thrusting through the "empty" desert, which, since there was "nothing there," could be used for nuclear testing. This writing is a "word to word fight for defining / whose symbolic dominates whose." The "negative" images of women and of lesbians are reclaimed on the train by two poets "thriving outside The Gaze," who have turned the gaze around, looking out through the moving window as through a camera lens at the outside world, but also realizing that the world looks back at them as "night turns the lens around," the gazes of emus eyeing them. The film image is repeated in Cheryl Sourkes' three negative collages which superimpose words, photographs and aboriginal images. The collages divide the book into three sections. Reel 1 consists of poems, each titled by the name of a place along the line and the time the train passed through. The next section, called Crossing Loop, is a three-page conversation written after the trip about both the experience and the difficulties of rewriting the world from a feminine perspective. Here Warland talks of finding the desert a site for lesbian rewritings, as in Jane Rule's novel *The Desert of the Heart*. The third section, Real 2, consists of prose passages, relating the reel to the "real," bringing in more social and political concerns. The desert, in male economic terms, is "not worth developing." But the book reiterates that the boundaries that divide worthwhile from worthless are artificial, arbitrary signs of power:

> "Welcome to Western Australia" the sign said
>
> the desert on either side
> identical

Words are our boundaries, "but what if the boundary goes walking." Women have been the negative that defines the positive term "man" for too long, and now go walking in the desert, getting off the train, at first blinded by 360 degrees of light, but recovering:

> then a gradual sensation
> of the Great Wheel rolling under us
> of the Great Womb we call earth

not solid not still
but an ever turning threshold

The train journey is over, but the poem still unreels, unrealing the world we've taken for granted for so long.

Fred Wah was one of the founders of *TISH* in 1961; Marlatt's association with that magazine began in 1963. Both, influenced by the poetics of the American Black Mountain School, are interested in the corporality of language and in pushing at the limits of syntax. The formal difficulty of Wah's *Waiting for Saskatchewan*, which won the Governor General's Award in 1985, was eased by its theme, the search for father and ancestors typical of many prairie writers. *Music at the Heart of Thinking*, as the title suggests, is much more theoretical. In it Wah is grappling with an issue at the forefront of literary theory — how to use reason when it has been implicated in so much that is negative about Western culture. "Scientific objectivity" has been discredited, as has a "male" rationality that represses "female" emotion. What will replace it (whose symbolic will dominate whose?) is in the process of being worked out. Thus he begins, "don't think thinking without heart." Instead he is developing, as he puts it, "a critical poetic that sees language as the true practice of thought." Thought, if theorized as separate from the world, can be hallucinated as "pure," "absolute," "disengaged"; Wah resists, seeing language as material, irrevocably in the world, tangled in a web of etymological, intertextual, and social connections, touched by all the forces that move people, including their hates, their loves, their delusions. What Marlatt has said about her own work fits Wah's: "I had definitely abandoned the textbook notion of sentence as the container for a completed thought, just as writing open form poetry had taught me the line has no box for a certain measure of words, but a moving step in the process of thinking/feeling, feeling/thinking." This is the way Wah puts it:

SENTENCE THE TRUE MORPHOLOGY OF SHAPE OF THE
mind including a complete thought forever
little ridges little rhythms scoping out the total
picture as a kind of automatic designing device
or checklist anyone I've found in true thought
goes for all solution to the end concatenates
every component within the lines within the
picture as a cry to represent going to it with the
definite fascination of a game where the number
of possibilities increases progressively with
each additional bump Plato thought

Occasionally, this becomes hard to bear: I was at first irritated, but later fascinated by Wah's constant refusal to stop dislocating his own meaning, "or as you say in

this story / you rip up your own street." He does occasionally pander to old-fashioned tastes:

> Now I know the names to measure
> in this language stream:
> whatever rhymes with no sense
> keys the dream.

Ultimately, however, what Wah writes can, more easily than what Marlatt and
Warland write, be co-opted into an avant-garde tradition that has little ultimate
impact, however revolutionary its ideas. Perhaps this difference is simply the sheer
scandal of their position, their need to ground their writing in their bodies, to oppose the conventional at *every* social level, not just at the level of language. As
Shirley Neuman has said of Lola Lemire Tostevin's work, "one of the great strengths
of the double discourse of feminist writing. . . [lies in] the difference it introduces
into the dominant literary discourse [which] is not so much one of style — male
writers use many of the same rhetorical strategies and women writers often learn
from them — as one of ideology, an ideology of difference."

CL 126 (Autumn 1990)

Richard Cavell

Personae

Glenn Gould is at once central and marginal to Canadian culture: central because
of his concern with such topoi as the North; marginal because of his refusal to
work with traditional forms. Otto Friedrich reads this paradox as one of personality; rather than attempting to pin Gould down, he approaches Gould through a
metaphor derived from the recording for which Gould is most famous — Bach's
Goldberg Variations. This choice recommended itself all the more strongly to
Friedrich because Gould's career opened and closed with recordings of this work,
and the Variations were written for a Count Keyserling, who, like Gould, was an
insomniac. Chapters are devoted to The Prodigy, The Virtuoso, The Composer, The
Conductor, and so on, all of whom are seen as variations on the enigma of Gould,
who enacted his public and private lives through a half-dozen personae, including

Dr. Herbert von Hochmeister, Fine Arts critic from the Arctic Circle, and Ted Slutz, New York cab driver. Friedrich's refusal to impose closure on this multifarious personality further influenced the form of his biography, *Glenn Gould: A Life and Variations*, and the chapters often reproduce transcripts of interviews with persons who knew Gould, revealing in all their nakedness the impossibility of the task Gould's executors had set Friedrich. "Gerry Graffman recalls meeting Gould several times in Berlin," writes Friedrich, "because the two pianists were both practicing in the Steinway building."

Q: But he often said that he practically never practiced at all.
A: He was practicing a lot.
Q: He was practicing a lot?
A: He was practicing a lot.

The variations on a personality which is always absent — an absence hypertrophied by Gould's withdrawal from the stage at the height of his career — include the child who started a newspaper called "The Daily Woof"; the virtuoso who, in 1957, gave triumphant recitals in Moscow and Leningrad; the hypochondriac addicted to Valium; the businessman who invested (sans broker) with extraordinary success; the technologist whose recordings were a myriad of splices; the legendary interpreter of Bach; the devotee of Strauss and Scriabin; the composer of quartets/documentaries/operas/fantasies; and the eccentric whose charge for dangerous driving was dismissed by the judge after Gould explained that his hands had not been on the wheel because he was conducting Mahler. The complete separation of these personalities is conveyed in a story told by Bob Phillips, whom Gould had invited to participate in the recording of "The Idea of North." When the session was over, Phillips asked, "Excuse me, Mr. Gould, but are you related to the pianist?" The complexity of Gould's talent is also illustrated by the catholicity of his discography, here compiled by Nancy Canning, and by the photographs of Gould. One of the Goulds about whom Friedrich writes with considerable restraint is the media star, with all the attendant questions about drugs and sex. This inclusion is less to be lamented, however, than the omissions Friedrich makes. Principal among these are Gould the intellectual and Gould the Canadian, omissions all the more egregious because so intimately interrelated and so utterly central, as "The Idea of North" makes abundantly clear. Friedrich's admission, in the "Note on Sources," that on "the general subject of Canada, I have done my best to rise from a characteristically American state of abysmal ignorance to one of merely woeful ignorance" is accurate but inadequate. And to assess Gould's writing (based on a youthful sample) as the work of "an intelligent but rather inhibited literary amateur" ignores the fact that pedantry was always balanced by play. The 500 pages in *The Glenn Gould Reader* comprise an intricate body of musical and communication theory to which Friedrich does not address himself. Nor has Friedrich followed up the references made in the course of his interviews to Marshall McLuhan, who had a profound influence on Gould, or availed himself of the suggestion in the Cott interviews that Gould saw his enterprise as Brechtian.

That Gould should return to the Goldbergs (the second version issued two weeks before his death in 1982, aged 50), that he should repudiate his 1955 recording of them, and that the second recording should be so radically different, is perfectly consistent with the refusal of interpretive mastery which characterizes Gould's *oeuvre*, a refusal which contradicts Friedrich's claim that Gould's ultimate concern was with control. Gould had in fact written, in "The Prospects of Recording," that, in "the best of all possible worlds," the "audience would be the artist and their life would be art." That the refusal of mastery extended, finally, to Gould's own life by no means supports Friedrich's contention that Gould is to be found only in his music. On the contrary: he is only to be found in his listeners.

CL 127 (Winter 1990)

7. LISTENING POSTS

Margaret Laurence

Illusions of Simplicity

"A modern novel of the Congo," the dust-jacket says. But Ralph Allen's latest novel *Ask the Name of the Lion* really tells us more about the dilemma of a western liberal whose lifelong attitudes of tolerance and goodwill no longer seem to have much relevance in the midst of the horrors and irrationalities of the Congo situation. Richard Grant, a Canadian doctor and a man of intelligence and compassion, goes to the Congo for the Red Cross, having sacrificed a brilliant career (in a somewhat overly noble fashion) for the sake of working where he feels his work is most needed. When the political situation explodes after Independence, some Congolese soldiers attack the isolated hospital. Grant escapes, with the others who happen to be there — Mary Kelvin, a Canadian nurse; Sierra, the U.N. representative; Songolo, an African *évolué* and a cabinet minister; Chartrand, a Belgian plantation owner; and Astrid Mahamba, Chartrand's African mistress. They are pursued by the soldiers, led by Sergeant Albert Tshibangu, who calls himself Nkosi, the Lion, and who has proclaimed himself president of Mgonga province.

Sierra directs the escape. He is all hero — the man of steel, veteran of many wars, putting his faith in action, but acutely sensitive as well (an art lover and once a talented musician). Always with Sierra there is the twisted inner grin — he knows he is dominated by the hungry "I." But he dares and dares again, and finally manages to wrest a pirogue away from an evil old witch of a Congolese bush woman. There follows a short and puzzling triumphal scene. "'*Mon Dieu, monsieur*,' Chartrand said in total homage." The others gaze at him in adulation, and even Dr. Grant murmurs "You are a great man, Monsieur Sierra." Whether we are meant to take this hail-Caesar sequence seriously or not, I was unable to decide.

When the rampaging soldiers catch up with the party, Astrid, who is portrayed appealingly as a mixture of naïveté and cunning, saves the situation by offering herself to the Sergeant and his men. Ultimately the drunken renegade soldiers are captured by U.N. forces, but not before they have killed the two men who could most have helped the Congolese people — Sierra and Songolo. The bitter irony of these deaths is movingly and convincingly shown.

The effect, unfortunately, is marred by the subsequent arrival of the Fourth Nigerians to the rescue, led by a British major who says "Dr. Grant, I presume?," quickly followed by "Sandwiches in a jiffy" and brandy in silver cups. The staunch major, unlike the Congolese soldiers, can hold his liquor and keep his head. Thank God for the English.

But these occasionally jarring notes do not represent the essence of the book. The real journey is not the outer one through the jungle but the inner one of Dr. Grant, a journey away from innocence. In the beginning, when a reporter tells him "even if these people were white, yellow or God-damned emerald green, they'd still only be one step ahead of the baboons," Grant is shocked. But gradually he discovers the Congolese are not what he thought they would be. The Congolese soldiers really are "drunk and doped and illiterate and crazy and full of hate." He has wanted to think the best of Africans, and now can no longer do so. His sense of despair and futility grows, until he comes to the conclusion that the reporter was right. He knows the standard reasons for the country's collapse — the Belgians' past brutalities, the cruel exploitation of the Congolese, their total lack of political and educational preparation for independence. But do these factors adequately explain the atrocities committed by such men as Tshibangu? Grant feels they do not.

> I never cut off anybody's hands. . . . None of us ever ran a slave ship.
> . . . We've all tried a little bit to repair the sins of the past, sins not our
> own, and here's how our grateful black brothers reply. The black
> brothers have just killed Sierra, a good brave man, for trying to lend
> his services to the brotherhood. They've killed Songolo, another good
> brave man, for trying to rise above their chapter of the brotherhood
> and lift the chapter with him.

Disillusioned, angry at himself for his former idealism, Grant decides to leave the country. At the last moment, however, he changes his mind. As he contemplates an African ivory carving, he makes his decision. "The human figure, with its short spear poised for combat, was unlike any living Congolese he had ever seen; it bore no relation to the weak, diseased, braggartly, and half-starved tribesmen he had known, and yet it was as relevant to their condition and their dreams as is the hidden god that dwells in every man." He will stay and do what he can in his miserably inadequate hospital. Fair enough. Or is it?

For Dr. Grant to have lost the first fine careless rapture of the essentially patronizing do-gooder is unquestionably, one feels, a step in the right direction. And for the author to have expressed very clearly the fact that we need not feel hag-ridden with guilt or menaced by the spectre of racial prejudice if we happen to find some Africans repulsive — this, too, is a good thing to have stated, if only as an antidote to the false liberalism of those who conscientiously condemn Dr. Verwoerd for silencing his opposition but are quite prepared to excuse Dr. Nkrumah for doing the same thing. Most of all, this novel is worthwhile because it frankly points out that for Europeans or Americans going to work in such countries as the Congo, goodwill is a very flimsy defence against the bewilderment, revulsion and anger which they will inevitably experience at some time or other.

Nevertheless, there is a glibness about this book which disturbs me. Dr. Grant is too ready to take things at their face value, too ready to accuse the Africans of ingratitude without determining whether or not *they* feel they have anything to be grateful for, and apparently without recognizing that his own cry of outraged justice ("here's how our grateful black brothers reply") is at least partly the cry of someone who has hungered for the Africans' gratitude more than he could have realized when he started out and who is almost childishly piqued when it isn't there.

Only once, it seems to me, does he touch upon what may be the true diagnosis. "I'm beginning to wonder if at least some of the problem out here isn't a psychiatric problem. . . . They're scared, always have been, always had good reason to be. . . ." I wish this line of enquiry had been followed further. In the main, however, the Congolese soldiers are shown only as they undoubtedly appeared on the surface — drunken, stupid, irresponsible, murderous. Tshibangu is a sadistic ape-man, snatching eagerly at power, but clownishly unaware of what power means. He boasts constantly of his physical strength, of his courage, of his education (which has actually been pathetically slight), but where the author might have used this boasting to reveal inner stresses, I get the impression instead that he views Tshibangu's pretensions only with disapproval and distaste, as though he really did not suspect at all the vulnerability that might lie behind them. Tshibangu's men are portrayed as dangerously cruel children, gleefully fondling the toys of war. They are all motivated only by lust — for drink, for women, for power.

I wonder if they can really have been so uncomplex and so easily explained? I have known a number of tribal and semi-tribal people in East and West Africa, and while I certainly do not claim to have understood them, I know at least that not one of them could have been called simple.

It is, of course, exceedingly difficult for us to comprehend the motivations of tribal and semi-tribal people. By semi-tribal I mean those who no longer live within their tribes but whose concepts and values are still largely those of the tribe. The Congolese soldiers appear to be in this group. Tribal man differs from individual man in needs and values as much as it is possible for humans to differ one from another. This is not, I need hardly say, a racial difference; on the contrary, it explains why many educated and de-tribalized Africans are so lonely — their wide educational differences from their own people are slight when compared with their psychological differences.

The best outline of the tribal personality which I have seen is to be found in O. Mannoni's *Prospero and Caliban: the Psychology of Colonization*, in which, incidentally, the description of the Madagascar uprising in 1947 bears an uncanny resemblance to the Congo situation. "When faced with a serious difficulty," Dr. Mannoni says, "the typical European tends to rely on his self-confidence or his technical skill. His main concern is not to prove *inferior* either to his own idea of himself or to the situation. But the main concern of the Malagasy, when his security is threatened, is not to feel *abandoned*. He has practically no confidence in himself and very little in technique, but relies on certain protective powers without which he would be utterly lost."

The same could be said of most parts of Africa, although anything which is said in a general way will obviously be an over-simplification. Tribal man never stands alone. He is guided from his earliest childhood by the tribal customs and by the tribal elders, who in turn are guided by what they consider to be the voices of the ancestors. Past, present and future are thus seen as a continuum. The individual has little or no sense of his separate identity, and cannot even contemplate a life apart from the tribe. He depends for his sense of security on the observance of rituals and on the essentially magical or spiritual power of protectors, the elders and chief, the ancestors and the gods. When the European enters the picture, breaks all the local taboos and apparently gets away with it, he frequently takes on the role of protector. This dependence relationship has nothing whatsoever to do with personal likes or dislikes. To the tribal man, what matters is not whether he likes his protector, but the degree of power that the protector is believed to possess. Significantly, as Dr. Mannoni points out in regard to the Malagasy uprising, and as subsequently happened in the Congo, it is not when the European is the most stern that the revolt occurs, but when he has suddenly decided to be more liberal. In giving a greater degree of responsibility to people who are utterly unprepared for it, he thrusts those with tribal concepts into a state of abandonment, the appalling uncertainties of which will be felt most keenly by those who have already once been uprooted from their birth-tribes and who have found substitute tribes within, say, the police or the army.

Many of the Congolese soldiers had been recruited forcibly, torn from their ancient protections and put into an army which must to some extent have taken the place of the tribe. Although they probably detested their Belgian officers, the officers were self-assured and capable of maintaining an order which must have had more ritual than military significance to the tribal mind. With the arrival of independence, the order of things, the patterns of propitiation, the most basic guarantees of inner security, must for the Congolese soldier have quite literally fallen apart.

I have no doubt that the soldiers were "drunk and doped and crazy and full of hate." But I also think it is possible that they were men filled with terrors which they did not begin to understand but which compelled them towards the false buoyancy of bottled courage or empty boasting and towards the momentary release found in violence, a violence which conveniently provided them with scapegoats for their own turmoil. I may be quite mistaken, and the true explanation may lie along other lines entirely. But whatever the explanation may be, I do not believe it is likely to be a simple one. A statement such as Dr. Grant's, "By God, they *are* just down from the trees," tells us nothing about the Congolese, although it does tell a good deal about a western observer who is bitterly disappointed at what he takes to be the ignoble savage. In fact, of course, both noble savage and ignoble savage are equally myths, creatures of our own imaginations. The reality of tribal men is not to be found in such subjective judgments as these.

As Dr. Grant in the end sets out stoically on his round of the wards, I have the feeling that unless he somehow begins to see the Congolese in terms of their own concepts and background, rather than his own, "the hidden god that dwells in every man" will very likely remain permanently hidden.

CL 14 (Augumn 1962)

Basil H. Johnston

One Generation from Extinction

Within the past few years Gregor Keeshig, Henry Johnston, Resime Aki-
wenzie, Norman McLeod, and Belva Pitwaniquot died. They all spoke
their tribal language, Anishinaubae (Ojibwa). When these elders passed
away, so did a portion of the tribal language come to an end as a tree disintegrates by degrees and in stages until it is no more; and, though infants
were born to replenish the loss of life, not any one of them will learn the
language of their grandfathers or grandmothers to keep it alive and to pass
it on to their descendants. Thus language dies.

In some communities there are no more Gregor Keeshigs, Henry John-
stons, Resime Akiwenzies, Norman McLeods, Belva Pitwaniquots; those
remaining have no more affinity to their ancestral language than they do
to Swahili or Sanskrit; in other communities the languages may not survive
beyond a generation. Some tribal languages are at the edge of extinction,
not expected to survive for more than a few years. There remain but three
aboriginal languages out of the original fifty-three found in Canada that
may survive several more generations.

There is cause to lament but it is the native peoples who have the most
cause to lament the passing of their languages. They lose not only the ability to express the simplest of daily sentiments and needs but they can no
longer understand the ideas, concepts, insights, attitudes, rituals, ceremonies, institutions brought into being by their ancestors; and, having lost the
power to understand, cannot sustain, enrich, or pass on their heritage. No
longer will they think Indian or feel Indian. And though they may wear
"Indian" jewellery and take part in pow-wows, they can never capture that
kinship with and reverence for the sun and the moon, the sky and the
water, or feel the lifebeat of Mother Earth or sense the change in her moods;

no longer are the wolf, the bear and the caribou elder brothers but beasts, resources to be killed and sold. They will have lost their identity which no amount of reading can ever restore. Only language and literature can restore the "Indian-ness."

Now if Canadians of West European or other origin have less cause than "Indians" to lament the passing of tribal languages and cultures it is because they may not realize that there is more to tribal languages than "ugh" or "how" or "kimu sabi." At most and at best Euro-Canadians might have read or heard about Raven and Nanabush and Thunderbirds and other "tricksters"; some may have even studied "Culture Myths," "Hero Tales," "Transformation Tales," or "Nature Myths and Beast Fables," but these accounts were never regarded as bearing any more sense than "Little Red Riding Hood" or "The Three Little Pigs." Neither language nor literature were ever considered in their natural kinship, which is the only way in which language ought to be considered were its range, depth, force and beauty to be appreciated.

Perhaps our Canadian compatriots of West European origin have more cause to lament the passing of an Indian language than they realize or care to admit. Scholars mourn that there is no one who can speak the Huron language and thus assist scholars in their pursuit of further knowledge about the tribe; scholars mourn that had the Beothuk language survived, so much more would be known about the Beothuk peoples. In mourning the extinction of the language, scholars are implicitly declaring that the knowledge derived from a study of snowshoes, shards, arrowheads, old pipes, shrunken heads and old bones, hunting, fishing, transportation, food preparation, ornamentation and sometimes ritual is limited. And so it is; material culture can yield only so much.

Language is crucial. If scholars are to increase their knowledge and if they are to add depth and width to their studies, they must study a native language and literature. It is not enough to know linguistics or to know a few words or even some phrases or to have access to the Jesuit *Relations*, Chippewa *Exercises*, Ojibwa *Texts*, or a *Dictionary of the Otchipwe Language*. Without a knowledge of the language scholars can never take for granted the accuracy of an interpretation or translation of a passage, let alone a single word; nor can they presume that their articles, tracts, treatises, essays bear the kind of accuracy that scholarship and integrity demand. They would continue to labour under the impression that the word "manitou" means spirit and that it has no other meaning. Superstitious nonsense, according to the white man. They do not know that the word bears other meanings even more fundamental than "spirit," such as, and/or pertaining to the deities; of a substance, character, nature, essence, quiddity beyond comprehension and therefore beyond explanation, a mystery; supernatural; potency, potential. What a difference such knowledge might have made in the studies conducted by Ruth Landes or Thomas B. Leekley, and others on the Anishinaubae tribe. Perhaps, instead of regarding "Indians" as superstitious for positing "spirits" in trees or in other inanimate or insensate objects, they might have credited them with insight for having perceived a vital substance or essence that imparted life, form, growth, healing, and strength in all things, beings, and places. They might have understood that the expression "manitouwan" meant that an object possessed or was infused with an element or a feature that was beyond human ken; they might have understood that "w'manitouwih" meant that he or she was endowed with extraordinary talents, and that it did not mean that he or she was a spirit.

Language is essential. If scholars and writers are to know how "Indians" perceive and regard certain ideas they must study an "Indian" language. When an "Anishinaubae" says that someone is telling the truth, he says "w'daeb-awae." But the expression is not just a mere confirmation of a speaker's veracity. It is at the same time a philosophical proposition that, in saying, a speaker casts his words and his voice only as far as his vocabulary and his perception will enable him. In so doing the tribe was denying that there was absolute truth; that the best a speaker could achieve and a listener expect was the highest degree of accuracy. Somehow that one expression "w'daeb-awae" set the limits of a single statement as well as setting limits on all speech.

There was a special regard almost akin to reverence for speech and for the truth. Perhaps it was because words bear the tone of the speaker and may therefore be regarded as belonging to that person; perhaps it is because words have but a fleeting momentary existence in sound and are gone except in memory; perhaps it is because words have not ceased to exist but survive in echo and continue on in infinity; perhaps it is because words are medicine that can heal or injure; perhaps it is because words possess an element of the manitou that enabled them to conjure images and ideas out of nothing, and are the means by which the autissokanuk (muses) inspired men and women. It was not for nothing that the older generation did not solicit the autissokanuk to assist in the genesis of stories or in the composition of chants in seasons other than winter.

To instil respect for language the old counselled youth, "Don't talk too much" (Kegon zaum-doongaen), for they saw a kinship between language and truth. The expression is not without its facetious aspect but in its broader application it was intended to convey to youth other notions implicit in the expression "Don't talk too much," for the injunction also meant "Don't talk too often . . . Don't talk too long . . . Don't talk about those matters that you know nothing about." Were a person to restrict his discourse, and measure his speech, and govern his talk by what he knew, he would earn the trust and respect of his (her) listeners. Of that man or woman they would say "w'daeb-awae." Better still, people would want to hear the speaker again and by so doing bestow upon the speaker the opportunity to speak, for ultimately it is the people who confer the right of speech by their audience.

ა

Language was a precious heritage; literature was no less precious. So precious did the tribe regard language and speech that it held those who abused language and speech and truth in contempt and ridicule and withheld from them their trust and confidence. To the tribe the man or woman who rambled on and on, or who let his tongue range over every subject or warp the truth was said to talk in circles in a manner no different from that of a mongrel who, not knowing the source of alarm, barks in circles (w'geewi-animoh). Ever since words and sounds were reduced to written symbols and have been stripped of their mystery and magic, the regard and reverence for them have diminished in tribal life.

As rich and full of meaning as may be individual words and expression, they embody only a small portion of the entire stock and potential of tribal knowledge, wisdom, and intellectual attainment; the greater part is deposited in myths, legends, stories, and in the lyrics of chants that make up the tribe's literature. Therein will be found the essence and the substance of tribal ideas, concepts, insights, attitudes, values, beliefs, theories, notions, sentiments, and accounts of their institutions and rituals and ceremonies. Without language scholars, writers and teachers will have no access to the depth and width of tribal knowledge and understanding, but must continue to labour as they have done these many years under the impression that "Indian" stories are nothing more than fairy tales or folklore, fit only for juvenile minds. For scholars and academics Nanabush, Raven, Glooscap, Weesaukeechauk and other mythological figures will ever remain "tricksters," culture heroes, deities whose misadventures were dreamed into being only for the amusement of children. Primitive and pagan and illiterate to boot, "Indians" could not possibly address or articulate abstract ideas or themes; neither their minds nor their languages could possibly express any idea more complex than taboos, superstitions and bodily needs.

But were ethnologists, anthropologists, linguists, teachers of native children and writers of native literature — yes, even archaeologists — to learn a native language, perhaps they might learn that Nanabush and Raven are not simply "tricksters" but the caricatured representations of human nature and character in their many facets; perhaps they might give thought to the meaning and sense to be found in Weessaukeetchauk, The Bitter Soul. There is no other way except through language for scholars to learn or to validate their studies, their theories, their theses about the values, ideals or institutions or any other aspect of tribal life; there is no other way by which knowledge of native life can find increase. Not good enough is it to say in hushed tones after a reverential description of a totem pole or the lacing of a snowshoe, "My, weren't they clever."

Just consider the fate of "Indian" stories written by those who knew nothing of the language and never did hear any of the stories in their entirety or in their original version but derived everything that they knew of their subject from second, third and even fourth diluted sources. Is it any wonder then that the stories in *Indian Legends of Canada* by E.E. Clark or in *Manabozho* by T.B. Leekley are so bland and devoid of sense? Had the authors known the stories in their "Indian" sense and flavour, perhaps they might have infused their versions with more wit and substance. Had the authors known that the creation story as the Anishinaubae understood it to mean was intended to represent in the most dramatic way possible the process of individual development from the smallest portion of talent to be retrieved from the depths of one's being and then given growth by breath of life. Thus a man and woman are to develop themselves, create their own worlds, and shape their being and give meaning to life. Had the authors known this meaning of the creation story, perhaps they might have written their accounts in terms more in keeping with the sense and thrust of the story. But not knowing the language nor having heard the story in its original text or state, the authors could not, despite their intentions, impart to their accounts the due weight and perspective the story deserved. The stories were demeaned.

ભ

With language dead and literature demeaned, "Indian" institutions are beyond understanding and restoration. Let us turn back the calendar two and a half centuries, to that period when the "Indian" languages were spoken in every home, when native literature inspired thought and when native "Indian" institutions governed native "Indian" life. It was then that a native institution caught the imagination of the newcomers to this continent. The men and women who founded a new nation to be known as the United States of America took as their model for their constitution and government the principles of government and administration embodied in The Great Tree of Peace of the Five Nations Confederacy. The institution of The Great Tree of Peace was not then too primitive nor too alien for study or emulation to the founders of the United States. In more recent years even the architects of the United Nations regarded the "Indian" institution of The Great Tree of Peace not as a primitive organization beneath their dignity and intellect, but rather as an institution of merit. There exist still "Indian" institutions that may well serve and benefit this society and this nation, not as dramatically as did The Great Tree of Peace the United States of America, but bestow some good as yet undreamed or unimagined. Just how much good such institutions may confer upon this or some future generation will not be known unless the "Indian" languages survive.

And what is it that has undermined the vitality of some of the "Indian" languages and deprived this generation and this society the promise and the benefit of the wisdom and the knowledge embodied in tribal literature?

In the case of the Beothuk and their language, the means used were simple and direct: it was the blade, the bludgeon, and the bullet that were plied in the destruction of the Beothuk in their sleep, at their table, and in their quiet passage from home to place of work, until the tribe was no more. The speakers were annihilated; no more was the Beothuk language spoken; whatever their wisdom or whatever their institutions, the whole of the Beothuk heritage was destroyed.

In other instances, instead of bullets, bludgeons, and bayonets, other means were used to put an end to the speaking of an "Indian" language. A kick with a police riding boot administered by a 175-pound man upon the person of an eight-year-old boy for uttering the language of a savage left its pain for days and its bruise upon the spirit for life. A boy once kicked was not likely to risk a second or a third. A slap in the face or a punch to the back of the head delivered even by a small man upon the person of a small boy left its sting and a humiliation not soon forgotten. And if a boot or a fist were not administered, then a lash or a yardstick was plied until the "Indian" language was beaten out. To boot and fist and lash was added ridicule. Both speaker and his language were assailed. "What's the use of that language? It isn't polite to speak another language in the presence of other people. Learn English! That's the only way you're going to get ahead. How can you learn two languages at the same time? No wonder kids can't learn anything else. It's a primitive language; hasn't the vocabulary to express abstract ideas, poor. Say 'ugh.' Say something in your language! . . . How can you get your tongue around those sounds?" On and on the comments were made, disparaging, until in too many the language was shamed into silence and disuse.

And how may the federal government assist in the restoration of the native languages to their former vigour and vitality and enable them to fulfil their promise?

The Government of Canada must finance the establishment of either provincial or regional language institutes to be affiliated with a museum or a university or a provincial native educational organization. The function of the "institute," to be headed by a native person who speaks, reads, and writes a native language, will be to foster research into language and to encourage the publication of lexicons, dictionaries, grammars, courses, guides, outlines, myths, stories, legends, genealogies, histories, religion, rituals, ceremonies, chants, prayers, and general articles; to tape stories, myths, legends, grammars, teaching guides and outlines and to build a collection of written and oral literature and to make same accessible to scholars, teachers and native institutions; and to duplicate and distribute written and oral literature to the native communities and learning institutions. The native languages deserve to be enshrined in this country's heritage as much as do snowshoes, shards, and arrowheads. Nay! More.

But unless the writings, the essays, stories, plays, the papers of scholars, academics, lexicographers, grammarians, etymologists, playwrights, poets, novelists, composers, philosophers are published and distributed, they can never nurture growth in language or literature. Taking into account the market represented by each tribe, no commercial publisher would risk publication of an "Indian" book. Hence, only the federal government has the means to sponsor publication of an "Indian text," either through a commercial publisher or through the Queen's Printer. The publication of an "Indian" book may not be a commercially profitable enterprise, but it would add to the nation's intellectual and literary heritage.

CL 124–125 (Spring-Summer 1990)

T.D. MacLulich

Canadian Exploration as Literature

The first three chapters of the *Literary History of Canada* can be seen as raising an interesting problem in literary theory: In what sense should the writings of the Canadian explorers be viewed as "literature"? Certainly exploration writing cannot be viewed as part of the literary mainstream. In fact, it is quite probable that the explorers are allotted their place in the *Literary History* more as auxiliaries to cultural history than as full members of the belle-lettristic community.[1] On the other hand, exploration writing exercises a considerable fascination over many readers. The writings of the explorers tell many exciting stories of adventure, relate many entertaining and even amusing anecdotes, and introduce the reader to a gallery of interesting and unusual characters. In some way, then, a number of conventionally "literary" qualities have found their way into the writings produced by the explorers. Nonetheless, to argue that exploration writing *is* literature simply on the grounds that it *can* be approached in a literary manner is surely to avoid the real issues. The pertinent questions are: Have the explorers' literary qualities arisen by accident or design? And are these literary qualities pervasive and consistent enough to constitute a set of literary conventions? In his well-known "Conclusion" to the *Literary History*, Northrop Frye roundly asserts that the explorers wrote with "no more literary intention than a mating loon." Frye's contention may be sound when we are dealing with explorers whose accounts were intended only as a rough diary of their journey, or as a private report to their European backers. But the situation changes when an explorer prepares his journal for publication. Then he faces the essentially literary problem of revising his original account of daily occurrences into a form which will maintain the attention of his prospective readers. As Victor Hopwood astutely points out, accounts

of exploration usually must be subjected to a considerable amount of revision before they are ready for publication:

> Exploration tends to be repetitive, and the fourth or fifth adventure
> with a bear, boring, at least in the telling. If journals are to become
> interesting to the ordinary reader, they need suppression of repetitive
> detail, expansion with incident and description and development of
> direction and purpose.[2]

The explorer must choose which events to record and which to omit; he
must select some events to stress and others to pass over lightly; he must
decide on the amount and kind of interpretive commentary he will offer;
and above all he must shape his account in accordance with his own sense
of the pattern inherent in his personal experiences.

The transformation which an exploration account undergoes before it is
published can be clarified by comparing the literary activity of explorers
with the literary efforts of historians. The comparison will be based on an
analysis of historical writing borrowed from Hayden White's massive
study of nineteenth-century historiography, *Metahistory*. White argues
that the bare chronicle of events which is the historian's starting point possesses no intrinsic shape or meaning. It is the historian who transforms a
mere chronological sequence of events into a "story" by associating particular events with "inaugural motifs," "transitional motifs," and "terminal
motifs." Before the historian goes to work, each event

> is simply "there" as an element of a series; it does not "function" as a
> story element. The historian arranges the events in the chronicle into a
> hierarchy of significance by assigning events different functions as
> story elements in such a way as to disclose the formal coherence of a
> whole set of events considered as a comprehensible process with a
> discernible beginning, middle, and end.[3]

But the historian does more than simply bracket a portion of the historical
record within a kind of verbal punctuation marks; he shapes each story in
a particular manner. According to White, the historian patterns the broad
outline of each historical story after one of the four *mythoi* identified by
Northrop Frye in *Anatomy of Criticism*. That is, the historian shapes his
stories as either Comedy, Tragedy, Romance, or Satire. This shaping of the
historical record into one of Frye's categories White labels "emplotment."

White's analysis of historical writing is relevant to a consideration of
exploration writing because the explorer is in fact a kind of historian. Like
the historian the explorer is engaged in imposing order on a set of events
which are given rather than imagined. White writes that the historian

confronts a veritable chaos of events *already constituted*, out of which
he must choose the elements of the story he would tell. He makes his
story by including some events and excluding others, by stressing some
and subordinating others. This process of exclusion, stress, and
subordination is carried out in the interest of constituting *a story of a
particular kind.*[4]

This description of the historical process is very similar to Hopwood's account of the changes an explorer's journal must undergo before publication. Both Hopwood and White describe a process of "exclusion, stress,
and subordination"; moreover, Hopwood's "development of direction and
purpose" is parallel with White's "emplotment" into a story of a "particular kind."

In applying White's concept of "emplotment" to exploration writing
only one change in White's analysis must be made: a different set of narrative categories must be used. Exploration accounts seldom, or never, fall
into the areas of Comedy or Satire. Moreover, although many exploration
accounts are emplotted in ways that resemble Romance and Tragedy, explorers do not possess the wide scope for action available to characters in
many works of the Romantic and Tragic modes. (In particular, explorers
are much less powerful than those Romantic heroes for whom the laws of
nature are suspended.) As a result, it is most convenient in the present discussion to use a typology of narrative which directly pertains to accounts
of exploration. It is the contention of this paper that most accounts of exploration are emplotted in one of three ways, either as *quests*, as *odysseys*,
or as *ordeals*.

When an explorer sets out on a journey, he usually has a specific goal in
mind. If his journey is successful, it is quite natural to make the attaining
of the goal the central theme of the ensuing narrative. The result will be an
account in which every episode will have a clear relationship to the explorer's progress towards his goal, an account structured as a successful
quest. Events and people will be mentioned only insofar as they either help
or hinder the attainment of the goal. The dangers and hardships encountered will be emphasized. The journey will be portrayed as a succession of
crises, in each of which some obstacle is overcome, rising to a climax with
the final attainment of the goal. This authorial strategy results in a swiftly
moving, straight-line narrative, focused on limited issues. The explorer
himself appears as a determined and forceful hero, a conqueror. Such heroic explorers tend to resemble each other, all displaying bravery, physical
strength, resourcefulness, and unflagging determination.

There is, of course, the possibility that an explorer may fail to complete
his journey, due to circumstances beyond his control. The obstacles may
be too great or he may lack the requisite resourcefulness and strength of

character. Such a failure is usually accompanied by great suffering and hardship; in extreme cases the explorers may die. (Accounts of an exploring party's extinction have been preserved because in some cases the explorer's diary — notably Scott's — has been recovered after his death.) When an explorer tells a story of disaster or near-disaster, his account may aptly be termed an *ordeal*. The action of an ordeal will focus on the attempts of the exploring party to ensure their survival, and the thematic focus will fall on the human capacity to endure privation. A further thematic emphasis will grow out of the means by which rescue or escape is achieved, whether Providential, fortuitous, or brought about by human means. The climax of the account will be the eventual rescue or escape itself — or the final scene of disaster.

A third possibility arises when the explorer's goal is only of secondary importance in comparison with his desire to obtain an overall view of the unknown regions he is traversing. Then, the incidental details of the journey become the main focal point of the account. The explorer describes the things seen and the experiences undergone for their own sake rather than simply as adjuncts to a quest for some specific place or object. Such an explorer often gives extensive descriptions of the lands and the peoples he encounters, and may describe his own gradually growing understanding of a non-European way of life. Focusing on incidental details in this way results in a loose and digressive structure, which may be described as an *odyssey*. Like Homer's wanderer the explorer will often seem more interested in his immediate surroundings than in reaching his distant objective. Such odyssean explorers display a greater range of personality traits than do heroic travellers or sufferers. The personal interests of an odyssean traveller determine the centres of attention of his narrative; individual characteristics are allowed a greater expression than in a quest or ordeal.

CB

The three forms of exploration account do not correspond directly to Frye's typology of narrative forms, but they can be related to an overlapping, but less inclusive, set of fictional categories. A heroic quest-explorer, who succeeds either by mental or physical force in overcoming all difficulties, will emerge as an inflexible and indomitable proponent of a fixed scheme of values, rather like some of the righteous heroes of certain quest-romances. On the other hand, an explorer who undergoes an ordeal emerges as an enduring sufferer, rather like the heroes of certain simple tragedies. Most explorers who depict their journeys as either quests or ordeals cling to the values of their society of origin, and seek to impose themselves and their purposes on both their own subordinates and on the native peoples they encounter. In contrast, an odyssean explorer adapts himself to the non-European conditions with which he is surrounded; his account depicts a learning process analogous to the education or initiation undergone by the central characters of many novels. Thus, the correspondences among the three forms of exploration account and ordinary forms of fictional narrative may be summarized in a simple diagram:[5]

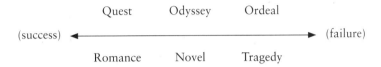

As the diagram suggests, the three kinds of exploration account are not absolutely distinct categories, but rather are convenient labels to identify portions of a literary continuum. Quest and ordeal are the extreme points, polar opposites. An account emplotted as a quest emphasizes the explorer's success in attaining his goal; an account emplotted as an ordeal stresses difficulties and suffering which are not redeemed by success. The odyssey falls between the two extremes; an odyssean explorer places less emphasis on his desire to reach a particular goal, and pays more attention to the incidental details of the journey. Moreover, the three forms are not necessarily mutually exclusive, but may exist in combination. For example, an account may combine the traits of quest and odyssey, or of odyssey and ordeal. Or an odyssey may contain incidents emplotted as a quest or as an ordeal — and so on.

Nonetheless, in any individual account one of the three forms will dominate. To explain why, we can again appeal to White's analysis of historical writing. White remarks that historians' stories fall into simple pre-existing patterns

> precisely because the historian is inclined to resist construction of the complex peripeteias which are the novelist's and the dramatist's stock in trade. Precisely because he is not (or claims not to be) telling the story "for its own sake," he is inclined to emplot his stories in the most conventional form. . . .[6]

Like the historians described by White, explorers are also relatively unsophisticated storytellers, who tend to emplot their stories in a simple manner. Once an explorer has decided how he interprets his journey (a decision which may be either consciously or unconsciously made), he normally presents the details of his journey in a way that supports his overall vision of what he has accomplished.

The emplotment of an explorer's story in one of the three forms is signalled principally through large-scale structural features; that is, the explorer expands or otherwise emphasizes those scenes and incidents which reinforce his interpretation of his experiences, and compresses or omits scenes which do not contribute to his chosen interpretation. However, he may also explicitly signal his intentions by attaching verbal motifs to certain events and at times by making overt authorial statements of purpose. For example, in *Voyages from Montreal* Alexander Mackenzie clearly warns his readers to expect the undeviating, relentless movement of a quest account:

> I could not stop to dig into the earth, over whose surface I was
> compelled to pass with rapid steps; nor could I turn aside to collect
> the plants which nature might have scattered on the way, when my
> thoughts were anxiously employed in making provision for the day
> that was passing over me. I had to encounter perils by land and perils
> by water; to watch the savage who was our guide, or guard against
> those of his tribe who might meditate our destruction. I had, also,
> the passions and fears of others to control and subdue. To-day, I had
> to assuage the rising discontents, and on the morrow, to cheer the
> fainting spirits of the people who accompanied me. The toil of our
> navigation was incessant, and oftentimes extreme; and in our progress
> over land, we had no protection from the severity of the elements, and
> possessed no accommodations or conveniences but such as could be
> contained in the burden on our shoulders, which aggravated the toils
> of our march, and added to the wearisomeness of our way.[7]

In contrast to Mackenzie, David Thompson allows his attention to wander freely away from the actual progress of his travels, and expands incidental happenings until they become the main features of his account. Thompson's awareness of this trait in his *Narrative* is indicated when he remarks, after delivering one of his most famous digressions (that on the two races, man and beaver), "From this long digression, I return to my travels in the Nut Hill."[8] Even when he inserts into his account a portion of his journal describing a mid-winter journey over the prairies, Thompson's purpose is not simply to describe his geographical progress, but to make clear the nature of the experience he has undergone:

> As my journey to the Mississourie is over part of the Great Plains, I
> shall give it in the form of a journal, this form, however dull, is the
> only method in my opinion, that can give the reader a clear idea of
> them.[9]

In these passages, and in others throughout the *Narrative*, Thompson's awareness of the odyssean nature of his account is clear to the attentive reader.

It should be apparent that the present argument does not support a theory of environmental determinism. It might seem that whether an explorer undergoes an "ordeal" or completes a "quest" is not a matter of authorial choice, but is the result of the actual physical conditions he encounters. Of course, the influence of external conditions cannot be disregarded. But subjective factors are also extremely important — one man's ordeal may be another man's Odyssey. For example, suppose we compare Luke Foxe's *Northwest Fox; or, Fox from the North-West Passage* (1635) with Thomas James' *The Strange and Dangerous Voyage* (1633). These books both describe expeditions made to Hudson Bay in the same year, yet they present very different pictures of the dangers and difficulties of such a navigation. The easy voyage experienced by Foxe and the difficulties encountered by James probably have as much to do with the personalities of the two captains as with the actual conditions encountered.

Examples drawn from the early records left by French travellers also help to illustrate how a writer's attitude can colour his presentation of his experiences. At one extreme is the trader and adventurer Pierre Esprit Radisson:

> I took my gun and goes where I never was before, so I choosed not one way before another. I went [in] to the wood some three or four miles. I find a small brook, where I walked by the side awhile, which brought me into meadows. There was a pool where were a good store of bustards. I began to creep [as] though I might come near. The poor creatures, seeing me flat upon the ground, thought I was a beast as well as they, so they came near me, whistling like goslings, thinking to frighten me. The whistling that I made them hear was another music than theirs. There I killed three, and the rest scared, which nevertheless came to that place again to see what sudden sickness befelled their comrades. I shot again; two paid for their curiosity.[10]

Surely Radisson has embroidered this scene more than is necessary merely to get his story told; the additional details reflect his zestful delight in the free hunting life. At the other extreme are many of the writers in the *Jesuit Relations*, who present life with the "savages" as a kind of penance, a purgatory on earth. "A soul very thirsty for the Son of God," writes Father Le Jeune, " I mean for suffering, would find enough here to satisfy it."[11] Lejeune's preconceptions, even more than actual physical conditions, seem to underlie this remark.

The wide applicability of the proposed classification of exploration writing can be suggested by undertaking a brief survey of some of the major Canadian accounts of exploration. Among the records left by the early northern voyagers, the ordeal is the predominant form. The nature of these

accounts is well indicated by Tryggvi J. Oleson, in his history of the early
exploration of territories now included in northern Canada:

> The annals of these expeditions are records of courage, perseverance,
> and almost incredible endurance amidst some of the harshest and most
> difficult natural conditions ever encountered by man. They are true
> tales of heroism, for the Canadian Arctic . . . can be the deadliest of all
> regions to those who bring little more than ignorance to the conquest
> of it. And this was the case with the great majority of those who, in the
> beginning of the seventeenth century, ventured to penetrate its ice, fog,
> and mists — in what can only be described as frail little barks, fitted
> for little more than coastal navigation or for sailing the high seas
> under the most favourable conditions.[12]

As Oleson's comments indicate, the keynotes of these accounts are danger
and hardship. Some of the accounts are one continuous succession of perilous experiences, brought on by the ice and storms of northern water.
Dionyse Settle's account of Frobisher's second voyage conveys the helplessness all of these navigators must have felt at times:

> the ship and barkes . . . were forced to abide in a cruell tempest,
> chancing in the night amongst and in the thickest of the yce, which
> was so monstrous, that even the least of a thousand had been of force
> sufficient, to have shivered our ship and barks into small portions, if
> God (who in all necessities, hath care unto the infirmitie of man) had
> not provided for this our extremitie a sufficient remedie through the
> light of the night, whereby we might well discerne to flee from such
> imminent danger, which we avoyded with 14. Bourdes in one watch
> the space of 4 houres.[13]

Although these accounts may often be, as Oleson says, tales of heroism,
the chief characters are not heroic in the usual sense. The early voyagers do
not strike the modern reader as determined and powerful, but as beleaguered and confused. Whatever discoveries they make seem fortuitous, as
their tiny ships drift at the mercy of wind and current. The voyagers may
be personally brave and at times reckless, but their stories illustrate the
small scope of man's knowledge and his helplessness in the face of natural
forces.

The presentation of a voyage as an ordeal is most pronounced in those
accounts which tell of enforced winterings in Hudson or James Bay. To the
dangers of northern navigation these accounts add the hardships of a long,
dark Arctic winter. Such misadventures befell Hudson in 1610–11, Bylot in
1612–13, Jens Munk in 1619–20, and Thomas James in 1631–32. James,

the last of the early seekers after a Northwest Passage, depicts his voyage
as beset by difficulties right from the time he left England. Once he reaches
Hudson Strait his difficulties are multiplied by the ice and storms he encounters there, so that on numerous occasions he writes as though destruction is imminent:

> All night, the Storm continu'd with Violence, and with some Rain in
> the Morning; it then being very thick Weather. The Water shoal'd
> apace, with such an overgrown Sea withal, that a Sail was not to be
> endur'd; and what was worse, there was no trusting to an Anchor.
> Now therefore we began to prepare ourselves, how to make a good
> End, of a miserable tormented Life.[14]

As well as describing such overt dangers, James has an astute eye for the
small personal details which make his men's plight more moving and immediate to the reader. His eye for the pathetic is well illustrated in his description of the last days of one of his men, injured when ice caused a
capstan to get out of control:

> The 19th, our Gunner, (who, as you may remember, had his Leg cut
> off) languish'd irrecoverably, and now grew very weak; desiring, that,
> for the little Time he had to live, he might drink Sack altogether; which
> I order'd he should.[15]

Throughout the account James goes out of his way to enlist the reader's
sympathies by describing the difficult conditions under which the men laboured, their poor equipment, and the weakness of their conditions as a
result of scurvy.

∝

In later years, when most explorers were either men connected with the fur
trade or had acquired experience in wilderness travel in some other way,
the chances of an expedition turning into an ordeal were lessened. However, when an inexperienced traveller ventured forth, especially into the
extreme conditions of more northerly regions, disaster could still strike. A
vivid example is the first overland journey of John Franklin, which records
the gradual disintegration of his party into starving near-skeletons, beset
by the twin spectres of death and cannibalism:

> We now looked round for the means of subsistence, and were gratified
> to find several deer skins, which had been thrown away during our
> former residence. The bones were gathered from the heap of ashes,

these with the skins, and addition of *tripe de roche*, we considered
would support us tolerably well for a time.

When I arose the following morning, my body and limbs were so
swollen that I was unable to walk more than a few yards. Adam was
in a still worse condition, being absolutely incapable of rising without
assistance. My other companions fortunately experienced this
inconvenience in a less degree, and went to collect bones, and some
tripe de roche which supplied us with two meals. The bones were quite
acrid, and the soup extracted from them excoriated the mouth if taken
alone, but it was somewhat milder when boiled with *tripe de roche*,
and we even thought the mixture palatable, with the addition of salt,
of which a cask had been fortunately left here in the spring. Augustus
today set two fishing lines below the rapid. On his way thither he saw
two deer, but had not strength to follow them.[16]

The stiffness of Franklin's language, his inability to convey an emotional
response to the situation he depicts, adds an ironic dimension to the account. The reader perceives that the self-control which is reflected in
Franklin's unflappable tone mirrors the rigidity of personality which is
partly responsible for the plight of the expedition.

Franklin's difficulties arise largely because he is a British naval officer
sent out by the Admiralty rather than an experienced northern traveller.
More typical of Canadian explorers are the two fur traders Alexander
Mackenzie and Samuel Hearne. Both of these explorers utilize Indian
methods of travel and rely to a great extent on Indian helpers. However,
their journeys represent two very different approaches to the explorer's
task. Hearne's method is to cut his party to the minimum — one man —
and place himself under the protection of a prominent Indian and allow
the Indians' normal wanderings to carry him into regions unknown to
Europeans. In contrast, Mackenzie forces his party ever onwards, in spite
of the frequent hostility of the natives and the occasional reluctance of his
own men. Hearne adjusts himself and his purposes to the Indian way of
life; Mackenzie, although necessarily using Indian methods of travel and
relying on the natives for much of his food, bends the natives to his own
purposes. In other words, Hearne presents his travels as an odyssey whereas Mackenzie presents his two journeys as successful quests.

In their books the two men create very different authorial personalities.
Mackenzie emerges as a heroic figure. He does not change in the course of
his travels; instead, he imposes his values on his companions and on the
Indians. There are no real digressions in Mackenzie's account; every event
is either a step towards the goal or a setback to the progress of his journey.
The recurrent theme of Mackenzie's account is the overcoming of an obstacle, whether human or physical. He emphasizes the danger and hard-

ship of his journeys, and makes it plain that his own personal efforts are the primary factor in overcoming the obstacles his party faces. Most often it is the natives he must manipulate into serving his purposes; but upon occasion it is the fears of his own men he must control:

> I brought to their recollection, that I did not deceive them, and that they were made acquainted with the difficulties and dangers they must expect to encounter, before they engaged to accompany me. I also urged the honour of conquering disasters, and the disgrace that would attend them on their return home, without having attained the object of the expedition. Nor did I fail to mention the courage and resolution that was the peculiar boast of the North men; and that I depended on them, at that moment, for the maintenance of their character.[17]

If Mackenzie is a hero, Hearne is more like an anti-hero or a picaresque figure. Hearne's virtues are endurance, adaptability, and tolerance rather than forcefulness and overbearing strength. In fact, Hearne's efforts to influence his Indian companions are often quite ineffectual. His strength of character emerges only indirectly from his story, for he seldom stresses the difficulty of the journey, and does not emphasize his own role in ensuring its completion. Rather, Hearne presents himself as a relaxed, inquisitive, and at times amused spectator of life among the Indians. He often gives the impression of enjoying their erratic, unplanned mode of existence:

> The little river lately mentioned, as well as the adjacent lakes and ponds, being well-stocked with beaver, and the land abounding with moose and buffalo, we were induced to make but slow progress in our journey. Many days were spent in hunting, feasting, and drying a large quantity of flesh to take with us, particularly that of the buffalo.[18]

The choice of pronoun here seems to indicate a tacit identification with the Indians. Hearne has adjusted completely to the Indians and to the natural environment. He implies that the world contains more than one way of looking at things; whereas Mackenzie admits only one correct viewpoint.

Mackenzie and Hearne have long been well known. But David Thompson, who is probably the most outstanding of all Canadian explorers, was for a long time a relatively neglected figure. In particular, only in the past fifteen or twenty years have the remarkable literary merits of Thompson's account of his travels come to be adequately recognized. Nonetheless, as Victor Hopwood insists, Thompson's book "belongs among such master works as Cook's *Voyages*, Darwin's *Voyage of the Beagle*, Doughty's *Travels in Arabia Deserta*, Bates' *Naturalist on the Rivers Amazon*, and Stefansson's *The Friendly Arctic*."[19] Thompson's *Narrative* is a good illustration of the literary problem posed by an odyssean account. When an explorer understands his journey as either a quest or an ordeal, many of his literary decisions are virtually made in advance, or at least are confined within narrow limits. But an odyssean explorer must choose his own thematic focus, and must organize a mass of details in a way that is both consistent and interesting. In general terms, there are two main themes which an odyssean explorer may emphasize: his own initiation into the ways of the wilderness and its peoples, or the nature of the native way of life as understood by the natives themselves. We might call these two themes the personal and the anthropological approaches.

In contrast to Hearne's personal emphasis, Thompson's *Narrative* stresses the anthropological approach. His *Narrative* tells the story of a lifetime spent in the Northwest as a fur trader and explorer, but also presents an extensive description of the geographical regions over which he has ranged and gives a sympathetic portrait of the native peoples of these regions. This wide range of subject-matter encourages a digressive structure, with many passages of summary and description inserted into the narrative, as well as many anecdotes illustrating features of native life. Frequently, too, Thompson gives insights into native life by assigning Indian characters the role of spokesman for the native way of life. Thompson succeeds brilliantly in combining his life-story with a "scientific" account of the Northwest and its peoples. He emphasizes the westward progression of his travels through various geographical regions, so that from one perspective his book is, as John Warkentin points out, a skillful regional geography of the Northwest.[20] As well, he adds an ethical dimension to his portrayal of the Indian. The details with which Thompson fills out his personal story — Indian legends, anecdotes of Indian life and history, details of Indian belief and customs, descriptions of the animals he sees and the land he traverses — are all designed to expound the nature of Indian life, and to make clear the tragic decline of the Indian as a result of contact with Europeans. Thus, Thompson's account, by portraying the extinction of a vital and harmonious non-European culture, has the ultimate effect of presenting an implicit critique of European society.

The element of social commentary is common in odyssean accounts. For example, Vilhjalmur Stefansson's *The Friendly Arctic* also presents an alternative to the usual European way of seeing the world. In this case, it is Stefansson himself who embodies the alternate vision. To the Eskimo's methods of northern survival Stefansson adds a few scientifically based contributions of his own and presents himself as a kind of improved Eskimo, combining the native's adaptation to northern conditions with the European's rationality and freedom from superstition. Stefansson's ostensible purpose in the book is to prove a thesis about methods of Arctic travel. Stefansson believes in the existence of game in the unexplored regions of the polar lands and ocean, and he believes in his ability to secure food by hunting this hypothetical game. He does not want to arrive at some particular place so much as to prove that it is possible to travel more or less indefinitely, with a minimum of supplies and equipment, by obtaining food from the land. Therefore, he need not organize his account as a quest, but can adopt the looser, more digressive, odyssean approach. In fact, a description of the daily life of his party is his principal means of proving his thesis. However, from this near-idyllic description of northern camp life emerges the implicit message of Stefansson's account, a critique of the over-complicated and artificial nature of civilized life.

Stefansson emerges as the hero of his account; but he is a hero with an odyssean slant. His prime attribute is not the ability to perform heroic deeds, but his superior knowledge of the Arctic regions and his skill in living there. Every detail in *The Friendly Arctic* is arranged to highlight what Stefansson refers to as his "polar-craft." Unlike the American explorer Robert Peary, with whom he contrasts himself, Stefansson does not marshall his intellectual and physical resources to direct a journey of conquest; his intelligence is used to come to terms with the environment, not to subdue it. "I have always been temperamentally inclined to deal with natural difficulties by adaptation and avoidance rather than by trying to overwhelm them," writes Stefansson.[21] His whole book supports this self-analysis.

One major conclusion suggested by the preceding survey of Canadian exploration writing is that over the years odyssean accounts have almost entirely supplanted accounts emplotted as either quests or ordeals. Such a change is only natural. Inadequate equipment and inexperience with northern conditions left the early explorers open to the difficulties which led them to present their experiences as ordeals. Increasing acquaintance with wilderness conditions, and especially the adoption of techniques borrowed from the Indians and Eskimos, enabled travellers to venture forth with greater safety and a greater chance of success. However, improved exploring techniques and a more complete understanding of the northern environment were not the only factors encouraging the production of odyssean accounts. Perhaps even more important were the gradual diminution of purely economic incentives for exploration and the spread of a scientific outlook throughout Western society. The scientific attitude encouraged a more disinterested and objective scrutiny of the remote regions of the world, which in turn was conducive to the writing of odyssean accounts of exploration.

This paper began with a question, to which we can now return. Certainly exploration writing cannot be viewed as "pure" literature in the conventional sense. But it is a form of writing into which literary considerations enter in important and systematic ways. An explorer chooses the form of his story from within a restricted set of literary strategies, and

he shapes his narrative throughout in conformity with the underlying thematic concerns entailed by his chosen way of understanding his travels.
Moreover, the three forms of the exploration account embody three of the
most hallowed of literary themes. The quests of the heroic explorers reveal
powers of mind and body beyond the reach of ordinary mortals; the wanderings of the odyssean explorers expose the reader to modes of behaviour
and of thought that are beyond the range of everyday experience; and the
ordeals undergone by those explorers who suffer a series of misadventures
show the incredible strength of man's will to survive. Thus, the three forms
of exploration account highlight respectively the explorer's achievements,
his education and initiation, and the testing of his faith and endurance.
These are themes whose enduring interest for readers has been proved time
and again over the years. In its own way, each kind of exploration account
tells a story which, like the stories told in so many conventional works of
literature, reveals an unexpected dimension of human possibility.

Notes

[1] In the "Introduction" to the *Literary History* the editors remark: "This book treats,
not only works generically classified as 'literature,' but also, chiefly in separate
chapters, other works which have influenced literature or have been significantly
related to literature expressing the cultural life of the country." *Literary History of
Canada: Canadian Literature in English*, ed. Carl F. Klinck et al. (Toronto: U of
Toronto P, 1965), xi.

[2] "Explorers by Land: To 1860," *Literary History of Canada*, 25.

[3] *Metahistory: The Historical Imagination in Nineteenth-Century Europe* (Baltimore:
Johns Hopkins UP, 1973), 7.

[4] *Metahistory*, 6, n. 5.

[5] The necessity to invoke the category "Novel" points up an omission in Frye's
typology of narrative. As White points out, Frye's "method of analysis works well
enough on second-order literary genres, such as the fairy tale or the detective story,"
but "it is too rigid and abstract to do justice to . . . richly textured and multi-levelled
works" (8, n. 6). Historically, more complex or "mixed" modes of narrative evolved
out of the simpler traditional forms when authors fused the characteristics of two
or more traditional forms, or when (as in *Don Quixote)* they subjected the
conventions of a traditional form to a sceptical or "realistic" examination. The end
point of this historical progression was the mode of narrative we loosely term
"Realism," of which the Novel is the prime representative. Therefore, in order to
cover the entire range of narrative possibilities, Frye's four modes must be
understood to cover a wide range of variations on the basic types he describes, and
the admittedly somewhat catch-all category "Realism" must be added to Frye's
scheme. White finds Frye's four categories adequate for his discussion. However,
White is dealing with nineteenth-century historians, and historical writing did not
become thoroughly "realistic" until the twentieth century. If White were to extend
his analysis to twentieth-century historians, he might well feel the need to invoke a
category of historical writing analogous to the Novel.

[6] *Metahistory*, 8, n. 6.

[7] *The Journals and Letters of Sir Alexander Mackenzie*, ed. W. Kaye Lamb
(Cambridge: Cambridge UP, 1970), 58–59.

[8] *David Thompson's Narrative, 1784–1812*, ed. Richard Glover (Toronto: Champlain Society, 1962), 154.

[9] *Narrative*, 161.

[10] *The Explorations of Pierre Esprit Radisson*, ed. Arthur T. Adams (Minneapolis: Ross & Haines, 1961), 126.

[11] *The Jesuit Relations and Allied Documents*, ed. R. S. Mealing (Toronto: McClelland & Stewart, 1963), 33.

[12] *Early Voyages and Northern Approaches* (Toronto: McClelland & Stewart, 1963), 161.

[13] *The Principal Navigations, Voyages, Traffiques and Discoveries of the English Nation*, 12 vols. (Glasgow: MacLehose, 1903–05), VII, 216.

[14] *The Dangerous Voyage of Captain Thomas James* (Toronto: Coles, 1973), 37–38·

[15] *Dangerous Voyage*, 51.

[16] *Narrative of a Journey to the Shores of the Polar Sea in the Years 1819, 20, 21, and 22* (Edmonton: Hurtig, 1969), 439–40.

[17] *Journals and Letters*, 299.

[18] *A Journey from Prince of Wales's Fort in Hudson's Bay to the Northern Ocean in the Years 1769, 1770, 1771 and 1772*, ed. Richard Glover (Toronto: Macmillan, 1958), 175.

[19] "Introduction," *Travels in Western North America, 1784–1812*, ed. Victor Hopwood (Toronto: Macmillan, 1971), 34.

[20] "Early Geographical Writing in English on British North America," in *Papers of the Bibliographical Society of Canada*, 12 (Toronto, 1974), 38–71.

[21] *The Friendly Arctic: The Story of Five Years in Polar Regions* (New York: Macmillan, 1921), 103.

CL 81 (Summer 1979)

Eli Mandel

George Grant: Language, Nation, The Silence of God

My most vivid recollection of first hearing about George Grant's political philosophy and his views of modernism is a lecture by Dennis Lee. Like most of my colleagues, I had some sense in the early 1970's that Grant was, if not a deeply admired, a much respected philosopher, an intellectual of considerable force, the author of at least two books that went some way toward redefining the terms by which Canada was to be understood and the conditions of contemporary life that called for a re-definition. But at the same time, like most of my colleagues, I was aware too of what seemed to me a certain crankiness in Grant's style and thought that made his best work painful and uneasy reading. A recent tribute to Grant "as Canada's foremost political philosopher" qualifies its position oddly by remarking that "one cannot but think that George Grant has become important without becoming influential" and that "Instead of reading his own works and participating in his relentless ethical quest, men of Grant's own generation have been content to make him a fellow of the Royal Society."[1] Some such qualification or unease may have been in my mind as Lee began to lecture to a large freshman class in a Humanities course on "Canadian Culture" about Grant's *Lament for a Nation* and *Technology and Empire*. Two strong, conflicting emotions possessed me during the lecture: one, embarrassment at Lee's obviously painful struggle to articulate a deeply felt but somehow complicated series of arguments; another, something akin to awe at the degree of conviction in his view that Grant's moral position was somehow absolutely and fundamentally right. The effect of the lecture was quite extraordinary in its odd mixing of obscure and hidden emotions with feelings as immediately authentic as testimony or religious witness. It was only later, when in fact I read Lee's brilliant "Cadence, Country, Silence,"[2] that I understood what it was I was hearing that day or why it should have had the effect on me — and I dare say on the class — that it did. Later too I began to understand the reason for the class's fascination with a writer who by all usual standards should have proved repellent to them.

Writing of Grant's political and social thought in his essay "Loyalism, Technology, and Canada's Fate,"[3] Ramsay Cook begins by pointing to two unresolved paradoxes which underly Grant's work: one is the combining of political polemic and political philosophy in *Lament for a Nation*,[4] perhaps a confusion rather than a paradox; the other is the development in Grant's thought of two ideas, both part of "an extremely important Canadian tradition," one "the moral unity of the English-speaking world," the other "a desire for full Canadian status."[5] The paradox, at least in its second and more fully formed version, develops out of both Grant's special view of the philosopher's role and his account or, rather more accurately, his interpretation of Canadian history; but given the history of his intellectual development, it has its meaning as well in his sense of how it is possible at all to speak of God in history, when it is necessary, and what sorts of reticence are called for. His work, in other words, calls at the very least for a theory of language, a political theory, and religious witness.

Those philosophers and theologians who attempt to write of his "thought in process," the development of his ideas and argument, begin with some apology about the difficulty, if not the impossibility, of finding points of view from which to approach Grant's work: "Because all Grant's ideas are interrelated, it is almost impossible to divide his thought into four categories, and the very nature of conversation precludes such simple categorization."[6] Having said so much, the writers proceed to present Grant from four points of view, "Canadian Politics," "Intellectual Background," "Theology and History," and "Philosophy." There is a certain symmetry and even inevitability in the pattern, as suggested by the roughly similar divisions indicated in the poet Dennis Lee's account, "Cadence, Country, Silence," and the historian Ramsay Cook's version, "Loyalism, Technology, and Canada's Fate." Grant's major argument, changing as it develops, revolves about the same polarities throughout: history and eternity; time and revelation; progress and transcendence; mastery and excellence; ancient and modern. Part of his complexity and even cranky obscurity stems from his willingness to shift the level of the argument without necessarily altering his vocabulary to adapt to the apparent demands of, say, polemics as opposed to theory; part from his unexamined assumption that vocabularies hold at all levels. The extent that it is not possible to speak of "Christ" and "the second person of the trinity" interchangeably does not seem to have concerned Grant. The point of beginning therefore seems appropriately the question of language, if not indeed theory of language.

ॐ

Grant "does not engage in merely intellectual exercises," observes Barry Cooper (citing Lawrence Lampert's "The Uses of Philosophy in George Grant," *Queen's Quarterly*, 81 [1974], 495), and consequently his "is philosophy in a sense that would exclude it from most philosophy journals."[7] On the one hand, as Cooper observes, Grant goes out of his way to avoid identifying his work as philosophy, saying *Lament for a Nation* is "not based on philosophy but on tradition" while *Technology and Empire* does "not presume to be philosophy" but is "written out of the study of history of political philosophy."[8] That is to say, it is not philosophy as we now think of that study, nor as we once thought of it, though it would aspire to the latter not the former. If it concerns itself with thought and reason, it has to do with the question of the good, with the idea of nobility, excellence, with truth, not linguistic philosophy or logical analysis. Equally, then, Grant would say "his work is essentially a practical affair," "addressed to specific questions of policy," though it hopes to transcend "the occasions that inspired [it]."[9] Not abstruse, but about "practical, common, lived experience" and therefore the real concern of real men, not the cynical interests of the learned and esoteric. It is with intent that Grant distinguishes "the condition common to the majority of men" and the concerns of "the clever" in *Lament for a Nation*. Philosophy, in its outcome, is addressed to the one; mere journalism to the other.

But though the noblest ideals of thought and imagination are thus addressed and genuine illumination may be sought, a question arises, a disturbing prospect presents itself. It is one thing to dismiss as beyond the concern of the majority of men the interests of the linguistic philosophers, say Moore or Russell and the whole of the gigantic enterprise which is *Principia Mathematica* and post-idealist thought. It is quite another not to address oneself at all to the questions of Wittgenstein or to find mere cynicism and cleverness in Russell. The closing passages of the *Tractatus*, George Steiner reminds us in *Language and Silence*, are among the most austere, the noblest, the most courageous in the language of philosophy. To put them aside is to open a way not to the best utterance, or that worthy of all men, but mere confusion. The questions raised by Grant's political theory may very well prove to be questions of language, terminology, not attitude. What, for example, is the meaning of "universal" in "universal homogenous state"? What is the significance of speaking of "Christian man" as "the finest flower of all western civilization has produced"? To what sorts of irony are we invited to address ourselves in rhetoric of this sort? "The vast majority of Canadians are a product of western civilization and live entirely within the forms and assumptions of that enterprise."[10] Consider the intent and the possibilities one might attend to in the use of a word like "entirely" in a sentence of such heavy import. Or in this version of contemporary art, what sort of critical precision is being given to the adjectives: "Even the *surest* accounts of our technomania — the *sperm-filled* visions of Burroughs — are themselves spoken from the shallowness they would describe."[11]

There are two large issues in Grant's argument here, not small weaknesses of diction or flavour in style. One has to do with the political subject Ramsay Cook raises when he speaks of one of the two main ideas in the development of Grant's thought, "the moral unity of the English-speaking world." The other has to do with Grant's view of what has been called post-modern art, a view related to his argument about the nature and significance of technology in contemporary society and hence his view of the nationalist state, the Canada of his imagination. Both have to do with linguistic as well as ethical concerns.

As a moral philosopher, Grant naturally assumes the position that the English-speaking British world of the nineteenth century offers a point of departure for his account of the nature of Canadian society, its history and development, and its present character as a defeated country. I say "naturally" since, as Ramsay Cook reminds us, there are historical and family reasons to account for Grant's position, though the historical justification offered by Cook, I think, should have been open to rather more rigorous criticism than Cook offers.

The tradition from which Grant derives his argument of the morality of the English-speaking world is, of course, the loyalist tradition in Canada. Its family roots lie in the work and thought of both his grandfathers, Principal G.M. Grant and Sir George Parkin, both as Ramsay Cook indicates "prominent British-Canadian intellectuals in the late nineteenth century . . . moral philosophers and theologians . . . leading imperial federationists" and both as well are particularly "liberal Christians who identified the progress of mankind with the preservation and spread of Anglo-Saxon civilization."[12] Grant's identification with the imperialist, loyalist tradition is established early in his writing and while, because of his family background and history, it comes as no surprise, it early commits him to a series of difficult contradictions and tensions. The moral bias of his thought is to be expected and remains a constant, but the question of mankind's progress becomes a vexed one as he increasingly sees it identified with technological advance, a problem that occupies him more and more as he turns to the question of the nature of technological society. The British character of Canadian society derives, Grant argues, from its rejection of the American revolution, its consequent conservatism and "emphasis on social order in contrast to the extreme individualism of the United States," and its Commonwealth connection.[13] Yet the American roots of Canadianism remain potent and indeed irritating to the Canadian loyalist in particular. A puzzling tension in

Grant's thought makes itself apparent here. *Home* itself, a key word in Lee's account of Grant's influence on poetic possibilities, is an ambiguous place and therefore in the end indefinable for Canadians: it is at once America (lost place), Britain (twice lost), and Canada (undefined). The paradoxes here we will explore later.

The moral defence of the imperial connection is, in Grant, the usual, that is to say the traditional and historical defence, but that is not without its vexations. In 1945 in a pamphlet entitled *Canada Must Choose: The Empire Yes or No?* Grant wrote,

> We cannot judge the British Commonwealth from our petty interests alone (however well these are satisfied) but on the highest criteria of political morality. For today in the modern world, with it more than with any other political institution, lies the hope of Christian man, of ethical man, of man the reasonable moral being who stands before God and history. One can indeed say that ethical man, reasonable man, is a last remaining fragment of the dark ages, and that the new man is one ruled by Marxian economics or Freudian sex — mankind, in fact, who is brutal and unreasonable, unethical and material, who is ruthlessly dominated by his appetites. Then we can disavow the British Commonwealth. But if we believe in Christian man, the finest flower of all western civilization has produced, then there can be no doubt that our chief hope in the survival of such values is the survival of the British Commonwealth. Canada has a vital responsibility. Canada must choose.[14]

It is difficult to believe the writer of those lines could have read Conrad's *Heart of Darkness* or that the word "colonial" could have had any meaning to him, other than the institutional context that enables him to speak of political morality in the terms he does. In the context of Canadian history, of course, some sense can be made of this argument, as Cook tries to do. But when the writer extends the argument to include the history of the middle ages and the development of modernism in the work of Marx and Freud, it becomes difficult, if not impossible, to understand the kind of "morality" involved. It is perhaps no accident that the only means open to Grant in his discussion of political philosophy is, finally, then, an attack on the institution of "empire," and that if the British could be subsumed to a nostalgic past, the American empire could become the focal point of contemporary evil. "A central aspect of the fate of being a Canadian," he has said, "is that our very existing has at all times been bound up with the interplay of various world empires."[15]

To turn from the political and moral questions in Grant's thought to aesthetic ones may seem an evasive and peripheral move, but indeed the ways into his thought at times are as apparently labyrinthine as the arguments themselves. Grant is not an aesthetic philosopher, any more than a linguistic one. His position is everywhere moral and ethical. But in part, as Dennis Lee's "Cadence, Country, Silence" makes clear and the later *Savage Fields* even more evident, Grant's account of modernism not only says a good deal about his view of modern culture, it suggests key links between technology, society, and culture, and because these in his argument are linked equally with both language and politics, the topic turns out after all to bear heavily on some of his major concerns. To a certain degree, some of his angularity of argument and style has to do with the oblique way he chooses to find his way into his most passionately held convictions. So it is that Dennis Lee finds his way to an account of his own poetics by means of Grant's politics, and then from that to an odd and deeply moving worldview that opens out to the perspective from which to offer a critique of contemporary barbarism under the guise of defending its brilliance and courage. Lee is of course profoundly sympathetic to what can be called Grant's eschatological methodism, though *he* would never call it that and something in the one character echoes in the other. *Civil Elegies* is the poetics of Grant's political lament; *Savage Fields* the critical ground of *Technology and Empire*. We shall have reason to develop this point later.

Interestingly, it is in the midst of a discussion of the so-called fact-value distinction, the closest Grant comes to an analysis of contemporary language and its implications, that he allows himself his most revealing critique of modernism in art. There is, as always in Grant, a kind of sombre grandeur in his attack, but that should not conceal the real nature of his argument.

> The languages of historicism and values which were brought to North America to be servants of the most advanced liberalism and pluralism, now turn their corrosive power on our only indigenous roots — the substance of that practical liberalism itself. The corrosions of nihilism occur in all parts of the community. Moreover, because our roots have been solely practical, this nihilism shares in that shallowness. The old individualism of capitalism, the frontier and Protestantism, becomes the demanded right to one's idiosyncratic wants taken as outside any obligation to the community which provides them. Buoyed by the restless needs of affluence, our art becomes hectic in its experiments with style and violence. Even the surest accounts of our technomania — the sperm-filled visions of Buroughs — are themselves spoken from the shallowness they would describe. Madness itself can only be deep when it comes forth from a society which holds its opposite. Nihilism which has no tradition of contemplation to beat against cannot be the occasion for the amazed reappearance of the "What for? Whither? and

What then?" The tragedy for the young is that when they are forced by its excesses to leave the practical tradition, what other depth is present to them in which they can find substance? The enormous reliance on and expectation from indigenous music is a sign of craving for substance, and of how thin is the earth where we would find it. When the chthonic has been driven back into itself by the conquests of our environment, it can only manifest itself beautifully in sexuality, although at the same time casting too great a weight upon that isolated sexuality.[16]

There is nothing new here, unless it is the tone. The same apocalyptic rumblings had been heard, in a variety of ways, from 1945 on. Mailer's "White Negro," Levin's "What *Was* Modern," Barth's "The Language of Exhaustion," Sontag's "The Aesthetic of Silence," Steiner's *Language and Silence* all develop from different perspectives accounts of modernism as the extremity of an aesthetic and cultural dilemma intensified by a virtually psychotic social condition. All, it is worth noting, go far beyond the crudely worked-out limitations of Grant's account of the problem in "the languages of historicism and values" and several even suggest there develops in the direction and character of contemporary modernism, quite unlike anything implied in Grant's account, a paradoxical resolution to the very barbarism it entails in its "nihilism."

What is the nature of an experimental action? It is simply an action the outcome of which is not foreseen. It is therefore very useful if one has decided that sounds are to come into their own, rather than being exploited to express sentiments or ideas of order. . . . Sound comes into its own. What does that mean? For one thing it means that noises are useful to new music as so-called musical tones, for the simple reason that they are sounds. This decision alters the view of history. . . .[17]

John Cage's bold re-thinking of sound as musical value is not unlike Sontag's re-thinking of silence as poetic value. Both offer possibilities closed off by Grant's ethical stance about sentiment and ideas of order. No depth from shallowness. No substance from thinness. But yet the world does not end. Nor does it close off precisely where Grant would have it closed. Perhaps the analysis of language could have been carried further than it seemed necessary to him. And indeed the same reservation might be offered to Grant's account of nationalism and technology, the political analysis to which he resorts when the cultural after all proves inadequate.

∽

Technology, in fact, receives a far more careful account in Grant than does language. He has read with extreme care those modern thinkers who have given thought to the subject, Ellul and Strauss in particular. Ellul's definition of technology or technique is the one adopted by Grant, probably because of its comprehensiveness and its clear implication: "Technique is ourselves."

"By technology I mean," Grant writes citing Ellul's definition from *The Technological Society* (London, 1965, p. xxxiii), "the totality of methods rationally arrived at and having absolute efficiency (for a given stage of development) in every field of human activity."[18] The definition, as Grant indicates in his preface, is "implied throughout 'In defense of North America'" and elsewhere, notably in "The University Curriculum" where it is given and in "Tyranny and Wisdom," all important essays in *Technology and Empire*. A curious addition to the initial defining sentence is given in "The University Curriculum" where to the question of rationally arrived at methodology two other motives, and very odd ones indeed, are added: one is *belief* and the other purpose: "the improvement of the race."[19] "The dynamism of technology," Grant tells us, "has gradually become the dominant purpose in western civilization because the most influential men in that civilization have believed for the last centuries that the mastery of chance was the chief means of improving the race."[20]

The kinds of question one might be tempted to raise in talking about Grant's account of an apparently inevitable process moving to a given kind of society differ strikingly if one looks only at an account of "methods rationally arrived at and having absolute efficiency" rather than if one considers "what the most influential men have believed" especially to the end of "the chief means of improving the race." About that last subject men have believed very odd things indeed, some of which appear in Grant's own argument.

In "Tyranny and Wisdom" Grant "attempts to introduce what is for me the most important controversy in contemporary political philosophy," presumably what Strauss and Kojève have written about, "whether the universal and homogenous state is the best social order"[21] — in other words, about the controversy between the ancient and the moderns on the "battle of books." Much of *Technology and Empire* is an account of the inevitability of the "universal and homogenous state," an aspect of that controversy, and Grant's own account of *Lament for a Nation* summarized in "Canadian Fate and Imperialism" tells us the degree to which the earlier book addressed itself to the same questions:

> A couple of years ago I wrote a book about the dissolution of Canadian
> sovereignty. These days when psychologizing is the chief method for
> neutralizing disagreeable opinions, my psyche was interpreted as a

harking back in nostalgia to the British Empire and old fashioned
Canada. This was the explanation of why I did not think that the
general tendencies of modern society were liable to produce human
excellence. In this era when the homogenizing power of technology is
almost unlimited, I do regret the disappearance of indigenous traditions,
including my own. It is true that no particularism can adequately
incarnate the good. But is it not also true that only through some
particular roots, however partial, can human beings first grasp What is
good. . .? What I said in that book was that the belief that human
excellence is promoted by the homogenizing and universalizing power
of technology is the dominant doctrine of modern liberalism, and that
the doctrine must undermine all particularisms and that English-
speaking Canada as a particular is wide open to that doctrine.[22]

The subtlety and power of Grant's argument has been fully evident in
the degree to which it spoke to Canadian nationalists and through the sixties gave vivid force to their views. Lee's defence of an ironic Canadian
poetic voice may be only the best example, particularly in his expression of
the means by which the Canadian writer must learn to speak of *our* loss
and deprivation. Yet at the same time the vivid and curiously ironic defence of particularities is shot through with a thoroughly unpleasant distrust of the very rootedness that Grant ostensibly defends, "the juice of
[those] roots which for most men sustain their partaking in a more universal good," while contemporary history itself renders his account of a raceless and classless society, the universal and homogenous state, as
meaningless as the history of the empires whose potency he "defends."
At the heart of Grant's argument is his assumption of "universality" in
technology and "contemporary" civilization: "Like all civilizations the
West is based on a great religion — the religion of progress. This is the
belief that the conquest of human and non-human nature will give existence meaning. Western civilization is now universal so that this religion is
nearly everywhere dominant."[23] Aside from the curious qualification in
"nearly everywhere," one notes the confident language of Western dominance is now qualified (in technological as well as other terms) by such
matters as the so-called energy crisis and new ecological assumptions
about the paradoxical effects of technological development. It is no longer
as easy as it was in the 1960's to believe, with respect to Africa and Asia
and South America, that "non-western nations have taken on western
means, both technological and ideological, as the only way to preserve
themselves against the West."
Curiously, at the very moment Grant speaks of a "raceless and classless"
state, nationalist and regional particularities manifest themselves in ways presumably rendered ineffective by the barren positivist cultures he writes of. The

definition of Canada, in its historical roots, appears now, for example, less a matter of the tension between English-Canadian nationalism and American continentalism than of the federal-provincial or centralist-regionalist polarities. In fact, the terms in which it is possible to speak of cultural identity and political structure in Canada have been significantly altered from those which Grant would apply to the ones Professor Frye offered at about the same time that *Technology and Empire* appeared. In 1971, in the preface to *The Bush Garden*, Frye developed an argument very like Ramsay Cook's in *The Maple Leaf Forever*. Cook depends on a distinction between nation-state and nationalist state, Frye on a distinction between "the political sense of unity and the imaginative sense of locality," a tension which, Frye says, "is the essence of whatever the word 'Canadian' means."[24] Historically, at least, the regional-national tension makes more sense now than the loyalism of Grant.

In the final analysis, Grant's account of nationalism and imperialism is vitiated by an odd kind of inflexibility in thought which makes for intense drama but less possibility than one might have hoped for from so profound a thinker. There are harsh judgments of men in this work, unyielding and uncharitable. Consider Grant's comment on the question of whether "later arrivals from Europe have so placed their stamp on North America as to have changed in essence what could come from that primal." What "later" means soon becomes clear: ". . . the obvious facts about the power of Catholicism in our politics, or the influence of Jews in communications and intellectual life, or the unexpected power for continuance shown by ethnic communities, mean only that recent traditions have coloured the central current of the American dream."[25] Whatever this means, it is clear "North America" means the United States, not Canada, for "Catholics" does not include the kind of French-Canadian politician of whom Hugh MacLennan has written at length, nor does "Jews" in "communications and intellectual life" allude to Innis, McLuhan, and Frye. The remark, in short, is not worthy of serious intellectual discourse. Elsewhere, too, Grant remarks that comedy is an art he has not mastered, evident surely from the bad joke that follows: "As for pluralism, differences in the technological state are able to exist only in private activities: how we eat; how we mate; how we practise ceremonies. Some like pizza; some like steaks; some like girls; some like boys; some like synagogue; some like the mass. But we all do it in churches, motels, restaurants indistinguishable from the Atlantic to the Pacific."[26]

And in the end, too, one becomes aware of other kinds of inflexibility in Grant. For all his talk of particularities, he does not accept the possibility of rootedness, not in North America, for he says we are not "autochthonous," of the earth. Yet if a man is not of the earth, where is he from? What is his place? At the other extreme, there is what Grant speaks of as "our only indigenous roots — the substance of . . . practical liberalism itself." The difficulty becomes apparent: thought is rooted, imperial; feeling is not.

And out of that paradox of rootless emotion and indigenous thought grows the whole web of ideas in which, as Grant would have it, modern man is entrapped. "The pure will to technology. . . gives sole content to [the] creating [of the world]."[27]

C3

No version of Grant's thought, of course, is complete if it does not take into account not only that which is said in his major works but equally that which is not said. He is one of those rare writers, indeed "spirits" may be the best word, whose work finally presents itself through a series of reticences and silences. That which is not said because it proves to be that which cannot be said. It is this irony, if that is the right word, which adds resonance to his work and which gives it its peculiar modernity. For the most part, but not solely, the silence has to do with God. In *George Grant in Process* there is a "conversation" during which he addresses himself to some of the questions that can be raised. He does give an account of his conversion, his acceptance of God, during World War II and he puts the point in these terms, describing the experience of conversion:

> Obviously, there is much to think about in such experiences. All the Freudian and Marxian questions (indeed, most: the Nietzschian questions) can be asked. But I have never finally doubted the truth of that experience since that moment thirty-six years ago. If I try to put it into words, I would say it was the recognition that I am not my own. In more academic terms, if modern liberalism is the affirmation that our essence is our freedom, then this experience was the denial of that definition, before the fact that we are not our own.[28]

This, one recognizes, is the essential George Grant: his hatred of modernism and its liberal definition of the self as its own freedom; the powerful resistance to technology and its attempt to rationalize the means of mastery of both the external world and the human being, man himself; the extension of his loyalist ambivalence about America and its dream of the self as free and self-assertive; the American Empire as the embodiment of modern liberalism and technology, and the Canadian surrender to that self-indulgent southern dominance. "We are not our own." One recognizes, in that, the definition not only of "conservatism" but also of the lost Canada he laments. Its definition is deprivation and the dignity by which one learns to live with that loss.

It is in the same "conversation" that Grant's revealing words about Simone Weil appear. He responds to the comment that "she's a mystic," said with some implication of lack of academic respectability.

That was much later, after her early life in the proletarian movement in France and in the Spanish war. She was taught by a very able Kantian, and then at the end of her short life understood Plato. She had an immediate and direct encounter with the second person of the Trinity. I take her writings as combining the staggering clarity of her French education with divine inspiration. I take them as perhaps occasionally mistaken in detail, and as sometimes beyond me, but as the great teaching concerning the eternal in this era.[29]

Perhaps the only way to account for the extraordinary lapse in rhetorical tact in this comment, notably in the comment on "an immediate and direct encounter with the second person of the Trinity" is to suggest a painful embarrassment in Grant's version of the subject. This is the subject about which he can say nothing, "great teaching concerning the eternal." If any writing would have made sense here, or elsewhere in Grant, it would be that which drew directly and immediately on the gospel. But that he will not do. For one thing, as David and Edwin Heaven suggest in their article on Grant and Weil, the better way is not articulated in Grant's work.[30] His task is conceived negatively as "The destruction of inadequate sources of hope," and only in a veiled way points toward affirmation.[31] In part, because of the great distance he feels between himself and "the great thinkers and saints"; in part, because even to write as he does of his task as a philosopher is not necessarily to have thought the good and certainly not to have loved the good. Once, as David and Edwin Heaven remind us, he summarized his position on this question, and in doing so raised with the kind of rigour one has come to expect of him, the intolerable question he must live with, the intolerable answer he must sustain, and the wisdom with which he is able to do so:

> Nevertheless, those who cannot live as if time were history are called, beyond remembering, to desiring and thinking. But this is to say very little. For myself, as probably for most others, remembering only occasionally can pass over into thinking and loving what is good. It is for the great thinkers and the saints to do more.[32]

Even to have said this much is to have gained a difficult way. Beyond that, George Grant does not propose to go.

Notes

[1]   Larry Schmidt, "Introduction" to *George Grant in Process: Essays and Conversations* (Toronto: Anansi, 1978), ix.
[2]   Dennis Lee, "Cadence, Country, Silence: Writing in Colonial Space," *Boundary* 2, 3, no. 1 (Fall 1974), 151–68.

[3] Ramsay Cook, "Loyalism, Technology, and Canada's Fate," *The Maple Leaf Forever* (Toronto: Macmillan, 1977), 45–67.

[4] *Ibid.*, 48.

[5] *Ibid.*, 49.

[6] Larry Schmidt, ed., *George Grant in Process*. See esp. "Part V. A Grant Bibliography" by Frank K. Flinn. The bibliography lists some 50 items which Flinn divides into three groups concerned with major phases of Grant's thought: 1) "The Time of Chastened Hope"; 2) "An Era of Retractions"; and 3) "The Face of Moloch"; that is, an early period of liberalism; a second phase of changes developed in Grant's account of modernity; and a third which with *Time as History* examines the dynamic willing of modernism.

[7] Barry Cooper, *"A imperio usque ad Imperium:* The Political Thought of George Grant," *George Grant in Process*, p. 22. "In a rather similar way, the study which still uses the name of 'philosophy,' has made itself into a particular science, with its own particular rigors, concerned with the analysis of language, methods, and thought." George Grant, *Technology and Empire* (Toronto: Anansi, 1969), 125.

[8] *Ibid.*

[9] *Ibid.*, 23.

[10] *Technology and Empire*, 64.

[11] *Ibid.*, 39. My italics.

[12] "Loyalism, Technology and Canada's Fate," 49.

[13] *Ibid.*, 51.

[14] Cited in Cook, 52. See also Carl Berger, "The True North Strong and Free," *Nationalism in Canada*, ed. Peter Russell (Toronto: McGraw-Hill, 1966), 3–25.

[15] *Technology and Empire*, "Canadian Fate and Imperialism," 63.

[16] George Grant, "In Defense of North America," *Technology and Empire*, 39–40. It is worth comparing here Grant's remarks on the "present" state of the humanities in the university in "The University Curriculum," 126–27, an equally controversial passage because of its narrowly conceived version of science and the language of objectivity.

[17] John Cage, "History of Experimental Music in the United States," *Silence* (London: Calder and Boyers, 1968), 68–69.

[18] "The University Curriculum," *Technology and Empire*, 113.

[19] *Ibid.*

[20] *Ibid.*

[21] "Tyranny and Wisdom," *Technology and Empire*, 81.

[22] "Canadian Fate and Imperialism," *Technology and Empire*, 68–69.

[23] *Ibid.*, 77.

[24] Northrop Frye, "Preface," *The Bush Garden* (Toronto: Anansi, 1971), iii.

[25] "In Defense of North America," 26.

[26] *Ibid.*

[27] *Ibid.*, 39–40.

[28] George Grant, "Conversation: Intellectual Background," *George Grant in Process*, 63.

[29] *Ibid.*, 65–66.

[30] Edwin B. Heaven and David R. Heaven, "Some Influences of Simone Weil on George Grant's Silence," *George Grant in Process*, 68.

[31] *Ibid.*

[32] *Ibid.*, 69. On the question of the "homelessness" of modern man, it is instructive to compare the views of particularity, rootedness, and "ancestors" in, say, Grant and Margaret Atwood. If there are no North American gods in Grant's world, they do appear in the shamanistic wilderness of Atwood.

Nasrin Rahimieh

Naïm Kattan, "Le discours arabe," and His Place in the Canadian Literary Discourse

In the course of his career in Canada Naïm Kattan has become known for his role both in the Canada Council and as a creative writer. Appellations such as those chosen for him by Jacques Godbout, "le fée des bourses [à Ottawa]" (12), and the anonymous author of a *Saturday Night* review, "Our only Arab-Jewish-French-Canadian Writer" (9), reflect a duality essential to Kattan. Those who believe the life of an artist incompatible with that of a bureaucrat have criticized his position in the Canadian literary institution — a charge which has not hindered Kattan from pursuing his two seemingly disparate realms of endeavour.

Whatever view Canadians might take of Kattan's "double existence," they have unanimously adopted him as the very model of cross-culturalism. They recognize him as a man who has gone beyond the fear of assimilation by refusing to cling onto a single identity. In Jacques Allard's words, he is "un voyageur du transculturel, soucieux de comprendre les rapports de l'Orient et de l'Occident et tout aussi bien ceux des groupes ethniques canadiens. Juif d'Arabie, Arabe de la judéité, oriental d'Occident, occidental d'Orient. . . ce francophone québécois est toujours ailleurs que là où on le fixe" (7). It is this willingness to exist on the borders of many nations and languages which makes Kattan an enviable character in a polarized Canadian society. Kattan's very presence in Canada is a stern reminder of the need for a Canadian cultural plurality. This perception is often articulated by Kattan's critics, for instance in the title of I.M. Owen's review: "Why an Arabic-speaking, Baghdad-born Jew is a perfect guide to the modern Canadian experience" (5) or in Alexandre Amprimoz's assessment: "Naïm Kattan is an international writer. Social integration into the Canadian society is a very difficult thing. But paradoxically, the loneliness and the isolation of Kattan's caracters [sic] make them rather similar to the other heroes of contemporary Quebec literature" (82).

That Kattan fits within the Canadian literary mosaic is self-evident (the 1976 edition of the *Dictionnaire des auteurs québécois* lists him, albeit as a "critique littéraire," and *The Oxford Companion to Canadian Literature* presents a comprehensive survey of his literary production). What is less frequently discussed is the manner in which Kattan finds his voice within the various Canadian patterns. Is he a Canadian writer or an immigrant writer whom a historical accident has brought to Canada? It is the extensions of Kattan's transcultural spirit in his literary works which I wish to examine in the following argument. My contention is that while the ease with which Kattan moves in and out of languages and cultures affords him a high degree of artistic sensitivity, it also poses a constant threat to his literary voice. By refusing total integration, Kattan risks becoming "marginal." Yet, he has manipulated this same marginality into an art.

Let us begin with Kattan's choice of literary languages in Canada and elsewhere. Although fluent in English,[1] and in spite of the fact that English Canadians have found an affinity with his work, he insists on writing in French. For Kattan, English appears to be associated with the British occupation of Iraq, while French created a link, however illusory, with freedom and "authentic" self-expression. That is perhaps why to this day, his choice of literary language remains firm: "It was so painful for me to change from writing in Arabic to writing in French — and it cost me 15 years of silence — that I don't think I will ever be able to make a change again. I am satisfied writing in French, since there's a public for what I say in that language. I can write in French without feeling that I am exiled" (Simpson 36). What goes unnoticed by Kattan's interviewer, who is intent upon fitting him into a "Canadian" pattern, is the allusion to his mother tongue, Arabic. This closing statement of the interview reveals, if only indirectly, the essential in understanding Kattan — what I will call the need to exist on the margins.

Although born into the Jewish community of Baghdad and educated both in Hebrew and Arabic, he consciously opted for Arabic and its literary heritage. His first short stories and critical pieces were published in Arabic: "je me suis rendu compte que pour moi ce qui comptait c'était écrire en arabe. C'était de ma langue maternelle que j'étais fier" (Allard 12). This duality of vision is even reflected in his name, which is at once Arabic and Hebrew: "En hébreu, le nom *Kattan* veut dire *petit*. C'est une description, comme dans toutes les langues il y a des noms des gens petits. Mais *Naïm* veut dire charmant, agréable. Alors il y avait cette double signi-

fication. Du côté arabe le mot *Naïm* est encore plus élogieux. C'est paradi-
siaque. C'est la grande fortune d'être dans un climat de paradis. Et *Kattan*
veut dire cotonnier" (Allard 11). However, the balance between Arabic
and Hebrew is not as undisturbed as it first appears: "Enfant, parlant avec
les musulmans de ma propre ville, dans leur dialecte plutôt que dans le
mien, j'ai pressenti la condition minoritaire et je ne l'ai pas acceptée" (*Le
Réel* 182). In the opening chapter of *Adieu Babylone*, Kattan's semi-auto-
biographical novel, the reader glimpses this same clash of identities. The
protagonist's Jewish friend, Nessim, insists on communicating with Mus-
lims in his own dialect of Arabic. In contrast, the protagonist chooses silence, before arriving at another solution: "Je choisis un moyen terme. Mes
mots n'étaient ni ceux des juifs ni ceux des Musulmans. Je m'exprimais en
arabe littéraire, coranique" (*Adieu* 12). The compromise reached by the
protagonist and, by extension, Kattan is one which avoids simple polarities and insists upon complex inter-relationships. Recalling an incident in
his earlier years, Kattan points to what has become a conviction throughout his life:

> Il y avait quelqu'un qui m'a dit. . . . De quelle nationalité vous êtes? Je
> lui dis irakienne. Alors il me dit: oui, mais c'est quoi ça Irakien, vous
> êtes Musulman? je dis: non, alors il me dit: vous êtes de nationalité
> juive? je dis: Ce n'est pas une nationalité, il me répond: Il fallait le dire,
> pourquoi vous n'allez pas chez vous? Il fallait, et c'était un choix à
> l'époque, me dire que j'étais refusé par tout le monde ou me dire c'était
> ma chance d'appartenir à personne. (Allard 24)

The only mould into which Kattan's affinities can be fit is that of a cross-
cultural man. The title of his recently published novel, *La Fortune du passager*, aptly emphasizes his vagabond spirit. The historical necessity of
wandering across cultural barriers becomes clear in the light of Kattan's
biography.[2] But its implications for his literary endeavours still remain
obscure.

☙

While writing in French and identifying with its literary traditions, Kattan
refuses to suppress a past closely linked with Arabic and Hebrew. He
claims that his style of writing, which leaves much to the imagination of
the reader, is derived from Arabic narrative techniques. Quite often, essential details remain unsaid. In *Adieu Babylone*, for instance, the protagonist
is never named and although we recognize an autobiographical speaker in
the text, he remains a shadowy figure throughout. This creates a sense of
distance not usually associated with biographical narratives.

Kattan attributes this style of composition to what he calls *le discours arabe;* in the interview with Allard, in answer to a question regarding the prudish air of his texts, Kattan explains:

> Je ne peux plus dire à cet égard que je suis tout à fait Arabe. Il y a
> deux aspects de ce discours arabe qui expliquent un peu peut-être mes
> écrits. D'abord on parle beaucoup mais l'essentiel, ce qui est le plus
> fragile, quand il est encore fragile en nous, on ne le dévoile pas parce
> qu'on a honte de cette fragilité. . . . Dans le discours arabe, il y a
> beaucoup de mots, les gens parlent beaucoup mais l'essentiel est très
> peu dit . . . le deuxième élément dans le discours qui vient de mon
> enfance et qui est de ma culture, c'est de dire aux autres ce qui leur fait
> plaisir, même si c'est pas tout à fait vrai. (15)

The crucial elements in this description, at least in so far as it applies to Kattan's texts, are the cryptic and highly codified nature of language. There is a strong sense of the alien and the unutterable in *Adieu Baby-lone,* very little dialogue, and the characters are barely outlined and are not introspective. To borrow Kattan's own words, the essential is never said. Some of this effect can be attributed to cultural differences. Kattan himself encourages this type of interpretation through the notion of *le discours arabe.* Some critics have taken the same route. For instance, Spettigue speaks of "cultural differences difficult for Westerners to understand," which then develop into communication barriers between author and reader:

> One does not question the authenticity of the representation; but the
> result is to deepen the shadow-effect. All seems disembodied, unreal,
> except in moments of sordid and commonplace reality. . . . Socially
> and politically we are filled in on the current movements,
> journalistically, and this helps, but at the same time it reinforces the
> feeling that with the protagonist we inhabit a world of shadows. . . . It
> is not that *Farewell, Babylon* is unconvincing at all, but that it is exile
> literature, essentially colonial, recording marginal people for whom
> everything important happens somewhere else. (510)

What creates the "shadow-effect" in *Adieu Babylone* and Kattan's other works of fiction is not merely a function of his exile. In fact, his thematic preoccupation seems to be immigration rather than exile. I would suggest that the roots of what some critics have regarded as narrative unease are in Kattan's medium of expression. This is not to say that by choosing French he has denied himself and his creative works accessibility to Western audiences, but rather that the constant juxtaposition of languages in which Kattan has been immersed has created a narrative style devoid of "signifying" stability.

For an understanding of Kattan's notion of languages, we must turn to his essay *Le Réel et le théâtral* in which he outlines the differences between Eastern and Western cultures in terms of their relationship to "reality." He argues that for the Semites there exists no mediation between man and reality. In the West, on the contrary, man achieves the same relationship through the theatrical and the illusory. In a passage reminiscent of early German Romantic thought, he explains his understanding of the East-West dichotomy in the following manner:

> . . . . C'est l'homme qui établit une alliance avec Dieu pour sinon
> contrôler la nature, du moins prévenir sa menace. Cette forme de
> rapport se manifeste dans la langue elle-même. Dans la langue
> hébraïque et dans la langue arabe, il n'y a pas de séparation entre les
> mots et les choses. L'objet vit parce qu'il est nommé. (16)

On the level of linguistic and poetic expression, Kattan implies that Semitic languages have an immediate power of evocation which the West cannot grasp or recreate because of its own preoccupation with modes of mediation. Clearly, Kattan's notion of *le discours arabe* is based on the same theory: what appears as unspoken and implicit to the Western readers of his novels would have much clearer and more concrete significance for an Arab reader. This perspective allows us a partial understanding of the writer's own linguistic vision, but we must recognize the extent to which Kattan's own Judeo-Islamic heritage is fragmented from within.

ɔʒ

Throughout *Adieu Babylone*, the protagonist speaks of linguistic exile in his homeland. To belong, he must imitate the accent of his Muslim compatriots. That is to say, for the protagonist, as for the young Kattan, the most conventional form of speech becomes a mark of internal exile. When Kattan assures us that he considers Arabic his mother tongue, we must understand the statement in its proper context. Not only did he learn Hebrew and Arabic simultaneously, but also he mastered the transposition of the two. In this process, both languages are forced to undergo such transformations that ultimately they exist in complete neutrality. In fact, they create a new linguistic system.

In a chapter of *Adieu Babylone*, the narrator describes the use of the Hebrew alphabet for writing Arabic. This cryptic language, *Souki*, creates a bridge between the two languages. At the same time, however, it empties both of their internal logic of significance. For the Jewish teenagers who are employed by Muslim officials to decipher documents written in *Souki*, the language offers a glimpse of power: "Les Musulmans exprimaient ouvertement leur envie à l'égard des Juifs qui disposaient de cette écriture secrète" (129). The narrator does not further explore the implications of the simultaneous process of mutilation and conflation of languages, but Kattan's own sensitivity to the emptied-out medium surfaces in one of his short stories, "Le Gardien de l'alphabet."

The protagonist of this story, Ali Souleyman, leaves his homeland, Turkey, at the time of Ataturk's reforms, to find support for the preservation of the sacred alphabet of his language. He believes that the Latin script which has been chosen to replace Arabic threatens the very identity of his nation. Ironically, his convictions take him increasingly further away from his own land. He reaches total exile in Edmonton where he diligently rewrites new texts in the old alphabet. His zeal gradually obscures his goal; he copies and catalogues texts without ever reading them. Like the protagonist of *Adieu Babylone*, Ali Souleyman is estranged from the language he desperately wants to preserve: "Souvent, Ali était pris de vertige. Allait-il s'arrêter? Quand et où?" (119). Both protagonists suffer from a cultural alienation which is rooted in their medium of communication. The mother tongue itself is a vehicle for fragmentation of the self. In "Le Gardien de l'alphabet," this linguistic disorientation is accompanied with physical exile. The more fervent Ali Souleyman becomes in the preservation of his alphabet, the further he is removed from his own language and culture.

This analysis can also be extended to Kattan's own situation of the permanent migrant. Like the characters of his fictional works, he too is distanced from his mother tongue. In his interview with Allard, Kattan narrates an episode which is symptomatic of his linguistic dilemma:

> Il y a deux ans, il y a un Musulman, en Israël, qui a lu *Adieu Babylone* et a décidé d'en traduire un chapitre en arabe. Il l'a fait et me l'a envoyé après. Et j'ai lu *Adieu Babylone* qui se passe dans un pays arabe traduit en arabe. C'a été une expérience très dure et très étrange. Dure tout de même parce que je ne m'y suis pas reconnu, écrit dans ma langue maternelle. (Allard 16)

The inability to recognize himself in Arabic points back to his pluralist approach to all languages and cultures. In *La Mémoire et la promesse*, he writes: "l'individu existe et son appartenance à une culture, à une langue doit être un choix libre et cette liberté comprend celle de changer de culture et de langue" (158–59). What he resists is the possibility of being firmly placed in one linguistic system: "J'ai opté pour une langue que j'invente à chaque moment. J'ai choisi un lieu que je dote de présence en y inscrivant mon invention" (*Le Réel* 188). When translated into the language of fiction, this linguistic plurality poses a number of difficulties to the readers. Hence, the narrative unease remarked upon by the critics and the reviewers. The linguistic realm created by Kattan is one which maintains a critical relationship with all languages which enter it. As explained by the Moroccan writer and critic Abdelkebir Khatibi, this relationship is essential to all bilingual or multilingual writing:

> . . . la langue étrangère, dès lors qu'elle est intériorisée comme écriture effective, comme parole en acte, transforme la langue première, elle la structure et la déporte vers l'intraduisible . . . la langue dite étrangère ne vient pas s'ajouter à l'autre, ni opérer avec elle une pure juxtaposition: chacune *fait signe* à l'autre, l'appelle à se maintenir comme dehors. (186)

Kattan consciously adopts such a model in his creative works. Because he insists that elements of Arabic, Hebrew, French, and English be preserved in his writing, he is never entirely within one given linguistic or even literary system. In this sense it is neither *le discours arabe* nor a particular "Canadian" discourse which gives him his unique style of composition, but rather a transcultural discourse "qui parle *en langues* se mettant à l'écoute de toute parole d'où qu'elle vienne" (Khatibi 63).

Notes

[1]   "J'avais le choix entre le français et l'anglais comme deuxième langue, c'était à parité. J'apprenais autant l'anglais que le français et j'ai choisi le français parce que pour moi l'Occident libérateur était francophone" (Allard 13).
[2]   For a short biographical note, see Richard Hodgson, "Naïm Kattan," in *Dictionary of Literary Biography*, vol. 53: *Canadian Writers since 1960*, first series, ed. W.H. New (Detroit: Gale, 1986), 238–40.

Works Cited

Allard, Jacques. "Entrevue avec Naïm Kattan." *Voix et Images* 11.1 (1985): 7–32.
Anonymous. "Our Only Arab-Jewish-French-Canadian Writer." *Saturday Night* 94.1 (1979): 9.
Amprimoz, Alexandre. "Quebec Writers: The Anatomy of Solitude." *The Tamarack Review* 72 (1977): 79–87.
Dictionnaire pratique des auteurs québécois. Montréal: Fides, 1976.
Godbout, Jacques. "Ces Voyages qui forment la jeunesse." *Le Maclean* 4.16 (1976): 12.
Kattan, Naïm. *Adieu Babylone.* 1975. Montréal: Leméac, 1986.
——. "Le Gardien de l'alphabet." In *La Traversée.* Montréal: Editions Hurtubise, 1976.
——. *La Mémoire et la promesse.* Editions Hurtubise, 1978.
——. *Le Réel et le théâtral.* Montréal: Editions Hurtubise, 1970.
Khatibi, Abdelkebir. *Maghreb pluriel.* Paris: Denoël, 1983.

Owen, I. M. "Bridge of Tongues: Why an Arabic-speaking, Baghdad-born Jew is a
    Perfect Guide to the Modern Canadian Experience." *Books in Canada* 12.5 (1976):
    5–6.
Simpson, Leo. "A Conversation with Naïm Kattan." *Quill and Quire* 42.17 (1976):
    9–10, 36.
Spettigue, D.O. "Farewell, Babylone." *Queen's Quarterly* 84.3 (1977): 510–11.

CL 127 (Winter 1990)

Robert Kroetsch

The Grammar of Silence: Narrative Pattern in Ethnic Writing

What I am setting out to do here is simply this: I want to ask if there is a characteristic narrative of the ethnic experience.[1] More exactly, I am asking, is there, at the point where literature and ethnicity meet, a characteristic narrative structure? Assuming that such a structure does exist, what are some of its elements? Or, as I prefer to put it, what is the *grammar* of the narrative of ethnic experience?

Behind this specific intention, I am asking for a theory of ethnicity, a theory which I would locate in the idea of narrative. There is, possibly, a story that repeats itself, with significant variations of course, whether we are describing and exploring the ethnic experience as sociologists, as psychologists, as novelists and poets, or as literary critics. Not only am I limiting myself to the literary expression of that narrative — I am, outrageously perhaps, working explicitly out of two literary texts.

Frederick Philip Grove is perhaps the most complex and most instructive ethnic writer yet to appear on the Canadian literary scene. As you know, he was a writer who arrived in Canada in the early part of this century and who gave the impression that he was a Swedish aristocrat who had fallen on hard times while visiting in Toronto. He went out to the prairies and set about becoming a Canadian writer, working in English, and by the time of his death in 1948 he had succeeded to a remarkable degree, though, as we shall see, he insisted throughout his career on calling himself a failure. Only in recent years have we discovered that Frederick Philip Grove was not a Swede but rather a German writer of bourgeois background, Felix Paul Greve, who faked his suicide and migrated to Canada and became, under his assumed name, a central figure in Canadian writing.

I am going to work with two of his numerous texts. In his novel, *Settlers of the Marsh* (1925),[2] a novel that he began in German and finished in English, he tells the story of a Swedish immigrant, Niels Lindstedt, who goes to the frontier in Manitoba to make a new home. The story is a love triangle. Niels falls in love with a Swedish girl, Ellen Amundsen, who has sworn an oath not to marry, because of the horrible example of her parents' marriage. Niels then marries a Canadian widow, Clara Vogel, and ends up murdering her. After a period in prison, he returns to his community and marries Ellen.

In his "autobiography," *In Search of Myself* (1946),[3] Grove purports to give an account of how he himself left Sweden and came to North America and, while living in Manitoba, set about establishing his career as a teacher and writer, after years of working as a farm labourer. He marries a Canadian woman, a teacher from a Mennonite background, and sets about his heroic effort to establish himself as a writer, against what seem to be impossible odds of poverty, poor health, and publishers' indifference.

∞

We have here, that is, two narratives of the ethnic experience, one using the conventions of the novel, the other using the conventions of autobiography (and I might add that the chapters of *Search* are titled, "Childhood," "Youth," "Manhood," and "And After"). What is interesting is the elements that occur in both. Both are stories about the migrating generation. The experience of the migrating generation, it seems to me, is granted privileged status in this literature (even while those same immigrants might have experienced a violent silence in actual life). The migrating generation is often seen in heroic terms by the later generations. Importantly, here, in the writings of Grove, we have narratives written by the person who experienced the migration.

Grove's principal characters in *Settlers*, Niels and one of the two women to whom he is attracted, Ellen, are from backgrounds that came close to making them serfs in Sweden. The hero of *Search*, on the other hand, perceivable as Frederick Grove himself, comes from a background of extreme wealth; he might indeed have become master of the kind of estate on which his fictional characters were potentially serfs. Grove imagines these two extreme possibilities, and yet both Niels and Phil (the hero's name in *Search*) come to the same narrative predicaments, often seen in binary patterns. Let me list a few of them.

There is an extreme tension between ideas of success and ideas of failure. Niels labours for years to build a large house that he believes is the emblem of success. Yet, in that same house, he discovers how totally he has failed in the new world: his wife, Clara, becomes a figure of death, haunting that house, and reminding him constantly of the failure of what he calls his vision.

Writing *Search* twenty-one years later, Grove is even more obsessive about the idea of failure. At one point, in speaking of his literary career, he says, "I tried; and I shall shortly discuss why I was bound to fail, as I had failed in everything that I had ever undertaken with an economic aim in view; this book is the record of a failure; and its explanation: a double failure, an economic and a spiritual one, for ultimately the one involved the other." It seems apparent, after awhile (and the word failure is used obsessively in the second half of the book), that the idea of failure has become a generative force in the narrative and in Grove's own life.

The immensity of his failure becomes a measure of his success. His very failure is not only his own; it becomes a measure of and a criticism of the society into which he has entered. Like that supreme master of creative failure, Malcolm Lowry, Grove is able to force himself into heroic bouts of writing by meditating on his failure, by recording it carefully, by listing the titles of failed manuscripts and the growing total of rejections. And, like Lowry, he goes on imagining for himself ever more ambitious projects.

Where the appearance of failure might be an act of rebellion or a naturalistic element in traditional Canadian writing, for the ethnic writer it harbours darker and more complex and possibly more exciting possibilities. As in the case of Grove, it becomes the single word by which he judges both himself and the society into which he has entered. That word can be or is made, at times, to lose its traditional meaning and come to signify success.

cs

Another essential and related binary is that of ideas of inferiority and ideas of superiority. Neils Lindstedt, from the opening page of *Settlers*, is paired with a kind of double, a fellow immigrant, Lars Nelson, a giant of a man who with ease makes a good marriage and becomes a successful farmer. Nelson has succeeded by the standards of the materialistic society around him, but it is obvious that he is, for Grove, morally and spiritually the inferior of Niels Lindstedt. Lindstedt is the superior man who brings to bear on experience the possibilities of and demands for relevance and meaning. He confronts the idea of signification. And yet it is he who commits a murder.

Phil Grove, in *Search*, represents the pinnacle of European culture. He has been everywhere, he has studied everything, he has met everyone of artistic consequence in Europe. Then he begins his years of work as a farm labourer on the Great Plains of North America. He tells at some length of pairing up with a Pole who like him looked disreputable but who, like him also, "spoke half a dozen European languages." At one point they begin to discuss French poetry while pitching bundles into a threshing machine. "It was done ostentatiously, with the pointed intention of making the other hoboes open their mouths. He [the Pole] even dropped his perfect American speech and changed to French; and in doing so, he adopted what, in these raw surroundings, might have passed for aristocratic society manners, handling his pitch-fork with the nonchalance of a fop, parodying that nonchalance by its very exaggeration."

European culture has been reduced to a parody of itself, and that largely by means of language acts. Grove and his friend are at once superior and inferior. And on this occasion they are shortly hauled in by the local police and fleeced of all their cash, in the final carnivalization of what they and their values represent in this new world.

Thirty pages later Grove can write, "I wanted to be in touch with the finest and highest thought of my age. Instead, I was being rubbed the wrong way, day in, day out, by those who, for the moment, were my social equals — whom others would have called the scum of the earth. . . ." Half a page later he can write, "I was no longer a 'good European'; let Europe take care of her own troubles; I was rapidly becoming extra-European, partly because on account of my failure to take a sixth trip to Europe. Europe, to me, had suddenly ceased to exist."

By the end of the book this arrogant extra-European can say, "As I have said, I was suffering from an inferiority complex." The tension between superiority and inferiority must either destroy him or make him write. Grove, moving from class-conscious Europe into the North American ideal or illusion of democracy, is *unsettled*. Again, in a situation where signified and signifier do not cohere, he might be totally destroyed, or he might become the truly creative individual.

ભ

There are other binary patterns that Grove establishes as basic to the ethnic experience: revelation and concealment, integration and resistance, forgetting and remembering. But behind all these is the basic tension between signifier and signified. In a painfully moving passage Grove observes "That the artist is not a hunter constitutes him a cripple, physical or mental, and therefore an object of contempt as well as, paradoxically, of a reluctant admiration. For his work partakes of the nature of a miracle . . . the work of art becomes a fetish endowed with the functions of magic."

In the new world, the magic seems to falter. For the heroes of *Search* and *Settlers* it becomes difficult, even impossible, to tell failure from success, to tell superiority from inferiority. A gap opens between word and object. In the Europe of their past — as Grove's characters remember it — it was possible to define and locate connections. In the abrupt change to this new world, a chasm opens.

Niels Lindstedt believes he can attach the right woman to the word "wife." The Canadian widow, Clara Vogel, is in his perception seductive and evil. The immigrant girl, Ellen Amundsen, is innocent and desirable. He brings with him a paradigm that makes of women whores and virgins. Somehow he manages to set a trap for Ellen and get caught by Clara. He stumbles into an immense chasm between word and object, and compounds the space by becoming a murderer, not the farmer, the nurturing man, he wants to be.

The gap in *Search* is equally catastrophic. The single-minded hero of that autobiography that might be fiction and might be fact (another threatening binary in the ethnic experience) confesses a few pages from the end of the book, "I have often doubted whether there is anything that I can legitimately call I." This narrator, completing an autobiography, confesses that he cannot locate the "I" that is the subject of the book. The gap between signifier and signified has become the subject itself, a question mark over what it is we mean by the act of writing. Grove (or Greve), the bourgeois man from Germany, in writing the autobiography of the Swede, Phil Grove of Manitoba, announces a contemporary predicament and grounds it in the narrative of ethnicity.

❦

How do these patterns of binary opposition get turned into narrative? How do we avoid a kind of paralysis with characters caught between two worlds — caught, if you will, in silence. If we take departure and return as the basic or archetypal design of the journey, then the ethnic story immediately becomes problematic in that the traveller buys a one-way ticket.

If the elements in the binaries are the nouns in the grammatical set, what are the verbs that set things in motion? How do we articulate the silence?

A principal way to establish or re-establish narrative coherence in the face of the gap between signifier and signified is through a re-telling of stories. In ethnic writing there is often an attempt at healing by the rewriting of myths. The myth most often retold, at least on the surface of ethnic writing, is the garden story. Niels Lindstedt is obviously in search of a new version of Eden. Two major scenes take place in a garden or bower. The garden is set in contrast to the house. And further, the image of the garden recalls the question of naming that is so central to the Genesis story. I want to conclude, later, by looking at those two scenes.

Phil Grove in *Search* is also aware of this model. When he finds himself feeling like an exile in North America, he does not dream of a return to Europe. Rather, he explains, "A new nostalgia arose . . . I would build a

shack on some hillside overlooking a stream and the woods." He even decides on the location of this edenic place: "it was in the Pembina Mountains, on the Canadian side, not very far from the little town of Manitou
in Manitoba."

In his choice of place he is able to unite the Indian spirit of place, or at
least of the place-name, with his dream of paradise. In actual fact, of
course, as Grove establishes so vividly in the prologue to *Search*, he struggled in vain toward that paradise, and ended up trying to run a dairy farm
in rural Ontario. That prologue begins: "It was a dismal November day,
with a raw wind blowing from the north-west and cold, iron-grey clouds
flying low — one of those Ontario days which, on the lake-shores or in a
country of rock and swamp, seem to bring visions of an ageless time after
the emergence of the earth from chaos, or a forebodying of the end of a
world about to die from entropy."

Grove, on his way by car to pick up a girl to work as "a household
drudge," is painfully aware that there is only one thing you do in this paradise — and that is work. And work, in this new world, is another version
of silence. Grove is remarkable in his portrayal of the silencing effect of
work. Even the obsessive writer, in *Search*, seems to be silenced by his own
heroic efforts. He writes and he writes, and his very effort cuts him off
from all chance of being heard. And, not inappropriately, he himself begins
to be afflicted with deafness.

And yet this silence is enclosed in a larger silence. Grove's travelling
heroes are caught between the "silenced" old version of the garden (European in this case) and the not-yet-speaking new one. And, it seems to me,
behind the not-yet-spoken garden, there is another myth trying to speak
itself.

While the garden myth is often present on the surface of a narration of
the ethnic experience, I suspect the concealed story is that of the necessary
death — the death, that is, out of one culture, with the hope that it will
lead to rebirth in another.

Grove faked his own death. And yet in a symbolic way there was nothing fake about it: he died out of one culture and into another.

ॐ

Death and rebirth is a recurring pattern in *Search*. Phil Grove is ill to the
point of death and wonders if it wouldn't have been better if he had died,
because in that case his manuscripts would have been destroyed and the
struggle to write would have been over. But the most moving and ironic
death is that of his young daughter, May. A few sentences after reporting
her death, Phil Grove remarks, "And now, as if we had at last paid our dues
to the fates, break after break seemed to come for me."

Niels Lindstedt, after shooting and killing his wife Clara, goes to his barn and kills a gelding in a curious scene that can only invite symbolic interpretation: the death of the horse is the symbolic death of the unmanned man, Niels Lindstedt. His process of rebirth is startling in its effect. After six and a half years in prison, Lindstedt emerges a man reborn. Grove himself had served a prison term. The threat of another led to his "suicide" and his movement from German into English as a writer. Perhaps the death in ethnic narrative is, explicitly, a death out of one language into another. (And this, beyond the example of Grove, would seem to hold true even for the person who moves with apparent convenience from an English-speaking place to an English-speaking place.)

Another way to bring signifier and signified back into conjunction is through a change of story model.

In the opening of *Settlers* the two men, Lindstedt and Nelson, are struggling blindly through a November snowstorm, moving from the edge of civilization, into the Big Marsh. As they struggle the narrative voice says, "Both would have liked to talk, to tell and to listen to stories of danger, of being lost, of hairbreadth escapes: the influence of the prairie snowstorm made itself felt. But whenever one of them spoke, the wind snatched his word from his lips and threw it aloft."

It is as if the old story forms are no longer adequate to the new experience. Silence has reasserted itself. Grove himself spoke of the "tragedy" of Niels Lindstedt, attempting to assert the appropriateness of a traditional mode. Yet he gives his story a happy ending that surprises many readers — an ending that many readers protest but that few would change. It turns out that we allow the tragedy to transform itself into something approaching comedy, in the name of a revisioning of the novel itself as form.

Grove's *Search* sets out to be an autobiography. By the end it too has become something else, with the author commenting in the middle of the book, "I felt an exile. I was an exile. I did not live among people of my own kind; among people who, metaphorically, spoke my language. . . ." In the next sentence he adds, "The only sort of what, with a stretch of the imagination, could be called literary art with which I ever came into living contact, consisted of the 'tall' tales of the west; and they stood out in flagrant contradiction to the squalid reality I saw all about."

The offended Mr. Grove, in *Search*, has written one of the finest tall tales in the literary history of the west. If Mark Twain admitted to stretching the story a little, Frederick Philip Grove could be said to stretch it just about as much, while admitting nothing. He explains that at one time he was sending out as many as a dozen unpublished works, each one "copied out in six copies of fine, copperplate handwriting. Let me say that there were twelve volumes in all; then there were seventy-two manuscripts; and each of them had been sent out and received back at least three times, more likely five times a year. So that I had made, on an average, three hundred and sixty shipments a year, or one a day." And this, he adds, has gone on for sixteen years.

Grove, in the course of that stretching, found a story model that enabled him to speak, eloquently and validly, of what he had experienced. Language had become that literal and that isolated for him. He had transformed himself into a great hoard of repeating and circulating and unread manuscripts.

ça

If there is a gap between word and object, the final question is language itself, and the question of naming. Perhaps the completion of the narrative is made possible, not primarily by the surface story, but rather by a narrative movement that entails a changed sense of language, a movement from the old language, through silence (a silence that might be imagined even as a death) into a new language.

Grove says, in *Search*: "Thus, in the attempt to set down my vision, I realized that I had at bottom no language which was peculiarly my own. In a way this was an advantage to me; I had half a dozen instead. But in another way, it was a disadvantage and even a misfortune: I lacked that limitation which is best for the profound penetration of the soul of a language. I ground my teeth in my struggles; and, for the moment, all my struggles were with words."

The turning point in Phil Grove's life comes when he is seen in a railway station by a French priest in North Dakota reading a copy of Baudelaire's *Fleurs du mal*. Of the priest Grove says, "He was an immigrant himself; he was French, not, as I had supposed, French-Canadian." This European priest talks to Grove of his circumstances and says to him, "Why didn't you teach?" The priest, shortly thereafter, is killed in a railway accident — he is another double and a representative of European civilization and he dies the necessary death. Grove goes to Manitoba to begin his long and hellish struggle with story and language. He is ready to unname himself as European and to struggle to rename himself as Canadian.

This erasure of names is a part of the experience of migrating peoples, and part of the narrative of that experience. And that erasure becomes palimpsest, it leaves its trace — as it did when Greve changed his name to Grove, at once concealing and changing who he was and leaving a trace that would enable us to complete the task of renaming that he had initiated.

That moment of unnaming with its potential for renaming occurs twice in *Settlers*, and this in the marshland itself, that unshaped, unmapped, unnamed space. In paired scenes, one in the middle of *Settlers*, one at the end, the two adults, Niels and Ellen, are transformed into "boy" and "girl," and the story's past tense gives way to present tense. In both scenes the nameless "children" approach a schoolhouse and pass it up for the natural world of berry bushes and singing birds. Both scenes end with awkward and painful attempts at naming.

At the end of the first, Niels realizes that Ellen is going to refuse marriage:

> The realization of a bottomless abyss shakes him.
> "Ellen," he calls with an almost breaking voice.
> The girl slowly rises. "I know," she says. "Don't speak."

He speaks with a *breaking* voice. She speaks to command silence — "Don't speak." Having been named herself, she then goes on to name the man in return: "Oh Niels, I am going to hurt you deeply." It is as if the speaking of a name is, at this point in the story, the breaking of a taboo. That breaking of the taboo brings about tragedy.

Ellen refuses to marry Niels. We move immediately to a death scene. We see old man Sigurdsen dying: "Sigurdsen lay in his clothes, not on the bed, but on the floor, his head reversed, his legs curved back, sprawling. . . ." Niels watches the man die in what is a grotesque parody of sexual fulfilment and the narrative reports of Niels: "Quietly he got up and drew a blanket over it that had been he."

Niels has entered into his death journey. He is *fooled* into marriage with Clara Vogel — the Canadian woman. He is unable to understand her — he cannot understand any of her names — as Clara Vogel, as widow, as district whore, as victim of frontier morality, as an experienced woman whose dimensions mock his own fatal innocence — and now, in an explosive reversal of convention, it is the European who is innocent, the Canadian who is experienced. The paradise Niels presumed to locate by building a house turns into hell. He completes his journey into silence by murdering his wife.

Niels Lindstedt goes to prison and in that version of silence earns (too easily for some readers) a kind of redemption. But Grove is not interested here in recording the literal prison experience. Prison has been a theme since the book opened. Grove is interested, rather, in Niels' return from the prisonhouse of silence to the world of speech.

ଓଃ

At the end of the book Niels earns parole and returns to his farm and goes to meet Ellen. Again they meet, as they did in the middle of the novel, in "that natural bower in the fringe of the bush." This scene is at once a repetition and a reversal of the scene in the middle of the novel. Again the narrative moves into present tense and again the two figures become nameless

— they become simply the man and the woman. Again, he speaks her name, his voice almost failing him. Again she says, "I know. . . . Don't speak."

But now she wants Niels to be quiet so that she can speak. Speech, finally, is possible. At this point the old names have been stripped of all prior meaning. They can be spoken now as new names, as a beginning. Ellen, at last, can forswear her oath not to marry.

The repetition of the two scenes suggests a ritual unnaming and a re-naming into new lives in a new world. And the paradox here is that the new names are exact homonyms for the old ones. The signifier sounds as it always sounded. But the signified has shifted radically. Now it can be joined again with its signifier; name and object come together, the new life is possible.

A genuine settling is not so much described as proposed at the end of this narrative. In the last line of the text, a paragraph that is a single, short sentence, a "vision" arises between the two lovers, and this time it is "shared by both." A grammar of the narrative of ethnic experience has begun to assert itself. The silence is finding a way to transform itself into voice.

Notes

[1] This talk was delivered as the introductory lecture in a series, "Ethnicity and Literature: Canadian Perspectives on Language, Silence, and Translation," University of British Columbia, 26 September 1984.

[2] Frederick Philip Grove, *Settlers of the Marsh* (Toronto: McClelland & Stewart, 1966). All quotations are from this edition.

[3] Grove, *In Search of Myself* (Toronto: Macmillan, 1946). All quotations are from this edition.

CL 106 (Fall 1985)

8. GALLERY FOUR

Laurie Ricou

Especially into History

For Jack Hodgins, inventing a world has never been simply a matter of recording (or exaggerating) the peculiarities of folk culture and local speech patterns, as important as forms of island are to his fiction. He realizes his Vancouver Island not so much by the usual methods of comparison and contrast, but by layering. When he stretches the lines of his fiction across Georgia Strait, or across the Atlantic or Pacific Ocean, he superimposes other worlds upon — or recognizes them within — his potentially depthless new world. *Innocent Cities* extends the method by pushing an accident of naming into a strategy of fictional mapping. The novel is set in Victoria, capital city of the colony of Vancouver Island since 1848, and in an antipodean Victoria, the state in southeastern Australia legally defined since 1851. The Gold Rush mentality of one ("this tiny city of exalted hopes") turns out to animate the migrants from the other; the paradoxical fauna of one ("a world where birds are the size of pigs") mutate into the strangely twisted flora of the other. As this geographical arabesque — and the dust jacket — so blatantly announces, Hodgins has written "the ultimate Victorian novel."

Ultimate, in this instance, signals both an extreme — conventions of plot and character pushed to their limit — and a form basic and original. Hodgins' mock Victorian novel rests on a plot that might have played at the Theatre Royal in 1890. James Horncastle, comically cocky gambler, operates, with his wife and family, Victoria's The Great Blue Heron Hotel. Until the arrival of Kate Jordan from the other Victoria, married to Horncastle years earlier in Victorian England. Add to the mix Kate's two sisters, with their own designs on Horncastle, or on Logan Sumner, the local builder, who pines for Adelina, Horncastle's daughter, etcetera and so on. But in the Victorian novel, as in the Victorian parlour, decoration and overstuffed upholstery are often more interesting than narrative. Hodgins crowds his fictional world with as much bric-à-brac as will fit. Like his hotel, which keeps expanding, and incorporating its earlier forms, so the plot embraces set pieces of courtroom confrontation, a half dozen revenge motifs, a deathbed vigil, and a suspense mystery. Like Dickens, he pursues the singular oddities of his characters until their absurdity is indelible: Logan Sumner is never seen without his yardstick, with which he unconsciously measures everything within reach; Horncastle seldom speaks a sentence which contains a subject. Like the serial novel which it remembers, it wanders into other forms — into the epistolary at one point, into the journalistic, into the self-reflexive, into history.

Especially into history. *Innocent Cities* is Hodgins' most obviously "researched" novel. Sometimes neatly, sometimes a little awkwardly, it incorporates bits of Victoria's history, be they the excitement of a Royal Visit, or the brand of shaving soap on display at the Agricultural Fair. Hodgins seems to have combed the archives carefully to convey, in the midst of his parody, the texture of life in the nineteenth-century colonies. But, again, the sense of history is not limited to Vancouver Island vignettes (although I recognized a confidence in evoking the Victoria where he now lives that is not matched by the details of the Victoria where he is still a tourist). In good measure, at least, the whole world's history is entered into the mix by the global circling of the geography. To be sure the world's wider history is often mentioned only to point up how determinedly it is ignored by Vancouver Island's Victorians. Thus, of course, Hodgins quietly investigates the peculiar culture of a city determined to become what Victorian Britain had long since ceased to be, and thus to mask the brawling, unprincipled extraction of resources which was its economic mainstay. As Logan Sumner intones at one point, "tidy histories tell more lies than messy ones." Hodgins has used the capaciousness of the Victorian novel to create a decidedly messy one.

The landscape seems to complement this twisted circuitry: "individual pines and scrub oaks, isolated from other trees, created strange paradoxical shapes out of their tensions: trunks thrust south toward the source of light, while limbs strained north away from the winds of the strait — each tree struggling as though to pull itself apart." As with the historical detail, Hodgins devotes more space in *Innocent Cities* to establishing the peculiar topographies of local settings, to the biological details of typical flora and fauna. And yet it is a bemused regionalism, pulled apart by the "naked passion" of another region of windmill palms, frangipani, and shrieking whip-birds.

Immersed in this "jungle of names," Kate Jordan "could almost smell the earthy green scents emanating from the sounds themselves," "could easily imagine the sounds of the tree-names sending down extra sets of aerial roots." Such passages, which direct the reader's attention to the "intimacy" of words, are the most surprising feature of this crowded, rambunctious novel. *Innocent Cities* is Hodgins' post-Saussurean novel. Often he writes as if he had just set aside one of the L=A=N=G=U=A=G=E poets to wonder how "to translate into the language of another place." This interest centres, fittingly, in Zachary Jack, Sumner's native assistant, who lives among four languages: bits of his mother's language, a comic-book pidgin, Chinook, and a briskly colloquial English. In the washed up debris of a shipwreck are pieces of board with words, in several languages, printed on them. Zak gathers these to cover up the cracks in his shack, until he has what appears to be "a building constructed entirely out of words." Words — without context, without meaning — just a jumble of clumsy words such as Logan hears himself recite when declaring his love for the lovely Adelina. Sumner also tries to give words a more permanent form, by erecting beside his wife's grave marker, his own tombstone. What's set in stone is, for Logan, alterable: to the original one-word expression of his grief, "inconsolable," he keeps adding phrase after phrase, and stone after stone to record his current and shifting emotional state. Eventually Sumner is required to demolish his "ridiculous palace of fantastical words," by which time he cannot remember why it had once been important to him. And so, in such motifs, Hodgins' plot and setting and character live uneasily amidst questions of what is meaning, and of how it is produced, and of what ideological content is masked by language use, and of what is the *physical* status of language itself, as sound and hieroglyph. So the ultimate Victorian novel becomes the a-Victorian novel and the post-Victorian novel, its anti-narrative seeming to erase its narrative. But then Victoria itself can be seen as "the absolute end of everything." And at that limit, beyond language, float still the dreams — of the perfect match of cricket, of the whispers of the séance, of the flying machine modelled after the great raven, which flies with the inspiration of people who have had "centuries of experience inventing devices to make the impossible easy."

CL 136 (Spring 1993)

Patricia Merivale

Portraits of the Artist

Montreal Anglophone Jewish writing is the literary 'bridge' between the two more notorious Canadian solitudes, suggests Michael Greenstein in *Third Solitudes*. Robert Majzels' novel, *Hellman's Scrapbook*, seems to have been written expressly to confirm this generalization.

Hellman's Scrapbook is ludically but unintimidatingly postmodern in its narrative tricks and strategies, several of which are hinted at by the title. It is the Bildungsroman of a self-conscious, politically sensitive young Jewish Montrealer, David Hellman, whose "Bildung" must be put together by the reader of his antiphonally structured "scrapbook," constructed in that home-away-from-home of the Canadian postmodern narrator, an insane asylum. (*Prochain épisode* and *The Studhorse*

Man come to mind, for starters.) It is a growing-up-in-Montreal story, with many echoes and elements of its predecessors, both (Jewish) Anglophone (like Richler) and Francophone (like Victor-Lévy Beaulieu), and numerous relatives abroad, such as Alexander Portnoy. David's re-telling of, in order to come to grips with, his father's sufferings in a Nazi concentration camp presents interesting parallels with Art Spiegelman's son-of-a-survivor story, the two-part comic-strip novel, *Maus*.

The episodic autobiography of David, as child, adolescent, and young man, is (on one level) set into motion by and (on another) alternates with, the narrative shadow of his parents' awful past. He explicitly (although inconspicuously) claims his father's stories as a main ingredient in his own cripplingly creative neurosis. The biographical and the autobiographical are rapidly interleaved within the frame story, the "self-begetting novel" of Hellman in the asylum, putting himself together by means of this journal-like series (dated from March 10 to May 31, 1980) of "letters to his father." Parody, pastiche and cliché: Hellman is "trapped in the [Oedipal] Jewish joke" of the third, or Portnoy, generation.

The "scene of writing" is everywhere, although it must be furtively concealed from the prying eyes of Antoine, the Gothically (or Nabokovianly) sinister asylum attendant (is he friend or foe?), and thus from the eyes of David's psychiatrist, Dr. Caulfield (like Portnoy's Dr. Spielvogel) is a blackly comic stand-in for those other ambiguously benevolent torturers of Jewish youth from the Old Testament through Portnoy, the hero's parents, as well as a grotesque figure whose mission of "extracting confessions," resonantly echoes, in Hellman's mind, the interrogators of the concentration camps. His name metamorphoses in every episode. It may be "really" Caulfield, but soon becomes "Crackfile," "Coldfeel" or "Clayfeet," and another twenty-one phonetic yet significant variations pile up into a comically cumulative liturgy towards the end of the story.

While Hellman resists, by way of the Scrapbook, the psychiatric attempt to box him into a fixed identity, when he needs a running, jumping, dodging, fluid, and polymorphous one, Majzels does not stint us of plot. There are such satisfying set pieces as a World-of-Wonders-like episode in one of the seamier carnival corners of the 1967 World's Fair, where our adolescent hero, playing the picaro, runs into "real [low] life" head-on. Here he meets Annie, a walking, yet three-dimensional, cliché of the Older Woman with a Heart of Gold who introduces our hero to love and, inevitably, to his own capacity for haplessly betraying her. David's experiences as a (bilingual) factory worker introduce his political commitments; his encounters with Oscar the Frathouse hippie, a joyous specimen of the bizarre, eccentric, doomed and drug-soaked loner as Québécois — albeit anglophone — literary type, provide the heart of the book's blackest (and funniest) comedy. A fourth textual element, further reifying the "scrapbook" image, is made up of clippings from current Montreal newspapers, which Hellman tapes *over* the texts of his stories to conceal them. These antitexts, printed as if on darker paper, obscure most, but not all, of the underlying texts, from us as well as from Antoine and Crackfill; we try (maddeningly, in vain) to make sense out of the more interesting narratives underneath. The main stories are *de facto* fragmented by them; yet these rather anodyne, allegedly random news items are full of palimpsestically antiphonal implications for Hellman's text, of which they are (of course) an integral part. This becomes particularly clear towards the end, where the major antitext, moving slowly into the frame, introduces David's Philippine adventures, the climax of his autobiography, and perhaps the weakest segment of the book. David's account of being on the politically correct side of the people's war in that vividly steamy corner of the third world is interrupted by a recasting (corresponding to the newspaper intertexts of the earlier sections), from historical journal accounts (Magellan's and others, shaped into a sort of *Lord Jim* plot), of the early exploration and conquest of the Philippines. This, the longest antitext, is the only one detachable into a narrative of its own. The sources of all the anti-texts are given at the end, both out of obligation and courtesy (real-world) and mock-accuracy (text-world). This interesting, if peripheral, device is at least unsentimental, while the "magic" (that is the Magic Realism) of David's telepathic hand-holding, an image of his imaginative forays into other people's lives and hearts, suggests the exhaustion of those images of authorial empathy employed with such vigour by Grass and Rushdie.

From the beginning, the discrete and distinct narratives are smoothly juxtaposed to suggest subtle parallels; by the end, they segue into low-key phantasmagoria, moving in and out of each other, while leaving their traces on, and leaking unmistakeably into, the asylum narrative proper. It never becomes wholly clear what prompted David to burn his hands and thus incite his incarceration in the Hochelaga Memorial Institute: an Einsteinian sense of responsibility for the sufferings of the world? (See the Einstein quote among the epigraphs.) Or the deaths of his own friends? "I've killed them all," he says, like Grass's Oskar Matzerath, who also mulled over, from an asylum bed, his responsibility for history and the lives of others.

The writing therapy which makes up this fairly long (perhaps slightly too long?) novel, Hellman playing with his memories in order to make artifacts of them (self-reflexive imagery is seldom far to seek, but most of it is subtler and more effective than the "magic" hands, or even the burnt ones), seems to be therapeutically as well as aesthetically successful. At the end, the main characters from his memory-stories come together in his cell in narrative harmony, to give their blessing to his reconciliation — through 'real' magic this time — with his parents, and thus with his own life. "Give me your hand" are the last words of the book.

Hellman's Scrapbook is one of the liveliest and most substantial novels of the 1992 Canadian season.

Lawrence Mathews

Charlie's Choice

Subtitled *A Memoir*, Wayne Johnston's *Baltimore's Mansion*, a hard-headed lyrical reading of the Newfoundland psyche, largely through the prism of his own family, might as accurately have been called *An Elegy* — not so much for the country that Newfoundland once was, but for the mode of understanding that privileges notions of nationality over the levelling (or liberating) ideas of modernity.

The crucial historical event is the referendum of 1948, in which Newfoundlanders voted by the slimmest of margins to confederate with Canada. Johnston's father, Arthur, is strongly anti-confederate throughout his life, maintaining a romantic vision of a nation rooted in traditions that are, in some unspecifiable way, superior to those that would supplant them. Johnston's grandfather Charlie, a blacksmith in the Southern Shore community of Ferryland (the site of Lord Baltimore's attempt to establish a colony in the New World), might be assumed to represent the same sentiments.

But in a powerfully imagined scene near the end of the book, Johnston reveals what has been broadly hinted at almost throughout. In the voting booth, Charlie Johnston, inexplicably inspired by a "solitary impulse," marks his ballot for confederation: "He will wonder later if his hand was God guided to do what to him seemed and always will seem wrong. . . ." We are given no direct information about the source of the "solitary impulse." Elsewhere Charlie is consistently associated with integrity, good sense, and hard work; some of the most striking passages describe his labours at the forge. Further, as blacksmith, he occupies a central, almost priestlike role in his community. Is his action completely arbitrary, a comment on the irrationality of the Newfoundland spirit? To draw such a conclusion is to be reductively ironic. Perhaps Johnston's subtler point is that Charlie's act reflects the ability of Newfoundlanders to adapt intuitively to changing circumstances, an ability that has allowed "Newfoundland" to survive as a cultural entity from Lord Baltimore's time to the present. Much earlier in the book, Charlie has the foresight to warn his son, *circa* 1940, that, although there have been Johnston blacksmiths in Ferryland since 1848, "[t]here'll be no more need for blacksmiths soon. . . ." The claims of tradition will not prevail against the current of social change.

As a character in the book, Wayne Johnston himself is self-effacing, taking centre stage only when it becomes absolutely necessary for narrative coherence. In places, though, his own position crystallizes. In one section, Wayne (aged 10) and his father take a trip on the trans-Newfoundland railway. The year is 1968, and the train is in the process of being replaced by buses — faster, cheaper, the wave of the future. The train is identified by Arthur Johnston (and many others) with "the old

Newfoundland." At one point in the journey, Wayne can see a bus on the highway running parallel to the tracks:

> I found myself now treacherously rooting for that single silver bus. I was impressed by how much faster it was moving than we were. The bus looked like a sleek, wingless plane, and, in comparison with the many-sectioned train, seemed so heroically singular, so self-sufficient. . . . The weathered, wooden train, the wooden, black tarred ties, the rusting rails, the ancient railway bed . . . all seemed to blend in with the landscape, an unobtrusiveness that to some was one of its merits, though it did not seem so to me.

This passage is central to *Baltimore's Mansion*'s implicit argument. "The weathered, wooden train" may symbolize the archaic notion of collective identity that Arthur Johnston espouses relentlessly and that Charlie Johnston, at one significant moment, repudiates definitively.

Certainly when one looks for tangible evidence of the glories of "the old Newfoundland" cherished by Arthur, the findings — apart from the character of Charlie himself — seem pathetically thin. In fact, Arthur's Newfoundland is only the Avalon Peninsula (the rest of the island voted two to one in favour of confederation), more particularly that region's Catholic working class, which had little political and economic power either before or after union with Canada. What was lost with confederation seems more a dream than a reality.

This dream is epitomized by such phenomena as the superstitious piety associated with the Virgin Berg, "an iceberg hundreds of feet high and bearing an undeniable likeness to the Blessed Virgin Mary [that] appeared off St. John's harbour" in 1905. Catholics all along the Southern Shore collected barrels of fragments, which were transported to church basements "where they were kept like casks of wine, consecrated by a bishop and afterwards used sparingly as holy water. . . ." (Johnston's account of this incident is devastatingly deadpan.) But some forty years later, as Charlie Johnston nears death, he thinks, touchingly, of the water and the possibility that the "priest might prescribe . . . one healing ladleful." And we are reminded of what is authentic in the tradition he represents and what is chimerical.

Arthur, coming of age around the time of confederation and wounded like his mythic namesake, does not think about the possibility of healing. He expresses his bitterness in childish ways, as when he forces the young Wayne to recite, for the amusement of visitors, a "catechism" in which Joey Smallwood (leader of the confederate party) is ridiculed as "him, who toad-like, croaks and dwells among the undergrowth" and who leaves "behind him as he goes a trail of slime." Arthur is not unique, merely an extreme manifestation of a generation that "had in part defined themselves by their opposition to Joey. . . . Now, in their early fifties, they were no less bewildered than they had been back then. They had followed the river of what should have been, knowing it led nowhere."

As Wayne grows up, he feels the attraction of his father's quixotic romanticism but keeps his distance from it. At one point Arthur tells him the possibly apocryphal story of Newfoundlanders living abroad at the time of confederation who opted neither to return home nor to get new passports from Canadian embassies. Wayne's judgment is both generous and dismissive: "Citizens of no country, staging their futile, furtive, solitary protests that were at once so grand and so absurd." For Wayne Johnston's generation, "the very existence of the country known as Newfoundland was just a story." *Baltimore's Mansion* will rank as one of the most delicately written and powerfully felt retellings of that complex and enigmatic tale.

CL 170–171 (Autumn-Winter 2001)

Eva-Marie Kröller

Why Family Matters

In a 2002 edition of its *Books* supplement, the *Globe and Mail* heralded the arrival of yet another set of Canadian books that broadly fall under the heading of historical fiction, among them novels by Guy Vanderhaeghe on the 1870s West, Austin Clarke on 1950s Barbados, and Katherine Govier on the nineteenth-century naturalist James Audobon. Equally remarkable, however, is the re-emergence of another nineteenth-century genre with a strong historical backbone, the "family saga," in which characters must cede to their children their seemingly assured places in the generational hierarchy, and adjust to a changing world while they are at it. Indeed, one comes away from Rohinton Mistry's remarkable *Family Matters* with the conviction that the old are required to undergo changes at least as revolutionary as the young, and that they must do so despite failing mental and physical strength.

Set in Bombay, Mistry's novel tells the story of Nariman Vakeel, a retired professor of English literature gradually deteriorating from Parkinson's disease, and his children who take turns looking after him. At first, this is the duty of his step-children Coomy and Jal, who share his spacious, if dilapidated flat with him; then, after he injures his ankle and requires bedrest, he is unceremoniously passed on to his daughter Roxana who cares for him in an apartment already so overcrowded that one of her children must sleep under a make-shift tent on the balcony when Nariman occupies the settee. Not until the last few pages of the novel do we find out that Coomy's apparently gratuitous callousness towards her helpless stepfather is triggered by her recollection of a liaison from which he found it impossible to extricate himself even while he was married to her mother, and by the trauma of her accidental death together with her husband's deranged former lover. This late and sensational revelation urges the reader to reconsider Coomy's character and brings into sharp focus the ways in which leisurely story-telling allows Mistry's cast a complexity that cannot be determined by any one factor, such as age or gender or class. Indeed, some characters completely reinvent themselves over the course of the novel, especially Roxana's husband Yehad who first recoils fastidiously from the old man's bodily functions and then tenderly attends to his needs, while at the same time transforming himself from a nonchalant Parsi into an obsessive one. Most of the novel is told in the third-person omniscient mode, but the epilogue features the first-person narrative of one of Yehad's adolescent sons who observes how his father's religious fanaticism is beginning to push his older brother into the same sort of confrontation that, the reader knows, ruined their grandfather's first love.

The characters' cultural environment is similarly mixed, and Mistry's humour shines in his virtuoso descriptions of several traditions grafted on top of each other. "All along the street, establishments seemed to have taken their cue from the Bombay Sporting Goods Emporium," he writes apropos of Christmas in Bombay: "The Jai Hind Book Mart featured a barefoot Santa in padmasana, an English translation of the Bhagavad-Gita open in his lap; perched upon his nose were half-moon reading glasses. Rasoi Stainless Steel had an aproned Santa stirring a large cooking utensil. The Bhagat Opticals Santa wore stylish reflector sunglasses." The book abounds with allusions to Parsi culture that sometimes only the initiated will understand, but on nearly every page there are also allusions to western culture, both high and popular: the children read Enid Blyton and learn Tennyson by heart, their grandfather cites Shakespeare and listens to Bach, while others whistle tunes from *Fiddler on the Roof* or *White Christmas*, causing Yehad to erupt with irritation — "Don't you have any Indian sources to quote, for a change?" — when his eccentric boss Mr. Kapur cites *Othello* one time too many. Sometimes, the symbolism called upon to synthesize some of these interconnections (the jigsaw puzzle, the spider-web, the letter-writing, the historical photos) is a little creaky, but these moments are richly compensated for by others in which Mistry's purpose couldn't be clearer. Thus, while the narrative lingers lovingly over some of the more outlandish hybridities of Bombay, Mistry has as little patience with the policing of purity as he has with the rhetoric of multiculturalism. One of the stories his sons like to hear concerns Yehad's unsuccessful application for immigration to Canada, a bitter and eloquent commentary on the emptiness of its official policies. Indeed, together with Carol Shields's *Unless*, this may be one of the angriest books of 2002, Mistry's trademark burlesque humour notwithstanding. It is also one of the most exceptional novels of 2002, and I read through the night to finish it.

Susan Fisher

Colonial Confessions

Through a long night in 1952 on the "Wessindian" island of "Bimshire" (i.e., Barbados), Mary Gertrude Mathilda Bellfeels confesses to murder. She has summoned Percy, the local police sergeant, to take down her official statement. But in Austin Clarke's Giller-prize winning novel, *The Polished Hoe*, Mary takes a long time to get to the bloody climax of her confession. Each time she begins to narrate her crime, Mary and the investigating sergeant find themselves digressing. Their separate reveries lead us away from that evening, back into their intertwined histories. Only in the final pages do we find out what work the polished hoe has done.

Since she was eight or nine years old, Mary has belonged to Bellfeels, the plantation manager. She returns on several occasions to the memory of a Sunday afternoon when she was seven or eight: Bellfeels ran his riding crop down her body, assessing her and claiming her for his own. From that day forward, she was his, not available to any other man. In exchange for her services to Bellfeels, Mary has lived in a comfortable house, and her son Wilberforce has been educated in England. Bellfeels has been Mary's lover and protector and the father of her son; he has also been her jailer and her violator. Now, in middle age, she has taken her revenge.

Percy's memories also take up considerable space in *The Polished Hoe*. He has known and loved Mary since childhood. He remembers his first glimpses of her; he remembers especially the shattering realization, when they were just twelve or thirteen, that Mary was Bellfeels's possession. (As various anecdotes from village history make clear, the punishment for coveting the manager's woman would have been, at the very least, a brutal beating.) The sergeant relives the details of his long affair with Mary's servant Gertrude and their trysts in the canefields. He remembers his advancement through the police force, an investigating trip to Trinidad, and his work as a spotter during the war.

Through Percy's memories and Mary's, Clarke reconstructs not just two individual lives, but also the colonial society that contains them. In Bimshire, Englishness — in religion, literature, speech, and blood — represents the only kind of legitimacy. Mary, with her church going, her reverence for literature, and her quiet decorous ways surely "knows Englund by heart." Throughout her memories and Percy's, music, in the forms of American jazz and English hymns, signals their complex allegiances, both to other African-Americans and to the anglicized world of Bimshire. Her son Wilberforce, who as a young man and scholarship winner went off to study in England, has returned as that most respectable of colonials, a doctor of tropical medicine. Wilberforce is a mimic man, fully schooled in English values and tastes but neither "white" nor "native." He is still the son of a black woman, and he knows that his precious Englishness is only the respectable face of the violence and arbitrary power that dominate life in Bimshire. The hoe, the murder weapon Mary wields in her act of revenge, was "mannifactured up in Englund."

This novel demands a great deal of its readers. It requires patience with Mary and Percy's Shandyesque inability to get to the crime that is the novel's pretext. It also demands a certain effort (at least for those unacquainted with West Indian speech) to understand the dialect Clarke uses. And what does it take — patience or a sense of humour — to accept his random references to Canada (reminiscent of those mandated allusions to Canada in American motion pictures of the 1940s)? Canada, for example, is the source of potatoes (from PEI); it is also mentioned in passing as a country where, over the long winters, sex-starved homesteaders turned to their daughters instead of their worn-out wives.

But readers who persist, despite these obstacles, will be rewarded. Mary is an admirable creation. She is an archetypal colonial victim, whose violation symbolizes all the violence of the slave system; at the same time, she seems a thoroughly believable individual. And when she tells us why she has killed Bellfeels, we, like the sergeant, have no choice but to listen, no matter where her story leads us.

CL 178 (Autumn 2003)

Jerry Wasserman

Hollywood Not

Vancouver's identification as Hollywood North has become such a cliché that no self-respecting Vancouverite would repeat it today without at least a smirk of self-conscious irony. The city rocketed to its status as North America's third or fourth largest production centre over the course of little more than a decade beginning in earnest in the mid–1980s. When the video boom, a proliferation of new American cable channels, and the Fox network's inaugural seasons triggered an increased demand for "product," Vancouver and environs answered the call. Only a quick plane ride up the coast from Los Angeles in the same time zone, the region offered a variety of spectacular locations, compliant unions eager for the work, and local governments anxious for the economic spin-offs and glamour that the industry brings. Along with a rapidly weakening Canadian dollar, it all added up to major savings for American companies. In 1987, Hollywood producer Stephen J. Cannell built a large studio in North Vancouver to accommodate his new TV shows such as 21 *Jump Street*, and the floodgates opened.

By the year 2000, according to Mike Gasher (in *Hollywood North: The Feature Film Industry in British Columbia)*, film and television were contributing over a billion dollars annually to the provincial economy compared with only $12 million in 1978. By that time too, the locals had started to become blasé about the whole deal. People would joke that practically everyone in the city had at one time or another been seen on *The X-Files*, and location fatigue began appearing in neighbourhoods where film trucks had become as common as Starbucks. Given the typical pattern of British Columbia's boom and bust economy, many expected that the crash would soon follow. Although it hasn't yet, production has fallen steadily over the past few years for a variety of reasons, and the Hollywood North label increasingly smacks of colonial cringe.

Gasher's earnestly informative book, focusing on feature film production, argues that this recent history differs only in degree from British Columbia's position in the North American film industry during most of the past century. Gasher identifies a number of interrelated elements that have characterized the BC filmmaking experience: the branch-plant nature of its economic base; an emphasis on foreign rather than domestic location production; its alienation from the institutions of central Canadian film financing and production; an industrial rather than cultural conception of cinema; and, accordingly, provincial government film policies heavily skewed toward regional industrial development. He provides a late chapter that looks briefly at local colour in such made-in-BC movies as *The Grey Fox*, *My American Cousin* and *Double Happiness*: "indigenous films [that] particularize and diversify British Columbia [and] render the province a distinct historical, political, social, and cultural entity." But ultimately, he argues, the shapers of provincial film policy have been more interested in the industry than in the films, more eager to present the province as a cinematic *tabula rasa* that can double for anywhere than as a source of cultural identification or art. "This land is your land. . . . We can give it to you for a song," boasts a BC Film Commission promotional brochure. Cast as a cheap commodity, no wonder British Columbia remains more of a stand-in than a star in its own movies. A former film commissioner suggests that its most notable role has been "Nowheresville, USA."

Not that British Columbians haven't responded to that role with an ambivalence typical of Canadian relationships with the US. As early as 1920, the province began trying to balance its share in the profitability of American movie-making with a halfhearted maintenance of indigenous cultural defences. While encouraging American companies to shoot and screen their movies in BC, the government also established the British Columbia Patriotic and Educational Picture Service which required that BC theatres open every show with fifteen minutes of films and slides depicting the "wealth, activities, development, and possibilities" of the province. By 1924 BC's fifteen minutes of legislated fame were no longer being enforced but the American movies remained. When Britain established a preferential quota in 1927 for films made within the Empire, Hollywood studios moved into BC to make "quota quickies" for the British market. In 1937 the BC film censor — the first in Canada — banned 50 films for displaying US flags. But long after British quotas and BC censors were gone, American quickies, flags, and money remained. By 1995 total spending on film and television production in BC had leapt to over $400 million, a mere 8 per cent of it local investment.

Although Gasher steers clear of political finger-pointing, his analysis reveals a depressing lack of concern for homegrown cultural development by the "free enterprise" governments that have run BC for most of its history. At the start of the film boom in the mid–1980s, British Columbia accounted for a minuscule 1.3 per cent of total provincial government spending on film and video production in Canada. When the Social Credit government of the day committed $10.5 million to help finance local films, it would only justify the fund in terms of economic diversification and tourism. Alberta had had a cultural branch and Saskatchewan an arts board since the 1940s; Quebec, Ontario and Manitoba added theirs in the 1960s; but British Columbia had to wait until 1995 for an NDP government to establish the BC Arts Council. Not that it had much effect. In 2004 the provincial Liberals eliminated a $4 million fund to encourage local film production.

Despite all this, British Columbia has profited much more than it has suffered from being a northern satellite of the Hollywood empire. As multinational industries go, this is exploitation on a very minor scale. The Americans have not set up film *maquiladoras* along the border. They may pay less well than they do in L.A. and treat locals with the polite condescension they reserve for all foreigners. But the regional economic benefits are indeed substantial, the reflected glamour is harmless fun, and the industry is a whole lot cleaner than pulp mills, sweatshops, or mines. The absence of a thriving feature film culture is hardly unique to the westernmost province, nor can it be blamed on crass Hollywood moguls elbowing out plucky local artists. The problems of funding and distribution are endemic across Canada (at least outside of Quebec), and the dark shadow cast by American cultural hegemony transcends all national borders. Only when we begin seriously to distinguish between film as *culture* and film as *cultural industry* will the branch-plant mentality of Hollywood North cease to be a concern for anyone outside the Ministry of Regional Development.

CL 185 (Summer 2005)

Adam Dickinson

Figuring Wisdom

Giorgio Agamben proposes in *Stanzas* that one of the great unquestioned assumptions of Western culture is the acceptance of the scission between poetry and philosophy as natural. So ingrained is this split, Agamben points out, that it was old news even for Plato. Jan Zwicky's *Wisdom & Metaphor* is an attempt to address and question this split as a means not simply of fusing poetry and philosophy but of demonstrating that to love wisdom is also to be wise to the paradoxical tensions alive in poetic apprehensions of the world. A central claim in the book is that metaphorical and analytic ways of making sense respond to different aspects of how things mean, and neither must be reduced to systematic procedures for determining truth. One of the problems with analytic philosophy for Zwicky is its assumption that clarity is singular — to be clear is to eliminate ambiguity. By emphasizing the plurality of contexts simultaneously present in thinking metaphorically, and by formally presenting her arguments in resonant relation to an archive of other texts taken from philosophical, mathematical, poetic, musical and other traditions, Zwicky demonstrates that to think clearly, to be wise, is to recognize that "different wholes occupy the same space."

Wisdom & Metaphor is in part an extension of Zwicky's 1992 work *Lyric Philosophy*. In fact, key terms in *Lyric Philosophy* such as "lyric" (an integrative mode of thought stemming from the desire to escape the confines of language) and "domesticity" (being at home with the tension between the objectification of linguistic thinking and lyric wordlessness) also function centrally in *Wisdom & Metaphor*. Moreover, both works are formally constructed in a similar way — the author's text is aphoristically presented on the left-hand page while the right-hand page collects an archive of one or more excerpts from other authors and artists such as Ludwig Wittgenstein, Simone Weil, Herakleitos, Henri Poincaré, Lao Zi, and Charles Simic. The form of the book enacts the relational dynamic at stake in its content. In an attempt to depart from philosophy "pursued as an unbroken series of arguments," Zwicky turns to the aphorism and its capacity to evoke resonant connections between divergent contexts: "An aphorism invites its reader to look at things a certain way; a collection of them invites her to see connections for herself. — That is, aphoristic writing cultivates our ability to see-as."

"Seeing-as" is a pivotal concept in *Wisdom & Metaphor*. Borrowing from Wittgenstein, Zwicky develops the idea as an expression of the moment of sudden insight that characterizes genuine understanding. To experience patterns fitting together and to comprehend a metaphor are both moments of "seeing-as," and they involve, Zwicky argues, gestalt shifts between perceptions and re-perceptions of a whole. The relational dynamic intrinsic to "seeing-as" is a breaking and a joining; it is an articulation between "is" and "is not," between the language of distinct objects and that which exceeds language. This attentiveness to paradox, to being at home among the simultaneous expressions of irreducible contexts, is "seen as," by Zwicky, coterminous with what it means to be wise. Wisdom, she writes, "has to do with the grasp of wholes that occupy the same space, yet are different. This life as opposed to that. ('Oh, I see now how it is for you!')."

Wisdom & Metaphor is a study of and in resonance. Think of resonance in the musical sense of harmonics and overtones where integrated components may be sympathetically attuned. Through the concept of "seeing as," Zwicky links metaphorical understandings to the sudden insights conveyed by geometrical proofs, to the ways in which a laundry basket, a porch, a day strike us in their utter particularity. The experience of this particularity, or "*this*ness," for Zwicky is "the experience of a distinct thing in such a way that the resonant structure of the world sounds through it." Attention to resonance, therefore, has a political dimension: it is the necessary acknowledgement that difference inhabits any connection — things are particular and distinct and yet cannot be reduced to a single context of meaning.

The wide-ranging scope of this book is remarkable (we move at once from Pythagorean Theorem to Japanese poetry and beyond). The beautiful design by Gaspereau Press is consistent with the concerns of the text by allowing for large pages with considerable open space — the aphorisms and the borrowed quotations glitter, enacting their own gestalt shifts. In doing so, the practice of philosophical inquiry explored by Zwicky as an exercise in attention is reflected in the attention demanded by each page.

Jan Zwicky is a unique poet and philosopher, and *Wisdom & Metaphor* is an important book. This work has much to offer not just poets and philosophers, but anyone who has struggled with what it means to understand something in the terms of something else.

CL 191 (Winter 2006)

9. RELATIVE POSITIONS

Janice Kulyk Keefer

Another Country

One evening, not long ago, I came into the possession of an envelope —
plain, brown, 8 x 12 — on which two words were marked, in my dead
grandmother's handwriting. A foreign language, a different alphabet. Yet
however much of my Saturday-school Ukrainian I'd forgotten, I couldn't
fail to know these words by heart. They were the reason translation was
necessary in the first place — translation from one country, language, future into another. "Moyèh pöleh: my fields."

Paszport: Rzeczpospolita Polska — contents inscribed in Polish and
French. In Latin, official recognition of private life: *Testimonium copulationis: Thomas Solowski, aetas 20, Helena Lewkowycz, aetas 18.* A map
of fields narrow as piano keys: the land my grandparents still own in a
vanished country. From the Polish Transatlantic ·Shipping Company, a
Notice to passengers Helena Solowska (34) and daughters Natalja (14)
and Wira (12). Disclaimer of responsibility — in English, Polish, Ukrainian, German, Finnish, Lithuanian, Latvian, Roumanian, Czechoslovak,
Serbian, Yiddish, and Croatian. And finally, on cream-coloured, durable
paper: Certificate of Canadian Citizenship, Helena Solowska. Address,
Toronto, Ontario, Canada. Place of birth: Poland. Distinguishing Marks:
None.

Confirmation in paper, ink, official stamps of a world I know only as
memories and stories: a country as different from my own as "Rzeczpospolita Polska" and the crowned eagle is from Canada and its·scarlet maple
leaf. The land with which I've been obsessed ever since I was old enough
to know how to remember.

☙

Where to begin with something that's as much a web of gaps and silences as words? Thanks to the envelope I have, at last, something definite, concrete: Pid-Volochiska, the name of the village, though it may now be called by another name. I know that my grandfather, Tomasz Solowski, was Polish: my grandmother, Helena, Ukrainian. And I know from history books that Ukrainians living in Poland weren't allowed to speak or read their mother tongue, that the language had to survive underground, in the fields and in the home. The village in which my mother grew up was then on the border between Poland and Russia: my grandmother told me of how she once went to market in the nearby town and bought a fine pair of pigs only to have them run away and end their days as Russian bacon. More than pigs escaped — young men were always being shot at the border, trying to cross into the worker's paradise. My aunt has stories of how she and my mother would play "mourner," draping themselves in black scarves, following the coffins to the burial ground; eyes streaming for strange young men buried with no more ceremony than if they'd been dead birds or barn cats. And there were *Liebestods*, as well — I have heard of the beauty of the young men, and that of girls in shifts stiff with blood-red embroidery, their long braids glistening, roped around them. Dead because their parents had forbidden them to marry, dead because nothing but landlessness, the kind of poverty which means starvation, could come of love. They'd hang themselves or slit their throats: I have been told about the open coffins the whole village would parade to see: protruding, purple tongues cut off; chins propped, necks scarved: that's how it was then, that's the kind of thing which happened there.

Unless, like my grandparents, you spat in Death's face. The story of their meeting I have heard and reheard, embroidered so that I can't tell, and do not wish to ask, what I've made up and what is memory. My grandmother, a mere fifteen, the youngest in a family of girls where only sons were wanted. My grandfather, a soldier, a cavalry man, going to a dance in the village. Tomasz Solowski: uniformed, handsome, tall — the girls a storm of doves around him. Of them all, he asks my grandmother to dance. She is wearing a kerchief on her head, even though young, unmarried girls may wear their long hair loose and unconfined. And while she is dancing with Tomasz, the girl who was her best friend runs up to them and whips the kerchief from my grandmother's head. Instead of thick, wheat-coloured hair, there is just a downy fuzz, like that of baby chicks: she has had Typhus — her hair is only beginning to grow in. Shamed, she runs into the garden — would there have been flower gardens in a Polish village? Never mind, I want a garden here, a river, nightingales and pear blossom. . . . Tomasz follows her, his uniform kindled by the white-fire moon. He comforts, kisses her. They are married within the next month.

Against both parents' wishes. She was to have been matched with a farmer whose lands were adjacent to her father's: he was to have married his step-sister, so that the land would not go out of the family. All this is true, and yet I have embroidered, misheard: I have their marriage certificate now, from the envelope — the *Testimonium copulationis*. They were not fifteen and eighteen, as I'd always believed, but eighteen and twenty. I also have the photograph — whether it really is of my grandmother's mother I do not know, but it is her only possible likeness: a woman encased in a black dress, with a black scarf clamped round her head, cutting off her forehead, the way a nun's coif would do. And with no band of white for relief: just black, even the shadows out of which her stone eyes peer. My great-grandmother, come to witness my mother's birth: I have been told that she sat with folded arms outside the room in which her daughter screamed. Sat, and spoke only once, saying, "You wanted Tomasz: you've got Tomasz." I've also been told that my grandmother spent only a few hours resting after her labour. She had to get back into the fields — there was planting to be done, and no money to hire help on the land.

The land, always the land: moyèh poleh. Thin strips marked out on the tissue paper map, snipped ribbons of land, scattered through the village, handfuls of earth to be halved and quartered between what was to have been four children: my mother and her sister and then the twins who would die before they were a year old, for whose sake, the day after their birth, my grandfather went off to Canada. I have my grandfather's Certificate of Immigration, earned by a voyage, third class, on *The Empress of France*, to earn Canadian dollars and buy a few more strips of Polish land. And here, another story, one that people tell me cannot possibly be true; one that I've entirely invented. That the man in the sepia photograph stapled to the immigration card was shipped from Quebec to Saskatoon, and found himself forced to work for a farmer who treated his labourers worse than he did his livestock. How my grandfather, who'd not been a farmer back in Poland, but a soldier, set out in October to walk east to the city, any city. And through freezing rain, tempests of snow, walked all the way to Toronto, where he found work in a foundry, a place no less hellish than the farm he'd abandoned. Somewhere in my mother's house is a memento of his days in that foundry: a metal nutcracker he cast, in the shape of a dog: you press the tail down and the jaws smash whatever's caught between them.

⋈

I picture my grandmother and her daughters, leaving the port of Gdynia, bound for a country that's no more than a foreign word, the stamp inside a passport. The crossing — my grandmother sick as a dog in her stifling, third-class berth — while her daughters dance to the accordion music sailors play on tilting, windy decks. Young girls coming down to their mother, calling her to wake up, dance, look at the moon's face, or nets of sunlight on the waves, and she'd push them away, groaning in the belly of that reeking, rolling ship. For my aunt and my mother, a time of the first leisure, the first freedom they have ever known, or would know for a long time after. No schoolwork and no farmwork, but dancing, careering round and round the decks. Until the day they dock, and officials come aboard to inspect the cargo. The blunt, purple stamp of the Health Officer on my grandmother's immigration card. And my mother remembering this: a room full of naked women, women forced to strip to the skin to assure their new countrymen they carry no hideous disease, bear no contagion. My mother thinking that the older women are all wearing aprons, until she looks again, and sees that the aprons aren't cloth but flesh: sagging breasts and bellies of women worn and wrung out like scrubbed clothes, hung on the racks of their own bones to dry.

Now it is the dockyards at Halifax, the porter who helps them onto the train. My mother cannot say please or thank you — not just because she doesn't know any English, but because she is dumb with fear. For this man is black, she has never seen a black person before, and the village priest has told them only devils are black. This man with his uniform, his jaunty whistle and wide smile, this is the devil helping them onto, shutting them into a train bound for what, where? How did they survive that journey, sitting upright in the coaches whirling past a landscape indecipherable as the language of its people? Of the journey, my mother has told me only one thing: how she stepped out of that hot and smoky train into the night of a strange city, to find not stars but letters scrawled across the sky. Fiery, enormous, unfathomable: Sosa Sola, Sosa Sola. When she learned to read them not in the Cyrillic but the Latin alphabet; when she read them, not in electric letters on the sky, but round a coca-cola bottle, were they more or less meaningful? What sort of clue did they furnish to this place where nothing grew — where you had to go to the store for bread and milk and eggs? So that my grandmother would lock herself in the bathroom of their rooming house (having had to patiently queue for her turn). Would let the taps gush in order to cry without being heard — cry for everything she had left behind, the orchard filled with pear trees, the cows and geese and chickens, fields of wheat and rye, root cellars stocked with potatoes, onions, beets.

I remember my grandmother remembering how she'd wept: how, the only time I asked her if she wished she'd never taken that boat to Halifax, she couldn't answer me, as if my question were not only meaningless, but lunatic, like asking if you wished to be unborn. I remember for myself the backyard of her house on Dovercourt road, the narrow strip of grass at the back, bordered by prodigally fertile earth: roses and zinnias and phlox and asters; beans and tomatoes and garlic which, once harvested, would hang in wreaths on the cellar joists; cucumbers for pickling; raspberry canes and strawberry beds her grandchildren were free to harvest. That narrow strip of garden fed my aunt's family as well as my own — could the land my grandmother had left behind in Poland, those paper fields, have ever produced so much? Could that earth have been any richer, blacker?

Blacker, yes, because the dead were there, my mother's sister and brother, twins who'd died in infancy. For years the ghosts of that unknown aunt and uncle haunted me: I would scour the old albums and find pictures of babies which I'd persuade myself were them, Ivan and Marusha, even though the photos were taken on Centre Island or at Niagara Falls, and these children had died in another country. For a long while I only knew that they'd died young. I hugged this mystery to myself, half-shocked and half-enchanted: nobody else I knew possessed this kind of ghost, was singled out in such a distantly macabre way. And then, much later, information came without my asking. When I was pregnant my mother told me, for the first time, that Ivan had died only a few days after his birth: that Marusha had suffered all her short life, from epilepsy. They couldn't afford doctors, there was no hospital nearby, and so to keep the baby from harming herself they would put her into the trough used for kneading dough, holding her body straight until the fits had passed. And then my mother told me of the night her year-old sister died: the open coffin, no bigger than a cradle, being placed on a high shelf, and my mother, curious, not understanding, reaching up to where the baby lay. Finding something impossibly cold and small, something which she still cannot believe had been her sister's hand. Years later, my mother recounted a dream my grandmother had had, the night before Marusha's death. Something evil had come into the house — something long, snakelike, thick as felt in the mouth. She'd had to roll up this evil thing in her arms, roll it up like a carpet and then push it outdoors. When she woke she'd found herself standing outside, arms pressed against the fence, her feet and fingers stiff with snow.

CB

I have in my possession a plain brown envelope stuffed with tissue paper documents the colour of dead leaves. I have, too, a set of stories, memories of other people's memories. And an obsession with a vanished country, a landscape of differences and mirrors, prodding me to link scraps and pieces into something durable, before silence undoes all the strings. My grandparents' lives haunt their photographs and signatures on those dead passports stamped with heraldic eagles. The faces of my mother and my aunt reflect the faces in their Polish passport photos the way a gibbous moon reveals the new. Sometimes new stories are disclosed — things I can't imagine and don't know how to ask for. Not long ago I spoke on a radio programme to do with Ukrainians and war crimes about the need to face and respond to, not just "transcend" the past. I spoke of how the children of immigrants had never been told the necessary things, how any history of complicity and guilt had been hidden from us. And received, some weeks later, a letter from my aunt, who'd happened, by pure chance, to have heard me speak. It was a very ordinary, affectionate letter, full of news of her children and questions about mine. But she began by speaking of the radio interview and by telling a story of what had happened to a cousin of hers, who'd been a young boy when she left Poland in 1936. During the war, Nazi sympathizers in his village had gouged out his eyes, cut out his tongue, while his mother was forced to watch. Relatives had written, after the war, recounting this. And now my aunt wrote to me, not in anger, but in perplexity: "We never wanted to burden you children with this — how could we have told you? Is this what you really want to know?"

Not want, but have to know, along with all the stories of lovers in a garden, memories of neon stars and epic journeys by boat and train and foot. The stuff that my particular obsession feeds on, threading images and words through ever-larger silences.

CL 120 (Spring 1989)

Claire Harris

Sam Selvon, 1923–1994

Sam dead. Sam Selvon, he dead, yes. An' is born the man born only in 1923, so he just seventy. He gone home to Trinidad for visit, little business an' thing, next you know he dead. He dead wrap in he language. In what Selvon call "the rhythm an' lilt" he use to make he own version of Trini-talk. An' is giving this brand o' English the authority of narration, an' is seeing in he gut that a man is how an' what he talk, that is so you pull you world 'round you shoulder, all this is what make Selvon a bossman in the Caribbean literary revival what begin in Britain in the fifties.

Sam. Sam Selvon, he do so many things, an' do them mostly with grace an' courage an' he real self on he lips. He begin writing in Trinidad while he working as wireless operator for the Royal Navy. Was during the war, an' he tell me heself he start with poetry.

Sam: "Girl, I start so too, but is why you don't stop with that chupidness an' write a novel? You can't live on poetry you know?"

Me: "Look man, novels go on for ever."

Sam: "Girl, you siddown an' write it. Stop when you done."

But that was much later. Then, he try journalism for the *Trinidad Guardian*, till restless for the great world, he gone up to Britain in 1950 like thousands an' thousands others. Is up there in London he meet up with all them from those other islands — Brathwaite, Lamming, Salkey, Wilson Harris, Mittelholzer, Naipaul. As he say heself they meeting "not as island-ers but as black immigrants" what writing. An' he get serious about novels, an' he take he place. He write ten in all. Was Moses in *The Lonely London-ers* what make Sam Selvon name. Everybody, everybody, even critic, recog-nize that this Moses was a true-true character what take London an' make it he own. He an' he friends, "the boys liming in Moses room" an' their "oldtalk" an' "kiff-kiff at a joke" make a London, you could touch, with its smells, its snail adjustment, an' the crack-up, mamaguy lives of Black Britons. In 1975, there follow *Moses Ascending*, an' in 1983 *Moses Migrating*. By that time Sam Selvon tongue firm in he cheek, an' was for him to write Sam Selvon tongue firm in he cheek, an' was for him to write he doubleness an' for reader to find out. Like Moses, he migrate. An' he come here, to Canada, in 1978, too.

Is an amazing thing. Sam Selvon one of the few what write about that racially, culturally mix-up place that Trinidad is, like is a racially, culturally mix-up place. He mainly East Indian, but he write a slice of real creole culture. Everybody jam side by side in his books. A rare thing: he inscribing a version of we culture without pretence or curry-favor. Now is to let Selvon say in he own words why he come to Canada. But first try an' imagine for this gentle, sensitive, gregarious man, this man what never try to bamboozle anybody with the 'author business,' what it must have been like in Enoch Powell's Britain, all his writer friends gone home. He spend half he life in Britain, an' it was time to get back to the West. If not to the source of he language, to a place which seem nearer home. "There is a new world feeling (in Alberta, Canada) whereas living in Britain was an old world feeling. So this is really what I went over there to try and get into. And living in Canada which is a developing country, I feel almost part of, going along with the development, whereas in England I felt there was already so much tradition established here, that I was imposing on it, where as in Canada I feel I am actually helping to build it." (Interview with Susheila Nasta, for the BBC April 1984. Printed in *Wasafiri*, Spring 1985.)

Sam dead. Sam Selvon. But before that, he work as writer-in-residence at the University of Calgary, the University of Alberta, the University of Victoria, an' a few other places too. He also work as janitor at the University of Calgary. All the while he writing plays, essays, reviews, short stories, beginning a new book (unfinished) to add to he collection since from *A Brighter Sun* (1952). To add to the television plays he write in Britain, to the radio plays he write here, to *Pressure* (1978) what was the first black feature film make in Britain. All the while he traveling, picking up prizes, honorary doctorate, Guggenheim Fellowships. All what go with a writer what change something, so can't really ever dead. So Sam dead, this Spring 1994, in Trinidad. Sam Selvon, he dead, yes. But he work so important to this Americas, he living still. Living in the books he leave, and in his children. Living in all them new 'nation-language' writers what flooding out of the Caribbean. In all them what young, an' black or brown or white come out of the islands to make home in Britain, in Canada, in the United States, an' putting worlds, language in the mouth, in the veins of the work like Sam Selvon. In them he living still.

Norman Levine

Why I Am an Expatriate

On a hot June day in 1949 I sailed from Montreal. I stood by the rails on the deck of the British freighter that was taking me to Newcastle. From the first mate's cabin a record was playing *Bye, Bye, Blackbird*. I remember watching the Mountain, the Sun Life Building, the Jacques Cartier bridge, and wondering when I would see all this again.

I had left Canada once before, in 1944, on a troopship. Then I took it for granted that I would come back. This time I was far less certain.

I was leaving for a stay in England of at least two years. For I had just received a five thousand dollar fellowship with which to continue post-graduate work at London University on my proposed thesis: "The Decay of Absolute Values in Modern Society." But I knew, even then, that I had no great interest in the academic. It was, mainly, just the means of getting me over. And I wanted to get over because of the English girl who sat beside me at McGill and took the same courses as I did and who was returning home, to London, after graduation; and also, because I had in my Gladstone bag the manuscript of my first novel. The publisher in Toronto had read it and said I would have to get it published in New York or London; then he would look after the Canadian market.

These were, as I remember them, my immediate reasons for sailing down the St. Lawrence on the freighter. But why I stayed on in England and became an expatriate goes back much further, and may account for the mixed sentiments I had leaving Canada on that hot June day.

It began, I imagine, when I was five; when my mother took me one morning from the house on St. Joseph in Ottawa, crossed St. Patrick and walked to York Street, and left me at the public school to begin my first day. I could not speak a word of English.

I was brought up in an orthodox Jewish home. My parents, and those who came to visit them, spoke only Yiddish with a few Polish or Russian words thrown in. Everyone else in that street, and those surrounding it, was French Canadian. The hostility and indifference of this neighbourhood, and the close-knit set-up of the small Jewish community, tended to keep us children fairly immune from any contact with Canadian society, except for going to school — but that was close to home, and remained Lower Town.

It wasn't until I went to High School that I began to leave Lower Town. (Although there had been the odd sortie: like going for blotters to the stores on Rideau, Sparks, and Bank — selling exhibition tickets opposite Zeller's on Saturdays — or once, when I was around nine or ten, running away from home by hitch-hiking with a friend to what is Uplands Airport today but what used to be farmland, and being brought back by the police.)

The best thing about High School was getting there — riding in the early mornings, especially in the fall along the Driveway, by the Canal, on the blue CCM bicycle with the handlebars turned inside out, until you came to the Avenues, on the opposite side of the city. Otherwise it had little attraction. We went to that particular High School because our parents couldn't afford to send us to university. And we remained there until, legally, one was free to leave; then we would go and work in the government.

For the two and a half years that I went there I spent my time doing shorthand, bookkeeping, filing, typing, and writing business letters. In spare hours we had some English, very bitty; some geography, and Canadian history. We were also taught penmanship and everyone came out of there with that easy-to-read mass-produced commercial style. (I rebelled against this to such an extent that I can hardly read my writing today.) Then we had salesmanship. We had to go in front of the class and pretend we were selling something — a car, a house, or life-insurance — to a classmate, while our teacher criticized our technique.

Although I wasn't getting much of a formal education at High School I did get one from a different source. I became a member of a left-wing Zionist youth movement. Originally it consisted of my friends who now lived in the neighbourhood, around Murray Street. We had built a ping-pong table together and used to go out skiing in the Laurentians or swimming at Britannia and Hog's Back. Then someone older came from Montreal and invited us to join the youth movement. We wore grey-blue shirts with green kerchiefs at the neck, just like Boy Scouts. But our immediate aim was to end up in Palestine and live and work on one of the *kibbutzim*.

We rented a clubhouse — a bare room above a shoe-store on Rideau Street — and we would come here at nights, on weekends, whenever we were free. We drew up schedules, and read Marx, Adam Smith, Dos Passos, Steinbeck, Hemingway, Veblen, and gave lectures in front of each other. We pooled our spending money. We ate pork on the Sabbath. We sang *Ballad for Americans*. And we argued about religion, free love, capitalism and communism, Hedy Lamarr, The Book of The Month Club selections, *Gloomy Sunday*, and girls.

As soon as I could, at sixteen, I left High School, and worked in the government as an office boy until I was eighteen. The year was 1942. So I joined up as aircrew with the RCAF, and after training out west graduated as a pilot officer and eventually ended up with 429 Squadron at Leeming, Yorkshire.

The kind of life I suddenly found myself leading in England was completely different from what I had known in Canada. All the time in Ottawa I was conscious of living on Murray Street, Lower Town, but that one didn't belong; the appeal of the left-wing Zionist youth movement was that it recognized the fact that to be Jewish here in Canada meant that you were excluded from feeling that you belonged to what was going on in the country. In England I found myself being attended to by a series of batmen, all old enough to be my father. We ate in a fine mess. A string quartet played for us while we had our Sunday dinner. And on the wall above us was the *Rokeby Venus*. We lived well. We had lots of money to spend. The uniform gave us admission to all sorts of places. And perhaps because one was twenty, I suddenly found myself absorbed in "living," where before it seemed one was just hanging around, marking time.

Occasionally I would be made to realize the distance that had grown between myself and my background. My father, though he was able by this time to speak a hesitant English — was unable to read or write it. And by the time I went overseas, though I could with difficulty make myself understood in Yiddish — I was unable to read or write it. Consequently we were unable to communicate and had to keep silent.

∞

I remember not long after the war was over going to see a film, "The Best Years of Our Lives." I don't remember it as a particularly good film. But it did touch on that feeling that one had when returning to Lower Town — to the banner on the wooden verandah saying WELCOME HOME SON; the peddlers' horses and wagons parked on both sides on the street; the eyes of middle-aged women staring from behind lace curtains — that one could not go back to this past. Whatever issues the war had been fought over, I now found myself fighting a personal battle as well.

At first this took strange forms. I found myself pretending that I didn't live in Lower Town. I would get off the street car on Laurier in order to walk through Sandy Hill, rather than take one to let me off on St. Patrick, which was only a block away from home. I began to live in a fantasy world:

pretending that I wasn't Jewish, giving myself fictitious parents. And I started to write, a novel, set in Austria. (Needless to say I had never been to Austria — but had read the week before a book about Vienna that was lying around the house.) The clubhouse, politics, going to Palestine, didn't interest me. The rift the war had opened up was too violent for me to pretend to forget that other way of living which seemed so much freer and less provincial. The price I had to pay, I could not have realized at the time.

But the war was over, and something had to be done. I decided to go to university — mainly to postpone the decision of what to do. I did not want to return to work in the government. I decided on McGill partly because I have always liked Montreal: for us from Ottawa it meant 'the big time'. And I remembered as a child fruit-peddling with my father, crossing over the small bridge by Lansdowne Park and seeing — when the wagon came up to the rise — the Redmen playing rugby in the stadium. It was only a glimpse, but long enough to decide me on McGill.

At university I was in my element — mainly because I could not take it seriously. I graduated with two degrees, first class honours, various prizes, a scholarship, and the five thousand dollar fellowship. Even at the end, I was unable to take any of this seriously because I considered all along that my presence there was something in the nature of a fraud.

The only reason I was able to be there in the first place was because of the Veteran's Act; fifty per cent of my flying class was killed. And on top of that, on my first day I was asked to fill in a registration card. They wanted to know my entrance qualifications — Junior Matric. Not having it, I filled in the first figures that came into my head. Had anyone bothered to check up, that presumably would have ended that. But they didn't. Since then I have always nourished a soft spot for the academic when it deals with human nature.

At McGill I continued to play out this fantasy. It was, on the whole, very pleasant. I found myself going to magnificent houses with clinging vines, sloping lawns, flower beds and rock gardens. From their windows I could see the city below with its churches and bridges and factory chimneys. Occasionally I did make a gesture. I took a room in an old cellar on Dorchester Street, next to the boiler. The slot of a window faced the railway lines. The room was narrow, dingy, and there was always a film of grit on the walls and my face when I woke up. My friends would come here in their fathers' cars, have a good look — they put this down to some perversity on my part — then we would leave and drive comfortably away to the cottage with the period furniture; the top flat with the butler; or cocktails at the Berkeley. But throughout this, and the dinner-dances, the nice people, the lectures, the talk, and the all night balls: "There was," as Sir Thomas Browne has said, "another man within me that's angry with me."

By the time I left McGill I was pretty confused. Things seemed so far to have fallen in my lap, as long as I continued to play this game — which was, for me, just a series of pretenses. The postponement of any decision, which I got by going to university, was now up. The choice I had to make was either to continue the way I had, and it seemed all too easy and attractive to do so — or else try to come to terms. I didn't think I could do this by living in Canada, where I would always feel a sense of betrayal.

I had by this time also realized that all I wanted to do was write. And I knew that this would be easier, at the beginning, away from home. Writing, in the immediate circle of relatives and friends, was resented; even though they paid lip service to it. Mainly because I did not follow their own ways of existence. It shocked them that I should try to 'make a living' from something so precarious as writing poems, stories, or novels. They would have said nothing against me if I had gone door to door selling life insurance.

So I came over to England.

But postwar England came, at first, as something of a surprise. Wartime England meant for me a life of abundance, care-free good times, new experiences. Now, it meant sharing with another Canadian a peeling flat that was falling to bits; queueing up once a week for the cube of butter, the small Polish egg, the bit of cheese, the few rashers of streaky bacon, the ten cigarettes under the counter. And also, perhaps for the first time in my life, I began to accept my past, and to understand myself; by some irony, the closer I came to that, the closer I began understanding my fellow-man.

CB

Now, I like going back to Montreal, Ottawa, Lower Town. After I have lived in England for a few years, I feel it necessary for this reminder; it somehow puts certain things right for me; and I enjoy being back. Whether I live in Canada or not, that doesn't seem so terribly important at present. I find it exciting whenever I return, while I don't find that about England. I guess I could live in England another ten years without feeling any compulsion to write about it. But I find it a good place to live and work — I feel pleasantly anonymous. What happens when I have run dry of my Canadian things? I don't know. That is the price one has paid for living away. But it doesn't concern me as yet, and in any case one always falls back on the personal. A British novelist who read *Canada Made Me* said, "You know I think what you really would like to have been was an orthodox Jew." Perhaps. But that is impossible in the world I know. And, although my parents could not have known it, it all began with the sound of a schoolbell on that first morning when I was five. What followed was inevitable.

CL 5 (Summer 1960)

Rudy Wiebe

Passage by Land

I never saw a mountain or a plain until I was twelve, almost thirteen. The world was poplar and birch-covered; muskeg hollows and stony hills; great hay sloughs with the spruce on their far shores shimmering in summer heat, and swamps with wild patterns burned three and four, sometimes five feet into their moss by some fire decades before, filled with water in spring but dry in summer and sometimes smoking faintly still in the morning light where, if you slid from your horse and pushed your hand into the moss, you could feel the strange heat of it lurking.

In such a world, a city of houses with brick chimneys, telephones, was less real than Grimms' folktales, or Greek myths. I was born in what would become, when my father and older brothers chopped down enough trees for the house, our chicken barn; and did not speak English until I went to school, though I can't remember learning it. Perhaps I never have (as one former professor insists when he reads my novels); certainly it wasn't until years later I discovered that the three miles my sister and I had meandered to school, sniffing and poking at pussy-willows and ant hills, lay somewhere in the territory Big Bear and Wandering Spirit had roamed with their warriors always just ahead of General Strange in May and June, 1885. As a child, however, I was for years the official flag raiser (Union Jack) in our one-room school, and during the war I remember wondering what it would be like if one day, just as I turned the corner of the pasture with the cows, a huge car would wheel into our yard, Joseph Stalin emerge and from under his moustache tell my father he could have his farm back in Russia, if he wanted it. Then I would stand still on the cow path trodden into the thin bush soil and listen, listen for our cowbells; hear a dog bark some miles away, and a boy call; and wonder what an immense world of people — I could not quite imagine how many — was now doing chores and if it wasn't for the trees and the curvature of the earth (as the teacher said) I could easily see Mount Everest somewhere a little south of east. Or west?

My first sight of the prairie itself I do not remember. We were moving south, leaving the rocks and bush of northern Saskatchewan for ever, my parents said, and I was hanging my head out of the rear window of the hired car, vomiting. I had a weak stomach from having been stepped on by a horse, which sounds funny though I cannot remember it ever being so. Consequently, our first day in south Alberta the driver had me wash his car and so I cannot remember my first glimpse of the Rocky Mountains either. It was long after that that anyone explained to me the only mountain we could see plainly from there was in the United States.

But sometimes a fall morning mirage will lift the line of Rockies over the level plain and there they will be, streaked black in crevices under their new snow with wheat stubble for base and the sky over you; you can bend back forever and not see its edge. Both on foot and from the air I have since seen some plains, some mountains on several continents; jungles; the Danube, the Mississippi, even the Amazon. But it was north of Oldman River one summer Sunday when I was driving my father (he had stopped trying to farm and he never learned to drive a car) to his week's work, pouring concrete in a new irrigation town, that we got lost in broad day-light on the prairie. Somewhere we had missed something and the tracks we were following at last faded and were gone like grass. My father said in Low German, "Boy, now you turn around."

I got out. The grass crunched dry as crumbs and in every direction the earth so flat another two steps would place me at the horizon, looking into the abyss of the universe. There is too much here, the line of sky and grass rolls in upon you and silences you thin, too impossibly thin to remain in any part recognizably to yourself. The space must be broken somehow or it uses you up, and my father muttered in the car, "If you go so far and get lost at least there's room to go back. Now turn around." A few moments thereafter we came upon a rail line stretched in a wrinkle of the land — the prairie in Alberta is not at all flat, it only looks like that at any given point — white crosses beside rails that disappeared straight as far in either direc-tion as could be seen. We had not crossed a railroad before but the tracks could no more be avoided here than anything else and some connecting road to the new town must be eventually somewhere beyond.

In that wandering to find it is rooted, I believe, the feeling I articulated much later; the feeling that to touch this land with words requires an archi-tectural structure; to break into the space of the reader's mind with the space of this western landscape and the people in it you must build a struc-ture of fiction like an engineer builds a bridge or a skyscraper over and into

space. A poem, a lyric, will not do. You must lay great black steel lines of
fiction, break up that space with huge design and, like the fiction of the
Russian steppes, build giant artifact. No song can do that; it must be giant
fiction.

The way people feel with and live with that living earth with which they
are always labouring to live. Farmers or writers.

CL 48 (Spring 1971), revised in *River of Stone*, 1995

George Ryga

The Village of Melons: Impressions of a Canadian Author in Mexico

Asked some years ago as to my most memorable impression of my months in Mexico, I involuntarily and with lingering fear recalled the village of melons.

It was an arid village, somewhere south of Tepic along the west coast of the country. We drove into it late in the afternoon. We had driven since dawn without food, and were looking forward to a family meal and a rest from the heat and highway stress of the day. Entry into the village was through a narrow lane surrounded by peeling adobe walls enclosing shops and houses. The lane was cool and gloomy, sheltered overhead by palms and banana fronds. Then suddenly the lane ended, and we entered the dazzling light of the village square, crowded with stalls of melons. There were all manner of melons — from vegetable squash to sweet pumpkins, gourds, honeydew, musk and watermelons. On the far end of the square beside the steps to the church, a small cluster of stalls displayed vegetables. But these stalls were dwarfed by the melon stalls in the square. That was my first impression on entering the square.

The second was fearful. For the stalls were run by women and children with distended bellies and blank faces which revealed no animation whatsoever. Despite this cornucopia of melons, the people of this village were starving to death.

I drove quickly out of this village, over the protests of my children, for I was chilled by a spectre I was in no way prepared to face — that of a slow death within an illusion of wealth and abundance.

Over the days following, and over subsequent years, this impression became a disturbing metaphor. It troubled me for a variety of reasons, both personal and sociological. No sooner would I reconcile myself to one face of this image, then another visage, more gaunt and distressing than the first, would turn to confront me with contradiction of the spirit.

Personally, I was distressed by my initial but enduring horror at the seeming inevitability of things. And the dawning realization that I on my own could do nothing to alter events shaping before my eyes. Coming out of a culture whose paramount feature is mobility — the ability to change geographic location easily in pursuit of self-betterment — as well as the ability to flee horizontally from disaster — what I had seen that afternoon was unthinkable. I could not reconcile myself to such fatalism. To the death of will, or so it seemed to me.

Yet even in those moments in the village, serious contradictions began to bedevil me. I was old enough and travelled enough to realize that a purely mechanistic approach to problems of cultures and traditions was immature and prone to miscalculations. Perhaps I had only half-seen the village and its calamity. Or maybe I had seen more than was really there — and had added details to observations singularly my own. How could I tell?

The fabric of commerce, culture, and spiritual values in an ancient landscape is dense and extremely complex. From the standpoint of my own references, which are historically so youthful as to weigh lightly in such matters, the problems in the village of melons appeared quickly evident and easily resolvable.

Simply this: the agricultural soil off which the village survived was either nutritionally depleted, or seriously contaminated and therefore no longer capable of providing nourishing food. Therefore the village should, for reasons of survival, abandon the fields and village and migrate elsewhere to re-establish another village and farmlands from which they could produce health-giving vegetables, cereals, and fruit. It was a simple and practical solution, evident to anyone coming from a nation of people to the north where each individual can change geographic and provincial residence twice in one year in pursuit of career, education, or satisfaction of restless whims. Where it is not unusual to meet people daily who have bought and sold homes four or five times in their lifetimes — and who, when asked, would define "home" as a dimly remembered address on a dimly remembered street of a city to which often as not they had only the vaguest stirrings of affection or belonging.

The village of melons had likely existed on its present site for five hundred or a thousand years. In all probability it was built on the ruins of one or more previous ancient villages of which there is no longer memory or record. The cobbled streets over which I had driven so quickly would hold some memory of my passing, as they harboured the mute echoes and minute imprints of ten million footfalls of people and animals relentlessly coming and going through the nights and days of a hundred and a thousand years. And in antiquity prior to that. Here people had loved, laboured, murdered, fled pestilence and returned, died and been reborn in a baffling panorama of time and history which I could only guess at. The stones and fields were hallowed by the endless procession of people, shaping and re-shaping the earth to survive. All this I could only guess at, from evidence no more substantial than silent echoes of the walls.

So the simple resolution was meaningless. Even measured against the horror I had seen, the death of history would be far more profound than the possible extinction of a hundred villagers through starvation. It would be an outrage to suggest these villagers had arrived at this decision through considered personal choice. Had there been a choice, the village might have been abandoned when we came.

ᘓ

So I hurried out of the village of melons, while the villagers remained, numbed and bloated, victims of vague and complicated emotional and spiritual inter-actions of which I knew nothing. I parked on the outskirts of the village, lis-tening to complaints of my children and watching a bent young woman approaching on the dusty road, leading a burro laden with dried corn husks.

And as I watched her approach and move past our vehicle, the nature of my visit to Mexico changed. I was a writer, but this time I was not re-searching or writing. I had come for the sun and a rest, leaving behind all my notes on pending work. My family and I had already swum in the warm waters of Mazatlan, had seen our first shark, had tasted our first fresh coconut, which had fallen overnight beside our van in the camp-grounds. But actively writing or not, I was still busy harvesting impres-sions. On the outskirts of the village of melons, I was confronted with a dilemma which required all the resources I had honed over the years as an author before I could go anywhere ever again.

Confronting me was a conditioned reaction rising out of my own cul-ture, which is so ego-centred with the maintenance of physical comforts. Posed against my welling emotions was a different cast of mind and spirit — one which appeared to willingly accommodate frailty, aging, and even-tual death of people and things as inevitable and necessary. With the vil-lage smoldering behind me in the heat of late afternoon, I struggled against the deepening sensations of moral helplessness and pain.

In my mind I scrambled into my own early country upbringing — know-ing that a village must have a well for water and surrounding fields for an economical supply of food. That would suffice in Canada. Our prairies are dotted with such hamlets.

But in Mexico, the village square and the church are equally essential, for this civilization is more gregarious than mine. Man and God live in close proximity here, in a natural relationship which northerners find disturbing, but somehow reassuring. People walk in this hot desert country, covering distances slowly. They carry burdens on their heads and shoulders. The aged and very young share much in common — know of each other's existence and shortcomings. The old person lifts the infant to its feet for the first time. The infant in time leads the old person through the streets by the hand, conscious of the elder's faltering footsteps and declining days of life.

Despite this reduced alienation of people from people, life is far from benign. Only a fool or insensitive brute would fail to notice drudgery, minimal schooling, inadequate health care and other social shortcomings as highly visible components of the landscape. I marvel to this day at how a well-fed, indulged northerner in good health can sit in a cantina and stare into the street through an open archway and see virtually nothing except that his money buys more than at home. This indifference and detachment separating us from them has entered all too easily into popular myth.

It is not the role of the writer to deepen such divisions created by ignorance and calcified personality traits. The world is better served through facing and carefully exploring the reasons for such differences, even if such an exploration creates personal cultural or moral distress. Again, one does not choose the time or place for such decisions. One is thrust upon them willynilly, and seldom in the best of circumstances. To flee from such turmoil and confrontation of the spirit is not admirable, unless one has already opted for a gloomy and cynical withdrawal from faith in human potential.

Responding to my own cultural conditioning, my first impulse was to flee from the village of melons. But pausing on the outskirts of the village, I could not escape the metaphor of this chance encounter with devastation and what it implied. It was not something as isolated and alien to me as I would have wished it to be. There were many parts of the scenario I already knew of, yet dared not assemble, concentrating instead on better craftsmanship in my work.

From my craftsmanship I had learned long ago that studying another language strengthens understanding of one's own language. Extending that truism further, it should be possible to comprehend one's own culture in a new way by entering another. Particularly an ancient culture, so close to us geographically. Yet as I write these lines, I am deluged by recollections of acquaintances who went to Mexico over the years, and the surprisingly narrow focus of their observations, their tastes and preferences. They spoke highly of the whore-houses in the border towns, the spicy food, the beggars, the availability and low cost of textiles and leather goods.

Even Malcolm Lowry can be faulted for a consumer fascination with this ancient world, even though his consumerism was tortured and burdened with heavy demons of the heart and mind. Unlike Lowry, my friend the bee-keeper settled for one good dinner and getting himself laid. Hardly a seasonal accomplishment, yet complete in its own dimension. So what is left to do then? Turn the car around and head for the American border and the familiarity of the Western Hotel chain? And on return home, add to the restless myth dividing peoples by dwelling in conversations on the other's poverty — making that the total distinction between ourselves and them on racial, economic, social — and eventually human worth values?

It is such a simple and unfulfilling tack to take. Repeated over the years and generations, it must invariably lead to a deepening gulf between civilizations. An indifference and a faltering of curiosity which enters into the very language that we use. The designation "banana republic" is not so much derisive as it is cynical. For it implies that some people are capable only of producing bananas. Their languages, songs, what they think and feel, count for nothing. Such a dismissal of human worth may have little effect on the peoples against which it is directed, for human worth matters little in economic exploitation — either for its architects or its victims. But it is a disastrous reflection on the cultures from which it originates, for it tarnishes them with decadence and raises the spectre of another kind of eventual decline and death.

An artist in our time can turn and flee from all this — rush away to some patch of earth reasonably insulated from the drumbeats of ongoing history. Here you can, if you wish, select the birds you wish to sing in your trees by shooting down those whose songs you do not wish to hear. You can build a house with irregular walls if you wish, and spray-paint your lawn some different colour from the universal green. All it takes is money and an extra burst of energy, both of which we have in abundance compared with the villagers in the tropics. You can create, with modern technology and some electrical current, your own environment of sound and light to mirror the growing madness festering in your skull. Yes, you can turn and flee. Flee from the village of dreadful illusions. . . .

CB

But that is not the only choice. There is another method of approaching this uncompromising dilemma. And that is to continue on into the desert, accepting what is there as a distressing fact of life, and losing garments of personal culture in the process — memories and attitudes — all the real and cosmetic dressings of what I and you once were — approaching nearer and nearer to the abyss of revelation about what it is to be human in a universal sense. It is not a journey for the timorous. One must brace for anguish and self-denial. One must be free to receive — to allow new language and metaphor to filter into oneself through osmosis of food, climate, pacing, humour, fear. Even the theft or loss of personal possessions and surface trimmings on the vehicle you drive are inconsequential. They were only surplus acquisitions to begin with. And they will be replaced by late night rituals and processions of worship as alien to the national Catholic church as they would be to any foreign influence attempting to penetrate and redirect one of the world's oldest civilizations. You will hear folk songs whose language and nuances reveal a new dimension of dramatic and emotional expression. You will discover explosive humour and profound introspection. You will experience legends such as those incorporated by the folk writer, Azuela, that transcend death in moving the human person-ality into a nether-world populated by the spirits of those departed and those to come in a complex and dynamic relationship, struggling out of the morass into something more just and moral than the life of streets and fields in the endless procession of nights and days.

You may, if you are fortunate, stumble into a primordial darkness of spirit. And engage in spiritual and physical slavery wrestling with yearn-ings for fascism, socialism, a craving for vengeance against the oppressors who came with Cortes. And left only yesterday morning in a Toyota Celi-ca, its trunk loaded with crafted Tasco silverware which they acquired for less than the market value of the metal.

You will bear witness to the darkness and the light, the skies crackling and exploding as faceless horsemen and their women appear racing from near shadows into distant gloom, the horses trailing sparks beneath their pounding hooves. Celebrations of simple food and passionate discussions, laced with timeless hatred for the mendacity of those who rise from among the people only to betray their trust, race, and history.

And through this fierce vortex will pass the men with rifles — the rob-bers, the corrupt police and militia — the warriors cut loose from com-mand or personal discipline, surviving on the fear they generate. Through this fierce vortex will pass the revolutionaries, bandoliers across their shoulders and guitars in hand, linked to the people more through emotion than political consensus. Brilliant, god-like, tragically foolish — all grouped into a common body of fatal heroism from which the legends and folk-songs of the future will erupt.

Through it all I recall how the light pales and darkens. In the fields, the corn matures and is gathered by the shawled, black-clad women. In a small town where I lived a while, the most beautiful young woman I had ever seen is scandalized by her husband, her children taken from her, and is driven out to survive in the streets as a scavenger and a whore. It was all a brutal joke. The entire town became smaller for it. While in the fields, the corn aged and was gathered.

And in the mountains, young boys wearing large sombreros — my sons among them — poach wood, returning home under cover of darkness. I sit in a doorway with my friend and watch them pass by silently, their slight shoulders burdened with bundles of twigs and branches. They vanish in the darkness and my friend and I speak of Emilio Zapata, who could not read or write — and Hidalgo, who could. And my friend sings two fragments of songs he remembers of the time.

ଓ

I have not returned to the village of melons. But in a way, I have never left it. My seasons in Mexico altered me, more profoundly than any comparative event of like duration in my entire life. I abandoned my intent at a holiday and began writing again, feverishly and late into the night. Around me in the darkness, the restless animals in the hamlet called to each other. Children cried fitfully in their sleep. Drunkards sang raucously and off key and rang the churchbells in the square. I heard the cries of birth and the low moans of the dying as I completed final work on *Paracelsus*. Then in a happier state of mind, began writing *A Portrait of Angelica*.

And as I wrote and listened in my pauses to the sounds of the dusty streets around me, the village of melons took its place in a deepening mosaic of observations which defied the sequences of time and chronology. Pressing new questions began to preoccupy me: since life and human destiny were so uneven and full of surprises, what validity should I give to the traditional demands of order and progression in my work — particularly my dramatic writings? Was not life itself a revolutionary process, with its own fluid and everchanging discipline? Did I not learn this from the folk procedures of Azuela, when he took my imagination into impossible places with the authority and ease of someone documenting a commonplace event?

On our return to Canada, I was startled by the austere visions I had somehow acquired during my time away. And reminded in a different way of the village of melons. For here food was overabundant, housing sumptuous and airtight. Our own home was suffocating with the clutter of needless accumulations gathered as a family over the years. These illusions of plenty baffled even my children, and for days we wandered through rooms and over grounds of our garden. We missed adversity, and the fine edge of despair which made all the seconds and minutes of life so precious and memorable. We had everything we needed once again, and yet we collectively experienced the haunting realization that we had nothing. All this surrounding us was transient, destructible and a purely material and cosmetic assurance of security against a savage climate and the loneliness of a young culture barely finding its own feet. We had yet to rediscover the medical and social security systems of our country — those great and reasoned achievements of our society that commit us to help one another in times of hardship.

Some days later, I was called by Judy LaMarsh to appear on her radio talk show in Vancouver, to speak of my impressions from my visit to the south. She was a representative of the Canadian establishment — authoritative, confident, glacial in spiritual inflexibility. I have my problems with establishment, not unlike problems I have with God: namely — with such credentials, why are they so prone to mistakes? She questioned me, and I recalled with rising animation what I had seen and confided my conviction that despite all the problems of poverty, armaments and the oppression of peoples, the human will to live and perfect itself would prevail. Even as I spoke, I was aware she had become distant and dull eyed. . . .

And in the parking lot of the radio studio that morning, I again remembered the village of melons and the vendors I had seen, starved of will, staring uncomprehending at something distant and visible only to themselves.

CL 95 (Winter 1982)

Ven Begamudré

Greetings from Bangalore, Saskatchewan

We have a saying in the city of my birth: "Those born in Bangalore can never live anywhere else." Much can be read into this, much that is mystical and romantic and rife with metaphor, but its origin is straightforward. The saying refers to climate. Bangalore lies on a plateau of the Deccan Peninsula, an imperfect catenary dangling between the Arabian Sea on the west and the Bay of Bengal on the east. (Completing this picture is Sri Lanka, a teardrop-shaped pearl fixed off-centre.) At 1000 metres above sea level, Bangalore boasts a pleasant year-round climate. People move there from across India. As a result, Bangalore has become one of India's fastest growing cities, with all the problems such growth brings. These things happen.

Around the turn of the century this American tourist was taking the train across Canada to go see the Rockies and it stopped in this prairie city. So she gets down to have a stretch and asks a porter, "Excuse me, y'all, but where are we?" The porter says, "Regina, Saskatchewan." So the tourist says to her girlfriend, "Ain't that cute? He don't speak English." I heard this long before I settled here. I came for a month in 1978 and stayed. That first winter was especially cold; temperatures often hit minus 38 degrees Celsius. It was the first time I saw ice coating the inside of windows. Robert Service might as well have written of me in "The Cremation of Sam McGee." Was it only coincidence that he was called "the Canadian Kipling"?

On a map, Bangalore can be found between 75 and 80 degrees east longitude. Regina can be found near 105 degrees west longitude. One is roughly halfway around the world from the other. Much can be read into this, much that is mystical and romantic and rife with metaphor. Here are random notes — greetings — from my true home: Bangalore, Saskatchewan.

On Homelands and Blood

> Like a satellite unable to escape the gravitational pull of the earth, my
> life continues revolving about my father's district of Nanjangud. This
> is not meant to be a complaint; it is merely an observation. Indeed, an
> American tour operator told me, while reminiscing about his quaint
> midwest town, "You cannot go home again."
>
> Why anyone would wish to do so, I cannot guess. And yet I know it
> is foolish to attempt to leave the past behind, for however long ago or
> far away that past may feel, it remains with us always.

My own life, like that of the unnamed narrator of this story,[1] also continues revolving about India. Not all of India; only the South, and that's why
I claim to be from South India. India is a subcontinent, after all. To say I'm
from India would be like an Austrian saying he's from Europe; it would be
true but not specific. From the South, then. Which part? All of me, of
course.

Another joke, yes, but not really. My father's family is from a state now
called Karnataka (once Mysore); my mother's family is from a state called
Andhra Pradesh. I'm Kanarese on one side, Andhra on the other. Caste?
Brahmin on both sides, my mother's a higher sort of brahmin than the
other; my father's side more orthodox and so more proud. There's more.
On my father's side we're not simply brahmin but Madhva brahmin, nom-
inal followers of Madhva Acharaya (Madhva the Teacher), who lived in
the thirteenth century. Like him we're Vaishnavites, followers of Vishnu,
the Protector among the three great gods who compose the Hindu Triad.
And still more. Though we're from the South, we're lighter-skinned than
some Southerners because we're actually of mixed blood. Dating back farther than the thirteenth century, it's true, but still mixed: Aryan on the one
hand, Dravidian on the other; light on the one, dark on the other.

Can any of us truly say what we are? It depends on the time, on the
place, on the context. It depends on who asks the question and why.

On Exile and Entrapment

It's uncomfortable becoming an exile after one's parents adopt a new home
— in my case, Canada. I won't romanticize the lot of exiles because there's
nothing romantic about it. I used to bemoan my lot; now I revel in it for it
allows me to view my homeland with detachment. For example I've learned
that India, like Canada, is less a country than a construct; that even the
name *India* was given to it by non-Indians, who couldn't pronounce names
like *Bharat*. Alberto Manguel best describes the exiled artist's task in a

book of photographs by Rafael Goldchain, a Latin American photographer who now lives in Canada. Manguel writes,

> The exile's task is twofold: to procure for himself an image of the absent country that will allow him a constant point of reference, and to procure for others an image of that same country that will not lend itself to easy clichés and mere local color.[2]

How to procure those images? Here we come to the task of a writer. It's a common task whether one hails from India or Canada.

The last time I attended a function in Regina's Indian community, someone said, "Your father tells me you write stories. What do you write about?" "Sometimes about India." "How old were you when you came over?" "I was six." The man looked at me then and said, "Oh, well, but you're not a real Indian then?" My first thought was, "Good for you; you're as bigoted as the rest," meaning other Canadians. Not a generous thought, that. Now I realize he was genuinely bewildered. How *do* I write about India? I do it the same way one writes about anything. Not all writers; those who make traditional fictions.

I write about what I know. What I don't know I research. What I can't research I make up. Even when I'm doing this, I try to make sure I'm writing about things I understand. There's much I don't know about my heritage, but I'd like to think there's much I understand; that even if I don't understand something, I shall always be willing to acknowledge this. My belief in genetic imprinting helps. Even this belief is inherited. Once a Hindu, always a Hindu.

Here's a story of a different kind of exile, one as uncomfortable as it is permanent. It's a retelling of a legend in which we can read much that is mystical and rife with metaphor:

TRAPPED BETWEEN HEAVEN AND EARTH

Trishanku, King of Ayodhya, wanted to enter heaven in his mortal form. He wanted to live there like a god or a sage and so he asked his guru, Sage Vasishta, to help him.

Vasishta claimed Trishanku's dream was hopeless for he was a mere king — neither god nor sage. Vasishta was a brahmarishi, a brahmin sage who had pleased the gods with austerities and worship. He knew much.

Trishanku travelled south to the hermitage of Sage Vasishta's sons. Since their father had refused to help the king, so did the sons. He declared he would seek the help of some other sage.

Furious with the king for turning his back on their father, Vasishta's sons changed Trishanku into a chandala, an outcaste. Black and ugly, he wandered along confusing paths through desolate lands until he came upon Sage Vasishta's rival, Visvamitra.

Now Visvamitra had his own dream. He wanted to become a brahmarishi like Vasishta. But Visvamitra had been born a warrior and become a king and so he had become a rajarishi, a noble sage, inferior to one born brahmin. Visvamitra decided that if he could gain Trishanku a place in heaven he, Visvamitra, would be hailed as greater than Sage Vasishta.

And so Visvamitra's disciples invited all the pious and learned men to a great sacrifice. Only the sons of Sage Vasishta refused to attend. They said being near a chandala would defile them. Visvamitra cared nothing for this. He officiated at the rites and poured ghee into the fire until it began to smoke from the butter and oil.

"Oh, devas," Visvamitra called to the gods, "come down from the skies and lead the great King Trishanku into heaven!" No gods appeared even after Visvamitra repeated his prayer; even after he poured so much ghee on the fire it sent up pillars of smoke. He decided to lift Trishanku into heaven with his own powers.

Such power Visvamitra had! While everyone watched open-mouthed, Trishanku rose into the sky, up through the clouds, and past the clouds to heaven's very steps.

Indra and all the gods stood firmly in the way. Indra said, "Heaven holds no place for a king cursed by his guru's sons. Fall — to the depths of the earth!"

Trishanku fell off heaven's steps. He fell back toward the clouds. Even as he fell, head downward, he cried for help.

Visvamitra could not admit defeat; not even by the gods. "Stop where you are!" he called.

Trishanku stopped halfway between heaven and earth, just above the clouds. He hung there upside-down.

"I shall create a heaven around you!" Visvamitra declared. He created around the king the Saptarishis, seven stars. They circle the earth to this day.

You know them as the seven stars of Ursa Minor, the Great Bear.

On Reading Others

Ruth Prawer Jhabvala is, to my mind, the greatest Indian writer of the 20th century. She's not a "real Indian," though what makes a real Indian is clearly debatable. She was born in Germany of Polish parents and moved to England when she was twelve. She's likely best known for two things: her novel *Heat and Dust*, which received the Booker Prize in 1975; and her numerous screenplays for such films as *Shakespeare Wallah* and *The Bos-*

tonians. What makes her Indian? She married an Indian, calls her children Indian, and has lived in India for most of her adult life.

Other writers have affected me more strongly than she has. In the novels of R.K. Narayan I rediscovered an India I thought I had lost; I began accepting that maxim "Once a Hindu, always a Hindu." Among my contemporaries, Rohinton Mistry holds a special place. His short story collection *Tales from Firozsha Baag* marked a turning point in Canadian literature precisely because most of it is not set in Canada. Without meaning to, he gave other writers of our generation permission: not to write about Canada yet be Canadian writers. Perhaps there were books before *Tales from Firozsha Baag* which unwittingly gave us this permission. None I'd read were by a fellow Indian.

And yet it's in the novels and short stories of Ruth Prawer Jhabvala that I find most pleasure, emotional and intellectual — especially novels like *The Nature of Passion* and *The Householder* and short stories like "A Course in English Studies." In the introduction to her book *How I Became a Holy Mother and Other Stories*, she writes this:

> Sometimes it seems to me how pleasant it would be to . . . give in and wear a sari and be meek and accepting and see God in a cow. Other times it seems worth while to be defiant and European and — all right, be crushed by one's environment, but all the same have made some attempt to remain standing. Of course, this can't go on indefinitely and in the end I'm bound to lose — if only at the point where my ashes are immersed in the Ganges to the accompaniment of Vedic hymns, and then who will say that I have not truly merged with India?[3]

On Language

Here is an excerpt from a work-in-progress, a nebulous (as in vague or confused) rendering of my visits to India. It's written in English since that's the language in which I think, read and write; yet it contains an occasional passage like this, a "found poem":

MARKETTINALLI
"Badanekayige bele enu?"
"Badanekayi kiloge aivaththu paise."
"Badanekayi chennagideya?"
"Chennagideri!"
"Ardha kilo kodu."
"Thegedukolli."
"Gorikayi bele enu?"
"Gorikayi. . . eppaththu paise."

What happens if a writer doesn't speak his native tongue or tongues? Since my father had decided I would be raised North American, he arranged for me to speak English first. And so, although I didn't come here until I was six, I quickly forgot my father tongue, which is called Kannada, and my mother tongue, which is called Telegu.

When I started writing seriously about India, though, I discovered I didn't speak the languages my main characters spoke. I wanted to use Kannada and Telegu in my Indian fiction — not to add local colour, which Manguel warns us against, but to preserve my heritage. And not to preserve it like some dusty artifact but to preserve it because my ashes, too, will one day be immersed in a river. Using Kannada and Telegu hasn't been a problem in the work I've done these past ten years. I used my memories and phrasebooks. Here's a translation of what appears above:

> IN THE MARKET
> "What is the price of eggplant?"
> "Eggplant is fifty paise per kilo."
> "Is the eggplant good?"
> "It is good, sir!"
> "Give me half a kilo."
> "Take it."
> "What is the price of bean?"
> "Bean is . . . seventy paise."

As a writer of traditional fiction my job is, among other things, to invent or re-invent characters and situations so they *seem* real. A difficult task in itself which needs no complications. Then recently one of my cousins by marriage asked, "How can you truly understand village and townspeople unless you speak their language?" He meant I needed to understand such people because, although our families had lived in cities for much of this century, our roots are in villages and towns. It's not a matter of inventing some bucolic past; it's a matter of history. He and his wife started teaching me Kannada. We laughed a lot but, by the end of the afternoon, I wandered about practising phrases like "Snana madtiya?" It means, "Do you want to make a bath?" Not *take* a bath; *make* a bath.

No matter how conscientious I am about learning Kannada, though, I'll keep losing it in the same way as I've lost so much of my French. What to do? A French-speaking writer unwittingly offered a solution, or at least a compromise. The Québécois poet Madeleine Gagnon once told a largely American audience, "Listen to the music of the language." She went on to say that if we did this we might begin understanding the person who spoke it.[4] This made me wonder: do I really need to learn the native tongues which were never truly mine in the first place? What if it's enough to remain open to Kannada and Telegu rhythms; to listen to the music of the language?

Of course it's debatable how authentically we can write about the people we left behind without speaking their language. If I were a poet, I would invent a new language. Even that's not necessary. Whether one is in rural or urban India, Indians don't speak some rarefied, pure form of their native tongue; they speak a language full of phrases from other tongues, especially English. Witness the term "kilo" in that marketplace dialogue.

The South Indian novelist Raja Rao faced a somewhat different problem. Let me quote at length from his 1937 foreword to the classic novel *Kanthapura:*[5]

> The telling has not been easy. One has to convey in a language that is not one's own the spirit that is one's own. One has to convey the various shades and omissions of a certain thought-movement that looks maltreated in an alien language.

He is asking how a person can write about his own culture in a language which lacks enough words to describe that culture. He continues:

> I use the word "alien," yet English is not really an alien language to us. It is the language of our intellectual make-up — like Sanskrit or Persian was before — but not of our emotional make-up. We are all instinctively bilingual, many of us writing in our own language and in English. We cannot write like the English. We should not.

This is a bold statement but hardly a surprising one, coming as it did from an Indian nationalist. Yet he immediately surprises us by saying:

> We cannot write only as Indians. We have grown to look at the large world as part of us. Our method of expression therefore has to be a dialect which will someday prove as distinctive and colorful as the Irish or the American. Time alone will justify it.

Time has justified it. At the 1989 PEN Congress in Toronto, Anita Desai spoke of her attempts to convey everyday shoptalk in her novel *Baumgartner's Bombay.* She called her attempts an experiment, with all the hope and trepidation the word implies.[6] Even as she spoke it amazed me: how much groundwork our predecessors have laid, so we who are writing now can take such experiments for granted; so we can mix English and other languages freely and think little of it. Let me end these random thoughts — these greetings from Bangalore, Saskatchewan — with another piece from that still nebulous work-in-progress:

TECHNICOLOUR

I am discovering speech under equatorial skies. My father lives in America and plans to raise me there, so he asks my grandmother to teach me English instead of their mother tongue. That's why when I later live with my mother, while we wait to rejoin him, she takes me to only American movies. Dumbo learns to fly. The Swiss Family Robinson races ostriches, battles pirates. The Sleeping Beauty sleeps under blue American skies. But I want to see an Indian movie, a film. What happens in films? Swearing me to secrecy, my grandmother takes me. The film is in her mother tongue. It's in black and white. In one scene, Lord Krishna reclines on a window ledge and plays his flute. Villainous guards vainly swing their swords at him, perhaps even through him. In the final scene warriors on horseback assemble in a courtyard while the evil king, mortally wounded, crawls to his death. The warriors cheer their new king, and fireworks burst over the palace. White fireworks in a black and white sky.

Notes

1 "A Planet of Eccentrics" in *A Planet of Eccentrics* (Lantzville: Oolichan Books, 1990): 22.

2 Alberto Manguel, "Rafael Goldchain: The Memory of Exile" in *Blackflash*, Saskatoon: The Photographers Gallery, 6:3 (Fall 1988): 6.

3 Ruth Prawer Jhabvala, *How I Became a Holy Mother and Other Stories* (Markham: Penguin Books, 1984): 16.

4 Madeleine Gagnon, Reading at "The Literatures of Canada," U of North Dakota, Grand Forks, March 21, 1991.

5 Raja Rao, *Kanthapura* (New York: New Directions Paperbook, 1967): vii.

6 Anita Desai, Reading at "The 54th World Congress," PEN, Toronto, September 24, 1989.

CL 132 (Spring 1992)

Contributors

Margaret Atwood is a celebrated novelist, essayist, poet, and short story writer, perhaps most famous internationally for her dystopia, *The Handmaid's Tale*, and her Booker Prize-winning *The Blind Assassin*; her recent books include *The Penelopiad*, *Moral Disorder*, and *The Door*. She is active in PEN International, and lives in Toronto.

Réjean Beaudoin is Associate Editor of *Canadian Literature* and the author of numerous studies of francophone writing, including *Le roman québécois*.

Ven Begamudré, novelist and memoirist, divides his time between Regina and Bali; his story collections include *A Planet of Eccentrics* and *Laterna Magika*.

Gérard Bessette was a Kingston-based novelist and critic whose influential publications include the novels *Le libraire* (tr. as *Not for Every Eye*) and *La garden-party de Christophine*, and a literary commentary, *Une littérature en ébullition*.

Clark Blaise, noted especially for his short stories (*Montreal Stories*), for *Time Lord* (a biography of Sir Sandford Fleming), and for *Days and Nights in Calcutta* (a memoir he wrote with his wife, the novelist Bharati Mukherjee), directed the U of Iowa International Writing Program until retiring to San Francisco.

E.D. Blodgett, currently the Poet Laureate of Edmonton (author of *Arché/Elegies*), is a comparative literature critic (*Configurations; Five Part Invention: A History of Literary History in Canada*) who writes about Anglo-French interrelationships and theories of cultural representation.

George Bowering, Canada's first Poet Laureate, is noted for such collections as *Kerrisdale Elegies* and for his postmodern fictions (*Burning Water*; *Caprice*) and his vernacular histories of British Columbia and the Prime Ministers of Canada; author of more than 80 books, he lives in Vancouver.

Robert Bringhurst has translated works by the major Haida poets Skaay and Ghandl; in essays (*The Elements of Typographical Style; Everywhere Being is Dancing*), poetry (*The Calling; Ursa Major*), and books of cultural engagement (*A Story as Sharp as a Knife*), he writes about writing as an act of thinking.

Richard Cavell has served as Director of the International Canadian Studies Centre at the U of British Columbia, and is Series Editor for *Cultural Spaces*; the author of *McLuhan in Space: A Cultural Geography*, he has edited, with Peter Dickinson, *Sexing the Maple*, an historical anthology of Canadian writings on sexuality and gender.

George Elliott Clarke, a native of Nova Scotia, is a poet, playwright, critic, librettist, currently E.J. Pratt Professor of Canadian Literature at the U of Toronto; his writings include *Whylah Falls*, *Beatrice Chancy*, and *Execution Poems*, in which he dramatizes the lives of Nova Scotia's Black community.

Wayde Compton teaches creative writing at Simon Fraser U and elsewhere; he has written the innovative poem sequence *49th Parallel Psalm* and other works, and edited *Bluesprint*, an anthology of Black literature and orature from British Columbia.

Glenn Deer is Associate Editor of *Canadian Literature*; a specialist in the rhetorical representation of Asian Canadian culture, he has published widely on Asian North American literature and on the culture of diversity.

Adam Dickinson is a graduate of the U of Alberta, where he studied ecocriticism; he teaches poetics at Brock U, and his books of poetry include *Cartography and Walking* and *Kingdom, Phylum*.

Sandra Djwa taught until recently at Simon Fraser U; she has edited the poetry of E.J. Pratt and the writings of F.R. Scott, among others, and has written extended biographies of F.R. Scott, Roy Daniells (*Professing English*), and P.K. Page.

Margery Fee became the Editor of *Canadian Literature* in 2007; she has written books on Margaret Atwood and Howard O'Hagan, and (with Janice McAlpine) published *Canadian Guide to English Usage*.

Susan Fisher teaches at U of the Fraser Valley; she was Acting Editor of *Canadian Literature* from 2002 to 2004, and has written on war writing and on Japanese-Canadian literary connections.

Sherrill Grace chaired Academy I of the Royal Society of Canada for three years. The editor of Lowry's *Letters* and author of *Canada and the Idea of North* as well as books on Expressionism, Atwood, Pollock, and women's theatre, she teaches at the U of British Columbia.

Claire Harris, born in Trinidad, has been active in Alberta literary circles since 1966; her award-winning volumes of poetry include *Fables from the Women's Quarters*, *Drawing down a daughter*, and *Travelling to Find a Remedy*.

Iain Macleod Higgins, poet (*Then Again*), critic (*Writing East: The 'Travels' of Sir John Mandeville*), was poetry editor of *Canadian Literature* from 1995 to 2003; he is Director of the Medieval Studies Program at the U of Victoria.

Linda Hutcheon, University Professor of English and Comparative Literature at the U of Toronto, is a leading literary theorist, author of such books as *A Theory of Parody*, *The Canadian Postmodern*, *Irony's Edge*, and (with Michael Hutcheon) *Opera: Desire, Disease, Death*.

Basil H. Johnston, Anishnaabe writer, storyteller, and ethnologist, long affiliated with the Royal Ontario Museum, writes to preserve and explain Ojibway language and mythology in such books as *Tales the Elders Told*, *The Star-Man*, *Ojibway Heritage*, and *Indian School Days*.

Manina Jones teaches Canadian Literature at the U of Western Ontario; she is the editor (with Marta Dvořák) of *Carol Shields and the Extra-Ordinary*, and the author of a study of "documentary collage" and (with Priscilla Walton) *Detective Agency*.

Janice Kulyk Keefer teaches literature and theatre at the U of Guelph and is noted for her critical writings (*Under Eastern Eyes; Reading Mavis Gallant*), her fiction (*Constellations; The Green Library*), and her inquiry into her Ukrainian heritage (*Honey and Ashes: A Story of Family*).

Thomas King, of Cherokee and Greek/German descent, teaches Native Literature and Creative Writing at the U of Guelph. Along with editing an anthology, *All*

My Relations, he has written such novels and stories as *Medicine River; Green Grass, Running Water;* and *One Good Story, That One.*

Susan Knutson is Dean of the Faculty of Arts and Sciences at U Sainte-Anne in Pointe-de-l'Église, Nova Scotia; founding editor of *Port Acadie*, she has written *Narrative in the Feminine* (on Marlatt and Brossard) and several studies in Acadian literary history.

Robert Kroetsch, poet, critic, and novelist, currently lives in Winnipeg. Among his internationally celebrated works are *The Studhorse Man, Badlands, Seed Catalogue, Completed Field Notes, The Lovely Treachery of Words, A Likely Story,* and *The Man from the Creeks.*

Eva-Marie Kröller won the 2004 Distinguished Editor Award of the Council of Editors of Learned Journals for her work as Editor of *Canadian Literature* (1995–2003). Author of books on Canadian travel writing, Bowering, and the 1960s, she has edited *The Cambridge Companion to Canadian Literature* and (with Coral Ann Howells) *The Cambridge History of Canadian Literature.*

George Kuthan was a lino-cut and wood engraver, born in Czechoslovakia; his gallery exhibitions ranged from landscapes to erotica; many of his graphic designs have appeared regularly in *Canadian Literature* and are now held in the UBC Library.

Louise Ladouceur, after a career in theatre (in a Radio-Canada téléroman, *Mont-Joye*, and on stage in Montreal), is now affiliated with the Faculté Saint-Jean at the U of Alberta; her book *Making the Scene* studies translation practice in Canadian drama.

André Lamontagne chairs the Department of French, Italian, and Hispanic Studies at the U of British Columbia; he writes about contemporary topics, from Hubert Aquin (*Les mots des autres*) and *Le roman québécois contemporain* (on language and voice) to *Le tribunal parallèle.*

Margaret Laurence, one of the leading Canadian novelists of her time, championed women's rights and young writers. While her early work grew out of her experience living in Africa, she remains best known for her "Manawaka cycle," set largely in Manitoba, including *The Stone Angel, The Fire-Dwellers, A Bird in the House,* and *The Diviners.*

Norman Levine, born in Ottawa, lived most of his life in England and France, and was admired for the stylistic precision of his fiction; his *Selected Stories* (1985) was followed by such collections as *The Lower Town, Why Do You Live So Far Away,* and *Champagne Barn.*

Dorothy Livesay, social worker, teacher, autobiographer (*Right Hand Left Hand*), and pre-eminent poet (*The Self-Completing Tree*), worked in Zambia and throughout Canada before retiring to Victoria. Her socially conscious poetry addresses economic disparities and (e.g., in *The Unquiet Bed*) her "personalist" sense of womanhood.

T.D. MacLulich wrote widely cited articles on Leacock, the Romance, exploration narrative, and other topics in Canadian criticism; his books include *Hugh MacLennan* and *Between Europe and America: The Canadian Tradition in Fiction.*

Laurent Mailhot, long affiliated with U de Montréal, is a writer, anthologist, and historian of literature in Québec; among his many books are *Le théâtre québécois, La poésie québécoise des origines à nos jours, La littérature québécoise depuis 1960,* and *Plaisirs de la prose.*

Eli Mandel, Saskatchewan-born poet, editor, and essayist, was much admired for his gift of metaphor; in addition to a study of Irving Layton and several anthologies of poetry and criticism, he wrote a memoir (*Out of Place*) and nine volumes of poetry, selected under the title *Dreaming Backwards*.

Gilles Marcotte, novelist, historian, teacher, and critic, is a major figure in Québec literature; his scholarly 4-volume *Anthologie de la littérature québécoise* established a canon, and among his influential critical volumes are *Une Littérature qui se fait*, *Le Roman à l'imparfait*, *Écrire à Montréal*, and *Le Lecteur de poèmes*.

Joyce Marshall, long a resident of Toronto, wrote four books of fiction and translated several works by Gabrielle Roy, Thérèse Casgrain, Eugène Cloutier, and Marie de l'Incarnation. Her selected stories, *Any Time at All*, appeared with an Afterword by Timothy Findley.

Lawrence Mathews, editor, critic, and fiction writer (*The Sandblasting Hall of Fame*), lives in St. John's, where he was a founding member of the Burning Rock Collective, a group of Newfoundland writers that includes Michael Winter and Lisa Moore.

Thelma McCormack is Professor Emerita in Sociology at York U; she has published in such journals as *Sociological Inquiry*, *Social Research*, and *Gender and Society*, where her work focuses on the mass media, gender relations, and violence against women.

Robin McGrath is a journalist, poet, scriptwriter, writer of fiction for both adults and young adults (*Donovan's Station*, *Gone to the Ice*), and an internationally recognized authority on Inuit culture. She lives in Newfoundland and Labrador.

Kevin McNeilly, critic, poet, teacher, edited the Anne Carson issue of *Canadian Literature* in 2003; he writes on critical theory and on a range of contemporary media, from television and jazz to the politics of postmodern music.

Patricia Merivale is an emeritus professor at the U of British Columbia and the author of books on the myth of Pan and the metaphysical detective story; her comparatist work on Aquin and Hébert has led her to study the elegiac romance and the apocalyptic artist parable.

William New edited *Canadian Literature* for 17 years; his more than fifty books include critical studies such as *Borderlands: How We Talk About Canada*, *Grandchild of Empire*, *Land Sliding*, *A History of Canadian Literature*, *Encyclopedia of Literature in Canada*; and eleven volumes of poetry, including *Vanilla Gorilla* (for children) and *Underwood Log*.

Laura Potter, who worked as an undergraduate intern and editorial assistant with *Canadian Literature* in 2007, is planning to pursue doctoral studies.

Al Purdy, poet, anthologist, raconteur, and friend of Charles Bukowski, Margaret Laurence, and George Woodcock, wrote and edited more than fifty books; he was celebrated especially for his command of vernacular rhythms, as in *The Cariboo Horses*. *Beyond Remembering*, his collected poems, appeared in 2000.

Nasrin Rahimieh, author of *Oriental Responses to the West* and *Missing Persians*, served as Dean of Humanities at McMaster U before accepting an endowed chair in Persian Studies at the U of California (Irvine); she specializes in Iranian film, women's writing, and encounters between Iran and the West.

Laurie Ricou, one of the leading ecocritics in Canada, edited *Canadian Literature* from 2003 to 2007. Noted for his studies of prairie and Pacific Northwest Coast writing, he has published *A Field Guide to "A Guide to Dungeness Spit,"* *The Arbutus/Madrone Files*, and *Salal*.

Herbert Rosengarten was Associate Editor of *Canadian Literature* for several years, before becoming Chair of English and Assistant to the President at UBC; his publications include Oxford editions of novels by Anne and Charlotte Brontë.

Malcolm Ross, a powerful influence on 20th-century Canadian culture, served variously with the National Film Board, the Canada Council, universities in Winnipeg, Toronto, Kingston, and Halifax, and as the first editor of the New Canadian Library; his books include *Our Sense of Identity* and *The Impossible Sum of Our Traditions.*

George Ryga, playwright, novelist, radio and television scriptwriter, was one of the foremost figures in anglophone Canadian theatre, noted especially for his use of contemporary idiom and his fierce attention to social politics, as in *The Ecstasy of Rita Joe*, *Grass & Wild Strawberries*, his novel *Hungry Hills*, and his collected essays, *Summerland.*

Andreas Schroeder, poet (*The Ozone Minotaur*), novelist (*Dust-Ship Glory*), autobiographer (*Shaking It Rough*), and journalist (*Fakes, Frauds, and Flimflammery*), chaired the Writers' Union of Canada in the 1970s, and currently holds a Chair in Creative Nonfiction at the U of British Columbia.

Stephen Scobie, Scots-born poet, critic, helped found Longspoon Press in Edmonton and taught at the U of Victoria. His more than twenty books include such poems as *McAlmon's Chinese Opera* and *The Ballad of Isabel Gunn*; studies of bp Nichol, Leonard Cohen, and (with Douglas Barbour) concrete and sound poetry; and *Signature, Event, Context.*

Norman Shrive, known for his work in Ontario conservancy groups, headed the English Department at McMaster U; as editor and critic, he was an early champion of 19th-century Canadian literature, writing *Charles Mair: Literary Nationalist* and other historical studies.

Antoine Sirois, professor and administrator at U de Sherbrooke, has written extensively on such writers as Claude-Henri Grignon, Gabrielle Roy, Anne Hébert, Louis Dantin, and Ringuet, and with David M. Hayne compiled numerous bibliographic aids to the comparative study of francophone and anglophone literatures in Canada.

David Solway, poet, anthologist, critic, educational theorist, is the author of over 25 books; his poetry includes *Paximalia*, *Franklin's Passage*, and (as Andreas Karavis) *Saracen Island*; among his books of prose are the assertive essays of *Director's Cut* and a travel account, *The Anatomy of Arcadia.*

Donald Stephens was Associate Editor (with George Woodcock) of *Canadian Literature*; a prize-winning teacher, celebrated in *Inside the Poem*, he wrote on the work of Bliss Carman and others, and edited both *Writers of the Prairies* and John Richardson's *The Canadian Brothers.*

Philip Stratford, poet, editor, critic, was Professor of English at U de Montréal. His books include *All the Polarities*, a comparative study of francophone and anglophone writing in Canada; numerous translations of Québécois and Acadian writings; *Olive: a dog* (for children); studies of Graham Greene; and poems, including *The Rage of Space.*

Ronald Sutherland, critic, Professor Emeritus at U de Sherbrooke, was an Advisory Editor with *Canadian Literature* during George Woodcock's editorship. A comparatist, he is the author of such pioneering studies as *Second Image* and *The New Hero.*

Warren Tallman, critic, mentor, taught poetics at the U of British Columbia, and is best known for organizing a 1963 poetry conference which brought together Allan Ginsberg, Charles Olson, Robert Duncan, and Margaret Avison, influencing Bowering, Davey, and other *Tish* poets; his essays are collected in *Godawful Streets of Man* and *In the Midst.*

Audrey Thomas, novelist, short story writer, radio playwright, is known for her linguistic *brio* and sharp insights into behaviour; her novels — set in Africa, Canada, and elsewhere — include *Intertidal Life*, *Coming Down From Wa*, and *Isobel Gunn*, and her selected stories appeared as *The Path of Totality*. She lives on Galiano Island and in Victoria.

Lola Lemire Tostevin, a native of Timmins, is a poet, novelist, and translator who now lives in Toronto. Her facility with languages not only enables her to translate Hébert into English and Ondaatje into French, but also informs her own writing, as in the poem sequence *The Color of Her Speech* or the novel *The Jasmine Man*, set partly in Tunisia.

Jerry Wasserman, New York-born actor and professor of English and Theatre at the U of British Columbia, has performed in over 200 television and film roles. He writes about blues music and about Canadian theatre history, as in *Modern Canadian Plays* and a 400th anniversary edition of Marc Lescarbot's *Theatre of Neptune in New France*.

Tom Wayman, poet, teaches at the Kootenay School of the Arts; co-founder of the Vancouver Industrial Writers' Union, he has published numerous volumes of poetry (selected in *Did I Miss Anything?*), together with essays (*Inside Job*) and anthologies (*East of Main*, with Calvin Wharton) that focus on literature, work, and working people.

Robert Weaver, radio producer, anthologist, editor, and literary catalyst, joined CBC radio in 1948, creating innovative programs that highlighted such writers as Mordecai Richler, Alice Munro, Leonard Cohen, and Timothy Findley. He also founded *Tamarack Review*, and edited several Oxford volumes of short stories and *The 'Anthology' Anthology*.

Rudy Wiebe, novelist, is Professor Emeritus at the U of Alberta. Passionately committed to understanding Native lives and histories (as in his novel *The Temptations of Big Bear* and his narrative biography *Stolen Life*, with Yvonne Johnson), he has also written of Mennonite history (*The Blue Mountains of China*) and Arctic landscapes (*Playing Dead*).

George Woodcock ("Anthony Appenzell," pseud.), man-of-letters (celebrated in *A Political Art*), edited *Canadian Literature* for its first 18 years. Winnipeg-born, he grew up in Shropshire, became the friend of George Orwell and other British literary figures, returning to Canada in 1948. A political libertarian (as expounded in his history *Anarchism*), he helped establish the charitable organization CIVA, supported the Writers' Trust, and devoted much of his writing (some 145 books in all) to marginalized peoples (Métis, Doukhobors, Haida). His other books include histories (*Canada and the Canadians*), studies of literary figures from MacLennan to Merton, travel books (on India, China, the South Pacific, South America), scripts of radio plays, and poetry (*The Cherry Tree on Cherry Street*).